A History
of
The Royal Regiment of Wales
(24th/41st Foot)
*
1689-1989

A History of The Royal Regiment of Wales (24th/41st Foot) and its predecessors

*

1689-1989

by

J.M.BRERETON

With a Foreword by
HRH THE PRINCE OF WALES, KG, KT, GCB, AK, QSO, ADC
Colonel in Chief

CARDIFF
PUBLISHED BY THE REGIMENT
1989

Published by
Regimental Headquarters
The Royal Regiment of Wales (24th/41st Foot)
Maindy Barracks
Cardiff
South Glamorgan

Copyright © 1989 The Royal Regiment of Wales (24th/41st Foot)

First Published in 1989

ISBN 0 9513397 0 2

All rights reserved. No part of this publication may be
reproduced, stored in a retrieval system, or transmitted
in any form or by any means, electronic, mechanical,
photocopying, recording or otherwise, without prior
permission of the Publishers.

Designed by Jim Reader
Design and production in association with
Book Production Consultants, 47 Norfolk Street, Cambridge CB1 2LE
Typeset by Cambridge Photosetting Services, Cambridge
Printed in Great Britain by Butler and Tanner Ltd, Frome

Contents

Regimental Battle Honours vii
Dedication ix
Foreword by HRH The Prince of Wales, KG, KT, GCB, AK, QSO, ADC,
   Colonel in Chief xi
List of Subscribers xiii
List of Illustrations xvii
List of Maps xxv
Introduction xxix

Chapter One	1689	Birth of a Regiment	1
Two	1689–1701	Prentice Years	13
Three	1701–13	Marlborough's Men	23
Four	1713–82	41st and 69th	41
Five	1782–1811	Honours for the 69th	53
Six	1809–16	The 24th and 69th with Wellington	67
Seven	1814–31	Nepal, North America, Burma	87
Eight	1841–9	Afghanistan, Chilianwala	107
Nine	1844–73	The First VCs. Welcome to Wales	129
Ten	1874–9	Isandhlwana, Rorke's Drift	151
Eleven	1881–95	The South Wales Borderers, The Welch Regiment	179
Twelve	1899–1914	The Boer War and After	191
Thirteen	1914–18	The Great War	219
Fourteen	1919–39	Interlude	251
Fifteen	1939–45	The Second World War, Part I	285
Sixteen	1944–5	The Second World War, Part II	321
Seventeen	1945–68	End of an Era	347
Eighteen	1969–78	The Royal Regiment of Wales	395
Nineteen	1978–89	To the Tercentenary	421

Appendix One	The Victoria Cross	451
Two	Titles of the Regiment	453
Three	Colonels of the Regiments	455
Four	Commanding Officers 1945–88	459
Five	The Chilianwala Colours	461
Six	Regimental Music	467
Seven	Regimental Customs, Traditions and Affiliations	475
Eight	Sport	487
Nine	Regimental Association	497
Badges of the Regiment		498
Index		507

Battle Honours

(Those in bold are borne on the Colours)

Blenheim, Ramillies, Oudenarde, Malplaquet, Belleisle, Martinique 1762, St. Vincent 1797, Cape of Good Hope 1806, India, Talavera, Bourbon, Busaco, Fuentes D'Onor, Java, Salamanca, Detroit, Queenstown, Miami, Vittoria, Pyrenees, Nivelle, Niagara, Orthes, Peninsula, Waterloo, Ava, Candahar 1842, Ghuznee 1842, Cabool 1842, Chillianwallah, Goojerat, Punjaub, Alma, Inkerman, Sevastopol, South Africa 1877-8-9, Burma 1885-87, Relief of Kimberley, Paardeberg, South Africa 1899-1902

The Great War

Mons, Retreat from Mons, **Marne 1914**, Aisne 1914, 18, **Ypres 1914, 15, 17, 18**, Langemarck 1914, 17, **Gheluvelt**, Nonne Bosschen, Givenchy 1914, Gravenstafel, St Julien, Frezenberg, Bellewaarde, Aubers, **Loos, Somme 1916, 18**, Albert 1916, 18, Bazentin, Pozieres, Flers-Courcelette, Morval, Ancre Heights, Ancre 1916,18, Arras 1917, 18, Scarpe 1917, Messines 1917, 18, **Pilckem**, Menin Road, Polygon Wood, Broodseinde, Poelcappelle, Passchendaele, **Cambrai 1917, 18**, St Quentin, Bapaume 1918, Lys, Estaires, Hazebrouck, Bailleul, Kemmel, Bethune, Scherpenberg, Drocourt-Queant, Hindenburg Line, Havrincourt, Epehy, St Quentin Canal, Beaurevoir, Courtrai, Selle, Valenciennes, Sambre, France and Flanders 1914-18, Struma, **Doiran 1917, 18, Macedonia 1915-18**, Helles, **Landing at Helles**, Krithia, Suvla, Sari Bair, Landing at Suvla, Scimitar Hill, **Gallipoli 1915-16**, Egypt 1915-17, **Gaza**, El Mughar, Jerusalem, Jericho, Tell'Asur, Megiddo, Nablus, Palestine 1917-18, Aden, Tigris 1916, Kut al Amara 1917, **Baghdad**, Mesopotamia 1916-18, **Tsingtao**

The Second World War

Norway 1940, **Normandy Landing, Sully**, Odon, **Caen**, Bourguebus Ridge, Mont Pincon, Souleuvre, Le Perier Ridge, **Falaise**, Risle Crossing, Antwerp, Nederrijn, **Le Havre**, Antwerp-Turnhout Canal, Scheldt, **Lower Maas**, Venlo Pocket, Zetten, Ourthe, Rhineland, **Reichswald**, Weeze, Hochwald, Rhine, Ibbenburen, Aller, Arnhem 1945, **North-West Europe 1944-45**, Benghazi, Gazala, **North Africa 1940-42**, Sicily 1943, Coriano, **Croce**, Rimini Line, Ceriano Ridge, Argenta Gap, **Italy 1943-45, Crete, Canea**, Withdrawal to Sphakia, Middle East 1941, North Arakan, **Mayu Tunnels, Pinwe, Kyaukmyaung Bridgehead**, Shweli, Myitson, Maymyo, Rangoon Road, **Sittang 1945**, Burma 1944-45

Korea 1951-52

This Book is dedicated to the soldiers of The Regiment, and also to their wives who have given much to an Army to which we are devoted. In particular we remember those who have lost their lives or suffered serious injury in the service of their Country, over the past three hundred years.

> Major General L. A. H. Napier, CB, OBE, MC, DL
> (Colonel of the Regiment)

His Royal Highness, The Prince of Wales KG, KT, GCB, AK, QSO, ADC, Colonel in Chief.
BY AUBREY DAVIDSON – HOUSTON 1988

KENSINGTON PALACE

The Royal Regiment of Wales was formed when The South Wales Borderers (24th of Foot) and the Welch Regiment (41st of Foot) amalgamated at an impressive parade in Cardiff Castle in June 1969. However, the history of these fine Welsh regiments goes back to 1689, and since then they have a distinguished record of service to this Country throughout the world.

This comprehensive History, covering 300 years, is a splendid account of dedicated achievement which must surely be an example to all those who follow.

I have been extremely proud to be Colonel-in-Chief of The Royal Regiment of Wales since its formation and I am sure it will continue to maintain its reputation as one of the most outstanding regiments in the British Army, and one with a distinct Welsh flair.

Charles

Subscribers to the Regimental History Appeal

This history has been made possible by the generosity of many friends and members of the Regiment. The names of major subscribers appear below.

Lieutenant Colonel J. Q. Adams, MBE
Major J. Quinton-Adams
Major R. H. T. Aitken
Lieutenant Colonel G. I. Amphlett,
    MVO, MBE
Lieutenant Colonel R. J. Ashwood
Captain M. J. Bartlett
Major J. E. Benny, MBE
Captain M. J. Betteridge
Major J. T. Boon, CBE
G. B. Borwell, OStJ, CBIM
Captain S. Boulton
R. J. Brayshaw
Lieutenant Colonel G. Brett,
    DSO, OBE, MC
Lieutenant A. D. C. Bromham
Colonel D. de G. Bromhead,
    LVO, OBE, FRGS
Major T. M. E. Brown
Lieutenant Colonel T. S. Brown, OBE
Lieutenant Colonel A. T. A. Browne,
    MM, TD
Colonel T. U. Buckthought, TD, DL
Lieutenant Colonel R. J. Burford
Major K. C. Carpenter, TD
Captain R. M. Carpenter, MC, TD
Captain A. Cave-Browne-Cave, DSO

Lieutenant Colonel The Rt. Hon. Lord
    Chalfont, OBE, MC, PC
Colonel R. Chapman, OBE, DL
Colonel A. J. Chaston,
    CBE, MC, TD, DL
Major I. D. Cholerton, BA (Econ)
Major D. E. Collins
Lieutenant Colonel A. G. Comer, MBE
Brigadier B. T. V. Cowey,
    DSO, OBE, DL
Brigadier C. F. Cox, OBE
Lieutenant Colonel D. E. Cox,
    LVO, MBE
Lieutenant Colonel R. S. Cresswell,
    OBE, DL
Colonel J. O. Crewe-Read, OBE
Lieutenant Colonel R. O. Crewe-Read,
    MC
Captain A. R. Cullimore
Major P. L. Cutler, MBE, JP
Major A. Davey
Brigadier K. J. Davey, CBE, MC, DL
C. P. David
Major A. J. Davies
Major J. G. Davies
Lieutenant Colonel M. Davies, JP
Major P. Davies

Subscribers to the Regimental History Appeal

Major P. G. Davies
Captain R. Tudor Davies
Brigadier E. M. Davies-Jenkins, OBE
Major G. N. Dawnay
Lieutenant Colonel A. J. de Lukacs-
                  Lessner de Szeged
Captain G. R. Deakin
Brigadier H. H. Deane, DSO
Major E. J. Deeble
Major T. H. Delahaye
Colonel C. H. Diamond
Major D. O. Dowdeswell, TD
Lieutenant Colonel R. C. Edger, OBE
Major A. M. Edwards
Colonel I. C. Edwards, CVO, OBE, TD
Major R. O. J. Edwards
Major G. J. B. Egerton, JP, DL
Lieutenant Colonel B. W. T. Elliot
Lieutenant Colonel C. H. Elliot
Major G. B. Evans
Major J. Evans
Lieutenant Colonel J. R. Evans, TD, DL
Major O. A. Evans
Captain S. G. Evans
Major V. H. Evans, TD
Major M. J. Everett, TD
Lieutenant Colonel A. R. Evill
Lieutenant Colonel F. S. Field, OBE
Sir Graeme B. Finlay Bt, ERD
Major B. Fitzgerald, TD
T. H. Flower
Major T. J. M. Flower TD
Major A. V. Ford
Captain N. P. N. de Rouen Forth, TD
Captain L. D. Freeman
Lieutenant Colonel J. C. M. Garnett
Major P. A. J. Garnons-Williams
Captain K. Gill
Captain M. I. Gittins
Lieutenant Colonel I. G. B. Goad
Lieutenant Colonel R. H. Godwin-
                  Austen
Major R. C. Goodall
Lieutenant Colonel P. L. Gooderson, TD

Lieutenant Colonel J. N. Goodwyn
Captain M. F. T. Green, BSc
C. F. Griffin, ERD, JP, FRAI
Major M. C. C. Griffin
Colonel J. M. Grundy
Major W. G. Gulley
Lieutenant G. S. Hammond
Colonel R. Hanbury-Tenison, JP
M. J. G. Hann
Major General L. A. D. Harrod, OBE
Major K. R. Harry, TD
Lieutenant Colonel M. J. H. Harry
Lieutenant Colonel P. D. Harry, OBE
Captain P. M. Hart
Colonel W. P. Howells, CBE, TD, DL
Lieutenant Colonel R. I. Hywel-Jones,
                  MC
Major J. H. Jessop
Colonel B. T. John, CBE, TD
Major General B. D. Jones, CB, CBE
Lieutenant Colonel C. B. Jones
E. B. Jones
Captain F. H. Jones
Major H. T. W. Jones
Major J. Glyn Jones, TD
Captain R. G. Jones
Major A. P. Keelan
Lieutenant Colonel G. P. Kerruish
Major D. I. Kilmister
Major J. C. St. J. Kilmister
Major D. W. Knight
Colonel J. E. J. Lane
Brigadier C. J. Lee, CBE
Captain S. N. Lee, BA
Colonel M. T. O. Lloyd, OBE
Major W. R. Lloyd
Lieutenant Colonel I. W. Lloyd-Jones,
                  MC
Major E. D. Lloyd-Thomas, JP
Captain M. J. Maguire
Lieutenant N. G. Mann
Major H. D. Margesson
Lieutenant Colonel J. E. Margesson, MBE
Colonel J. S. Martin, OBE

Subscribers to the Regimental History Appeal

Colonel P. J. Martin
Major P. J. Matthews, MBE
Captain R. J. A. McGregor, BA
Colonel I. D. B. Mennell, OBE
Major J. A. Ll. Mitchley
Major H. P. Monkley
D. Mordecai
Colonel C. Morgan, OBE
Lieutenant Colonel D. G. Morgan, TD
Colonel D. R. Morgan, OBE, TD, DL
Colonel G. F. K. Morgan,
    OBE, MC, TD, DL
J. G. Morgan-Owen, CB, MBE, QC
J. G. Morris
Major D. S. Mortimer
Major General L. A. H. Napier,
    CB, OBE, MC, DL
Lieutenant Colonel Sir Joseph W. L.
    Napier, Bt, OBE
Lieutenant P. M. L. Napier
Brigadier V. J. L. Napier, MC, OStJ
Major A. C. Nash
Captain G. J. J. Neale, CBE
Major P. Norrington-Davies, LLB
Major P. J. Norrington-Davies
Major C. R. V. Norris
Captain A. G. O'Connor
Major T. E. Orpin, CBE
Major R. T. Parkinson, TD
Lieutenant Colonel C. R. Parrish, TD
Lieutenant Colonel W. J. Parsons, MBE
Major P. J. R. Poncia
Major A. D. Powell, CH, CBE
Major C. H. N. Poyntz, BSc
Captain A. E. Price
Brigadier R. E. C. Price, CBE, DSO
Major T. Price, MBE
Captain J. A. Pritchard
Colonel A. H. Protheroe, MBE, TD
Captain I. E. Pugh, DL
Major R. L. Pugh, TD
Major D. M. Randell, MBE, MC
Captain E. J. K. Rees, DL
Major T. J. Van Rees, ED

Major J. M. Reid
Lieutenant Colonel D. L. Rhys,
    OBE, MC, DL
Captain D. J. Richards
Captain J. Spencer Richards
Colonel A. G. Roberts, DSO
Colonel J. R. Vaughan Roberts,
    CBE, TD, DL
Lieutenant Colonel M. G. R. Roberts,
    MBE
Colonel N. O. Roberts
Major H. B. Rodge, TD
Major P. M. Rossiter, TD
Captain G. C. Rowland-James
Colonel H. Morrey Salmon,
    CBE, MC, DL, DSc
H. R. H. Salmon, MA
Major N. H. Salmon
Colonel R. M. Scott, TD
Lieutenant Colonel A. K. Sharpe, OBE
Major R. P. Smith
Captain M. R. Snook, BA
Brigadier Sir Nicholas Somerville, CBE
Major T. Wilson Stephens, MBE, TD
Colonel S. R. A. Stocker, OBE
Major R. C. Taverner, MBE
Lieutenant A. J. Terry
Captain M. D. Terry
D. W. Thomas
Captain J. A. Thomas
Colonel D. E. Thornton, CBE, ERD
Major H. A. Todman
P. C. Tudball
N. A. McMahon Turner
Brigadier A. C. Tyler, CBE, MC, DL
Captain R. H. Tyler
Colonel W. R. D. Vernon-Harcourt,
    OBE
Major C. J. Vivian, DSO, MC
Major J. E. Walliker, MC
R. A. Warnes
Colonel B. J. Watkins, TD, DL
Major D. J. M. Watkins
Captain E. T. Watkins, MBE

Subscribers to the Regimental History Appeal

Lieutenant Colonel J. A. Watkins, MC, ERD, BA
Major The Rt. Hon. Sir Tasker Watkins, VC, PC, DL
Major T. P. Wheadon
B. Whelan
Major C. W. Wilks, BSc

Colonel P. D. Williams, OBE, TD, DL
Captain R. Williams, MC
Lieutenant T. L. Williams
Captain J. G. G. Wilson
Major S. H. Windsor
Lieutenant Colonel W. T. D. Wood, MBE
Major G. S. T. Woods, MBE

1st Battalion PRI
1st Battalion Corporals' Mess
1st Battalion Sergeants' Mess
1st Battalion Officers' Mess
1st Battalion Commanding Officers Fund
3rd (Volunteer) Battalion Officers' Mess
4th (Volunteer) Battalion Officers' Mess
The South Wales Borderers and Monmouthshire Regiment Museum
The Welch Regiment Museum

List of Illustrations

Black and White

Chapter One 1689 – Birth of a Regiment
The Church at Pluckley 2
Colonel Daniel Dering 5

Chapter Five 1782–1811 – Honours for the 69th
Battle of the Saints, 1782 54
Lieutenant General Sir Ralph Abercromby 57
The Naval Crown 57

Chapter Six 1809–16 – The 24th and 69th with Wellington
The Duke of Wellington 69
The Waterloo Medal 82

Chapter Seven 1814–31 – Nepal, North America, Burma
Field officer's Gold Medal, Detroit 92
The Battle of Queenstown, 1813 93
Lieutenant Colonel Sir Edmund Williams 100
The 'Welch' letter 103

Chapter Eight 1841–9 – Afghanistan, Chilanwala
Brecon Barracks, c. 1900 108
Officer's coatee, late 18th century 109
Brigadier John Pennycuick 121
Chilianwala grave 123
Chilianwala memorial tablet 124

Black and White Illustrations

Chapter Nine 1844–73 – The First VCs. Welcome to Wales
Lieutenant Colonel Julius Goodwyn and officers of the 41st Regiment, Sebastopol 134
Lieutenant Colonel Hugh Rowlands, VC 137
Lieutenant Colonel Hugh Rowlands and officers of the 41st Regiment, 1870 141
Assistant Surgeon Campbell Douglas, VC 144
Private David Bell, VC 145
Private Thomas Murphy, VC 145
The Royal Glamorgan Light Infantry, 1871 147
Officers of the 2nd Battalion the 24th Regiment, 1871 148

Chapter Ten 1874–9 – Isandhlwana, Rorke's Drift
Lieutenant Edric Gifford, VC 152
Major General Sir W. Penn Symons, KCB 155
Lieutenant Teignmouth Melvill, VC 161
Lieutenant Neville Coghill, VC 161
Lieutenant Gonville Bromhead, VC 165
Private John Williams, VC 166
Private Henry Hook, VC 166
Private Robert Jones, VC 167
Private William Jones, VC 167
Corporal William Allen, VC 169
Private Frederick Hitch, VC 169
The roll of those present at Rorke's Drift 170–1
The Wreath of Immortelles 174
Lieutenant Edward Browne, VC 175
Rorke's Drift Memorial 177

Chapter Eleven 1881–95 – The South Wales Borderers, The Welch Regiment
Letter regarding territorialisation of the 69th Regiment 181
Maxim Gun Section, Mounted Infantry 183
Cap badges 187
1 Welch, Malta, 1894 189

Chapter Twelve 1899–1914 – The Boer War and After
1 Welch disembarking at Port Elizabeth, 1899 193
Gwilym Jenkins – Taffy III 194
NCOs Mounted Infantry, The Welch Regiment, 1903 196
The surrender at Paardeberg, 1900 197
A call for volunteers, 1899 198
1 Welch entering Pretoria, 1900 205
SWB Regimental arch, 1906 208
SWB Corps of Drums, 1936 209
2 Welch, Wet Canteen, Pembrokeshire, 1910 210

Black and White Illustrations

Married Quarters, Pembroke Dock	211
A selection of uniforms worn by 2 Welch, India, 1906	213
Officers of 2 SWB, 1907	214
SWB Private wearing the Brodrick hat	215
Isandhlwana memorial	216

Chapter Thirteen 1914–18 – The Great War

Captain Mark Haggard	221
Lance Corporal William Fuller, VC	221
The death of Captain Mark Haggard	222
'Stick it The Welch'; Maindy Barracks, Cardiff	223
2 SWB landing at Laoshan Bay, 1914	225
2 SWB at Laoshan Bay, 1914	225
2 Mons, Ypres	226
2 Welch, Neuve Chappelle	227
Officers of 2 Welch, Givenchy	228
Cape Helles, Dardanelles	229
Suvla Bay, Dardanelles	232
Fatigue parties at West Beach, Dardanelles	233
2 SWB, Montsuban, 1916	234
The Mametz Wood memorial	235
Private James Finn, VC	236
2nd Lieutenant Kinghorn Myles, VC	236
Captain Angus Buchanan, VC	238
Corporal H. W. Lewis, VC	238
Sergeant Albert White, VC	240
Sergeant Ivor Rees, VC	240
Cambrai, 1917	242
WO2 John Henry Williams, VC	246
Lieutenant Colonel D. G. Johnson, VC	246
Colonel C. V. Trower, 24th Regiment	247

Chapter Fourteen 1919–39 – Interlude

Reforce Christmas card, 1927	252
HRH Edward, Prince of Wales	254
1 SWB Egypt, 1930	255
1 SWB Colour Party, Egypt, 1930	256
1 SWB, Mena Camp, Egypt, 1930	257
The Havard Chapel, Brecon Cathedral	259
The Cenotaph, Maindy Barracks, Cardiff	260
Lieutenant General Sir Alexander Cobbe, VC	261
Major General Sir Thomas Marden	262
Church parade, Aldershot	264
View of Landi Kotal	266

Black and White Illustrations

1 Welch, Waziristan, 1923	267
Transport lines, Waziristan, 1923	268
Pitching bivouacs, Waziristan, 1923	268
Laying up of 1 SWB Colours, 1934	271
1 SWB Colours	272
The Museum, Brecon	275
Buglers of 1 Mons, 1936	276
Guard of Honour of 1 Mons, 1937	277
Kit laid out for Inspection, 1937	278
Boy-Soldier Hill, 2 Welch 1937	279
Rail-armoured car, 2 SWB; Palestine, 1936	281
'The South Wales Borderers' locomotive	282

Chapter Fifteen 1939–45 – The Second World War, Part I
Mobilisation Telegram, 1939	285
2 SWB before embarking for Norway, 1940	287
2 SWB landing in Norway, 1940	288
Suda Bay, Crete	294
Tobruk, 1942	296
Sample of Jon's humour	299
6 SWB, 24th Tunnel, Burma	309
6 SWB on parade, 1944	312
6 SWB's 40th annual reunion dinner, Newport, 1986	315

Chapter Sixteen 1939–45 – The Second World War, Part II
Major Tasker Watkins, VC	332
Corporal Edward Chapman, VC	340
5 Welch casualty	341
5 Welch at Reichswald Forest	341
89th Quartermaster Battalion, US Army	343

Chapter Seventeen 1945–68 – End of an Era
Visit of Princess Elizabeth to Cardiff	348
RSM A. E. Visick	349
A Company, 1 Welch; Korea, 1952	353
Hill 355; Korea, 1952	355
1 Welch, Korea; St David's Day, 1952	356
1 Welch, Korea, leek eating; St David's Day, 1952	357
A Group of 1 Welch officers; Korea, 1952	358
Major General Sir A. Reade Godwin-Austen	359
Colour Party at Freedom of Brecon Parade, 1948	360
Major General C. E. N. Lomax	361
Lieutenant General Sir Charles Coleman	362
SS *Dilwara*, 1955	363
1 SWB; Malaya, 1955	365

RN helicopter, Malaya 366
Lieutenant Colonel R. C. H. Miers and Captain J. A. Ll. Mitchley, Malaya 367
Major J. E. Margesson, Second-in-Command, Malaya 368
Major A. Gwynne-Jones 369
The new cap badge, 1958 370
National Servicemen; Brecon, 1957 371
The Welch Regiment Chapel, Llandaff Cathedral; interior 372
The Welch Regiment Chapel 373
Cwrt-y-Gollen, Crickhowell, circa 1960 376
The three Colonels of The Welsh Brigade Regiments 378
1 SWB; Ma'alla Aden, 1967 383
1 SWB; Aden, 1967 384
Lieutenant General Sir David Peel Yates 387
Major General F. H. Brooke 388
1 Welch on Public Duties; London, 1969 390
Lieutenant Colonel L. A. D. Harrod with Taffy 391
Welch Regiment Group at Maindy Barracks, Cardiff 392

Chapter Eighteen 1969–78 – The Royal Regiment of Wales
Colonel in Chief, 1969 396
Presentation of Queen's Colour, 1969 397
The Colonel in Chief with Taffy 398
Training, 1970s 403
Northern Ireland 405
Rededication Tablet, St Cadoc's Church, Trevethin, Pontypool 412
2 Mons Chapel, St Cadoc's Church, Trevethin, Pontypool 413
The new cap badge, 1975 415
1 RRW; Belize, 1977 417
Major General L. A. D. Harrod 419

Chapter Nineteen 1978–1988 – To the Tercentenary
Normandy Barracks, Aldershot 422
3 RRW, training with SA 80 425
3 RRW, training; 12-ft wall 425
1 RRW on Public Duties; London, 1980 427
Graffiti; Northern Ireland 430
Northern Ireland, 1981 431
Northern Ireland, 1981 432
Northern Ireland, 1983 432
Major General and Mrs L. A. H. Napier 435
Recruits Training at Cwrt-y-Gollen 436
Civic Luncheon Group, Cwrt-y-Gollen, 1986 437
4 RRW at Freedom of Dinefwr parade, 1985 440
Northern Ireland, 1986–7 444
Northern Ireland, 1986–7 445

Appendix Five
Major General Morgan-Owen 463

Appendix Seven – Regimental Customs, Traditions and Affiliations
First mascot, 1855 476
The massive Tirah goat, 1899–1905 478
Taffy IV 479
3 RRW, Eating the leek 481
The Eversleigh Star 484

Appendix Eight – Sport
2 Welch, Army Champions, 1912 488
2 Welch, Army Champions, 1924 489
1 SWB, Army Champions, 1924–8 490
A selection of internationals, Welch Regiment 491
1 SWB, Army Champions, 1969 492
2nd Lieutenant W. D. J. Carling 493
RSM Richards 494
1 RRW boxing team; Lemgo, 1987 495

Badges of the Regiment
Badges and insignia, 24th Regiment of Foot 499
Badges and insignia, The Welch Regiment 501
Badges and insignia, 41st and 69th Regiments of Foot 503
Badges and insignia, The Monmouthshire Regiment 505

Colour Illustrations

Colour

Frontispiece
HRH the Prince of Wales, KG, KT, GCB, AK, QSO, ADC, Colonel in Chief
  (by Aubrey Davidson-Houston, 1988)

Between pages xxxii and 1
Sir Edward Dering, 3rd Baronet of Surrenden
The Coat of Arms of Sir Edward Dering
The Duke of Marlborough

Between pages 32 and 33
The Battle of Blenheim
Private of 41st (Invalids) Regiment, c. 1751
Regimental In-Pensioners, 1988

Between pages 64 and 65
Lieutenant General The Hon. Edward Cornwallis
The Death of Brigadier General Simon Fraser

Between pages 96 and 97
The Battle of the Saints, 1782
69th Foot, Cape St Vincent, 1797

Between pages 128 and 129
Regimental Colours of the 41st Regiment, 1747 and 1816
Colour of the 4th US Regiment
Russian Drums captured at Sebastopol

Between pages 160 and 161
Lieutenant Colonel Robert Brookes
The Battle of Chilianwala, 1849
The Battle of Goojerat, 1849

Between pages 192 and 193
Sergeant Ambrose Madden, VC
Friendly Power in Egypt

Colour Illustrations

Between pages 224 and 225
The Battle of Isandhlwana
The Defence of Rorke's Drift

Between pages 256 and 257
Section of Mounted Infantry
South Africa, 1900

Between pages 288 and 289
Gheluvelt, 1914
The 2nd Battle of Ypres, 8th May 1915

Between pages 320 and 321
D Day, 1944
The Memorial at s'Hertogenbosch

Between pages 352 and 353
Taffy VII in Berlin
The Amalgamation Parade, 11th June 1969

Between pages 384 and 385
The First Colours of The Royal Regiment of Wales
Freedom Scroll, City of Cardiff

Between pages 416 and 417
Infantry Equipment, 1988

Between pages 448 and 449
1 RRW Band and Drums on Parade, Lemgo
The Goat Major with Taffy III, 1987

Between pages 480 and 481
Regimental Silver
Regimental issue side drum
The Regimental Association Service Medal

List of Maps

Chapter 3
Marlborough's Campaigns 1704–1709 26
The March to the Danube 1704 27
The Schellenberg 1704 28
The Battle of Blenheim 1704 31
The Battle of Ramillies 1706 34
The Battle of Oudenarde 1708 36
The Battle of Malplaquet 1709 37

Chapter 4
Belleisle 1761 47
Warburg 1760 48
Canada 1776–81 – Burgoyne's Advance 50

Chapter 5
The Battle of The Saints 1782 55
India 1805 61

Chapter 6
The Peninsula War 1809–14 68
The Waterloo Campaign 1815 78
The Battle of Quatre Bras 1815 79
The Battle of Waterloo 1815 80

Chapter 7
North America 1812–14 91
Burma 1824–26 99

Maps

Chapter 8
The First Afghan War 1839–42 111
The Second Sikh War 1849 111
The Battle of Chilianwala 1849 119

Chapter 9
The Crimea 1854 133
The Battle of Inkerman 1854 135
The Andaman Islands 1867 143

Chapter 10
The Zulu War 1879 153
Isandhlwana 1879 158
Rorke's Drift 1879 164

Chapter 11
Egypt 1888–89 186

Chapter 12
S Africa 1899 192
Jacobsdal and Paardeberg 1900 195
The Orange Free State and SW Transvaal 1900 201

Chapter 13
The Great War – Europe 1914–18 220
Tsingtao 1914 224
The Great War – Middle East 230
The Gallipoli Campaign 1915/16 231

Chapter 15
Northern Norway 1940 286
Narvik 1940 291
Crete 1941 295
The Middle East 1941–42 298
Italy 1943–45 302
Burma 1944–45 307

Chapter 16
D Day 1944 323
NW Europe 1944–45 328

Chapter 17
Korea 1952 352
Malaya 1955–58 364
Cyprus 1957–58 375
Aden 1967 382

Chapter 18
N Ireland 1969–87 406

Introduction

It is a truism that the backbone of the British Army has always been the stolid, footslogging, pack-humping infantryman of the Line; the redcoat of Marlborough's day, the PBI of the Old Contemptibles. Not without good reason was the accolade 'Queen of the Battlefield' bestowed on the infantry. At Waterloo the élite of Napoleon's Army broke and were shattered on the staunch squares of British infantry. In the trenches of France and Flanders, in the Burmese jungles, among the mountains of Korea, it was the foot-soldier who bore the brunt of everything.

The sophisticated infantryman of the 1980s may no longer slog weary miles on his own feet, nor hump all his possessions on his back, but his essential rôle has changed little. Guns and aircraft may batter an enemy strongpoint, tanks may overrun or bypass it. The infantryman, dismounting from his APC, must then go in and finish the job. If armour cannot assault a position, the infantry must and will. They remain the essential combat arm. It was always the infantryman who dug in and doggedly held the threatened sector, who met his enemy face to face at 'the sharp end', fighting in the narrow streets, thick jungle, swamp, craggy mountains, terrain where only the soldier on his feet can go. And when not on night or sentry duty, the infantryman must bivvy as best he can, often in a waterlogged hole in the ground. No wonder he became 'the Poor Bloody Infantry'.

The mystique, or 'glamour', acquired by certain special forces, such as the Special Air Service and the Parachute Regiment, sometimes tends to overshadow the deeds of the conventional infantry of the Line. Yet few battles could have been won without them, and throughout their centuries of service the infantry regiments have acquired their own mystique, compounded of heroic devotion to duty, staunchness in the face of fearful odds, and that special 'tribal loyalty' or *esprit de corps* – terms which will appear many times in the following pages.

This then, is the story of an infantry Regiment which by the time these words appear in print will, under various titles, have served Kings, Queens and country for 300 years. It is really the story of four Regiments, for The Royal Regiment of Wales is an amalgam of three previous Regiments, The South Wales Borderers (or 24th

Regiment) and The Welch Regiment, itself the result of merger of the 41st and the 69th Foot. It is a fitting honour that since its creation in 1969, The Royal Regiment of Wales should have as its Colonel in Chief HRH the Prince of Wales, whose foreword and picture grace this work.

Any historian, if honest, must confess that he has filched much from others who have laboured before him in the same field. Between them, The South Wales Borderers and The Welch Regiment have amassed a large corpus of previous regimental histories, all of which have provided valuable grist to my mill, and which I am glad to acknowledge:

> *Historical Records of The 24th Regiment from its Formation in 1689.* Edited by Colonel George Paton, Colonel Farquhar Glennie, Colonel William Penn Symons, Lieutenant Colonel H. B. Moffat (London, 1892).
> *The South Wales Borderers, 24th Foot, 1689–1937.* By C. T. Atkinson (Cambridge, 1937).
> *The History of The South Wales Borderers 1914–1918.* By C. T. Atkinson (London, 1931).
> *History of The South Wales Borderers and the Monmouthshire Regiment 1937–1952.* By Lieutenant Colonel G. A. Brett and others (5 parts; Pontypool, 1953–6).
> *A History of the Services of the 41st (the Welch) Regiment (now 1st Battalion the Welch Regiment) from its Formation in 1719 to 1895.* By Lieutenant and Adjutant D. A. N. Lomax (Devonport, 1899).
> *A Narrative of Historical Events connected with the Sixty-Ninth Regiment.* By W. F. Butler (London, 1870).
> *The History of The Welch Regiment.* Part I, 1719–1914, by Major A. C. Whitehorne. Part II, 1914–1918, by Major General Sir Thomas O. Marden (Cardiff, 1932).
> *The History of the Welch Regiment 1919–1951.* Based on the original work of Captain J. de Courcy and amplified and enlarged by Major General C. E. N. Lomax (Cardiff, 1952).
> *A Short History of The Royal Regiment of Wales (24th/41st Foot).* Anon. (but compiled by Lieutenant Colonel John Margesson) (Halesowen, 1977).

The regimental historian must lean heavily on the resources of regimental headquarters and museums, and it is my very pleasant duty to record the immense debt I owe to Colonel N. O. Roberts, Regimental Secretary and his assistant, Major P. L. Cutler, MBE, at Cardiff, Major R. P. Smith, Assistant Regimental Secretary at Brecon (and Curator of The South Wales Borderers Museum), and Lieutenant Bryn Owen, RN (Retd), Curator of The Welch Regiment Museum. Despite the multifarious duties of their appointments, these officers have veritably been my pillars of strength over a period of nearly three years, responding promptly and effectively to my constant barrage of queries and providing much essential source material from Regimental archives. In addition, they relieved me of the chores of hunting down original drawings, paintings and other illustrative requisites for the plates in this book. For their unstinted co-operation my gratitude cannot adequately be expressed.

The true originator of this history was the Colonel of the Regiment, Major General L. A. H. Napier, CB, OBE, MC, DL. It was he who initiated the project and secured the funding. It was also he who throughout my labours has retained a close interest in their progress, commenting on the drafts and proffering valuable suggestions.

My later chapters, from World War II onwards, have benefited from the recollections of former officers of The South Wales Borderers, The Monmouthshire Regiment and The Welch Regiment, who are too numerous to name. But I thank them all for correcting errors and adding much-needed detail. And as always, I am grateful to the staff of the Powys County Library, especially Mr Roger Foulkes of the Llandrindod Wells Headquarters and Mr Christopher Price of Brecon. Research at the Public Record Office, resulting in the acquisition of valuable unpublished material, was undertaken by Mr Richard Wright of The Authors' Research Services, London. Finally, I pay tribute to my typist, Mrs Trevor Harris, of Clyro near Hay-on-Wye, whose customary expertise produces immaculate typescripts from chaotic manuscripts.

Note It must be clearly understood that where views are expressed on political matters, such as the Northern Ireland problem, these views are entirely the author's own and must not be ascribed to the present Regiment.

JMB

Sir Edward Dering, 3rd Baronet of Surrenden, Kent. He raised the 24th Regiment on 28th March 1689, and died at Dundalk, Ireland in September 1689.

The Coat of Arms of Sir Edward Dering, 3rd Baronet of Surrenden, Kent.

John Churchill, 1st Duke of Marlborough, Colonel of the 24th Regiment, 1702–4.
PHOTOGRAPHED BY JEREMY WHITAKER AND REPRODUCED BY KIND PERMISSION OF HIS GRACE THE DUKE OF MARLBOROUGH

CHAPTER ONE

Birth of a Regiment (1689)

To many infantry soldiers of today the name 'Brecon' means hard slogging over the rugged peaks of Pen-y-Fan and Corn Du, live-firing exercises and tactical schemes on the moorlands of the Sennybridge ranges, and much wrestling with theoretical problems. Since 1973 the NCOs' Tactical Wing of the School of Infantry has been located in a complex of barracks discreetly hidden away on the eastern outskirts of the town, and known as Dering Lines.

It is a fair surmise that of the thousands of platoon sergeants and corporals who have become familiar with Dering Lines, only a select few have any idea of the name's significance. The choice was, in fact, an appropriate one: it perpetuates the memory of Colonel Sir Edward Dering who in 1689 raised the 24th Regiment of Foot, senior component of the amalgam which became The Royal Regiment of Wales, a Regiment with which the town of Brecon has long been proud to be associated. In the squat Cathedral near the remains of the Norman Castle hang the tattered remnants of the Colour carried by the 24th at the Battle of Chilianwala in 1849, and the Wreath of Immortelles presented to the Regiment by Queen Victoria after its heroic actions at Isandhlwana and Rorke's Drift, where nine VCs were won. Here also are memorials to 6,819 officers and soldiers who fell in the two World Wars. The old 19th-century barracks, now housing Headquarters Wales, boast one of the Army's finest Regimental Museums, that of The South Wales Borderers, which title the 24th assumed in 1881 and bore until amalgamation with The Welch Regiment in 1969.

Sir Edward Dering came of an ancient Kentish family who had owned the manor of Surrenden, near Ashford, since mediaevel times, and had been granted a Baronetcy by Charles I in 1627. Edward (one of seventeen children) was born in 1655 and succeeded to the title as 3rd Baronet on the death of his father (also Edward) in 1684. Unhappily, little is known about Sir Edward, apart from the facts that, like his father and grandfather before him, he represented his county in Parliament, and had seen no military service before being commissioned Colonel, except possibly as an officer in the local Militia. Many landed gentlemen dallied with this mild form of part-time soldiering, if only to bolster their egos and their authority among the peasantry.

The Church at Pluckley where the Dering family tomb is situated.

However, it seems that Sir Edward had earned some notability (or notoriety), for Charles Dalton in his *English Army Lists and Commission Registers*[1] tells us that he was known as 'the Black Devil of Kent'. What sort of picture of our founding Colonel this sobriquet was intended to convey can only be left to the imagination, for no explanation is forthcoming.

In 1688 the despotic Catholic monarch, James II, was ousted by the Dutch Protestant, Prince William, in the 'Glorious Revolution'. Although the great majority of 'Dutch William''s subjects welcomed him as the deliverer from abhorred popery, the new King was not allowed to rest peacefully on his throne. His arch-enemy, Louis XIV, was threatening his native Netherlands; and in Scotland the Jacobites were fomenting opposition to the foreigner who had usurped their own Stuart sovereign. Then in March 1689 came intelligence that ex-King James had landed at Kinsale, and with the ready connivance of cousin Louis was busy recruiting the Irish Catholics in a bid to regain power.

In the face of these threats even the anti-military lobby in Parliament conceded that the defence forces must be augmented, and orders went forth for the raising of twenty-five new regiments of Foot, besides several of Horse. Of the twenty-five, only six were to survive subsequent disbandment, and one of these was ranked as the 24th

Birth of a Regiment 1689

Regiment of Foot.[2] By an odd coincidence, its immediate senior, the 23rd Foot, was to become The Royal Welch Fusiliers, now the only sister-Welsh Line Regiment to The Royal Regiment of Wales.

Accordingly, on 8th March, 1689, Sir Edward Dering was commissioned Colonel and ordered to raise 'by beat of drume or otherwise as may be fitte' a regiment of Foot, to consist of thirteen companies, each of three sergeants, three corporals, two drummers and sixty 'private men'. Besides the Colonel, the officer establishment was to be one Lieutenant Colonel (as Second-in-Command), one Major, nine Captains, nine Lieutenants and two Ensigns. One chaplain and one 'chirurgeon' were also allowed, but although enjoying officer status, these held no military rank.

The business of recruiting and equipping the Regiment was arranged by an Agent appointed by the Colonel. In the 24th Regiment's archives at Brecon is a manuscript copy of the original Articles of Agreement 'Between Sir Edward Deering of Surrenden in the County of Kent, Bart, Colonel of our here mentioned Regiment of Foot' and 'Richard Harnage of the Parish of St. Pauls Country Garden in the County of Middx'. The said Richard Harnage contracted to:

> ... furnish and provide and to equip eight hundred private sentinells or souldyers of or belonging, or to be belonging, to the said Regiment, therefore shall sell parcels of goods and clothing and accoutrements hereafter mentioned, and that is to say, eight hundred hatts; eight hundred pairs of stockings; eight hundred pairs of shoes; sixteen hundred shirts; sixteen hundred cravets; eight hundred swords; eight hundred belts ...

The cost of the clothing and accoutrements amounted to £1,520, which sum Sir Edward Dering was to pay Richard Harnage on or before 20th May 1692. By that date, however, Sir Edward was dead and, as will be seen later, his unfortunate Agent may not have been fully reimbursed.

To us it seems odd that a young civilian with no military training or experience (other than perhaps some very 'irregular' diversion with the Militia) should be instantly appointed to raise and command a regular regiment of some 900 all ranks for active service. But in the 17th century (and later) there was nothing out of the way in this practice. The fact is that the capacity of a Colonel's purse, and his social standing, were of equal importance to any military prowess or qualifications he might possess. Although Government funds were allotted for the recruiting, clothing and quartering of a regiment, these were seldom adequate (especially if the Colonel had extravagant tastes in dress), and as just noted, the Commanding Officer would need to dip into his own pocket for the honour of serving his King and country. And, of course, all officers had to pay not only for their commissions, but also for their own uniforms, accoutrements, and even arms (and chargers, where authorised). That many Colonels dipped into their soldiers' pockets by filching their pay with unauthorised 'stoppages' shows that not all were imbued with the true spirit of an officer and a gentleman.

Sir Edward's commission is dated 8th March 1689, but the Regiment has always celebrated the 28th as its birthday, and Atkinson[3] says this was probably the date when officers and men were first mustered. The original Muster Roll cannot be traced, but if the latter date is correct, it betokens some very energetic effort by Dering (or his Agent) to recruit, kit out, arm and parade nearly 900 men within less than three weeks. In these tasks he was assisted by his younger brother, Daniel, who was commissioned Lieutenant Colonel in the Regiment. Unlike Sir Edward, Daniel was already an experienced officer, both naval and military. In 1679 he was a Lieutenant commanding a frigate in the Mediterranean; two years later we find him as Captain of the Grenadier company in one of the Foot regiments on the Irish Establishment. With the purge of Protestant officers and soldiers perpetrated in Ireland by James II's toady, the Earl of Tyrconnel, Daniel fled to England, where his elder brother was only too pleased to have him as Second-in-Command. Not only did he contribute some military expertise, but he brought with him several officers who had served with him in Ireland, including one Alexander Ramsay, who was appointed Major. It is probable that Daniel brought some 'purged' Irish soldiers as well.

At this point the reader must be reminded that the Colonelcy of a regiment then bore little resemblance to the honorary post of today, where the incumbent is more often than not a retired general officer. Until the mid-18th century, the Colonel was the *de facto* Commanding Officer, with all the training and administrative responsibilities of that appointment, including active command in the field. Moreover, the 17th-century Colonel enjoyed (and, alas, often abused) far greater power and authority than the modern Commanding Officer. The expenditure of Government funds for the clothing, quartering and pay of his unit was left entirely in his hands, as was the disciplining and punishment of his officers and men. Although he was, of course, officially bound by the new Mutiny Act and the Articles of War,[4] and was answerable to the Commander-in-Chief and through him to the sovereign, in practice he was left very much to his own devices in the 'management' of his command.

Very shortly after mustering, the new 24th Regiment was on the march from Kent to the Midlands where, as was the practice, the companies were widely scattered, from Lichfield and Rugeley to Warwick and Coventry. There were then no barracks in the kingdom, other than those of such royal fortresses as Dover, the Tower of London and Edinburgh, and the men were billeted in 'Inns, Livery Stables, Ale-houses, Victualling-houses . . .' as laid down in the Mutiny Act. The dispersal of troops throughout the country was a necessary provision for the maintenance of law and order, for there was no constitutional police force and soldiers had always to hold themselves in readiness for that distasteful duty 'in aid of the Civil Power'. This could mean anything from quelling pub brawls and hustings fracas to opening fire on riotous assemblies. Such duties did nothing to endear the soldier to the civilian populace who, since the days of Cromwell's military dictatorship, had associated him with iron-fisted oppression. For almost 200 years the Army's public relations were to suffer.

And now what of the men of Colonel Dering's Regiment of Foot? What of the character of this prototype of The Royal Regiment of Wales? Unhappily, we have

Colonel Daniel Dering. He took over command of the 24th Regiment in September 1689 when his brother died, and he himself died in Ireland in 1691.

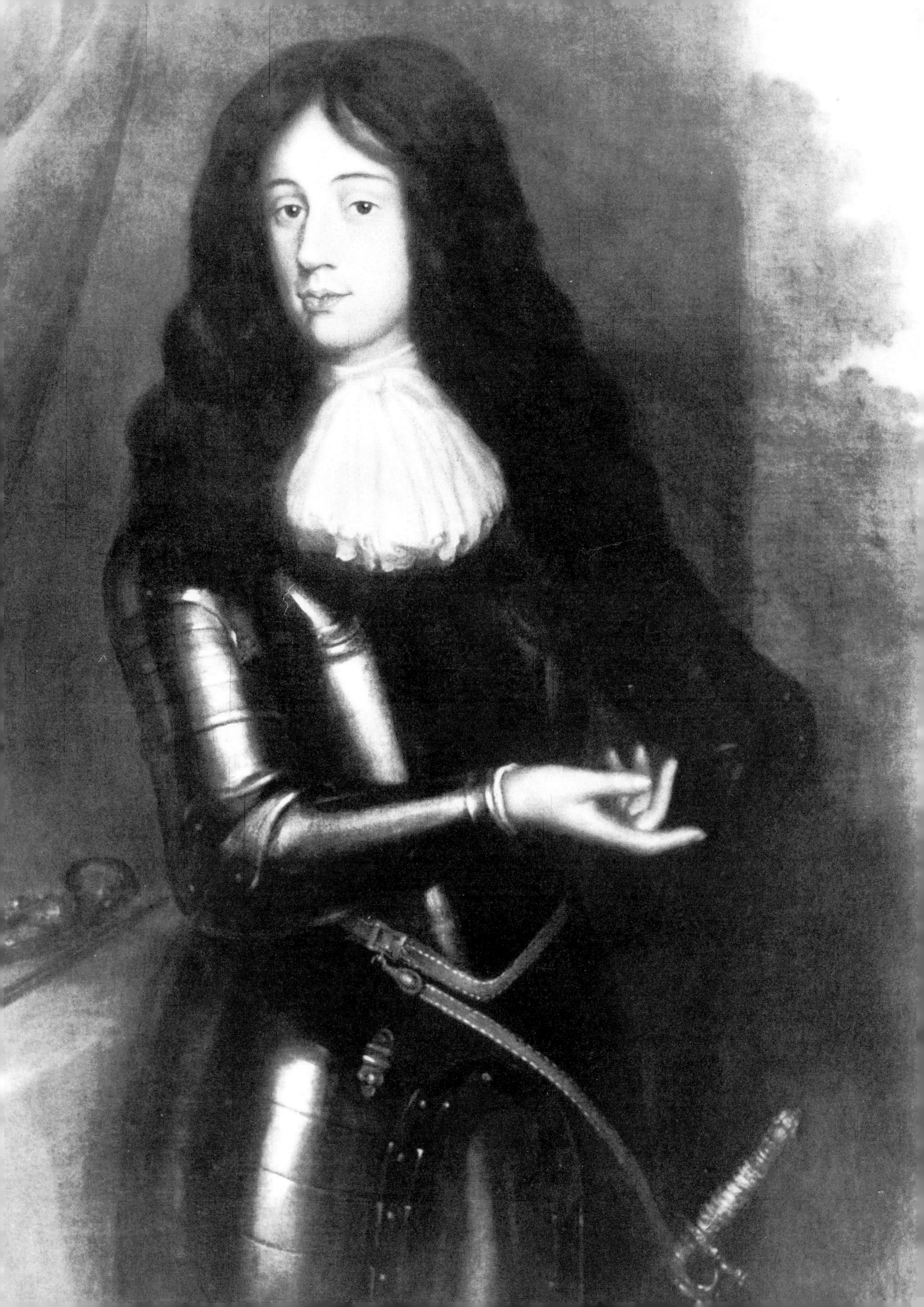

nothing to go on: no glimpses from diaries or memoirs, not even a contemporary Muster Roll. We can only conjecture. It seems logical to assume that the rank-and-file were preponderantly 'Kentish men' or 'Men of Kent',[5] husbandmen, as the term was, which embraced various classes from yeomen and tenant farmers down to humble, labouring peasants. 'Our armies have been raised by Gentlemen of Figure and Estate among their Tenants, among their Husbandmen and the farmers' sons, the Cottagers and the poor Plebi of the Country.' Thus wrote Daniel Defoe in 1698.[6] Doubtless many of Dering's men came from his own estates, while there was probably a leavening of townsmen from Maidstone, Ashford and other centres, besides the Irish 'refugees' brought over by Daniel Dering. Perhaps some few recruits would have drifted south from London, but the capital was the preserve of the Guards and of the Royal Regiment of Fusiliers, and poaching was not encouraged. Of one fact we can be reasonably certain: the Regiment which was to become essentially Welsh, and proud of it, could not have paraded a single Welshman on its first muster – or for generations afterwards.

Very few, if any, of the 'Private Men' could read or write, and most of them would remain illiterate throughout their service; not until the 19th century was any serious thought given to education of the rank-and-file. While platoon sergeants and some senior corporals might laboriously inscribe nominal rolls and copy out battalion or company orders, all that was demanded of the humbler ranks was that they should understand verbal orders and drill commands and act upon them automatically. The soldier was not expected to think for himself. To encourage him to do so by cramming his mind with book-learning was not only a waste of time, but might jeopardise good order and military discipline. The educated soldier was a potential discontent. At least, such was the attitude of authority then.

One of the unique, abiding characteristics of the British soldier has been his loyalty, a loyalty not so much to his country, or to the sovereign to whom he has sworn allegiance, but more immediately to his regiment – *The* regiment. No matter how far it is down the Army List, his regiment is peerless, superior to all the other 'mobs'; he is as fiercely jealous of its achievements in battle as he is of its idiosyncrasies of customs and traditions, and even of the minutiae of its dress. The regiment is his family; no soldier was worth his cap badge who was not ready to black the eye of a 'foreigner' who dared to utter insulting gibes in a garrison canteen.

But this 'tribal loyalty' or *esprit de corps* is a plant that needs cultivating; traditions, like Battle Honours, are acquired only with years of service. It would be naïve to claim that the men who enlisted in Dering's Regiment were imbued with any such spirit: like those of the other newly-raised units, they were merely a co-opted motley of civilian labourers and rustics who had donned uniform and exchanged the tools of their trades for musket and pike. It was much later that a man might boast of his Regiment's heroics under 'Corporal John' at Blenheim or elsewhere.

Even after a regiment had earned renown and distinctions, there was another factor which must have militated against a true 'family' spirit, and that was the curiously transient practice of designating all units by their Colonel's name. Whenever there was a change of Colonel, which, of course, could be quite frequent, the regiment was obliged to adopt a new title, new insignia, very often new customs, and even variations in dress. Thus the recruit who joined Colonel Dering's Regiment in 1689 would find himself in Venner's by 1691; four years later he would be in the Marquis de Puisar's; another six years and he would owe allegiance to Colonel Seymour. If he survived twenty years' service he would see eight changes of title and badges. Our sister-Welsh Regiment, the 23rd, underwent five such changes in the first four years of its existence. Whether all this impermanency could foster a genuine sense of 'belonging' is doubtful.

If we have only vague notions about the original soldiers of our Regiment, at least we know roughly what they looked like on parade. All ranks wore a long cloth coat reaching to the knees and buttoned up to the neck, round which was tied a cravat of white lace for officers, or a simple neck-cloth for other ranks. The coat was lined with baize (a coarse woollen material) and was reasonably weatherproof, though heavy. For fatigues and drill it could be doffed to reveal a stout waistcoat of similar material. Nether limbs were clothed with kersey knee-breeches, woollen hose and square-toed shoes (termed 'straights'), which were interchangeable between feet. Oddly enough, not until the mid-18th century was it conceded that the marching infantryman needed stouter footwear; then ankle boots were substituted. The common headgear for musketeers and pikemen was a wide-brimmed hat of black beaver or felt. At first it was turned up, or 'cocked', on one or both sides; but by Marlborough's time it had become cocked on all three sides, to give us the familiar tricorn or cocked hat which can still be seen adorning the heads of the Chelsea Pensioners on their ceremonial parades.

Each company consisted of two-thirds musketeers and one-third pikemen. The latter, wielding 16-ft pikes, were picked from the tallest and strongest men, their task being to protect the musketeers from attack while they went through their complex drill of loading and 'giving fire'. By 1689 the prestige of the pikemen was being usurped by the grenadiers (usually the 13th Company) who became the élite of the battalion – the tallest and smartest, and examples to the rest. The grenadier was armed with a short musket, bayonet, sword, hatchet, and three hand-grenades carried in a leather pouch. In contemporary artwork he is easily distinguished by his tall mitre cap which replaced the broad-brimmed felt hat. The latter would obviously have hindered his motions in slinging his musket and hurling his grenades.

For centuries the term 'redcoat' has denoted the stolid British infantryman. But when Colonel Dering raised his Regiment there was no regulation colour for uniforms, just as there were no 'sealed patterns'. It is true that many regiments, including the prestigious Horse, were already clothed in red (or scarlet, or crimson) this being traditionally regarded as the martial hue. However, we know that several newly-raised units wore blue coats, and according to the authoritative Carman,[7] Dering's was one of them (together with Lord Herbert's – the 23rd). It is said that this choice was out of deference to King William, all of whose Dutch regiments were dressed in blue exclusively. Coat cuffs were turned up, and when on the march skirts were buttoned back, thus exposing the lining, or what (rather illogically) became termed the 'facings'. The colour of these facings was left to the whim of the Colonels, who usually adopted that of their own livery, but we do not know Dering's preference. Although the Regiment had certainly adopted its distinctive 'willow-green' facings by 1742, exactly when these came into wear cannot be determined. 'Willow-green' eventually became 'grass-green', but exactly when it is not possible to say.

Officers' dress was similar to the mens', the only distinctions being a profusion of gold or silver lace on the coat, a silk sash or 'scarf' worn round the waist, and, of course, better quality material. In addition, all officers wore a small crescent-shaped gorget-plate of metal suspended from the neck and covering the top of the chest. This relic of plate armour served no practical purpose, but merely indicated commissioned rank. When the gorget was finally abolished in the 1830s, the coloured patch of cloth underneath it was retained and eventually emerged as the red tabs on the collar, and later the lapels, of the staff officer.

The only fire-power of the battalion was, of course, the musket. When first raised, Dering's men, and the rest of the Foot, carried the primitive matchlock, a cumbersome weapon, 5 ft 2 in. long and weighing nearly 13 lb. As its name implies, it was fired by igniting the charge with a slow-burning 'match', a length of treated hemp, which the musketeer carried coiled round his waist or stowed in his hat. About one round a minute was the maximum rate of fire. By 1690 the improved flintlock had been issued to the Guards and Fusiliers, but it was not until after King William's Irish campaign that all the Foot were so armed. Even the flintlock weighed 12 lb., while the fully-trained soldier could not achieve more than two rounds a minute. There was a lengthy, rigid drill for loading and firing this weaponry, and lest it be thought that the enemy obligingly stood easy while the several 'motions' were performed, firing was carried out by successive ranks: when the front rank had delivered their volley they filed to the rear to reload, while the second 'gave fire'. And the enemy did likewise. Use of cover was unheard of. There was only one firing position, and that was bravely standing erect, to give as good as was received. Accurate marksmanship was totally unnecessary: with opposing ranks seldom more than 100 yards apart, often closer, a regular succession of volleys into the mass was all that could be desired.

Besides their muskets, all the soldiers carried both bayonet and sword. Until about 1700 the former was the 'plug' type, fitting into the muzzle of the musket, so that the weapon could not be fired with fixed bayonet, but after that date the socket or 'ring' bayonet was introduced, obviating such a drawback. Although the sword remained part of the private soldier's armoury until 1768, there is little evidence that he was drilled in its use as an offensive weapon. More probably it was regarded as a last resort if he were bereft of his musket and bayonet in a hand-to-hand encounter. The pikemen's 16 ft weapons would have been little more than a hindrance in close-quarter fighting, but firmly planted at an angle in the ground they constituted a very effective form of *chevaux de frise* when cavalry (or charging infantry) threatened.

As we have seen, officers were distinguished by their gorgets and finery, but there was also a nice distinction in their personal weapons. Field officers, when not mounted,[8] carried a 'half-pike', that is, one 9 ft long; Captains had an 8-ft pike or spontoon; Lieutenants and Ensigns had a similar pike but with a plainer head. The only officers to carry firearms were those of the Grenadier company, who had a short, light musket, but no pike.

Since 1747, infantry regiments have been allowed only two Colours per battalion, the King's (or Queen's) and the Regimental, but on Dering's early parades a multitude of 'flags' would have fluttered above the ranks. In those days a regiment was permitted to carry one Colour for the Colonel, one for the Lieutenant Colonel, one for the Major, and one for each of the thirteen company commanders. All were of different hues, all bore varied devices. In naval parlance, the regiment on parade with all its Colours could veritably be described as 'dressed overall'. Naturally, the Colonel's Colour was accorded supreme honour; its design was left to him, and he usually took the liberty of incorporating in it his family crest and the colour of his livery.

There is no record of what device Sir Edward displayed: possibly it was his own crest: a black horse, *passant*, upon a coronet. Samuel Milne's work, *The Standards and Colours of the Army*,[9] is usually held to be definitive, but although he details, and illustrates, the standards of every cavalry regiment and the Colours of most of the infantry, the 24th is one of the few omissions. The only reference in the whole work (covering the period 1661–1881) is a passing mention of the jettisoning overboard of the 1st Battalion's Colours to avoid capture when their transports were attacked by the French off Mauritius, in 1810. The same author contributed an appendix on Colours to the *Historical Records of the 24th Regiment* by Colonel Paton *et al.* (1892), but could find little to add, except to conjecture that the earliest Colonel's Colour '*may* have been of green silk, with the crest of some device from the coat of arms of Sir Edward Dering (its first Colonel) in the centre'. It would be satisfying to claim that the Regiment's traditional green facings originated with their first Colonel, but even Milne could offer nothing but supposition.

In addition to adding their 'colourful' display on parade, the Colours served strictly practical purposes: not only were they carried in battle to identify regimental and company Headquarters and to serve as rallying posts, but in quarters they were hung outside the field officers' and company commanders' billets so that orderlies and others might know where to report. Being essentially utilitarian 'accoutrements' (as they were termed), they were not then accorded the same veneration and honours as in later years.

Rates of pay for the Army had been established by a Royal Warrant of James II in 1685, and with successive parsimonious Governments, these continued unchanged until George III made some meagre increases in 1783. In the early days of Dering's Regiment, the Colonel himself received 12s. per day as Colonel, plus a sinecure of 8s. as 'captain' of his company, which was actually commanded by a 'Captain Lieutenant'; the Lieutenant Colonel got 7s. rank pay plus 8s. for his company; the Major had 5s. plus 8s. Captains, Lieutenants and Ensigns received flat rates of 8s., 4s. and 3s. respectively. A sergeant got 1s. 6d. (there were then no Warrant Officers), a corporal 1s. and the humble private 8d.

These rates may seem niggardly pittances, but as always when dealing with monetary matters, we must remember relative values then and now. In theory, the soldier on 8d. a day, or 4s. 8d. a week, was almost affluent compared with his civilian counterpart of the labouring classes. Beveridge states that the average earnings of a contemporary farm labourer were not more than about 3s. 6d. *per week* – out of which he had to find all his living expenses, while, unlike the soldier, he enjoyed no job security.[10] On paper the pay rates now seem quite generous. But the recruit was seldom told that he would actually see only a minimal fraction of his entitlement. Out of the total pay the swingeing stoppage of 6d. a day was docked as 'subsistence money' to pay for his rations and lodging; from the balance, termed 'gross off-reckonings', there was a deduction of one day's pay a year for the Chelsea Royal Hospital, and a 5% stoppage for the pocket of that Whitehall functionary, the Paymaster-General himself. What remained was styled 'nett off-reckonings' and a proportion of this went to the Colonel for the clothing of the regiment. Thus the private soldier was lucky if he were left with more than a penny or two per week as spending money. Whether the Colonel strictly observed the Pay Regulations was a matter for his own conscience, and as already noted, not all Colonels were conscientious. It was tacitly accepted that the 'proprietor' of a regiment should make a profit out of the business of running that regiment, and if this involved cheating his soldiers (and the Government), blind eyes were turned.

As for the officers themselves, their own pay was not inviolate either. Besides regulation deductions for the Royal Hospital, the Paymaster-General, the Commissary General of Musters, auditors and others, there were fees to be paid to the Exchequer, and even fees for the issue of their own pay warrants. Apart from the 'subsistence money', supposed to be paid in advance, anything left over was paid yearly in arrears, often very much in arrears.

In addition to all this, the officer had to pay for his commission itself. Charles II had attempted to abolish the purchase system, but without success, and the contentious practice flourished for another 200 years. We may read that Sir Edward Dering was 'granted' his Colonelcy. In fact, he had to put down £6,000 for the privilege of serving his King and country (and of losing his life). Of course, prices varied according to rank: a humble Ensign paid £200; a Captain and company commander, £1,000; a Major, £1,800; and a Lieutenant Colonel, £2,400. Obviously, the term 'officer and gentleman' implied the possession of considerable private means as well as good breeding. Not only was the initial commission purchased, but so were the steps up the promotion ladder. We often come across subalterns with perhaps fifteen or more years' service, simply because they could not afford to buy a Captaincy. The nominal rolls of the 24th provide several examples, such as John Gardiner, who bought his Ensigncy in 1693 and retired as Lieutenant in 1722. Henry Berkeley, Ensign in 1792, had only reached Captain when he sold out thirty-eight years later.[11]

The only way by which promotion might be gained without purchase was by waiting for dead men's shoes: if an officer were killed in action, or died of wounds, the next senior might step into the vacancy (provided the Colonel approved). Very rarely, however, a step up might be granted free in recognition of some signal act of gallantry in the field, but such cases had to be submitted to the King for his personal approval.

The pros and cons of a system whereby a young man with few qualifications other than money could be granted a position of trust and responsibility in the Army were periodically debated in the House and elsewhere for two centuries. But unjust or not, the purchase system produced some of the British Army's greatest leaders, Marlborough, Wellington and Moore among them, not to mention five of the present Regiment's VC heroes. In addition to the authority and prestige which it brought, a commission was overtly regarded as an investment. Although regulation prices were laid down from time to time, these were ignored, and when an officer sold his commission he would do so at a profit – usually selling to the highest bidder. The Government was quite happy to condone such trafficking, for it saved the Treasury the expense of providing officers' pensions. When a man finally sold out, the sum realised was regarded as an adequate substitute.

Included among the officers of Dering's Regiment were the chaplain and the doctor, but these were officers by courtesy only. They held no military rank, and were engaged by the Colonel in much the same way as sutlers and contractors. While the padre might be adequately qualified to conduct the regular services of worship enjoined by authority, and to deliver periodic homilies to the paraded soldiery on the evils of the flesh, the devil and drink, the doctor's skills were limited. The contemporary state of his art being what it was, he was capable of little more than sawing off limbs, applying home-made salves and ointments, and, of course, performing that clinical panacea, blood-letting. If the sick or wounded soldier could not be cured by such therapy, he died.

There has always been a caste system in the British Army, with its class distinctions between officers and men forming a barrier that until modern times was insurmountable. In the 17th century, and for long afterwards, this distinction was rigid indeed. As we have seen, the officers came exclusively from the moneyed land-owning classes, the county families, or the aristocracy itself; most, if not all, had enjoyed the formal classical education incumbent on a gentleman, while some – such as Edward Dering – had held positions of authority and responsibility in civilian life. The men, on the other hand, were just as exclusively from the lowest orders, which in those days meant that they were uneducated, if not totally illiterate, rude in their habits and foul mouthed (barrackroom language has venerable origins). Even 200 years later the poet could describe the private soldier as 'Poor, reckless, rude, low-born, untaught . . .'.[12] To put it bluntly, most of the 17th-century soldiers were what we might now regard as uncouth oafs. Obviously, there was no common meeting-ground between the officer and his men, apart from the fact that both had undertaken to serve the King as soldiers.

Notes

[1] Six volumes, 1892–1904 (reprinted 1960).

[2] Numbers were allotted merely to denote order of precedence, or seniority, and at that date were in no sense regarded as titles.

[3] *The South Wales Borderers 24th Foot 1689–1937.*

[4] Articles of War had been in force since mediaeval times, but, as the title implies, were applicable only in time of war. As a result of the mutiny of Colonel Dumbarton's Regiment (1st Foot) in March 1689, Parliament passed a bill governing the conduct and discipline of the Army in peacetime, and on 3rd April 1689 the first Mutiny Act became law. This was an historic event, for it was the first time that Parliament formally recognised the existence of a standing army in time of peace.

[5] Traditionally, 'Kentish men' were those born west of the Medway, and 'Men of Kent' those born east of that river.

[6] Defoe, Daniel. *An Argument for a Standing Army* (1698).

[7] Carman, W. Y. *British Military Uniforms . . . Henry VII to the Present Day* (1957).

[8] All infantry field officers (and Adjutants) were entitled to chargers until the 1930s.

[9] Only 200 copies were printed, in 1893, and this authority is now exceedingly scarce.

[10] Beveridge, Sir William: *Prices and Wages in England from the Twelfth to the Nineteenth Century.*

[11] These and others are to be found in the Roll of Officers reproduced in Atkinson's history, Appendix I.

[12] Doyle, Sir Francis. *The Private of The Buffs.*

CHAPTER TWO

Prentice Years (1689–1701)

Less than five months after the first muster parade, Colonel Dering's Regiment found itself on active service. In August 1689 King William despatched an expeditionary force of 15,000 all arms to deal with the menace of his father-in-law, ex-King James, whose Catholic rebels had overrun virtually the whole of Ireland. Commanded by the veteran Huguenot refugee, the Duke of Schomberg (in his 74th year), King William's force included all the newly-raised Foot, among which, besides Dering's, was Lord Herbert's Regiment. So the two that were later to emerge as sister-Welsh regiments endured their baptism of fire together.

Unless hunting elusive forebears, readers of regimental histories are apt to be wearied by recurring nominal rolls of long-forgotten officers,[1] but an exception is warranted at the present juncture. Not only was the Irish campaign the first major operation in the history of the British Army, but it saw the ancestors of The Royal Regiment of Wales confronting an enemy for the first time. The names of at least some of those ancestors are worthy of recording. The following notes are taken from Charles Dalton's *English Army Lists and Commission Registers* and refer to the roll on p. 14.

It will be seen that the Regiment was still short of establishment by two Lieutenants and ten Ensigns. If the Colonel's experience of soldiering was minimal, he enjoyed a welcome leavening of officers who had previously seen service in Ireland before the Tyrconnel purge. In addition to his brother, Daniel, already noted in Chapter I, eight of the company commanders had held previous commissions, as had Captain Lieutenant Wray. Of the soldiers we know nothing, except that, as earlier remembered, some of them were undoubtedly brought over from Ireland with the above 'Irish' officers to re-enlist in the new Regiment.

On 13th August the Regiment landed at Bangor on Belfast Lough. There was no opposition, for the Jacobites had prudently withdrawn, leaving a strong garrison in Carrickfergus near the mouth of the lough. Schomberg immediately laid siege, and while we know that Dering's was one of the twelve Foot regiments engaged in the week-long operation, no details are forthcoming, not even of casualties. This is a pity; for although Carrickfergus would hardly warrant a Battle Honour, it goes on record as

Colonel Sir Edward Dering's Regiment of Foot (24th)
(c. August 1689)

Captains	*Lieutenants*	*Ensigns*
Sir Edward Dering (Colonel Commanding)	**Christopher Wray** (Capt.- Lieutenant Commanding the Colonel's Company)	**William Kingsley**
Daniel Dering (Lieut. Colonel 2nd-in-Command)		**Matthew Barrow**
Alexander Ramsay (Major)	**Edward Fitz-Simmons**	**Herbert Humphreys**
Archibald Clinkard (Capt. Grenadier Coy.)	**John Clark**	
William Delaune (Capt. Coy. Commander)	**Edward Shirley**	
Patrick Meade (Capt. Coy. Commander)	**Philip Griffen**	
Charles Alcock (Capt. Coy. Commander)	**Benjamin Tichborne**	
Finch Humphrey (Capt. Coy. Commander)	**Robert Menzies**	
Robert Napper (Capt. Coy. Commander)	**Edmund Harris**	
George Twistleton (Capt. Coy. Commander)	**Daniel Bright**	
Richard Slaper (Capt. Coy. Commander)	**George Crofts**	
Adam Purdon (Capt. Coy. Commander)	**Francis Jeffreys**	
Thomas Oldfield (Capt. Coy. Commander)		

Adjutant Lieut. **Benjamin Tichborne**
Quartermaster Lieut. **Philip Griffen**
Chaplain **William Jephson**
Surgeon **Gerald Lisle**

the Regiment's first action. The sad fact is, neither past nor present historians have been able to unearth anything worthwhile about the services of Dering's Regiment in William's Irish campaign. The well-known contemporary sources, such as George Story's *Impartial History of the Wars in Ireland* (1693) and Schomberg's own despatches and letters preserved in the Public Record Office, reveal little but bald statements about movements, parade states and so forth, interspersed with some not very flattering comments on the officers.

In September Schomberg advanced his base to Dundalk, and it was here that his troubles began – though not through enemy action. First, it had become painfully obvious that the English regiments were ill-trained, ill-disciplined and ill-led. In one of his despatches he complained that 'scarce twenty men in a company' could handle their muskets properly, while they were woefully ignorant of drill movements. Then sickness struck, aggravated by logistical bungling. The camp was badly sited in low-lying, boggy ground; rain fell in torrents; the men had no tents and no provisions. Bread and meat lay in plenty at the Belfast base; and there they rotted, for the Commissariat had not bestirred itself to provide any means of transport. Schomberg ordered makeshift huts to be erected, and though his seasoned Dutch and Huguenot troops complied, the raw English soldiers were either too inexperienced or too idle to exert themselves, and they lay exposed to the elements. Shamefully, their officers did little or nothing to ameliorate such privations, preferring to look after their own welfare. In a letter to the King, Schomberg averred that 'if all were cashiered that deserve it, few would remain . . . If the leave asked for by all the officers was granted, the greater part of the army would be without officers. Sickness is only feigned by them: they are only tired of being here.' More shocking strictures came in a confidential report on all regiments compiled by Schomberg's Quartermaster General in December. For example: 'Colonel ill, and as incapable as are almost all the other officers, who are usually absent and are so greedy of money that the soldiers can scarce get paid . . .'; 'officers . . . are the most negligent that can be imagined', and the Commanding Officer was often the only one present.

By comparison the report on Dering's Regiment was mild: 'The regiment has fine men and fairly clothed: but except the Major [Ramsay] the rest of the Officers *n'est pas grand chose*, and know nothing of their Companies . . .'.

By early November 1689, when the Army moved back to winter quarters around Belfast, many of the English regiments had been decimated by dysentery, influenza or sheer debility. In two months Schomberg had lost 6,400 men out of the 14,000 at Dundalk, while scores of survivors were still ineffective through sickness.

It seems that Dering's 'fine men' had endured better than most, for a return of 28th October, just before leaving Dundalk, shows that only 1 officer and 49 soldiers had died, while 6 officers and 183 soldiers were on the sick list, leaving 31 officers and 503 soldiers present and effective. This compares very favourably with the other English regiments, some of which could not parade more than 200 fit men. If we are to believe that the officers were no more conscientious than the rest, their men must have been able to fend for themselves.

Fate decreed that the Regiment's first recorded casualty should be the founding Colonel himself. George Story's *Impartial History* states that Sir Edward Dering died of a fever (probably dysentery) at Dundalk on 27th September (1689) '. . . much lamented by all who knew him'. He was in his 34th year, and was buried in Dundalk churchyard. The Colonelcy was now assumed by the Second-in-Command, brother Daniel, though when (or, indeed, if) he actually took command is problematical. Daniel in fact seems to have been curiously undecided about which service claimed his prior duties, the Army or the Navy; for although he was certainly appointed Lieutenant Colonel in the Regiment on its raising, the confidential report quoted above reveals that as late as December he was 'always absent (being Captain of a vessel)'. Possibly the *de facto* command was assumed by the new Lieutenant Colonel, one Samuel Venner, for whom no previous commission is traceable. Dalton conjectures that he had probably seen service with William's Dutch forces. We shall hear more of him.

After the customary winter recess, King William, with reinforcements, arrived in Ireland in June 1690 and took over supreme command from the aged Schomberg. In July he soundly trounced James's forces at the Battle of the Boyne, James himself fled back to cousin Louis at Versailles, and apart from mopping-up operations the Irish campaign was over. Daniel Dering's Regiment played no part in the Boyne victory, and contemporary sources reveal little enough of its doings during the rest of the campaign. However, Story and Dalton record the bald fact that Daniel died in June 1691, and so after only twenty months the Regiment lost its second Colonel. Where or how he died is not revealed, whether on board his ship or with his 'land' command, nor do we know where he was buried. The Dering family had now lost three brothers in the King's service. The third was John, who was commissioned Cornet in Princess Anne of Denmark's Regiment of Horse in 1685, and who, according to Story, died as Captain 'at Tanderogee' (Tandragee, Armagh) in 1689. He was probably a victim of the sickness epidemic.

On Daniel Dering's death, Lieutenant Colonel Samuel Venner was promoted Colonel, and took command. This was in June 1691, and as Venner's Regiment the 24th were actively engaged in hunting down the marauding gangs of guerrillas, or 'rapparees', and in the siege of the Jacobites' last stronghold of Limerick, which capitulated on 28th September. Having decisively defeated his father-in-law, and, as the English people fondly imagined, secured permanent peace and law and order in Ireland, King William was now free to confront his arch-enemy, *Le Roi Soleil*, on the Continent. Thus all but the necessary garrison troops were withdrawn from Ireland, to prepare for a war with France that was to see generations of British soldiers earning renown, and death, in the cockpit of Europe over more than one hundred years.

Venner's Regiment returned to England in December 1691, but it was not until the following July that their services were called upon. While the main operations went ahead in Flanders, it was resolved to mount a diversionary raid or 'descent' on the enemy coast at St Malo, and on 26th July 14,000 troops, including Venner's Regiment, were embarked at Portsmouth to join the naval force. However, the upshot of this expedition was not so much a clash with the enemy as one between naval and military commanders. The former declared that they could not hazard their ships within range of the St Malo guns unless the defences had first been 'softened up' by a land attack. The military officers were equally adamant that it would be madness to attempt a landing unsupported by the naval armament. An alternative proposal to attack Brest or Rochefort was then debated, but this was vetoed since it was considered that 'the summer was too far spent' for such an enterprise. And so the whole force returned ignominiously whence it had come, 'to the astonishment and disgust of the whole nation', wrote Lord Macaulay.

Just a month later, however, the Regiment made their first landing on Continental shores when (together with Sir John Morgan's 23rd Regiment) they were detailed to join a force of twenty-five battalions tasked to seize Dunkirk. Disembarking at Ostend on 27th August, the force advanced unopposed to Dixmude, which they found evacuated. The troops were then employed in repairing the defences until the end of September, when '... in view of the lateness of the season it was resolved that an attack on Dunkirk would not be propitious' (Macaulay). And so, without firing a shot, the task force returned to England and Venner's spent an unprofitable winter in billets at Portsmouth.

By now morale must have been at a low ebb. The war in Flanders had been raging for two years, with the young regiments of the Army displaying at Steinkirk and elsewhere the stolid valour which was to be the hallmark of the British redcoat. All this had happened while Venner's men had not even confronted the enemy, but had been subjected to humiliation in two abortive operations that added nothing to their name or their spirit. And it seems that the Colonel himself did little to raise the tone. In March

1692 he was court-martialled on a charge of defrauding the Agent. In defence he claimed that the Government itself was guilty of a similar offence: there was, he said, an accumulated sum of £6,000 owing for arrears of pay. This was probably true, for the Paymaster-General and his minions were notoriously lax in their duties. But the Colonel's conduct was evidently in dispute within the Regiment: the contemporary chronicler, Narcissus Luttrell, records that in March three of Venner's officers who supported him actually fought duels with three others opposed to him. Evidently Venner escaped lightly, for not only did he retain his command but, according to a note in Dalton's *English Army Lists*, in 1693 he was also appointed Director of Hospitals in the Low Countries. Which of the two posts now claimed his prior attention is not known.

However, there was soon a temporary change of role for the Regiment. In May 1693 they were embarked as marines in ships of the Grand Fleet (as were what had now become Colonel Ingoldsby's Regiment – the 23rd Foot). There was nothing unusual in such duties: until the formation of the permanent Corps of Royal Marines in 1755 (and for some time afterwards), it was necessary for infantry regiments to provide soldiers for 'sea service' when naval operations were undertaken, their duties being to add musketry fire-power in close-quarter engagements, to board enemy vessels, and, of course, to effect landings.[2] Detached by companies among ten ships, Venner's spent some four months at sea escorting merchantmen bound for the Mediterranean, but yet again they saw no action and merely had to endure short rations and the discomfort of cramped shipboard quarters.

A sterner test was soon to come. In June 1694 another 'descent' was planned on Brest, and Venner's was among the ten battalions embarked at St Helens under command of Lieutenant General Tollemache ('Talmash' to the troops). As usual, security about the operation was lax, and the French were well prepared. As soon as the ships made into Camaret Bay they were assaulted by cross-fire from shore batteries, which sank one vessel and severely damaged others. The first wave of the assault force was led by Tollemache himself with the combined grenadiers of the battalions in the landing-craft of the time – long-boats crewed by seamen – the rest of Venner's following in support. Before they could reach the shore they suffered withering musketry-fire from unsuspected enemy entrenchments, and when the leading craft hesitated, Tollemache bravely plunged into the surf and with some 150 men gained cover behind rocks on the beach. When another 200 men had landed, their General, although by now wounded with a musket-ball in the thigh, once more led a desperate rush up the beach. But now squadrons of French cuirassiers appeared, and it was only after entreaties by his staff that Tollemache was persuaded to concede the day and retreat to the boats. Those who did not reach them were cut down or captured by the charging horsemen.

This Brest operation not only failed in its objective but cost heavy casualties. Lord Berkeley, the naval commander, reported a total of 1,100 killed and wounded, with one ship sunk and three badly damaged. The gallant Tollemache died of his wound before the survivors reached Spithead. Unfortunately, Venner's casualties cannot be established, for Berkeley's return lists the troops merely by the ships carrying them, not by their regiments. But since the Grenadier company took part in the first assault and the rest of the Regiment was in close support, their losses must have been as heavy as any.

After a brief respite for refitting, in June the Regiment was again at sea for attacks on Dieppe and Le Havre, but this time no landing was undertaken. After a naval bombardment the force returned to St Helens, and Venner's found themselves routed back to the Regiment's birthplace – around Maidstone and 'adjacents' in Kent. While for many, no doubt, this meant reunion with kith and kin, there still seemed little prospect of displaying martial valour with King William and his Army of the Grand Alliance, and in November such prospects receded further when the Regiment was posted to London for guard and garrison duties. There it remained for the next four months, preoccupied with spit-and-polish, pipeclay and drill rather than real soldiering in the field. However, the monotony of such duties was soon broken by a Regimental crisis, provided by the Colonel himself. We have already seen Venner tried by court martial three years previously: now, on 12th March, the observant Narcissus Luttrell recorded, 'Saturday last Colonel Rowe[3] and Colonel Venner were suspended by a court martial upon complaint by some officers, and 'tis said will be broke.' Unhappily, the chronicler reveals nothing of the charges, nor of the sentence, but the fact remains that both Rowe and Venner disappear from the Commission Registers after March 1695.

With uncustomary error, Luttrell goes on to relate (on 16th March) that 'Colonel Venner's regiment is given to Colonel Brudenell'. In fact, Lieutenant Colonel Thomas Brudenell (ancestor of Lord Cardigan of Balaclava fame) took over as Colonel of Rowe's Regiment, while Venner's vacancy went to one of the several Huguenot refugees, with the resounding name of Louis James le Vasseur Cougneé, Marquis de Puisar. His commission is dated 13th March. In Dalton's work the title appears as 'Puizar', while Paton *et al.* in their *Historical Record* add an alternative, 'Puissar'. Whether the men ever learned to get their tongues round the full names and title of their new Colonel (the fourth in six years) is doubtful, but we shall now refer to the Regiment as de Puisar's.

De Puisar's tenure lasted five years – longer than any of his predecessors – and the Regiment spent the first eight months of his command at sea once more, with Admiral Russell's Mediterranean Fleet. But again they saw no action: an unopposed landing force at Palamos, near Barcelona, was hastily withdrawn when Intelligence reported that a strong French Fleet was about to give battle. The report proved false, and there was neither land nor sea battle. Thus unblooded again, the Regiment returned to England, no doubt heartily sick (physically as well as metaphorically) of being confined in the orlop decks of heaving and pitching men-o'-war, with nothing but salt pork and ships' biscuits for rations, and monotonous spells of duty on watch on forecastle and poop. One compensation, however, was the extra pay authorised for all soldiers on 'sea service' with the Fleet: in the case of a private this was 3s. 6d. per week, while a sergeant got 6s. But as always, the Paymaster-General was laggard in his duties, and it took de Puisar nearly three years to extract arrears of £1,172 'sea-pay' owing to his Regiment.[4]

All this happened while other regiments had been distinguishing themselves with King William's forces in Flanders and the Netherlands, several of them earning what was to be their earliest Battle Honour, 'Namur'; but still the 24th seemed to be denied any real campaigning. Instead they resumed their dreary peregrinations by 'march route', this time through Gloucestershire and into Herefordshire and Monmouthshire, before coming to rest again in their home county of Kent in 1696.

Until the erection of permanent barracks, and the establishment of a civilian police force, regiments not employed overseas were constantly on the march through the length and breadth of Britain. The primary object of scattering troops throughout the country was, as we have seen, a necessary precaution for the preservation of law and order: but in authority's view a not unimportant secondary motive was that the constant footslogging from station to station kept the soldier occupied and out of mischief, besides maintaining fitness. The familiar term 'route march' – familiar, that is, to the pre-1939 marching infantryman – had its origin in the 17th-century 'march route', which was exactly that. Whenever a unit changed stations, a detailed itinerary was issued from the Quartermaster General's office, specifying the exact route, the several halting places, and the time in which the route was to be covered. A day's march seldom exceeded twelve miles, which may not seem very demanding, but the pace was governed by the slowest element in the column, which in the case of a battalion was the lumbering baggage train of horse-drawn wagons with hired civilian drivers. The days of properly established regimental transport and a B Echelon under the Quartermaster lay a long way ahead. And there was then no Band, nor even a Corps of Drums, to enliven the trudging column. Each company's two drummers took it in turn to beat out the pace with monotonous taps of their side-drums, varied perhaps with an occasional three-pace roll for effect. Fifes had long been in existence, of course, but there was no attempt to organise a marching ensemble of drums and fifes until the next century.[5]

It was rare for the Colonel to subject himself to the exertions and privations of a march route. Unless he was unusually conscientious, he made his own arrangements and travelled ahead in his own or a hired carriage, leaving his Second-in-Command, the Lieutenant Colonel, to look to the marching column. However, this officer did not have to trudge with the men: all field officers and company commanders were officially allowed horses, even though they had to provide them, and all forage, out of their own pockets.

The soldiers probably had mixed feelings about the constant footslogging from one district to another. On the one hand, there was relief from the interminable parade-ground drill and 'postures' and spit-and-polish and pipeclay, which were their daily lot in quarters; and country lads who had never set eyes on their next-door villages, let alone the next county, must have felt themselves in another world when they beheld the teeming streets of such cities as Bristol or of the metropolis itself. That publicity slogan of the 1930s, 'Join the Army and see the World', was surely even more apt in the 17th century. But, of course, marches spelt hardship such as slogging in all weathers along unmade, muddy 'roads', with the almost certain knowledge that the night's halt would offer little comfort, even if there was a weatherproof roof. As we have seen, the new Mutiny Act laid down that the troops were to be billeted in available public houses, which could be anything from a well-appointed inn to a sleazy wayside ale-house. The publicans were obliged to provide the soldiers with 'dry lodgings . . . Fire and Water, and necessary Utensils to dress their Meat'. The cost thereof, and of the 'meat', was paid for out of the soldiers' subsistence money. Not surprisingly, the innkeepers were unwelcoming hosts, for not only did they make little profit out of the business, but the very presence of the unpopular soldiery often drove away the regular customers. There are instances recorded of some publicans removing their inn-signs as soon as they learned that troops were in the vicinity.

In May 1697 de Puisar's command was scattered in detachments between Sandwich and Woolwich when the Marquis received orders to assemble at the latter place and prepare for embarkation. At long last the Regiment were to join King William in the field. They duly landed at Ostend on 5th June, and after a march of some sixty miles joined the main Army in camp at Cockleberg near Brussels. But yet again they were thwarted of action. Wearied of the protracted hostilities which had been dragging on for nearly eight years, Louis was already resigned to negotiations, and on 11th September the Peace of Ryswick was concluded, by which the 'Sun King' grudgingly acknowledged William as King of England and was forced to make territorial concessions. And so after three months' bloodless 'campaigning', de Puisar's Regiment returned with the rest of the British contingent to England.

King William was received in London as the conquering hero, with bells pealing and fireworks exploding in Green Park. A day of public rejoicing was appointed, on which the Archbishop of Canterbury conducted a thanksgiving service in St Paul's. Meanwhile, Parliament set about the customary arrangements for thanking the soldiers who had gained the King his triumph. At the conclusion of hostilities the strength of the British Army amounted to some 87,000 all ranks; with the return of peace it was conceded that the country could not afford to maintain such a huge standing Army. But in December 1697 there was shocked disbelief when the House voted that all regiments raised since 1680 should be peremptorily disbanded. If this 'piece of malignant folly', as Fortescue described it, had been put into effect, the Army would have been slashed to a pitiful minimum of Household troops and some half-dozen each of Dragoon and Foot regiments. And this history would not have been written.

For the next few months a running battle ensued between the King and his supporters and Parliament, and finally in March 1699 (after William had threatened to abdicate) a compromise was reached: an establishment of 7,000 men was allowed for England, 12,000 for Ireland and 4,000 for Scotland. But a total of thirty-one regiments of Horse, Dragoons and Foot were 'broke'. The redundant officers were granted half-pay, as a sort of retaining fee, but the soldiers were virtually cast adrift to fend for themselves. They were generously allowed to take their clothing and knapsacks with them, and were granted ten days' subsistence money – amounting to 3s. 4d. for a private.

Although the 24th was one of the junior Foot regiments, and several of its seniors fell to the axe, it escaped. Atkinson surmises that its retention was owed to the Colonel, for the Marquis de Puisar had always been *persona grata* at Court since he had married one of the ladies of the royal household. But his influence did not save his Regiment from what was regarded as 'exile' on the Irish Establishment, where it arrived in December 1698. Until the Act of Union in 1801 the Army in Ireland was administered quite separately from that in England, having its own Commander in Chief,

Commissariat, Paymaster and other functionaries. Since supplies were cheaper than in England, rates of pay were lower, and thus to Parliament it made sense to keep as many regiments as practicable on the Irish Establishment. Such a posting was not popular with the troops, for not only did it mean cuts in pay, and more primitive conditions, but there was constant danger of raids and ambushes from 'bog-trotters', or rapparees and other rebellious factions who resented English rule. Terrorism was rife in Ireland long before the IRA gangsters began to perpetrate their outrages.

If the 24th was spared disbandment, it did not escape inviolate. Reductions in strength followed immediately after it joined the Irish Establishment, and by March 1699 it had become little more than a skeleton, with two companies cut and the remaining eleven reduced to only forty-one NCOs and men instead of the previous hundred. This gave a total strength of 451 rank-and-file and 37 officers, the lowest establishment yet seen. But as always, Parliament was soon to rue the surgery it had performed on the Army.

The Regiment's three years of Irish 'exile' were unremarkable, except for a change of Colonel and with it, of course, of title. In February 1701 the Marquis de Puisar was reported 'died', believed drowned on passage to Ireland, and in March the vacancy was filled by Colonel William Seymour. Although they were to be known as Seymour's Regiment for only one year, the 24th were now commanded by the most experienced officer they had yet seen. Son of the Devon Baronet, Sir Edward Seymour, the Colonel had served in a number of 'Holland' regiments in the Dutch service since 1674. In 1686 he was Captain in the Royal Fusiliers; in 1692 he was Lieutenant Colonel of the Coldstream; and in 1694 he took over as Colonel of Lord Cutts's Regiment of Foot, which three years later emerged as Colonel Seymour's Regiment of Marines. This suffered in the Parliamentary purge of the Army after the Peace of Ryswick, and the Colonel went on half-pay until his appointment to the 24th. With twenty-seven years' service, Seymour was a hardened campaigner, having fought in the Low Countries for Prince William of Orange and with the same as King William in Flanders; he was wounded at Landen and commanded his Regiment in the final siege of Namur.

Within two months of assuming his new Colonelcy, William Seymour received orders to recruit his Regiment up to 833 all ranks and to hold it in readiness to embark for the Netherlands. The involved power politics that set off the War of the Spanish Succession and brought glory and renown to the British Army under one of its greatest Captains, the Duke of Marlborough, need not be detailed here. Suffice it to say that the treacherous arch-enemy of Protestant Europe, Louis XIV, not only flouted all his treaty obligations about the succession to the vast Spanish Empire, including the possessions in the Netherlands, but on the death of ex-King James II he was impertinent enough to proclaim that monarch's son ('the Old Pretender') as the rightful heir to the English throne.

William Seymour would undoubtedly have led the 24th with distinction on their first Continental campaigning, but it was not to be. By the time the Regiment was in action, it had become honoured with the name and title of the great Captain General himself.

Notes

[1] Those avid for such detail will find a complete roll of the 24th's officers, from 1689 to 1937, in Atkinson's history.

[2] A unique exception to the practice of employing foot-soldiers occurred when two troops of the 17th Light Dragoons (later Lancers) served in a ship of the Line in the West Indies; hence the term 'Horse Marines'.

[3] Henry Rowe was Colonel of an Irish regiment of Foot, disbanded in 1697.

[4] Quoted by Paton *et al.* from Treasury Papers, Vol. XIII.

[5] Full details of musical matters will be found in Appendix 6.

CHAPTER THREE

Marlborough's Men (1701–13)

After a fortnight's sea voyage from Cork, the 24th arrived at Breda in July and went into camp with the other twelve infantry regiments making up the reinforcements for the Allied Army in the Netherlands. Theoretically the Regiment was now on active service, but there was to be no fighting for many months. A state of war was not actually declared until May of the following year, and meanwhile the advent of winter meant the close season for campaigning, as we have seen.

It was tacitly accepted that during the 'recess' officers might find urgent private business that needed attention at home, and very often no officers but junior subalterns were to be found in the battalion's winter quarters. The Colonel of the 24th evidently felt his presence was required in England, for in December 1701 the ever-observant Luttrell noted '... Brigadier Soames and Coll. Seymour are lately arrived in Whitehall from Holland'. However, some officers returned on bona fide recruiting duties, for the establishment had now been increased to three sergeants and sixty privates per company, with seventy in the Grenadier company. While some of the recruits were old soldiers turned adrift after the Peace of Ryswick four years earlier, the majority were what Fortescue describes as 'the sweepings of the gaols and the streets'. Since sufficient volunteers were not forthcoming, magistrates were empowered to round up all able-bodied men 'without lawful calling or employment', while gaolers were directed to empty their establishments of debtors. By 1702 the net had been cast wider (or lower): convicted felons were offered pardons on condition that they enlisted. Just over a century later Wellington was to describe his soldiers as 'the scum of the earth'; when Colonel Seymour and his officers beheld the latest drafts from England, their reaction was probably similar.

One of their recruits was the notorious Peter Drake, an Irish rogue who made a practice of enlisting in and deserting from successive regiments – each time with the usual bounty. Having already received £5 to enlist in the 9th Foot, he made a better bargain of £8 with Seymour's recruiter in London during the winter of 1701–2. Arriving in Holland, he picked a quarrel with a fellow-Irishman and was wounded in the subsequent duel. He then chanced to encounter the same sergeant who had enlisted him for the 9th, and was promptly arrested as a deserter. Evidently some native blarney saved him from being shot, for he claimed that on learning that the 9th were bound for the West Indies he switched to the 24th because he was determined to fight for King and country in Flanders. He was pardoned by Colonel Seymour, but neither the 24th not the King enjoyed his services for long. A month or so later he disappeared after an altercation with one of his Company Sergeants, and Seymour's were probably glad to see no more of him. This time he exchanged not only regiments, but Armies, for he subsequently joined a French regiment of Foot.[1]

There were no regimental Depots or recruit training centres at this period, and we can only marvel that the motley rabbles were soon transformed into the staunch, disciplined redcoats that earned so much renown for Marlborough and the British Army. We must remember, however, that soldiering was then a very simple business. The infantryman especially was little more than an automaton, marching, drilling and performing his 'postures' entirely by word of command. Initiative was neither necessary nor expected; individual expression, or personality, was suppressed by the machine in which the private soldier functioned as a cog. All that was demanded was physical fitness and a degree of moral fibre that enabled a man to stand in the ranks and go through the automatic drill of loading, ramming and firing while his comrades fell mutilated and dying around him.

All this was based on discipline, which was really synonymous with punishment. The soldier knew that if he committed an offence he would suffer for it, often severely, with penalties that to modern minds seem more reminiscent of the Gestapo than the British Army. Although the 'Reign of the Lash' did not commence until after Marlborough's day, soldiers coud be freely beaten by their NCOs or officers for minor peccadilloes, while there were Draconian penalties for serious crimes. The Articles of War specified capital punishment for twenty-five offences, ranging from mutiny, striking a superior officer and cowardice in the face of the enemy, to robbery and rape. For 'uttering blasphemous speech' a soldier's tongue was bored with a red-hot iron; for insubordination or 'disgraceful conduct', which could be merely a dirty turnout on parade, he might be sentenced to the Gauntlet, in which he was marched between two ranks of his comrades who belaboured his naked back with stout canes. Alternatively he would enjoy a ride on 'the Wooden Horse', on which he was mounted astride two planks joined like an inverted 'V', with weights such as roundshot or muskets attached to his legs to increase the pressure on his crutch. Even more painful was the Picket: the victim was suspended from a post by his wrists, with his bare feet just touching sharp-pointed stakes driven into the ground.

If there was plenty of stick for the soldier, there were few carrots. The only reward a smart and conscientious private could expect was normal promotion up the ranks, possibly to Lieutenant and Quartermaster after perhaps twenty years' service. There was no good conduct pay and there were no decorations or medals for gallantry in the field. It is true that on rare occasions a man might be granted an Ensign's commission for an act of signal bravery, but such cases were rare indeed. Until the abolition of the purchase system for officers in 1871, the soldier's prospects of achieving a commission were negligible.

We now come to February 1702. On the 14th of that month Luttrell recorded: 'The later brigadeer Trelawney's regiment is given to Coll. Seymour, who resigns his to the earl of Marlborough.' This change of Colonelcy was actually gazetted on the 12th, and it must have caused some surprise, as well as gratification, to Seymour's officers and men, who now rejoiced in the title 'Earl of Marlborough's Regiment of Foot'. It was perhaps understandable that William Seymour should exchange into a senior regiment. Trelawney's was in fact the 4th or Queen's Own Regiment (later The King's Own Royal Regiment (Lancaster)), and moreover it was earmarked for conversion into Marines, which probably attracted Seymour, for he had already commanded his own Regiment of Marines, and sea service seemed to be to his liking.

As for the Captain General himself, he had previously held the Colonelcies of such élite units as the 3rd Troop of Horse Guards, the (1st) Royal Regiment of Dragoons and the 7th Foot (Royal Fusiliers). Without being derogatory it must be admitted that the 24th was in no sense distinguished at this date, and was relatively junior in the Line. Why Marlborough should have chosen to honour it with his name is something of a puzzle. However, although the Regiment was to earn its first resounding Battle Honour, 'Blenheim', under the accolade of the Commander in Chief's title, there is nothing to suggest that the new Colonel took any particular interest in 'his' Regiment. Quite obviously, his position precluded any pretence of assuming actual command – this was left to the Lieutenant Colonel, William Tatton – but in the whole of his published letters and despatches there is only one passing reference to the 24th, as a component of a brigade. Similarly, Winston Churchill's three-volume biography[2] has no mention of the Earl's assumption of the Colonelcy, although the Regiment appears as 'Marlborough's'.

Very shortly the Regiment found itself owing allegiance to a new monarch as well as a new Colonel. In March 1702 King William, who had bravely led his troops in Ireland and the Netherlands, succumbed to a fall from his horse while hunting in Hampton Court park, and was succeeded by Anne, second daughter of his erstwhile enemy, King James II. The Queen's first act was to confirm John Churchill, Earl of Marlborough, as 'Captain-General and Commander-in-Chief of the forces to be employed in Holland in conjunction with the troops of Her Majesty's Allies'. Once more a Grand Alliance was formed, comprising England, the Netherlands, Austria and the Protestant states of Germany, and in May war was formally declared on Louis XIV and his Catholic friends.

Marlborough now had some 60,000 troops under his command, among which about 22,000 were British soldiers. The next two years saw him displaying his generalship in a military chess match of manoeuvre and siege in the Netherlands, during which he was sorely tried not so much by the enemy, but by the hidebound bureaucrats of his masters, the States General, whose deputies dogged him in the field, vetoing his more aggressive plans and curbing any show of boldness. However, by the spring of 1704, most of the Spanish Netherlands had been won back from the French, who had surrendered the fortresses of Venloo, Liège and other strategic strongpoints. We know that the 24th were engaged in all these operations, but details are lacking, and not even casualties are recorded.

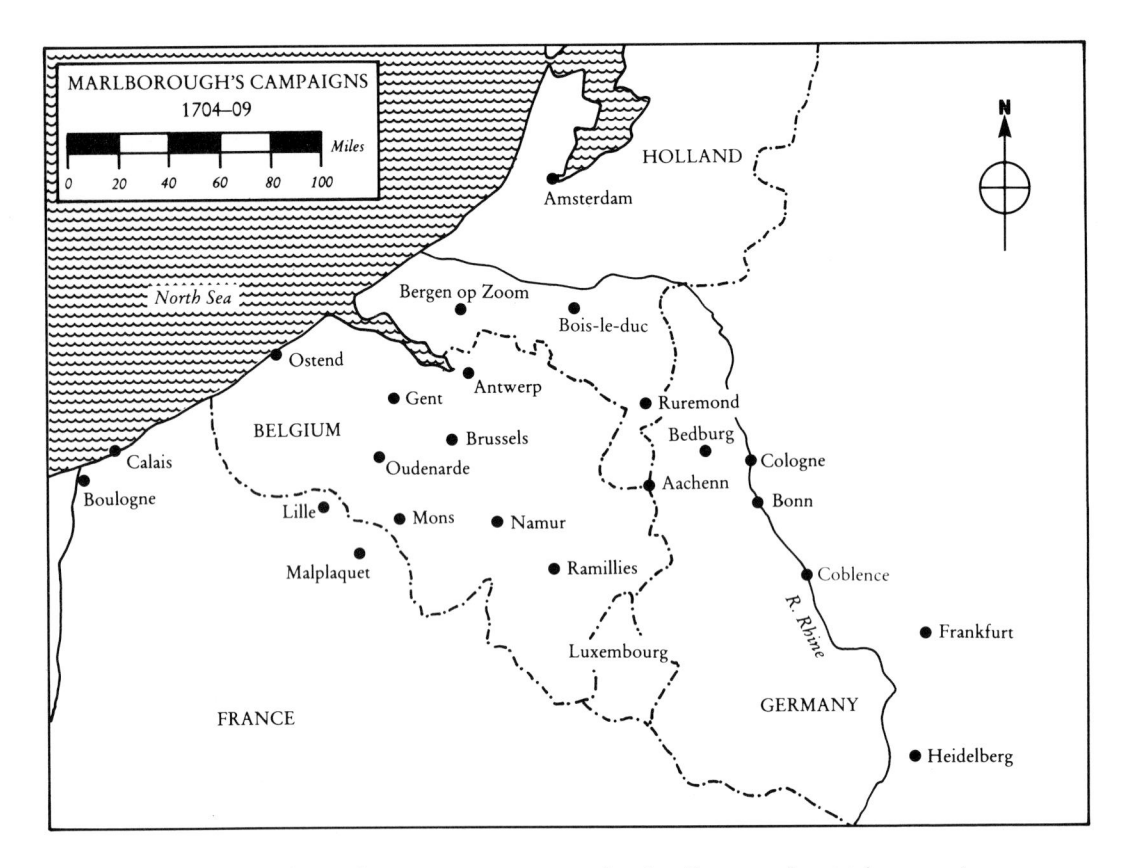

With the end of another winter's recess, in April 1704 the 24th were in camp at Bois-le-Duc ('Boiled Duck' to the soldiers, and now 'sHertogenbosch) when they were ordered to march some seventy miles to a place called Bedburg, near Cologne. 'To what purpose is not expounded', wrote Captain Pope of Schomberg's Horse, who rode ahead of them. Bedburg was reached on 7th May and here they found the whole of the British contingent, awaiting review by their own titular commander, who had now become the Duke of Marlborough. The grand ceremonial took place two days later, and was probably the first time that the Duke had beheld 'his' Regiment on parade. On 18th May orders were issued for the entire force to march at 5 a.m. the next day. The objective and the plans were still 'not expounded'.

This was in fact the beginning of Marlborough's celebrated march to the Danube, in which he moved his Army some 400 miles in 40 days, to culminate in the victory of Blenheim. Early that spring the powerful Elector of Bavaria had thrown in his lot with Louis, and together with the forces under Marshal Tallard – a combined Army of some 90,000 all arms – was posing a threat to Vienna, the capital of the Holy Roman Empire. Though the Empire was neither Holy nor Roman, Vienna was its Achilles heel and its fall would be not only a military catastrophe for the Alliance, but its moral effect among the Protestant peoples of Europe would be incalculable.

THE MARCH TO THE DANUBE 1704
━▶━▶━▶━▶━▶ LINE OF MARCH

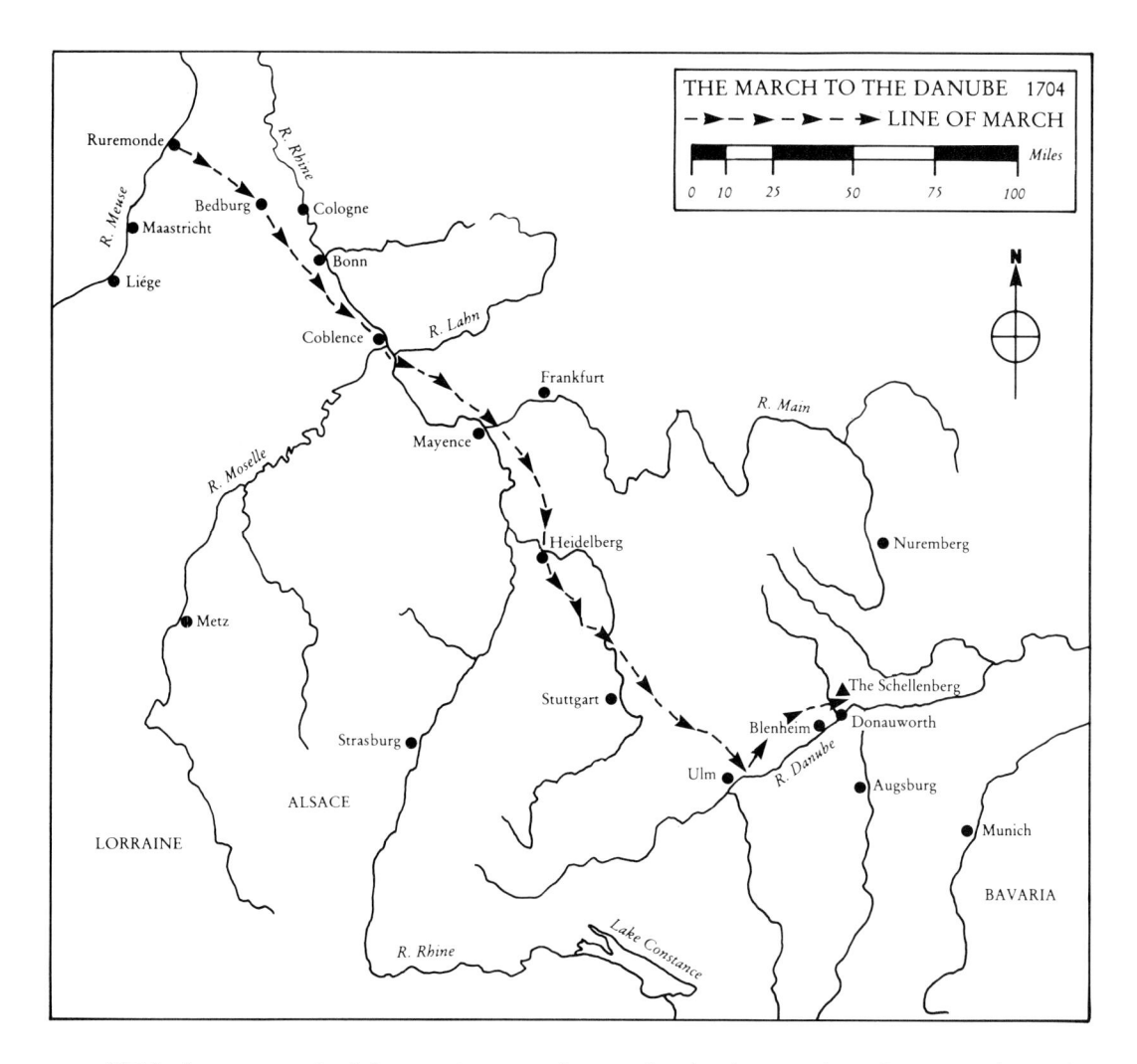

With the approval of Queen Anne and an enthusiastic promise of support from the brilliant soldier-Prince Eugene of Savoy, Commander in Chief in Austria, Marlborough determined to counter the Franco–Bavarian threat on the Danube. All planning and preparation were carried out with strictest security, in order to deceive not only the enemy, but also the overcautious Dutch burghers of the States General, whose Deputies would have been aghast at such a madcap scheme. Hence they were told that the advance would be merely as far as the River Moselle, when Marlborough was to drive west to Paris.

In December the previous year Marlborough had written thus to his newly-appointed Quartermaster General, Colonel William Cadogan:[3]

You do well apprehend that good order and military discipline are the chiefest essentials in an army. But you must ever be aware that an army cannot preserve good order unless its soldiers have meat in their bellies, coats on their backs, and shoes on their feet. All these are as necessary as arms and munitions. I pray you will never fail to look to these things as you may do to other matters.

Marlborough's genius for organisation and logistical detail was never better exemplified than in his marathon march to the Danube. Each day's route was carefully planned in advance, and at the halting places the troops found plentiful supplies of bread, meat and forage secured by the Quartermaster General and paid for with good English gold. At the half-way stage Cadogan had arranged for 12,000 new pairs of shoes for the infantry and quantities of 'fitt iron for the horseshoes'. Captain Parker of the Royal Irish Regiment (18th) wrote:[4]

As we marched through the countries of our allies Commissaries were appointed to furnish us with all manner of necessaries for men and horse; these were brought to the ground before we arrived, and the soldiers had nothing to do but to pitch their tents, boil their kettles and lie down to rest.

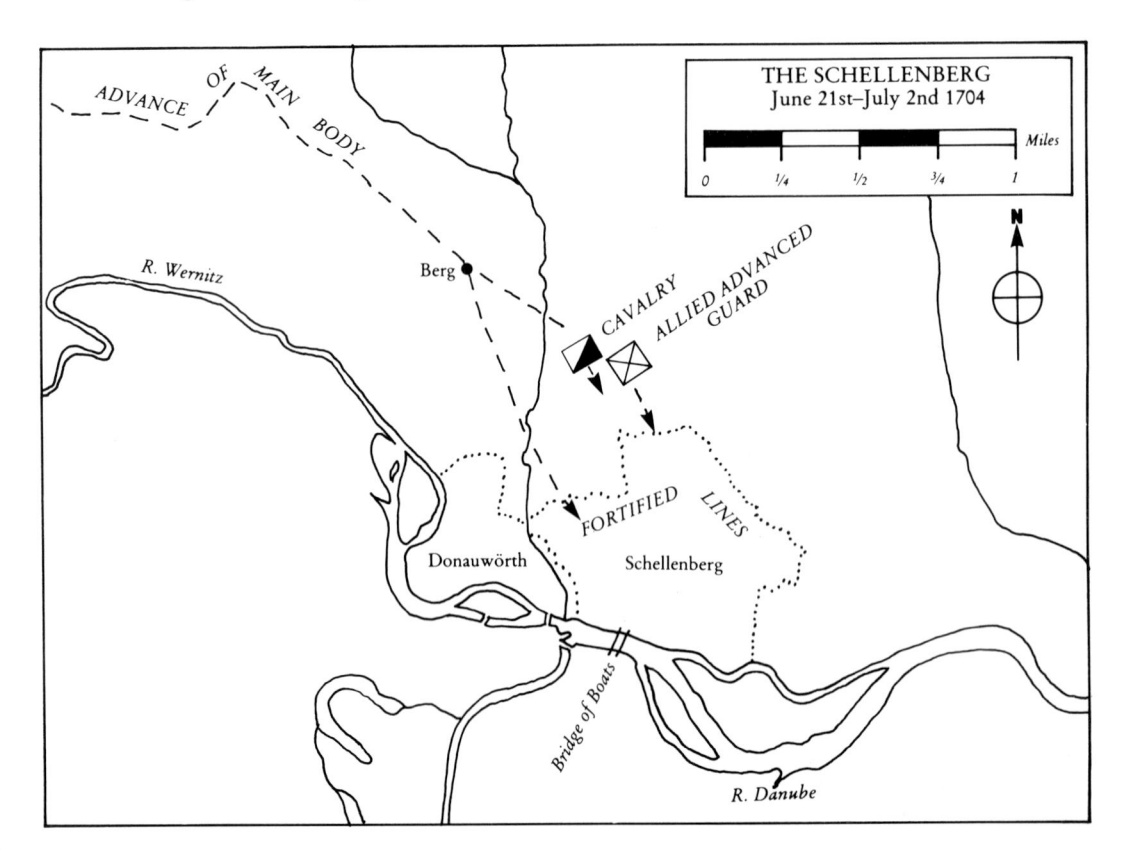

Surely never was such a march carried on with more order and regularity and with less fatigue, both to man and horse.

It was Marlborough's genuine concern for the well-being of his troops, as much as his prowess in battle, that earned him their respect, even their affection. To them he became 'Corporal John'. The soldiers of the Peninsula and Waterloo would never have bestowed any such compliment on the Iron Duke.

By the end of June the 'scarlet caterpillar', as Fortescue described it, was approaching the Danube where, towering above the river rose the seemingly impregnable Schellenberg fortress on its 500-ft scrub-covered heights, the town of Donauworth nestling below. So far there had been no let or hindrance, for the cunning manoeuvre had initially outwitted the enemy. But now it was learned that the Schellenberg was held by some 12,000 hardened troops under the redoubtable Bavarian General, Count d'Arco, while Intelligence reported that Louis, having at last got wind of the situation, was diverting reinforcements to this key point. The Schellenberg was in fact the key not only to Bavaria but to Vienna itself. It could not be bypassed.

Marlborough had now been joined by Prince Louis, Margrave of Baden, with his Imperial infantry, and on 2nd July the attack went in. The 24th were commanded by Lieutenant Colonel Tatton and formed the right-flank Battalion of the second line of the 6,000-strong assault force. The first line, including the 1st Guards, Royal Scots, 23rd and 37th, was led by a 'forlorn hope' of fifty guardsmen. 'Forlorn' they were: within sixty yards of the breastworks they were met by murderous volleys of musketry and only seventeen of the fifty stumbled back down the slope on the advancing first line. These men carried fascines with which to cross the trench protecting the breastworks, but mistaking a lower gully for the trench, they cast their fascines therein, and on reaching the actual trench had no means of crossing. At close quarters they were mown down and the survivors retreated in some disorder.

Meanwhile the second line, with the 24th on their right, were already struggling up through the scrub and rocks, losing men as they went. Rallying the shattered battalions, they pushed desperately up to the very parapets with bayonets fixed. Now followed a carnage. A French Colonel in the thick of the fight wrote afterwards:[5]

> The English infantry led the attack with the greatest intrepidity, right up to our parapet, but there they were opposed with a courage at least equal to their own. Rage, fury and desperation were manifested by both sides. The little parapet ... became the scene of the bloodiest struggle that could be imagined ... We were all fighting hand to hand, pushing them back as they clutched at the parapet; men were slaying or tearing at the muzzles of muskets and at the bayonets which pierced their entrails.

Once more the attack failed and, grievously mauled, the survivors withdrew to cover in the gully, musket-balls still humming over them and inflicting casualties on the British cavalry awaiting their opportunity on the lower slopes. But Marlborough's ally, Prince Louis, now launched a diversion. His Imperial infantry scrambled up to a sector where the entrenchments were incomplete and, thus heartened, the British line again advanced. In the face of this assault in front and flank, the staunch defenders at last gave way. Streaming down from the heights they were smitten by the charging squadrons of British Horse and Dragoons and harried all the way to the bridge of boats across the Danube. Under the press of fugitives this collapsed and hundreds were swept away, to add to the French casualties. The brave Count d'Arco himself managed to swim his horse across the river, and escaped.

The capture of Schellenberg was a heavy blow for Louis. Not only had he lost some 8,000 of his most tried and trusted troops, but with his enemy's occupation of the strategic focal point of Donauworth, the heart of Bavaria now lay under threat. But Marlborough paid a high price for the victory. His total killed and wounded amounted to 4,000 while the British troops alone lost 1,500 officers and men killed. The 24th escaped relatively lightly, with one officer and twenty-nine killed, three officers and forty-four men wounded.

By 12th August Marlborough had advanced unopposed through Bavaria and joined forces with his gallant ally Prince Eugene at the village of Munster on the Danube. They knew that Marshal Tallard had concentrated his Franco–Bavarian Army of 56,000 troops some six miles upstream, with their strongpoint in a village at the junction of the Danube and its tributary the Nebel. The locals called this Blindheim, but as Battle Honours of British regiments testify, to us it has become celebrated as Blenheim.

A personal reconnaissance by Marlborough and Eugene showed the enemy in a formidable position. Their front, stretching some four miles from the very banks of the Danube below Blenheim as far as Lutzingen, was protected by the Nebel stream, no great obstacle in itself, but its course was bounded by treacherous swamp, hazardous alike to horse and man. The allied commanders could see that battalions of infantry and batteries of guns were in position across the far bank of the Nebel, while on the steeply rising ground behind were massed squadrons of cuirassiers and dragoons, who would surely swoop down on any attackers who managed to pierce the front. Spies reported that the village of Blenheim was strongly fortified with palisades and breastworks and held by twenty battalions with twelve squadrons of dragoons in support.

It was a daunting situation for the two Allies. Not only did the enemy enjoy a tactical advantage in their position, but their 56,000 strength gave them a numerical superiority over the 52,000 combined allied forces.

In the small hours of 13th August Marlborough deployed his squadrons and battalions along the near bank of the Nebel, while Prince Eugene led his Imperial Horse and Foot on a wide flanking movement to attack the enemy's position around Lutzingen on the left of their line, which was held by the Elector himself, Prince Maximillian of Bavaria. The attacks were planned to go in simultaneously.

The assault on the key point of Blenheim village itself was entrusted to Lieutenant General Lord Cutts ('Salamander' Cutts) with his three brigades of British infantry and one of Hessians.[6] The 24th, or Marlborough's Regiment, were posted to Brigadier General Archibald Row's Brigade which also included, besides his own Regiment (the Royal Scots Fusiliers), the 1st Foot Guards (Grenadiers), the 10th Foot (Lincolnshire)

BLENHEIM
August 2nd–13th 1704

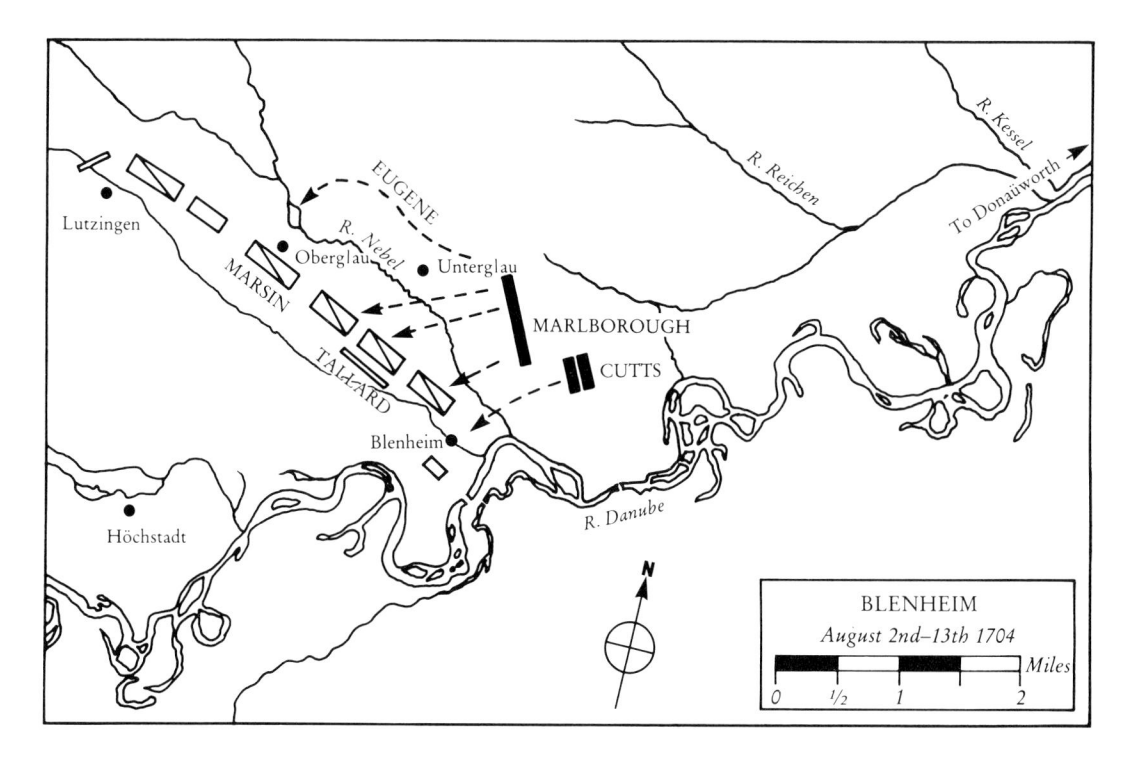

and the 23rd (Royal Welch Fusiliers). The 24th were about to earn their first Battle Honour in company with their future fellow-Welshmen. Owing to the difficult terrain, Prince Eugene and his right-wing forces were delayed in deploying, and it was only at 12.30 p.m. that Marlborough was able to order the advance.

Row's five battalions led the attack on Blenheim village, with the 24th between the 23rd and the Guards on the right of the line. The Brigadier had given strict orders that there should be no halting to fire: the advance must go on unchecked until he himself had struck the palisades with his sword. As the line came within range, at about 100 paces, a storm of musketry depleted the ranks, but the survivors pressed grimly on, 'with undaunted courage and intrepidity ... on the muzzles of the enemy', wrote a sergeant of the 18th Foot in the second line.[7]

The gallant Brigadier reached the breastworks unscathed, but as he smote the palisades with his sword he fell mortally wounded. The men fired a volley and then flung themselves on the defences with bayonet and sword. But as Marlborough's Chaplain General, Dr Frances Hare, recorded in his Journal, 'the superiority of the enemy and the advantages of their position rendered that mode of attack unpracticable'.[8] Having lost nearly a third of its strength, the Brigade was forced to retire to cover in some dead ground. Here they were assaulted by squadrons of charging *Gens d'Armes*, but thanks to the noble fire-support of the Hessian Brigade and a counter-attack by British squadrons, these were driven off.

Reinforced by Ferguson's Brigade of four fresh Battalions (Royal Scots, 15th, 26th and 37th), together with the Hessians, the 24th and their own mangled Brigade made another desperate assault. This time they succeeded in forcing back some of the defenders from the breastworks, but such was the overwhelming fire of twenty-seven battalions now confronting them that it was impossible to surmount the defences and enter the village itself. Once more suffering heavy casualties, the Brigades withdrew. Although they could not know it, the French sector commander, alarmed by the threat to this vital flank, had diverted seven of the battalions from the centre to reinforce the garrison, so that Blenheim was now held by some 12,000 men. While General Cutts was preparing to hazard yet a third attack, Marlborough's aides had informed him of the seemingly impregnable position, and he thereupon ordered the 'Salamander' to desist. The plan now was simply to 'contain' this left-flank stronghold by surrounding it with troops, and thus to prevent Tallard's reinforcement of his centre. This was achieved: the defenders were securely pent up in the village and 'could not rush out without getting on the very points of our bayonets', wrote Captain Parker. Although the attacks on the village had failed, and cost heavy casualties, the fact that Marshal Tallard effectively lost the twenty-seven battalions penned down there for the rest of the day was a significant contribution to his defeat.

Since this is essentially a regimental history, there is little point in giving a detailed account of the subsequent course of the battle.[9] Consigned to the investment of Blenheim village, the 24th and the rest of Cutts' force had no part in the struggle that raged along the banks of the Nebel. It is sufficient to say that after attack and counter-attack and heavy artillery pounding, Tallard's centre (bereft of the battalions in Blenheim village) was weakened, and by 4 p.m. Marlborough was able to order the final advance. Some 80 squadrons of allied cavalry smashed through the massed ranks of 12,000 cuirassiers and then cut down nine battalions of Foot. Meanwhile Prince Eugene had penetrated the Lutzingen defences and the Elector, seeing his front collapsing and his right flank threatened, withdrew in some panic towards the fortress of Ulm.

The valorous garrison of Blenheim village was still holding out, and now were assaulted by shot and shell from the British Batteries.[10] Their encirclement was complete, for battalions of English Foot and squadrons of Dragoons blocked any escape to the Danube or to Höchstadt in rear. Aware of the situation elsewhere, the garrison awaited orders: for a desperate attempt to break out, or to surrender. But no orders came. Their commander, the Marquis de Clerembault, was being swept down the Danube, having left his men to their fate, and attempted to swim his horse across the river. He was drowned.

Deserted by their General, their rear defences pierced, the garrison laid down their arms. By dusk the Battle of Blenheim was over and Marlborough was able to send off an ADC to Sarah at home: 'I have not time to say more but to beg you will give my duty to the Queen, and let her know her Army has had a Glorious Victory . . .'.

It was indeed 'glorious'. Not only was Blenheim the most decisive defeat yet suffered by *Le Roi Soleil* in the 61 years of his reign, but it shattered the myth of French 'invincibility', and cost the King 38,600 of his veteran officers and soldiers, including Marshal Tallard himself, who surrendered to Marlborough. The whole of Bavaria was now in allied hands, and the threat to Vienna was dispelled. But victories are only won

The attack on the village of Blenheim, 13th August 1704.

Private of the 41st Regiment of Invalids, 1751.

Some of the Regimental In-Pensioners, Chelsea Hospital, 1988.

at a price. Marlborough and Eugene lost a total of 4,600 killed and 7,600 wounded, the heaviest casualties suffered by the Grand Alliance in the present campaigning.

As usual at this period, it is difficult to establish accurate figures for the 24th's losses. Both Atkinson and Paton agree that five officers were killed; the former says eight officers were wounded and eighty other ranks were killed. Paton puts the latter figure at 115, but can only hazard that the wounded were 'in the proportion of something like two to one to the killed'. Charles Dalton is his 'Blenheim Roll'[11] lists only three officers killed and ten wounded, but adds a note that two of the latter subsequently died of their wounds. C. B. Norman's *Battle Honours of the British Army* (1911) puts the total of other ranks killed at eighty-four, but gives no figure for wounded.

The name 'Blenheim' has pride of place among the present Regiment's Battle Honours; but incredibly enough the 'Glorious Quartet' of Marlborough's great victories were not officially authorised to be borne on Colours and appointments until 1882. Until that date Battle Honours had been awarded to certain regiments in a curiously arbitrary fashion, often to the exclusion of many who were entitled (one suspects that the Colonels of the latter were not very energetic in pressing their claims). In 1881 the whole matter was formalised after deliberation by a War Office committee, and so, after 173 years, the regiments who fought with Marlborough were granted their awards.

Before leaving Blenheim, and with proper chronology ignored, mention must be made of a later 'March to the Danube' carried out by the 24th Regiment. In July–August 1961 B Company, 1st Battalion The South Wales Borderers, retraced the entire route from Bedburg to Blenheim. Led by Captain N. L. G. Robinson, sixty-five officers and soldiers marched on foot, averaging some twenty miles a day. But unlike their predecessors, they enjoyed the advantage of a mechanised administrative party who made arrangements at each night's halt, and were available to pick up any stragglers (of which there were none). They also enjoyed lavish hospitality and ceremonial welcomes throughout Bavaria. At Gross Heppach, where Marlborough had met Prince Eugene, they were marched in by the town band and lunched by the Burgermeister in the Gasthaus Lamm where the two commanders had dined. Donauworth, below the Schellenberg, was dressed out with Union Flags and bunting. Here the marchers were the guests of a Panzer Grenadier battalion, whose members showed them where the original 24th had struggled up the heights of the Schellenberg. At Blenheim the hosts were officials of the Bavarian State Government, and the Company was joined by the Battalion's Band and Drums and Colour Party, motoring in from Minden. On 13th August, the 257th anniversary of the battle, a ceremonial parade was held, with speeches by the Burgermeister and Company commander, wreath-laying ceremonies, and the sounding of Last Post and Reveille by the Battalion's buglers.

It was generally agreed that this second 'March to the Danube' had been a huge success. Not only was the reception everywhere heart-warming (sometimes almost embarrassingly so), but for the soldiers a few pages of their Regimental history had been brought to life. There was only one disappointment: it was originally proposed

Map: Ramillies, May 12th–23rd 1706

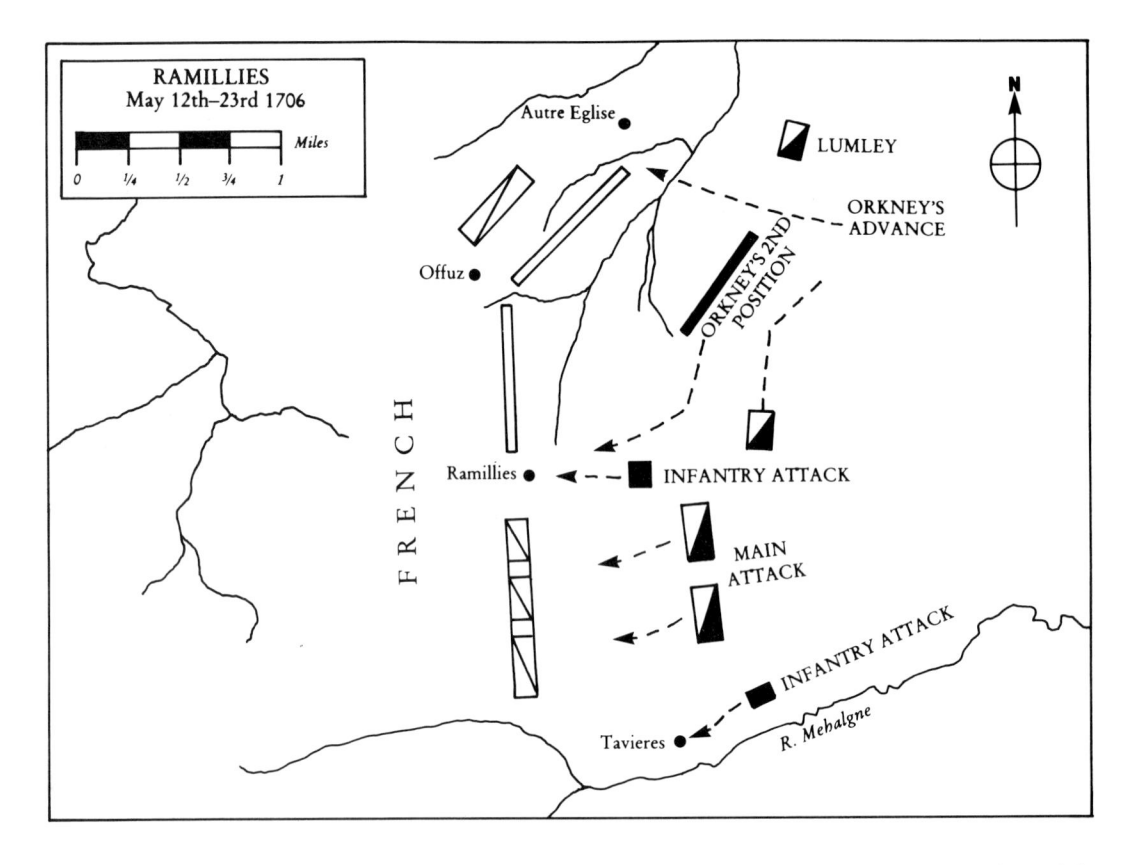

that a detachment of their comrades of the first march, the 23rd Foot (Royal Welch Fusiliers), should join them, but sadly commitments elsewhere rendered this impossible.

To return to the original 24th, there is little operational detail worthy of recording for the next two years. But meanwhile the Regiment had relinquished the distinctive title of 'The Duke of Marlborough's Regiment'. As one of his rewards for his great victory, on 25th August 1704 the Duke was granted the Colonelcy of the 1st Foot Guards (Grenadiers), and on the same date Lieutenant Colonel William Tatton (who had been in active command since 1702) was appointed Colonel of the 24th in his place. Hailing from Cheshire, Tatton had bought an Ensign's commission in the 9th Foot (Norfolk Regiment) in 1685. Having fought with that Regiment in Ireland and Flanders, he had risen to Lieutenant Colonel by 1695, when he became Second-in-Command of the 24th (or Venner's Regiment).

Inconclusive skirmishings, feints, marching and counter-marching were the lot of Tatton's Regiment until May 1706 when the next confrontation in force took place. This was the Battle of Ramillies where, on the 23rd of the month, Marlborough's allied force of 62,000 all arms faced 60,000 French under Marshal Villeroi (who had replaced the captured Tallard). Tatton's Regiment was brigaded with the 1st (Royal Scots), 10th (Lincolnshire), 18th (Royal Irish) and 29th (Worcestershire), and together with two other British brigades was posted on the extreme right flank where a rivulet, the Little Gheete, protected the enemy's left-wing position in the village of Autre Eglise. After the usual artillery cannonade by both sides, the British redcoats were ordered to attack. Struggling across the stream, they drove back the enemy outposts and were about to storm Autre Eglise with the bayonet when to their astonishment an ADC galloped up with Marlborough's orders to withdraw to their original position. With customary cunning, the Captain General had planned the right-wing operation merely as a feint, hazarding that in the face of the threat Villeroi would divert troops from his centre. This is what happened, and for the rest of the day Tatton's men and the other nineteen battalions of redcoats lay in position across the rivulet, still posing a threat, but taking no offensive action. Until evening it was a repeat of the Blenheim situation. But then, as the cavalry wrought havoc elsewhere, the 24th and their comrades at last resumed their broken-off attack and advanced almost unopposed into Autre Eglise. The demoralised garrison fled. The village of Ramillies in the centre was quickly overrun by another British brigade, and then Marlborough launched a massive attack by some eighty squadrons of British and Dutch cavalry, which shattered the French line and sent the survivors fleeing in a rabble. Among the defeated infantry was that 'amiable renegade', ex-Private Peter Drake of the 24th, now a Captain, and his comments on his latest comrades were scathing: 'They indeed acquitted themselves shamefully and fled, with great precipitation, like frightened sheep.' He saw four battalions of the élite *Regiment du Roi* 'lay down their arms like paltroons and surrendered themselves prisoners of war. In short, they all left the field with infinite disgrace . . .'.[12]

Although not as costly as Blenheim, Ramillies cost the French 8,000 killed and wounded, with some 7,000 made prisoner. Marlborough lost just over 1,000 killed and 3,600 wounded, of which only a few hundred were British soldiers. Records of regimental casualties do not appear in any of the authorities, but it seems that the 24th with their comrades of the right-flank brigades suffered hardly at all.[13]

The year 1707 was one of frustration for Marlborough: most of his plans were vetoed by the Dutch Deputies and there was little fighting but minor skirmishes between reconnaissance patrols and foraging parties. And in an unusually wet summer there was much footslogging for the redcoats through flood and mud, as like chess-board pieces they were moved from one sector to another.

The spring of 1708 saw yet another change of Colonelcy in the 24th. On 9th March William Tatton, now Brigadier General, transferred to the 1st Foot Guards as senior or '1st' Major and Company commander. This may seem to be demotion, but in the Guards regimental rank did not correspond with Army rank, and he retained his seniority (the former Company commander, though 'Major' in the Regiment, was actually a Major General). Tatton went on to become Lieutenant General and died in 1737 as Colonel of The Buffs.

There was now an infusion of Guards blood in the 24th, for Tatton was succeeded (on 9th March) by Brigadier General Gilbert Primrose, who had been 2nd Major in the 1st Guards and had fought with them at Schellenberg, Blenheim and Ramillies. Scarcely had he taken over his new command when on 26th March the Regiment and ten others were ordered to Ostend, there to embark for Tynemouth. At sea they learned that their

OUDENARDE
June 30th–July 11th 1708

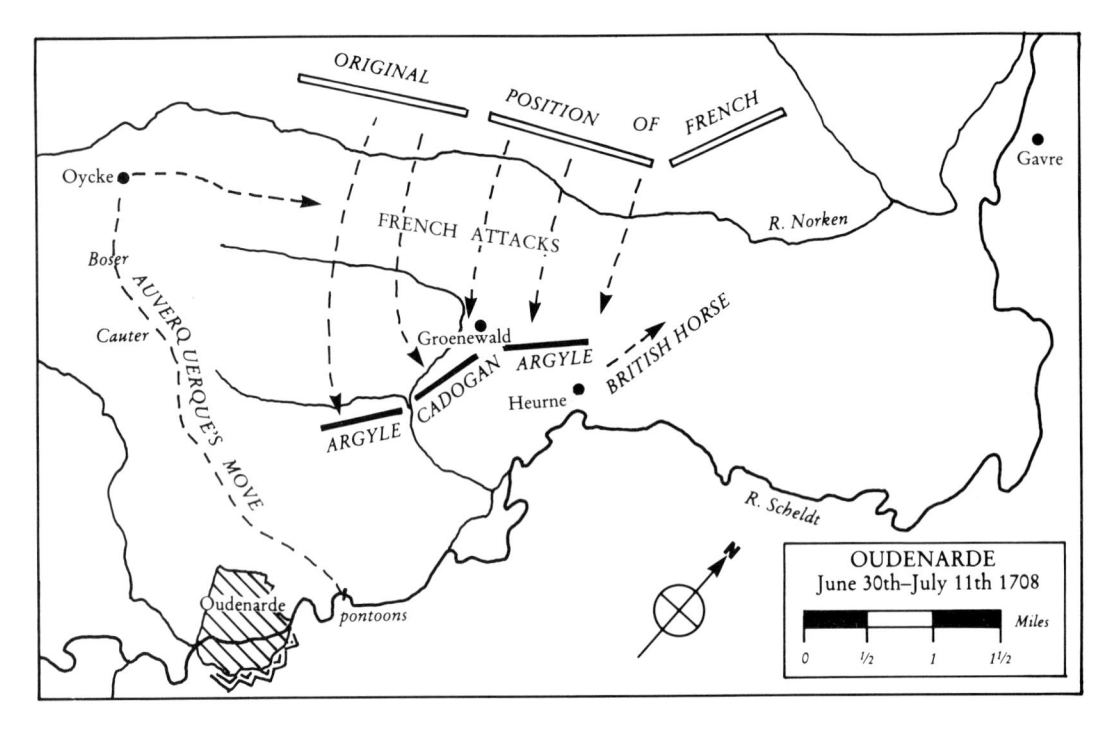

task was to oppose a rumoured French invasion on the Scottish coast in an attempt to stir up a Jacobite rebellion. However, their services were not needed. Deterred by a naval squadron, the French Fleet withdrew, and after spending a miserable month of confinement on board ship, the ten battalions returned to Ostend and reunion with Marlborough's Army at Ghent.

Some fifteen miles south of that city is the modern Belgian town of Audenaarde, but the name emblazoned on Standards and Colours of the British Army is 'Oudenarde'. It was here, on 11th July 1708, that Marlborough achieved the third of his quartet of victories.

By a series of forced marches, on 11th July he had brought the French to bay on the heights above Oudenarde and the River Scheldt. The numerical odds were even this time, for both sides deployed some 80,000 all arms; but the French command was shared between the young Duke of Burgundy and the veteran Marshal Vendome. Inevitable friction between the two proved their undoing. Marlborough also had a co-commander, but there was no friction here, for the latter was his trusted ally, Prince Eugene.

The 24th were brigaded with The Buffs and the 16th under their own Colonel, Gilbert Primrose, and formed an element of the centre 'division' under the Duke of Argyll. In the early hours of the morning General Cadogan with thirty squadrons and twelve battalions crossed the Scheldt near Oudenarde to make a feint against the French right flank. The inexperienced Duke of Burgundy ordered a retreat, but after some confusion was overruled by Vendome, who launched an attack against the advancing

MALPLAQUET
Aug 31st–Sept 11th 1709

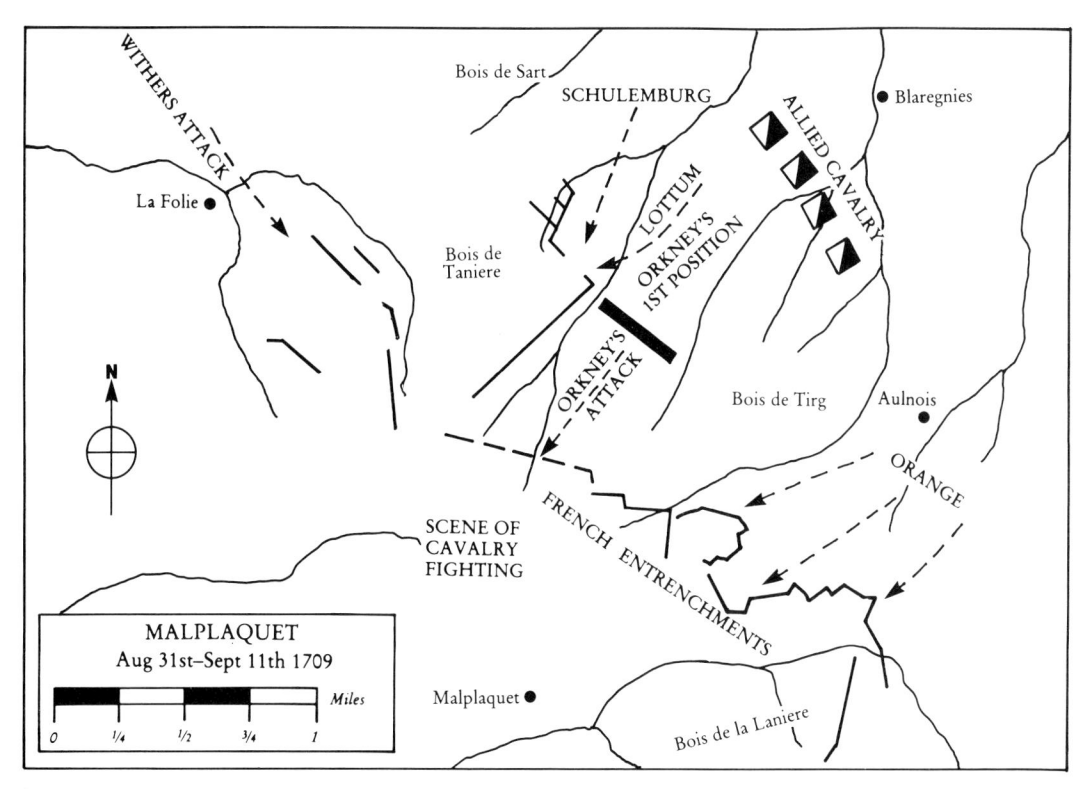

lines of redcoats under Argyll who had now pushed across the river. A fierce and confused infantry fight followed among the difficult terrain of copse and hedgerow, with the 24th in the thick of it. 'We drove the enemy from ditch to ditch, from hedge to hedge, and from out of one scrub to another, in great hurry and disorder', wrote Sergeant Millner of the 18th. This indecisive struggle continued for several hours, until Marlborough sent the Dutch General Overkirk with twenty battalions and all the left-wing cavalry on a wide turning movement round the enemy right flank. At the same time Prince Eugene attacked their left. By 9 p.m. the whole French position was practically enveloped; but dusk was falling, and fearing that the converging allied troops would slay each other, Marlborough ordered a cease-fire. Burgundy and Vendome made good their escape with the survivors of the fight, and as night fell the exhausted redcoats camped on the battlefield. They had marched some fifty miles in sixty hours and had been in action for ten hours. The French lost 6,000 killed and wounded while 9,000 were made prisoner. Writing (as always after a battle) to Sarah, Marlborough declared: 'I thank God the English have suffered less than any of the other troops...'. Their casualties were in fact astonishingly light: out of the total of 3,000 allied killed and wounded, only 53 British officers and men were killed and 177 wounded. There are no details of the 24th's casualties, but they must have been minimal. Oudenarde was Marlborough's cheapest victory.[14]

His next objective was the capture of the great fortress of Lille, a bastion of the

French defences in Flanders. This he entrusted to Eugene, reinforced by five British Battalions, among which were the 23rd and 24th. The fortress was held by 16,000 men under the redoubtable Marshal the Marquis de Boufflers and was protected by numerous outworks. The siege commenced on 17th August, but such was the stoutness of the defence that little progress could be made, the storming parties being repeatedly beaten back with heavy losses. By September Eugene had lost 2,600 of his 40,000 troops. He himself was wounded leading an assault, and Marlborough took over. The citadel was in fact never taken, but with ammunition and food almost exhausted, de Boufflers was forced to surrender the town on 10th December. The gallant old Marshal (aged 65) and the 8,000 survivors of his 16,000 garrison were allowed to march out with the honours of war.

Although Lille does not appear in any regimental Battle Honours, its four-month siege cost Marlborough and Eugene nearly 15,000 killed and wounded – five times the total of casualties at Oudenarde. While there were no official figures for the 24th's losses, a contemporary newspaper reported 1 officer and 68 men killed, 6 officers and 202 men wounded.[15]

Nine months later Marlborough and Eugene again confronted the veteran de Boufflers and Marshal Villars on the field of Malplaquet. This battle, the last of the famous 'Quartet', was fought on 11th September 1709 and, wrote Captain Parker of the 18th Royal Irish, 'was the most obstinate and bloody battle that had been fought in the memory of any then living'. It also saw the strongest concentration of opposing forces in any encounter on European soil until World War I: the Allies fielded 110,000 men, the French about 100,000. Marlborough disposed his British infantry – eighteen battalions – in the centre under Lord Orkney, and the 24th were posted on the left of the first line, brigaded with the 8th, 18th and 21st.

The French were in a strong position, their flanks secured by two dense woods, the gap between them protected by entrenchments, redoubts and batteries of guns. After the customary artillery prelude, the battle opened at 7 a.m. with attacks by Eugene's Prussians and Danes on the flanking woods. After several hours of attack and counter-attack, the impetuous young Prince of Orange disregarded orders by launching his entire force of Dutch infantry and cavalry into a holocaust of fire on the left flank, losing 5,000 men in some 30 minutes. Villars now began to threaten the Allies' exposed flank by diverting battalions from his centre, and seeing this manoeuvre Marlborough ordered Orkney to advance with his British infantry. They carried the entrenchments and drove back the defenders. Then, through the gaps, pounded Dutch and British Cuirassiers, Horse and Dragoons, and there developed the greatest cavalry clash yet seen since the days of Gustavus Adolphus – some 30,000 horsemen charging, rallying, and charging again. All this took place while they were nobly supported by the fire of Orkney's battalions (the 24th among them), support which Orkney himself subsequently put on record: 'I really believe, had not the foot been there, they would have drove our horse out of the field . . . such a pelting at one another I never saw the like.'[16] But the French Horse were not finally 'drove out' until Prince Eugene personally led his forty squadrons of Austrians into the mêlée. It was now 3 p.m.; Marshal Villars had been carried off wounded; the French centre had collapsed; and de Boufflers, seeing his flanks enveloped, conceded the day. This time there was no rout. The old Marshal withdrew his troops in good order, and Marlborough was too humane to order his mauled and battle-weary regiments to follow up.

Malplaquet was no Blenheim. Although the French had retired, they had not been decisively beaten, while the allied casualties were more than twice the number of the enemy's. They amounted to 24,000 killed and wounded; the French lost only 9,000, with 3,000 taken prisoner. Yet again we have no details of the 24th's casualties. Even the industrious Charles Dalton's 'Malplaquet Roll'[17] merely lists officers present by regiments, without noting casualties as in his 'Blenheim Roll'.

There were no further pitched battles for Marlborough and his men, only a succession of sieges, which cost more lives. In June 1710 the strategic fortress of Douai was captured after two months' investment, the 24th being one of eight British battalions involved (together with the 23rd). According to Lediard,[18] this cost 1,900 all ranks killed and wounded, the 24th's share being 1 officer and 35 men killed, 9 officers and 148 men wounded.

With the forcing of the *'ne plus ultra'* lines and the capture of Bouchain in August 1711, Marlborough's campaigning, and his military career, were at an end. George Bernard Shaw once wrote: 'the British soldier can stand up to anything except the British politician'. Marlborough's soldiers were incredulous and then outraged when in December they learned that their great Captain General, their 'Corporal John', had been dismissed his command and recalled. The political machinations that led to trumped-up charges of 'extortion', 'embezzlement' and 'waste of his soldiers' lives' need not concern us; suffice it to quote Fortescue: 'This vindictive persecution of Marlborough was an insult to a brave army as well as a shameful injustice to a great man . . .'.

Further insults were to be suffered by that brave Army. In January 1712 came the infamous 'Restraining Order' by which the British forces were forbidden to take any offensive action, and the final indignity followed in July when the newly-appointed Captain General, the Duke of Ormonde, was ordered to withdraw the entire British contingent back to Ghent, leaving their Hanoverian, Dutch and Prussian allies dumbfounded. And so the 24th, who had played their part in establishing the British Army on its pinnacle of renown, ended their first Continental campaign in humiliation.

Notes

[1] Drake's diary, entitled *Amiable Renegade, The Memoirs of Capt. Peter Drake 1671–1753*, was published in 1960 (Oxford), but not surprisingly he says little about the 24th.

[2] *Marlborough – His Life and Times* (Harrap, 1934).

[3] *The Letters and Despatches of John Churchill, First Duke of Marlborough, from 1702 to 1712*, ed. Gen. Sir George Murray (1845).

[4] Parker, Captain Robert. *Memoirs of the Most Remarkable Military Transactions from the Year 1683 to 1718* (1747).

[5] de La Colonie, Jean-Martin. *The Chronicles of an Old Campaigner*, translated and edited by W. C. Horsley (1904).

[6] At this period there were no permanently established operational brigades (or higher formations). They were formed on an *ad hoc* basis in the field, and like the regiments, were designated by the names of their commanders.

[7] Millner, Sergeant John. *A Compendious Journal of Marches . . . 1701–1712* (London, 1733).

[8] Quoted in *Letters and Dispatches of John Churchill, First Duke of Marlborough*.

[9] Apart from Waterloo, Blenheim is the most fully documented battle in British military history. Fortescue gives it twelve pages in his history of the Army, and more recently a complete book has been devoted to it: *The Battle of Blenheim* by Peter Verney (Batsford, 1976).

[10] It is strange that Marlborough did not order any artillery 'softening up' of the position before the initial costly infantry attacks went in.

[11] Reproduced in Vol. V of his *English Army Lists and Commission Registers*.

[12] *Amiable Renegade*, op. cit.

[13] In his *Battle Honours of the British Army* (1911), C. B. Norman usually details casualties by regiments. But in the case of Ramillies there are blanks.

[14] As an aside, it is worthy of record that the young Prince George, Elector of Hanover, gallantly led a charge in one of the cavalry actions and had his horse shot under him. Thirty-five years later, as King George II of England, he became the last British sovereign to lead an Army in battle – at Dettingen.

[15] *Daily Courant*, quoted by Atkinson.

[16] 'Letters of the First Lord Orkney'. *English Historical Review*, XIX, 1904.

[17] Published in his *English Army Lists and Commission Registers*, Vol. VI.

[18] Lediard, Thomas. *Life of John Duke of Marlborough* (1736).

CHAPTER FOUR

41st and 69th (1713–82)

The Treaty of Utrecht in 1713 brought the inevitable Parliamentary clamour for the reduction of the armed forces. Twenty-two regiments of Foot were immediately disbanded, and those that survived found their strengths cut to thirty-seven NCOs and men per company. Thus reduced, the 24th were posted to the Irish Establishment, where they remained for many humdrum years. The only diversion was a brief raid on the coast of Spain at Vigo in September 1719, which ended after a month with the tame surrender of the Spanish commander.

By now the 24th had acquired a new Colonel (and title). In September 1717 Gilbert Primrose died, as Major General, and the vacancy was purchased by Colonel Thomas Howard of the 33rd. He had served in Spain and Portugal, twice being captured, but was exchanged, as was then the custom with officer-prisoners. The 24th were to remain Howard's Regiment for twenty years – the longest span yet without a change – and during this period the nickname 'Howard's Greens' became current. This at least offers evidence that the green facings (often described as 'willow-green') had been adopted by 1717.[1]

And now we must temporarily leave the 24th, to record the birth of their future partner. With the outbreak of the Jacobite Rebellion of 1715, Parliament had cause to rue the late wholesale pruning of the Army. Several new regiments of Dragoons and Foot were hastily raised, and in order to relieve existing regiments of garrison duties it was resolved to re-employ some of the Out-Pensioners of the Chelsea Royal Hospital who, while not fit for active service, were reckoned capable of performing the undemanding duties of garrison troops. Accordingly, in 1715 twenty-five independent companies of these Pensioners were formed to release regular battalions for field service. On the suppression of 'the Fifteen' the following year, the scheme seemed to have proved itself, not only to the advantage of the regulars but also to that of the Royal Hospital, which had been relieved of the issue of some 1,500 pension payments. In 1719, therefore, it was decided to form a complete regiment of 'invalids', as they were termed, and on 11th March Colonel Edmund Fielding was ordered to raise ten companies and take command. Each company was to have two sergeants, two corporals, one drummer and fifty private soldiers, with the normal establishment of officers. Styled 'Colonel Fielding's Regiment of Invalids', the new unit was later to emerge as the 41st Regiment of Foot, and subsequently, as The Welch Regiment.

To us the title 'Invalids' may seem distinctly droll, but in those days an 'invalid' soldier was not necessarily a sick one, but simply a pensioner, whether disabled or not. If none of Fielding's men were fit enough for active service, they were all trained soldiers, many of whom had fought with Marlborough, and were well used to military discipline. The fact that only five days after Fielding's warrant, three complete companies were able to take over garrison duties from the Foot Guards at Portsmouth betokens a smooth and speedy mustering.

Edmund Fielding, of East Stour, Dorset, was neither aged nor infirm. Now 43, he had purchased his Ensigncy in the 1st Foot Guards in 1696, had seen service under Marlborough, and had been Colonel of a regiment of Foot which was disbanded in 1713, when he retired on half-pay.[2]

Not surprisingly, the early history of the 'Invalids' is unremarkable, being monotonous years of garrison duties at Portsmouth, with detached companies at Plymouth. The records show little but changes of Colonel and title. Edmund Fielding died as Lieutenant General in 1743 and was succeeded by Colonel Tomkins Wardour, whose family hailed from Whitney-on-Wye, Herefordshire. He had previously served with the Queen's Regiment of Horse (King's Dragoon Guards) and the Horse Guards, and after his death in 1752 (aged 64) was buried in Westminster Abbey. Why he should have been so honoured is not known. Wardour was the last Colonel to bestow his name upon the Regiment, for in 1751 a Royal Warrant directed that henceforth all regiments were to be designated simply by their numbers, or ranking, in the Line, and not by their Colonel's name. Thus Wardour's became the 41st Regiment of Foot, though as they were still a garrison-only unit, the suffix '(Invalids)' was added.[3]

By 1767 it seems that the Regiment had become one not so much of 'invalids' as of geriatrics. An Inspection Return by General the Earl of Pembroke, dated 18th May of that year, recorded that 'the officers are old, mostly wounded and infirm, and many have lost limbs'. The senior Major was aged 82; there was a Lieutenant of 80 (who was 'stone blind'); one Ensign was 79, another was 71 (and also 'stone blind'); and most of the other officers were in their 60s. Of the soldiers, twenty-seven were totally unfit for the lightest duties and the majority were described as 'stout'.

In 1787 the almost farcical pretence of employing the aged and infirm as 'soldiers' was at last abandoned. On 11th December the 41st's Colonel, now Major General McNab, was informed by Horse Guards (War Office) that his Regiment was to be removed from the establishment as a corps of invalids and was 'to serve in the line upon the same footing in every respect as His Majesty's other regiments of infantry'.

The Regiment was in fact born anew. All the aged and infirm officers were generously retired on full pay, and the soldiers were discharged with normal pensions as Out-Pensioners of the Royal Hospital. This change took place on Christmas Day 1787, and the following year's Army List showed all but one of the officers as transferred from other regiments of the Line. The exception was Major General McNab, who was allowed to continue as Colonel. Archibald McNab had in fact been

Colonel of the 41st since 1784. Aged 60, and having seen active service with the 32nd and 88th Foot, he was to retain his present appointment for only three years, for he died in 1790.

In January 1788 an 18-year-old youth was posted in as Lieutenant, having been commissioned Ensign in the 73rd Highlanders the previous March. In the contemporary Army List he appears as 'Hon. Arthur Wesley', but his name was later to become more familiar as Wellesley. However, the 41st saw little of the future Duke of Wellington, for shortly after joining he was whisked away by influential friends to the staff of the Lord Lieutenant of Ireland in Dublin Castle, and six months later he was nominally transferred to the 12th Light Dragoons (who saw even less of him).

The establishment of the reconstituted Regiment was ten companies, including the Grenadier Company and the newly-formed 'Light' Company,[4] the total strength being 30 officers and 432 other ranks. As 'Invalids' the Regiment had worn dress similar to that of the Chelsea Pensioners, but now they conformed to the rest of the Line infantry, with the regulation red coat, white waistcoat, white breeches and black spatterdashes. The head-dress was still the 'Marlborough' cocked hat. As before, officers were distinguished by finer quality dress, with silver lace and the gorget. Officer of field rank wore a silver epaulette on each shoulder, others a single epaulette on the right shoulder. Sergeants also had better quality material than the men, and wore a red-and-white sash round the waist, but junior NCOs bore no rank distinctions. It may as well be mentioned here that the familiar chevrons for NCOs were officially introduced in 1802, with four for sergeant majors (not then classed as Warrant Officers), three for sergeants and two for corporals, all worn only on the right arm.

We now revert to the 24th, whom we left in 1729 as Colonel Howard's Regiment. A recruit enlisting in that year would spend the whole of his service without confronting an enemy, for until 1741 the Regiment's lot was the uneventful one of home service, in Ireland, England, and Ireland again. There was a change of Colonels in 1737 when Thomas Howard, now Major General, exchanged to The Buffs and Major General Thomas Wentworth took over. He had been Colonel of the 39th since 1732 and had acted as Adjutant General from 1722 to 1733. By this time a regimental Colonel was rarely the actual Commanding Officer, as he had been in Marlborough's day. Nearly always a general officer, he was usually found some staff appointment which supplemented his pay as Colonel; without such appointment he received no pay of General's rank. And so the active command of the regiment was left to the Lieutenant Colonel, as it has been ever since.

The Regiment's next experience of active service was to prove disastrous. In October 1740 they sailed with an expedition under Lieutenant General Lord Cathcart to capture the port of Cartagena (in what is now Colombia) from the Spanish, who were threatening British maritime trade in the Caribbean. From the first, calamity followed calamity. By the time the ships, with 9,000 men aboard, had reached the South American coast, 617 had died from scurvy and dysentry while 1,500 were sick. Then, Lord Cathcart himself succumbed[5] and was succeeded in command by the 24th's Colonel, Thomas Wentworth. In his long career (he was commissioned in 1704) Wentworth had never heard a shot fired in anger, and his succession did nothing for the fortunes of the expedition. After the landing there followed unseemly wrangles between him and the naval commander, Admiral Vernon, the latter demanding aggressive action, the former pleading sickness and 'difficulties' and requesting reinforcements of sailors, which were refused. After some three weeks of inaction, except acrimonious correspondence between Admiral and General, Wentworth was at last persuaded to attack the fortress of Cartagena. Having lost their way in the night approach march, the troops, including the 24th, found themselves confronting the strongest sector of the defences and were beaten back with heavy casualties. Of the 1,200 men engaged, only 560 survived, the 24th losing 1 officer and 36 men killed, 94 wounded. This repulse decided the issue. The remnants of the forces were withdrawn to the transports, where they lay idle for ten days, awaiting a favourable wind. Sickness now struck again, and scores of men went down with 'local distempers' – dysentery, malaria and scurvy. By the time the Fleet made into port in Jamaica, the total British strength was down to 1,400 effectives. When the 24th finally returned to Plymouth in December 1742, they had lost 10 officers (including the Commanding Officer, Lieutenant Colonel Sandford), and 781 other ranks. The vast majority of these casualties were due to sickness rather than enemy action.

In 1744 infantry regiments were for the first time allotted specific recruiting areas, and the counties of Devon, Cornwall and Somerset were assigned to the 24th. The Regiment itself was now quartered in the West Country, at Exeter, Plymouth and Bristol, where it remained until Prince Charles Edward, the Young Pretender (or Bonnie Prince Charlie) fomented the 2nd Jacobite Rebellion in 1745. The Regiment was hastily routed (by sea) to Scotland, but by the time the men had disembarked at Leith, the Prince had been defeated at Culloden and 'the Forty-Five' collapsed. Meanwhile, in June 1745, Thomas Wentworth moved on (and up) to the 2nd Horse (later 5th Dragoon Guards), whom he graced as Colonel for barely two years before his death in 1747. The 24th's next incumbent was equally short lived: Brigadier General Daniel Houghton, founder of the 45th Foot (Sherwood Foresters) in 1741, took over on Wentworth's demise, only to pass on himself two years later.

Now the Regiment welcomed as Colonel the second (and last) peer of the realm in its history, though this one was not as distinguished as his predecessor, the Duke of Marlborough. William Henry Kerr, Earl of Ancram, purchased the vacancy in December 1747, and was to remain the titular commander until 1752. He had been Lieutenant Colonel (and Commanding Officer) of the 11th Dragoons, with whom he was wounded at Fontenoy, and as ADC to the Duke of Cumberland he was again wounded at Culloden.

For the remainder of their stay in Scotland the 24th were employed in the preservation of law and order among the Highland clans, and this saw them toiling as road-building labourers. The opening-up of the Highlands by General Wade's military roads had been undertaken between 1725 and 1740, but communications in some districts were still inadequate for policing duties. Thus in 1746 the soldiers of the Regiment heaved, broke and rammed stone to construct a five-mile road over the formidable Pass of Glencroe,[6] linking Arrochar with Inveraray, in Argyllshire. Today the summit of the pass is named on the maps as 'Rest and be Thankful', and the

Regimental Records state that on reaching this point the Regiment erected a stone seat with that inscription, continuing: 'This road was made by soldiers of the 24th Regiment in 1746. Lord Ancram, Colonel.' There is some discrepancy here, for as we have just seen, Lord Ancram did not become Colonel until the following year. Perhaps it was he who later arranged for the seat to be built; at all events it has long since disappeared, and only a stone now marks the site.

In July 1751 King George II signed a Royal Warrant' which regularised the Colours and dress of all regiments in the Regular Army. In fact, there was little change from the earlier Warrant of 1747, except for such distinctions as facings. The 24th still wore the knee-length red coat, white breeches and gaiters, and the cocked hat, but for the first time the facings were specifically directed to be of 'willow-green': previously they had been described as 'olive-green'. There was nothing particularly distinctive in green facings as such, for eleven other regiments of Foot and four of cavalry wore them, in varying shades. But only the 24th wore 'willow-green'. The infantry Colours, like the dress, were now 'uniform' throughout the Army. They were to be 6 ft 6 in. flying and 6 ft 2 in. on the pike, and it was reiterated that the display of Colonels' arms, crests or livery was 'expressly forbid'. The 1st, or King's, Colour was the Union Flag with the number or ranking of the regiment in Roman characters in the centre. The Regimental Colour was in the facing colour, with a small Union Flag in the upper canton and the central number as in the King's. It was not until 1784 that Battle Honours began to appear on Colours.

As we have seen, another effect of the 1751 Warrant was the final abolition of Colonels' names as regimental titles and the substitution of numbers. Thus Colonel Ancram's Regiment became officially the 24th Regiment of Foot, a title which they continued to cherish even after they had emerged as The South Wales Borderers, and which still appears as a suffix to the present Regiment's name.

Less than a year after these changes (in February 1752), Lord Ancram returned to his old Regiment, the 11th Dragoons, as Colonel, being succeeded by the Hon. Edward Cornwallis from the 40th Foot, who had been lately Governor of Nova Scotia. Then relatively young, 41, Cornwallis was to remain Colonel of the 24th for twenty-four years – a record unsurpassed in the history of the Regiment.

In June 1752 the Regiment, commanded by Lieutenant Colonel William Rufane, was posted to the Mediterranean island of Minorca, which in those days was reckoned to be as strategically important as Gibraltar. Besides the 24th, the garrison in the citadel of Fort St Philip included their old comrades of Marlborough's wars, the 23rd, together with the 4th and 34th. None was up to establishment, the total strength being 2,800 all ranks. In April 1756 the French mounted an attack in force, and the Governor, Lord Tyrawley, being absent as usual, full responsibility fell upon the Lieutenant Governor, George Blakeney, who was now aged 82 and crippled with gout.

The French under Marshal Richelieu landed on 17th April and laid siege to Fort St Philip, where, outnumbered by three to one, the aged Governor had withdrawn all his troops. Then followed weeks of artillery bombardment and ferocious attacks on the bastions and redoubts which the four steadily weakened battalions drove off, inflicting heavy casualties. On 19th May the garrison's morale was boosted by the appearance of a British Fleet from Gibraltar, led by Admiral Byng; but hopes of relief were dashed when, after firing a few token shots, the Admiral turned about and left the astonished defenders to their fate. The inevitable finale came after more than two months of constant attacks and unremitting pounding by howitzer and gun. By 27th June the garrison, reduced by killed, wounded and sick, were in a desperate state, with rations dwindling, water supplies failing, and many of the defences battered down. Seeing no prospect of relief, and loth to sacrifice any more of his brave soldiers, Blakeney surrendered. Marshal Richelieu was probably glad to agree to terms, for he had already lost 2,400 men, but he was chivalrous enough to accord his adversaries full honours of war as they marched out, and to grant them free passage to Gibraltar in his own transports. Although some 500 of the garrison were stricken down with sickness, actual battle casualties were remarkably light, thanks to the strength of the fortifications: 126 were killed and 306 wounded. The 24th lost fourteen killed or died of wounds and fifty-four wounded.

The British flag never again flew over Minorca, and while there was fulsome tribute to the staunch garrison,[8] Parliament was shocked and indignant at the loss of such a valuable Mediterranean strongpoint. A scapegoat had to be found, and, as is well known, Admiral Byng was court-martialled and shot on his own quarterdeck.

While at Gibraltar, on 26th August 1756, the 24th learned that they and fourteen other infantry regiments were to be augmented by ten companies, the additional ten to be formed into a 2nd Battalion. What we must therefore (if only temporarily) call the 1st Battalion returned home in November, to find that the 2nd had already been recruited and mustered in Lincolnshire under Lieutenant Colonel the Hon. Charles Colville. However, the Battalion as such were to see no active service, for on 23rd April 1758 all the newly-raised 2nd battalions were separated from their parents and formally constituted as regiments in their own right. Thus the 24th's offspring became the 69th Regiment of Foot, eventually to merge with the 41st as the junior partner of The Welch Regiment.[9] On 28th April Colville was promoted Colonel and appointed Colonel of the Regiment. Aged 68, this first Colonel of the 69th was a Scot and a veteran campaigner, having fought at Malplaquet, in the 1727 siege of Gibraltar, and at Dettingen, Fontenoy, Culloden and Lauffeldt. At Fontenoy he commanded the 21st Foot (Royal Scots Fusiliers) and was severely wounded.

It fell to the 69th to earn the fifth Battle Honour that appears in the present Regiment's roll, gained for the little-known action of Belleisle in 1761. This island (now Belle Ile) lay off the French coast, some twenty miles from the mouth of the Loire, and its capture would provide a useful base for any subsequent operation, besides compensating in some measure for the humiliating loss of Minorca. On 8th April, the 69th under Lieutenant Colonel Teasdale with eleven other battalions effected a landing, but were forced to withdraw to the ships in the face of fierce opposition. There was then a lull until sea conditions permitted the landing of heavy siege guns to support an attack on the heavily fortified citadel. After a week's bombardment the infantry went in with the bayonet, Captain Benjamin Bromhead of the 69th[10] capturing three redoubts with his Company. By now the fortifications had been pounded into rubble, and having lost more than 1,200 men, the French commander capitulated. British casualties amounted to 780 killed and wounded out of the 7,000 engaged. The 69th's losses were light: only twenty-eight soldiers were killed or died of sickness, while four officers and eighteen soldiers were wounded.

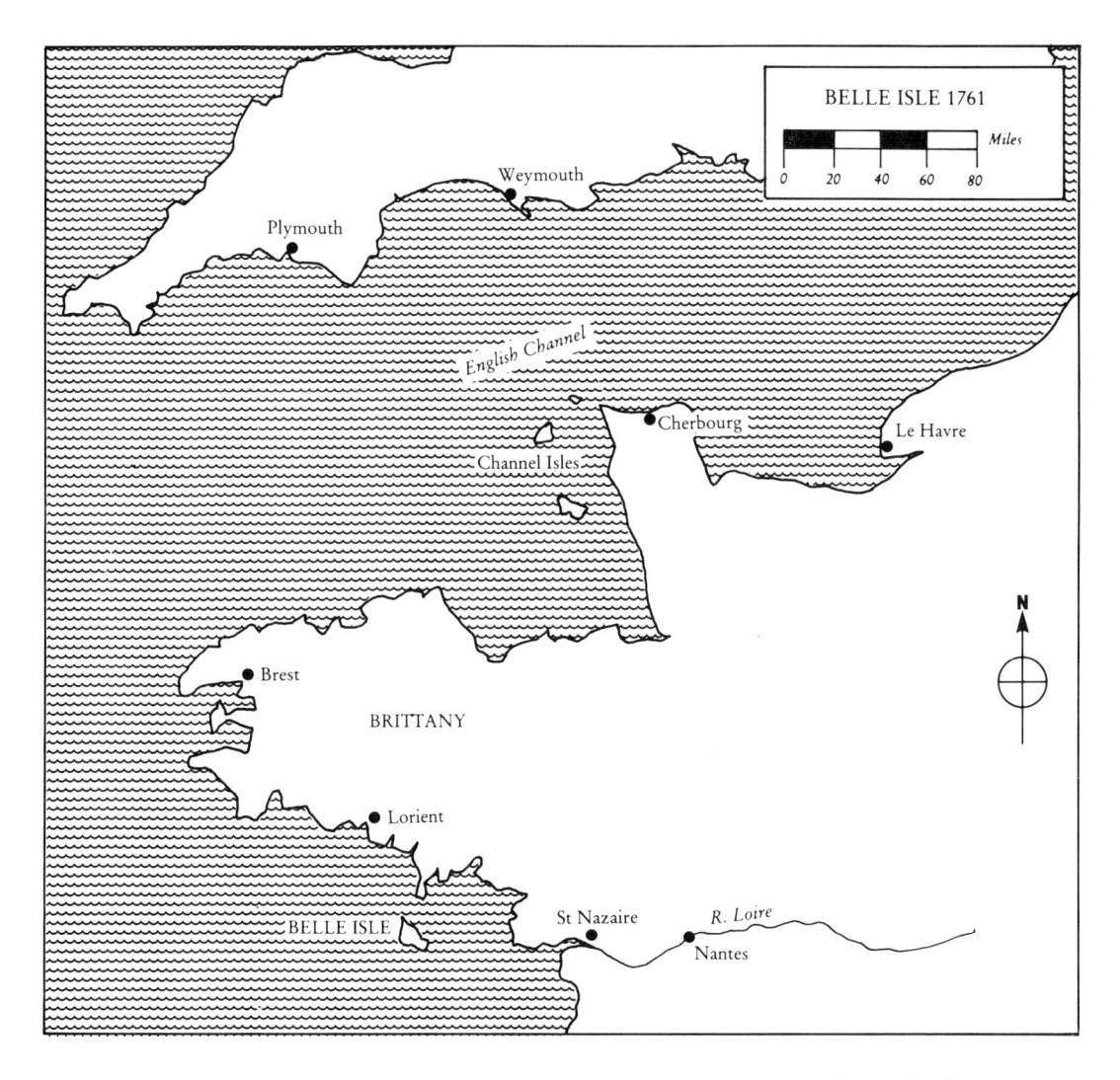

The seizure of Belleisle was hailed with rejoicing at home and laudatory addresses in the House; but the satisfaction was short lived, for two years later the island was ceded back to France under the Treaty of Paris, which concluded the Seven Years War. It was only in 1951 that The Welch Regiment and seven others were granted the Battle Honour 'Belleisle'.

Before the Treaty, however, the 69th had added another Honour. With the wresting of Quebec from the French, Britain was able to concentrate on driving them out of the West Indian territories, which included Martinique, the northernmost of the

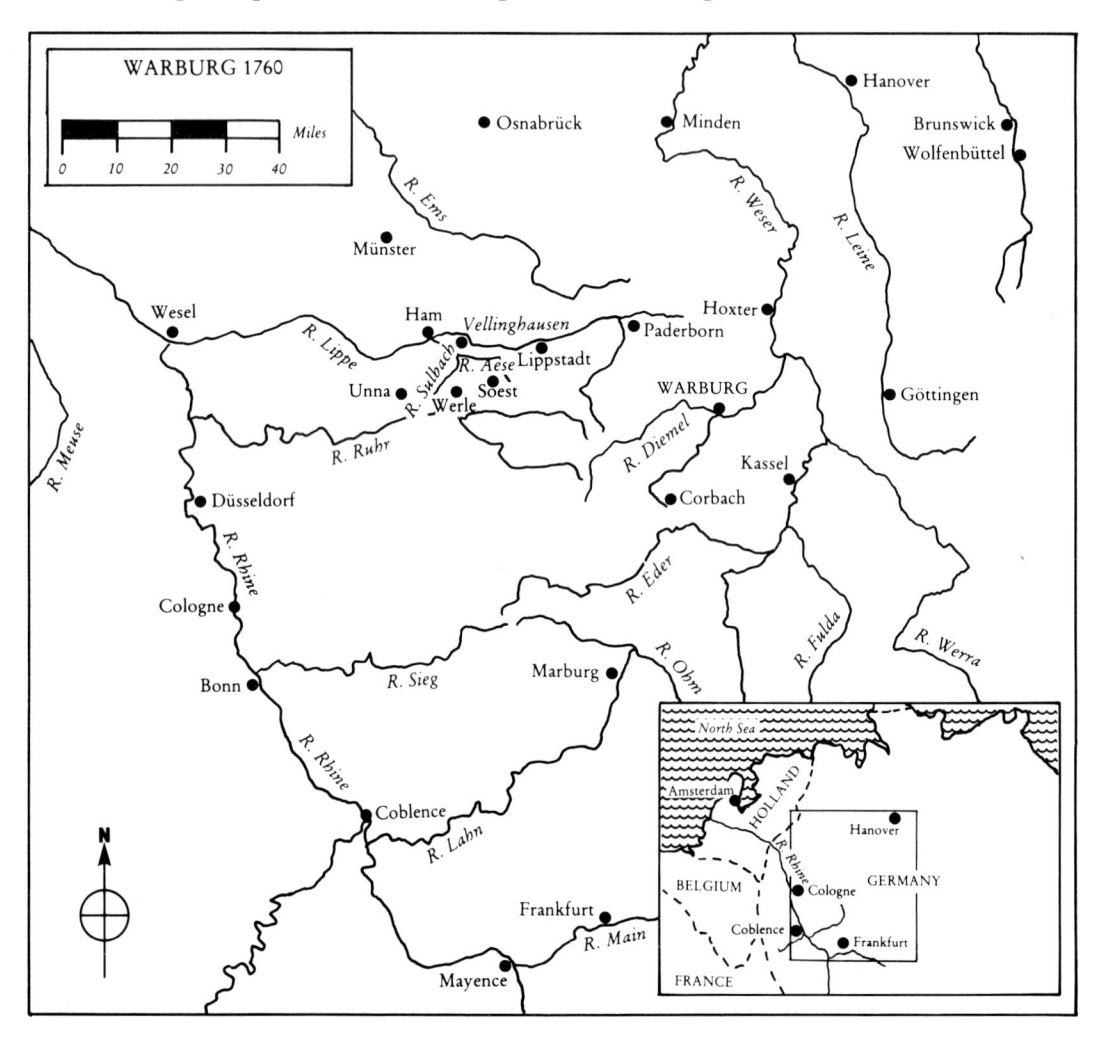

Windward Islands. The task force totalled some 8,000 infantry and detachments of artillery, among them the 69th and three of their comrade-battalions of the Belleisle venture, brigaded together under the 24th Regiment's former Commanding Officer, now Brigadier Rufane. The landing was successfully effected on 16th January 1762. Heavy fighting ensued, with the French being gradually pushed back into the citadel of Fort Royal, where after a three-week siege they finally surrendered. According to Fortescue, the total British losses were 383 all ranks killed and wounded, while Norman,[11] quoting from a contemporary issue of *The London Gazette*, gives the 69th's as a minimal 2 soldiers killed and 6 wounded. Unaccountably, the same author details casualties for the '41st Welsh', which is an obvious error, for the 41st were most certainly not present. It seems he confused the 1762 expedition with that of 1794, when the 41st did participate in the second capture of Martinique from the rebellious French, losing one officer wounded, one soldier killed and six wounded – the exact figures erroneously given by Norman for the earlier capture.

We must now go back to 1760 when the Seven Years War was still raging in northern Europe. In May of that year Prince Ferdinand of Brunswick, commanding the Allied Army, called for British reinforcements, and six battalions were accordingly routed from England. Described by Pitt (the Prime Minister) as 'six of our best battalions', these included the 24th Regiment. They all joined the British contingent under the Marquis of Granby near Kassel at the end of May, the Regiment being brigaded with the 33rd, 50th and 51st.

Their first action was the Battle of Corbach in July, when Ferdinand's impetuous young nephew, the Heriditary Prince (unmindful of the dictum that 'time spent in reconnaissance is seldom wasted') attacked what he imagined to be a weak detachment, only to be confronted by the entire French Army. Hastily withdrawing, he was saved from disaster by the staunchness of his four British battalions, who, wrote Granby in his despatch, '. . . showed the greatest eagerness to engage and in the retreat the greatest firmness and discipline'.

On 31st July Ferdinand himself commanded at the Battle of Warburg, where he utterly routed a French force of some 30,000 troops, slaying 1,500 and taking 1,900 prisoners. Today Warburg is chiefly remembered as a cavalry action, for it was the Marquis of Granby and his regiments of British Horse and Dragoons who carried the day with shattering charges.[12] But in the early stages the infantry also played their part, all the Grenadier companies, including those of the 24th, putting in a wide flanking movement which resulted in a four-hour struggle of fire and movement, while the battalion companies were heavily engaged in a musketry duel in the centre and on the other flank. The victors' losses were relatively light, at 1,200 killed and wounded, of which only 600 were British. In the 24th one officer and seven soldiers were killed, one and twenty-four wounded.

The Battle Honour 'Warburg' was granted (in 1909) only to the cavalry regiments who galloped with Granby; why the infantry who bore the brunt of the initial fighting should still be denied this distinction is a puzzling anomaly.

The year 1760 passed with much skirmishing and minor engagements, resulting in little advantage to either side, and no casualties but sickness for the 24th. Their next serious action came on 15th July 1761 when 100,000 French attacked the combined 50,000 of Ferdinand and Granby around the village of Vellinghausen. After a desperate struggle among hedgerows and copses the enemy were routed with the loss of 6,000 men. Again, allied casualties were fewer – no more than 1,600 killed and wounded – but 470 of these were British redcoats. The 24th lost their Commanding Officer, Lieutenant Colonel John Cook[13] and forty-seven men killed, with one Lieutenant and eighty men wounded. Although Vellinghausen was a significant defeat for the enemy, and a signal example of the redcoats' prowess, no Battle Honour has ever been awarded – another anomaly. The battle was the last major engagement in the war, which had been dragging on since 1755. In November 1762 the troops heard rumours of negotiations and these were confirmed by the end of the month when all hostilities ceased. A month later the 24th were posted to Gibraltar, and there they remained until 1769, when they were transferred to the Irish Establishment.

The next six years were spent in the unwelcome Irish 'exile', with reduced pay for the soldiers and no prospect of home leave. Whether the Regiment was involved in any skirmishing with the raparees or sundry other 'dissidents', we cannot tell for no records have survived.[14] However, we do know that in January 1776 the Regiment saw a change of Colonel. In that month Lieutenant-General Cornwallis died, after twenty-four years' tenure of the appointment, and was succeeded by Major General William Taylor. This officer had served in the 9th and 32nd Foot and for the past year had been Colonel of the 3rd Battalion, 60th Foot (the 'Royal Americans', and later The King's Royal Rifle Corps).[15]

As already observed, a regimental Colonel was no longer the *de facto* Commanding Officer, and it was the lot of Lieutenant Colonel Simon Fraser to lead the 24th at the outset of one of the most politically humiliating campaigns fought by the British Army. When Fraser took command the Union Flag flew over the whole of North America, from Hudson's Bay to Florida. But in 1775 the American colonials revolted; two years later their *ad hoc* forces had compelled the surrender of a British field Army of regular soldiers, and in 1783 Britain finally lost what became the United States of America.

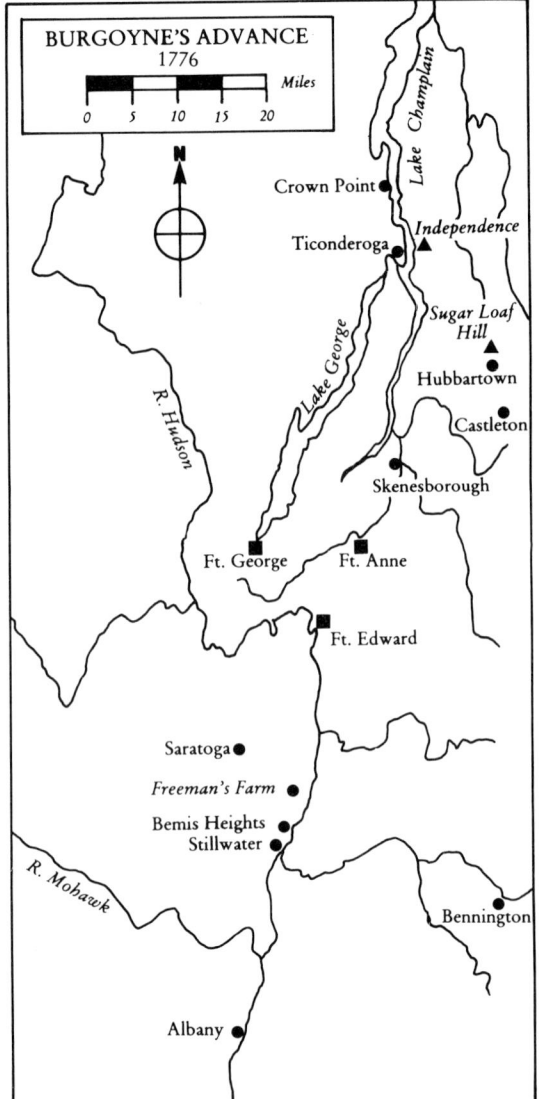

The 24th, together with seven other battalions, sailed for Canada in April 1776, and were thus too late to take part in the recapture of Quebec from the rebels. The following eighteen months of almost continuous fighting, often in difficult, wooded terrain, against a wily enemy well accustomed to fieldcraft and guerrilla tactics, cannot be fully detailed here.[16] It is sufficient to say that the Regiment acquitted itself with honour in every action, while Colonel Rufane, promoted Brigader, particularly distinguished himself at the capture of Ticonderoga. By October 1777, General Burgoyne's British force had been decimated by battle casualties and sickness and were facing overwhelming odds at Saratoga. Denied the reinforcements he had pleaded for and with his men almost starving, Burgoyne surrendered on 17th October. Of the 7,000 men originally under his command, only 3,500 were fit to march out. By the terms, these remnants were to be allowed free conduct to Boston, there to be shipped to England; but to the lasting shame of the newly-formed American Congress the terms were dishonoured, all the survivors being kept prisoner until 1781.

It has proved impossible to establish the exact battle casualties of the 24th during the campaign. But we know that 30 officers and 567 other ranks had embarked for Canada in 1776. A return of prisoners in May 1780 showed 23 officers and only 187 other ranks; by the time the Regiment returned to England in July 1781, the strength was down to 8 officers and 106 rank-and-file. Thus it is clear that in 5 years the Regiment had lost 22 officers and 461 men. How many of these were killed in action, or succumbed to sickness, or simply 'disappeared' while prisoners-of-war, is unknown. But one of the battle casualties to be officially recorded was the gallant Brigadier General Simon Fraser, who was killed by a sniper at Saratoga.[17]

Just a year after the 24th's survivors returned to England, on 31st August 1782, the Commander in Chief directed that all infantry regiments except those already bearing some titular distinction were to adopt a 'territorial' or county subtitle. This was an early attempt to foster a bond between regiments and counties, and thus, it was hoped, to stimulate recruiting. Initially the individual Colonels were asked for their preferences, but as the majority seemed to have none, while some were actually antagonistic to the scheme, the titles were allocated in an entirely arbitrary fashion.

It might be thought that the 24th with its Kentish origins, might have been associated with that county, but not so. In September 1782 they found themselves styled '24th (or 2nd Warwickshire) Regiment of Foot'. Apart from the fact that they had lately been recruiting around Tamworth, their connections with Warwickshire were minimal. Much the same applied to the 6th Foot, who were ordered to add '(1st Warwickshire)'. Preoccupied with a landing on St Kitts in the West Indies, our other Regiment, the 69th, were probably oblivious of the fact that they were now titled the '69th (or South Lincolnshire)'. As for the 41st, they remained barren of any subtitle, county or otherwise, until 1831 – one of only five regiments to be so 'distinguished'.

Notes

[1] In 1738 Thomas Howard's kinsman, Colonel the Hon. (later Sir) Charles Howard, took over the Colonelcy of the 19th Foot. They also wore green facings and, to the confusion of many, became known as The Green Howards – their present title.

[2] His son, Henry Fielding, achieved a celebrity denied to Edmund. Besides being a prolific playwright, he is acknowledged as the first of the great English novelists: his novel *Tom Jones* (1749) was a best-seller in its time, was recently adapted for television, and is compulsory reading for students of English literature.

[3] In some earlier warrants the title 'Royal Invalids' had appeared but, as Whitehorn points out in

his *History of the Welch Regiment*, this was quite unofficial and there is no 'Royal' in the 1751 Warrant. It is suggested that the unauthorised usage arose through the Regiment's association with the Royal Hospital and its wearing of a uniform slightly modified from the Chelsea Pensioners' uniform.

[4] Light companies were added to all infantry of the Line during the 1770s. Like the Grenadiers, they were regarded as élite elements of the battalions, enjoying 'superior intelligence' and performing scouting, patrolling and skirmishing tasks. They were the forerunners of the Light Infantry regiments.

[5] Fortescue adds the footnote that his death was due 'to an overdose of Epsom salts'.

[6] Not to be mistaken for the better-known Pass of Glencoe.

[7] *Regulations for the Colours, Cloathing, &c., of ye Marching Regiments of Foot and for the Uniform Cloathing of ye Cavalry, their Standards, Guidons, Banners &c.* This historic warrant is now preserved in the Public Record Office (Ref. WO. 7/25).

[8] In his *Naval and Military Memoirs*, Beatson observed: 'The terms on which the fort was at last surrendered by a handful of men, so distressed, so shattered and so neglected, remains a lasting monument to their honour.' The gallant old George Blakeney was made a KB and given an Irish peerage. Lieutenant Colonel Rufane of the 24th was rewarded with a brevet as Colonel.

[9] Their immediate seniors, the 68th Foot, had originated as the 2nd Battalion of the present Regiment's fellow-Welshmen, the 23rd Foot or Royal Welch Fusiliers.

[10] Bromhead was an ancestor of the VC hero, Major Gonville Bromhead, of Rorke's Drift fame.

[11] *Battle Honours of the British Army*, op. cit.

[12] Leading the attack himself, Granby lost first his hat, then his wig, and so went 'bald-headed for the enemy'.

[13] Cook had succeeded Lieutenant Colonel Rufane only the previous year when the latter (after thirty-nine years with the Regiment) exchanged to the 76th Foot.

[14] There is a woeful dearth of British military archives from Ireland, resulting from the destruction by artillery fire of the then Irish Public Record Office in Dublin during the 'Troubles' of 1922.

[15] Atkinson incorrectly states that he had been 'Lieutenant Colonel of the 9th Foot' when appointed Colonel, but that historian did not enjoy the advantage of Leslie's definitive *Succession of Colonels of the British Army* (1974) in which Taylor's previous Colonelcy is given as above. At that period the 60th had four battalions, each with its own Colonel.

[16] Fortescue devotes seventy-three pages to this campaign (Vol. III), while Atkinson covers seventeen pages in recording the 24th's actions.

[17] Two hundred years later, as an adventure training exercise, a platoon of C Company, The Royal Regiment of Wales, marched the entire route of the 24th's campaigning, through Ticonderoga to Saratoga, where they were fêted and televised on the spot where Simon Fraser had been killed.

CHAPTER FIVE

Honours for the 69th (1782–1811)

Few but naval historians, and members of The Royal Regiment of Wales, are likely to have heard of 'The Battle of the Saints'. This action took place on 12th April 1782, off the West Indian island of Dominica, when Admiral Rodney's thirty-six Sail of the Line roundly defeated an equally strong French Fleet, thus destroying France's naval domination of the Caribbean and securing the safety of Jamaica and other British possessions. While perhaps the saints were watching over Rodney, the name is derived from the straits known as Passage des Saintes in which the engagement was fought. Serving as marines aboard the British ships were the 69th Foot, who had been posted to the West Indies the previous year. The two Fleets closed for action at 8 a.m. and it was not until sunset, some ten hours later, that the French Admiral hauled down his Colours. All this long day the soldiers manned forecastles, poops and fighting tops of their men-o'-war, adding their musketry volleys to the naval shot and shell as the enemy vessels came within range. The Battle of the Saints was hailed as a great victory for the Royal Navy, but it also brought distinction for the 69th and their successors.

On 22nd May 1782 both Houses of Parliament passed a Vote of Thanks to Admiral Rodney and his Fleet, the 69th Foot being specifically mentioned. In recognition of their services, the Regiment were authorised to display a laurel wreath (similar to that of the Royal Marines) around the regimental number on the Colours, while the officers could wear miniature wreaths on their epaulettes. But for reasons never explained, these distinctions had lapsed by 1836, and when the then Commanding Officer, Lieutenant Colonel Monins, approached the War Office for their restitution, he was refused 'owing to the lapse of time which has occurred'.[1] However, official recognition did again materialise, though by that time the 69th had ceased to exist as such. In 1909 Army Order No. 312 directed that The Welch Regiment should bear upon its Colours 'A Naval Crown superscribed 12th April, 1782'.

In February 1797 a detachment of the 69th found themselves distinguished as marines, this time under Lord Nelson at the Battle of Cape St Vincent, in which he defeated the Spanish Fleet and gained one of his greatest victories. In his despatches

Battle of the Saints, 12th April 1782: the general action.
NATIONAL MARITIME MUSEUM, GREENWICH

Nelson singled out the Regiment for especial praise: 'The soldiers of the 69th, with an alacrity which will always do them credit, and Lieutenant Pierson of the same regiment, were always the foremost in this service' – by which he refers to the boarding of the Spanish flagship. The 69th's detachment consisted only of Lieutenant Charles Pierson and sixty-three other ranks, and perhaps because of this weak strength the War Office refused to award a Battle Honour when application was made in 1880.[2] In 1891 the matter was brought to the personal attention of the Queen, who overruled Whitehall's decision, and so after ninety-four years the Honour 'St Vincent' was granted to The Welch Regiment.

Thus with the award of the naval Crown in 1909, the Regiment was proud to become the only unit in the British Army to display two Naval honours, a distinction which has been inherited by The Royal Regiment of Wales since 1969.

While the 69th's detachment was earning Honours at sea, the 41st were engaged in suppressing a French-backed rebellion in the West Indies, where between 1794 and 1796 they suffered more from sickness than from enemy action. Described by Fortescue as 'the graveyard of British soldiers', the West Indian islands became notorious for the horrifying death tolls resulting from yellow fever, typhus, malaria and other tropical diseases, of which at this time the medical profession was largely ignorant. During their two years in San Domingo the 41st were virtually destroyed by these afflictions, losing a total of 754 rank-and-file. It then became the turn of the 69th

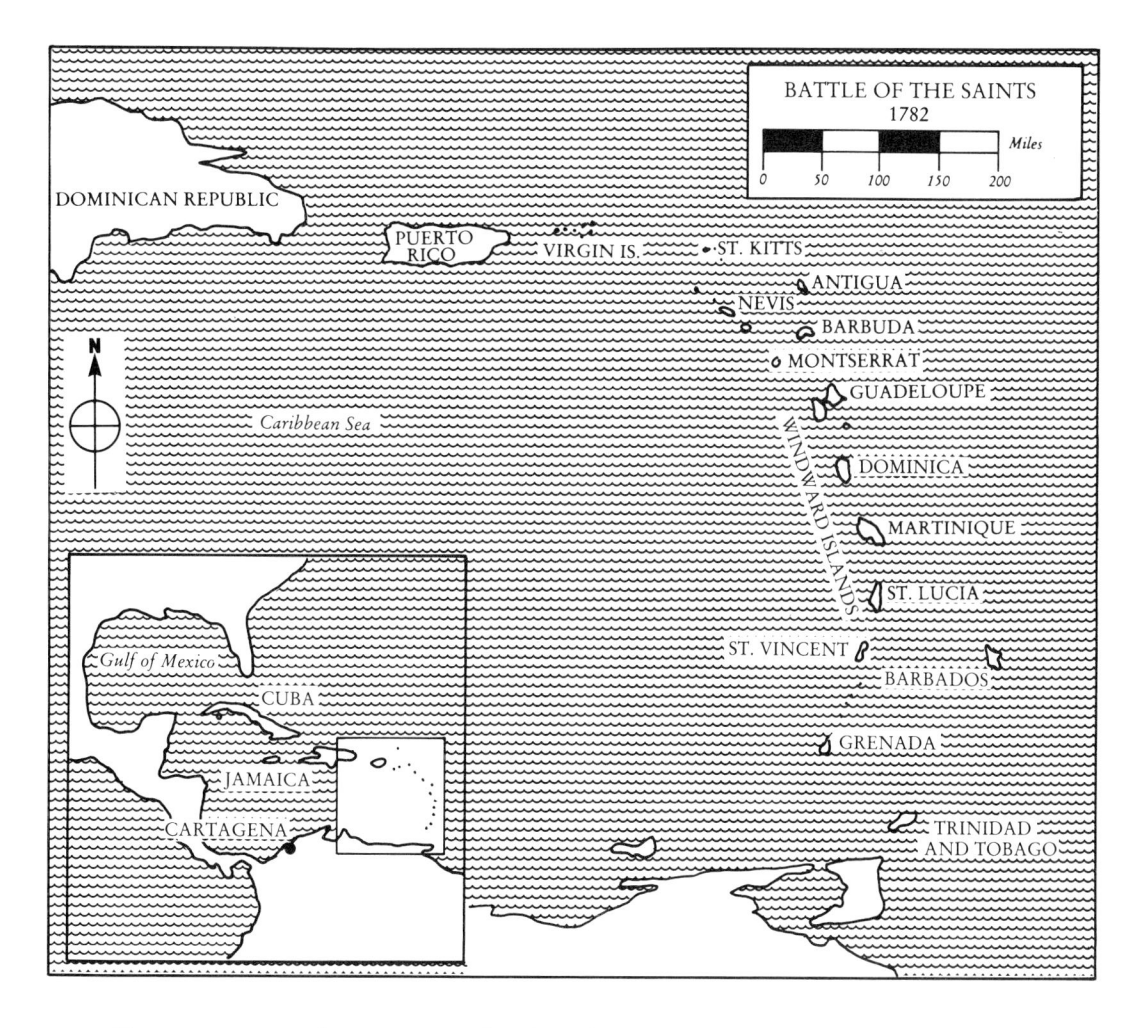

Map: Battle of the Saints 1782 — showing the Caribbean with Dominican Republic, Puerto Rico, Virgin Is., St. Kitts, Antigua, Nevis, Barbuda, Montserrat, Guadeloupe, Dominica, Martinique, St. Lucia, St. Vincent, Barbados, Grenada, Trinidad and Tobago, Windward Islands, Caribbean Sea; inset showing Gulf of Mexico, Cuba, Jamaica, Cartagena.

to suffer even worse losses. Less the detachment serving with Nelson's Fleet, they arrived in San Domingo just after their future partners had left, and when the island was finally evacuated in 1798 they had buried 25 officers (including the Commanding Officer, Lieutenant Colonel George Legard) and some 897 other ranks.[3] The 'graveyard' of the West Indies continued to swallow up thousands of British soldiers until the peace of 1815, when the defence of the islands was taken over by the native West India regiments. Of the 97,000 all ranks who served there between 1793 and 1815, approximately 70,000 were carried off by disease.[4]

One of the 41st's officers who survived the West Indian ordeal was Lieutenant Colonel Coote Manningham, whose name is today revered by The Royal Green Jackets as the founding Colonel of their earliest ancestors, The Rifle Brigade. After service in the 45th, 39th and 105th Regiments, Manningham was appointed second Lieutenant Colonel of the 41st in September 1795,[5] but while in the West Indies he acted as

Adjutant General to Major General Forbes, commanding in San Domingo, so that the Regiment probably saw little of him. Soon after returning to England he was promoted Colonel and appointed ADC to King George III. In January 1800 Colonel Manningham was selected by the Duke of York, Commander in Chief, to raise and train a novel unit of lightly-equipped skirmishing and scouting troops armed with the recently introduced Baker rifle, and known as the 'Experimental Corps of Riflemen'. The Corps was made up of drafts from fifteen regiments of Foot, among which were three officers and thirty-three other ranks from the 69th (the 41st were unable to contribute, having been posted to Canada the previous year). In 1809 Manningham, now Major General, commanded a brigade under Sir John Moore in Spain, and as a result of his sufferings in the arduous withdrawal to Corunna he contracted an illness from which he never recovered. He died in August 1809 at the relatively early age of 44.

Few readers will need reminding that the Experimental Corps of Riflemen became the 95th (Rifle) Regiment, and in 1816, The Rifle Brigade. The ancestors of The Royal Regiment of Wales can fairly be claimed to have played their part in the creation of the distinguished 'Left of the Line'.

With the advent of the 19th century it is appropriate to glance at a few changes and innovations. In 1800 the time-honoured cocked hat of Marlborough's day gave way to a shako of black felt, with a badge comprising a gilt plate with the Royal Cypher and the regimental number — the prototype of the present-day cap badge. This first shako (termed 'cap') was not welcomed by the soldiers: a cylindrical erection with miniature peak, it was unsecured by chinstrap or other means, and was apt to fall off in a high wind or energetic motion, while it gave no protection from sun or rain. From its unsightly appearance it was dubbed 'stove pipe'. The red coat now had shorter skirts, hooked back to expose white or buff breeches, while knee-length black gaiters protected the lower limbs. Facings remained unchanged. It was only in 1802 that the soldier was granted an outer garment for wear in bad weather: the first greatcoat was made of heavy grey kersey, reaching below the knees, and had an extra cape over the shoulders; when not in use it was carried rolled on top of the hide knapsack (forerunner of the pack).

In the battalion companies the principal weapon was still the venerable flintlock 'Brown Bess' musket, though a shorter pattern with a 42 in. barrel was introduced in 1803. Swords for rank-and-file had been abolished in 1768, and the only cold-steel weapon was the 17 in. socket bayonet. Although, as noted above, a rifled firearm had been issued to the new 'Rifle Corps', the rest of the Line infantry had to wait until 1851 before they were similarly armed.[6]

What with pipeclaying accoutrements, polishing metalware and cleaning arms, the early 19th-century soldier had plenty to occupy his few leisure hours, but in addition he was afflicted by one of the most absurd and time-consuming chores to beset the fighting man. Since the 1760s the soldier (and his officer) had been obliged to undergo a ritual of hair-dressing almost as involved as the coiffure of a lady of fashion. The hair had first to be brushed, combed and well greased with tallow, then pulled tightly back to be twisted into a queue and secured by a rosette. Finally, the whole was dusted with white powder. All this could only be accomplished with the aid of a man's comrades, and the complete operation of 'queueing up' might take nearly half an hour. To the relief of all ranks, the ridiculous practice was abolished in 1808, when the soldier was allowed to grow his hair naturally '. . . at back not extending below the top of the collar'. It was only in the 20th century that the military 'short back and sides' style became obligatory.

Discipline was still founded on the bedrock of punishment, and although the old ordeals of 'the Wooden Horse' and 'the Picket' had been abolished, they were superseded by the even more brutal flogging with the flesh-searing cat-o'-nine-tails, or knotted lash. At the beginning of the 19th century a soldier who 'offered violence to his superior officer' might be awarded horrifying sentences of up to 2,000 lashes, spread over days, or weeks, and necessitating hospital treatment. In 1807, however, King George III was 'graciously pleased' to limit the maximum sentence to 1,000 lashes. Despite periodic dispute in the House, and outcry in the Press, the notorious 'Reign of the Lash' continued almost to the end of the century.[7] The Duke of Wellington was convinced that 'there is no punishment that makes an impression upon any body except corporal punishment', a view supported by most officers.

Almost without exception the rank-and-file were still recruited from the illiterate lowest stratum – what modern sociologists would term 'socially disadvantaged groups' – and they accepted the harsh discipline with the same stoicism that enabled them to face the hardships and hazards of active service.

Lieutenant General Sir Ralph Abercromby, KB; Colonel, 69th Foot, 17th September 1790– 25th April 1792.

A Naval Crown superscribed 12 April, 1782. Commemorates The 69th's action as Marines at the Battle of the Saints 1782 and St. Vincent 1797.

The first decade of the century brought more action, and distinctions, for the 24th and the 69th. In July 1801 the 24th joined General Abercromby's forces at Alexandria and took part in the brief campaign which finally drove Napoleon's garrisons out of Egypt. Cairo surrendered tamely, but it was not until the end of August that the defenders of Alexandria were forced to follow suit. As usual, sickness carried off more men than did French bullets. The 24th's battle casualties were a minimal four soldiers wounded, but four officers and thirty men died of disease. After two months in the country the Battalion could parade only 174 effectives out of a total strength of 506, the remainder being smitten with dysentery, sandfly fever and the endemic ophthalmia. In July the following year (1802) the King was pleased to direct that all thirty-one regiments who had rid Egypt of the French should bear on their Guidons and Colours the Honour 'Egypt (with the Sphinx)'. Down to amalgamation with The Welch Regiment in 1969 this device continued to figure in the badges of the 24th Regiment and The South Wales Borderers.

A further distinction for the 24th came in 1806 when, with five other regiments under Lieutenant General Sir David Baird, they forced the capitulation of the Dutch at Cape Town, thus securing the Colony for Britain, and for themselves the Battle Honour 'Cape of Good Hope 1806'. South Africa was to play a significant role in the lives (and deaths) of British soldiers over the next hundred years, and in 1879 it was to be the setting for two of the most memorable actions in the 24th's history (see pp. 151–178). Soon after the capture of the Cape, Sir David Baird was appointed Governor and a year later (in July 1807) the 24th found themselves honoured with his appointment as their Colonel in place of the recently deceased General Richard Whyte. A Scot and a distinguished soldier with some thirty years' service in Europe, India and Egypt, Baird was a stranger to the 24th before the Cape expedition, but he remained their Colonel for twenty-two years, and, after Marlborough, was arguably the most eminent holder of the appointment down to the 20th century. Having lost an arm during Sir John Moore's retreat to Corunna, Baird became Commander in Chief in Ireland, Governor of Fort St George, and, as full General, GCB, KC. He died in his 73rd year in 1829.[8]

In 1803 Britain was not only at war with Republican France (led by the 1st Consul, Napoleon Bonaparte), but heavily engaged in India against the Mahratta hordes. To augment the over-strained Army, Parliament authorised the raising of 2nd battalions of Line regiments, the scheme of recruiting being known as 'raising men for rank'. Under this, an officer could gain a free step in promotion according to the number of men he could persuade to enlist. Thus in July 1803 another 2nd Battalion of the 69th was formed, and in September the following year the 24th were similarly augmented. These 2nd Battalions had relatively short existence, for both had been disbanded by 1816 – but not before that of the 24th had gained nine Battle Honours under Wellington in the Peninsula.

To most British soldiers serving prior to 1947, India, or 'the Shiny', was a very familiar posting, as it was to the forebears of The Royal Regiment of Wales. The first of these to set foot in the subcontinent was the 1st Battalion of the 69th, who landed at Madras in July 1805. Following the successful campaign against the Mahrattas by Lord Lake and Sir Arthur Wellesley (late Lieutenant in the 41st), the Hon. East India

Company's Presidency of Madras enjoyed peace, and the 69th in their barracks at Fort St George foresaw little likelihood of any serious business. But exactly a year later they were to be involved in a traumatic episode which brought them honour but cost them dear. It can fairly be claimed that but for the gallantry of the 69th's officers and soldiers, and the initiative and daring of a British cavalry commander, the sepoy mutiny at Vellore might well have equalled the holocaust of 1857.

In February 1805 the newly-appointed Commander in Chief of the Presidency arrived from England. Lieutenant General Sir John Cradock had never served in India, was totally ignorant of the 'native' soldiers, their customs, castes and religions, and was not disposed to learn. A noted stickler for discipline and regulations, his displeasure was immediately aroused by the unmilitary appearance of the sepoys on parade, with their floppy, chapatti-like pagaris, naked legs and, worse, the variety of beards, moustaches, caste-marks, ear-rings and other adornments described as 'joys'. Thus in November 1805 he abolished the pagari in favour of a modified type of shako, and the following March saw new regulations forbidding all caste-marks and ear-rings, and restricting facial hair. To the Indian soldier all these were not merely 'joys' but carried deep religious and caste significance, while the new head-dress was especially objectionable as being similar to that worn by half-castes and the despised Christian Indians. There were mutterings that the British were attempting to force their religion on the Company's Army. In May 1806 a Battalion of Madras Native Infantry at Vellore flatly refused to adopt the shako. Cradock ordered a court martial, which sentenced the NCOs to be reduced to the ranks; other sepoys were awarded 900 lashes apiece and discharged from the service, while the Battalion was removed from Vellore in disgrace.

It was at this juncture that four companies of the 69th under Major James Coates were posted to the garrison of Vellore, which also comprised two other battalions of the Madras Native Infantry who had so far remained passive. In overall command was Lieutenant Colonel St John Fancourt, from the 34th Foot. Also in the strategic fortress of Vellore (some eighty miles west of Army Headquarters at Madras) were four 'political detainees', the sons of the great Mysore leader, Tippu Sultan, who had been slain in the capture of Seringapatam. Leading a life of indolent ease, with many privileges as befitting their rank, these Princes had ample leisure to reflect on the fallen splendour of their father's Empire, and to dream of the day when the Tiger Flag of Mysore would again be raised. They also had ample opportunity of intriguing with the Indian element of the garrison. Unsuspected by the Commander in Chief, Vellore was in fact a powder keg, and the companies of the 69th had arrived in time to become victims of the explosion.

The total strength of the four companies was 11 officers and 372 other ranks. The rest of the garrison consisted of six companies of the 1st Madras Native Infantry and eight of the 23rd (who had replaced the mutinous Battalion). Thus with some 1,800 Indian troops, the British element was outnumbered by a little over four to one. But this was normal in a 'mixed' brigade, and despite the disquieting rumours reaching Army Headquarters at Fort St George, the Commander in Chief did not consider it necessary to adjust the balance. The nearest military station to Vellore was sixteen miles away at Arcot, where the British 19th Light Dragoons and two Company cavalry regiments were stationed, all under command of Lieutenant Colonel Rollo Gillespie.

It was the usual practice for the Indian troops to sleep outside the fort in the 'native' lines, but when a field day was ordered, as it was for 10th July, they spent the previous night within the walls so as to facilitate a speedy turnout in the early hours. Thus on the evening of the 9th the whole Indian contingent marched in, under arms, and settled in their lines near the Princes' quarters. This was the opportunity awaited by the plotters.

Details for guard duties were taken from the 69th who provided two subalterns and fifty-three NCOs and men for the Quarter Guard, Magazine Guard and other guards. By midnight the rest of the 69th lay sweltering in fitful slumber on their charpoys. At 2 a.m. the acting field officer of the day, one Jemadar Sheikh Kassim of the 1st Madrasis, reported in from his rounds: *'sab thik hai'* – all is well. And so it was for the conspirators, of whom the Jemadar was the ringleader.

An hour later Sergeant Cosgrave of the 69th was puzzled to hear a tramping of feet and clink of arms approaching his Quarter Guard in the darkness. No patrol was due at this time, and he ordered his sentry to challenge. In reply came a fusillade of musketry which felled Sergeant and sentry; as the rest of the Guard came tumbling out they too were mown down, and the brave drummer-boy was bayoneted as he began to beat the General Alarm. The rudely awakened 69th soldiers in their barrack block had scarcely time to seize their weapons before a storm of musket-balls ripped through the reed matting over open doorways and windows and into the mass of bodies. Over in the officers' quarters Colonel Fancourt ran out of his bungalow straight on to stabbing bayonets. Lieutenant Eley of the 69th was shot with his infant son in his arms, and his wife was then bayoneted.

Having broken into the arsenal, the insurgents dragged out two 6-pounder guns and now concentrated their fury on the 69th's barracks. Many of the soldiers had been killed, many more were wounded; there were no officers with them, only some junior NCOs. But here were stolid British infantrymen of the Line, and having barricaded the doors they determined to sell their lives as dearly as possible, taking pot-shots through windows as roundshot brought bricks and roof-tiles showering upon them.

Meanwhile, a group of officers, headed by Captain Maclachlan of the 69th, together with Sergeant Brady, had managed to take refuge in an officer's quarter where they held out for two hours. One of the officers later related that while fleeing for his life he came upon a 69th sentry standing doggedly at his post near the magazine. He urged him to run for it, but the reply was 'I cannot, sir, I have not been relieved yet.' Subsequently the bullet-riddled body of this British 'Pompeii Centurion' was found still at his post. As Whitehorne observes (in his *History of the Welch Regiment*), 'it is sad that the name of this very splendid man should not have been handed down to us.'

Except for the 69th's barracks, still holding out, the whole of the fort was now in the hands of the mutineers, who had even flaunted the green Tiger Standard of Mysore on the flagstaff. By dawn the firing had abated, for most of the sepoys were indulging in an orgy of pillaging and looting, and Captain Maclachlan and his little band, now joined by Captain Barrow (also of the 69th), managed to dash for the comparative security of the barracks. The interior was a shambles: amid the rubble lay the bodies of fifty men, while as many wounded were crying out for water which could not be obtained. The survivors' ammunition was nearly exhausted, for, complying with normal practice, they had been issued with only six rounds per man the previous night.

Leaving some men to tend the wounded, Captain Maclachlan led about 150 fit survivors through the rear windows and on to the ramparts in a desperate attempt to reach the magazine and replenish ammunition: on gaining it they found nothing but blank cartridges. Shortly afterwards Maclachlan fell wounded and Captain Barrow took command. Leading another party to one of the bastions he too fell, and the 69th were left without a combatant officer. But Assistant-Surgeons William Jones and John Dean (of the Hon. East India Company) unhesitatingly took over, and under these gallant medical officers sixty-odd soldiers fought their way to the bastion above the main gateway. As they did so, Sergeant Angus McManus and Private Philip Bottom braved a heavy fire to reach the flagstaff and haul down the rebel Standard, which they bore back to their cheering comrades. Although some rounds had been picked up from dead sepoys, ammunition was still a problem; but, coming across bags of Arcot rupees scattered by the mutineers, the 69th turned them to a novel use with the blank cartridges collected earlier. There is a story that as an Irish private fired off a hail of silver coinage he yelled, 'I'll trouble ye for the change out o' that, ye black soor!'

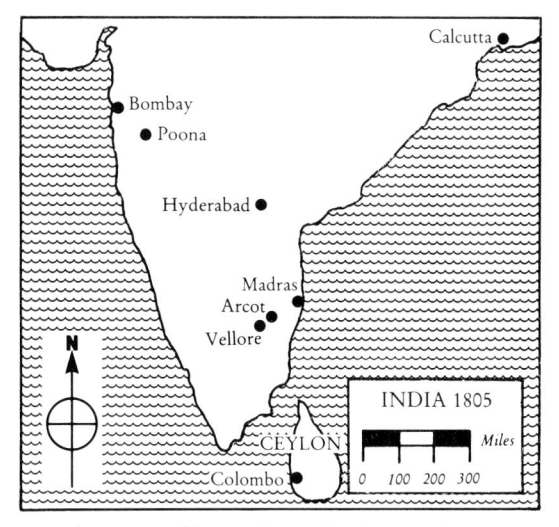

At this juncture a horrible act of barbarity was perpetrated by the sepoys. Dragging out fifteen sick men of the 69th from the hospital building, they shot and bayoneted them all in full view of their fellow-soldiers. Witnessing this atrocity, the latter swore they would wreak vengeance before they went down fighting; and such an end now seemed inevitable, for they had no inkling that relief was even then on its way.

Major Coates, commanding the 69th detachment, had not been involved with his men. As was the custom, he and other field officers not on duty had been sleeping in more comfortable quarters outside the fort, and when the mutiny erupted he was unable to join his command. But he did the next best thing, and sent a mounted officer galloping off to Arcot for help. It so happened that early the same morning Colonel Rollo Gillespie was riding from Arcot to pay a courtesy call on his friends, the Fancourts, at Vellore, and thus scarcely had he left the cantonment than he was met by the bearer of the shattering news. Spurring back to the cavalry lines, Gillespie turned out the duty squadron of the 19th Light Dragoons and a troop of the 7th Native Cavalry, and, ordering the remainder of the cavalry and two guns to follow, he led his little force to Vellore.

At about 9 a.m. the sixty-odd remnants of the 69th were still holding out in the gateway bastion, now almost down to their last round (and last rupee), when they were astonished to behold Gillespie and his troopers thundering up to the walls in clouds of dust. In their lust for slaughter the mutineers had omitted to raise the drawbridge, and the two outer gates were still open. Encouraged by Gillespie, Sergeant Brady and some privates lowered themselves down by means of their belts and contrived to open the third gate, but the fourth (inmost and stoutest) was beyond their powers. It could only be blown open by galloper guns, which had not yet arrived. Brigade commander or no, Gillespie was not the man to sit and await them. Having got himself hauled up to the bastion, he collected all the 69th men and led a bayonet charge on the guns covering the inside of the gateway. The mutineers fled and the guns were turned to face them. Though no ammunition was left, the mere threat of the muzzles and the glinting bayonets of the enheartened 69th soldiers were sufficient to gain a breathing space. At this critical moment the rest of Gillespie's cavalry with the two 6-pounder guns galloped up, and he ordered an officer of the Madras Engineers to blow open the innermost gate. This officer was Lieutenant (later Major) John Blakiston, who has left us an eye-witness account of what followed:[9]

> Finding the gun was already loaded with shot, I ordered the sergeant to discharge the piece, and that he might as well lay it for the bolt, pointing with my sword to where I thought it was. He did so, and the gate flew open. Colonel Gillespie now informed us that he should descend the rampart with the party of the 69th and ... in a few minutes after, the cavalry should gallop into the fort. Having given the Colonel a short start, we dashed sword in hand into the square ... The sepoys gave way in all directions, being closely pursued by the cavalry, numbers being cut down in the streets and on the glacis ... in short, no quarter was given. ... Shortly after, we passed over the bodies of the 69th sick, lying in their hospital clothing as they had been brought out and butchered. Upwards of a hundred sepoys who had sought refuge in the palace were brought out and by Colonel Gillespie's order, placed under a wall and fired at with cannister shot from the guns till they were all despatched.

The Vellore mutiny was over; the British flag again flew over the gateway, as it did until 1947. The 69th had lost two officers and eighty soldiers killed, while three officers and seventy-six soldiers were wounded. The recorded casualties of the mutineers were 350 killed and 100 wounded, but it was believed that many other wounded managed to escape to their villages. Colonel Gillespie was hailed as the 'Saviour of Vellore'. Fortescue avers that had it not been for his timely intervention and decisive action the consequences of the mutiny could have been catastrophic '... among them might well have been the loss of British India.'

On 20th July Colonel Gillespie wrote as follows to Army Headquarters Madras:[10]

> Colonel Gillespie begs leave to state ... to His Excellency the Commander-in-Chief the sentiments he entertains of the meritorious conduct of the

troops under his command, as well as that of the remains of His Majesty's 69th Regiment, who composed the garrison of Vellore on the 10th inst. To the officers of the 69th Regiment, who in the early part of the insurrection assembled their men to make head against the barbarous enemy, who were attacking them on all sides, too much praise cannot be given; and Colonel Gillespie has particularly to regret the gallant exertions of Captains Barrow and McLachlan Lieut. Mitchell and other wounded officers were too soon lost to the regiment, from those officers being unfortunately disabled so early in the day.

The remains of this valiant corps fought gallantly for several hours without an officer, and the Colonel begs leave to express his admiration of their undaunted resolution. Colonel Gillespie cannot help mentioning in terms of the highest approbation, Sergeant Brady, of the 69th Regiment, who so bravely followed him in the sally from the ramparts, and drove the enemy from their lurking places, previous to the charge of the cavalry.

After the subsequent enquiry Gillespie was awarded the then handsome sum of £2,500; Sergeant Brady of the 69th received £250 and was offered an Ensigncy, which he declined in favour of a Conductorship in the Ordnance Department. Apart from the somewhat niggardly grants of £18 to Sergeant McManus and £7 to Private Bottom, the staunch conduct of the remainder of the Regiment went unacknowledged. Sixty years later (and after another, greater, mutiny) the subject of Battle Honours came under War Office review, and the 69th applied for the grant of 'Vellore'. This was refused. It was held that the theatre Honour 'India', already granted, was sufficient, although this was also awarded to six other regiments who had never set foot in Vellore. Sir John Cradock, whose ill-judged and insensitive orders had sparked off the mutiny, was relieved of his post and sent home, as was also Lord William Bentinck, Governor of the Presidency.

The 69th continued to serve in the 'East Indies' for another nineteen years. By the time they returned to England, Wellington's Armies had driven the French out of the Peninsula, and the Battle of Waterloo had seen British soldiers fighting on the Continent of Europe for the last time until 1914. If the Regiment were deprived of any share in the Iron Duke's great victories, they earned distinction in lesser-known fields. In 1810 they formed part of a small expeditionary force which captured the island of Bourbon[11] (off Mauritius) from the French, and the following year saw them victorious in Mauritius itself. By a curious coincidence, the seizing of Mauritius effected the release of 11 officers and 375 men of the 69th's future associates, the 24th Regiment. Sailing for India from the Cape in June 1810, the 24th had been involved in a running sea battle with French frigates, and two of their transports were captured, crews and soldiers being interned in Mauritius. The Battle Honour 'Bourbon'[12] was granted in 1826, but oddly enough the capture of Mauritius went unrewarded. With the eviction of the French from this theatre, the East India Company was free to concentrate efforts on the wresting of Java from the Dutch, who it was feared, were under the influence of Napoleon. Commanded by Lieutenant General Sir Samuel Auchmuty, some 12,200

British and Indian troops were detailed for the expedition, which effected a landing near Batavia in July 1811. The 69th were led by Colonel William McLeod, who had taken over as Commanding Officer just before the Vellore mutiny, and their divisional commander was that 'Saviour of Vellore', Colonel Rollo Gillespie. The stolid Dutch proved formidable enemies, as did the terrain of jungle, swamp and thickly wooded mountain, and it was only after two months' heavy fighting that their General Janseens conceded defeat. Among the eighty-seven casualties of the 69th was Colonel McLeod, killed while leading his men on a strongpoint on the Batavia River. His 'distinguished gallantry' was mentioned in General Auchmuty's subsequent General Orders. The Battle Honour 'Java' was awarded in 1818, to be shared by the four other British regiments engaged.[13]

During the first half of the 19th century it was a general rule for regiments to serve not more than ten years overseas before being posted back for a five-year spell of home service. But the almost constant 'small wars' in the East and elsewhere played havoc with this practice, and as we have seen, the 69th were continuously abroad, on the East India Company's service, for almost twenty-one years. It was only in February 1826 that they were posted home.

Although there are no surviving statistics, only a handful of the young soldiers who had sailed for Madras in 1805 could ever have seen England again. Throughout the century British soldiers in India continued to be slain not only by Mahrattas, Sikhs, mutinous sepoys, Pathan tribesmen and other assorted foes, but by the endemic hazards of the country itself. As late as 1878 Field-Marshal Lord Roberts was writing: 'In the fifty-seven years preceding the Mutiny the annual rate of mortality amongst European troops in India was sixty-nine per thousand, and in some stations it was even more appalling'.[14] Dysentery, typhus and malaria, took their toll, but the most dreaded scourge was cholera, which was responsible for more fatalities than anything else. The medical profession was utterly ignorant of its causes, and there was no known cure. The swiftness with which it struck was terrifying: an epidemic could smite a fit battalion in the morning and leave twenty or thirty men dying in agony by nightfall. Only much later was it discovered that cholera was not an invisible, poisonous 'cloud', but a bacillus bred in unsanitary conditions and transmitted by contaminated water or food. Most soldiers in 'up-country' stations were crowded in primitive mud-built (*matti*) huts or 'bungalows', in which they ate their meals plagued with myriads of flies that had been feasting on the ordure of the open latrines nearby. There was no proper drainage system, and the wells or 'tanks' supplying drinking water were inevitably fouled. Although cholera fatalities for the 69th are not recorded, some idea of the horror can be gauged from the report of an epidemic in Karachi in June 1845, where within four days the garrison of eight regiments buried 763 officers and men.[15]

Another major threat to effective strengths was what the doctors then termed 'heat apoplexy', or heat exhaustion. Until after the Indian Mutiny the authorities gave no thought to providing the soldier with a tropical dress: he was compelled to march and fight in hot-weather temperatures soaring above 100° F clad in his home service attire of thick red coat, serge trousers, shako and constricting cross-belts. Small wonder that he suffered accordingly, and the sick list rose. During a ten-day march in southern India in

Lieutenant General the Hon. Edward Cornwallis, Colonel the 24th Regiment, 1752–76.

The death of Brigadier General Simon Fraser of Balnain. He commanded the 24th Regiment in America during the War of Independence. He was mortally wounded near Saratoga on 7th October 1777, when commanding the Advanced Corps of General Burgoyne's Army.

June 1839, forty-two men of the 84th Foot went down with 'the apoplexy', and five died.

If the West Indies of the 1790s proved the graveyard of the British soldier, the 'East Indies' of the 19th century ran it close.

Notes

[1] In the Regimental journal, *The Men of Harlech*, for November 1981, Lieut. Bryn Owen, Curator of The Welch Regiment's Museum, pointed out that as the distinction had been conferred by a vote of Parliament, it could only be rescinded by a similar vote, which was never taken. Theoretically, therefore, The Royal Regiment of Wales should still be entitled to bear the wreath.

[2] It was a general ruling that in order to qualify for a Battle Honour a regiment should have been present at an action with its Regimental Headquarters and at least one company (or squadron).

[3] The casualty figures for both the 41st and the 69th were derived by Whitehorne *(History of The Welch Regiment)* from Monthly Returns now filed in the Public Record Office (Refs. WO. 12/7695, WO. 17/151, WO. 17/190).

[4] 'The Destruction of the British Army in the West Indies, 1793–1815', by Dr R. N. Buckley *(J. Society for Army Historical Research*, Vol. LVI, 226, 1978). This deeply researched medical study supplements and corrects Fortescue's account.

[5] At this period all regiments were allowed two Lieutenant Colonels, the second or junior acting as Second in Command and deputy in the absence of the senior.

[6] The first British rifle, the Baker, was, of course, more accurate than the smoothbore musket, but it was still a muzzle-loader, and its disadvantage lay in the difficulty of ramming the bullet down the rifled bore. Hence the rate of fire was no more than one round per minute, compared with the three of the musket.

[7] The maximum sentences having been successively reduced to 200 lashes, flogging was finally abolished in 1881.

[8] A two-volume biography by Theodore Hook was published in 1832, while a complete summary of his life appears in *The Dictionary of National Biography*.

[9] *Twelve Years' Military Adventure* (published anonymously, 1829).

[10] Quoted in *A Narrative of the Historical Events connected with the Sixty-Ninth Regiment*, by W. F. Butler (London, 1870).

[11] Now Réunion.

[12] Only one other British regiment was awarded the 'Bourbon' Honour, this being the 86th Foot, now represented by The Royal Irish Rangers.

[13] It should be added that having again distinguished himself in Java, Major-General Robert Rollo Gillespie, KCB, fell at the head of his troops in the Nepal campaign of 1814.

[14] *Forty-One Years in India.*

[15] Heathcote, T. A. *The Indian Army. The Garrison of British Imperial India* (1974).

CHAPTER SIX

The 24th and 69th with Wellington (1809–16)

While the 69th were suffering from enemy action and climatic hazards on their Indian posting, the 2nd Battalion of the 24th were earning nine Battle Honours in the Peninsula. In his history of The South Wales Borderers, Atkinson devotes 5 chapters and 179 pages to their Peninsular campaigning, but the present author can afford no more than a digest of events.

Landing in Lisbon in April 1809, the Battalion joined Major General Mackenzie's Brigade, together with the 31st and 45th, forming part of Wellesley's[1] five divisions which were to confront the French in the first major encounter of Talavera. This hard-fought battle took place on 27th and 28th July. After indecisive attack and counter-attack by both sides, a critical situation developed on the 28th when the Guards Brigade were caught in the act of deploying and driven back in some disorder, carrying with them another brigade and exposing the whole of the British centre. Mackenzie immediately brought up his own Brigade, led by the 24th, and the pursuing French were checked, allowing the Guards and the rest to rally. The 'admirable steadfastness' of Mackenzie's men, as Fortescue describes it, proved the turning point of the day: Wellington was enabled to redeploy for his final attack which shattered the French line and cost them more than 7,000 casualties.

The 24th suffered severely for their staunchness: 51 men were killed and 278 wounded, of whom 46 later died of their wounds. These were the heaviest casualties of any British regiment engaged. Unhappily, the decisive action of their Brigade at first went unacknowledged, for Mackenzie himself was killed and no report of it reached Wellesley. Consequently the latter's despatch, published in *The London Gazette*, made no mention of the events. This omission was pointed out to Wellesley by Major Chamberlain (who had taken over the 24th when Lieutenant Colonel Drummond was wounded) and the Marquis then sent off a letter giving full credit to the 24th and their comrades. By ill fortune the packet carrying it was sunk by the French, and so the letter was lost. It was only in the next century, with the publication of Oman's definitive history of the Peninsular campaign,[2] that the 24th's gallant conduct was made public.

More than a year passed before British and French again came to grips, for while

The 24th and 69th with Wellington 1809–16

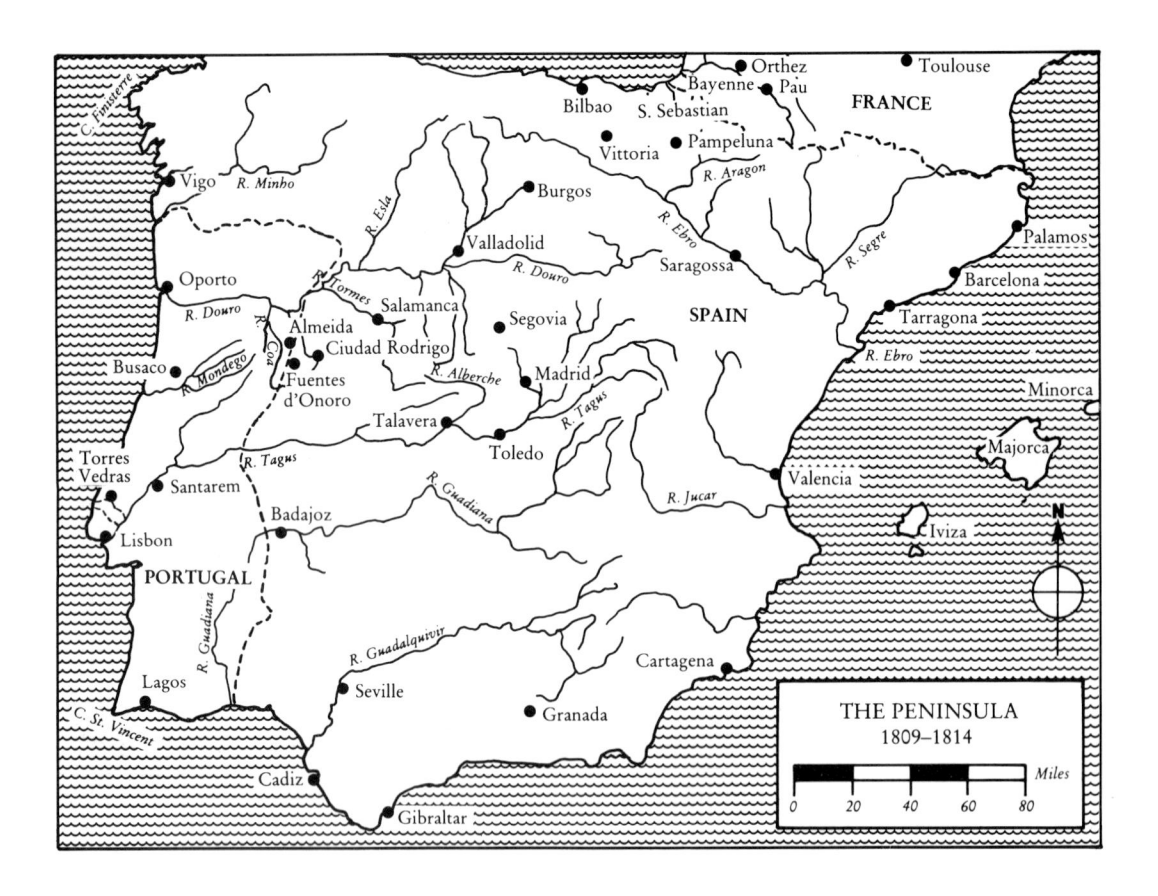

the latter were harrying the Spanish forces in Andalusia, Lord Wellington (as he had now become) was refitting and redeploying on the Portuguese frontier south of Badajos. The lull was much needed. The valley of the Guadiana River, in which the troops spent the summer and autumn, was notoriously unhealthy and the regiments were almost decimated by dysentery and 'fever' (probably malaria). The MS Regimental Records of the 24th state that in August the Battalion could scarcely muster 100 fit men, and by the end of the year nearly 600 of the 873 all ranks who had marched from Lisbon in May were lost through 'the Fever and Ague'. Sadly, Wellington's despatches reveal that another cause for concern was the abundant wine of the country which could be bought or stolen everywhere, and which had disastrous effects on unaccustomed stomachs.[3]

The 24th's soldiers were probably no better and no worse than the rest; drunkenness, whether on exotic wines, or home-brewed ale, or fiery spirits, remained the most prevalent crime throughout the Army during the whole of the 19th century.

Although Wellington could give credit when credit was earned, he was often scathing about the quality of the men who won his victories for him. His notorious utterance about 'the scum of the earth' was applied to those who fought at Waterloo,

Arthur Wellesley, Duke of Wellington.

but he could be just as uncomplimentary about his Peninsular troops. The army was 'a rabble', he declared in a despatch of May 1809: some had enlisted 'for having got bastard children – some for minor offences – many more for drink; but you can hardly conceive such a set brought together'. Nevertheless, with all their moral failings, the same 'rabble' drove the flower of Napoleon's Army over the Pyrenees, and time and again showed that when it came to a stand-up fight against odds the courage of the stolid British redcoat was unsurpassed. Wellington might scoff at the suggestion that his soldiers enjoyed any 'fine military feeling – all stuff – no such thing', but by now the burgeoning Regimental spirit or *esprit de corps* must have exerted some influence. The 24th had been in existence for 120 years, and although the 2nd Battalion was a newcomer, its officers and men bore allegiance to their parent. They wore the same green facings and badges, and were surely aware that their predecessors under the great 'Corporal John' had soundly trounced the same enemy they were now confronting, while the Sphinx on their shako plates bore witness to the fact that they had driven 'Boney' out of Egypt. Major Thomas Chamberlain, commanding, had served in the 24th since 1793 and had fought at Alexandria. Several other officers came from the 1st Battalion; all would have brought with them some gloss of the 'family' traditions.

During most of the period 1809–10 Wellington was on the defensive behind his lines of Torres Vedras, along the Portuguese frontier, and it was not until September 1810 that he ventured forth to bar Massena's advance across the ridge of Busaco. Although this battle saw the French repulsed with heavy casualties and, as Fortescue asserts, 'established the moral superiority of the British over the French soldier', only the Light Company of the 24th were in action, suffering the minimal loss of one officer wounded.

We now come to one of the earliest extant memoirs of any member of the present Regiment's ancestors. Lieutenant Joseph Anderson joined the 24th's 2nd Battalion in 1808 and served with it in the Peninsula until invalided home in 1811. His autobiography was written in later years, when he had become a retired Lieutenant Colonel, and although rather bald when dealing with the Battalion's doings in battle, it gives us some illuminating glimpses of life in the Peninsula, which deserve quotation.[4] Thus, after the Battle of Talavera:

> A fearful and distressing sight that field presented as we went over it, covered with thousands of the enemy's dead as well as our own, and thousands of wounded, numbers with their clothes entirely burnt off their bodies from the dry grass having caught fire from the bursting of shells during the action; there were many of the wounded who could not crawl away and escape . . . [after withdrawing] . . . Our marches on many days did not exceed ten miles and our provisions became very limited. We had much rain and our men suffered much sickness, fevers, agues and disentry [*sic*]; the latter was much increased by the quantity of raw Indian corn and wild honey which the country produced, and which the soldiers consumed in spite of every threat and order to the contrary. This retreat lasted three weeks, and I never remember seeing more general suffering and sickness. On crossing the bridge of Arzobispo we met a division of the Spanish army driving a herd of many

hundreds of swine. Our men broke loose from their ranks as if by instinct, surrounded the pigs and in defiance of all orders seized each pig and cut it up . . . so they each secured their mess for that day, then again fell into place in the ranks, as if nothing had happened . . . When we camped for the night our good soldiers sent a liberal portion of their spoil to each of their officers, nor were the generals forgotten! And they, like the youngest of us, were thankful, at that time, for so good a mess.

Sadly, it must again be said that Wellington was no Marlborough. His Commissariat Department was generally a shambles; the troops in the field often went days or even weeks without supplies, so that they were forced to live as best they could, off the country. The 'shoes' provided for the infantry were of such inferior quality that they quickly disintegrated, and there are instances of men having to march with makeshift footwear of bandages and straw.

While behind the lines of Torres Vedras, Anderson had the misfortune to lose his Company's ledger books and pay chest, and also those of another company which he was holding. All went astray when one of his baggage mules broke loose and disappeared with the lot. His only recourse was to ask every man in the two Companies to tell him their account balances, debit or credit, and thus to make up new books; though whether each man was truthful he had no means of knowing. He had given up hope of recovering the original books, and the money, when he received a note from a corporal of the 5th Dragoon Guards stationed nearby, stating that the errant mule with tin chest had turned up in his lines and had been handed over to two soldiers of the 24th, who had promised to return it. But no soldiers appeared, and as the corporal was positive he could remember the men, he was brought to the 24th's lines, where he picked them out on an identity parade. Eventually the two privates confessed: they had looted the money and hidden the chest. An inevitable court martial followed, at which they were sentenced to flogging and stoppages of pay. But this sad story had a happy ending. The chest was recovered with the pay ledgers still intact, so that Anderson was able to check the original figures with the verbal statements made by the men of the two Companies:

> And here comes the cream of my long story . . . To their honour, therefore, be it told, there was not a half-crown's difference between the ledgers and those given by each soldier from memory, the voluntary statements of no less than a hundred and fifty men! I consider this a great proof of the general honesty and integrity of the British soldier.

The campaign of 1811 opened with the withdrawal of Massena and the main French Army from Santarem, and Wellington in hot pursuit. The 24th were posted to what Anderson calls 'the Scotch Brigade', for the other two Regiments were the 42nd and 79th Highlanders (later Black Watch and Cameron Highlanders). During the pursuit there was distressing evidence of the atrocities perpetrated on the Spanish villagers by the retreating French:

> 'The scenes of destruction and murder . . . on our daily march were dreadful: houses and furniture burnt, men and women mutilated and murdered, lying about in the most disgusting and barbarous manner, some with their throats cut, some with their eyes and ears gone, and others cut up and most dreadfully exposed; all this for revenge, because they would not, or could not, supply the French army with provisions . . .'.

The pursuit went on for several weeks, with only intermittent skirmishing and exchanges with the enemy rearguard, and the usual hardships for the soldiers:

> We always took up our position each night in the open fields, without any covering except our blankets, and these were generally saturated with wet, for in Portugal rains are frequent, and dews and fogs unusually heavy during the night . . . It rained fearfully during the night. In the field which my brigade occupied we were up to our ankles in mud. It was one of the most trying nights we ever had; our men suffered so much from wet and cold that two or three were found dead on the ground when the assembly sounded next morning.

On 4th May Wellington and Massena clashed in force at the village of Fuentes de Oñoro, a name which the British Army has shortened to Fuentes d'Onor for its Battle Honours. For three days there was fierce fighting to gain possession of the village, which changed hands three times. The issue was decided on 5th May when the French were finally driven out after determined bayonet charges by the 24th with the 74th and 88th. This affair cost Massena more than 3,500 men, Wellington's casualties being only half that number, while the 24th escaped with only 1 officer and 9 men killed and 20 wounded. The officer was Lieutenant Edmund Ireland, 'a very dear friend' of Lieutenant Anderson, and the latter, with two other subalterns, determined to go and retrieve the body, now behind the French lines:

> So, accompanied by two of our soldiers carrying a blanket, and without leave, we moved boldly off to the French side until stopped by one of their sentries . . . A French officer and a dozen men then advanced and asked us who we were and what we wanted, and being told we came to look for and claim the body of an officer and friend of ours who fell that day on their ground, our brave foe said at once, 'Certainly, gentlemen, give me up your swords and I shall be happy to conduct you wherever you wish to go'. [After partaking of brandy and biscuits with the French officer, the party were escorted to the spot where Ireland had fallen.] We soon recognised him amongst heaps of slain, he was lying on his back stripped of all his clothing. He was shot right through the head, and must have died at once. We placed him in the blanket and carried him back with us, returning as we came, by the French officer's bivouac, there receiving our swords. In a quarter of an hour we were back in our own lines, without having been missed.

They duly buried their friend's body. But word of their unauthorised mission had got about, and the three subalterns found themselves summoned before the Commanding Officer, Lieutenant Colonel Kelly,[5] who gave them 'a most severe lecture on the impropriety of our conduct' in venturing without leave into enemy lines. If the French officer had not been so chivalrous, they might well have been captured, and it would have been difficult for them to prove they were not deserters. Later, however, they were told by the Second in Command that, 'although obliged to reprimand us, no one thought more highly of our conduct than our good Colonel Kelly'.

In winter quarters near Almeida, the troops inevitably suffered from exposure and disease. By the end of October the 24th had 134 men out of 380 on the sick list, one of them being Lieutenant Anderson who 'was attacked so severely that after some days' suffering without any covering or shelter, I was ordered to the rear and then on sick leave'. He was invalided home in December, and must now disappear from these pages, for he never rejoined the 24th.

In January 1812 (winter weather or no) Wellington determined on the capture of Ciudad Rodrigo and Badajos, two of only three strategic fortresses remaining in French hands. After a twelve-day siege the former capitulated on 19th January, the 24th being constantly engaged on the outworks. Twenty regiments took part in this siege, but only nine were awarded 'Ciudad Rodrigo' as a Battle Honour, and the 24th was not one of them. Apparently only those nine involved in the final storming of the breaches were singled out – a somewhat invidious decision, especially as some of the remainder suffered heavier casualties than those honoured. Badajos was captured in April, but this name does not figure in the Regiment's Battle Honours because the 24th were employed merely as part of the covering force and took no part in the siege. By now, thanks to the incompetence of Wellington's Commissariat, most of his troops were scarcely recognisable as 'Redcoats'. Their clothing had become so worn and so patched with whatever came to hand that it was anything but 'uniform', and little of the original red was visible. 'You would not believe what a rag-tag and bobtail lot we have become,' wrote a Lieutenant of the 88th,[6] 'some of our fellows look more like walking scarecrows than soldiers, with bits of sacking tied round their shoulders and waists. Others have purloined assorted oddments of apparel from the villages, so that they are clad in coats of many colours.' However, in February some urgently need replacements of clothing and necessaries arrived from England, where the authorities had thoughtfully provided a sponge for each soldier 'for the purpose of frequently washing his head' (lice, ticks and fleas commonly accompanied the troops wherever they went).

Wellington gained his great victory of Salamanca on 22nd July 1812, when his 30,000 men soundly defeated 40,000 French in 40 minutes.[7] The 24th were with the 1st Division, which was consigned to watching one flank and did not advance until, in fading evening light, they were pushed forward to complete the rout of a beaten and demoralised enemy. Not surprisingly, casualties were minimal in this Division: the 24th reported only five men wounded. Salamanca opened the road to Madrid, which Wellington (and the 24th) entered in triumph on 12th August, Napoleon's puppet King, Joseph Bonaparte, having fled.

For the next couple of weeks both officers and men enjoyed hospitality and entertainment from the Spanish citizens, who bore little love for the French and still less for the vanished 'King'. The Regiment was at first billeted in the gracious precincts of the royal gardens, but later they moved out to the more splendid Escurial Palace, summer seat of the Spanish monarchs, and here the officers luxuriated in the royal apartments. With them were those of the 1st Battalion, 23rd Foot, who had fought in the same actions during the previous two years.

Wellington's next objective was the capture of Burgos, the one remaining French-held fortress in northern Spain, and the attempt proved a humiliating anti-climax to the Madrid triumph. Weakened by previous battle casualties and sickness, the British and Portuguese force was no match for the overwhelming strength of the defenders and their fortifications, while Wellington was woefully short of siege artillery which, through lack of gun-team animals, had to be left behind in Madrid. The siege dragged on from 19th September to 22nd October, during which time the 24th's Battalion lost 22 men killed and 67 wounded out of their original weak strength of 198.[8] The heaviest of these losses were suffered in a brilliant little action which brought praise from Wellington himself. On 4th October he personally selected the 2nd/24th as the storming party to assault a breach made in the walls after the explosion of a mine. Captain William Hedderwick[9] led a bayonet attack through the debris. Desperate hand-to-hand fighting ensued, during which twelve men were killed and fifty-six wounded, but the hundred-odd survivors drove back the defenders and established themselves in a retrenchment, where they held on until, at nightfall, Wellington ordered them to withdraw. Describing the operation in his despatch of the following day, the Commander in Chief wrote: 'The conduct of the 24th regiment was highly praiseworthy, and Captain Hedderwick and Lieutenants Holmes and Fraser, who led the storming party, particularly distinguished themselves'. Hedderwick was immediately given a brevet Majority, while Holmes and Fraser were promoted Captains.

Having lost nearly 2,000 killed and wounded in the month's siege, and being now threatened by relieving French Armies, Wellington resigned himself to failure, and on 22nd October he began his withdrawal to the Portuguese frontier. In his later despatch he was to write that he had 'got clear in a handsome manner from the worst scrape I ever was in'. But in its appalling losses from privation and sickness the operation is almost comparable to the better-known disastrous retreat of Sir John Moore to Corunna, and 'handsome' is not the adjective the troops would have chosen. The weather was dreadful, torrential rain turning roads and tracks into quagmires through which the infantrymen struggled, often up to their knees in mud. There was seldom any shelter at night, and the exhausted soldiers had to snatch what rest they could in makeshift bivouacs, their clothing soaked. As usual, the Commissariat bungled: rations and forage went astray, so that man and beast were forced to glean what little they could from the countryside. The MS Regimental Records of the 24th reveal that the men resorted to taking pot-shots at the herds of wild pig, but since the incessant rain rendered cooking fires almost impossible, they were reduced to chewing raw flesh.

By the time Wellington had completed his 'handsome' withdrawal to the environs of Ciudad Rodrigo, after nearly a month on the run, he had lost 9,000 men from sickness, exposure and malnutrition, while 16,000 were on the sick list. Fortescue was a fervent admirer of Wellington, and it is with considerable restraint that he describes the retreat from Burgos as 'not one of the most creditable episodes in the history of the British Army'.

The winter of 1812–13 was spent in much-needed refitting and reorganisation. At home the Duke of York, Commander in Chief, proposed to withdraw the skeleton battalions from Spain and send out entirely fresh, up-to-strength replacements. But Wellington objected: 'Experience has shown', he wrote, 'that a soldier who has got through one campaign is of more service here than two, or even three, newly arrived from England', and he urged that six of the weakest battalions should be temporarily amalgamated. Even the Army's Commander in Chief could not argue with the Iron Duke, and so in December 1812 the 2nd/24th found themselves merged with their counterparts of the 58th Foot (later 2nd Northamptonshire Regiment) with the somewhat prosaic title of '3rd Provisional Battalion'. The combined strength of rank-and-file was now 489, and Colonel Kelly of the 24th was given command.

By the spring of 1813 the Allied Army had been augmented to 80,000 all arms and Wellington was ready for the final expulsion of the French from Spain. The first clash came on 23rd June when combined British and Portuguese forces encircled King Joseph Bonaparte's Army around Vittoria. The enemy put up a stout fight at first, but when Joseph learned that his line of retreat was threatened by a wide turning movement, he led his troops in a retreat which became a rout, leaving behind 8,000 casualties, the whole of his artillery, his treasury chest with five millions dollars in gold, his mobile harem of '*vivandières*' and his personal travelling coach.[10]

The 24th/58th (or 3rd Provisional Battalion) saw little of the action at Vittoria. They were attached to Wellington's 7th Division which was ordered to advance over mountainous terrain on the left flank, but the going was so bad that the accompanying artillery became stuck and caused a hold-up, so that by the time the Division had struggled to the scene of the main action, the French were fleeing. Needless to say, no casualties were suffered by the 24th this day. Nevertheless, their exertions on the approach march, if not in action, earned the 24th the Battle Honour 'Vittoria'.[11] And for Lord Wellington there was a Field Marshal's baton.

Demoralised and in disarray, the French were now on the run for the Pyrenees and their own 'sacred soil', but although there was still fighting to be done, as British regiments' Battle Honours testify, this was really little more than a series of rearguard actions on the part of the retreating army.

Having bypassed Pampeluna and pushed northwards, at the end of July Wellington came up against the redoubtable Marshal Soult whom Napoleon had sent hastening from the German theatre to replace the effete King Joseph. Soult had established himself in a formidable position among the rocky heights of the Eschalar Pass in the foothills of the Pyrenees. Although Wellington had only some 15,000 men to oppose Soult's 25,000, he determined to attack.

The 24th/58th were brigaded with the 6th and 82nd under Major General Barnes, and it was this Brigade which earned the accolade of high praise from the Commander in Chief. While the Light Division were working round the left flank, Barnes pushed forward unsupported, and with skilful use of fire and movement sent two whole divisions of the enemy fleeing from their entrenched positions. The Light and 4th Divisions then came up and completed the rout. If Wellington's mention of the 24th at the siege of Burgos had been complimentary, his despatch of 4th August 1813 was almost rhapsodical:

> Major-General Barnes' brigade was formed for the attack, and advanced before the fourth and light divisions could co-operate with them, with a regularity and gallantry which I have seldom seen equalled, and actually drove two divisions of the enemy, notwithstanding the opposition opposed to them, from those formidable heights. It is impossible that I can extol too highly the conduct of Major-General Barnes and these brave troops, which was the admiration of all who were witnesses of it.

Writing later to Lord Bathurst (Secretary of State for War) he added: 'I assure you some of the best battalions of the Army are the Provisional Battalions. I have lately seen two of them engaged, that formed of the 2nd Battalions of the Twenty-Fourth and 58th Regiments and that formed of the Queens and the 2nd Battalion, 53rd Regiment: it is impossible any troops could behave better.'[12]

The Eschalar affair cost the 24th/58th Battalion 17 killed and missing and 124 wounded. Among the latter was the 24th's Commanding Officer, Colonel Kelly, who had not long recovered from his previous wound. This time he was invalided home and his duties were taken over by the next senior officer available, the 27-year-old Captain William Le Mesurier.

The crossing of the Bidassoa River was effected at the end of August, without serious action by the 24th/58th, and by October Wellington's men were enduring blizzards in the Pyreneean mountains above the Nivelle. Apart from battle casualties, the Battalion suffered from sickness and exposure, for, as always, there was little in the way of supplies, and only bivouacs of branches and turves for shelter. The 24th's effectives numbered only 286 NCOs and men, while the 58th were even weaker with 200 all ranks. But there was no 'close season' for the troops that winter. Wellington was determined to keep up the momentum of the pursuit, whatever the elements, and in November he descended from the heights and drove Soult's Army across the Nivelle. Although the 24th/58th were heavily engaged in the centre of the attack, with the 7th Division, they escaped lightly: the 24th with only two officers wounded. The MS Regimental Records add 'and several men killed', but Norman merely lists five men wounded.[13]

For the Regiment, the last round of their long drawn-out campaign came at Orthes on 27th February 1814, the first major engagement on French soil, when Wellington inflicted 4,000 casualties on Soult and sent his survivors scurrying back to take refuge in Toulouse. The 24th/58th were again involved in the thick of it, among the streets and orchards of the village, where after a prolonged fire-fight they put in a final bayonet charge which drove the enemy out in disorder. Thanks to their good use of cover, the 24th element again escaped with remarkably light casualties: only one soldier was killed and three officers (including Captain Le Mesurier) and thirty-two other ranks were wounded.

The Peninsular War was now virtually at an end. On 10th April 1814 Soult made a last ineffectual stand at Toulouse, unaware that four days earlier Napoleon had abdicated and was on his way to exile on Elba. The 24th had no part in Wellington's final battle, for their 7th Division was held back in reserve near Bordeaux. Soult managed to escape on the capitulation of Toulouse, but when he learned of his chief's surrender he too gave himself up, and hostilities formally ceased on 19th April.

During their five years' campaigning with Wellington, the 2nd/24th had earned nine Battle Honours for the Regiment (as did their comrades of the 58th);[14] they had marched many thousands of miles, and besides the nine major engagements had fought innumerable minor actions, skirmishes and affrays. All this had cost them some 420 all ranks killed or died of wounds or sickness, and nearly 500 wounded.

But the Battalion received scant thanks for their endeavours. After enjoying a comfortable spell in billets around Bordeaux, the surviving officers and men were shipped to Cork and thence to Ramsgate, where the Regimental Depot had been established. Here in early October they learned that they and other 2nd battalions raised at the outset of the Peninsular War were to be disbanded; and thus on 24th November 1814, the 2nd/24th paraded for a valedictory address by Major General Sir Denis Pack, and were then formally struck off the Army List. Nineteen officers were retired on half-pay, 140 other ranks were discharged, and the remainder were posted to other regiments, including their parent the 1st/24th, then serving in India. Forty-four years were to pass before the 24th Regiment could parade another 2nd Battalion.

However, the 2nd Battalion of the 69th, together with others, were allowed a stay of execution, and this enabled them to participate not only in the assault on Bergen-op-Zoom, which ended in their capture (and subsequent release), but also in Wellington's supreme victory. By June 1815, Napoleon, having escaped from Elba, was once more threatening the Allies, with an Army of some 125,000 men, all eager to redeem France's military honour. On 15th June his main forces were concentrated around Ligny and Quatre Bras, south of Waterloo, and the Emperor decided to give battle simultaneously to Blücher and his Prussians at Ligny, and to Wellington at Quatre Bras.

The 2nd/69th, with 30 officers and 516 other ranks, were commanded by Colonel Charles Morice[15] and brigaded with the 2nd/30th, 1st/33rd and 2nd/73rd, under Major General Sir Colin Halkett, as an element of the 3rd Division. On 15th June the Brigade was in camp around Soignies, some twenty-five miles east of Quatre Bras. At the cross-roads village of Quatre Bras itself was a mixed division of Dutch and Belgians, and on learning that Ney was advancing on this sector, Wellington ordered his 3rd Division to reinforce them. Having marched the route in twelve hours, the Division arrived at Quatre Bras at 5 p.m. to find the Dutch-Belgians driven from their positions and Picton's 5th Division holding the left flank. No sooner had the 69th halted than Halkett received an urgent request from the commander of one of the 5th Division brigades for a battalion to reinforce his exhausted and mutilated squares. The 69th were selected, and so found themselves under the command of General Sir Denis Pack, the same officer who had recently presided over the disbandment of the 2nd/24th.

There then followed a disastrous incident. The terrain around Quatre Bras was completely open, with no natural obstacles – ideal for cavalry action – and as Colonel Morice could see glittering squadrons of Kellermann's cuirassiers deploying to his front, he ordered his companies to form square. The Regiment were in the midst of this complex evolution when up galloped a gesticulating officer who turned out to be none other than the 1st Corps commander, the excitable young Prince of Orange, who demanded to know what Morice was about. On being told he was forming square to receive cavalry, the Prince peremptorily bade him desist and deploy back into line. Though against his better judgement, Colonel Morice could only comply with his Corps commander's direct order.

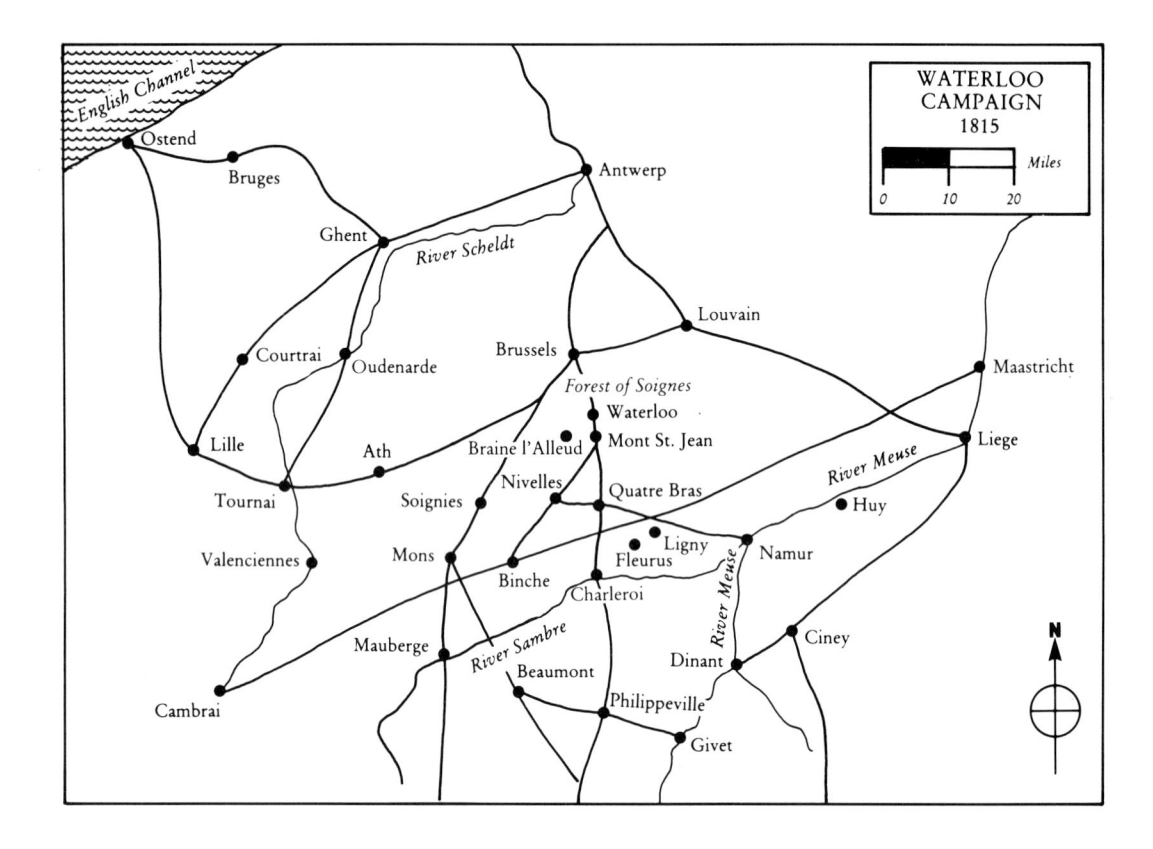

Meanwhile, the massed squadrons of cuirassiers, led by Kellermann himself, had attempted to ride down the 33rd Foot, but these were already in firm square and were not to be broken. Wheeling off, the 8th Cuirassiers then spotted the 69th in the act of changing formation and exultantly thundered down upon them. Once more Morice strove to get his men into square, but only two companies had time to form before the avalanche of steel-clad horsemen smashed into them. The two unformed companies were virtually destroyed; the two in square stoutly defended themselves with volleys of musketry, but in the face of repeated charges they were eventually forced to take refuge in the squares of the 42nd and 44th. By this time the 1st Guards Division had joined the although there was a sharp cavalry action at Genappe when Lord Uxbridge's rearguard became embroiled with advanced troops of Ney's Polish lancers. But then the elements took a hand, unleashing a violent thunderstorm which forced the infantrymen to flounder up to their knees in floodwater and mud. No rations had been forthcoming since dawn the previous day. At nightfall the soaked and weary soldiers had to make do with some sodden biscuit and hunks of meat, most of which remained uncooked, for it was almost impossible to kindle camp fires. Thus, unfed, caked in mud, shelterless, the troops that were to gain the British Army's supreme victory awaited the dawn of 18th June.

The Battle of Waterloo evoked, and continues to evoke, an unexceeded torrent of literature from historians, biographers, military theorists and others, even novelists. Fortescue spread himself over one and a half chapters and fifty-five pages in his blow-by-blow account of the ten-hour engagement. But we are concerned with just one small cog in Wellington's machine – the 69th Foot, who saw little and knew less of what went on beyond their own Brigade squares.

The Regiment was still in Sir Colin Halkett's 5th Brigade with the 2nd/30th, 33rd and 2nd/73rd.[17] The 69th mustered 30 officers and 511 other ranks, commanded by Colonel Morice. To confront Wellington's Allied Army of 67,660 men and 156 guns Napoleon had deployed 71,940 men with 246 guns. This huge concentration of nearly 140,000 troops with 30,000 horses and 400 guns was to fight it out on a battlefield of less than three square miles, an area which in later days might have been allotted to a single brigade of infantry with armour.

The 69th and their Brigade were positioned a few hundred yards north of the outposts of Hougoumont and La Haye Sainte and immediately to the left of the Guards Brigade. This position remained unaltered until Wellington's final advance, the only variations being changes of formation from line to square and back to line, as the situation demanded.

It was not before the sun had dispelled the thick morning mist, at about 11 a.m., that the battle opened with the customary overture of artillery cannonading, but this did little damage to the 5th Brigade taking cover below the reverse slope of the ridge along which the British line extended. Then followed Napoleon's first advance, which surged past Hougoumont and La Haye Sainte to threaten the British centre. Now moved up to the crest of the ridge and forming square with the 33rd, the 69th were heavily assaulted by waves of infantry and cavalry, and it was during this phase that Colonel Morice, already wounded in the shoulder, fell with a musket-ball through his head, so that command of the Battalion devolved upon Lieutenant Colonel George Muttlebury. Mauled by fire from the stolid British squares, the French were finally driven back by the celebrated charge of Ponsonby's 'Union Brigade' (Royal Dragoons, Scots Greys and Inniskillings). There was then a lull until just after 4 p.m., when Napoleon unleashed the flower of his cavalry, some 5,000 cuirassiers, dragoons and lancers, in a desperate attempt to smash through the redcoats' squares. Between the two squares of the 5th Brigade stood Major Lloyd's Battery of 9-pounder field guns. After firing volleys of grape and cannister at the advancing squadrons the gunners took refuge within the squares, while the latter, front ranks kneeling, met the horsemen with storms

The Waterloo Medal, 1815.

of musketry as they closed on their position. The Battle of Waterloo demonstrated a military fact of life that took a long time to be fully appreciated: no matter how brave and thrusting, unsupported cavalry were totally ineffectual against the disciplined fire-power of formed bodies of resolute infantry.

For nearly two hours successive waves of heavy cavalry thundered upon the British squares, only to be smashed to fragments, 'like waves beating against rocks', as Captain Mercer wrote, while the heaps of dead and wounded men and horses piled up within bayonet reach. Captain Gronow of the 1st Guards likened the storms of bullets striking breastplates to 'the noise of a violent hail-storm beating upon panes of glass'.

During one of the attacks Private Dooley of the 69th created a diversion by fighting a personal battle with a lancer who lunged at him and wounded him in the shoulder as he knelt in the front rank:[18]

> Being exasperated by this, he sprang out of the ranks and chased the lancer, but the latter . . . returned at full tilt, and although Dooley was at once ordered to take his place in the square, he faced his antagonist in the open. Everybody expected to see Dooley spitted like a hog, and the excitement was intense; it was soon over, however, for he dexterously caught the lance on his bayonet and threw the point clear, and the next moment the lancer was on the ground, pierced through the body; his horse galloped away riderless.

The repulse of his cavalry was a severe reverse to Napoleon, who was now being attacked by Blücher's Prussians on his right flank. Only his Imperial Guards could save the day. At 7 p.m. the Young Guard and Old Guard advanced on the British centre, to be met by the fire of Maitland's Guards and the 5th Brigade. After an initial setback when the 5th Brigade were driven back with heavy losses (the 73rd lost twenty-one officers out of twenty-five), the line reformed and the Imperial Guards wavered and turned tail. It was then that Wellington waved his cocked hat and ordered the general advance. The Prussians smote the fugitives in the flank and harried them far into the night. Napoleon narrowly escaped capture, but on 25th June, after debating the possibility of fleeing to the United States, he surrendered to the Captain of the British man-o'-war, *Bellerophon*, and sailed to captivity on St Helena.

'It was the most desperate business I ever was in . . .', wrote Wellington after the battle, 'Our loss is immense, particularly in that best of all instruments, the British Infantry. I never saw the Infantry behave so well.'[19] Truly that superb 'instrument' had suffered severely. In Sir Colin Halkett's Brigade alone, 21 officers were killed or wounded, Sir Colin himself being among the latter, while the total other ranks casualties amounted to 480. The 69th, who had already lost their Commanding Officer, Colonel Morice, and 153 others at Quatre Bras, suffered a further 6 officers and 64 other ranks killed, wounded and died of wounds.[20] In all, the allied casualties totalled some 22,000, while the French lost 25,000 besides 7,000 prisoners and 240 guns.

But for the British Army there was to be no more blood-letting on the Continent of Europe until 1914.

Apart from the Battle Honour 'Waterloo', granted on 8th December 1815, there were other awards for those engaged in the battle. On 23rd April 1816 the Prince Regent authorised the issue of a 'Waterloo Medal' to every officer, NCO and soldier who had been present. This was the first general service medal since that issued by Cromwell to his troops who gained the victory of Dunbar in 1650. All eligible NCOs and men were allowed to reckon two years' service towards pension, while subalterns were awarded a similar reckoning towards increase of pay. In addition, prize money was distributed to all ranks, from £433.2s.4d. for field officers to £2.11s.4d for privates.

In September 1815 the Companionship of the Order of the Bath was instituted, and among the first officers to be awarded the decoration was Lieutenant Colonel George Muttlebury of the 69th.

On 24th July the 69th entered Paris with the victorious troops, there to be reviewed by the Emperors of Russia and Austria and the King of Prussia. Encamped in the Bois de Boulogne in August, the 69th probably expressed little interest when they were joined by another Regiment of Foot, newly arrived from Canada. This was the 41st, whose experiences on the other side of the Atlantic will be outlined in the next chapter.

As with the 2nd/24th, the victories of the 2nd/69th under Wellington were to prove a swansong. With the inevitable reduction of the armed forces after Waterloo, all the remaining 'hostilities only' 2nd battalions were ordered to disband. Having been posted home in January 1816, the 2nd/69th was struck off in October of that year. Eight officers and 313 rank-and-file were absorbed by the 1st Battalion, then in Madras, the remainder being retired on half-pay or discharged.

Notes

[1] He was created Viscount Wellington after Talavera, his Dukedom following in 1814.

[2] Oman, Sir Charles. *History of the Peninsular War* (1902–30).

[3] 'No soldier can withstand the temptation of wine. This is constantly before their eyes in this country, and they are constantly intoxicated when absent from their regiments, and there is no crime which they do not commit to obtain money to purchase it, or if they cannot get money, to obtain it by force.' (Wellington to Adjutant General, 2nd November 1810.)

[4] Anderson was commissioned Ensign in the 78th Highlanders in 1805. After service in the 24th, he was transferred to the York Chasseurs and eventually commanded the 50th Foot. Retiring in 1848, he died in 1877. His autobiography, entitled *Recollections of a Peninsular Veteran*, was edited by his grandson, Captain Acland Anderson (3rd Dragoon Guards), and published in London in 1913. This volume is now very scarce: the Regimental Archives have no copy, and even the MOD Library denied all knowledge of it. The author was at length able to track down a copy in The London Library.

[5] Kelly, transferred from the 1st Battalion, had just taken over from Major Chamberlain.

[6] Macloughlan, P. M. *Letters from the Peninsula* (Dublin, 1823).

[7] It was at Salamanca that Major General Gaspard Le Marchant, founding-father of the Royal Military College, Sandhurst, fell leading his Heavy Brigade in a final charge.

[8] These casualty figures may be a little suspect. They are taken from the MS Historical Record, and it is not always clear whether figures quoted are cumulative totals or additional.

[9] Hedderwick was the senior effective officer available, the Commanding Officer, Colonel Kelly, and other field officers being either sick or wounded.

[10] This coach was captured by some troopers of the 14th Light Dragoon, who discovered among its fittings what was described as 'a silver utensil' – His Majesty's chamber-pot. Today this is preserved in the Mess of the 14th/20th King's Hussars ('The Emperor's Chambermaids') and does duty as a 'loving cup' on special Guest Nights.

[11] The Spanish have always preferred the spelling 'Vitoria', as it appears on modern maps and atlases, but ever since Wellington's day the British have unaccountably added the extra 't'.

[12] Despatches, 11th August 1813.

[13] *Battle Honours of the British Army*.

[14] 'Talavera', 'Busaco', 'Fuentes d'Onor', 'Salamanca', 'Vittoria', 'Pyrenees', 'Nivelle', 'Orthes', 'Peninsula'.

[15] In Whitehorne's history, and elsewhere, this name is spelt with two 'r's, and sometimes appears as 'Morris'. The above is the version given in the 1815 Army List.

[16] The Regimental Colour was valiantly defended by Volunteer Christopher Clarke, who survived twenty-two sabre wounds, and was immediately granted an Ensigncy in the 42nd Highlanders.

[17] Later the East Lancashire Regiment, Duke of Wellington's (West Riding), and Black Watch, respectively.

[18] *Reminiscences of Sergeant J. Hall*, 33rd Foot (quoted in *History of the Thirty-Third Foot, Duke of Wellington's (West Riding) Regiment*, by Albert Lee (1922).

[19] Letter, Wellington to his brother, Lord Mornington, 19th June 1815 (*Camden Miscellany*, XVIII).

[20] A complete nominal roll of the casualties is given in Whitehorne's *History of the Welch Regiment* (pp. 134–5).

CHAPTER SEVEN

Nepal, North America, Burma (1814–31)

'Welsh Regiment of Infantry'

On 3rd May 1986, an impressive ceremony was performed in the centre of Brecon. Before a throng of some 2,000 spectators, the 80-strong Gurkha Demonstration Company based in Dering Lines received from the Mayor an illuminated scroll conferring upon them Honorary Citizenship of the Town. As the Citation declared, this honour was accorded not only as a tribute to 'the gallant services and distinguished record' of all Gurkha regiments, but in recognition of the close and happy association which had existed between Brecon and the Gurkhas since 1973.[1]

For more than 170 years Gurkha soldiers have enjoyed the admiration and respect of their British comrades-in-arms. Their fighting qualities, steadfast loyalty, unquenchable cheerfulness in adversity and spirit of camaraderie, were all such that in the days of the Raj the British soldier was quite ready to fraternise with 'Johnnie Gurkha' to a degree he could never manage with the sowars and sepoys of India. With the creation of the British Army's Brigade of Gurkhas in 1947, this rapport has continued to the present day.

It was perhaps fitting that Brecon should be the first town in Britain to honour the Gurkhas, for it was Brecon that had for so long been the home of the 24th Regiment, and it was the 24th who were among the first British troops to encounter these doughty little warriors from Nepal. But it is ironic that they should have done so as enemies.

In 1814 the Hon. East India Company was becoming alarmed by the expansionist designs of the Raja of Nepal, who had been trespassing into the Company's territories in the Terai, bordering his independent mountain Kingdom. The crisis came in May when his troops seized some police posts on the frontier and slew a British officer. In those days such an affront could not go unpunished, and in November Lord Moira, Governor-General of Bengal, declared war on Nepal.

At this juncture the 1st Battalion of the 24th were stationed in the military cantonment of Dinapur, some 300 miles up the Ganges from Calcutta, whence they had moved in July. A force of 17,000 British and Indian troops, in four divisions, was detailed for the punitive operation, and the 24th had the misfortune to be posted to the easternmost Division, commanded by Major General Bennet Marley of the Hon. East India Company. This was tasked with the capture of Kathmandu, the Kingdom's capital. As a recent historian observes, the Divisional commander 'was not noted either for energy or initiative'.[2] Having divided his command into two columns, Marley moved off on 26th November, with the two companies of the 24th in one column and the remainder in the other, all the rest of the force being native infantry battalions. It took the columns nearly six weeks to cover the fifty or so miles to the region where the tangle of forest-clad foothills extended down from the Himalayas.

After these exertions Marley called a halt. He had not fired a shot (for he had not seen an enemy to shoot at) and was still some sixty miles short of his objective. On 1st January a surprise Gurkha attack drove in two of his outposts, and this so unnerved him that he withdrew his entire Division to the base-camp of Bettiah, whence he had started. Here he was assaulted not by Gurkhas but by Lord Moira himself, who in a scathing express demanded to know the reasons for the 'mischievous indecision'. This was too much for the Major General. Without a word to his staff, or anyone else, he abandoned his command and disappeared down country. After a month's inactivity the truant was replaced by Major General George Wood, also a 'Company' officer, who proved no more enterprising than his predecessor. Having led his 24th and Indian battalions on a hundred-mile trudge along the forest belt to no purpose other than the destruction of a few abandoned Gurkha stockades, he retired in peace to the camp near Bettiah. Meanwhile, over on the left of the British flank, an officer of very different mettle had led his Division to capture the Gurkha stronghold of Dehra Dun, and then laid siege to their hill-fort of Kalunga. This was Major General Sir Robert Rollo Gillespie, whom we have already met as the 'Saviour of Vellore' (and of the 1st/69th). Outnumbered by more than six to one, the 600-odd Gurkhas in Kalunga held out for nearly a month, and when they surrendered, out of ammunition and food, only 60 were left. But Gillespie himself was killed, together with 30 other British officers and 750 rank-and-file. It was here that British regard for these valiant little hillmen was born; after the campaign a small obelisk was erected, with the inscription: 'They fought in the conflict like men, and in the intervals of actual conflict showed us a liberal courtesy'.

The 24th did not set eyes on their future allies until a second campaign got under way in February 1816. Again they were detailed for the right-flank column, but this time it was commanded by an able, thrusting officer – their own Commanding Officer, Colonel William Kelly, who had lately arrived from the disbanded 2nd Battalion. Marching via an undefended pass through the wooded foothills, they came upon the strong Gurkha position of Hariharpur, and after some 'softening up' by the accompanying 3-pounder mountain guns, three companies of the 24th under Major Charles Hughes burst through the stockade and drove out the defenders with the bayonet. But Gurkhas do not readily admit defeat. Reforming, they counter-attacked with ferocity, and it was only the arrival of reinforcements with elephant guns that finally beat them off with the loss of 120 killed and 300 wounded. Kelly's men suffered sixty casualties, including Major Hughes and two other officers wounded, eight soldiers killed and twenty-seven wounded. On 6th March the Raja of Nepal sued for peace, and by July the 24th were back in their Dinapur cantonment.

British admiration for the erstwhile foe bore fruit in April 1816, when as a result of recommendations from officers who had fought in the campaign, Lord Moira approved the recruitment of a battalion of Gurkhas for service in the Hon. East India Company's forces. Today the descendants of this Battalion are known as the 2nd King Edward VII's Own Gurkha Rifles (The Sirmoor Rifles), and serve the Crown as an integral component of the British Army.[3] The next time the 24th saw Gurkha soldiers was as staunch comrades-in-arms during the Sikh War of 1848, and since then the antecedents of The Royal Regiment of Wales have fought alongside them in far-flung campaigns and in two World Wars. Curiously, the Regiment's Motto, *'Gwell angau na Chywilydd'*, means much the same as that of the Brigade of Gurkhas, *'Kaphar hunnu bhanda marna ramro'* – It is better to die than to live a coward.

The 24th remained in India until 1823, when after nearly seventeen years' overseas service they were posted home to Portsmouth. They may not have suffered severely in battle, but inevitably sickness had taken its toll. In the garrison Church of Dinapur, the 2nd Battalion The South Wales Borderers erected, in 1925, a memorial brass 'In Memory of 202 Officers, Non-Commissioned Officers, Men and Families of His Majesty's 24th Regiment who died at Dinapore 1816–1818'. While a proportion of these deaths was attributable to that dreadful scourge, cholera, many others resulted from the ever-prevalent malaria, dysentery and typhus, which continued to smite the British in India, soldier and civilian, down to the present century. Hence in any large cantonment the melancholy notes of Last Post sounding over some departed comrade were heard almost daily.

'The 41st is an uncommonly fine regiment', wrote Major General Isaac Brock, commanding the British forces in Canada in 1812. In that year the bulk of the British Army was heavily engaged in the Peninsula, and taking advantage of this preoccupation, the Americans declared war. This was in June, when the 41st, who had been serving in North America for almost thirteen years, were confidently expecting a home posting. Instead, they found themselves fully justifying their General's commendation in two years' campaigning, which added four Battle Honours to the roll.

With the Napoleonic war raging in Europe, the troops committed to the security of Canada were virtually a 'Forgotten Army': General Brock was allowed a pitifully small force of some 6,000 men to defend a frontier of 340 miles, and of these only 4 units were regular British infantry.[4] The remainder were local Militia and Fencibles, backed up with some very irregular loyal Indian braves. Having recently received a draft from England, the 41st were fully up to strength with 32 officers and 880 other ranks, commanded by Lieutenant Colonel Henry Proctor. This officer had been commissioned Ensign in the 43rd Foot (Monmouthshire) in 1781, and having purchased his steps up to Major, was given a brevet Lieutenant Colonelcy in January 1800. In October of that year he was appointed to command the 41st. A strict discipliarian, Procter gained his Regiment a high reputation for smartness of drill and turnout, but his leadership in the field became a matter of controversy. He was a devoted husband and father of three children, and as a previous historian gently puts it

'... his extreme affection for his household somewhat hampered the duty which as Lieutenant Colonel of a regiment he should have exercised'.[5]

The Regiment's first encounter with the enemy came on 26th July when they and some of the Militia were despatched to defend the town of Amherstburg, threatened by the American occupation of Detroit across the narrow neck of Lake Erie. The fighting was little more than a series of desultory skirmishes between advanced posts on the Aux Canards River, and would scarcely be worth a mention were it not for an incident that brought a laudatory General Order from the commander of the forces. After declaring that 'that the 41st Regiment have particularly distinguished themselves', General Brock went on:

> His Excellency wishes particularly to call the attention of the troops to the heroism and self-devotion displayed by two privates, who, being left sentinels... continued to maintain their station against the whole of the American force until they both fell, when one of them, whose arm was broken, again raised himself and opposed with his bayonet those advancing against him, until he was overwhelmed by numbers. An instance of such firmness and intrepidity deserves to be thus publicly recorded...

The two heroes were Privates Hancock and Dean; the former was killed, the latter wounded and taken prisoner. In 1842 Major George Richardson, ex-volunteer in the 41st during the American War, published his *War of 1812*,[6] in which he, like the other historians, recounts the above deeds and quotes the General Order. The copy of this scarce volume held in The Welch Regiment Museum in Cardiff has been copiously annotated by its original owner, Lieutenant James Cochrane of the 41st, who fought with the Regiment in the campaign. To Richardson's account he adds the following pencilled comment: 'Hancock and Dean, a double sentry from the advanced picket, were both *drunk and asleep* when the advancing enemy drove in the picket: and, in their stupid surprise, offered useless resistance when roused by the Americans. The first was killed, and the last made prisoner. Deane [*sic*] being released, was again captured in Oct. 1813 and eventually deserted the service....'.

Whether or not the two were rudely aroused from a drunken stupor, they must obviously have put up a stout, if 'useless', fight. On the capture of Detroit, says Richardson, 'the first act of General Brock was to enter [the fort] and liberate in person the gallant Dean, shaking him warmly by the hand and declaring that he was indeed an honour to the profession of a soldier'. This passage is allowed to pass without comment by Cochrane.

For the capture of Detroit, General Brock had detailed a force of 1,000 troops, but of these only 300 all ranks of the 41st, and 30 Gunners, were British regulars, the remaining being Canadian Militia and Indians. The American commander, General Hull, had a garrison of some 2,500, but Brock was not the man to be deterred by disparity of numbers, and he knew that his opponent's reputation was questionable. Having attired some of his Militia in British redcoats, Brock deployed his whole command in a show of force before the glacis, and sent in a summons to surrender. Not surprisingly, perhaps, this was refused. Then the British guns opened up, supported by fire from two ships anchored offshore. The bombardment continued well into the night, one lucky (or unlucky) shell exploding in the American commander's Mess and killing four officers. By next morning, 16th August, the 41st and their comrades were all prepared to carry the fortress by storm, but their efforts were not required. As Brock was deploying his troops, he was surprised to behold a parleying party under a white flag descending the glacis. General Hull had agreed to capitulate.

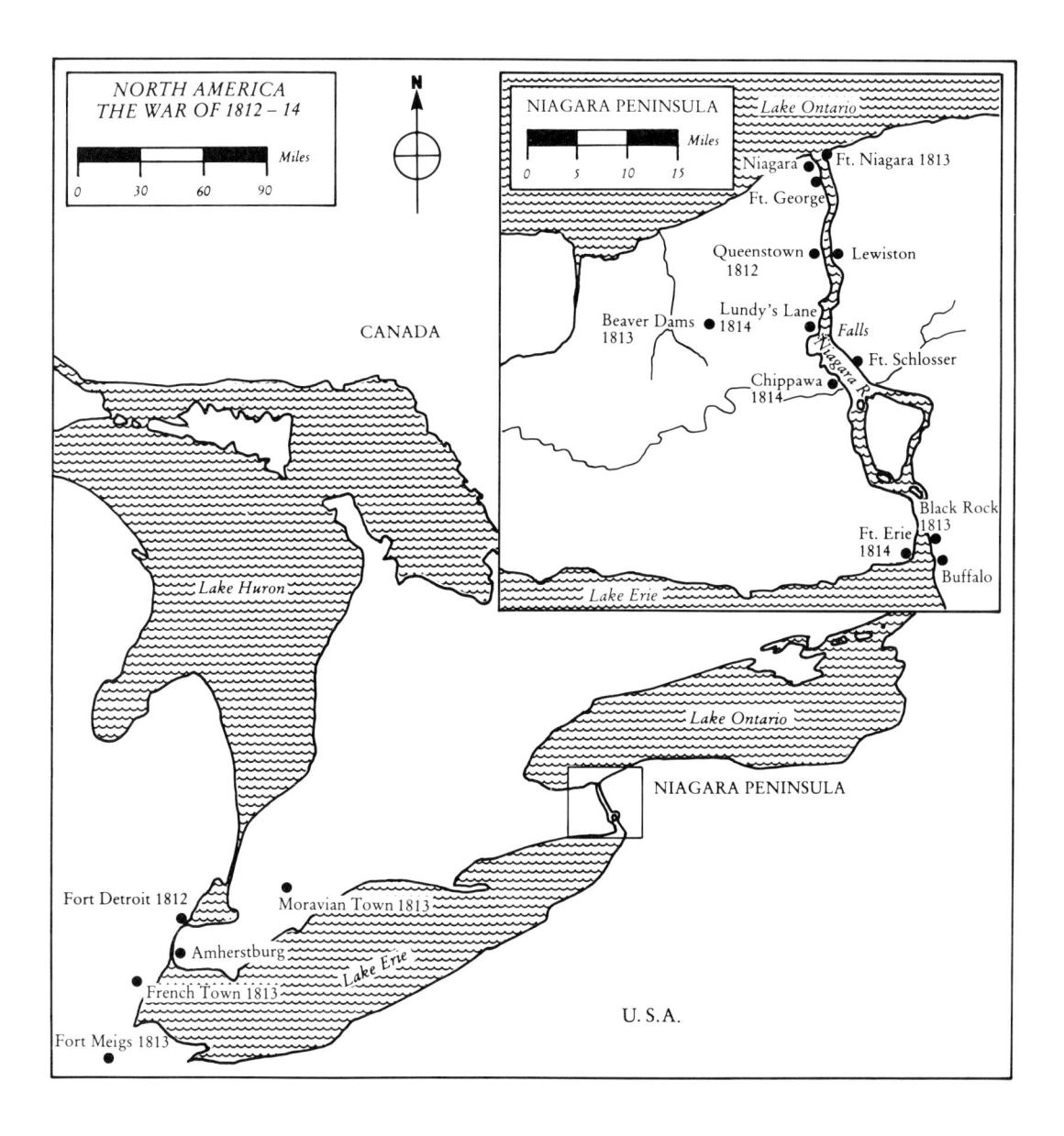

Field officer's Gold Medal, Fort Detroit, 1812; awarded to Captain Peter Latouche Chambers, 41st Foot.

Thus the capture of Detroit proved a completely bloodless victory: there was not a single casualty among the British force, while the Americans suffered only a few wounded by shell-fire, in addition to the four officers killed in the Mess. With the capitulation of Detroit, the whole of Michigan territory fell into British hands, together with nearly 2,500 prisoners and large quantities of arms, ammunition and stores. Also captured were the Colours of the 4th US Regiment of Infantry, which can today be seen in The Welch Regiment Museum. And The Royal Regiment of Wales takes pride in being the only unit in the British Army to bear the Battle Honour 'Detroit' (granted in April 1816). It was certainly the least costly of all their Honours.

Very shortly afterwards – on 13th October – the 41st earned another Battle Honour, this time in company with the 49th (later Royal Berkshire Regiment). Again supported by Militia and Indians, the 1,000-odd force attacked a strongly-held American position above Queenstown, near the Niagara Falls, and after a sharp fire-fight charged in with the bayonet. Some 300 Americans were killed and wounded, and 960 surrendered. The 41st escaped lightly with only two rank-and-file killed and ten wounded. But a much lamented casualty was the British commander, Major General Brock, who was killed at the head of his troops.

January 1813 saw the 41st involved in a costly action against General Winchester's force of some 900 Americans in position at Frenchtown on the River Raisin. The British were commanded by Colonel Proctor, now acting Brigadier, who had with him 243 of his Regiment, 250 Militia and 800 Indians, together with three light 3-pounder guns. A night march on 21st January brought the attackers within sight of the enemy encampment by dawn. Completely unsuspecting, General Winchester had not even bothered to post outlying picquets, and it seems that the whole camp was snugly asleep (as indeed was the General). The 41st were actually deployed in line and fully expecting to dash in with the bayonet. But Proctor was not one for bravado. Said Major Richardson: 'The conduct of Colonel Proctor on this occasion has ever been a matter of astonishment to me... The Americans were lying in their beds undressed and unarmed, and a prompt and forward movement of the line would have enabled us to have taken them with the bayonet at advantage...'.

Instead, the cautious Proctor brought up his 3-pounders, and by banging away

Battle of Queenstown, 13th October 1813. NATIONAL ARMY MUSEUM

with them effectively woke the slumbering enemy, who smartly manned their posts and delivered volleys of musketry upon the British line. Losing several men killed and wounded, the 41st were forced to take cover in some dead ground. Proctor now displayed bolder tactics, ordering the Militia and Indians to work round one flank, the 41st round the other. In the face of these simultaneous assaults, most of the Americans fled across the icebound river, to be pursued and captured by the Indians. Among them was General Winchester, still in his nightshirt. Some 400 of the more resolute enemy had established themselves in a strong blockhouse and were staunchly beating off attacks when they received a message from their captured General ordering them to surrender. This they obeyed, and the hour-long battle was over. But, largely owing to Colonel Proctor's initial hesitation, the British casualties were heavy. Out of the total of 500 engaged, 11 officers and 172 other ranks were killed and wounded. The Indians must have suffered too, but their losses were not recorded. In the 41st, two officers were wounded, fifteen privates killed and ninety-two other ranks wounded – nearly half of their total strength. Nevertheless, Frenchtown was a serious reverse for the Americans: 300 were killed and 522 made prisoner, while an unrecorded number were slaughtered by the Indians. In his self-congratulatory despatch of 26th January to Army Headquarters, Colonel Proctor was ungenerous enough to omit any reference to the noble efforts of the 41st, or their acting Commanding Officer, Major Joseph Tallon (who was wounded), although he singled out other units and individuals. For his own efforts, Proctor was promoted Brigadier General.

His next success came in May when his command of 1,000 troops, including the 41st, and an equal number of Indians, attacked General Harrison's garrison of Americans at Fort Meigs on the Miami River. Here the enemy took the initiative by detaching 800 men to capture British batteries in position on the river bank opposite the fortress. This they achieved, but disregarding orders to spike the guns and rejoin the garrison, they remained in position. Proctor immediately ordered three companies of the 41st, supported by Militia and Indians, to retake the batteries. Richardson was engaged in this counter-attack and described what followed:[7]

> The main body of our small detachment under Major Muir advanced against the American left and centre ... while Major Chambers whose gallantry in the field was ever remarkable, boldly attacked their right then occupying the principal battery. On approaching the position he threw away his sword, and seizing the accoutrements and musket of a soldier ... who had been shot dead a moment before, called out ... 'who'll follow me and retake the battery?' I was immediately behind him and as enthusiastically replied ... that I would. Lieutenant Bullock who had been wounded over the left eye a day or two before ... together with Lieutenant Clements (of the 41st also) were a few paces in rear, and these officers, followed by not more than a dozen men who happened to be near at the time, pressed eagerly forward ... It is a matter of perfect surprise to me, even at this hour, that our little force had not been annihilated to a man, for the Americans were in strength, and of course perfectly under shelter, and the easy conquest we obtained (for they fled as we drew near the battery) can only be attributed to the fact that their centre and left were being sorely pressed by the detachment under Major Muir, and the Indians under Tecumseh ... Driven from the batteries the enemy in vain sought for safety in the woods. The murderous fire of the Indians ... drove them back over their pursuers, until in the end there was no possibility of escape, and their army was wholly destroyed.

In this affair the 41st suffered 11 men killed and 1 officer (Lieutenant Bullock) and 38 men wounded: perhaps not too high a price for the recapture of three batteries and the taking of 450 prisoners – and 'vast numbers' of Americans killed, adds Richardson. In due course (April 1816) the Regiment was granted the Battle Honour 'Miami'. But it seems an odd anomaly that the more significant victory of Frenchtown went unrewarded.

The defeat of the Americans in the Batteries did not mean that their army was 'wholly destroyed', as Richardson boasted. On the contrary, the garrison of Fort Meigs stubbornly held out, and by 14th May Proctor was forced to abandon the siege, his men being smitten with dysentery and fever, and militiamen and Indians having vanished to homes and tribal encampments. After a disastrous attempt to take Fort Stephenson on the Sandusky River, when Proctor's already depleted command lost another ninety-six officers and men killed and wounded, a detachment of the 41st served as marines aboard a British Fleet confronting the American Commodore Perry on Lake Erie. The outcome was a humiliating defeat for the British (on 10th September) and the loss for the Regiment of 10 men killed and 183 captured. This proved Major General Proctor's *ne plus ultra*.[8] The Americans now enjoyed complete control of Lake Erie, and the British Right Division (including Proctor's command) was isolated from the Centre Division across the Niagara frontier. With more than 100 sick, his artillery captured, ammunition and supplies cut off, and fit men exhausted and in rags after months of marching and fighting, General Proctor was in a desperate position. Overruling Chief Tecumseh's urging to stand and fight, he resolved to retreat to the Thame River and the safety of the frontier. By 5th October his Column of troops, Indians and 'followers' had arrived in the wooded environs of Moravian Town.[9] This withdrawal, and Proctor's subsequent actions, have been justifiably criticised by Regimental and other historians. It seems that he remained totally unaware that some 6,500 Americans under the veteran General Harrison were following up; he did not trouble to destroy bridges nor even to detail any rearguard. Only when he learned that his baggage had been captured did he realise that the enemy was on his tail. Halted in a clearing within a few miles of Moravian Town (where there was a good defensive position), his men waited for orders while their General meditated on his next move. The initiative now passed to General Harrison, who flung in 1,500 of his mounted infantry. Twice these horsemen were repulsed by the hastily formed squares of the 41st, but a third charge broke them, and on their left flank the Indians were scattered by another 1,500 infantry who slew Chief Tecumseh. The 41st, with forty-eight killed and wounded, were surrounded. If they were expecting orders from their commander, none came, for General Proctor and his staff had galloped off to safety after the first attack.[10] Within 20 minutes the action was over, and 19 officers and 345 other ranks had been captured. All remained prisoners for nearly a year, until in July 1814 a convention agreed upon an exchange.

Having deserted his command, General Proctor proceeded to pen a scurrilous despatch to Army Headquarters at Montreal, in which he sought to mask his own shortcomings by laying the blame on his troops. However, after some acrimonious correspondence, he was brought before a court martial at Montreal on 21st December 1814, the most serious of five charges being that:

> ... he did not make the military disposition best adapted to resist the attack, and during the action and after the troops had given way, he did not make any effectual attempts to rally or encourage them, or cooperate with or support the Indians, he having quitted the field soon after the action commenced, such conduct betraying great professional incapacity, and being disgraceful to his character as an officer.

The court found him guilty on four of the charges; but leniency prevailed: he was merely ordered to be 'publicly reprimanded' and to lose six months' pay and seniority. But when the proceedings were reviewed by the Prince Regent at home, His Royal Highness expressed strong disapproval of the mild sentence and, though he could not order a retrial, he directed that his 'high disapprobation' of General Proctor's conduct should be made known. Thereupon a General Order was issued, severely reprimanding him and expressing 'His Royal Highness's regret that any officer of such length of service and exalted rank should be so extremely wanting in professional knowledge, and deficient in active and energetic decision required in one placed in such a responsible situation...'. This was to be read out before every regiment in the Army. Lieutenant Cochrane scribbled (in Richardson's history): 'This wretched man was of course never again employed. With this terrible reproof... he slunk away into obscurity and we never heard of him more.' Major General Henry Proctor died in 1822, unlamented by the Regiment he had once commanded.

Before the debacle of Moravian Town, the 41st had been reinforced by 150 men from the newly-raised 2nd Battalion at home. This Battalion, like those of the 24th and 69th, had been formed on an hostilities-only basis during the Napoleonic War, but as seen in the previous chapter, the 2nd/24th were not destined for Wellington's Army. Mustered at Winchester in August 1812, they were posted to Quebec the following day, and were soon in action. On 11th July a commando-style dawn raid was mounted on the American Batteries and stores at Black Rock on the Niagara River. The enemy were taken completely by surprise: barracks and warehouses were burned down, four guns were destroyed, and four others were captured, together with 177 muskets and huge quantities of stores and foodstuffs. All this for the loss of six men killed and ten wounded. No doubt good use was made of forty-six barrels of whisky carried off with the rest of the booty.

In December 1813 the remnants of the 41st who had escaped capture at Moravian Town were merged with the 2nd Battalion[11] and on the 18th of that month the Regiment was involved in the brilliant capture of Fort Niagara, another example of commando tactics. Having stealthily disposed of sentries and discovered the password in the small hours, the main assault force of two companies of the 41st succeeded in having the main gate opened to them. Overpowering the Guard, they swept in with the bayonet, while another attack went in on the eastern bastion. Thus rudely awakened, the befuddled Americans put up little resistance and within thirty minutes the fort was in British hands. So complete was the surprise that only six of the attackers were killed and five wounded, the latter including one private of the 41st. For this minimal price not only was the fort itself secured for the rest of the war, but with it were captured 27 guns, 3,000 small arms, and large stocks of ammunition, stores and clothing. The Americans lost 79 killed and wounded and 344 prisoners.

The British forces in Upper Canada were now commanded by Lieutenant-General Gordon Drummond, who was no stranger to the 41st, having served in the Regiment as Lieutenant and Captain from 1791 to 1794. Unlike his predecessor, Sir George Provost (who had joined in Colonel Proctor's slighting of the 41st at Moravian Town), Drummond was a man of strong character and powers of leadership. He was soon to display both in what proved to be the final engagements for the 41st.

At home the British public, rejoicing in Wellington's Peninsular victories, were totally unconcerned with the 'forgotten Army' in North America, and to this day the names 'Lundy's Lane' and 'Fort Erie' have little meaning to any but descendants of the 41st and a handful of other regiments who bear the Battle Honour 'Niagara'.[12]

In July 1814 the Americans were again concentrating on the Niagara frontier, and on the 25th of the month there came the strongest clash of opponents since the war

Breaking of the line, Battle of the Saints, 12th April 1782. NATIONAL MARITIME MUSEUM, GREENWICH

Soldiers of the 69th Foot (later 2nd Battalion The Welch Regiment) manning a fighting top on board HMS Captain *(Commodore Horatio Nelson, RN) during the Battle of St Vincent, 14th February 1797.*

began. Just a mile from the Niagara Falls was a low eminence traversed by three parallel roads, the central one being known as Lundy's Lane. Pushing forward from Fort Erie in the south, some 3,800 Americans under General Brown needed to secure this point before advancing northwards to attack the British bases of Fort George and Fort Niagara. In the late afternoon General Drummond with 1,700 British and Canadians, including the Light Company of the 41st, took up position on the hill just as the advanced elements of Brown's force arrived within artillery range. A few rounds from the British 6-pounders stirred the Americans into action: while their main body commenced a musketry duel in the centre, a column worked round the left flank and drove back the Militia and Light Dragoons, wounding and capturing Drummond's Second-in-Command, Major General Riall. They then launched fierce attacks against the centre, where stood the 41st Light Company with the Royal Scots, the 8th and the 89th. The repeated attacks 'were met with the most perfect steadiness and intrepid gallantry', wrote Fortescue, and having lost nearly 500 men, Brown drew off to reorganise. It was now 9 p.m. and darkness had fallen. But if the British imagined that the lull which followed heralded the withdrawal of their enemy, they were mistaken. Both sides had received hard-marching reinforcements, which brought their strengths nearly equal at about 2,800 all ranks. Again the Americans advanced, one body driving back the Gunners in the centre and turning the guns on the British. Drummond ordered up four more guns which engaged the captured pieces at pointblank range. There followed a series of desperate attack and counter-attack: 'All order was lost in the darkness, battalions, companies, and even sections became intermixed and the fight was carried on with the bayonet, with the butt, with any weapon that came to hand' (Fortescue). The confused mêlée lasted for nearly three hours until, at midnight, General Drummond managed to restore some order among his troops, and with the Light Company of the 41st leading, these put in a final charge before which the exhausted Americans gave way. The American General was now wounded, his force was severely depleted, his survivors had lost heart. After some desultory musketry exchanges, Brown gave up the fight and the British were left in possession of the Lundy's Lane field.

Casualties on both sides were heavy. The British and Canadians lost 873 killed and wounded; and while the Americans acknowledged a total of 860, Drummond put the true figure at 1,500. He himself was wounded. The 41st's Light Company lost nearly half their strength: three killed and thirty-four wounded out of the seventy who went into action.

The name 'Lundy's Lane' does not appear among any regiment's Battle Honours. Instead, by some rather tortuous reasoning, in October 1824 those who had fought so stoutly were awarded the Honour 'Niagara', although, as noted above, this distinction had previously been conferred on the flank companies of the 41st for their capture of Fort Niagara. Thus the single Honour now covered both victories. Lundy's Lane proved costly to the Americans not merely in casualties, but in morale. Taking over from the wounded Brown, General Ripley abandoned all plans for the northward advance to Fort Niagara and sought refuge in the formidable strongpoint of Fort Erie, on the northern shores of the lake.

After a spell for refitting and reinforcement (by, among others, the remainder of the 41st from Fort George), General Drummond resolved to deal with Ripley as he had dealt with his predecessor. On 13th August he opened an artillery bombardment on Fort Erie, which continued for nearly two days, but made little impression on the stout walls and bastions. This being so, Drummond decided to storm with the bayonet '... a weapon of which he seems to have been extremely fond', wrote Lomax. The assault commenced in the small hours of 15th August, with three columns advancing simultaneously. The two on the left met with fierce resistance and were temporarily checked, but the third, including the flank companies of the 41st, the 104th and some Marines, succeeded in occupying the bastions of the Old Fort, where they captured the guns and turned them on an American Battery which had been annoying the other columns. At this critical moment disaster struck. Under one of the captured bastions was the main magazine with huge stores of artillery and small-arms ammunition and powder. Whether by accident or design, this erupted in a devastating explosion which utterly destroyed the bastion and 500 of the troops in the vicinity. In the resulting panic and confusion the dazed survivors could only struggle back to the British lines, their retreat covered by the Royal Scots, whom Drummond sent forward.

Ten minutes earlier the capture of Fort Erie had seemed almost certain. Now with nearly a third of his force casualties, the General resigned himself to abandoning the operation. His total losses amounted to 905 killed and wounded, many of the latter subsequently dying. Out of their original strength of 140, the 41st lost 1 officer and 40 other ranks killed, 4 and 35 wounded, nearly all of these being incurred in the explosion.

Fort Erie was a setback, but elsewhere the British forces were victorious. On 24th August Major General Robert Ross defeated the Americans at Bladensburg on the outskirts of Washington, entered that city and burned all the public buildings, including the Capitol. By December 1814 both sides were making overtures for peace, and on Christmas Eve 'the War of 1812' formally came to an end with the Treaty of Ghent.

Meanwhile there had been no fighting for the 41st since the Fort Erie catastrophe. At the end of August reinforcements of battalions released from the Peninsular Army began to arrive in Canada, and these allowed General Drummond to relieve his own mauled units. Thus by September the 41st were withdrawn to Fort George. Any plans Drummond might have formulated for a second assault on Fort Erie were forestalled when the American commander evacuated it, having blown up the defences.

In October 1814, while en route for Quebec, the 41st learned that their 2nd Battalion was officially disbanded. This was of little more than academic interest, for the meagre remnants of the 2nd had been merged with the 1st after the Moravian Town debacle, as related above. The two years of campaigning had cost the Regiment 133 all ranks killed and 339 wounded. It had also earned them the Battle Honours 'Detroit', 'Queenstown', 'Miami' and 'Niagara'. We have seen that the Regiment was posted to Wellington's Army in June 1815, but it arrived too late to take part in the Waterloo triumph. However, eleven years later it was to earn another Battle Honour in a more remote field. After a spell of home service in Ireland and Scotland, the 41st were posted to India, arriving at Madras in July 1822.

What Fortescue described as 'one of the very greatest achievements of the British soldier', was the arduous two-year campaign in the fever-infested jungles and teak forests of Burma, or the Kingdom of Ava, whose rulers had been steadily encroaching on the East India Company's territories along the northern frontier. The ultimate provocation came in December 1823 when Burmese columns raided British posts around Sylket, only some 200 miles from the Company's seat of Government at Calcutta. Lord Amherst, Governor-General, declared war in February 1824, and a punitive force of 10,600 British and Indian troops, including the 41st, was despatched from Madras, landing at the mouth of the Irrawaddy on 10th May. The 41st, under Lieutenant Colonel Henry Godwin, totalled 27 officers and 692 other ranks. On the next day the Regiment were among the first to enter the city of Rangoon, which was secured within twenty minutes: the Burmese had fled. That night the men bivouacked within sight of the great gold-encrusted Shwedagon Pagoda, and were thus among the first Europeans to set eyes on what was to become a popular tourist attraction of the East.

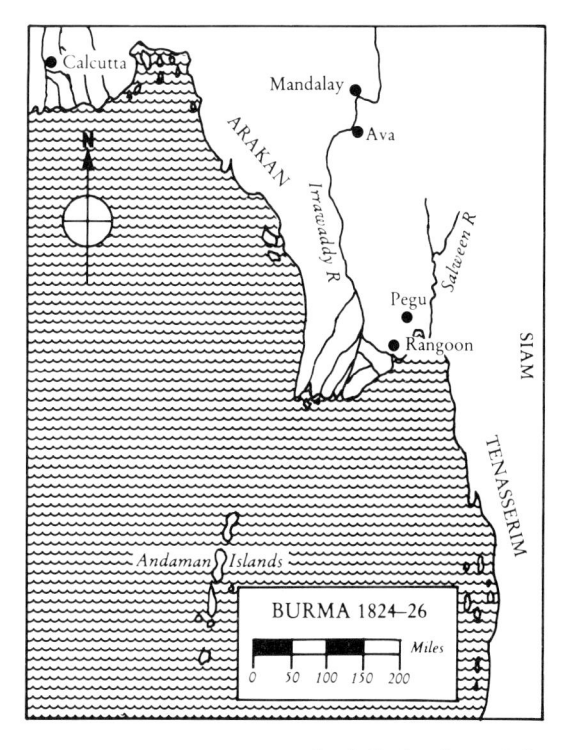

After a period of uneasy stalemate when the British, short of food and smitten with sickness, drove off sporadic attacks, General Campbell decided on a major offensive to capture the Burmese King's fortress-capital of Ava some 400 miles up the Irrawaddy, near to the town of Mandalay. Unlike Gurkhas, Sikhs, Mahrattas, Pathans and other Oriental opponents confronted by the British soldier, the Burmese were never noted for their martial spirit. Apart from guerrilla tactics of ambushing detachments in jungle familiar to themselves, their usual mode of opposition was to build formidable stockades of thick bamboo, behind which they would keep up a brave showing with fire from muskets and 'light artillery' or jingals – primitive weapons firing a ball weighing nearly 1 lb. If the stockade were penetrated by British guns, they did not stay to face the infantry bayonets. One such stockade was battered and carried by 450 men of the 41st under Major Peter Chambers on 10th June. As he entered the breach he was felled by a spear-thrust in the face, whereupon Private William Collier bayoneted his adversary and, gathering some soldiers, went on 'in the most daring fashion' to clear that sector of the stockade. In later years, Collier might have been rewarded with a DCM, but at that time gallantry in the field usually went unrecognised by authority. What the Burmese lacked in fighting spirit, they made up in numbers, though this availed them little. Time and again the British found themselves outnumbered by as many as twenty to one, as at Kokein, north of Rangoon, where 20,000 enemy abandoned a stockaded position and fled before the bayonets of 1,200 redcoats (including 100 men of the 41st).

Inevitably, battle casualties were far outweighed by those from the endemic diseases of the jungle. Malaria, dysentery and typhoid depleted the ranks, while another hazard was gangrene, or septicaemia. A tiny scratch from a thorn or sliver of bamboo would fester, and within a week a man's leg or arm would be covered with foul suppurating ulcers. Lacking antiseptics, all the doctors could do was amputate.[13] By March 1825 – after less than a year in the field – the 41st had lost 176 men from sickness and 'fever'

The decisive action of the campaign came in February 1826 with General Campbell's capture of Pagan, where his 2,000-strong force utterly routed some 15,000 Burmese. The 41st, now augmented by a draft of the 69th volunteers, carried the centre of the position with the bayonet. They suffered one man wounded. The British then advanced unopposed to within forty-five miles of Ava, and the King, alarmed for his personal safety, sued for peace. The treaty was signed on 25th February, and the British and Indian troops began to evacuate the country. By July 1826 the 41st had returned to their barracks at Fort St George, Madras.

The Burmese campaign was among the most costly fought by the British Army, with a shocking casualty figure of 3,115 dead out of an original strength of 3,586. But more shocking is the fact that only about 156 of these fell in action: the real enemy was disease. The 41st had landed in Burma with 692 NCOs and men; during the 2 years they received reinforcements (including those from the 69th) of 257, bringing the total who served to 939. Of these, 18 were killed in action or died of wounds; 223 succumbed to sickness.

The home authorities were remarkably swift in conferring distinctions: on 28th December, 1826 the Regiment was awarded the Battle Honour 'Ava'; Lieutenant Colonels Henry Godwin and William Smelt[14] were made Companions of the Order of the Bath, as was the wounded Major Peter Chambers. The latter was promoted Lieutenant Colonel and given command of the 41st, in succession to Godwin, in April 1827. But four months later he was smitten with cholera and died at Madras.

Lieutenant Colonel Sir Edmund Keynton Williams, KCB, KTS; Commanding Officer, 41st Foot, 9th August 1827–9th July 1837.

The 41st were not to see England until another seventeen years had passed and another three Battle Honours had been won (as related in the next chapter), but this span includes dates memorable for the legacies they have left to the present Regiment.

In 1831 the 41st were stationed at Arni, near Madras, with Colonel Sir Edmund Williams in command. Some time in March he received the following letter from the Adjutant General:

> Horse Guards
> 25th February 1831
>
> Sir,
> I have the honor to acquaint you, by direction of the General Commanding in Chief, that His Majesty has been graciously pleased to approve of the 41st Regiment being in future styled the '41st, or Welsh Regiment of Infantry'.
> I have, etc.
> *John Macdonald*
> A. G.
>
> The Officer Commanding,
> 41st Regiment,
> Madras.

Identical letters, dated 24th February, were sent to the Colonel of the Regiment (Major General the Hon. Sir Edward Stopford) and to the Secretary-at-War.[15] For the moment we can ignore the controversial spelling 'Welsh'.

Thus came about the Regiment's first link with Wales. But, one might well ask, why the 41st? Not once in their 112 years' existence had they set foot in the Principality, nor had they ever recruited therein, not even on the border. Although as in other English regiments, a few Welshmen would no doubt have found their way into the ranks, their number was so minimal that successive Inspection Returns did not deign to notice them, only English, Scots and Irish being enumerated.[16]

The fact that the new title was 'approved', leads one to surmise that some person or persons had applied for it; but unfortunately there is no trace of any such application in the Public Record Office files, nor, in fact, is there any previous correspondence on the subject. However, Lomax in his history states categorically that it was Colonel Williams who had previously 'made application' – though on what evidence is not revealed. While it may seem a transgression of protocol for the Commanding Officer rather than the Colonel to petition the King, the former had personal reasons for seeking to associate his Regiment with Wales.

Colonel Sir Edmund Keynton Williams, KCB, was the only officer in the Regiment to bear a Welsh name. His family hailed from Penhros in what was then Monmouthshire, and one of his ancestors, Sir Roger Williams, had been a distinguished soldier in Elizabethan times. Sir Edmund was proud of his Welsh descent, and moreover enjoyed the friendship of several influential personages in South Wales, among them Sir Digby Mackworth of Glanusk, near Caerleon. Apart from national feelings, there was another factor that could have motivated him. As we have seen, most infantry regiments had been given 'territorial' titles in 1782, but the 41st remained barren of any such distinction. In 1831 the Regular Army included, besides English regiments, fifteen Scottish and seven Irish, but only one represented Wales – the 23rd or The Royal Welch Fusiliers. If the 41st could also become 'Welsh' (or 'Welch') this would not only satisfy Sir Edmund's personal interest, but could do a little more justice to the Principality in the Army List titles.

Before the year was out, the Adjutant General despatched another gratifying letter, copies as before:[17]

                                            Horse Guards
                                  19th December 1831

Sir,
    I have the honor to acquaint you, by direction of the General Commanding in Chief, that His Majesty having been pleased to permit the 41st Regiment in February last, to be styled the 41st, or Welsh Regiment of Infantry, has also permitted it to bear on its Colours and Appoint-
      ments 'The Prince of Wales's Plume' with the Motto
         'Gwell angau neu Chwilydd'
        I have, etc.
          John Macdonald
          A. G.

The Officer Commanding,
41st Regiment,
Madras.

Whether the badge and Motto had also been applied for by Sir Edmund (or the Colonel) must remain conjectural, for there is no documentary evidence. But, at all events, the 41st had now acquired distinctions that were to be inherited by their successors down to the present day. And until the raising of the Welsh Guards in 1915, no other regiment of the Regular Army bore a Welsh Motto.

We now come to thorny questions of orthography, over which there has been confusion, dispute and embarrassment. First, was the original title 'Welch' or the more usual 'Welsh?' Since 1831 the 41st, and its descendants The Welch Regiment and The Royal Regiment of Wales, have fiercely maintained that the 'c' spelling is not only the correct version, but the one originally authorised. Their claim is based on a copy of the Adjutant General's letter of 19th December, 1831, now framed and displayed in The Welch Regiment Museum at Cardiff. In this the word is quite clearly 'Welch' (and someone has heavily underscored the 'c'). But as seen above, in the copy of the same letter held in the Public Record Office, the word is equally clearly 'Welsh', as it is in the copies sent to the Colonel of the Regiment and the Secretary-at-War, and also in the

> Horse Guards
> 19. Dec. 1831.
>
> Sir,
>
> I have the honor to acquaint you, by direction of the G.C. in C; that His Majesty having been pleased to permit the 41st Regiment in February last to be styled "The 41st or Welch Regiment of Infantry" has also permitted it to bear on its colours & appointments, The Prince of Wales' plume, and the motto,
>
> "Gwell Angau nen Chwilydd".
>
> I have —
>
> — Sir —
>
> Ed/ John Macdonald
> A.G
>
> The O.C.
> 41st Regt
> Madras.

The Copy Letter from the Adjutant General on which the 41st, later 1st Battalion The Welch Regiment, based its case to be styled 'The Welch'.

original letter approving the title. Moreover, there are significant discrepancies in the Museum's copy. Not only is this in a totally different (and seemingly later) hand, but there are abbreviations not present in the Public Record Office letter. For instance, 'General Commanding in Chief' has been rendered as 'G.C. in C'. On the face of it, the impression is that this copy was hurriedly and carelessly made by some later amateur researcher.

In the earliest history of the 41st (1899), Lomax reproduces the above letter with the 'c' spelling, his authority being the MS Regimental Records, which quote no sources. While the present author regrets his temerity in disputing Regimental traditions, he can only present facts. And one fact is indisputable: in all issues of the Army List down to 1920, the 's' spelling appears. Whitehall's stance seemed to be thus: whatever the Regiment claimed, their version was the correct one; the natives of Wales were Welsh, *ergo*, the Regiment was 'Welsh'. It was only with the publication of Army Order No. 56 of January 1920 that authority relented and 'The Welsh Regiment' became officially 'The Welch Regiment'.

This orthographical controversy is relatively minor compared with the embarrassment evoked by an error in the Motto. The correct version, *'Gwell Angau na Chywilydd'*, can be literally translated as 'Better Death, not Shame', but within the Regiment this has always been rendered as 'Rather Death than Dishonour'. However, as originally written in the above-quoted Adjutant General's letter, the word *'neu'* ('or') replaces *'na'* ('not'), so that the Motto carried the somewhat inglorious formula, 'Better Death or Shame'. Exactly when this dreadful blunder was rectified cannot be determined, though the Motto was being correctly printed with *'na'* in the Army Lists from the 1850s onwards. But the alteration of shako and helmet plates was another matter. According to documents in The Welch Regiment Museum, it was only after some unkind comments had been made in the South Wales Press that in 1895 the Member of Parliament for Merthyr was moved to put a question in the House to the Secretary for War, and as a result an order was issued for new helmet plates with the solecism corrected.

The reasons for the choice of the particular Welsh Motto are obscure. One theory is that Colonel Williams borrowed it from his friend Sir Digby Mackworth, whose family were said to have inherited it from the ancient Princes of South Wales. But the Motto had also been borne for many years by the venerable Royal Glamorgan Light Infantry Militia, and the Colonel may well have adopted it from them. On the other hand, this Motto seems to have been quite common. As Theophilus Jones records in his *History of Brecknockshire* (1805–9), the little Church of Crickadarn, near Builth Wells, contains a memorial to one 'Lewis Lloyd Esq. who died 2nd day of March, 1640'. Under his arms is the Motto *Gwell Angau na Chywilydd*'.

Whether the new distinctions meant anything to the English, Scots and Irish soldiers of the 41st away on their Indian posting in 1831, is debatable. They may have become 'Welch' (or 'Welsh'), with an unpronounceable Welsh Motto, but they were not to see anything of their adopted Principality for another thirteen years.

Notes

[1] Found by the Gurkha Rifles regiments serving in the UK, the Gurkha Demonstration Company was established at Dering Lines, Brecon, in 1973, as a unit of the NCOs' Tactical Wing of the School of Infantry.

[2] Pemble, John. *The Invasion of Nepal* (Oxford, 1971).

[3] On the abolition of the Hon. East India Company in 1858, all Gurkha regiments were absorbed in the (British) Indian Army. With the granting of independence to India in 1947, four of the ten existing Gurkha regiments were transferred to the British Army as the Brigade of Gurkhas, the remainder being incorporated in the (new) Indian Army.

[4] These were the 8th (later The King's Regiment (Liverpool), 41st (The Welch Regiment), 49th (Hertfordshire), 100th (Prince of Wales's Leinster).

[5] Lomax, D. A. N. *A History of the Services of the 41st (the Welch) Regiment.*

[6] This was published in Canada. The British Library does not possess a copy.

[7] *The War of 1812*, op. cit.

[8] Proctor's promotion was dated 4th June.

[9] In some histories the original Dutch version, 'Moravianstadt', is preferred.

[10] Lieutenant Cochrane's pencilled addition to Richardson's narrative adds '... an indifferent horseman, he [Proctor] never rode faster in his life ... within 24 hours he rode 70 miles!'

[11] According to Lomax and Whitehorne, only one officer (Lieutenant Bullock) and fifty men managed to evade capture at Moravian Town, but there may have been others on detachment or special duties, not present at the action. This is unclear.

[12] 15th/19th The King's Royal Hussars, the Royal Scots, the Royal Regiment of Fusiliers, The King's Regiment, The Queen's Lancashire Regiment, The Royal Irish Rangers.

[13] During World War II British prisoners-of-war working on the Japanese railway in Thailand suffered from exactly the same 'jungle ulcers', and many of them lost limbs.

[14] Smelt did not actually serve with the 41st in Burma, having been given command of a brigade.

[15] These are preserved in the Adjutant General's Letter Book at the Public Record Office, Kew; refs. WO. 3/82, WO. 3/431.

[16] Surprisingly, the Returns for the 1830s show a constant preponderance of Irishmen. In May 1831 they numbered 394, compared with 315 English and 37 'Scotch'.

[17] Public Record Office, Kew; ref. WO. 3/83.

CHAPTER EIGHT

Afghanistan, Chilianwala (1841–49)

The advent of the Victorian era in 1837 saw relatively few changes in the soldier's way of life, or his officer's. The latter was still obliged to pay for his commission and promotion (and his uniform), and with inflation the regulation prices had increased since Marlborough's day. The humble Ensign of Foot had to put down £450 for the privilege of serving his country (a Cornet of Dragoon Guards paid £840), while anyone aspiring to a battalion Lieutenant-Colonelcy needed £4,540. Little or no thought was given to education in the ranks: as yet there were no obligatory educational examinations, and thus no stimulus for a man to struggle with his three Rs rather than enjoy the bibulous attractions of the canteen. Indeed, some high-ranking officers, including the Duke of Wellington, viewed the schooling of soldiers with disfavour: they might develop ideas above their station, with a consequent threat to discipline. The common soldier's business was to fight, and all he needed for that was skill at arms, foot drill and blind obedience to orders.

In 1837 all soldiers enlisted 'for life', but ten years later a limited service scheme was introduced, whereby the infantry recruit could sign on for an initial period of ten years with the Colours, after which he could either take his discharge or re-engage for another eleven years. The basic rates of pay remained unchanged – the private soldier was still 'a shilling-a-day man' until after the Crimean War, when he was granted an extra penny. But in 1836 there came a niggardly allowance of good conduct pay: men of 'unblemished conduct' were awarded one penny a day extra after every five years' service.

Discipline was still firmly grounded on punishment, and punishment usually meant the 'cat'. But resulting from continual debate in the House and periodic outcry in the Press, sentences were steadily reduced from the savage thousand and more lashes of the previous century. In 1846 arose the case of a private of the 7th Hussars who had died after receiving 150 lashes. This created such a storm in the House and among the public, that the Government was forced to make a significant concession to the abolition lobby, and the maximum sentence by any court martial was reduced to fifty lashes.

Brecon Barracks, c. 1900.

    The contentious practice of billeting troops in public houses was virtually defunct by the time Victoria came to the throne. The erection of permanent barracks had begun in the 1790s and by 1840 there were more than 260 throughout England and Wales. In Brecon, the building which now houses the Museum of The South Wales Borderers was erected in 1805 as a magazine and armoury (previously the townsfolk had been alarmed by the storage of large quantities of ammunition and gunpowder in the Town Hall). Between 1842 and 1844 the Government engineer, Colonel Orde, designed and erected the barrack blocks which became the home of the 24th Regiment. The brick or stone-built barracks in the United Kingdom were an improvement on squalid ale-houses and taverns, but they were spartan in amenities. Few boasted proper ablution facilities, and sanitary arrangements were primitive: at night a common urinal tub was placed in each barrackroom, or on the verandah if there was one, to be emptied at Reveille by the unhappy soldiers detailed as sanitary orderlies. Barrackroom accommodation was not generous. In 1842 the Barrack Regulations specified a minimum of 450 cubic feet for each soldier; a convict in prison was allowed 1,000. But at least the soldier now had his own wooden cot, with straw-filled palliasse, and his stoutly-built barracks were weatherproof. Many of these early Victorian barracks (with later amenities) are familiar to grey-haired old soldiers of today.

    For the first couple of years of the new reign the infantryman's weapons remained unaltered, the venerable 'Brown Bess' flintlock and 17-in. socket bayonet continuing in service. But in 1842 a new percussion-system musket was introduced, to banish the flintlock.[1] The cap itself was almost identical with that seen on the base of a modern cartridge, and each soldier carried seventy-five caps in a leather pouch. Instead of the laborious business of pouring priming powder into the pan, it was a simple matter to slip a cap over the nipple at the base of the barrel. Nevertheless, the weapon was still cumbersome, measuring 4 ft 6 in. from butt-plate to muzzle and weighing 10 lb. 2 oz.

The period saw a few alterations in dress. In 1829 the skirted red coat gave way to an abbreviated coatee, a most unpractical garment for, like the battledress blouse of a later generation, it gave no protection to the loins or the thighs, while it had not a single pocket. Tight fitting, and adorned with white lace, it looked very smart, however, and to authority smartness was everything. The green facings of the 24th and 69th remained unchanged, but in 1822 the unique red of the 41st was altered to white at the specific request of the then Colonel, Major General Sir Edward Stopford. Several other regiments, cavalry and infantry, wore white facings and why the Colonel chose to abandon the former distinction is not recorded. In 1836 a new pattern of trousers was introduced, which for the first time displayed the now-familiar red welt down

Officer's coatee, worn by 24th Regiment, late 18th century

the side seams. They were also provided with a fly instead of the old flap opening, and were lengthened to reach well down over the heels. But since no gaiters were worn, the bottoms must have become uncomfortably wet and muddy in bad going. For home service the material was a stout serge known as 'Oxford mixture', but for tropical wear a lighter nankeen garment was issued.

We must now revert to the 41st Regiment ('of Welch Infantry') who in December 1841 were soldiering at Karachi, in India. Two years previously British phobia over the bogey of Russian domination of Afghanistan had reached a crisis when it was reported that the new Amir in Kabul, one Dost Muhammed, was 'intriguing' with a Russian envoy. Afghanistan had always been regarded as a convenient buffer state between the territories of the Raj and those of the Tsars, and its neutrality was all important. But this did not mean that its ruler should not look more favourably towards London and Calcutta than to St Petersburg. For more than twenty years that (deposed) ruler had been a refugee in India, enjoying British hospitality, and when Lord Auckland, Governor-General, learned of events in Kabul he resolved that this was the moment to itervene and reinstate the exiled Shah Shuja on his throne. Thus in 1839 began the ill-conceived, ill-managed and disastrous 1st Afghan War.

At first all went well. The British 'Army of the Indus' entered Kabul in August 1839, and Dost Muhammed having fled (over the Russian border, it was rumoured), Shah Shuja was installed with due pomp and ceremony. Fondly imagining that all would now be sweetness and light in Kabul, the Governor-General withdrew all but a token force of 4,500 garrison troops from the country. But the effete, vacillating Shah had never enjoyed any respect among his people, and they now resented having him foisted back on them by force of foreign bayonets.

The inevitable eruption came in November 1841, when the Afghans rose in revolt and murdered Sir William Macnaghten, the British envoy, his deputy Sir Alexander Burnes, and many others. Hopelessly outnumbered, the British could only agree to humiliating terms for complete evacuation. As they were again to discover in 1879 (and the Russians a hundred years later), Afghans do not take kindly to foreign intervention in their affairs. The Afghan leader (Dost Muhammed's son) promised safe conduct to Jalalabad, but this promise proved worthless. Marching in bitter January weather, the column of 4,000-odd troops, 12,000 'followers' and three dozen British women and children, were set upon by fanatical tribesmen as soon as they entered the snow-clad passes. On the third day the survivors were overwhelmed in the Khurd Kabul Pass and the remnants of the 44th Foot, with British Gunners of the Bengal Horse Artillery, went down fighting to the last. Only a single man, Dr William Brydon, escaped to reach General Sir Robert Sale's Brigade at Jalalabad. Some of the women and children, and half a dozen officers, were made prisoners and eventually incarcerated in a remote mud fort at Bamian in northern Afghanistan.[2] As for Shah Shuja, set on his throne by the hated Feringhis, he was hanged by his countrymen in the Great Bazaar of Kabul.

The shock-waves of indignation and dismay set up by this humiliating end to the Afghan venture resulted in the launching of 'the Army of Retribution' – but only after some nervous procrastination by the new Governor-General, Lord Ellenborough, who was at first inclined to sweep the whole nasty business under his carpet and forget it.

Not all the British troops had been withdrawn from Afghanistan. Brigadier General Sir Robert Sale and his 'Illustrious Garrison' were stoutly defending Jalalabad, fifty miles on the Afghan side of the Khyber, and in the south-west Kandahar was still occupied by Major General Sir William Nott. The plan was to advance to Kabul on two fronts: the Column under General Nott would advance from Kandahar, the other under General Pollock would force the Khyber, relieve Jalalabad and continue thence to the capital.

The 41st Regiment now enter the picture. Having been routed from Karachi to Quetta in February 1842, they were detailed to join the Scind Field Force which was to reinforce General Nott at Kandahar. The *de jure* Commanding Officer was Colonel Richard England, but since he was promoted brevet Major-General and given command of the Field Force, the actual command was assumed by Major Thomas Gore-Brown, and it was he who led the Regiment throughout the campaigning.

Their first brush with the Afghans came on 28th March when General England, advancing from Quetta, was surprised by a superior force of tribesmen employing their usual ambush tactics near the village of Haikulzi. Four companies of the 41st were engaged, among whom was Colour Sergeant David Haslock, whose diary is now in The Welch Regiment Museum. Here is his account of the action:

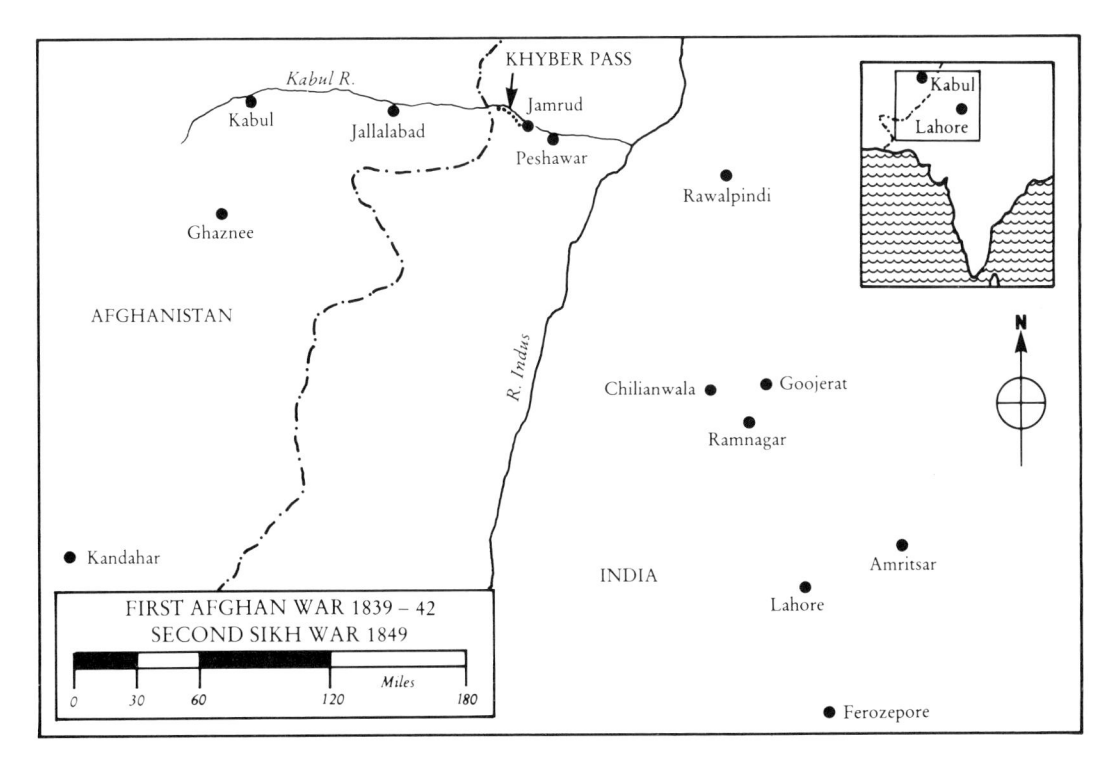

> On the 28th March, Easter Monday, we marched about 8 miles then came to Action in earnest and a sharp engagement took place, for the Enemy were strongly posted within stone breastworks on the hills in front and on each flank near Hykulzie [sic]. We stormed the main body twice but were repulsed each time as their cavalry charged on the rear of the storming party. We kept the fun up till dusk in the evening, then we took possession of an old Fort called Bogar. We were obliged to leave our killed on the Field of Honour where they received their death Wound. We were only a Wing of the 41st Regiment and a Company of Artillery and a Regiment of Bombay Sepoys, so we were but few to contend against such an Army that opposed us.

In fact, about 470 British and Indians were engaged, out of whom 27 were killed and 72 wounded. The 41st lost one officer and seventeen rank-and-file killed, fifty-one wounded. Among the latter was Sergeant Haslock, with a gunshot wound in the leg. Bivouacking that night in the ruined Bozar fort, the survivors were assaulted by a violent thunderstorm and torrents of rain. 'Rain is very uncomfortable for soldiers in Camp', wrote Haslock, 'but in this instance it answered our purpose right well...'.

Not only did it provide a much-needed water supply, but it effectively damped the matches of the Afghans' primitive *jezails*,[3] so that there was no sniping during the night. Next day Brigadier England withdrew his whole force to Quetta.

This abortive advance brought a stinging rebuke from the impatient General Nott in Kandahar, who demanded to know why England had not pressed on, and asserted that his tame withdrawal had done more harm to the Kandahar force 'than twenty thousand Afghans in the field'. He was sending a brigade to meet the Quetta Column at the northern end of the Khojak Pass on 1st May, and England was to be there by that date, Afghans or no Afghans.

Reinforced by, among others, the remaining four companies of the 41st from Karachi, England's Column of some 3,000 all arms set off again on 23rd April and, having buried the mutilated bodies of their dead still lying on the field at Haikulzi, joined General Nott's Brigade at the Khojak Pass and reached his garrison of Kandahar on 10th May. Though they had been harried by the inevitable snipers on the way, no serious opposition was met. Only eleven British soldiers were wounded during the march.

For nearly two months the combined force remained in Kandahar, allowing the other 'pincer', General Pollock's Army, to advance through the Khyber and continue to Jalalabad and Kabul. Apart from some desultory skirmishes outside the walls of Kandahar, this respite seems to have been passed pleasantly enough. 'We are very comfortable here', wrote Sergeant Haslock:

> ... There are some large vineyards near the city, and we are just in time for the beautiful, large ripe grapes. No Afghan is allowed near the place, so we live in the best houses and the Persians carry on their business as though there was not a conquering enemy in the place. In the splendid Bazar is sold commodities from all parts of the world, as the caravans of merchants from different parts stop here for a week or so. The City walls are very high with strong batteries and two carriages may pass each other on the ramparts... Over the crossing of the main streets a splendid dome is built by way of Market Hall and here is for sale the beautiful shawls from Cashmere, the rich silks and cloths from Persia and Buckhara. There is Arabian, Circassian Mogul and many other country traders living here, so we can buy anything we like best. The houses we live in have flat roofs made firm so that they can walk on them the whole length of the streets... It is the best place we have been in since we left England... We can buy cakes made from wheat flour as long as a tailor's sleeve board, also plenty of milk and good butter which is quite a treat for us... But we shall soon have to leave these niceties and beat a march, for there are more of Englands enemys to be subdued yet.

The march was 'beat' on 9th August when General Nott's force of 7,000 combatant troops with followers and baggage animals left Kandahar for Ghazni and Kabul.[4] The 41st, still led by Major Gore-Brown, were not accompanied by their true Commanding Officer, for Nott had ordered Brigadier England to return with a detachment to Quetta, 'to keep open the lines of communication'. The fact is, the two commanders had not been on the best of terms since the Haikulzi affair.

Apart from ever-present marauding tribesman, the real enemy was now the climate. In August the cruel sun-roasted plateaux of Afghanistan are at their cruellest: temperatures soar to 116° F or higher, with little relief at night. There was no shade for the marching columns and no escape from the stifling clouds of dust that enveloped them. With watercourses merely dry nullahs, raging thirst could only be tempered by a meagre ration from the bhisti's water-skins at the midday halt. In 1880, Robert's men were lightly clad in cotton drill with sun helmets, but Nott's British soldiers trudged in their serge coatees permanently soaked with sweat, while their useless round forage caps gave no protection from the relentless glare of the sun which beat back from sand and rock. Strangely, casualty figures for the Afghan campaign omit all mention of losses through heat exhaustion, but some must have been incurred.

There were sharp engagements between 27th and 30th August when the Afghans, having ambushed and cut up a squadron of Bengal cavalry, withdrew to a fortified village near Ghuain (or 'Goyain' as earlier historians have it). As the 40th and 41st and Native Infantry advanced to attack, some Afghans emerged protesting innocence, but as soon as the troops approached within range they were met with volleys of musketry. Thereupon the village was rushed with the bayonet and put to the flames. According to the Rev. I. N. Allen, chaplain to the 40th Foot, the British lost thirty-seven all ranks killed in this affair, but the 41st had only seven men wounded. The Afghans' killed were put at 'not less than 150'.[5]

On 30th August there was a fierce action at Ghuain itself when the fort was battered by Nott's 6-pounders and then stormed by 3,000 British and Indian soldiers, including the whole of the 41st. Among the spoil were vast quantities of British ammunition and two 6-pounders captured by the Afghans at Ghazni. In his diary Padre Allen noted: 'It is much to be regretted that no allusion was made in the public despatch even to the presence of the 41st Regiment in the field, though it had an equal share in the affair with all the other infantry corps present.' He seems to infer that General Nott's rancour against Brigadier England was now being visited upon his Regiment. The great citadel of Ghazni, captured in the 1839 offensive and then evacuated, was reached on 5th September. Built by the 'World Conqueror', Mahmud of Ghazni, in the 11th century, the fortress still looked impregnable, frowning from its isolated ridge and garrisoned, so it was said, by some 2,000 Afghan warriors.

At first, the enemy seemed disposed to offer battle when a motley force of infantry and horsemen sallied forth from the gates, but these were quickly dispersed by musketry from the 40th and 41st, supported by artillery fire. Then, just as the troops were pitching camp, the Afghans resorted to their secret weapon. Lieutenant de Blaquiere of the 41st wrote:

> The nearest post of our Line was better than an English mile from the walls... beyond the range of cannon of even the largest growth, but just as we were comfortably reclining after our morning's work, 'bang' went a report that seemed like the explosion of a mine or small magazine, closely

followed by a rushing whirr that gave fearful omen of crashing ruin. *Plump* it lobbed among the ropes of our Mess Tent, tumbling some 30 yards further and grazing only the rump of a dozing camel. The fall of a thunderbolt could not have excited greater astonishment... the idea of any human contrivance sending such messenger so far among us was incredible...

The 'messenger' was in fact a solid iron roundshot weighing some 52 lb. ('half a hundredweight', said de Blaquiere) and, as later discovered, it had been propelled by a monster brass cannon, 10 ft long with a calibre of 8 in. (at this period the heaviest British field-piece was a 24-lb. howitzer). *Zabar Jang* (Mighty in Battle), as the Afghans dubbed it, continued to lob its fearsome missiles, but the only casualties were a few camels unfortunate enough to lie in the field of fire. Nevertheless, it caused General Nott to move his camp.

The vaunted fortress of Ghazni fell tamely, without any assault. Next morning it was found that the entire garrison had fled, and after blowing up the defences the Column marched on for Kabul. Having fought off sundry attacks on the way, the troops on approaching their objective learned that the other half of the 'pincer' movement, General Pollock's force, had forestalled them and occupied the capital, which '... doubtless saved us some hot work but also deprived us of some chances of renown', as a 41st officer observed. On 17th September Nott's Column went into camp outside the walls of Kabul city and were put under command of General Pollock. Their 320-mile march from Kandahar, with numerous actions *en route*, had occupied nearly forty days.

The British were now determined to wreak vengeance for the treachery and humiliation suffered the previous January. On 26th September a punitive force of 4,500 troops under Major-General McCaskill set out for the fortified town of Istalif, some 40 miles north-west of Kabul, where Akbar Khan the instigator of the revolt, was reported to have fled with 14,000 of his followers. In this expedition the only British infantry regiments engaged were the 9th (Norfolk) and the 41st, each being brigaded with two Indian battalions. The capture and sacking of Istalif on 30th September was not an entirely honourable episode. Most of the Afghan warriors fled after the first assault, leaving behind the greybeards and women and children. It seems that the sepoys got completely out of hand and shot or bayoneted the hapless creatures before resorting to an orgy of looting. 'It was a pitiful scene', wrote Sergeant Haslock, 'to witness children crying beside their dead or dying fathers and mothers... some of the sepoys were so intent on revenge that they neither spared age nor sex.' The British soldiers did their best to prevent the slaughter, and some of the 41st actually escorted terrified parties of women and children to safety, but the carnage was shocking. The whole town was fired and left in ruins. The only Regimental casualty reported was Lieutenant William Evans, who was killed in the initial attack. Paying tribute to Major Gore-Brown and the 41st for their conduct, General McCaskill's despatch also commended 'the exemplary humanity' displayed by the Regiment towards the hapless families.

Further 'retribution' followed when the returning force sacked and burned the evacuated town of Chaikar, and finally the Great Bazaar of Kabul and other parts of the city were put to the flames. Having thus wrought destruction and taken their vengeance, the entire British force began their march back to India on 12th October. Their route was the same as that taken by the ill-fated Column in January, and when they entered the Khurd Kabul Pass, macabre reminders of the massacre met their eyes. An anonymous diarist of the 41st wrote:[6]

> ... A dreary route indeed, but rendered horrid to us by the spectacle of the mouldering remains of our slaughtered fellow soldiers, with which it is thickly strewn. Skeleton upon skeleton, they lie in frequent heaps, the parchment-like skin still stretched over the bones, and in every variety of posture, the result of violent and painful death. Our blood boiled as we gazed on these ghastly sights, and we deemed little enough had been done in vengeance...

The Afghans harried the Column throughout the twenty-five days' withdrawal, but the Sikh fort of Jamrud, at the Indian mouth of the Khyber, was reached without serious losses and on 7th November the 41st went into camp for a much-needed respite at Peshawar. Then they, with the rest of Pollock's force, marched into British territory in the Punjab, arriving at Ferozepur on 23rd December. Here the 'avenging Army' was feted with a public reception and review, and a grand ball for the officers. During the campaign the 41st had lost 2 officers killed and 117 other ranks killed and wounded, but, as Lomax hazards, 'A great number fell victims to exposure and fatigue' in their 2,000-odd miles of marching in extremes of climatic conditions. In August 1843 the Regiment was awarded the Battle Honour 'Candahar' and in the following June 'Ghuznee' and 'Cabool' were added.

Although it earned Honours and acclaim for the avenging Army, the 1st Afghan War achieved little for British prestige or influence in Afghanistan. All it had done was to leave the whole country smouldering with fierce hatred for the foreign interlopers who had attempted to impose their own puppet King – a hatred that was to explode with even greater violence and bloodshed thirty-seven years later.

After helping to put down an insurrection by the Amirs of Scind, the 41st embarked at Karachi and sailed for England in March 1843.

'Awful is the responsibility of those who have for so long maintained in command a General whose incompetence they have never hesitated to confess, and who have tendered the feelings of an obstinate old man at the expense of a carnage which has filled so many households with mourning, and deprived the British army of hundreds of its choicest soldiers.' Thus thundered *The Times* of 5th March 1849 on reporting the controversial Battle of Chilianwala in the Punjab.

The 'obstinate old man' was General Sir Hugh Gough, Commander in Chief in India, who only two years earlier had been acclaimed as a public hero and created a Baron for his victory over the Sikhs at Sobraon. Although Gough was now in his 70th year, he had lost none of his energy or his Irish zest for a scrap. Some of his superiors,

Wellington included, censured what they termed his 'Tipperary tactics' – a hot-blooded impetuosity and fetish for getting to grips with cold steel.[7] But his personal courage, hearty manner and picturesque native brogue made him a popular General. His troops were devoted to him.

The treaty with the Sikhs following Sobraon (1846) proved a fragile one. In 1848 there was insurrection at Multan; within a couple of months the Punjab was again seething with revolt and the new leader, Sher Singh, seemed determined on another trial of strength. The reluctant Lord Dalhousie, Governor-General, was at length persauded by Gough that force must be met with force, and in October 1848 he authorised the Commander in Chief to form the 'Army of the Punjab' and trounce the treacherous enemy once and for all. So began the 2nd Sikh War, in which the 24th Regiment was to play a conspicuous part.

At this date the Regiment was stationed at Agra, having been posted to India in May 1846. 'A splendid-looking corps', as a future Field Marshal described them,[8] the Battalion was fully up to strength with 27 officers and 1,071 other ranks. Lieutenant Colonel John Pennycuick, CB, KH, was commanding, and Lieutenant Colonel Robert Brookes was his Second -in-Command. Aged 60, Pennycuick had seen forty-two years' service, almost all of it in the East, but was a newcomer to the 24th, having succeeded to command from the 17th Foot in April 1848. Also in the Battalion was his 18-year-old son, Alexander, junior Ensign, and just commissioned from Sandhurst. 'We like the regiment very much', wrote Alex to his sister, 'it is a very fine one and the officers are a very gentlemanly set of fellows'.[9]

Having performed a remarkable forced march of 350 miles in 32 days from Agra, the Regiment joined Gough's Army of the Punjab at Ferozepur on 4th November. Here they were brigaded with the 25th and 45th Regiments of Native Infantry, as the 5th Brigade of the 3rd Division commanded by Major General Sir Joseph Thackwell. Since Colonel Pennycuick was the senior officer in the Brigade, he was given command, and Colonel Brookes took over the 24th. For the operations Gough had assembled a force of about 13,000 British and Indian troops with eleven 6-gun batteries of artillery.

The first encounter with the Sikh *Khalsa* (regular army) was at Ramnagar, where Gough managed to force the crossing of the Chenab River, but the 24th were not seriously engaged. Their recruits' baptism of fire came on 3rd December when at Sadulapur a Sikh rearguard action resulted in a lengthy artillery duel, in which neither side committed their infantry. But roundshot accounted for two men of the 24th killed and four wounded, two of whom subsequently died. Gough's Commissariat Department seems to have been little better than Wellington's in the Peninsula, for that night the troops found themselves with 'not a morsel to eat but what they had stowed in their knapsacks or could discover for themselves', as Lieutenant Mcpherson of the 24th recorded.[10] While he had to satisfy himself with some stale chapattis and cold tea, others fared better. The Major's charger had been killed by a roundshot, and the carcass was eagerly reduced to soup and steaks.

There followed a lull of three weeks while Gough's bellicosity was curbed by the cautious Lord Dalhousie. At length, on 10th January, His Lordship signalled his approval of a further advance, adding that a victory on the Jhelum would give him 'much pleasure'. Acknowledging, Gough expressed his hope that 'the enemy will fight for their salt, and I can get close to them'. Within three days that hope was realised, with results that cost him his command of the Army in India (if only temporarily).

In the early hours of 13th January the force of some 13,000 British and Indian troops marched out of their encampment at Dinghi, ten miles south of the River Jhelum, and, deploying into brigade columns, headed for Chilianwala, an insignificant huddle of mud hovels as yet unheard of by the outside world. It was not until after midday that this position was reached, and, a weak Sikh outpost having been driven off, Gough gave orders for the whole Army to encamp: '... the day being so far advanced I decided upon taking up a position in rear of the village in order to reconnoitre my front', as he noted in his subsequent despatch. Accordingly the soldiers piled arms, cavalry horses were unsaddled and picketed, and the complicated drill of laying out camp and erecting tents commenced.

North of the village lay about 500 yards of open plain, bounded on its far extremity by a dense belt of scrub jungle which extended some two miles back to the banks of the Jhelum. Completely invisible to the British, nearly 30,000 Sikh infantry and cavalry with 62 guns, under their Raja, Sher Singh, were deployed in that jungle. Their line, in fact, covered more than six miles from flank to flank, the left flank perched on a rocky eminence of hills and ravines near the village of Rasul.[11] The British Commander in Chief had only a hazy idea from spies that the Sikhs were somewhere on his front in force, but he made no attempt to 'reconnoitre my front'. Not a single patrol was sent forward as his troops settled down to cook their midday meal. 'I determined to postpone an attack until the following morning', he wrote, but the enemy confounded that plan. At about 1.30 p.m. Lieutenant Mcpherson and a couple of fellow-subalterns of the 24th clambered up a tree to spy out the ground in front. Flitting here and there among the far scrub white pagris were spotted. 'By Jove, the place is alive with them', exclaimed Mcpherson, and the three doubled back to their lines. As they did so there were flashes of gun-fire among the trees and roundshot came whirring and bouncing into the encampment. Bugles sounded the Alarm and General Assembly and the troops stood to. Gough now brought forward his own batteries, and for an hour or so there followed a furious artillery duel, which did curiously little damage to either side. The British Gunners had nothing to lay on but the erratic flashes in the jungle and drifting clouds of smoke, while their excited opponents were dropping most of their rounds short.

Later, Gough's critics claimed that the Sikh cannonade roused his 'Tipperary tactics' instinct and precipitated another of his wild 'get-at-'em' attacks. Others asserted that he had little choice: to withdraw without coming to grips was unthinkable; equally, to remain supinely in position was to invite enemy initiative. He ordered a deployment into line. By about 2.30 p.m. the line of battle was formed: on the extreme right flank a brigade of cavalry, then the two infantry Divisions, with another cavalry brigade covering the left flank. Batteries of artillery were interspersed in the intervals, with orders to 'accompany and support the infantry'. As seen in the accompanying plan, the 24th were almost in the centre of the line, with the 25th Native Infantry on their right and the 45th on their left, Colonel Pennycuick commanding the Brigade and

Lieutenant Colonel Brookes the 24th. Together with Brigadier Hoggan's Brigade, on their left, the two Brigades made up the 3rd Division, which was now commanded by Brigadier Colin Campbell (later Field Marshal Lord Clyde). The previous Brigadier, Joseph Thackwell, had been put in command of the whole of the cavalry, and was also Gough's Second-in-Command. The entire force of 13,000 troops included only six British Regiments – 3rd and 14th Light Dragoons, 9th Lancers and 24th, 29th and 61st Regiments of Foot.[12]

At about 3.30 p.m. Gough gave the order for a 'simultaneous advance' (as he wrote in his despatch). But in the days when a commander's sole means of relaying orders in the field were bugles and mounted staff officers, or 'gallopers', it was virtually impossible to launch a three-mile line into a 'simultaneous' advance, and it was from this moment that things began to go wrong, with some units moving off well in advance of others.

Mindful of the dense jungle ahead, General Campbell decided that it would be impossible for him to control both his Brigades, and so he attached himself to Hoggan's leaving Colonel Pennycuick to act on his own initiative. Before doing so, however, he gave orders that were later to arouse controversy and censure. Perhaps imbued with the Commander in Chief's cold-steel fetish, he stressed that should be 'no musketry' in the Brigade: '... the bayonet must do the work'. Some contemporary accounts claimed that the 24th were even forbidden to load their muskets, but Campbell himself later denied this.[13]

As soon as the wall of jungle was reached all semblance of formation inevitably vanished. Formed battalions disintegrated into companies and platoons, even sections. As might have been foreseen, the supporting artillery gun-teams were unable to keep pace through the scrub, and many batteries were outpaced, their potential 'support' being nullified, their fire masked. 'Every regiment was separated from the one next to it, and fought a battle for itself', wrote Lord Dalhousie to Wellington.

In the centre, the 24th's Brigade encountered some of the thickest scrub. Normally the Regiment's uncased Colours, bravely borne forward by Lieutenant Phillips and Ensign Collis, would have formed a centre guide, but they were invisible to any but the men on their immediate flanks. All along the front, the 'simultaneous' attack was developing into a confused series of individual engagements, during which some of the sepoys mistook their own comrades for Sikhs and exchanged volleys. The 24th had now outstripped their two Indian Battalions and were struggling forward unsupported, although they did not know it. So far nothing had been seen or heard from the enemy, but after a few hundred yards the Regiment came within range of the guns and a storm of roundshot, grape and cannister burst upon them. 'My Company was near the centre', wrote Lieutenant Mcpherson, 'we held the Colours and made a good target. One charge of grapeshot took away an entire section, and for a moment I was alone...'. Captain Blachford 'heard a cheer and on looking towards the centre, saw Colonel Brookes in front of the Colours, waving his sword over his head. The regiment came to the double.' By now whole platoons had been mown down, and the jungle clearings 'blossomed with mute redcoats', as Mcpherson put it. But doggedly the survivors stumbled on, never pausing to fire a shot, in compliance with their orders.

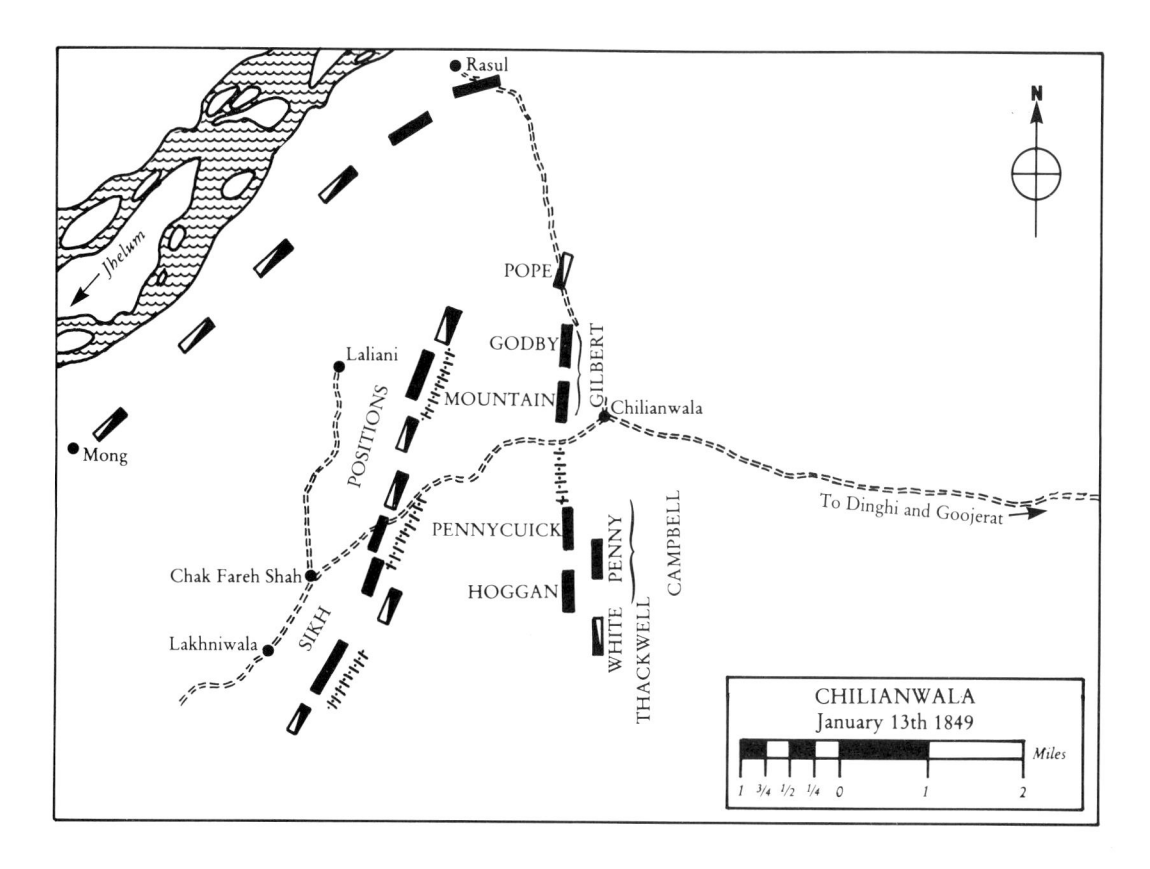

The first to reach the guns and charge in with the bayonet was the Grenadier Company, followed by the remnants of the others, '... with wild choking hurrahs' (Mcpherson). A fierce struggle ensued, Sikh tulwar against British bayonet, while from the rear of the enemy position came a hail of musketry from Sikh infantry who seemed unconcerned that they were firing on friend as well as foe. The guns were captured, and the bayonet had 'done the work'. Some of the men had been provided with 'spiking nails' to hammer into the vents of the pieces, but only two guns had been spiked when the Sikh infantry charged in a counter-attack. By now Colonel Pennycuick, Colonel Brookes and all the company commanders had been either killed or wounded, the two centre Companies had been practically destroyed, and the whole of the Colour Party killed. If the survivors were looking for succour from their Indian comrades, none came, for the two native Infantry Regiments were still struggling through the jungle, far behind. In the face of the fresh assault, the mauled remains of the 24th, virtually leaderless, withdrew in scattered groups. As they did so they met the laggard Native Infantry who, seeing the British soldiers repulsed, followed suit, and it was only when the jungle was cleared that the wreckage of the 24th was rallied and reformed by the senior unwounded officer, Captain Blachford (who had been acting as supernumerary field officer).

Although the Regiment had lost all but nine officers and nearly half its rank-and-file, Blachford led the remnant to join Brigadier Hoggan's left-flank Brigade, which, after a splendid action by the 61st Foot, had captured thirteen guns. But the 24th arrived only in time for the final pursuit of the retreating Sikhs and no more than a few shots were exchanged as the men were destroying some of the enemy ammunition wagons. However, this enabled the 24th to claim that it was 'thus the first and last regiment under fire on that memorable day' (Regimental Records).

In his *Memorandum*, already quoted, Sir Colin Campbell remarked: 'It is impossible for any troops to have surpassed H. M.'s 24th Foot in the gallantry displayed at the assault. This single regiment actually broke the enemy's line and took the large number of guns in their front ... a devotion to duty which has been rarely equalled and never surpassed.' In his despatch after the battle, Gough could not 'extol too highly the conduct of the 24th Regiment of Foot who, unfortunately without support, assaulted and took several of the enemy guns. My only regret is that their losses were severe, including the gallant Colonel Pennycuick and Colonel Brookes.'

Their losses were severe indeed. The Regiment had gone into action with 31 officers and 1,065 other ranks. Of these 13 officers were killed, 9 wounded; 225 NCOs and men were killed, 278 were wounded – a total of 525 casualties. These were the heaviest of all the regiments engaged.[14] As noted above, the entire Colour Party were lost, and so was the Queen's Colour. Lieutenant Colonel Matthew Smith, promoted from Major in the 29th, assumed temporary command of the 24th after the battle, and in a letter to the Colonel of the Regiment (Lieutenant General R. Ellice) he stated that: 'one of the men is reported to have wrapped the Colour round his body, but he was afterwards killed, and all endeavours to find any trace of it have hitherto been in vain'. No trace was ever found, but at least it did not fall into Sikh hands, as did some Native Infantry Colours. When Ensign Collis fell bearing the Regimental Colour, this was picked up by Private Richard Perry and safely brought in. Perry was promptly promoted Corporal and awarded a Meritorious Service Medal (now in the South Wales Borderers Museum). This 'Chilianwala Colour' remained in service until 1868, when (the Regiment still being '2nd Warwickshire') it was laid up in St Mary's Church, Warwick. The later battle between The South Wales Borderers and the obdurate church authorities to have it removed to the Regimental Chapel in Brecon Cathedral is related in Appendix 5.

The loss of Colonel John Pennycuick was a heavy blow to the Regiment, and the grieving family were also left to mourn the death of young Alexander as well. Some accounts say that when the Colonel fell, his son dashed to his aid and was cut down trying to defend him. But the true circumstances are set forth in a letter from Colonel Mathew Smith to Colonel Mountain (commanding the 29th's Brigade):[15]

Chilianwala: Brigadier Jonn Pennycuick (24th Regiment), commander of the 5th Brigade, and his son, Ensign Alexander Pennycuick, who were both killed by Sikh fire.
NATIONAL ARMY MUSEUM

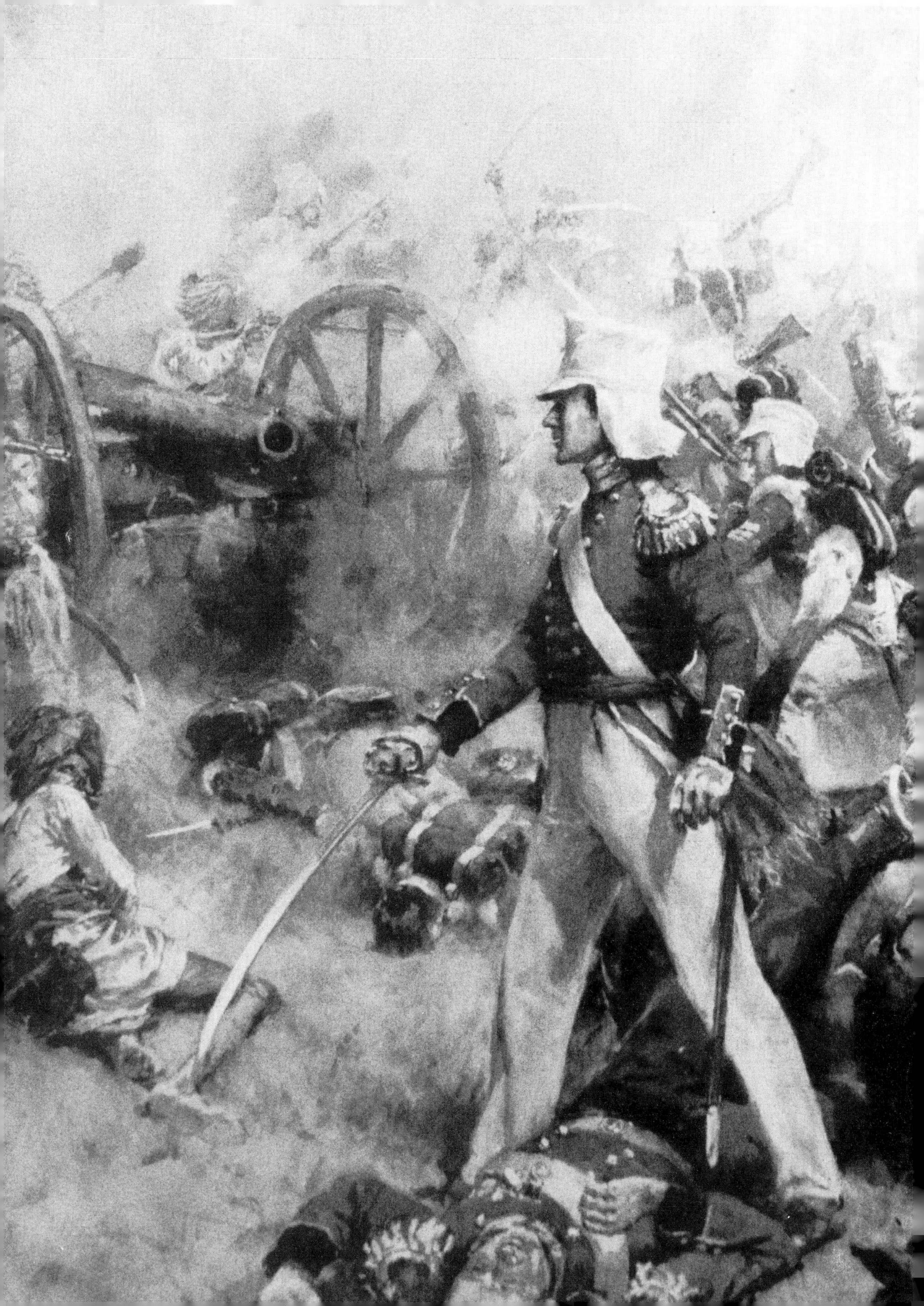

Wuzeerabad, 5th June '49

My dear Mountain,
    The sad tale of poor Brigadier Pennycuick's death & that of his son is brief.
    When the order was given for the line to advance, he continued near his own Regt. the 24th.
    For some cause or other, he was dismounted from his horse & went on, a little way in front of the 24th, on foot – the Regt. was at the charge pace – & when within some 50 yards of the guns, a Sergeant saw the Brigadier stagger and put his hand to his body, just below the breast. He & another went up to him to offer assistance – but he declined it saying – 'go on with the Regt.' Shortly after, a private soldier seeing that he was wounded went to him, & he accepted his assistance – two sergeants then joined him – & he said 'I am badly wounded, take me to the rear'. They saw that he was bleeding profusely – & rapidly losing strength – these three men conveyed him towards the rear, & shortly found that he was dead. They continued to carry the body but ... the Regt having reached the battery was over-whelmed – & after suffering immense loss, retired – they swept in confusion past the men carrying Pennycuick's remains – the Sikh cavalry following up and slaughtering all they got near. To save their own lives, therefore, & the poor Brigadier being no longer alive, they laid him down – took his handkerchief & keys from his pocket – & made the best of their way to the village, where the Regt. was rallied.
    Young Pennycuick, [who] had been on the sick list, was brought to the field in a dooly – there he insisted on going with the Regt. into action – he retired with it, after the repulse, and at the village, heard of his father's fate. Immediately, he went to the front in search of the body, & it would appear was killed by its side, for the two were found lying dead together ...

And so, gallant father and gallant son were laid side by side in the burial mound at Chilianwala.[16]
    Some of the wounded officers had remarkable escapes. Lieutenant George Williams was cut down and fell into a thorn bush, where he was continually hacked and slashed by Sikhs trying to finish him off. When found he had lost one hand, his skull was fractured, and he had suffered twenty other wounds from tulwar and lance. Miraculously he survived, and lived for another forty years.
    In those days regiments campaigned with as much of their peacetime comforts and amenities as they could manage (hence the enormous baggage 'tails'), and the 24th had even brought along a 39-ft Officers' Mess table. As Mcpherson recorded: 'In our Mess tent, on the table around which they had so often sat in mirth and merriment, were reverently laid the bodies of 13 of our officers, together with the remains of Sergeant-Major Coffee (commissioned in death).' Later, Major General G. F. de Berry

One of the three separate graves of soldiers of the 24th Regiment who were killed at Chilianwala.

(Lieutenant at Chilianwala), claimed that it was he who arranged for the bodies to be so laid out 'till I arranged with the Chaplain for their proper Christian burial on the mound near the village of Chilianwala'.

There were other more serious matters of contention about the 24th's actions at Chilianwala. Why were they ordered to attack 'without firing a shot'? The two other British infantry Regiments made full use of their muskets, and their casualties were slight compared with the 24th's.[17] Although Colin Campbell later admitted that he had ordered 'no musketry in the brigade', he did not explain why. It has been suggested that he was merely conforming to the Commander in Chief's well-known predilection for the bayonet, or 'Tipperary tactics'. If so, none of the other divisional commanders followed suit. There was criticism of Pennycuick for allegedly ordering the charge at too great a distance from the objective, thus further losing cohesion. This was categorically refuted in a letter to Major Kennedy from General Sir Charles Napier (published in *Life and Opinions of Sir Charles Napier*):

'All my enquiries satisfy me that Lieutenant Colonel Pennycuick did not order the change. That no man did. That it arose from a general impulse...

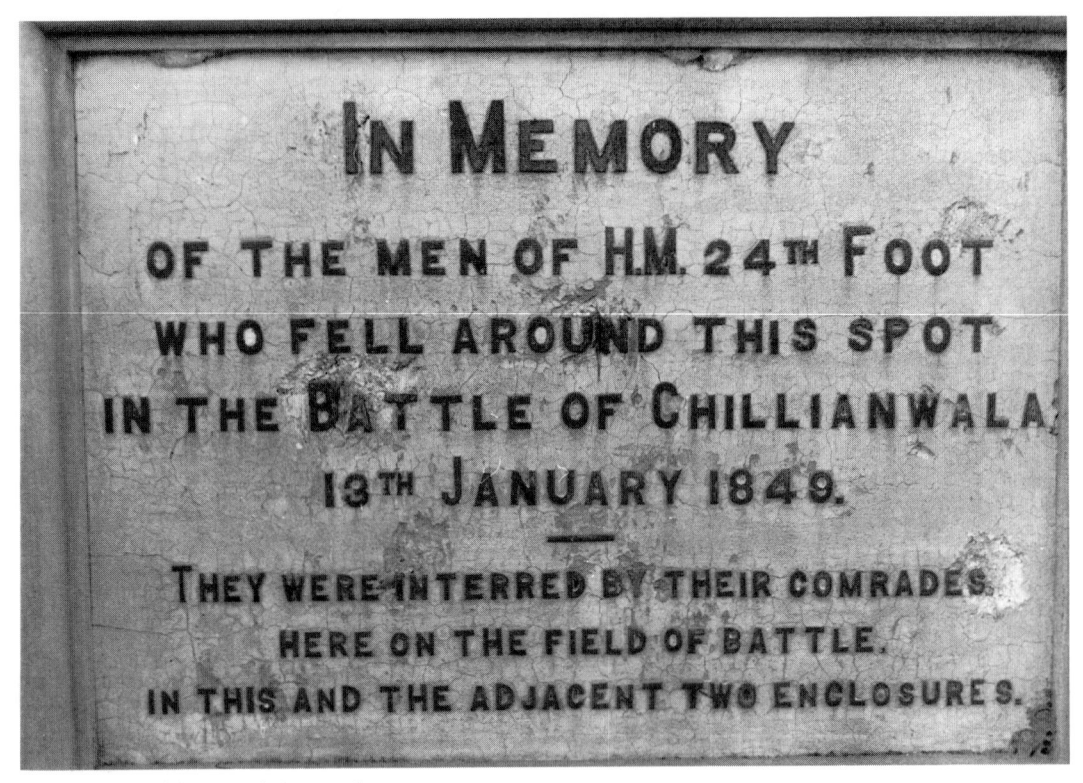

> IN MEMORY
> OF THE MEN OF H.M. 24TH FOOT
> WHO FELL AROUND THIS SPOT
> IN THE BATTLE OF CHILLIANWALA
> 13TH JANUARY 1849.
>
> THEY WERE INTERRED BY THEIR COMRADES
> HERE ON THE FIELD OF BATTLE.
> IN THIS AND THE ADJACENT TWO ENCLOSURES.

Memorial tablet at Chilianwala.

> the desire to close with the enemy, the cheers of the soldiers to encourage each other as they struggled through the jungle – all conduced to change an advance in quick time to a rush forward by a common impulse... There was nothing then for a brave and able commander to do but what Colonel Pennycuick did – dash forward, cheering on his men, and by his example supporting the impulse he could not check, and ought not to check. There were but two things to do – to run on, or to turn off: the 24th chose to nobler one.'

One may well imagine that the men, assaulted by the tormenting guns and forbidden to use their muskets, were only too eager to 'dash forward' and close with the enemy.

Gough claimed Chilianwala as a 'victory', but it was clearly a Pyrrhic one. In little more than two hours he had lost 89 officers and 2,350 other ranks killed, wounded or missing, out of a total strength of 13,000. Six guns had been captured and several Colours lost. Although Sikh casualties were also heavy (Gough reported about 2,000 killed), the British force had gained no tactical advantage: the Sikhs were still in position in the jungle and on the heights of Rasul (from where they flaunted the captured Colours).

It was not until early March that full reports of Chilianwala reached England, and when they did a storm of vituperation burst over the 'victor'. Gough was castigated for his 'reckless precipitation' and his 'contemptible generalship' (*The Times*), while Lord Dalhousie commented that 'the conduct of the battle was beneath the contempt of even a militia man like myself'. Members of the House (and the Press) demanded to know why he had impetuously launched his force into 'an impenetrable forest' against an unseen foe without any attempt at reconnaissance. Why had he entrusted the crucial right-wing Cavalry Brigade to an effete old man who had never led anything larger than a squadron in battle, and was so infirm that he had to be lifted into his saddle?[18] There was general condemnation of his handling of the artillery arm: his sixty-six guns (many of them heavy 24-pounders) should have been allowed to batter the enemy position more effectively before they were thrust with the rest of the line into the jungle, where they became virtually useless. Apparently no specific orders had been given to divisional or brigade commanders, other than that for 'a simultaneous advance'. The Commander in Chief had much to answer for. His losses were never again equalled in any other single battle on Indian soil.

The outcome was inevitable. On 17th March the ageing General Sir Charles Napier (conqueror of the Scind) was ordered out to replace Gough. But before the replacement could arrive at Calcutta, in May, the 'madcap profligate of of his soldiers' lives' (*The Illustrated London News*) had so far redeemed himself that he was once more a national hero, and vitriolic abuse was succeeded by laudatory enconiums and a Viscountcy. This redemption was achieved by his decisive (and indisputable) victory over Sher Singh and the *Khalsa* at Gujrat, on 21st February.

Here the Sikhs were in a strong position in front of the city, their flanks protected by dry nullahs. Gough's Army of the Punjab had made up the Chilianwala losses with reinforcements free to join after the capture of Multan, and he now deployed some 24,000 men with 96 guns. Still temporarily commanded by Lieutenant Colonel Smith of the 29th, the 24th had also been augmented by officers transferred from other units and by slightly wounded men now recovered, so that their strength was 29 officers and 665 other ranks.

This battle gave no cause for controversy. Gough employed his ninety-six guns to full effect, pounding the enemy lines for nearly three hours before allowing his infantry to advance, which they did not with bayonet only, but with skilful use of fire and movement, fully supported by cavalry on the flanks. The Sikhs fought valiantly, but the preliminary bombardment had severly depleted their ranks and silenced their own guns, and after nearly five hours they finally broke before the advancing British line. This time Gough could justifiably report 'a splendid victory'. He had defeated 60,000 enemy, the bulk of Sher Singh's *Khalsa*, inflicting on them some 12,000 casualties and capturing 40 guns, together with the Sikh strongpoint of Gujrat itself. His own losses were 802 all ranks killed and wounded, out of which 243 were British. For the 24th it was a bloodless victory: although initially subjected to heavy artillery fire, they lost not a single man killed or wounded.

The remnants of the *Khalsa* fled north to Peshawar where in early March they surrendered, and on the 14th Sher Singh formally accepted British rule at Rawalpindi.

The whole of the Punjab was now added to the territories of the Hon. East India Company.

The 2nd Sikh War had cost the 24th Regiment 22 officers and 509 other ranks killed and wounded, all but six of these at Chilianwala. But it also earned them the Battle Honours 'Chillianwallah', 'Goojerat' and 'Punjaub',[19] granted in March 1853.[20] For the British Raj there was another legacy. Just eight years later their erstwhile enemies were fighting loyally and staunchly alongside British soldiers in the Indian Mutiny, and the Sikhs continued to serve the Crown in Britain's Indian Army until 1947.

In April 1849 the 24th marched into the newly-established cantonment of Wazirabad, some twelve miles south of Gujrat, and here for the time being we leave them.

Notes

[1] The unlikely inventor of the percussion cap was a Scottish clergyman, the Rev. Alexander Forsyth, who patented the device in 1807.

[2] Among the captives was Florentia, Lady Sale, wife of the General at Jalalabad, and her *Journal of the Disasters in Affghanistan* (1843) has long been compulsory reading for students of the Afghan Wars.

[3] The *jezail* was a crude matchlock musket, made in Kabul, with an effective range of no more than about 150 yards. It remained the 'standard' firearm of the Afghan and Pathan tribesmen until superseded by looted British arms, which were then copied.

[4] By an odd coincidence, General Nott's march from Kandahar to Kabul began on the same day of the year as General Robert's more celebrated march in the opposite direction thirty-eight years later.

[5] *Diary of a March through Sinde and Affghanistan* (1848).

[6] The present author also passed this way in 1964, and the only reminder of the disaster was a rough stone cairn at the summit of the pass. But an Afghan villager claimed that bones and musket-balls were still being uncovered after 122 years.

[7] It is recorded that on learning his artillery was almost out of ammunition at Sobraon, he uttered the glad cry: 'Thanks be to God, now I can get at 'em with the bayonet!'

[8] Field Marshal Sir Henry Norman, then Adjutant of the 31st Native Infantry (in letter to Colonel W. P. Symons, co-author of *Historical Records of the 24th Regiment*.

[9] This letter, and others from father and son, are quoted in the memoir 'Lieutenant-Colonel J. Pennycuick CB KH', by W. S. Sampson, LLB, published in *J. Society for Army Historical Research*, L11, 212 (Winter 1974). The author is the great-great-grandson of Colonel Pennycuick.

[10] Lieutenant Alexander J. Mcpherson joined the Regiment in 1846 and fought throughout the 2nd Sikh War. Later, as Lieutenant Colonel, he wrote *Rambling Reminiscences of the Punjab Campaign*. He died in 1892.

[11] Coincidentally, just in rear of the Sikh position was the site of the battle where King Alexander of Macedon defeated the Indians under King Porus, 2,000 years earlier.

[12] Today, Queen's Own Hussars, 14th/20th King's Hussars, 9th/12th Royal Lancers, Royal Regiment of Wales, Worcestershire and Sherwood Foresters Regiment, Gloucestershire Regiment. There was another British regiment at Chilianwala, the 2nd Bengal European Regiment, but this belonged to the Hon. East India Company forces. It became The Royal Munster Fusiliers and was disbanded in 1922.

[13] In his *Memorandum on the Part taken by the Third Division . . . at the Battle of Chillianwala* (1851), Campbell described such allegations as 'almost too puerile to require contradiction'. Much later, General Blachford (Captain in the 24th at Chilianwala) alleged that Campbell had admitted to him after the battle that 'it would have been better to have sent in a volley or two before storming the guns'.

[14] A complete roll of all killed and wounded is given in *Historical Records of the 24th Regiment*, by Colonel Paton *et al.* (pp.164, 168–9).

[15] Quoted in Sampson, op. cit.

[16] Pennycuick's eldest son, also John, was commissioned in the Royal Artillery and after serving in the Crimea and the Indian Mutiny, died a General in 1888. His widow, Sarah, was given a grace-and-favour apartment at Hampton Court, where she died in 1878.

[17] Norman gives the following figures: 29th Foot – 4 officers wounded, 34 men killed, 203 wounded; 61st Foot – 3 officers wounded, 11 men killed, 100 wounded (*Battle Honours of the British Army*, op. cit).

[18] This was Brigadier General Pope, of the Hon. East India Company, whose vacillation in the face of the enemy led to the shameful 'Threes About' incident, when the 9th Lancers, 14th Light Dragoons and two Bengal Regiments turned tail and fled without striking a blow or firing a shot.

[19] These spellings are as they appear on the Colours.

[20] The site of the Battle of Chilianwala is now unrecognisable. Jungle clearance and irrigation have transformed it into an agricultural scene of sugar cane and maize. But outside the village a large obelisk marks the centre of the British position, and nearby are gravestones erected by Sarah Pennycuick in memory of her husband and son. In the grounds of The Royal Hospital, Chelsea, another obelisk commemorates the dead of the 24th.

Regimental Colour, 1747.

Regimental Colour, 1816.

Regimental Colours of the 41st Regiment, 1747 and 1816.

National Colour of the 4th American Regiment of Infantry, which, with the Regimental Colour, was surrendered to the 41st Foot at Fort Detroit in 1812.

The Russian drums captured at Sebastopol.

CHAPTER NINE

The First VCs Welcome to Wales (1844–73)

Little mention has been made of the 69th Regiment since Waterloo, after which the 2nd Battalion was disbanded. The 1st (and subsequently only) Battalion was then serving in India, where it remained until 1825, taking part in the operations against the Mahrattas (1816–19), for which it was awarded the theatre Honour 'India'. This was the last Honour that the 69th were to earn as such, and the plain fact is, they were given scant opportunity of distinguishing themselves before becoming the 2nd Battalion The Welch Regiment in 1881. The intervening decades were spent in humdrum internal security duties in the West Indies, Canada and Malta, with brief spells of home service.

However, while in Barbados, in 1852, the Regiment earned the graditude of the Royal Navy and Royal Marines. One morning in September the frigate HMS *Dauntless* made into port with officers and ratings so stricken with yellow fever that only one midshipman and a couple of sailors were left to work the ship. Heedless of infection, detachments of the 69th and the 34th, with their surgeons and orderlies, went on board and gave all the succour they could. Later, with the approval of the Admiralty, a piece of silver plate was presented to each Regiment, that of the 69th bearing the inscription:

> *Presented by the Officers of the Royal Navy*
> *and Royal Marines to the Officers of Her*
> *Majesty's 69th Regiment, in grateful remem-*
> *brance of the unbounded kindness and*
> *generous aid afforded by them to*
> *The Officers and Crew of*
> *Her Majesty's Ship Dauntless*
> *when suffering and disabled by Yellow Fever*
> *at*
> *Barbados 1852*

This plate is now in The Welch Regiment Museum, the 34th's having been inherited by The King's Own Royal Border Regiment.

Returning to the 41st, as seen in the previous chapter, this Regiment came home from the Afghan campaigning in 1843. In that year the Rebecca riots erupted all over South Wales, with 'Rebecca and her daughters' destroying turnpikes, vandalising tollhouses and attacking the property of unpopular magistrates and landowners.[1] The local constabulary were powerless to quell the disturbances, so that the Government was forced to send in troops.

Thus in June 1844 the 41st or 'Welsh Regiment of Infantry' first set foot in the Principality, with Regimental Headquarters and three companies posted to Brecon, the other companies being detached to Carmarthen, Newcastle Emlyn, Newton and Rhayader. Since we know that the Brecon barracks were completed in that same year, we can assume that the 41st (together with the 13th Light Dragoons) were among the first to occupy what was to become the Depot of their future partner, the 24th Regiment.

There are no records of the Regiment's actually being employed 'in aid of the Civil Power', but by the end of the year order had been restored and a Royal Commission removed most of the turnpike grievances. However, the contemporary *Cardiff and Merthyr Guardian* gives us the earliest reference to Welsh soldiers in the ranks of the 41st. Reporting the arrival of the Company under Captain James Vaughan at Carmarthen, on 6th July, the newspaper added: 'A great number of them are Welshmen, and some are natives of this town: they appear to be a fine body of well disciplined soldiers.' On 21st September a grand 'Race Ball' was held in Brecon's new Shire Hall, where, enthused the *Guardian*: 'The music of the splendid Band of the 41st lent additional charms to the fascination of the mazy dance . . .'.

The Regiment's sojourn in their adopted country lasted only a year, for in June 1845 they were placed on the Irish Establishment and posted to Dublin. But before leaving the Principality the Commanding Officer, Lieutenant Colonel Gore-Brown, and his Regimental Headquarters marched into Cardiff on 13th June, prior to embarkation. This, of course, was the first time that any antecedents of the present Regiment had visited the future Depot of The Welch Regiment. Brief associations with South Wales had now been formed, but another thirty-odd years were to pass before they became permanent links.

The 41st remained scattered in detachments in (southern) Ireland until 1851, a period that is largely barren of interest, for the records contain little but changes of station and Inspection Returns. Some of the latter were very complimentary, however, as was that recorded by Major General Sir Guy Campbell on 19th October 1846:[2]

> The 41st Regiment is in high order. Their appearance on parade at my inspection was soldierlike, very steady under arms, remarkably clean, and knapsacks and accoutrement well put on throughout. The regiment is young [there had been an influx of recruits] but they are tall, lathy fellows, and in a year or two will be as fine a regiment as any in the Service. The 41st has been very much detached, but the company officers have looked well after their men at the out stations, and the system and discipline of the corps has been maintained.

Oddly, although 'a great number of them are Welshmen', as the Press had reported, the Inspection Returns continued to ignore them, noting only English, Scots and Irish. By 1847 the preponderance of the latter had given way to Englishmen – 560, compared with 185 Irish and 16 Scots. Presumably the slighted Welshmen were still counted as 'English'.

A pleasant change from the rain-soaked hills and bogs of southern Ireland came in 1851 when the Regiment were sent to the Ionian Islands in the eastern Mediterranean. This was surely an idyllic posting. Strung out along the coast of Greece, the chain of islands from Corfu in the north to Zakinthos (or Zante) in the south had been under British protection since 1815, but they demanded little 'protection', for there was no enemy to threaten. The climate – later to attract the 'package' tourists – was delightful, and as the companies were detached among individual islands they were left very much to themselves, with little interference from authority, and none from the natives, who were friendly. But this *dolce far niente* existence was relatively brief. In 1853 the Regiment were moved to Malta, and in the autumn of that year were ordered to prepare for active service.

For some time there had been ominous sabre-rattling from Tsar Nicholas I, who had replaced Napoleon as the bogey of Western Europe. Having occupied the Danubian provinces of Turkey, he was now threatening Constantinople, and Western alarm rose to fever pitch when the Russian Fleet attacked and destroyed a Turkish squadron, and the Tsar began to build a naval base at Sebastopol. To Britain it seemed that the Russians were at their old game: with Turkey occupied, further expansion would surely follow through Persia and Afghanistan to the frontiers of India. In France, Napoleon III was no great admirer of Britain, the nation that had humbled his uncle's Empire at Waterloo, but he too feared the predatory designs of the Russian bear. And so, after centuries of enmity, Britain and France concluded an Alliance and on 28th March 1854 the two countries declared war on Russia.

By that date, the 41st, in Malta, had been brought up to establishment with 30 officers and 863 rank-and-file. They were commanded by Lieutenant Colonel George Carpenter, who had served with the Regiment since 1829, when he had exchanged from the 53rd as Captain. While at Malta the Regiment received a first issue of the new Minié rifle, supplied for service trials. Soon to replace the smoothbore percussion musket throughout the service, this rifled weapon was still a muzzle-loader, but of course was much more accurate, while the ingenious design of the bullet enabled it to be loaded as easily as its smoothbore predecessor.[3]

The British Army despatched to the Crimea in September 1854 numbered some 27,000 men in five infantry divisions, and one of cavalry. The 41st were brigaded with the 47th (later Loyal North Lancashire) and the 49th (Royal Berkshire), the Brigade commander being Brigadier General Adams, promoted from the latter Regiment. The Brigade was one of two forming the 2nd Division under Lieutenant General Sir de Lacy Evans.[4] As Commander in Chief of 'the Eastern Expedition', Horse Guards had selected an amiable old gentleman who was to prove not altogether equal to the rigours of command in the field. Lord Raglan was chosen because he was the only senior staff officer under the age of 70 – he was 68. As Lord Fitzroy Somerset he had served

Wellington dutifully on the Staff in the Peninsula, and had lost an arm at Waterloo. But he had never led so much as a company in action, and for the past forty years he had been desk-bound in Whitehall. Moreover, both his mental and his physical powers were long past their prime. Living incorrigibly in the brave old days of Wellington's victories, he was to cause frequent embarrassment at Headquarters by his habit of referring to the enemy as 'the French'. It seemed to many that the authorities had chosen the senior commanders and staff more for their aristocratic status than for any military distinctions. Neither Lord Lucan, commanding the Cavalry Division, nor his insubordinate subordinate, Lord Cardigan of the Light Brigade, had seen any active service, while it was public knowledge that the two brothers-in-law had long been sworn enemies. Of Lord de Ros, Quartermaster General (aged 69), it was said '. . . A more unsuitable officer for a position which combined the present-day duties of Chief of Staff with those of Quartermaster-General it would have been difficult to find. He not only lacked experience, but did not seem in the least anxious to acquire it. He was very fond of sunbathing.'[5] The prestigious command of the 1st Division (Guards and Highlanders) was given to a mere stripling of 35, the Duke of Cambridge, whose nearest approach to action had been when he led the 17th Lancers against some Chartist mobs in Leeds.

To minister to sick and wounded soldiers a 'Hospital Conveyance Corps' was formed at the suggestion of Lord Raglan. This was composed of some 300 aged pensioners who themselves quickly succumbed, either to privation or to the bottle, or both. The Commissariat Department was, as so often before, virtually useless. In charge was a humble civilian, James Filder, who at 66 had been recalled after a lengthy retirement from the Board of Ordnance.

Such was the Expeditionary Force with which the 41st sailed for the Crimea in April 1854.

In June the British and French Armies were concentrated around the Bulgarian port of Varna on the Black Sea, whence they were expecting to confront the Russians in the Danube basin. However, the Turks had managed to repel the enemy unaided, and despite some dispute in London and Paris, it was resolved to mount an attack on the Crimean peninsula, with the object of capturing the Russian naval base at Sebastopol. No one had troubled to find out that Varna and its environs were notoriously unhealthy, and before the combined forces could face the enemy they were assaulted by cholera and typhus. Within 6 weeks the French had lost 750 officers and men, with hundreds more sick. In the Coldstream eighty-two died, and the 5th Dragoon Guards were so depleted that they had to be temporarily amalgamated with the 4th. There are no statistics for the 41st, but it seems that they and their 2nd Division escaped lightly, having been in a separate camp.

On 14th September the force landed in the Crimea at Kalamita Bay, which the British soldiers dubbed 'Calamity' – unwitting presage of things to come. Kalamita lay some fifty miles north of Sebastopol and between stretched a totally unknown area of rolling plateaus and river valleys, said to be largely uninhabited. The only intelligence of the enemy was vague and conflicting: some reports put the Russian strength at 45,000; the French Commander in Chief, Marshal St Arnaud, believed 70,000 was nearer the mark; but British naval Intelligence hazarded at least 140,000 on the whole of the peninsula. The total allied force numbered 64,000, of which 27,000 were British.

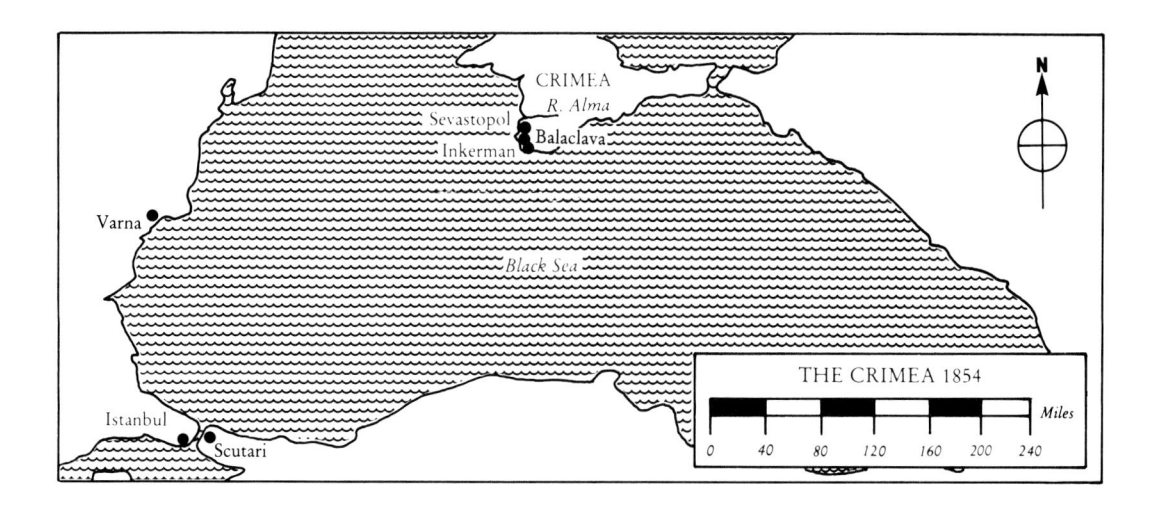

The operational plan was simple enough: the two Armies would march straight across the peninsula, French on the seaward flank, British on the inland, and then invest Sebastopol. Meanwhile the Navy would establish a base at the harbour of Balaclava, ten miles south of Sebastopol. The initial advance met surprisingly little opposition, the troops suffering more from the stifling heat in their unpractical kit[6] than from any enemy attention, and it was only when they reached the steep valley of the Alma, on 20th September, that they met the Russians in force.

Some 37,000 of the enemy had occupied the rugged heights on the far side of the river, and with fortified redoubts and numerous batteries the position looked impregnable. But whatever else Lord Raglan lacked, it was not the aggressive spirit. After some debate he obtained St Arnaud's agreement to a straightforward frontal attack, the French taking the right flank. Drums beating, Colours flying, the two Armies made a splendid showing as they deployed into line on their own side of the river – manoeuvring which evoked a prelude of artillery fire from the Russian guns. This did little hurt; the guns were firing at extreme elevation, and 'so plunging was the fire', wrote Captain Rowlands of the 41st, 'that I saw the head of a rear rank man shot off without touching the front rank man'.

The Alma River was forded without difficulty, and in the face of heavy fire the 41st struggled up the heights to occupy a position near Telegraph Hill, while the Light Division and the French drove off the enemy on the flanks. By now the British guns had come into action; severely mauled by their fire and threatened by the advancing bayonets, the Russians broke and fled, suffering more than 5,000 killed and wounded. Had the cautious Raglan not forbade his cavalry to pursue the fleeing army, the remnants might never have reached the safety of Sebastopol: as it was they were allowed to withdraw unmolested, to the extreme indignation of Lord Lucan and Lord Cardigan, whose horsemen had not even come into action. The allied casualties

Lieutenant Colonel Julius Goodwyn, CB, (CENTRE SEATED) and officers of the 41st (The Welch) Regiment of Infantry, and a Hussar guest at Sebastapol.
COPYRIGHT RESERVED. REPRODUCED BY GRACIOUS PERMISSION OF HER MAJESTY THE QUEEN

amounted to 2,000 all ranks killed and wounded, but the 41st escaped with only 4 men killed and 23 wounded.

Marching unhindered across the peninsula, British and French took up position on a plateau overlooking Sebastopol, which they felt confident of securing within a few weeks. It was now September, and another year was to elapse before this fond hope became a reality. On 25th October Lord Cardigan achieved his moment of glory (or notoriety) when he led his Light Brigade in the 'death ride' against the mistaken objective of the Russian batteries at Balaclava. The following day saw a relatively minor infantry clash in which the enemy's probe towards the Balaclava defences was easily repulsed by the British 2nd Division. Unfamiliar to any but students of the Crimean War, this Battle of Little Inkerman (not to be confused with the subsequent Inkerman) is memorable for The Royal Regiment of Wales, since it resulted in the earliest of the twenty-nine VCs won by their predecessors.

After six battalions of Russians had been driven back by artillery fire, four companies of the 41st and four of the 47th were launched in pursuit. Spotting some enemy ensconced in a stone quarry, Sergeant Ambrose Madden summoned Corporal

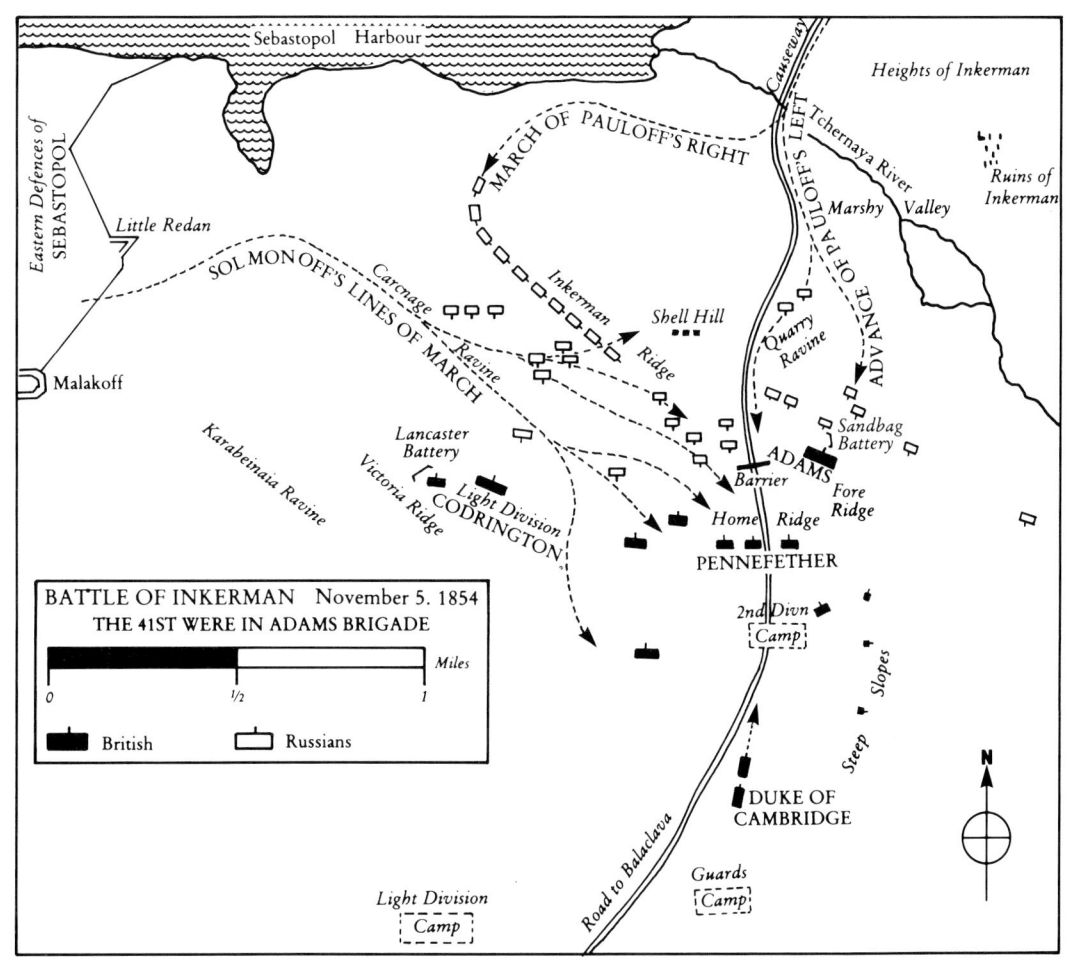

Crawford and a party of men, and with great dash and determination led them into the quarry, where one Russian officer and fourteen soldiers were captured, Madden personally taking three of them.

The Victoria Cross was not instituted until January 1856, so that Madden's award, gazetted on 24th February 1857, was retrospective. The Citation read: 'For having headed a party of men of the 41st Regiment, and having cut off and taken prisoner one Russian officer and fourteen privates, three of whom he personally and alone captured.'

Sergeant Madden, an Irishman from Cork, had enlisted in the 2nd Dragoon Guards (The Bays) in 1838, transferring to the 41st in 1845. Promoted Sergeant Major in 1856, he went with the Regiment to the West Indies the following year, so that he was unable to receive his VC from the Queen at the first Investiture in Hyde Park on 26th June 1857. Instead, it was presented to him by Major General E. W. Bell, Lieutenant Governor and GOC Jamaica, on 7th August 1857. Commissioned Ensign in 1858, Madden transferred to the 2nd West India Regiment in the same year, and continued to serve with that force in the West Indies and West Africa until he was smitten with yellow fever and died in Jamaica in January 1863, aged 43.[7] Sadly, his grave has never been located, and no memorial was erected. Thus the Regiment's first VC holder lies in some unknown 'corner of a foreign field'. But the VC itself is displayed in The Welch Regiment Museum.

Within ten days of the Little Inkerman affair the 41st were to gain their second VC, and the first of numerous DCMs. The action was the better-known Battle of Inkerman itself, in which, on 5th November, some 40,000 Russians fought desperately for the heights above Sebastopol against 16,000 British and French. This has been aptly termed 'the soldier's battle', for the terrain was a maze of ravines, gullys and rocky outcrops, while in the early stages thick morning mist restricted visibility to a few yards, often causing friend to be mistaken for foe, and vice versa.

Soon after dawn the 41st with their Brigade comrades the 47th were heavily assaulted by columns of Russians who forced them to retire. As they did so, Colonel Haly of the 47th was surrounded and dragged from his horse wounded, in imminent danger of death or capture. Seeing this, Captain Hugh Rowlands of the 41st's Grenadier Company dashed to his aid with a few of his men, and after a fierce hand-to-hand struggle rescued the Colonel. For this act of bravery, and his previous stubborn defence of a picquet, Rowlands was subsequently awarded the VC, gazetted together with that of Sergeant Madden on 24th February 1857.[8]

By 7.30 a.m. the 41st, joined by three companies of the 49th, had captured the Sandbag Battery and were preparing to move on. Meanwhile fresh Russian battalions had pushed forward, so that the little force of 700 British bayonets found themselves facing some 4,000 determined enemy. Having sent an aide galloping to the Duke of Cambridge for reinforcements from the Guards Division, Brigadier Adams (49th), was not disposed to sit and await their arrival, but ordered an immediate advance. There then followed a truly heroic struggle against overwhelming odds, the platoons of stolid redcoats halting only to pour disciplined volleys into the grey masses. With their Minié percussion rifles they enjoyed some advantage over the Russians, who had only the old smoothbore muskets. Driving in the opposing skirmishers, the two Regiments charged in with the bayonet and red and grey were mingled as the contest developed into a confused series of individual duels, every man for himself. Captain Edwin Richards was set upon by several Russians and summoned to surrender; he refused and went down pierced with bayonets, having shot four of his opponents with his revolver[9] and killed two more with his sword. Lieutenant John Swaby was wounded five times, but having emptied his revolver, felled a Russian officer with his sword before he too was bayoneted. Lieutenant Alfred Taylor died 'like a mediaeval hero' in single combat (Lomax). He fought a sword duel with a Russian officer while, as if by mutual consent, friend and foe paused to watch. The end came when each ran the other through simultaneously. During the fighting the 41st came upon the Russian 41st Regiment and captured three of their drums, which are now to be seen in The Welch Regiment Museum.

Lieutenant Colonel Hugh Rowlands, 41st (The Welch) Regiment of Infantry, VC, 5th November 1854, Crimea.

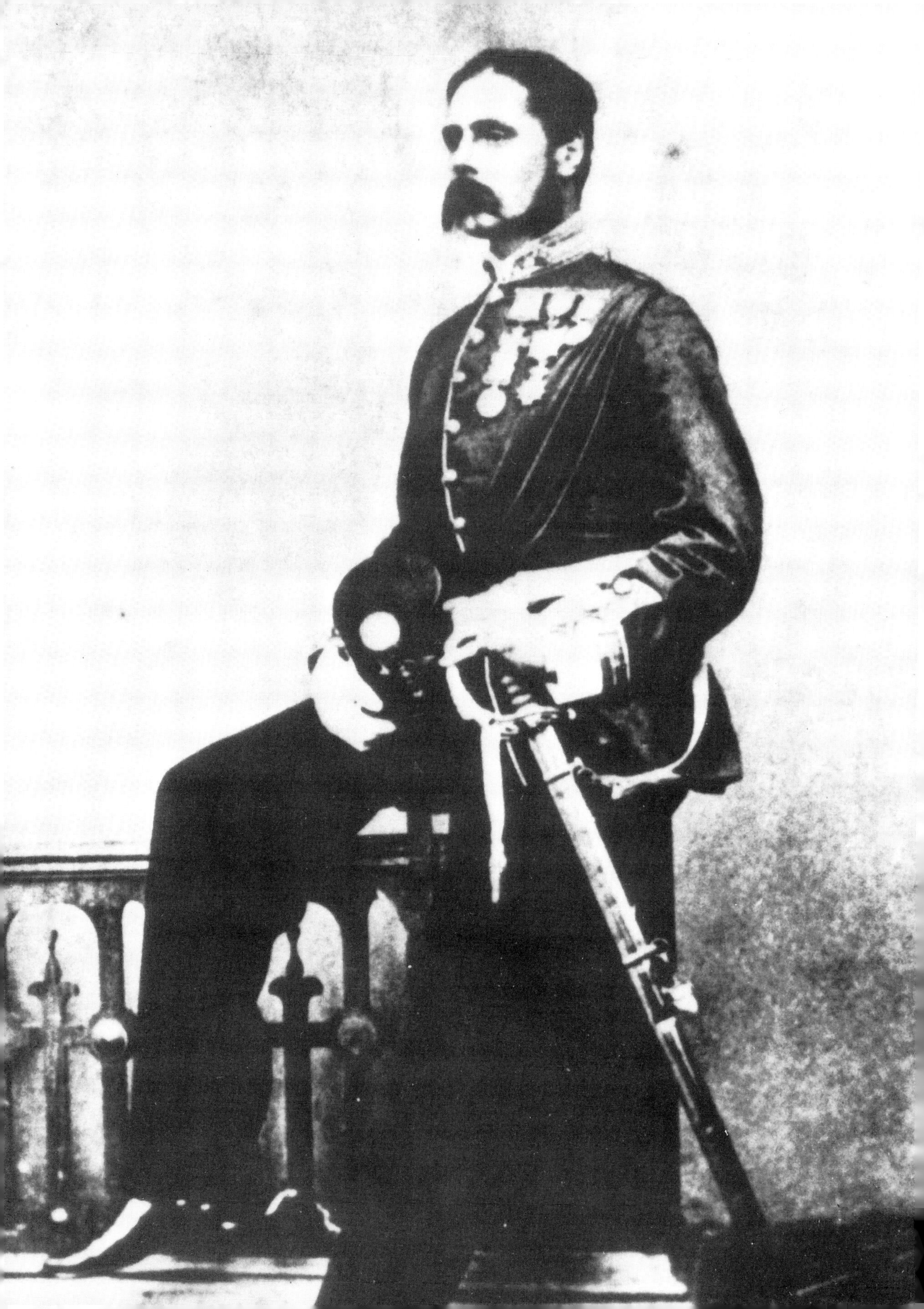

Incredibly, the puny force of British soldiers checked the advance of 4,000 Russians, but after more than an hour of the unequal contest, superior numbers told, and the 41st and 49th were forced to retire, leaving the enemy shaken but unbeaten. During this phase Lieutenant Colonel Carpenter was surrounded, dragged off his horse and desperately wounded with bayonet thrusts. He was rescued by Private Thomas Beach of the 55th and Private Patrick Hurley of the 41st, who fought off the Russians and carried the Colonel to safety. This gallant act earned a VC for Beach and a DCM for Hurley – the first to be awarded to the Regiment.[10] But Colonel Carpenter died shortly afterwards, and Major James Eman took over command of the 41st.

During the struggle around the Sandbag Battery, the Regimental Colour might have been lost but for the brave action of Sergeant Daniel Ford, who later received the Regiment's second DCM. Here is his own account of the incident:

> I was one of the sergeants acting as escort to the Colours of the 41st Regiment at the battle of Inkerman. Lieutenant Armar Lowry carried the Queen's, and Lieutenant Stirling the Regimental . . . when we were in front of the Sandbag battery, we got in the midst of a lot of Russians and, it being very foggy and a lot of firing was going on, it was difficult to see. A Russian fired at Lieutenant Stirling and shot him dead. The Colour fell from his grasp on the ground and I picked it up. As I did so a Russian seized the pole, and we had a regular tug of war, until I drove him through with my bayonet, when he let go. Another of the enemy came up and I drove the butt end of my rifle into his face. I then followed Lieutenant Lowry up the hill, when we met a staff officer who told us the Colours were to go to the rear . . .

Both Colours were eventually taken back to England and can now be seen in the Museum. After the struggle around the Sandbag Battery, the 41st, who had lost five officers killed and numerous men killed and wounded, were fragmented into small groups which were combined with similar groups from other regiments. For the rest of the battle the Regiment ceased to act as a cohesive unit.

The arrival of French reinforcements around noon decided the day, and by 2.30 p.m. the Russians, having lost 1,200 all ranks, withdrew from the Inkerman Heights to take refuge in the Sebastopol fortress. The British casualties were heavy: out of the 8,500 engaged, 43 officers and 589 other ranks were killed, while 100 officers, 1,778 men were wounded. In the 41st, besides the five officers mentioned above, thirty-four men were killed; six officers and ninety-one men were wounded.[11]

On 14th November a welcome draft of six Ensigns and 102 men arrived from the Depot in Ireland, to be greeted by the disastrous hurricane which smote the British encampment on the Inkerman Ridge. Tents were destroyed, stores scattered far and wide and many men injured, and the whole area became a quagmire of liquid mud. Down in Balaclava harbour ships foundered, with them much-needed warm clothing and supplies. Finally, the deluging rain turned to hail and snow.

This was but a prelude to the dreadful winter, 'our dire season of calamity' (Hamley), during which the troops suffered more from exposure, disease, and administrative bungling than from the attentions of the enemy. The Russians remained in force within their Sebastopol defences, but neither side was disposed to take the offensive before the winter was over. Meanwhile, the British soldiers succumbed in their hundreds. By December the death rate had risen to more than 100 per day with 8,000 sick in hospital at Scutari, where Florence Nightingale and her devoted band of voluntary nurses were hampered by lack of medical supplies. Even with the newly-arrived draft, the 41st could parade only 300 NCOs and men fit for duty. Privation, hardship and failure of logistics were nothing new to the British soldier; but previously his sufferings had gone unpublicised at home. The Crimean War saw the first accredited war correspondent in the field, and William Russell's fearless despatches to *The Times* shocked and horrified the nation. But still little was done until the spring, by which time more than 35% of the Expeditionary Force lay buried on the heights or at Scutari. If the Crimean War temporarily removed the Russian threat in the East, it also brought public recognition for the lot of the soldier, and through the efforts of Florence Nightingale and Sydney Herbert, the seeds of Army reform were sown.

By March 1885 casualties had been made up by drafts from home, the troops were accommodated in weatherproof huts, supplies were forthcoming and the siege of Sebastopol began in earnest. Now followed a protracted slogging match of attack and counter-attack and unremitting artillery bombardment by both sides. In June the enfeebled Lord Raglan succumbed to 'Crimean fever' and was succeeded by Major General James Simpson. On 8th September the 41st took part in the assault on the Redan which was driven back after nearly two hours' furious combat. Lieutenant Colonel Eman was killed leading one of the storming parties, as were Captain Every and most of the men. Meanwhile, however, the French had succeeded in capturing the Malakoff strongpoint and by dusk it was discovered that the enemy had evacuated the Redan. Next morning Sebastopol lay abandoned, the corpses of some 8,000 Russians and 5,000 British and French lying mingled in the smoking ruins.

The final assault on Sebastopol cost the British 158 officers and 2,026 other ranks killed and wounded. The 41st lost 3 officers killed (the two mentioned above and Captain Lockhart), and 6 wounded; 35 NCOs and men were killed, 125 wounded. Command of the Regiment now devolved on Lieutenant-Colonel Julius Goodwyn, previously Second in Command (and, later, Colonel of The Welch Regiment).

Although the Russians continued to occupy the heights inland from Sebastopol, the loss of that fortress (and of their Fleet) was a grave blow to their morale, and the winter of 1855-6 passed with little activity but desultory artillery exchanges and encounters between opposing patrols. Now adequately clothed, housed and fed, the British troops forgot the dreadful privations of the previous winter and settled down to an uneventful period of picquet duty, guards and fatigues. The Crimean War was virtually over; in February an Armistice was declared, and on 30th March the Treaty of Paris brought a formal end to hostilities.

In nearly two years' campaigning the 41st lost 10 officers and 145 other ranks killed or died of wounds; 15 officers and 436 other ranks were wounded, while 3 officers and 391 men died of disease. In addition, sixteen men were reported missing, believed dead. Thus the war had cost the Regiment a total of 1,016 casualties.

But it also earned the three Battle Honours authorised in October 1855: 'Alma', 'Inkerman' and 'Sevastopol'.[12] Sixteen NCOs and men were awarded the DCM.

The 41st arrived home in July 1856 and experienced their first journey by steam railway, from Portsmouth to the embryonic garrison town of Aldershot, where on the 29th they were reviewed by the Queen, who also visited their lines. While there, Her Majesty was introduced to Billy, the goat, a Russian animal that the Regiment had picked up and adopted as a pet at Sebastopol. The Queen took a keen interest in Billy and when he died in 1861 she arranged for a replacement to be presented from the royal herd at Windsor.

We left the 24th Regiment at Wazirabad in India, after the victorious 2nd Sikh War of 1849. In the fateful month of May 1857 the Battalion was stationed at Rawalpindi in the northern Punjab, peacefully occupied with the routine of drill, schemes and route marches. The previous year the men had received an issue of the new Enfield rifle to replace their old smoothbore muskets (the Minié weapon of the Crimean War did not reach India). The Enfield was still a muzzle-loader, but of course its rifling rendered it more accurate than its predecessor, while at just under 9 lb. it was the lightest weapon yet handled. Its effective range was about 250 yards. A novel feature was the cartridge of greased paper, the top of which was bitten off to empty the charge down the bore. No one could have foreseen that this Enfield cartridge was to lead to the holocaust of the Indian Mutiny.

When the rifles were issued to the sepoys of the Bengal Army, agitators spread the rumour that the paper was greased with the fat of cows and pigs, the former sacred to Hindus, the latter abhorrent to Muslims, thus affronting the caste and religious prejudices of both classes. There were other more deeply-seated grievances among the Indian troops, but this particular one sparked off a mutiny among a 'native' battalion in Bengal, and on 10th May the sepoys of Meerut mowed down officers and civilians and marched in triumph for Delhi.

During the year's carnage that followed, the 24th at 'Pindi remained remote from the upheaval in central and southern India. There was little trouple in the Punjab (where the Sikhs stood loyal and untainted), and only occasionally were detachments of the Regiment called out in mobile columns to 'show the flag' or to disarm potential mutineers among the few Bengal regiments. However, in July there came more serious business.

Trouble was reported among the 14th and 39th Bengal Native Infantry at Jhelum, and Lieutenant Colonel Ellice (Second in Command) was ordered there with three companies and three Horse Artillery guns. After a fourteen-mile march the Column arrived to find that the Bengali sepoys had fired on their British officers, killing several, and were defiantly barricaded in their lines. Ellice could deploy only some 320 all ranks of the 24th and three guns to confront about 1,000 well-armed mutineers, but this did not deter him. Supported by fire from the guns he led his men straight for the lines. This bold attack cowed some of the sepoys, who bolted into the darkness, but the remainder held out stubbornly and there was furious hand-to-hand fighting from hut to hut. Ellice himself was the first to reach the Quarter Guard, where a volley felled his horse and severely wounded him. Command now passed to Colonel Gerrard of the 14th Native

Lieutenant Colonel Hugh Rowlands, VC, and officers of the 41st (The Welch) Regiment of Infantry, Subathoo, c. 1870.

Infantry, Captain Spring leading the 24th. By dawn the mutineers were still undefeated and it seemed to Gerrard that the attack must be called off to await reinforcements. But just then a lucky shell from the Horse Gunners exploded the 39th's Regimental magazine, killing and wounding all the sepoys in the vicinity, and sending the survivors fleeing from their lines to take refuge in a nearby walled village. After giving his depleted and exhausted force some respite, Gerrard renewed the attack, but now the Horse Gunners ran out of ammunition, and having lost more men, he decided to suspend operations until the morning, so that the Gunners could send their limbers back for replenishments. Next morning, however, the village was found to be evacuated, and after pursuing for some miles and rounding up many prisoners Colonel Gerrard called a halt. The 24th's MS Regimental Records add that the prisoners were 'summarily executed'. A peculiarly horrific mode of execution was reserved for mutineers. The victim was lashed with his back against the muzzle of a field gun and a double charge of powder literally blew him to pieces – frequently scattering the gory fragments among the troops drawn up on three sides of a square.

This operation was costly to the 24th detachment. Twenty-five men were killed or died of wounds, and another forty-nine were wounded. As already noted, Colonel Ellice was severely wounded,[13] as were Lieutenant Chichester (who lost a leg) and Lieutenant Streatfield. Captain Spring was killed. The records state that 150 mutineers were killed, but many more wounded probably escaped to die later.

Apart from a few minor incidents, the rest of the Mutiny passed without notable action for the 24th, although those other hazards of Indian service, cholera and heat, carried off many. On a sixty-mile march from Attock to Rawalpindi in July 1857 twelve men died from *'coup de soleil'*, as the records have it, while at Amritsar in August twenty-five were stricken down with cholera.

In March 1858, while at Ferozepur, the Regiment learned that the Army was to be augmented by the addition of 2nd battalions to twenty-five infantry regiments, of which they were one. The 2nd/24th – the third to be raised – was to have a longer life than any of its predecessors, for it remained in being for nearly 100 years, until disbanded as 2nd Battalion The South Wales Borderers in the defence cuts of 1948.

Although in 1858 the 24th were still officially '2nd Warwickshire', they acknowledged few links with their titular county, and the new Battalion owed none at all, for it was chiefly recruited from Yorkshiremen. It was formally raised and mustered at Sheffield on 3rd June 1858, command being given to Lieutenant Colonel Charles Ellice, who had been invalided home after his wounds at Jhelum and was now recovered. A few officers were transferred from the 1st Battalion (and 124 men came from the Regimental Depot at Chatham), but the majority were posted in from other regiments or from half-pay.

One of the Lieutenants, Henry Marsack, is unique in being the only officer of the Regiment to have seen service with the French Foreign Legion. He enlisted as a Legionnaire in 1850 and fought in Algeria. Among the Ensigns was Charles Bromhead, who rose to command the Battalion and who was a brother of the Rorke's Drift hero, Gonville Bromhead, VC. On 3rd May 1859 the Battalion, with 32 officers and 779 other ranks, paraded at Sheffield for the presentation of its Colours by Susan, Lady Wharncliffe, wife of Baron Wharncliffe. These were the Colours that were to be lost in the debacle at Isandhlwana. Next month the Battalion entrained for Aldershot where they were expecting a lengthy sojourn. But this was not to be.

The fierce 'tribal loyalty' or *esprit de corps* that has always flourished in the British Army could sometimes lead to inter-regimental fracas. When soldiers of different units were stationed in close proximity, as at Aldershot, it was not unknown for jibes or insults in the Wet Canteen to set belts flailing and beer-mugs flying. On Christmas Day 1859 such an incident erupted in the Aldershot Garrison Canteen, when some men of the Tower Hamlets Militia cast aspersions on the 24th. Coming from mere Militiamen, this was doubly provocative, and a full-scale riot developed, quelled only by the intervention of the newly-formed Military Police. Perhaps the Militiamen should have borne some of the blame, but HRH The Duke of Cambridge, Commander in Chief, evidently considered that a regular unit should have displayed better discipline. The upshot was that the 2nd Battalion 24th Regiment was immediately removed from Aldershot in disgrace, and ordered abroad. It is said that on leaving the garrison the Battalion was addressed by the Duke in person, who concluded: 'If I could have my way, I would send you all to – well, a place not mentioned in Queen's Regulations, but as I can't send you there, you shall go to Mauritius for a spell.'[14]

The 2nd Battalion's 'spell' overseas was to last thirteen years, although only five were spent in Mauritius. In October 1865 the Battalion was ordered to Burma, and landed at Rangoon the following month. Although nominally self-governing, the country was occupied by British troops to safeguard commercial interests, and all was peaceful, so that the three-year posting passed off uneventfully for the majority of the Battalion. But some 200 miles off the southern tip of Burma lay the Andaman Islands, on the largest of which was a penal settlement for convicts from India. Among the detachments of British troops garrisoning the islands were three officers and 100 other ranks of the 2nd/24th, who, enjoying ample leisure to disport themselves with sea-bathing and fishing, could not have foreseen any chance of decorations for gallantry.

In May 1867 reports reached Port Blair (Headquarters of the 24th detachment) that a British merchantman, the *Assam Valley*, had run aground on the Little Andaman Island and that the crew had been massacred by the natives. A party of thirty NCOs and men of the 24th under Lieutenant W. T. Much, together with Assistant Surgeon Campbell Douglas, was sent to investigate. Arriving offshore at the reputed site of the massacre, the party manned two gigs, one of which made inshore while the other stood off to give any necessary cover. Despite a heavy surf, the first boat's crew managed to land and had just discovered half-buried remains of European bodies when they were assaulted by volleys of arrows from concealed natives. Lieutenant Much immediately recalled the landing party, but as they tried to embark their boat was swamped and capsized. The subsequent rescue of this party is best described in the words of the Citation for the awards of the VC:

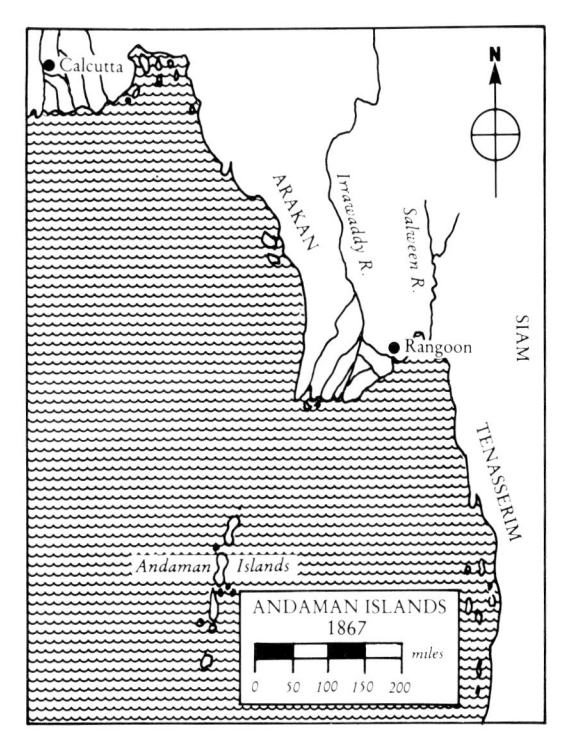

> The officer who commanded the troops on the occasion reports, 'About an hour later in the day, Dr. Douglas, 2nd Battn. 24th Reg., and the four privates referred to gallantly manned the second gig, made their way through the surf almost to the shore but finding their boat was half-filled with water they retired. A second attempt made by Dr. Douglas and party proved successful, five of us being safely passed through the surf to the boats outside. A third and last trip got the whole of the party left on shore safe to the boats. It is stated that Dr. Douglas accomplished these trips through the surf ... by no ordinary exertion. He stood in the bows of the boat and worked her in an intrepid and seamanlike manner, cool to a degree ... The four privates behaved in an equally cool and collected manner, rowing through the

roughest surf when the slightest hesitation or want of pluck on the part of any of them would have been attended by the gravest results. It is reported that seventeen officers and men were thus saved from what might have been a fearful risk, if not certainty, of death.

What the Citation omitted to mention was that throughout these heroic efforts the detachment was subjected to constant hails of arrows from the natives – though fortunately none found their mark. It was known that the Little Andaman inhabitants were cannibals, and had the 24th men been captured they would almost certainly have been slaughtered and devoured.

This episode resulted in the awards of five VCs' – then the largest number to be gained by one regiment for a single action, and not to be exceeded until the record number of nine were awarded for Rorke's Drift and Isandhlwana, again mostly to the 24th.

On 17th December 1867 *The London Gazette* announced the awards to:

Assistant Surgeon Campbell Mellis Douglas, 2nd Battalion the 24th Regiment; VC, 7th May 1867, Little Andaman Islands.

Assistant Surgeon Campbell Douglas
Private David Bell
Private James Cooper
Private Thomas Murphy
Private William Griffiths

In addition to his VC, Assistant Surgeon Douglas also received the Silver Medal of the Royal Humane Society, though none were awarded to the Privates. Campbell Douglas was a Canadian, born in Quebec in 1840, and was appointed Assistant Surgeon to the 2nd/24th in Mauritius in 1863. His 'seamanlike' handling of his boat might seem surprising for a medical officer, but he had always been an enthusiastic rower and canoeist. Before his retirement as Depot Medical Officer at Perth in 1902 he made several remarkable voyages in a Canadian canoe, including a single-handed crossing of the English Channel in 1895 and a similar voyage from New York to Boston in 1889. Douglas died at Horrington, near Wells, Somerset, in 1909.

Of the four Privates, three – Bell, Murphy and Griffiths – were from southern

Private David Bell,
2nd Battalion the 24th Regiment;
VC, 7th May 1867, Little Andaman Islands.

Private Thomas Murphy,
2nd Battalion the 24th Regiment;
VC, 7th May 1867, Little Andaman Islands.

Ireland; Cooper was a Birmingham man. Griffiths was the only one to continue in the 24th until the Zulu War of 1879, when he was killed at Isandhlwana.

In 1869 the 2nd/24th left Rangoon for Secunderabad in Southern India, and three years later its foreign tour came to an end with a posting home to Warley in Essex.

Meanwhile, the 1st Battalion had also completed its Indian tour, leaving Ferozepur in March 1861 and arriving at Portsmouth in July. With the 41st also at home, posted back from Jamaica and Barbados in 1860, this is a convenient moment to review some domestic details and developments.

As we have seen, the Crimean War resulted in Parliamentary and public agitation for some improvement in the lot of the 'common soldier'. Barracks were modernised and new ones built with proper sanitation and ablution facilities; reading rooms and coffee shops were provided as counter-attractions to the Wet Canteen, and efforts were made to substitute more appetising menus (prepared in adequately equipped cookhouses) for the soldiers' monotonous diet of boiled beef, potatoes and soggy cabbage. There were significant reforms in medical matters: an Army Medical School was set up at Chatham and all regimental doctors now had to pass professional examinations. By 1879 large military hospitals had been established at Woolwich, Netley (near Southampton) and Aldershot, all of which were to remain familiar to sick and wounded soldiers until after World War II.

Until 1860 little attention had been given to the education of the soldier, for he still tended to be regarded as little more than an automaton, functioning by reflex response to orders. But in that year the first Army Certificates of Education were introduced, and men were encouraged to study for them – in their spare time. There was no compulsion to do so, and the only incentive was ambition for promotion. There were three Certificates: the Third demanded nothing more than an ability to read and write simple passages and to do elementary sums; the Second and First were rather more advanced and were obligatory for promotion up to Warrant Officer. These three Certificates of Education (with steadily raised standards) remained in force until superseded by the current Education Promotion Certificates in 1971

Discipline was, of course, founded on punishment, but the latter half of the century saw victory for the humanitarian lobby who had so long been campaigning against the notorious cat-o'-nine tails. In 1868 flogging was restricted solely for offences committed on active service, and then only up to a maximum of fifty strokes. Finally the revised Army Act of 1881 expressly forbade any form of corporal punishment, in war or peace, and so after nearly 300 years the barbaric 'Reign of the Lash' was ended. The besetting crime of drunkenness was now punished by fines, other misdemeanours by confinement to barracks ('CB'), extra drills, or, for more serious offences, a term in one of the newly-established military prisons or detention barracks, such as the notorious 'Glasshouse' at Aldershot.[15]

In December 1868, Gladstone appointed Edward Cardwell as Secretary of State for War, and it is his name that is linked with the organisational and other reforms which transformed the Victorian Army, and the infantry in particular, into the force which crossed the Channel in 1914 and which remained structurally unchanged until after World War II. Such changes belong to a future chapter, but a reform of more direct concern to the soldier was the Army Enlistment Act of 1870, under which a recruit could sign on for a six-year period instead of the previous twelve. After the expiration of this term, he could either take his discharge to the Reserve (for six years) or extend his Colour service to the full twelve years. The dedicated and suitably qualified man could re-engage for twenty-one years if he so desired.

But Cardwell's most revolutionary, and controversial, act was to abolish the age-old purchase system for officers. No longer did a young gentleman have to put down large sums for his first commission and subsequent steps up the promotion ladder. The Army Regulation Act came into force in July 1871, and predictably it unleashed a storm of protest and criticism among the diehards who held that the possession of personal means, *ergo*, breeding, was of as much importance as any military aptitude. And, especially among the more fashionable regiments, there was apprehension that the Mess would now be invaded by types whom the Colonel could never have brought himself to interview as his potential officers. As it turned out, these fears proved quite groundless; even though he might not have to pay for the privilege of receiving the Queen's

The Royal Glamorgan Light Infantry, (later 3rd Battalion The Welch Regiment) at drill on Maindy Field Cardiff, summer 1871.

Commission, the young officer could not hope to pay his Mess bills and other expenses (such as uniform replacements) and play his part as a regimental officer unless he could supplement his not over-generous pay of rank. In 1870 an Ensign (2nd Lieutenant after 1871) received 5s. 3d. a day, which in some regiments scarcely covered Mess bills, Band subscriptions and the rest. The fact is, until 1939 the officer corps in the cavalry and infantry (and to a lesser extent in the supporting arms) continued to be drawn almost exclusively from the 'public school class', among which finance was seldom a problem. If it were, there would be little prospect of affording the three years' boarding and tuition fees at the Royal Military College, Sandhurst, which all potential cavalry and infantry officers now had to enter as 'Gentlemen Cadets'.

Whatever else Cardwell achieved, he did nothing for the soldiers' rates of pay. In 1865 a private got 1s. 2d. a day, a corporal 1s. 8d., a sergeant 2s. 4d. and the RSM 5s. These rates remained static until 1914 – as did all the stoppages.

The period brought several changes in dress, the most welcome of which was the introduction of the tunic to replace the tight coatee with its abbreviated skirts. The red tunic with its coloured facings[16] remained the regulation attire until superseded by khaki service dress after the Boer War, and then continued as Full Dress order for ceremonial occasions. The modern Full Dress tunic (no longer paid for out of public funds) is little changed from that worn by the 24th Regiment at Isandhlwana and Rorke's Drift. The dark blue, red-striped trousers remained unaltered, but by the 1870s black gaiters had been adopted to protect the nether limbs in the field. Numerous patterns of shako were introduced, found wanting and replaced, until in 1878 this futile

Officers of the 2nd Battalion the 24th Regiment, Secunderabad, 1871.

form of head-dress gave way to the Prussian-model blue helmet which, with a few modifications, remains the Full Dress article of today.

Turning to arms, the 1860s saw the demise of the venerable muzzle-loading musket or rifle. In 1866 the breech-loading Snider was issued to the regular infantry, and at once the trained soldier's rate of fire was increased from two to ten rounds per minute. Then in 1874 came the Martini-Henry, which with its .44 in. calibre proved a formidable weapon, and weighing only 8 lb. 10 oz. was the lightest rifle yet issued. It did yeoman service with the 24th Regiment in Zululand. Officers still carried their swords in the field, though not surprisingly they preferred to rely on their Smith & Wesson or Webley revolvers – now of course breech-loading.

One of the most radical of the Cardwell reforms took place in April 1873 with the reorganisation of the infantry of the Line. Under this scheme pairs of single-battalion regiments were 'linked' (but not yet amalgamated), the home-based regiments providing drafts for their partners overseas. Each pair established a common Depot, known as 'Brigade Depot' and consisting not only of the Depot Companies of each regiment, but also of two local Militia battalions. Thus for the first time in the Army's history, regiments enjoyed a permanent, static centre or 'home', firmly associated with a territorial area or county. Since at this date the 24th had two battalions, the linking scheme did not apply to them. But despite the fact that they were still the '2nd Warwickshire', they found themselves allotted a Depot at Brecon, in the same barracks that had been briefly occupied by their future partners, the 41st, in 1844. As their recruiting territory they were given the counties of Brecon, Radnor, Cardigan and Monmouth.

The 41st Welsh (or 'Welch') Regiment were linked with the 69th, each having only one battalion, and their 'Brigade Depot' was established at Fort Hubberstone near Haverfordwest (Pembrokeshire).

It so happened that when these changes took place all three Regiments were scattered far and wide. The 1st/24th were in Gibraltar, the 2nd in Aldershot; the 41st were in India and the 69th in Bermuda. None of their soldiers and few of the officers were to see their new 'homes' until more sweeping reforms brought about the amalgamations dealt with in a future chapter.

Nevertheless, the Principality had now said a firm *'Croeso i Gymru'* to the ancestors of The Royal Regiment of Wales.

Notes

[1] 'Rebecca', the instigator, was a Pembrokeshire man and the 'daughters' were groups of disgruntled farmers and other countrymen disguised in women's clothing. They were campaigning against the excessive number of turnpikes and exorbitant tolls levied on farm produce and necessities, such as lime.

[2] Public Record Office; WO.3/469.

[3] Invented by Claude Etienne Minié, a French infantry Captain; the conical-nosed bullet fitted loosely in the bore, but a soft iron plug inserted in the base was expanded by the force of the explosion, tightly engaging the rifling. Thus the projectile could be dropped down the bore and rammed home as rapidly as the smoothbore musket-ball.

[4] The 3rd Division was commanded by Major General Sir Richard England, former Commanding Officer, and later Colonel, of the 41st.

[5] Hibbert, Christopher. *The Destruction of Lord Raglan* (1961).

[6] Some units, probably the 41st included, discarded their useless shakos and marched in their forage caps.

[7] These details are taken from *The VCs of Wales and the Welsh Regiments*, by W. Alister Williams (Wrexham, 1984).

[8] Hugh Rowlands was commissioned Ensign in the 41st in 1849. Having commanded the

Regiment as Lieutenant Colonel, 1866–75, he served as Brigadier in South Africa and India, was promoted Major General in 1881, Lieutenant General in 1890, and died in 1909 as General Sir Hugh Rowlands, VC, KCB, Colonel of The Duke of Wellington's Regiment. He lies buried in St Michael's Church, Llanrug, near Caernarfon.

[9] The Crimean War was the first in which officers were armed with the revolver, or 'revolving pistol'. There was no regulation pattern, but most carried the Adams or Colt, which were five- or six-shot muzzle-loaders of .44 in. or .50 in. calibre.

[10] Instituted in December 1854, the Distinguished Conduct Medal was the first decoration for 'distinguished service or gallant conduct in the Field'.

[11] These figures are taken from the official return of British casualties forwarded to Whitehall by Major General Estcourt, Adjutant General to the force (PRO. WO1/370).

[12] The common English version is 'Se*b*astopol', but in Russian a 'b' is pronounced 'v', so that the Battle Honour version is more accurate.

[13] He survived to become General Sir Charles Henry Ellice, GCB, Colonel of The South Wales Borderers.

[14] These words are quoted, without source reference, by Atkinson in his history.

[15] This establishment, dreaded by generations of errant soldiers, was erected in the 1860s and was so called because the roof over the main block of cells was entirely of glass. In due course the epithet came to be applied to most military prisons.

[16] Grass-Green for the 24th; white for the 41st and Lincoln-green for the 69th.

CHAPTER TEN

Isandhlwana, Rorke's Drift (1874–79)

'The terrible disaster that overwhelmed the old 24th Regiment will always be remembered not so much as a disaster, but as an example of heroism like that of Leonidas and the three hundred Spartans who fell at the Pass of Thermopylae.' This apt tribute was paid by General Sir Reginald Hart, VC, when he unveiled the 24th's memorial at Islandhlwana in March 1914. For displays of sheer courage and fortitude the Battles of Isandhlwana and Rorke's Drift in the Zulu War of 1879 surely have few equals in the annals of the British Army. Isandhlwana may have been a disaster, but it was also a noble example of the British soldier's stubborn refusal to concede defeat in the face of overwhelming odds, while the defence of Rorke's Drift by its tiny garrison against similar odds was a feat of arms that has become part of the mythology of warfare. Both names are for ever linked with that of the 24th Regiment of Foot, or The South Wales Borderers,[1] and ever since 1879 Rorke's Drift Day has been celebrated by that Regiment and its present descendants.

The 1st/24th had arrived in South Africa in 1875 and two years later were engaged in the operations against the Kaffirs in the Transkei. In March they were joined by the 2nd Battalion from home, so that for the first time the two Battalions of the Regiment were operating in the same theatre and under the same command. The Kaffir tribes were subdued with minimal losses: the 24th had only two officers wounded and one private killed. But they were soon to confront a much more formidable enemy.

Before entering on the Zulu War, however, mention must be made of the little-known Ashanti campaign of 1873–4, when a British force under Major General Sir Garnet Wolseley overcame the rebellious Ashanti tribesmen who had been committing atrocities. None of the present Regiment's ancestors was engaged, but among the many officers who volunteered for service on the Staff were Captain C. J. Bromhead and Lieutenant Lord Gifford of the 24th. The latter, an ADC to Wolseley, was given command of a mounted scouting detachment which not only elicited valuable intelligence on forays into the bush, but actually penetrated the tribal stronghold of Becquah ahead of the main assault force. For his initiative and leadership in these operations Lord Gifford was awarded the VC in March 1874.

The Transkei and Ashanti tribesmen were little more than naughty 'niggers' compared with the redoubtable Zulu warriors under their King Cetywayo,[2] who in 1878 were threatening the northern frontiers of Natal. Founded by their venerated King Chaka in 1815, the Zulu Army was acknowledged to be the best-trained and best-disciplined tribal force in southern Africa. In many respects it resembled the British Army: it was divided into *Impis* or regiments, each under its own *Indula* or Commanding Officer, each with its own distinguishing marks or 'badges' on its warriors' shields, and each with its fierce 'regimental spirit'. But unlike British soldiers, the warriors were sworn to celibacy until they had 'washed their spears' in the blood of an enemy. Lightly armed with assegais and short stabbing spears, they were adept at fieldcraft, and, superbly fit, could cover as much as fifty miles a day at their jog-trot. In attack they invariably adopted their crescent or 'horn' formation, from the massed centre of which the two 'horns' spread out to engulf the enemy. Behind were the 'loins', more massed ranks ready to replace any fallen and to add impetus to the final rush. In their years of conflict with the Boers they had learned never to attack well-armed European foes in entrenched positions: they should be lured into the open where they could be rushed and overwhelmed by the crescent. It is generally agreed that among all the 'savage' enemies the British soldier had encountered in his far-flung campaigns, the Zulus were supreme in courage, discipline and tactics.

Lieutenant Edric Frederick Gifford, 3rd Baron Gifford, 2nd Battalion the 24th Regiment; VC, 1873–4, Ashanti War (particularly at Becquah).

When Britain annexed the Transvaal from the Boers in 1877, she inherited the long-standing border dispute with Cetywayo. A Commission set up to arbitrate found in favour of the Zulus, but Sir Bartle Frere, British High Commissioner, was nevertheless determined to curb the bellicose King – that 'irresponsible, bloodthirsty and treacherous despot', as he wrote. On relaying the Commission's findings he added his own humiliating conditions: the splendid Zulu Army should be disbanded, the warriors should renounce their vows of celibacy, and heavy fines should be paid for the several Zulu outrages in Transvaal territory. As Sir Bartle well knew, Cetywayo was not the man to submit tamely to such terms: confident that his 40,000 fighting men

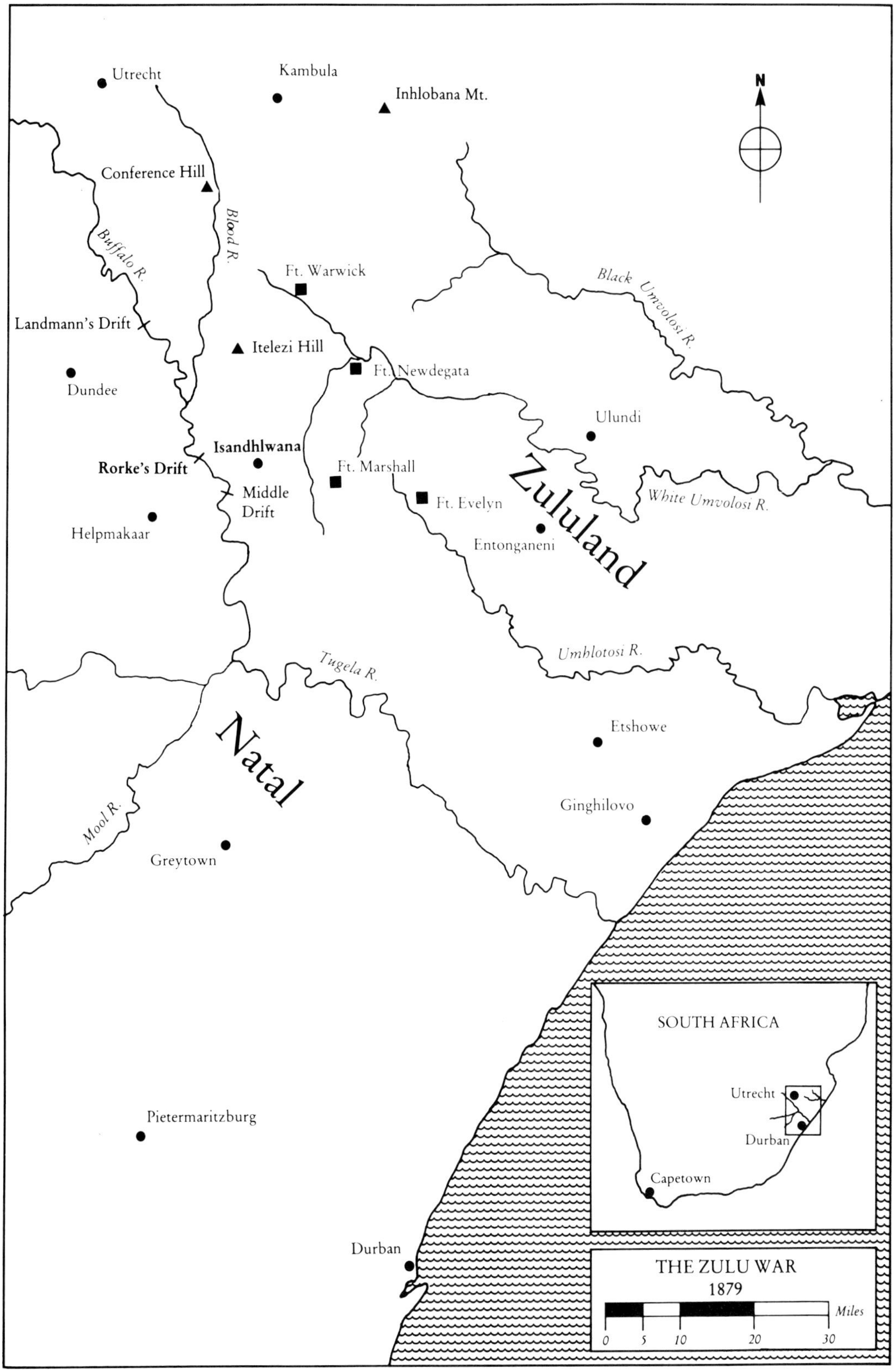

Utrecht
Kambula
Inhlobana Mt.
N
Conference Hill
Blood R.
Buffalo R.
Ft. Warwick
Black Umvolosi R.
Landmann's Drift
Itelezi Hill
Ft. Newdegata
Dundee
Ulundi
Isandhlwana
Rorke's Drift
Ft. Marshall
Zululand
Middle Drift
Ft. Evelyn
White Umvolosi R.
Helpmakaar
Entonganeni
Umhlotosi R.
Tugela R.
Etshowe
Natal
Ginghilovo
Mool R.
Greytown
SOUTH AFRICA
Utrecht
Durban
Pietermaritzburg
Capetown
Durban
THE ZULU WAR
1879
Miles
0
5
10
20
30

were a match for any of 'the white men in red coats', he contemptuously ignored the thirty days' ultimatum and made his own plans. And so, without troubling to consult London, Sir Bartle Frere launched a British force into Zululand on 11th January 1879.

The Field Force consisted of some 16,000 troops, of whom only 5,000 were regular British infantry. Artillery support was limited to nineteen 7-pounder field guns of the Royal Artillery. Command was given to Major General Lord Chelmsford, Commander in Chief in South Africa. As a veteran of the Crimea, the Indian Mutiny and the Abyssinian campaign, Chelmsford was an officer of wide experience in the field; but his new command was to do nothing for his reputation. The force's objective was the capture of Cetywayo's 'royal kraal', Ulundi, some sixty miles from the assembly point of Helpmakaar, and for the advance Chelmsford divided his command into four columns.[3] The two Battalions of the 24th were detailed for the central, or No. 3 Column, which also included N Battery Royal Artillery (six guns) and detachments of the Natal Native Contingent, Natal Mounted Police and other native levies. With a total strength of 4,200 all ranks it was the strongest of all the columns, and as senior British officer, Colonel Richard Glyn, CB, of the 1st/24th was appointed to command. The two Battalions of the 24th were not fully up to strength, having detached companies for duty at various bases in rear. The 1st Battalion paraded only five companies, totalling 16 officers and 375 other ranks; the 2nd, under Lieutenant Colonel Degacher, CB,[4] had 7 companies, with 23 officers and 748 other ranks.

Instead of establishing an independent force Headquarters, General Lord Chelmsford took the strange decision to attach himself and his staff to Colonel Glyn's Column. Although he assured the Colonel that he had no intention of usurping the latter's independence of command, he nevertheless reserved the right to control the line of advance and to take the principal tactical decisions. No doubt with misgivings, Colonel Glyn could only accept this curious demarcation – about which there was subsequent dispute and recrimination. The other columns were widely separated from No. 3, and as their doings are not relevant to this account, they must be ignored.

Having detached B Company of the 2nd/24th to watch the ford of Rorke's Drift on the Buffalo River, the Column pushed forward into Zulu territory. The British soldiers marched in their normal field service attire – red serge tunics, blue trousers with black gaiters and buff leather equipment. The only difference from home service dress was the cloth-covered cork helmets introduced for Indian service by Lord Wolseley, later to become familiar as the 'Wolseley topi'. Each man carried seventy rounds of .45 in. ball ammunition for his Martini-Henry rifle. With his valise (or pack) and two days' rations, his marching load was about 57 lb.

The initial advance met surprisingly little opposition: a few bands of Zulus were easily driven of and it seemed that the much-vaunted enemy was not so formidable after all. More obstructive was the difficult terrain of deep drifts, dongas and rock-strewn tracks which had to be made passable for the ox-drawn supply wagons – 110 of them, each with a span of 16 or 17 oxen. Thus it was not until 20th January that the Column had managed to cover the fifteen-odd miles from Rorke's Drift to a camp site beneath a curious natural feature. This was an isolated rocky eminence rising some 700 ft from the plain and with a sheer southern hump or escarpment, likened by some to a couchant lion. To the men of the 24th, however, it seemed to bear a remarkable resemblance to their Sphinx badge. Its Zulu name, they learned, was Isandhlwana.

When all the lumbering wagon train had arrived, the oxen were outspanned and coralled, neat lines of tents erected, and the men set about camp chores of digging latrines, collecting firewood and parading for picquet duty.

'Every one turned in early that night', wrote Captain Penn Symons of the 2nd/24th, 'not dreaming of what was in store for the morrow. Indeed, so far the invasion had been as autumn manoeuvres in pleasant but hot weather in England.'[5]

There were unconfirmed reports of Zulus massing in the hills to the northeast, and Colonel Glyn suggested that some patrols might be sent out on reconnaissance, but Chelmsford considered this 'unnecessary'. Glyn also proposed to dig entrenchments and form a laager with the wagons, but again he was overruled. The consequences of dual command were becoming evident. Earlier there had been reports of Zulus in the south-eastern hills, and thither Chelmsford had sent out a detachment of the Natal Native Contingent with some mounted levies under Major Dartnell of the Natal Mounted Police. Just after midnight this officer reported that the Zulus were in force on his front and he urged that two companies of the 24th be sent to support him. The force commander now took a decision which was to have disastrous results. Instead of despatching two companies, he detailed the whole of the 2nd/24th (four companies – the fifth was on picquet duty), nearly all the mounted levies and four of the six guns. This amounted to nearly two-thirds of the total strength at Isandhlwana. Having thus split his command, Lord Chelmsford abrogated his role as force commander and took personal command of the reinforcement, which marched out at 4 a.m. on the 22nd.

Major General Sir W. Penn Symons, KCB, in full dress of a Captain of The South Wales Borderers, 1890. He escaped from Isandhlwana. NATIONAL ARMY MUSEUM

Remaining to defend the Isandhlwana camp were about 1,800 all ranks: 426 of the 1st/24th, the Picquet Company of the 2nd; 60 Gunners with two guns, and some 800 Natal Native Contingent levies, plus a few details. Lieutenant Colonel Pulleine of the 24th was left in temporary command: he had just arrived from special duties at Pietermaritzburg. Before departing, Chelmsford had given written orders to Pulleine, stressing that he was 'to keep his men in camp, to act strictly on the defensive, draw in the infantry and extend the cavalry picquets'.

Chelmsford's reinforcement, with the 2nd/24th, reached Major Dartnell's sector, ten miles away, soon after 7 a.m. 'We then saw the enemy in scattered bodies of from 10 to 500, dispersing and retreating in front of us', wrote Penn Symons. The 24th Companies managed to kill thirty hiding in caves, but there was little evidence of any serious confrontation, for, as later revealed, this manoeuvring on the Zulu's part was merely a feint. At 9.30 a.m. Chelmsford received a despatch sent off by Colonel Pulleine at 8.05 a.m., reporting large bodies of Zulus massing in the hills north-east of the camp. The General was quite unperturbed: 'There is nothing to be done on that', he remarked, and settled down to breakfast. However, he ordered Captain Penn Symons and another officer to take signaller's telescopes and clamber up a nearby kopje from which the Isandhlwana camp was visible. All seemed quiet, and clearly there was no fighting in the vicinity. This being so, Chelmsford decided to bivouac for the night in his present position, but as his men were without tents and supplies, he sent a party back to Isandhlwana with orders for Colonel Pulleine to pack and despatch the necessary tents and rations. This party included Lieutenant and Adjutant Dyer of the 2nd/24th and the Transport Officer, Sub-Lieutenant Griffiths. They reached the camp at about 11 a.m., in time to meet their fate.

At about 10.30 a.m. Chelmsford gave permission for the Battalion of Natal Native Contingent, under Commandant Brown, to return to Isandhlwana: these native levies had been on the move for nearly twenty-four hours and were exhausted and out of rations. Brown had covered some six miles when he spotted large bodies of Zulus on his right flank, apparently heading for Isandhlwana. He immediately sent back a report to Chelmsford, who received it at about midday. Said Penn Symons: 'The General was asked by his Military Secretary, Colonel Crealock, in the hearing of several officers, if this would not alter his plans. He said "No, not at all"'. Advancing another couple of miles, Commandant Brown observed three columns of about 3,000 Zulus marching straight across his front in the direction of Isandhlwana, and cutting him off from the camp. He then despatched a mounted officer to the General with a more urgent message: 'For God's sake send every many back to camp, it is surrounded and will be taken unless helped at once.' This alarming intelligence reached Lord Chelmsford just before 1 p.m. The only action it prompted was a little personal reconnaissance as the General and his staff rode up a neighbouring kopje to spy out the camp with their glasses. They could see nothing amiss: the neat rows of white tents were plainly visible and there was no evidence of either Zulus or fighting. Therefore, coming from a 'native' source, the message was palpably untrue, or had been grossly exaggerated. If there had been an attack, it was obviously repulsed. But the truth was shortly to be confirmed in all its horror.

Among the Natal Native Contingent officers who had set out with their battalion for Isandhlwana was Commandant Lonsdale who, anxious to make advance arrangements for his exhausted men, had ridden on well ahead of Commandant Brown and the Column. He too was fatigued and weak from hunger, and was actually half-asleep in the saddle as his pony negotiated a donga in front of the camp. He therefore sensed nothing untoward in a red-coated figure emerging from one of the tents. It was only as he drew closer that he was shocked fully awake. The figure was not a British soldier, but a Zulu who had donned the torn and blood-stained tunic. Then other Zulus appeared, some wearing British cork helmets, and his pony began to snort at the stench of death as it came upon the mutilated bodies of the 24th Regiment. Wheeling about, Lonsdale miraculously escaped a shower of assegais and galloped horrified back up the trail.

Lord Chelmsford could hardly dismiss Lonsdale's eye-witness report. Stung at last into action, he collected the 2nd/24th and addressed them thus (according the Penn Symons): 'Twenty-fourth, whilst we have been out yonder the enemy has outflanked us and taken our camp. They are probably holding it now. At any cost we must take it back tonight and cut our way back to Rorke's Drift. This means fighting, but I know I can rely on you.' The men answered with a cheer.

As it turned out, there was no fighting. Although the cautious Chelmsford ordered his guns to loose off some shells as the 'relieving' Column neared the camp, there was no response, and as the 2nd/24th fixed bayonets and deployed into line 'all was still as death...' (Penn Symons). It was now about 8 p.m. and darkness had fallen. 'As we approached the camp we stumbled constantly, horror upon horror, over the hacked, gashed and ghastly bodies of our late comrades... We formed an oblong, guns and horses in the centre and lay or sat down in the ranks. It was bitterly cold. The mutilated dead were around us and in our midst. No one slept that night.'

Of the 1,600-odd men who had remained at Isandhlwana, not one was living. All had been assegaied or shot, and then stripped and disembowelled, following normal Zulu practice. Even the oxen and horses not carried off were lying slaughtered. In one spot the ripped-open body of a young drummer-boy hung from a hook like the carcass of a butchered calf. Although tents were still standing, everything had been looted: wagons were wrecked or overturned, ammunition boxes and medicine chests smashed open. Pathetic personal possessions, letters, pipes, toilet articles, were scattered among the corpses. But there were few weapons. The Zulus had gleefully seized the prized Martini-Henry rifles, and had also dragged off the two field guns.

As we have seen, when Lord Chelmsford had marched away nearly two-third of his command at 4 a.m. that morning, he had left Lieutenant-Colonel Pulleine in temporary command at Isandhlwana, now his main base camp. But he had also ordered up from Rorke's Drift Colonel Durnford, Royal Engineers, with a reinforcement of about 500 Native Horse and Natal Native Contingent, together with a Rocket Battery RA, manned by a Gunner officer and eight men of the 1st/24th. This force joined Pulleine's at about 10 a.m., and Durnford, as senior officer, took command. The garrison now consisted of the five companies of the 1st/24th, amounting to 426 all ranks, the Picquet Company of the 2nd/24th (about 170), 60 Gunners with two guns, and some 800 native levies – a total force of about 1,470 officers and men.

Although there had been a Zulu threat at 8 a.m., occasioning Pulleine's first message to Chelmsford, this had melted away, but soon after Durnford's arrival there were firm reports of more Zulu concentrations in the hills to the south-east. Engineer officer or no, Colonel Durnford was of an aggressive nature, always spoiling for a fight, and he promptly decided to take out his force of natives to meet the threat. According to contemporary reports, there was now some dispute between the two commanders. Pulleine's written orders from Chelmsford stressed that he was to remain 'strictly on the defensive' and to keep all his men in hand for the security of the camp. Thus it was surely contravention of these orders to detach a portion for offensive action far beyond the perimeter. But Durnford's seniority could not be disputed: he overruled Pulleine. Moreover, he requested two companies of the 24th to support him. After further objections from Pulleine, a compromise was reached: a company under Captain Younghusband would be sent to occupy a ridge some 1,500 yards north of the camp. And so at 11 a.m. Durnford with 500 Basutos and the Rocket Battery disappeared among the north-eastern ridges and kopjes.

Shortly afterwards heavy firing was heard from that direction, and Durnford's staff officer, Captain Shepstone, galloped into the camp, begging reinforcements: Durnford's Basutos were hopelessly outnumbered by huge masses of Zulus – 'the whole Zulu army is advancing!' Reluctantly Colonel Pulleine sent out Captain Mostyn's F Company to support A on the northern ridge and ordered the remainder to stand to.

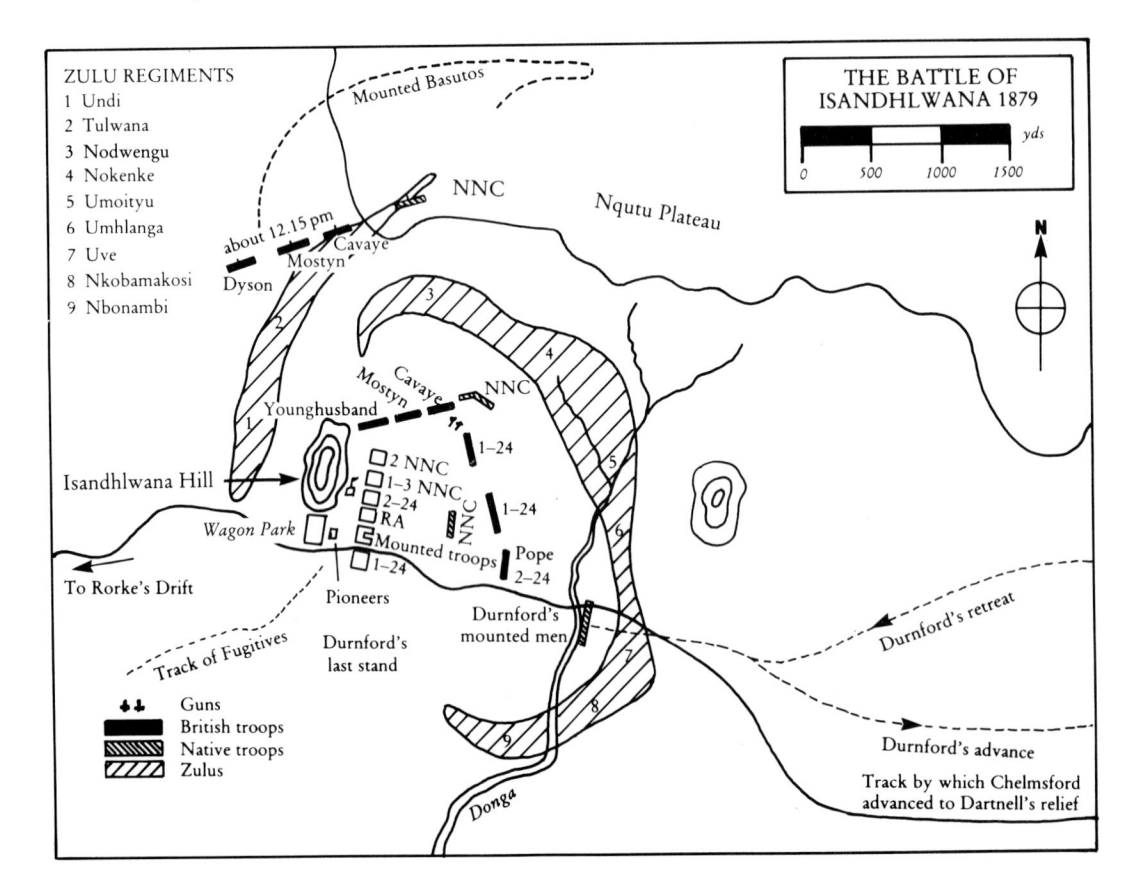

At this juncture the officers from Chelmsford's detachment arrived with orders for the despatch of tents and rations. Pulleine could only reply that as an attack seemed to be developing, there would be some delay in complying with the order. Later Chelmsford denied having received this message.

An attack was indeed developing. Durnford's men were driven back, his Rocket Battery overrun. Black masses of Zulus appeared to the north, where the two Companies of the 24th opened fire at 800 yards. But as the leading ranks fell, others took their place and the 'horn' (for such it was) began to envelope the left flank. C Company (Captain Cavaye) was pushed out to support the other two, while E of the 1st/24th (Captains Porteous and Wardell) and Captain Pope's G Company of the 2nd took up positions in shallow dongas facing east. As seen opposite, Pulleine's position was now in the form of an inverted 'L', with three companies on the north, three facing east, the NNC natives behind them, and the two guns of N Battery in the right-angle of the two lines. Now the Zulus' left horn began to curve round to the east, where it finally cut up and routed Durnford's force. To the men of the 24th it certainly seemed that 'the whole Zulu army' was attacking them: from left to right the dark hordes came on without a check. One of the warriors who was later captured stated that their *impis* totalled 20,000 men, and this tallies with British estimates. Only once did the attack falter, when soon after midday an eerie, unnatural dusk fell over the field. By a curious coincidence there was a brief eclipse of the sun at that hour, and the superstitious Zulus feared that the gods were deserting them. But when the sun shone forth again, so did their courage, and within half an hour they were hurling their assegais and stabbing with their spears. Running short of ammunition, outnumbered by nearly twenty-to-one, the defenders were slaughtered where they stood.

'It was a swirling shouting fight as we carried the redcoats forward with us right into their camp', recalled a Zulu warrior:[6]

> They fought with lungers (bayonets) swords and clubbed rifles among their little white houses and wagons, and even on the slopes of Isandhlwana itself until not a single one of the soldiers was left. We saw one tall man high up on the mount shake hands with his comrades and then run down towards us, climb on to a wagon and go on fighting so hard that none dared go near him. We all said what a brave man he was. It was lucky that some of our warriors had brought muskets to Isandhlwana, for only with one of them was he killed. Two of the bravest redcoats had glass in their eyes, they fought back to back for a long time and I think they were the last to die. [The bodies of Lieutenants Godwin-Austen and Pope were later found lying together. Both officers wore monocles.]

A few survivors of the battle managed to ride for their lives along the aptly-named 'Fugitives' Trail' leading south from the camp to the Buffalo River, four miles off, and among these was Lieutenant Melvill of the 1st/24th, bearing the Queen's Colour (the Regimental Colour had been left at Helpmakaar). When the end seemed inevitable, Colonel Pulleine ordered Melvill to take the Colour and endeavour to escape with it to Rorke's Drift. On his way, dodging Zulus, Melvill was joined by Lieutenant Coghill,

1st/24th, who, having injured his knee, had remained at Isandhlwana when his Battalion marched off with Chelmsford. Both were mounted on Basuto ponies, and, hotly pursued, they managed to reach the steep banks of the Buffalo. By coincidence, the Zulu narrator quoted above arrived at the same spot almost simultaneously, and it was here that he witnessed an incident that puzzled him:

> ... One of the redcoats trying to get across the river on his horse was carrying a long stick to which was attached a piece of cloth, coloured blue and red with a white cross. I have seen a cloth like this before at Krans Kop, which the white men used to pull down a pole and blow bugles as the sun went down. The stick this officer was carrying kept snagging in the bushes in the water, and as he swam the soldier seemed very tired. We thought he would surely sink, but then he was swept on to a big rock and hung on to it with one hand ... Then I saw one of the civilians in a blue coat who had reached the safe bank of the river, turn his horse back ... and swam it to the man stranded in the middle of the river.
>
> Afterwards I stood watching them both as they tried to carry the stick with the coloured cloth across the river again, but they were very weary and after a little time the river carried the stick away. The two men reached the river bank together and staggered up the hill until they could go no further; then they rested with their backs against a large rock. It was very easy for us to stab them.

Later, when Zabange related this story to Cetywayo, the Chief was annoyed that the 'cloth' had not been retrieved and brought back to him. Zabange replied that it was torn, 'and far too gaudy for you ever to have worn'.

The above account is reasonably accurate, but there is some doubt about the 'civilian' in a blue coat. Coghill was wearing his blue patrol jacket and this may have confused the Zulu eye-witness, but also with the little band of fugitives was a Mr Brickhill, civilian interpreter, in a dark blue or black coat, whose own account has been preserved.[7] As they approached the river:

> ... a little further on I met Mr. Melvill carrying the Colour. We proceeded some way when Mr. Melvill said 'Have you seen anything of my sword back there?' I replied that I had not ... Going down to the river we had some very bad country, so bad that we all dismounted and led ... I kept my horse back to enable Mr. Melvill to get down, as it was a very dangerous place. Mr. Coghill was just behind me and said 'Get on your horse Mr. Brickhill, this is no time to be leading a horse'. I did not know then that he suffered from an injured knee and could not walk. As we got down to the bed we had to slide down a bank 8 or 9 feet high. Mr. Melvill shot under a large tree and was nearly unhorsed by a branch which caught him on the right shoulder ... The Buffalo was very high, but there was no time to choose a crossing. The Zulus were making for a crossing higher up. I plunged in, my horse being at once

Lieutenant Colonel Robert Brookes, killed in action at Chilianwala while commanding the 24th Regiment.

The Battle of Chilianwala, 13th January 1849.

The Battle of Goojerat, 21st February 1849.

*Lieutenant Teignmouth Melvill,
1st Battalion the 24th Regiment;
VC, 22nd January 1879, Zululand
(posthumously awarded in February 1907).*

*Lieutenant Neville Coghill,
1st Battalion the 24th Regiment;
VC, 22nd January 1879, Zululand
(posthumously awarded in February 1907).*

off his legs ... A waterfall was just below us in which three riderless horses were struggling. Mr. Melvill crossed safely, but his horse could not climb the opposite bank. My impulse was to go to his assistance but his horse gave a plunge and I thought seemed to be climbing out.

Brickhill then galloped off under fire, and so did not witness the end. Melvill's horse slid back into the river; he was swept out of the saddle and, still encumbered with the Colour, was dashed against a rock to which Lieutenant Higgenson of the NNC was clinging. Struggling against the fast current, both men lost their grip, the Colour was swept out of Mr Melvill's hand and they were forced to swim for it, under a hail of musket-balls and assegais from the Zulus on the bank. Meanwhile Coghill had managed to swim his horse to comparative safety, but seeing his comrades' plight, he gallantly plunged his mount back into the current. At that instant it was shot and he too had to swim. The three men struggled together on to the Natal bank, here so steep that Coghill with his injured knee could not scale it. Higgenson, ahead, mounted a Basuto pony and rode off, but Melvill stayed with his brother-officer. Both were now utterly exhausted, and when the Zulus rushed '... it was very easy for us to stab them'.

Lieutenant Melvill and Lieutenant Coghill were the last of 600 officers and men of the 24th to die that day.

In England the Press had been preoccupied with General Roberts's victories in Afghanistan, and it was not until 15th February that *The Times* and *The Illustrated London News* published initial reports of 'a terrible disaster to the British troops in Zululand'. The nation was shocked to learn that 52 British officers and 806 soldiers, together with 471 'natives', had perished in a single morning at the hitherto unheard-of Isandhlwana. The casualty list reported no 'wounded', no 'missing'; only 'killed'.

For the 24th, this was the heaviest single day's toll they had ever suffered, far worse than Chilianwala, and one not to be equalled even in the holocaust of the Great War. The 1st Battalion lost 16 officers, including Colonel Pulleine, and 407 NCOs and men; the whole of the 2nd Battalion's Company under Lieutenant Pope perished – 5 officers and 127 other ranks. The Zulu losses were estimated at some 3,000 killed.

Reporting 'a very disastrous engagement' in his despatch of 10th February, Lord Chelmsford observed 'it seemed that the troops were enticed away from their camp, as the action took place about one mile and a quarter outside it'. He overlooked the fact that he himself had 'enticed' nearly two-thirds of his force away from that camp on a fruitless errand that morning, while in fact the main line of defence was not more than 1,500 yards from the camp. There is a vast body of literature dealing with the Isandhlwana debacle,[8] and most of it is critical of Chelmsford. Why was the General obsessed with the supposed threat to the north-east, and why did he not even trouble to investigate the reports of Zulu concentrations on the south-east? Why, when asked to send just two companies to reinforce Dartnell did he take himself and the greater part of his command? Why did he ignore the messages from Isandhlwana until it was too late?

But the deceased Colonel Pulleine and Colonel Durnford also came in for criticism (*de mortuis . . .* or no). Although the former had been ordered to take defensive measures in the camp, nothing had been done. No entrenchments were dug, no sangars were built, no attempt was made to laager the wagons. As for Durnford, some held that he should bear the greater blame for having by his independent action effectively dispersed the force into small groups.

While the Commander in Chief himself might not have been entirely blameless, his first despatch of 27th January had included a passage with which subsequent critics agreed:

> Had the force in question taken up a defensive position in the camp itself and utilised there the materials for a hasty entrenchment which lay near to hand, I feel absolutely confident that the whole Zulu army would not have been able to dislodge them. It appears that the oxen were yoked to the waggons three hours before the attack took place, so that there was ample time to construct that waggon-laager which the Dutch in former days understood so well . . . Rumours reached me, however, that the troops were deceived by a simulated retreat and, in their eagerness to close with the enemy, allowed themselves to be drawn away from their line of defence.

When news of the Isandhlwana disaster reached England it was accompanied by reports of the heroic defence of Rorke's Drift, and this tended to soften the blow. As *The Illustrated London News* of 1st March observed in its editorial, 'the tragical fate which befell a portion of Colonel Durnford's Column may now be viewed as an isolated reverse'. An official enquiry held at Helpmakaar on 27th January merely elicited facts and forbore to express any opinions about the causes of the debacle, or to apportion blame.

On that morning of 22nd January all was quiet at the post of Rorke's Drift where the trail from Helpmakaar crossed the Buffalo into Zululand. Left to defend this important link in the line of communications were B Company of the 2nd/24th, a company of the Natal Native Contingent and a few details – a total of eight British officers and 141 soldiers. Lieutenant Gonville Bromhead commanded B Company, which mustered eighty-one effectives, others being sick in the hospital building. Also present were eleven details of the 1st/24th. In charge of the ferry-boats, or ponts, at the drift was a subaltern of the Royal Engineers, Lieutenant John Chard, and as he was senior to Bromhead he assumed overall command of the post.

Until January 1879 Rorke's Drift had been a remote little Lutheran missionary post run by a Swede named Otto Witt, comprising two brick-built and thatched buildings, one being used as a 'Church', the other the missionary's dwelling. When the military took over, the Church was converted into a storehouse for ammunition and supplies, and the missionary house was commandeered as a hospital. In the compound between the buildings the soldiers' tents were set up and wagons parked. Another missionary, the Rev. George Smith, a South African white from Estcourt, acted as chaplain to the troops, while the sick were tended by Surgeon-Major James Reynolds of the Army Medical Department, with his three orderlies.

Although sounds of distant gunfire were heard during the morning, there was no cause for alarm until about 3.15 p.m., when an officer of the NNC at Isandhlwana arrived on his jaded mount, bearing dreadful news of the massacre. Thousands of victorious Zulus were now advancing towards Rorke's Drift, he said, and of the rest of Chelmsford's force there was no news. Chard and Bromhead immediately set about preparing defences. Among the stores were hundreds of heavy wooden biscuit-boxes and sacks of mealie, and these were formed into a 4-ft-high breastwork connecting the two buildings; windows and doors were barricaded and loopholes knocked through the brick walls; tents were struck. While this was going on, about a hundred NNC fugitives from Durnford's defeated force arrived and were posted in observation along the river bank.

Scarcely an hour later, the first attack developed with some 500 Zulus advancing on Durnford's men. After firing a few shots, the latter fled, followed by their officer, and did not stop until they reached Helpmakaar. This example demoralised the hundred-strong company of their fellow-NNC natives who vanished in the same direction. Now all that remained to confront the massing hordes were 131 soldiers of the 2nd/24th under Lieutenants Chard and Bromhead, the Medical Officer and five Commissariat officers. Deployed behind the makeshift breastwork, the men opened fire at 500 yards, steadily lowering their sights as the Zulus advanced on the southern perimeter. But although the Martini-Henry rifles with their man-stopping .45 in. rounds did terrible execution, they could not stem the rush before the leading *impi* was within fifty yards of the breastworks. Here the Zulus came under enfilading fire from the loopholes of the storehouse, and were temporarily checked. Some took cover behind the cookhouse, keeping up harassing fire with their muskets, but the bulk swerved round the back of the hospital in a bold attempt to rush the north-west defences. Now desperate hand-to-hand fighting took place, assegai and spear against bayonet, courage of defenders matched by that of attackers. Some Zulus tried to wrench off the soldier's bayonets before they went down with point-blank shots. A few glistening black warriors actually leaped the parapet, to be stabbed by half a dozen bayonets. By about 4 p.m. the situation became even more desperate as thousands of fresh Zulus appeared, completely surrounding the perimeter, and Lieutenant Chard ordered a withdrawal into a 'last ditch' position within an enclosure formed by a wall of biscuit-boxes extending round the stores building. This left the hospital isolated, like the poop of a vessel overrun by pirates. As the men in the enclosure poured volley after volley into black waves dashing against the biscuit-box wall, some of the Zulus managed to fling lighted brushwood on to the hospital roof and soon the thatch was blazing.

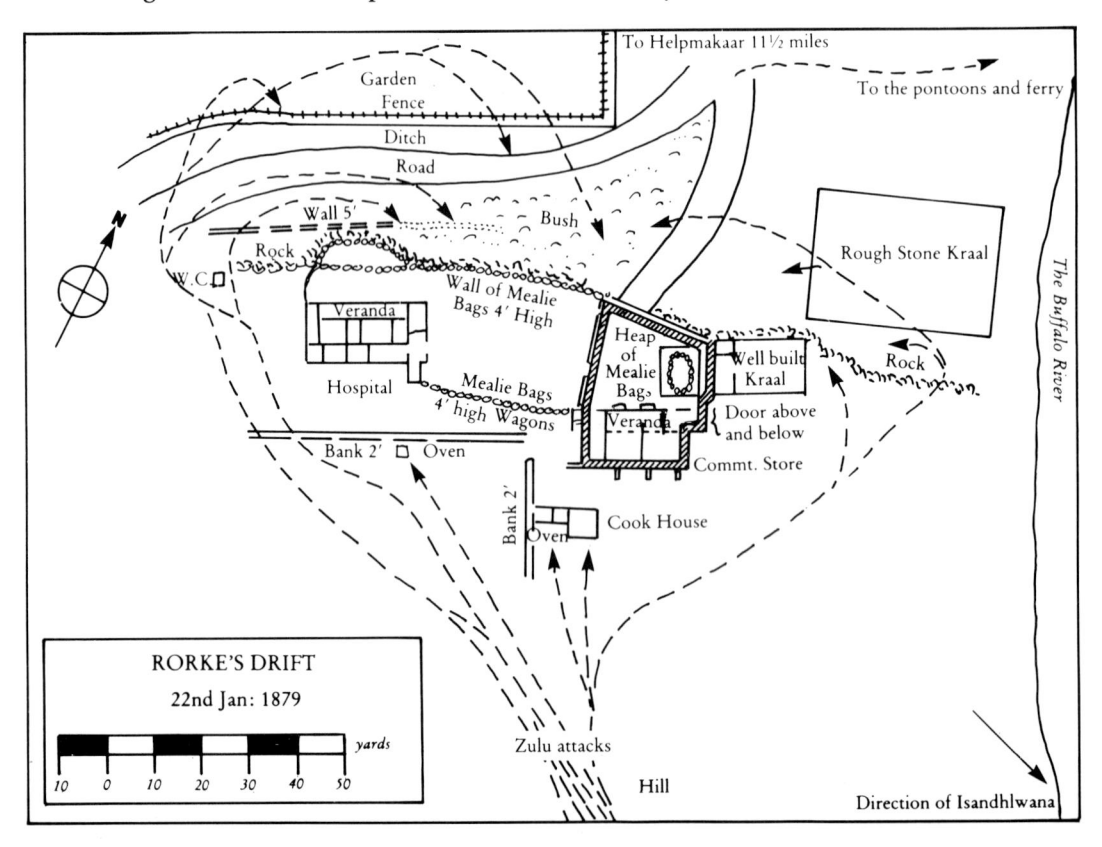

'The garrison of the hospital defended it room by room', wrote Lieutenant Chard in his subsequent despatch, 'bringing out all the sick that could be moved before they retired; Privates Williams, Hook, R. Jones and W. Jones, 24th Regiment, being the last men to leave, holding the doorway with their bayonets, their ammunition being expended. From the want of interior communication, and the burning of the house, it was impossible to save all. With most heartfelt sorrow, I regret we could not save these poor fellows from their terrible fate.'

Private Henry Hook survived to write his own graphic account of the ordeal in the hospital, and since he received a well-earned VC, his story deserves to be quoted in full:[9]

> From the very first the enemy tried to rush the hospital, and at last they managed to set fire to the thick grass which formed the roof. This put us in a terrible plight, because it meant that we were either to be massacred or burned alive, or get out of the building. To get out seemed impossible; for if we left the hospital by the only door which had been left open, we should instantly fall into the midst of the Zulus. Besides, there were the helpless sick

Lieutenant Gonville Bromhead, 2nd Battalion the 24th Regiment; VC, 22nd–23rd January 1879, Rorke's Drift, Natal.

Private John Williams, (Army name; his correct name was Private John Fielding), 2nd Battalion the 24th Regiment; VC, 22nd–23rd January 1879, Rorke's Drift, Natal.

Private Alfred Henry Hook, 2nd Battalion the 24th Regiment; VC, 22nd–23rd January 1879, Rorke's Drift, Natal.

and wounded, and we could not leave them. My own little room communicated with another by means of a frail door like a bedroom door. Fire and dense choking smoke forced me to get out and go into the other room. It was impossible to take the native patient with me, and I had to leave him to an awful fate . . . I heard the Zulus asking him questions, and he tried to tear off his bandages and escape.

In the room where I now was there were nine sick men, and I was alone to look after them for some time, still firing away, with the hospital burning. Suddenly in the thick smoke I saw John Williams, and above the din of battle and cries of the wounded I heard him shout, 'The Zulus are swarming all over the place. They've dragged Joseph Williams out and killed him'. John Williams had held the other room with Private William Horrigan for more than an hour, until they had not a cartridge left. The Zulus then burst in and dragged out Joseph Williams and two of the patients, and assegaied them. It was only because they were so busy with this slaughtering that John Williams

Private Robert Jones,
2nd Battalion the 24th Regiment;
VC, 22nd–23rd January 1879,
Rorke's Drift, Natal.

Private William Jones,
2nd Battalion the 24th Regiment;
VC, 22nd–23rd January 1879,
Rorke's Drift, Natal.

and two of the patients were able to knock a hole in the partition and get into the room where I was posted. Horrigan was killed. What were we to do? We were pinned like rats in a hole. Already the Zulus were fiercely trying to burst in through the doorway. The only way to escape was the wall itself, by making a hole big enough for a man to crawl through into an adjoining room, and so on until we got to our inmost intrenchment outside. Williams worked desperately at the wall with the navvy's pick, which I had been using to make some of the loop-holes with.

All this time the Zulus were trying to get into the room. Their assegais kept whizzing towards us, and one struck me in front of the helmet. We were wearing the white tropical helmets then. But the helmet tilted back under the blow and made the spear lose its power, so that I escaped with a scalp wound which did not trouble me much then, although it has often caused me illness since. Only one man at a time could get in at the door. A big Zulu sprang forward and seized my rifle, but I tore it free and, slipping a cartridge in, I shot him point-blank. Time after time the Zulus gripped the muzzle and tried to tear the rifle from my grasp, and time after time I wrenched it back, because I had a better grip than they had. All this time Williams was getting the sick through the hole into the next room, all except one, a soldier of the 24th named Conley, who could not move because of a broken leg. Watching for my chance I dashed from the doorway, and grabbing Conley I pulled him through the hole. His leg got broken again, but there was no help for it. As soon as we left the room the Zulus burst in with furious cries of disappointment and rage.

Now there was a repetition of the work of holding the doorway, except that I had to stand by a hole instead of a door, while Williams picked away at the far wall to make an opening for escape into the next room. There was more desperate and almost helpless fighting, as it seemed, but most of the poor fellows were got through the hole. Again I had to drag Conley through, a terrible task because he was a very heavy man. We were now all in a little room that gave upon the inner line of defence which had been made. We (Williams and Robert Jones and William Jones and myself) were the last men to leave the hospital, after most of the sick and wounded had been carried through the small window and away from the burning building; but it was impossible to save a few of them, and they were butchered. Privates William Jones and Robert Jones during all this time were doing magnificent work in another ward which faced the hill. They kept at it with bullet and bayonet until six of the seven patients had been removed. They would have got the seventh, Sergeant Maxfield, out safely, but he was delirious with fever and, although they managed to dress him, he refused to move. Robert Jones made a last rush to try and get him away like the rest, but when he got back into the room he saw that Maxfield was being stabbed by the Zulus as he lay on his bed. Corporal Allen and Private Hitch helped greatly in keeping up communication with the hospital. They were both badly wounded, but when they could not fight any longer they served out ammunition to their comrades throughout the night.

Having dealt with the hospital, the Zulus now concentrated their fury on the storehouse enclosure: 'several assaults were attempted and repulsed' reported Chard, 'the vigour of the attack continuing until after midnight; our men, firing with greatest coolness, did not waste a single shot, the light afforded by the burning hospital being of great help to us'. The eerie glare also revealed the mounting piles of Zulu corpses around the ramparts, but these in no way deterred the seemingly inexhaustible reserves leaping over the bodies with their battle-cry of *'Usutu! Usutu!'* One brave warrior actually manage to clamber on to the storehouse roof and was about to fire the thatch when a fusillade of shots felled him. By about 1 a.m. the attacks began to slacken, and the defenders, continuously in action for some eight hours, were able to ease their parched throats with tepid water from the carts in the enclosure and to munch dry biscuits from the boxes that had protected them. The hospital had now burnt itself out,

Corporal William Allen,
2nd Battalion the 24th Regiment;
VC, 22nd–23rd January 1879,
Rorke's Drift, Natal.

Private Frederick Hitch,
2nd Battalion the 24th Regiment;
VC, 22nd–23rd January 1879,
Rorke's Drift, Natal.

but in the darkness desultory firing continued all round the perimeter, though the mad rushes ceased. It was only with the coming of dawn around 4 a.m. that for the first time in twelve hours a strange silence fell over Rorke's Drift. The only Zulus to be seen were the massed corpses: the rest had vanished. Chard and Bromhead sent out some cautious patrols, but they found nothing but scores of discarded muskets and assegais. The exhausted little garrison took stock.

Between 4 p.m. the previous day and 4 a.m. the next morning 139 soldier had held off unremitting attacks by some 4,000 Zulus, yet their losses were no more than 17 men killed or died of wounds, and 12 wounded. The 1st/24th lost three privates killed; the 2nd, one sergeant (R. Maxfield) and eight privates killed. Nine more were wounded.[10] Chard reported that 'about three hundred and fifty' dead Zulus lay around the perimeter, but in the following few days another 100 were found between the post and the river, together with numerous blood-stained shields which the Zulus customarily used to carry off their casualties. No living wounded were found, but as the Zulus always made every effort to bear them away, it was hazarded that their number probably ran into many hundreds.

Roll of Officers, Non Com. Officers, and M[en]
January 2[?]

General Staff
1. Sergt Maybin

Royal Artillery
2. Bomb. J. Cantwell (WOUNDED)
3. " Lewis
4. Gunner Evans
5. " Howard

Royal Engineers
6. Lieut. J. R. M. Chard (IN COMMAND)
7. Priv. Robson

3rd Buffs
8. Sergt. Milne

1-24th Regt.
9. 56 Sergt. Edwd. Wilson
10. 625 Priv. Edwd. Nicholls (KILLED)
11. 1083 " Jenkins
12. 1861 " W. Horrigan (KILLED)
13. 560 " Desmond
14. 312 " Paton
15. 104 " Turner
16. 449 " Waters (WOUNDED)
17. 841 " Jenkins (KILLED)
18. 129 " R. Bakett (WOUNDED SINCE DIED)
19. 1502 " R. Joy

2-24th Regt.
20. Lieut. Bromhead (Comdg. B Compy.)
21. 2459 Col Sergt. Frank Bourne
22. 81 Sergt. Hy. Gallagher
23. 1387 " Geo. Smith
24. 735 " Jos. Windridge
25. 1328 Lance Sergt. Thos. Williams (WOUNDED SINCE DIED)
26. 1240 Corp. W. Allen (WOUNDED)
27. 582 " John French
28. 1112 " John Lyons

2-24th Regiment Contd.
29. 849 Corp. Alf. Saxty (B Compy.)
30. 2067 Drum. Pat Hayes
31. 2381 " Jas. Keefe
32. 973 Priv. Jas. Ashton
33. 918 " Wm. Bennett
34. 1257 Lance Corp. Wm. Bessell
35. 991 Priv. Chas. Bromwich
36. 1524 " Jos. Bromwich
37. 1184 " Thos. Buckley
38. 2350 " Jas. Bush
39. 1181 " Wm. Camp
40. 1241 " Thos. Chester
41. 755 " Thos. Clayton
42. 801 " Thos. Cole (KILLED)
43. 1396 " Thos. Collins
44. 1323 " Jas. Connors
45. 2310 " Arth. Connors
46. 1467 " George Deacon
47. 1357 " Michl. Deane
48. 1634 " Wm. Dicks
49. 971 " Thos. Driscoll
50. 1421 " Jas. Dunbar
51. 922 " Geo. Edwards
52. 969 " John Fagan (KILLED)
53. 2429 " Ed. Gee
54. 798 " Jas. Hagan
55. 1282 Lance Corp. Wm. Halley
56. 1062 Priv. John Harris
57. 1362 " Fredk. Hitch (WOUNDED)
58. 1373 " Henry Hook
59. 1061 " Jno. Jobbins
60. 593 " Wm. Jones
61. 716 " Robt. Jones (WOUNDED)
62. 970 " Jno. Jones
63. 1179 " Jno. Jones
64. 1428 " Evan Jordan
65. 2437 " Peter Judge
66. 972 " Pat Kears
67. 1386 " Michl. Riley
68. 1528 " Hy. Lines
69. 1176 " Thos. Lockhart
70. 1409 " Dav. Lloyd
71. 1504 " Joshua Lodge
72. 964 " Jas. Marshall

2-24th Regiment Contd.
73. 756 Priv. Hy. Martin (B Compy.)
74. 1254 " Chas. Mason
75. 1527 " Michl. Minehan
76. 968 " Thos. Moffatt
77. 525 " Fredk. Morris
78. 1342 " Aug. Morris
79. 1371 " Thos. Morrison
80. 602 " Jas. Murphy
81. 1279 " Wm. Neville
82. 1480 " Wm. Osborne
83. 1186 " Saml. Pitt
84. 1256 " Thos. Robinson
85. 1185 " E. Savage
86. 1618 " Geo. Sherman
87. 777 " Thos. Stephens
88. 1512 " Wm. Tasker (WOUNDED)
89. 889 " Thos. Taylor
90. 973 " Fredk. Taylor
91. 1280 " John Thomas
92. 1394 " John Thompson
93. 641 " Pat Tobin
94. 1281 " Wm. J. Todd
95. 1315 " Robt. Tongue
96. 1497 " John Wall
97. 977 " Alf. Whetton
98. 1395 " John Williams
99. 1398 " Jos. Williams (KILLED)
100. 1187 " Wm. Wilcox
101. 1316 " Caleb Woods
102. Drum. Pat Meehan (A Compy.)
103. 1441 Priv. Jno. Lyons
104. 2404 " Arth. Pears
105. 1731 " John Manley
106. " Scanlon (KILLED)
107. Drum. Pat Galgey (D Compy.)
108. Priv. Cheek (KILLED)
109. " Adams (Do.)
110. " Hayden (Do.)
111. 82 Lance Sergt. J. Taylor (E Compy.)
112. 934 Priv. Williams
113. 2453 " Wm. Cooper (F Compy.)
114. " Cole
115. 623 Sergt. Robt. Maxfield (G Compy.) (KILLED)
116. 106 Priv. Connolly

Contd.
117. Priv. Pa[?]
118. " Eva[?]

90th L[?]
119. Corp. [?]

Commiss[ariat]
120. Asst. Com[missary]
121. Asst. Com[missary]
122. Asst. Com[missary]
123. Lance Co[rp.]

A. M[?]
124. Dr. Re[ynolds]
125. Pears[on]
126. Corpl. [?]
127. Priv. [?]
128. " Lud[?]

Ch[aplain]
129. Rev. Geo. [Smith]

Natal
130. Troope[r]
131. [?]
132. [?]

Natal N[ative]
133. Lieut. [?]
134. Corpl. W. [?]
135. " J. S. [?]
136. " C. S. [?]
137. " W. [?]
138. " F. [?]
139. " J. M. [?]
140. Danie[l]
141. NATIVE [?]

The roll of those present at Rorke's Drift.

...sent at the __Defence__ of __Rorke's Drift__, — ... 23rd 1879. —

	Officers	N.C.O and Men	Sick Officers	Sick N.C.O and Men	Total
Staff		1			1
Royal Artillery		1		3	4
Royal Engineers	1	1			2
3rd Buffs		1			1
1 - 24th Regiment		6		5	11
2 - 24th Regiment, B. Compy and 17 Casuals Sick	1	81		17	99
90th Light Infantry				1	1
Commissariat and Transport Department	3	1			4
A. M. D.	1	4			5
Chaplain	1				1
Natal Mounted Police				3	3
Natal Native Contingent	1			7	8
Ferryman		1			1
	8	97		36	141

The following is a list of the "__KILLED__":—

Sergt Maxfield; Privates — Scanlen; Hayden; Adams; Cole; Fagen; Chick; 1398 Williams. — 2 - 24th — Privates — Nicholls, Horrigan and Jenkins. — 1 - 24th — Mr Byrne, Commissariat Dept, Trooper Hunter of N. M. P.; Corpl Anderson and Native, of N. N. Contingent. Total 15.—

Twelve wounded of whom two have since died — viz. Sergt Williams, 2 - 24th Regiment, and Private Beckett, 1 - 24th Regiment, making a "__total killed__" of __17__. —

I have the honour to be,
Your Obedient Servant
(Sigd) Jno. R. M. Chard
Lieut. R.E.

To Colonel Glyn C.B.
Commanding 3rd Column.

Rorke's Drift, 3rd February 1879.

At about 8 a.m. there was a scare when large bodies of Zulus were seen to the south-west, and the garrison braced itself for yet another onslaught. but unaccountably the formation wheeled away and disappeared. In fact, these *impis* had observed a large column approaching from Isandhlwana, and having just learned the wisdom of King Cetywayo's caution never to attack Europeans in a well-defended position, deferred to discretion.

After the dreadful night among the carnage of Isandhlwana, Lord Chelmsford marched his Column for Rorke's Drift at dawn. Approaching the post they beheld the column of smoke from the smouldering hospital, and feared the worst. But as they drew near, the men of the 2nd/24th spotted the red tunics of their comrades and heard shouting and cheering. In a few moments they had joined the survivors 'of as gallant a defence as the annals of the British Army have ever known' (Whitton). Official recognition of this gallantry came with the publication of *The London Gazette* on 2nd May 1879, announcing the awards of the VC to:

Lieutenant John Chard	Royal Engineers
Lieutenant Gonville Bromhead	2nd/24th Regiment
Corporal William Allen	,, ,, ,,
Private Frederick Hitch	,, ,, ,,
Private William Jones	,, ,, ,,
Private Robert Jones	,, ,, ,,
Private Henry Hook	,, ,, ,,
Private John Williams	,, ,, ,,
Surgeon Major James Reynolds	Army Medical Department
Asst-Commissary James Dalton	Commissariat and Transport Dept.
Corporal Ferdinand Scheiss	Natal Native Contingent

Eleven VCs gained in a single twelve-hour battle is a record never surpassed. In addition, Colour Sergeant Frank Bourne of the 2nd/24th and Private William Roy, 1st/24th, received the DCM, while Chard and Bromhead were given brevet Majorities. The Rev. George Smith received a chaplain's commission.

Twenty-eight years later two more VCs were added to the 24th's roll. Colonel Glyn, as Commanding Officer of the 1st Battalion, had strongly commended the deceased Lieutenants Coghill and Melvill for their efforts to save the Colour after the Isandhlwana massacre, and the Duke of Cambridge (Commander in Chief) agreed that had they lived they would have been recommended for the award of the VC. But at that date there was no provision for posthumous awards. Instead a 'Memorandum' was published in the *London Gazette* for 2nd May 1879, stating that the two officers 'would have been recommended to Her Majesty for the Victoria Cross had they survived'. After the Boer War, however, this anomaly was rectified, and in January 1907 King Edward VII approved the awards, which were gazetted retrospectively on the 15th. It must be added that the King had been averse to posthumous awards, fearing that they 'would open the door to many recommendations'. He was finally swayed by Mrs Sarah Melvill, the Lieutenant's widow, who took the bold step of approaching His Majesty personally.

Now with nine VCs earned within twenty-four hours, the 24th's record became unsurpassed by any regiment, and remains so to the present day.[11]

Meanwhile, a further cherished distinction was gained by the Regiment. On 3rd February Major Wilsone Black determined to locate the bodies of Coghill and Melvill and to search for the Queen's Colour for which they had given their lives. Accompanied by Lieutenant Harford of the 99th Regiment, he scoured the banks of the Buffalo River at Fugitives' Drift. Eventually the two came upon the bodies lying where they had fallen, assegai wounds in stomach and chest, but unmutilated. Around lay several dead Zulus. But there was no trace of the Colour. Darkness was falling, and having piled a rough cairn over the two bodies, Black and Harford returned to Rorke's Drift. Next morning the two officers and some mounted NNC men returned to the site for a further search. There was excitement when Lieutenant Harford discovered the Colour case lying in a shallow, and almost immediately a pole projecting a few inches above the water caught his eye. Captain Harben of the NNC then waded in and heaved up the lost Colour. An involuntary cheer from the covering party brought up Major Black 'in the wildest state of delight'; the Colour was replaced in its case and borne back to Rorke's Drift in triumph.

Next morning arrangements were made to transfer the Colour to the two Companies of the 1st/24th at Helpmakaar. A mounted sergeant of the 24th was detailed to carry it, with Major Black and Lieutenant Harford acting as escort. Just before reaching the base there was a touching interlude when Major Black handed over the Colour to Lieutenant Harford, saying that it was he who had discovered it, it was no more than his right to bear it to its destination. 'And so', wrote Harford, 'I had the very great honour, probably unique, of an officer belonging to another regiment carrying the Queen's Colour of one of the most distinguished Regiments in Her Majesty's service.'[12] At Helpmakaar the Colour was received with a Royal Salute and 'trooped' along the ranks of the two companies.

The 1st Battalion returned home, to Gosport, in September 1879, and in the following July the Queen intimated her wish to see the rescued Colour. Accordingly on the 28th Lieutenant Colonel J. M. G. Tongue, with two subalterns and four Colour Sergeants, took the revered silk to Her Majesty at Osborne House. It was then that the Queen bestowed a unique honour on the Regiment by personally placing on the pole of the Colour a Wreath of Immortelles, desiring that facsimile wreaths should always be borne on the Queen's Colours of both Battalions, to commemorate the devoted gallantry of Lieutenants Melvill and Coghill and the heroic defence of Rorke's Drift.

The original wreath was subsequently set in a decorated casket and placed in the Regimental Chapel in Brecon Cathedral, where it has remained ever since.[13] Today the replica is borne on the Queen's Colour of The Royal Regiment of Wales – a distinction still unique in the British Army.

It 1973 the well-known military historian, Michael Barthorp, visited the sites of Rorke's Drift and Isandhlwana, and his description was published in the *Journal of the Society for Army Historical Research* for autumn 1976. Here are some extracts:

To reach Rorke's Drift . . . near Helpmakaar a sign indicates a turning to the

The Wreath of Immortelles, the Regimental Chapel, Brecon Cathedral.

left. One then follows a dirt track road ... rough in parts, but reasonable going, until the scattered buildings and trees of Rorke's Drift come into sight. There is a considerable Swedish mission station still there, and one has to drive up among the buildings, on the left of the track, before finding any evidence of the battle. The first object one finds is a stone obelisk, painted silver, and surrounded by a low stone wall. On the front of the obelisk is a cross, with below it the Roman numeral 'XXIV', and below that, the words: 'Rorke's Drift/22nd January, 1879'; on either side are the names of the men who fell there ... Standing with one's back to the memorial and looking slightly right, about 150–200 yards away one will see a low building with a red, corrugated-iron roof, surrounded by bushes and trees. This occupies the exact site on which stood the original hospital, burnt down and evacuated during the fight... The position of the defences has been delineated with care and precision by boulders which can be found in the grass... Only when one actually stands on the perimeter, and recalls the epic twelve-hour struggle to hold the post, does one really appreciate how tiny the area was, and one cannot but be amazed how the 100-odd defenders were not overrun...

The field of Isandhlwana can hardly have changed in 94 years. A small mission station now stands at the foot of the spur, up which the companies of Mostyn and Cavaye were sent to delay the Zulu advance at the beginning of the battle... In the area of the saddle, where the wagon lines were situated, are various memorials, including that to the 24th Regiment. Across the saddle, on the slopes of the stony kopje, due south of Isandhlwana hill itself, is a small modern structure which contains a diorama of the battle and some show-cases, displaying the shields and weapons of the various Zulu regiments and some items of British clothing and equipment. The whole battlefield is covered with cairns of whitewashed stones, which are said to mark where the remains of the casualties were subsequently buried... Apart from these few additions to the landscape, the scene must be very much as it first appeared to the Centre Column in January 1879. As one stands at the foot of the hill, one is astonished at Pulleine's decision to deploy his companies so far out into the plain, away from the camp and the wagon lines tucked in under the hill.

Barthorp did not visit the site of Melvill and Coghill's graves at Fugitives Drift, where in April 1879 a marble cross was erected, in the presence of Sir Bartle Frere and his staff.

When the 2nd/24th marched out of Isandhlwana camp with Chelmsford's force on that morning of 22nd January, they left both their Colours behind in the Guard tent, and both had vanished after the massacre. The Colours themselves were never found, but in March a wood-cutting party from the 2nd Battalion discovered one Crown, which had been

Lieutenant Edward Stevenson Browne, 1st Battalion the 24th Regiment; VC, 29th March 1879, Zululand.

unscrewed from its pole: it was lying near a farm four miles from Rorke's Drift. A little later one of the cases was found nearby. In May, during a reconnaissance, an officer of the King's Dragoon Guards came upon one of the poles in the ruins of a kraal two miles for Isandhlwana. In 1880 these relics were presented to the Queen, who desired them to be placed in the armoury at Windsor Castle. There they remained until 1923 when King George V graciously restored them to the Regiment for safe keeping alongside the 'Isandhlwana Colour' of the 1st Battalion in the Memorial Chapel at Brecon.

Before the final defeat of the Zulu nation and the capture of King Cetywayo at Ulundi in July 1879, the 24th were to gain yet another VC. During the second advance on the royal kraal, Lieutenant Edward Browne was commanding a detachment of mounted infantry from the 24th, who on 29th March became involved in a sharp mêlée with a Zulu band near Inhlobana, and were forced to retire. Seeing one of his men unhorsed in the rear, Browne promptly galloped back, heaved him on to his own mount and, narrowly escaping assegais and bullets, brought him out of action. His award of the VC was gazetted on 17th June 1879. In the same action Private John Power distinguished himself in covering the retirement and was awarded the DCM.

The campaigning in South Africa between 1877 and 1879 had cost the Regiment 22 officers and 677 other ranks killed and died of wounds or sickness – the vast majority, of course, being lost at Isandhlwana. After the heroic, unparalleled defence of Rorke's Drift some felt that such a feat of arms should be recognised by the granting of a Battle Honour. But perhaps because only one company was engaged, and Regimental Headquarters were elsewhere, this was not to be. Instead, the Regiment had to remain content with the theatre Honour 'South Africa 1877-8-9', shared with fourteen others. It is a pity that the name of one of the most celebrated battles in the history of the British Army should be absent from the Regiment's Colours, and from the Army List rolls.

Notes

[1] The 24th did not, of course, become The South Wales Borderers until 1881, but with the passage of time and the blurring of public memory, it is the later title that has gained popular currency.

[2] This is the accepted spelling, but the name sometimes appears at 'Cetewayo' or 'Cetshwayo' – the latter being the Zulu pronunciation.

[3] A fifth column, detailed to watch the western frontier of Zululand, was commanded by Colonel Hugh Rowlands, VC, of the 41st (Welch) Regiment, who had volunteered for service in South Africa.

The 24th Regiment's memorial at Rorke's Drift.

KILLED
Pte HORRIGAN.W. 1st
 , JENKINS.J.   ,,
 , NICHOLAS.E. ,,
Sgt MAXFIELD.R. 2nd
Pte ADAMS.R.   ,,
 , CHICK.J.   ,,
 , COLE.T.   ,,
 , FAGAN.J.   ,,
 , HAYDEN.   ,,
 , SCANLAN.   ,,
 , WILLIAMS.J. ,,
DIED OF WOUNDS
Pte BECKETT.W. 1st
Sgt WILLIAMS.T. 2nd

RORKE'S DRIFT
22nd JANy 1879

[4] His brother, Captain W. Degacher, was serving in the 1st Battalion. Both officers had changed their name from Hitchcock in 1874.

[5] Captain William Penn Symon's unpublished account of his experiences with the 2nd/24th in the Zulu War is preserved in The South Wales Borderers Museum at Brecon. Much of what follows is taken from his account.

[6] The dictated account of Zulu warrior Zabange was published in *Blackwood's Magazine*, September 1970, and republished in *The Men of Harlech*, May 1971.

[7] Included in the Penn Symons account, op. cit.

[8] Among the more modern sources may be mentioned: *Zulu Battle Piece, Isandhlwana* (Sir Reginald Coupland, 1948); *The Zulu War: Isandhlwana and Rorke's Drift* (Rupert Furneaux, 1963); *The Washing of the Spears* (Donald R. Morris, 1965); 'Isandhlwana 1879: The Sources Re-examined' (F. W. D. Jackson, *J. Society for Army Historical Research*, 43, 1965); *The Zulu War* (Angus McBride, 1976).

[9] The account was first published in *The Royal Magazine* for February 1905, and later appeared in *The Red Soldier. Letters from the Zulu War*, by Frank Emery (Hodder & Stoughton, 1977).

[10] There are some discrepancies in the various accounts, but the above figures are taken from Lieutenant Chard's official despatch of 25th January 1879.

[11] The nearest approach was at Gallipoli on 25th April 1915, when the 1st Battalion The Lancashire Fusiliers earned six VCs 'before breakfast' in what became known as 'the Lancashire Landing'.

[12] In 1923 Harford, then Lieutenant Colonel, published his account of the finding of the Colour in the *Natal Mercury*.

[13] Except for one unhappy interval. On 16th May 1980 it was discovered that the wreath and casket had disappeared from their resting place. Smart detective work by the local police tracked down the thief within two weeks. He was a Brecon youth, wanted for other thefts, and he had hidden his spoils under a culvert near Christ College, Brecon. He was sentenced to eighteen months' imprisonment. Sadly the wreath was damaged – the flowers had been completely destroyed – but skilful restoration work was completed by craftsmen of the Victoria and Albert Museum.

CHAPTER ELEVEN

The South Wales Borderers, The Welch Regiment (1881–95)

In the previous chapter we glanced at the reforms introduced by Edward Cardwell in the 1870s. But Cardwell had also proposed the actual amalgamation of pairs of single-battalion regiments to form new 'corps' with new titles. Such heretical tampering with the hallowed traditions and loyalties of the regimental system predictably met with fierce hostility, not least from the die-hard Commander in Chief, the Duke of Cambridge, who roundly declared that such a radical reorganisation was 'unnecessary: all that is required can be done without it'. Thus Cardwell's brainchild was stillborn, and it was left to his successor to effect the transformation. This was Hugh Childers, who as 1st Lord of the Admiralty had carried out sweeping reforms in the Navy; on his appointment by Gladstone as Secretary for War, he immediately set about the Army.

The result of General Order 41 of 1st May 1881 was that eighty-two single-battalion infantry regiments were amalgamated by pairs, thus emerging as forty-one new two-battalion regiments with new titles. To ministerial minds this reform seemed a logical step, simplifying the Army's organisation and the Army List. But some of the 'married' pairs had other views. Many 2nd battalions found themselves junior to 1st battalions far younger than themselves, while what logic could there be in the fusion of the 30th (Cambridgeshire) and the 59th (2nd Nottinghamshire) Regiments as the 'West Lancashire Regiment'? And deeply resented by all, amalgamated or not, was the loss of the venerable numerical titles, ordered to be replaced by the novel 'territorial' or county designations.

The 24th Regiment, already with two Battalions, was spared the trauma of a forced marriage with a strange partner, but it found that from 1st July 1881 it was to become known as 'The South Wales Borderers'. Perhaps this made sense, for its Depot had been located at Brecon and it had recruited in South Wales for the past eight years. But whatever their masters may dictate, regiments doggedly cherish tradition, and although 'The South Wales Borderers' was soon to become an honoured title, its members and ex-members even down to modern times have preferred to say they served in 'the 24th'.[1] Oddly enough, the new title was adopted from one of the local Militia battalions, The Royal South Wales Borderers Militia, formed in 1876 and sharing Depot and administration with the 24th Regiment in Brecon. This now became the 3rd (Militia) Battalion of The South Wales Borderers, while The Royal Montgomery Militia became the 4th Battalion. Why the 'Royal' prefix was not inherited by the regular regiment is not satisfactorily explained, but a note in the Regimental Journal of April 1942 recounts the legend that the privilege was declined because it would have entailed breaking the Wreath of Immortelles on the badge to insert a Crown. This is surely an unlikely story!

As for our other two Regiments, the 41st and 69th with only single battalions were obliged to submit to amalgamation. It might seem strange that a 'South Lincolnshire' Regiment should be incorporated with a Welsh, but as we have seen, the two had been linked for draft-finding and recruiting purposes since 1873. The 41st must have been gratified to find that their own subtitle now became the title of the new entity, 'The Welsh Regiment', they themselves forming the 1st Battalion. The 69th were the losers, for both numeral and subtitle disappeared and, being the junior partner, they became the 2nd Battalion. The new Depot of both Battalions was established in Maindy Barracks at Cardiff, thus forging the firm links with that city, and with South Wales, that have continued to the present day. As pointed out earlier, when the 41st were granted their subtitle in 1831 the official spelling was 'Welsh', but the Regiment obstinately preferred 'Welch'. The same applied in 1881: the Army Lists continued to print 's', but the Regiment persisted with the 'c'. And, deferring to Regimental custom, from now on the present author will conform.

All this reshuffling of regiments and titles posed some delicate problems, about regimental Colonels, badges, Battle Honours, regimental Marches and so on. For The South Wales Borderers, however, who had merely adopted a new title, there was little to worry about. The veteran General Pringle Taylor (aged 80) had been appointed Colonel of the 24th in 1861, and continued as such until his death in 1884. The badge with its Sphinx and Wreath of Immortelles remained, but as it was obviously inappropriate for a Welsh Regiment to march past to the tune 'Warwickshire Lads', the Regimental Quick March was altered to 'The Men of Harlech'. This in itself seems a curious choice, for Harlech, in Caernarvonshire (as it then was) had little association, territorial or otherwise, with South Wales or the border. Maybe this was in retaliation for The Royal Welch Fusiliers' choice of a South Wales melody, 'War March of the Men of Glamorgan'! The only alteration that caused some heart searching was the ruling that the uniform's time-honoured grass-green facings were to be changed to white, the regulation colour for all non-'Royal' infantry of the Line.[2]

With the fusion of the 41st and 69th, more changes were inevitable. The 69th lost their Lincoln-green facings and adopted the regulation white (but as the 41st already wore white, they were not affected). The 69th were also the losers with their Regimental March, 'The Lincolnshire Poacher', which gave way to the 41st's traditional Welsh melody *Ap Shenkin* (more correctly, *Ap Siencyn*). The problem of the two Colonels was allowed to resolve itself by default, both continuing in office until one or other resigned or departed this life. Thus General Julius Edmund Goodwyn, CB, of the 41st shared the appointment with General David Elliot Mackirdy of the 69th, until the

Genl Thewen
69 Regt
Lincolnshire

Sir/

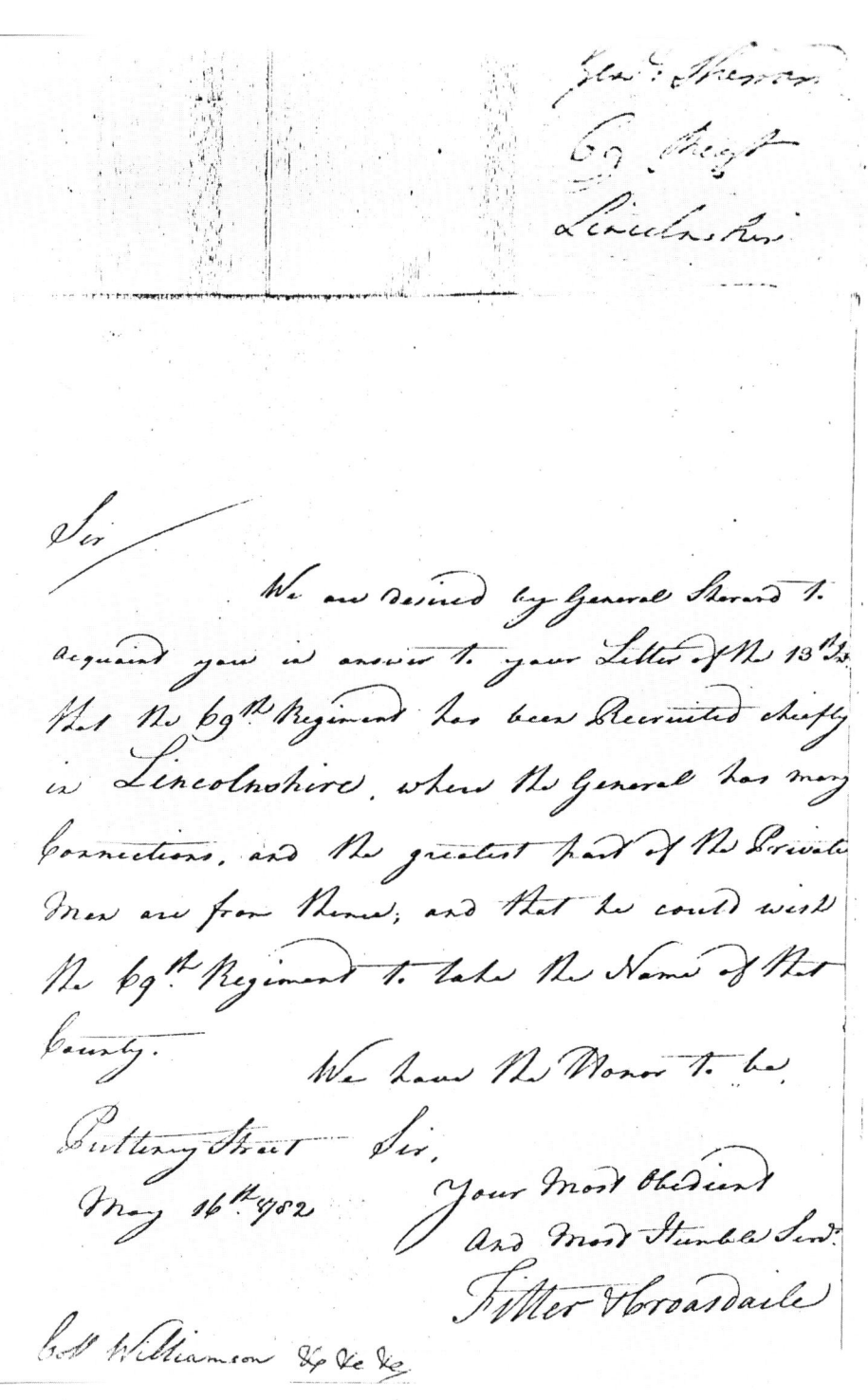

We are desired by General Sherard to acquaint you in answer to your Letter of the 13th that the 69th Regiment has been Recruited chiefly in Lincolnshire, where the General has many Connections, and the greatest part of the Private Men are from thence; and that he could wish the 69th Regiment to take the Name of that County.

We have the Honor to be,

Pulteney Street
May 16th 1782

Sir,
Your Most Obedient
And Most Humble Servt
Fitler & Croasdaile

Coll Williamson &c &c &c

Letter regarding territorialisation of the 69th, linking it with Lincolnshire.
FROM THE ORIGINAL HELD BY THE PUBLIC RECORD OFFICE

former died in 1883, leaving the latter as sole Colonel of The Welch Regiment. As for Battle Honours, the solution was quite simple: the new Regiment would inherit all those of its predecessors. The old 69th could only add five to the 41st's eleven.

As Welsh Regiments, it was natural that both should acquire *Y Ddraig Goch* or the Red Dragon among their badges. Apparently the 24th were a little doubtful about the true conformation of this beast, for they were aware that The Buffs (3rd Foot, Royal East Kent Regiment) had long displayed a dragon, which surely could not be of Welsh breeding. An enquiry to Garter King of Arms elicited the fact that the Welsh creature's tail had a loop in it, whereas The Buffs' did not.[3]

The 1881 reorganisation found all three original Regiments widely separated. Of the 24th, the 1st Battalion was stationed at Colchester, the 2nd at Gibraltar; the 41st was serving in South Africa; the 69th at Sheffield. Thus there were no ceremonial parades or other functions, and in fact, the changes had little impact on the soldiers who, as already seen, had been drafted between the 'linked' pairs since 1879. They merely had to remember new titles and polish new cap badges.

Readers will recall that when the 41st acquired the subtitle 'Welsh' (or 'Welch') they also adopted the Welsh Motto that caused so much trouble in spelling (and in pronunciation). In 1884 Lieutenant Colonel Alexander Tulloch took over command of the 1st Battalion The Welch Regiment, and he promptly resolved to simplify matters:[4]

> The Welsh regimental motto on the plate was long and difficult to pronounce; so I gave the regiment another which was easy for everyone, 'Cymru am byth!' ['Wales for ever!'] This caught on, and the men were regularly drilled to use it when charging, which they did in grand style. My orders also were that whenever any man got into difficulties he was to shout 'Cymru am byth!' and everyone hearing him was at once go to to his assistance.

This may well have 'caught on', especially with the Welsh majority of soldiers in the Battalion, but it was quite unofficial and never supplanted the authorised tongue-twister. It seems to have lost currency after Colonel Tulloch's handing over of command in 1888.

The last decade of the 19th century saw the infantry soldier armed with a weapon which, with a few improvements and modifications, was to outlast successive generations down to the latter half of the next century. The original pattern was the Lee-Metford rifle, introduced in 1888. The first magazine, bolt-action weapon, the calibre was standardised at .303 in. The magazine held eight rounds, and the trained soldier could fire off twelve aimed shots per minute. Modifications in 1895 allowed a larger magazine holding ten rounds, and as the service weapon was produced in the Government small arms factory at Enfield, the name was changed to Lee-Enfield. In 1902 a shorter and lighter pattern was issued (25 in. barrel, 8 lb. 2 oz. weight), to become the famous Short Magazine Lee-Enfield. This remained familiar to British, Indian and Commonwealth soldiers as the SMLE through the two World Wars and for more than fifty years, until superseded by the Belgian Self-Loading Rifle, or SLR, in 1954.

Another result of burgeoning weapons technology was the Maxim machine gun,

Maxim Gun Section, Mounted Infantry, 1st Battalion The Welch Regiment; commanded by Lieutenant W. E. L. Stewart. (c. 1899)

adopted by the British Army in 1891. This was the invention of the American genius, Hiram Maxim, and was the first truly automatic weapon in the history of firearms.[5] With the then devastating, and unprecedented, rate of fire of 600 rounds per minute, the Maxim added enormously to the close-support firepower of infantry battalions, who were each equipped with two (horse-drawn) guns. By 1912 the Vickers armaments group had taken over Maxim's invention, and as the modified Vickers Medium Machine Gun (no longer horse-drawn) the weapon, like the SMLE, remained in service for more than half a century. It was only in 1963 that it was replaced by the GPMG, or General Purpose Machine Gun.

If the march of progress was to be seen in the soldier's weapons, there were few commensurate developments in his drill, tactics or dress. The 'thin red line' complex still reigned; battalions, and whole brigades, spent hours deploying into line, forming square as at Waterloo, and deploying into line or column again. Except in The Rifle Brigade with their revolutionary ideas, the infantryman remained virtually ignorant of fieldcraft, or the use of cover. Such tactics would have been nullified, anyway, by the brave scarlet uniforms, white pipeclay and polished brass buttons, which occupied so much of the soldier's 'leisure hours'. It was not until after the Boer War that more realistic views of warfare prevailed.

There were no changes in the actual dress. Although khaki drill had been authorised for tropical field service, elsewhere red serge was the order. However, in 1888 the much simplified Slade-Wallace pattern of infantryman's equipment was introduced. Officers now wore the brown leather Sam Browne belt, but the original pattern had twin shoulder straps, supporting the Webley revolver on the right and the sword opposite.[6] At this date the only provision for the soldier in wet weather was his heavy serge greatcoat (though officers were now purchasing their Burberrys). It was during the Great War that the troops were issued with the light waterproof cape-cum-groundsheet.

Officers continued to be drawn almost exclusively from 'the public school class', that is, from moneyed parents. Once commissioned as 2nd Lieutenant (from Sandhurst), the infantry officer was paid 5s.3d. a day (his cavalry equivalent received 6s.8d.), but since he had to pay for all his uniform (and his Wilkinson sword), his messing, Band subscription and other 'contingencies', it will be readily understood that he had small prospect of doing so unless he could fall back on the customary allowance from father. After some three years the 2nd Lieutenant could expect his second pip, when his pay was raised to 6s.6d. The successive basic rates were: Captain, 11.7d., Major, 13s.7d., Lieutenant Colonel 18s. For Colonel and above pay depended on staff appointment as well as rank. A Brigadier received £1,500 a year, a Major General £1,700 and so on up to full General Commanding in Chief who enjoyed £4,500.

Just as the officers were from the upper middle classes, so the soldiers continued to be from the humblest. A return by the Army Medical Department in 1903 showed that the make-up of the rank-and-file was hardly changed from Wellington's day (even if they were no longer regarded as 'the scum of the earth'). Out of a total of 84,402 recruits examined 52,022 had been 'labourers, servants, husbandmen, etc.', while 18,922 were artisans, mechanics or 'shopmen'. Only 827 were found to be students with a 'superior degree of education'. The total also included 2,431 boys under 17, enlisted as trumpeters, drummers or band-boys.[7]

The basic pay of a private in the infantry had been raised from 8d. a day to 1s. in 1794. Incredibly, 100 years later this was still his emolument. But now he could look forward to an extra penny a day for each Good Conduct Badge earned. The first badge could be gained after two years' 'exemplary conduct', and subsequent ones could be gained at six-year intervals thereafter, up to a maximum of twenty-eight years' service, when a total of six chevrons were worn on the left forearm. There was also extra pay for 'proficiency', which included a First Class or Marksman classification in musketry, and the passing of the Second Class Education examination. But all this totalled only 1s.3d. per day. A corporal got 1s.8d., a sergeant 2s.4d., and the RSM 5s. – only 3d. a day less than a 2nd Lieutenant. And since the RSM had fewer expenses to meet, he was better off than his subaltern superior.

The 'small wars' of the still-expanding Empire continued to provide active service in far-flung theatres, such as Burma, where King Theebaw had been deposed and the country annexed. But not all the Burmese were willing to submit to British rule, and marauding gangs of dacoits were making life hazardous for the Bombay-Burma Trading Company. It took some 24,000 British and Indian troops nearly three years to subdue the discontents and restore law and order. Among the force was the 2nd Battalion The South Wales Borderers, who arrived in Rangoon from India in May 1886 and were immediately split into detachments for up-country operations.

As the 41st had discovered in the campaign of 1824–6, the wily enemy never offered pitched battle, preferring their native guerrilla tactics in the jungle terrain highly favourable to such methods. Consequently, the troops were subjected to weeks and months of arduous marching and patrolling, seldom coming to grips with the elusive dacoits, except when they ran into unsuspected ambushes. In many respects the operations were very similar to those undertaken by a later generation of The South Wales Borderers hunting the Malayan Communists seventy years on. Only now the men had no training in jungle warfare, while their dress was hardly conducive to rapid movement in thick jungle. Nevertheless, some of the 'movable columns' achieved remarkable success in tracking down large gangs and inflicting heavy losses. In October 1887 Major John Harvey led a fighting patrol of forty men of the 2 SWB and some of the Bombay Native Infantry in pursuit of the notorious Bho Shwe, one of the most wanted dacoit leaders. Within twenty-four hours the patrol covered a remarkable thirty miles of jungle tracks, in pelting rain, to pounce upon the unsuspecting Bho and his gang. Completely taken by surprise, these put up only the feeblest of resistance: the Bho and ten others were killed, several were wounded, and the rest captured, together with forty muskets and large quantities of ammunition. For this exploit Major Harvey received a well-earned DSO – the first to be awarded to the Regiment.[8]

By the end of the year the insurrection had petered out and the 'Upper Burma Field Force' was withdrawn to Rangoon. The two and a half years' operations cost 2 SWB fifty-seven NCOs and men, the vast majority succumbing to cholera, malaria and dysentery. The actual numbers killed in action are not recorded. In November 1888 the Battalion returned to India, and was to see no more fighting until the outbreak of the Boer War.

Meanwhile, in the same year that 2 SWB had embarked for Burma, 1 Welch left South Africa for Egypt, where they soon found themselves in action against the rebellious 'Fuzzie-Wuzzies' or Sudanese dervishes under their Mahdi, who had recently slain General Gordon at Khartoum. In December 1888 a British force under Colonel (later Field Marshal) Kitchener attacked a large concentration of dervishes entrenched around Gemaizah near Suakin, on the Red Sea flank. The position was valiantly assaulted by troops of the Egyptian Army under Kitchener, but the half-Battalion of 1 Welch gave valuable support with disciplined volleys of musketry from their Lee-Metfords. Their services were acknowledged in the force commander's despatch:

> The half-battalion of the Welch Regiment are seasoned soldiers, and whatever I asked them to do, they did well. Their marksmen at Gemaizah Fort and the remainder of the half-battalion on the left fired steady section volleys,

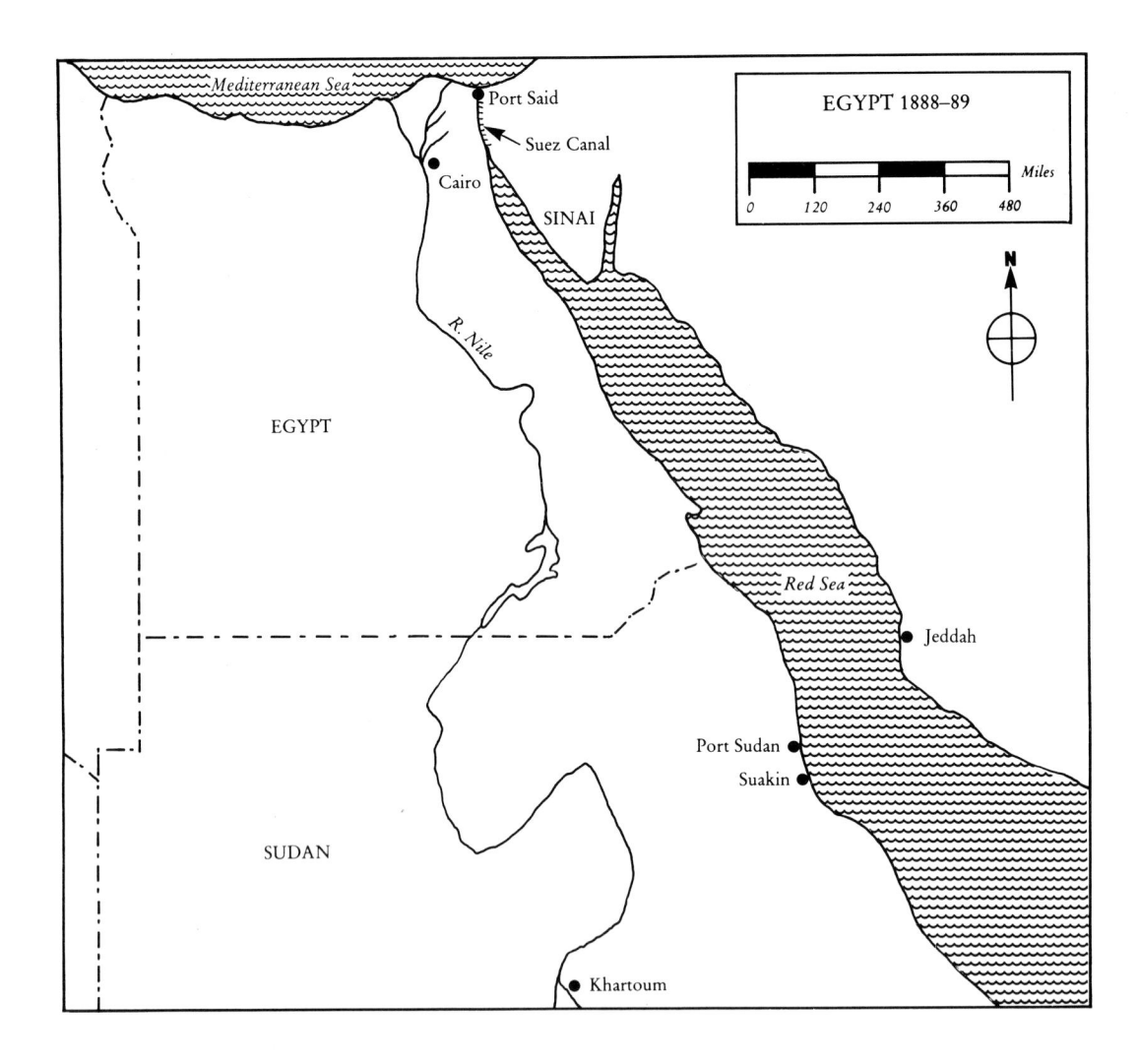

driving the Dervishes from their right position and inflicting severe punishment upon them when in the open; they were ably commanded by Lieutenant-Colonel Smyth . . .

Although the dervishes lost 500 men in this action, British casualties were remarkably slight: only 6 men killed and 46 wounded out of a total of some 4,000. The Welch, however, lost not a single officer or man.

As a point of detail it may be remarked that these operations marked the first time that any ancestors of The Royal Regiment of Wales had worn the new khaki drill uniform. On arrival in Egypt, The Welch had been issued with the 'dust coloured' cotton drill tunics and trousers, together with a khaki cloth cover for their helmets.[9]

Meanwhile 1 Welch and 1 SWB were both soldiering uneventfully in India, while the 2nd Battalion of the latter Regiment returned to the UK after an unwelcome year's posting among the barren rocks of Aden. After taking part as a street-lining unit in London for the Queen's Jubilee (22nd June 1897), the Battalion moved by rail to Newport (Monmouthshire), and on 12th July set out on a 136-mile march to their new station at Pembroke Dock. The route took them to Brecon where they spent two days in the barracks which had been their Depot since 1873, and for most of the officers and men this was the first time that they had set eyes on the Regiment's 'home'. They received a warm welcome not only from the Depot staff, but also from the people of Brecon, who thronged the streets to 'cheer our gallant Regiment who covered themselves with glory at Rorke's Drift', as *The Brecon County Times* reported. The rest of the fortnight's march, via Llandovery, Llandeilo and Carmarthen, was almost a triumphal progress, with streets decked with bunting and welcoming arches and crowds greeting their entry, while the local Volunteers turned out to provide guards of honour.

Since this was The South Wales Borderers' first entry into their own territory as a formed body, it was all very heart-warming. But as the real motive behind the march was a recruiting campaign (an early form of KAPE tour), the actual results were not so satisfactory: only twenty young South Walians came forward to enlist. At that period the coal and steel industries were at the height of their prosperity in the valleys, with good steady jobs available for the asking. Besides that, from Carmarthen onwards The South Wales Borderers were really poaching on the preserves of The Welch Regiment whose recruiting area included the whole of Carmarthenshire and Pembrokeshire, and whose 1st Battalion had carried out their own recruiting march only two years previously.

In January 1898 a memorial brass commemorating the 655 officers and men killed at Isandhlwana and Rorke's Drift was dedicated in the Priory Church at Brecon. The

The South Wales Borderers Cap Badge, 1898 *Cap badge, The Welch Regiment c. 1900*

serving Regiment was represented by Lieutenant Colonel R. A. P Clements, commanding the 2nd Battalion, with two other officers of the Battalion and the Band, while among the Old Comrades were seven of the thirteen VCs, including five Rorke's Drift heroes and one of the Andaman Island recipients.[10] Perhaps the most remarkable old soldier present was the 80-year-old Colour Sergeant William Thompson who had enlisted in the 24th in 1839 and had fought (and been wounded) at Chilianwala. He claimed to be the last survivor of that battle.

On May 25th 1898 The South Wales Borderers lost their Colonel, General Edmond Wodehouse, who had held the post since 1888. He was one of the few Colonels to have spent all their regimental service in the 24th, having been commissioned Ensign in the 1st Battalion in 1837. As Lieutenant-Colonel he commanded the Battalion from 1860 to 1867 and was the first commander of the 24th 'Brigade Depot' at Brecon. He missed the Chilianwala battle, being then in command of the Depot at Chatham. Wodehouse was succeeded by Lieutenant-General R. T. Glyn, CB, CMG, who as Colonel had commanded the centre Column on that fateful advance to Isandhlwana in 1879.

The Welch Regiment still paid respect to General David MacKirdy (late of the 69th), but in February 1890 he died aged 83, and General William Allan assumed the Colonelcy. Like Wodehouse, he was one of 'the family', for he had received his Ensigncy in the 41st in 1850 and had served in the Regiment for thirty-two years.

In June 1899 The South Wales Borderers were issued with a new cap badge, consisting of a Wreath of Immortelles encircling the Sphinx on a tablet inscribed 'Egypt', and over the lower part of the wreath the letters SWB. The wreath was, of course, a facsimile of that presented by Queen Victoria in commemoration of Isandhlwana and Rorke's Drift. This was the badge worn throughout the Boer War and the two World Wars, until it was reluctantly given up on the formation of 'The Welsh Brigade' in 1958 (see p. 369). The Welch, meanwhile, continued to wear the Prince of Wales's Plumes and Motto, surmounting a scroll inscribed 'The Welsh'. Officialdom still refused to recognise the 'c' spelling.

Since the amalgamation of 1881, the two Battalions of The Welch had seen nothing of each other, being stationed far apart. But in September 1892, when the 1st were in Malta, the troopship *Serapis* steamed in carrying the 2nd Battalion en route for India, and there was a get-together on board 'which was the occasion of much cordiality', as the records reported. The two Bands played 'suitable airs' and when the *Serapis* steamed out again there were 'hearty cheers for the gallant old 69th on its voyage to foreign service.'

Two years later the 1st Battalion returned home to Pembroke Dock, and there on St David's Day (1st March) 1895 a disastrous fire destroyed the Officers' Mess. At about 2 a.m. a sentry noticed flames issuing from the roof: he roused the guard commander and the bugler sounded the fire alarm. Very promptly officers and soldiers dragged out the fire engine from its hut and hoses were soon playing on the building. But water pressure (from wells) was low, and within an hour the building was completely gutted. Soon after the alarm was raised, Sergeant Curnow (Mess Sergeant) and Corporal Downes managed to seize both the Queen's and the Regimental Colours,

1st Battalion The Welch Regiment mounting guard at Governor's Palace, Valetta, Malta, 1894.

and also the Crimean Colours, from the blazing room, and throw them out of the window. Then they saved the Russian drums captured at Inkerman. Together with some of the Mess waiters, they next attempted to rescue the silver, but only a couple of pieces had been retrieved when the roof collapsed and the building became an inferno. Next morning a fatigue party searched the smouldering ruins, but all they found was molten silver which 'filled thirteen large buckets and one bath' (Lomax). The sale of this silver and the insurance payment enabled copies of many of the old pieces to be purchased. What remained of the monies was invested in a silver centrepiece and a pair of candelabra. It might be thought that the bravery of the two NCOs in rescuing the Colours would have been recognised by the granting of some award, but none is recorded. Later the Crimean Colours of the old 41st were laid up in Llandaff Cathedral, where they are to be seen today.

To conclude this chapter on a sad note, while 2 SWB were stationed at Allahabad, India, in 1891, they suffered the loss of their Rorke's Drift hero, Major Gonville Bromhead, VC, who died of enteric fever on 2nd February, and was buried in the British cemetery. Among the many telegrams of sympathy received by the Commanding Officer was one from the Commander in Chief himself, Field Marshal Lord Roberts, VC:

> Please let all ranks of the South Wales Borderers know how much the Chief sympathizes with them in the loss of Major Bromhead, V.C., who behaved with such conspicuous gallantry at Rorke's Drift, and so well supported the reputation of this distinguished regiment.

It was typical of 'Bobs' to concern himself with such details as condolences.

Notes

[1] This spirit is today even more fiercely maintained by the 22nd. The Army List has long insisted that they are simply The Cheshire Regiment, but its members are equally insistent that they belong to 'The 22nd (Cheshire) Regiment'.

[2] Greatly to the satisfaction of the Regiment, the cherished grass-green was restored in 1906, to be inherited by the present Regiment.

[3] The letter from Garter King of Arms, dated 29th September 1881, together with sketches, is reproduced in the MS Regimental Records.

[4] Tulloch, Major General Sir Alexander, KCB, CMG: *Recollections of Forty Years' Service*.

[5] Maxim settled in London in 1883 and his prototype machine gun was first demonstrated, to the Duke of Cambridge, and others, at the unlikely address of a basement in Hatton Garden, London. Having taken out British citizenship, Maxim was knighted in 1901.

[6] Contrary to popular belief, General Sir Sam Browne invented his belt *before* he lost his arm (and gained a VC) in the Indian Mutiny, and it was not until officers gave up carrying swords on active service that the second shoulder brace was discarded.

[7] It is worthy of mention that the youngest winner of the VC was a boy-soldier, Drummer Thomas Flinn of the 64th Foot, who gained the award during the Indian Mutiny, 1857, aged 15.

[8] The Distinguished Service Order was instituted by Queen Victoria in September 1886, and Harvey's award was gazetted on 12th November 1889. He had been commissioned in the 24th in 1865, served in the Kaffir and Zulu Wars, and as Lieutenant Colonel died of cholera in India, in July 1890.

[9] The word 'khaki' was derived from the Hindustani *khak*, meaning 'dust', and was first applied to the unmilitary attire of the Corps of Guides raised by Harry Lumsden on India's North West Frontier in 1846. Seeking a suitable 'camouflage' for his guerilla-type operations against the Pathan tribesmen, he had his soldiers dye their cloth garments with mulberry juice.

[10] The Rorke's Drift men were Privates F. Hitch, H. Hook, R. Jones, W. Jones and J. Williams; the Andaman Islands VC was Private D. Bell.

CHAPTER TWELVE

The Boer War and After (1899–1914)

In October 1899 Paul Kruger, President of the Boer Republic of the Transvaal, launched a force of 24,000 commandos into the 'Uitlanders' territory of Natal, laying siege to the garrison of Mafeking and the 'Diamond City' of Kimberley, while other Boers rode into Cape Colony to raise the Cape Dutch. Thus began 'the last of the gentlemen's wars', and the one which was to exert a profound effect on the training and tactics of the British Army.

In London it had long been known that the Boers could put some 50,000 men in the field, well armed with Mauser rifles and Krupp field guns; but still the total of British soldiers scattered all over South Africa was kept at only 12,000 men. Of course, in Whitehall circles it was equally well known that the Boers were no more than rabbles of irregulars, 'Bible-thumping farmers on scraggy ponies'. They could never stand up to well-trained, disciplined British regular soldiers. As so often in the past, the military hierarchy made the fatal mistake of underestimating their enemies. The Boers may have been 'irregulars', but they had been accustomed to practising fieldcraft from boyhood, were superb marksmen, and could cover astonishing distances on their 'scraggy ponies', over intimately-known territory. In short, they were what the British soldiers had never been, consummate guerilla fighters.

Only in November was the pitifully small British garrison in South Africa reinforced by the hasty despatch of troops from Britain and India, and General Redvers Buller, VC, was appointed to take command in the field. Among the reinforcements were the 1st Battalion The Welch Regiment who had been mobilised at Aldershot. They disembarked at Port Elizabeth on 26th November parading 28 officers, 823 other ranks and 'one machine gun and the Goat', as Whitehorne records. They were commanded by Lieutenant Colonel R. J. F. Banfield, a former 69th officer.

The Battalion remained inactive at Port Elizabeth for the next six weeks, while Generals Buller and Lord Methuen were vainly attempting to relieve Ladysmith and Kimberley. Their efforts resulted in 'the Black Week' of early December, in which some 30,000 regular British troops were defeated by the Boers, suffering 2,000 killed and wounded and some 500 taken prisoner.

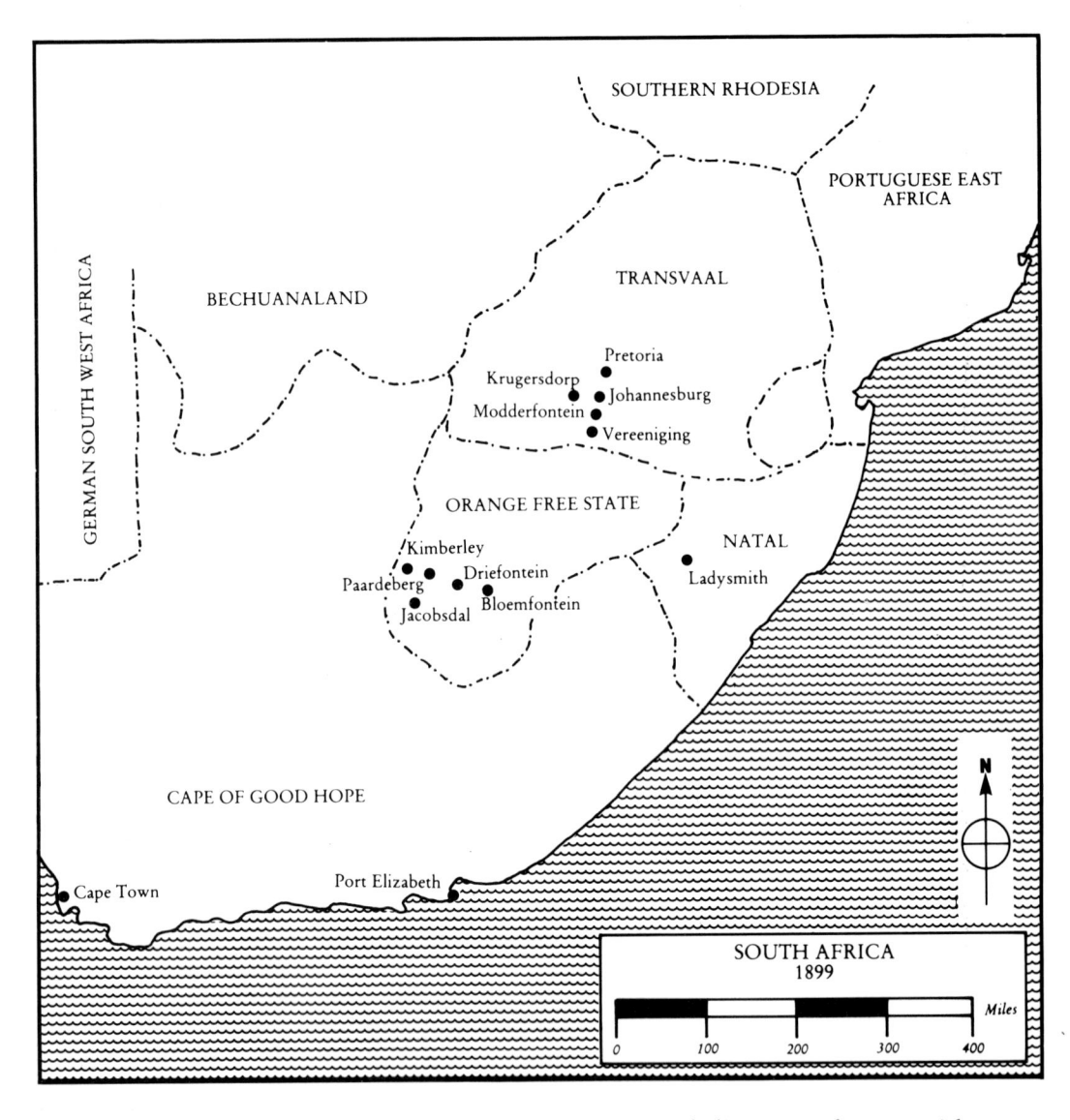

Such a shocking reverse aroused consternation and dismay at home, with angry questions in the House, and in January of the New Year the 68-year-old Lord Roberts was sent out to replace Buller. It was not until February that he had reorganised and made his plans, and by that time fresh reinforcements had arrived from England, among them the 2nd Battalion The South Wales Borderers under Lieutenant Colonel U. de R. Roche. Before leaving Aldershot the Battalion had learned of the death in Natal of their former Commanding Officer, Major General Sir William Penn Symons, KCB (from whose Zulu War account we quoted in Chapter Ten). He was mortally wounded while gallantly leading an attack at Talana Hill on 20th October.

*Sergeant Ambrose Madden, 41st (The Welch) Regiment of Foot,
VC, 22nd October 1854, Crimea.*

Friendly power in Egypt: 1 Welch Band in Muski, Cairo, 1888.

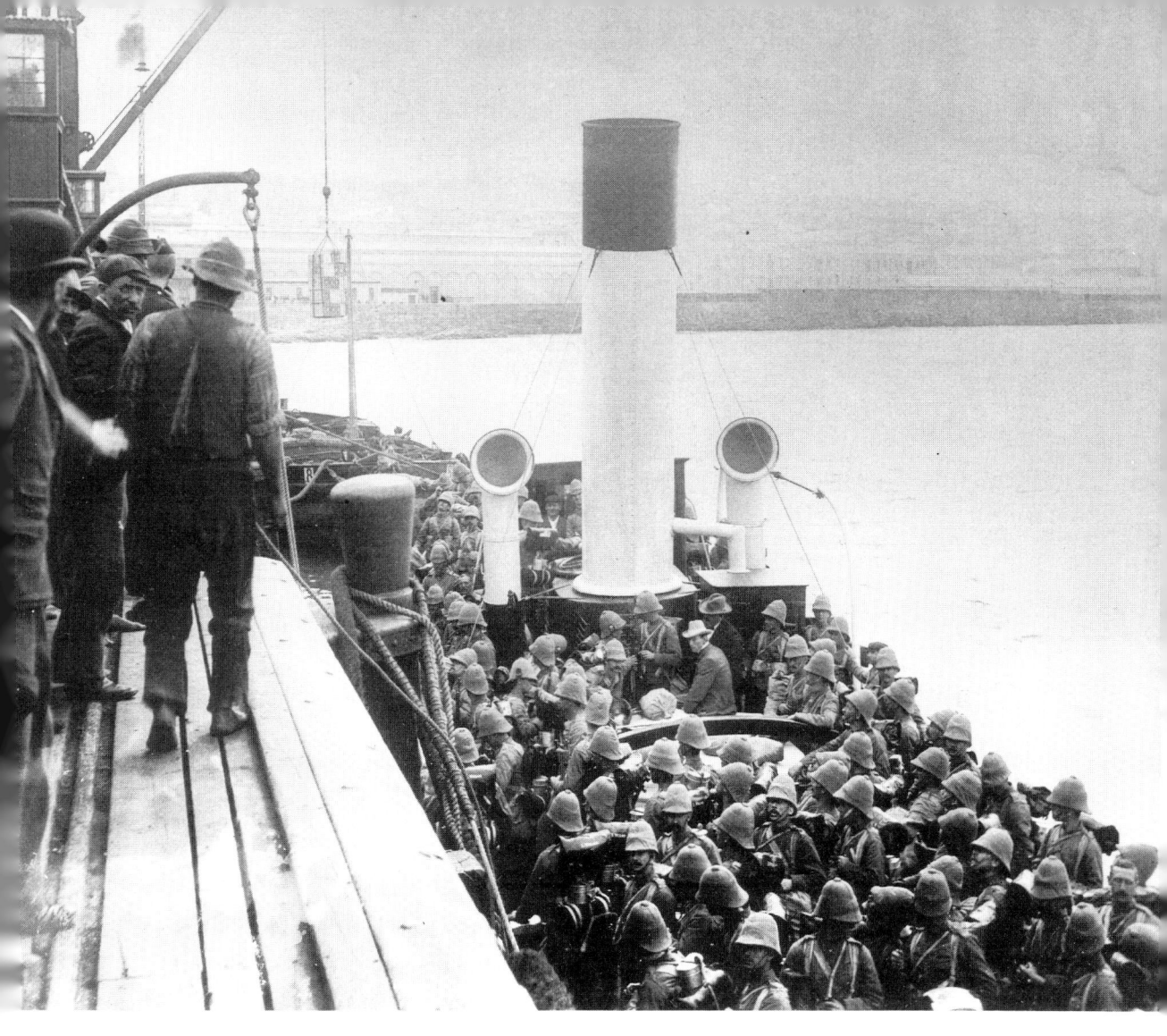

1st Battalion The Welch Regiment disembarking at Port Elizabeth, South Africa, 26th November 1899.

An innovation of Lord Roberts's was the formation of mounted infantry units, which were to play a valuable role in chasing the elusive enemy. Thus 2 SWB and 1 Welch each provided one company of volunteers who either claimed some experience in the saddle, or were willing to submit to a 'crash course' in equitation on a motley assortment of country-bred ponies and cobs.

Lord Robert's first objective was the relief of Kimberley. After a brilliant advance of General French's Cavalry Division, supported by three Infantry Divisions, this was achieved on 15th February. The Boer leader, Piet Cronje, now withdrew along the Modder River towards Bloemfontein: French's Cavalry Division swept round the west flank to cut him off, while the 6th Infantry Division completed an encircling movement on the other flank. With this Division were 1 Welch, and their baptism of fire came on the 18th when Cronje's laager was attacked at Paardeberg on the Modder.

This confused, long-drawn out engagement lasted from 6.30 a.m. until nightfall at around 6.30 p.m. – some twelve hours of bitter attack and counter-attack, neither side gaining any decisive advantage. At a critical phase, about 4 p.m., three companies of The Welch and four of the Essex were ordered to attack a strong Boer entrenchment across the river. Lieutenant Robins was commanding F Company (Captain Jones being wounded), and he afterwards described his experiences:

> We crossed the drift up to our waists in water as a starter: we had had no food since midday the day before. I led the way with 'F' Company in the firing line, 'B' Company second line and 'E', with Angell, in the third line, and the Essex in support. The Boers opened fire on us at about twelve to fourteen hundred yards off . . . We advanced by half company rushes – fired volleys, until we got within 600 yards, then we began independent firing. I have only

Gwilym Jenkins – Taffy III. It was Regimental goat no. 7 of the 1st Battalion The Welch Regiment and accompanied the Battalion to South Africa in 1899. It died on active service, 1900.

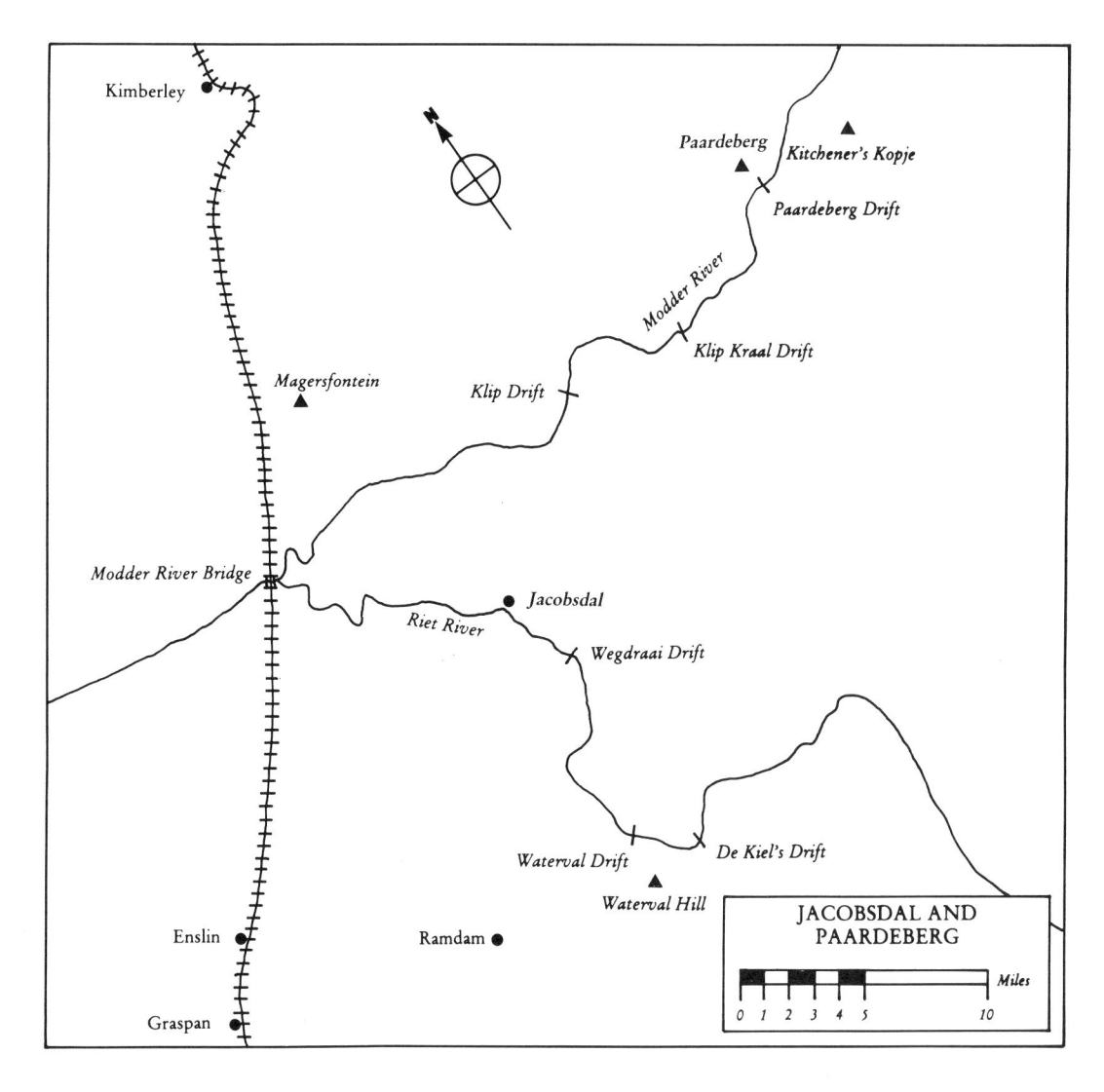

a hazy notion of what followed, we fired away and the left got within 500 yards of the trenches, then I got my men to rush up level with them; Angell and Major Ball were in the second line when they got hit... I got a bullet through the side of my helmet... we could not move a foot after this on either flank, as the Boers had got us under a cross fire, and the bullets simply whistled past. I wonder anybody escaped alive at all. We were under this heavy fire about two hours I should think. We were ordered to retire at sunset: our chaps did not want to retire... I did not know in the least what to do or where to retire to, but I found a lot of our men among some trees with some of our wounded, but no officer. I heard that the Colonel was still

NCOs Mounted Infantry, The Welch Regiment, South Africa, 1903.

lying out on the veldt; I went out with a Sergeant to look for him. On the way I met the D.A.A.G. of our Brigade. He told me the Colonel had been found, and all the wounded collected. [After withdrawing across the drift, the companies bivouacked for the night in a cattle laager] . . . It was bitterly cold and our clothes were still damp . . . Six of the Welch companies are commanded by subalterns of less than six months' service.

In his despatch to Lord Roberts, the Divisional commander, General Kelly-Kenny, drew attention to 'the very gallant conduct of the 1st Battalion of The Welch Regiment

The Boer War and After 1899–1914

who were on our right flank', while *The Times* correspondent wrote of 'their reckless bravery'.

But the Battle of Paardeberg cost the British 1,270 casualties, The Welch losing one officer and 18 men killed, five officers (including Colonel Banfield) and 65 men wounded. The senior surviving officer was Captain C. B. Morland, who now assumed command of the Battalion. The 2nd Battalion The South Wales Borderers were represented in this action by their Mounted Infantry Company, who lost six men killed and eight wounded during the closing stages. The Welch gained the Battle Honour 'Paardeberg', but this was denied to The South Wales Borderers since they had only the single Company present.

Although the day's fighting had been indecisive, it marked a turning point in the operations. Running short of ammunition and supplies, Cronje was forced to capitulate, and on 27th February he surrendered to Lord Roberts with 4,100 of his men. The Paardeberg diversion enabled Buller to relieve Ladysmith on 28th February, and a fortnight later 'Bobs' led his Army into Bloemfontein, capital of the Orange Free State.

It was on this advance that fierce opposition was met from the commando leaders

General Cronje surrendering to Field Marshal Lord Roberts at Paardeberg, 1900.

NATIONAL ARMY MUSEUM

> **3rd Vol. Battalion The Welsh Regt.,**
> Aberdare Detachment.
>
> ## TRANSVAAL WAR.
>
> Applications are invited AT ONCE from Members of the Aberdare Detachment desirous of Volunteering for Active Service, in accordance with the Order issued by the Secretary of State for War. All Applications must be made not later than the Church Parade on Sunday next, December 24th.
>
> Particulars may be obtained from the SERGEANT-INSTRUCTOR at the Armoury, or the undersigned.
>
> By Order.
>
> **W. D. PHILLIPS, Captain,**
> Officer Commanding Detachment.
>
> Dec. 22nd, 1899.

A call for volunteers to serve with the Volunteer Service Companies of The Welch Regiment in South African Boer War 1899–1902.

De La Rey and Piet De Wet at Driefontein on the Modder River, and The Welch once more found themselves in the thick of the fighting. The battle, on 10th March, was almost a repeat of that at Paardeberg, with the Boers in well-entrenched positions on a cluster of kopjes with open ground to their front, their infantry well supported by artillery on the flanks. Together with The Buffs, Essex and Gloucesters, The Welch were again committed to a frontal attack on the centre of the position, struggling up the rocky slopes under a hail of small arms and pom-pom fire.[1] Advancing by short bounds from cover to cover, constantly losing men, The Welch, Buffs and Gloucesters simultaneously reached the crest of their objective, paused to regroup, then fixed bayonets and charged. This enemy sector was valiantly held by the regular South African police or 'ZARPS' and there was fierce hand-to-hand fighting before they finally broke and fled down the reverse slope to their horses, leaving scores of dead and wounded in the trenches.

Lord Roberts singled out The Welch for handsome tribute in his despatch after entering Bloemfontein on 13th March: 'The storming of the Alexander Kopje by The Welch Regiment was the finest piece of work I have seen. The Welshmen showed marvellous skill in securing every particle of cover while advancing.' British losses at Driefontein amounted to 438 killed and wounded, The Welch suffering the heaviest of the battalions in the final assault. They lost two officers and 28 NCOs and men killed, five officers and 114 other ranks wounded.

One of the officers killed was Captain and Adjutant D. A. N. Lomax who fell while cheering on his men in the bayonet charge. David Lomax was the author of the earliest history of The Welch Regiment – the source of so much of the present historian's information.[2] This work was published in a limited edition of 250 copies at Devonport in 1899, only a few months before its author sailed with his Battalion for South Africa. Lomax entered the Regiment as 2nd Lieutenant in 1888, was promoted Lieutenant in 1890 and became Captain and Adjutant in 1899. The fact that in the midst of all his duties as a regimental officer, and latterly as Adjutant, he nevertheless managed to carry out all the laborious original research and write up a detailed history of 421 pages, replete with illustrations, is a very remarkable achievement, and one for which the Regiment and subsequent historians will always be in his debt.

The defeat at Driefontein sapped the Boers' morale to such an extent that they evacuated Bloemfontein and the city was entered without a shot being fired.[3] The Welch marched in with 11 officers and 654 other ranks – and '7 horses and 1 Machine Gun', adds Whitehorne, but he omits mention of the goat.

The 2nd Battalion the South Wales Borderers meanwhile had seen only a minor brush with the enemy at Jacobsdal on 15th February (when they lost one private killed and five wounded), but on 29th March they were involved in a sharp engagement with some 800 Boers dug in along a line of kopjes near the Karree railway station. Their commanding position covered the wreck of a blown bridge over the Modder, and to enable the British advance to continue it was essential that the Boers should be ejected and the bridge repaired. Deployed into line of five companies, The South Wales Borderers were launched against the centre kopje, with the East Lancashires attacking on their left, The Cheshires on their right. They at once came under heavy rifle and pom-pom fire, but, as an eye-witness recorded, 'the men behaved very steadily, advancing and lying down under fire like an Aldershot field-day'. When they were within about 500 yards of their objective the fire became so fierce that the troops were forced to halt under what cover they could find. Happily at this juncture one of the supporting Field Batteries dropped into action in rear and opened up with HE and shrapnel. Then some cavalry and mounted infantry began working round the right flank. Under this threat, and discouraged by shells bursting among and over them, the Boers did not stay to fight it out: they were seen to be scrambling over the crest to their ponies (as always, ready for quick withdrawal) and The South Wales Borderers, bayonets fixed, charged up the slope. But by the time they had reached the summit all they could do was to fire a few volleys into the dust clouds that masked the retreating enemy. Despite the fire they had endured during the initial advance, the Battalion escaped with remarkably few casualties: three men were killed, one officer and twenty-three wounded.

While the two regular Battalions of The South Wales Borderers and The Welch Regiment were in action, at home there had been a call for the Militia to be embodied and sent out to South Africa. At Brecon and Cardiff there was an immediate response. Almost to a man, the 3rd Battalions of both Regiments volunteered for active service, and in March 1900 they arrived at Cape Town. In addition, to replace casualties in the regular Battalions, a number of volunteer service companies were formed early in 1900, that of The South Wales Borderers joining their parent in March, three of The Welch Regiment arriving between March and April. The Militia Battalions were given little chance to show their mettle, being chiefly employed as 'L of C troops' (lines of communication) or as escorts to supply convoys. There were no death or glory opportunities here perhaps, but duties nonetheless arduous, and essential.

After the occupation of Bloemfontein the way was open for Roberts's advance to President Kruger's capital of Pretoria. All were confident that if this could be taken, and with it the 'Gold City' of Johannesburg, that would be the end of the war. Both The South Wales Borderers and The Welch Regiment took part in this operation, but although both were in the central Column under Roberts himself, the former were part of the 7th Division, the latter of the 11th, and they saw little of each other. The advance from Bloemfontein to Johannesburg and Pretoria was one of the most remarkable in the history of the British Army. In 26 days columns totalling some 44,000 troops marched 299 miles over broken terrain, enduring extreme heat by day and bitter cold by night, with limited rations and fighting several actions en route.

Lieutenant Colonel Banfield of 1 Welch had recovered from his wound at Paardeberg and was thus able to resume command of his Battalion for the start of the march on 3rd May. He subsequently wrote a detailed account of the operations which was published in the *Cardiff Times*, and a few extracts are worthy of quotation here. After crossing the Val River on 5th May:

> The marches now became, if possible, more trying than those we had already gone through, the sun intensely hot, blistering faces and hands and causing a terrible thirst, the water bottle being soon emptied. Any small spruits

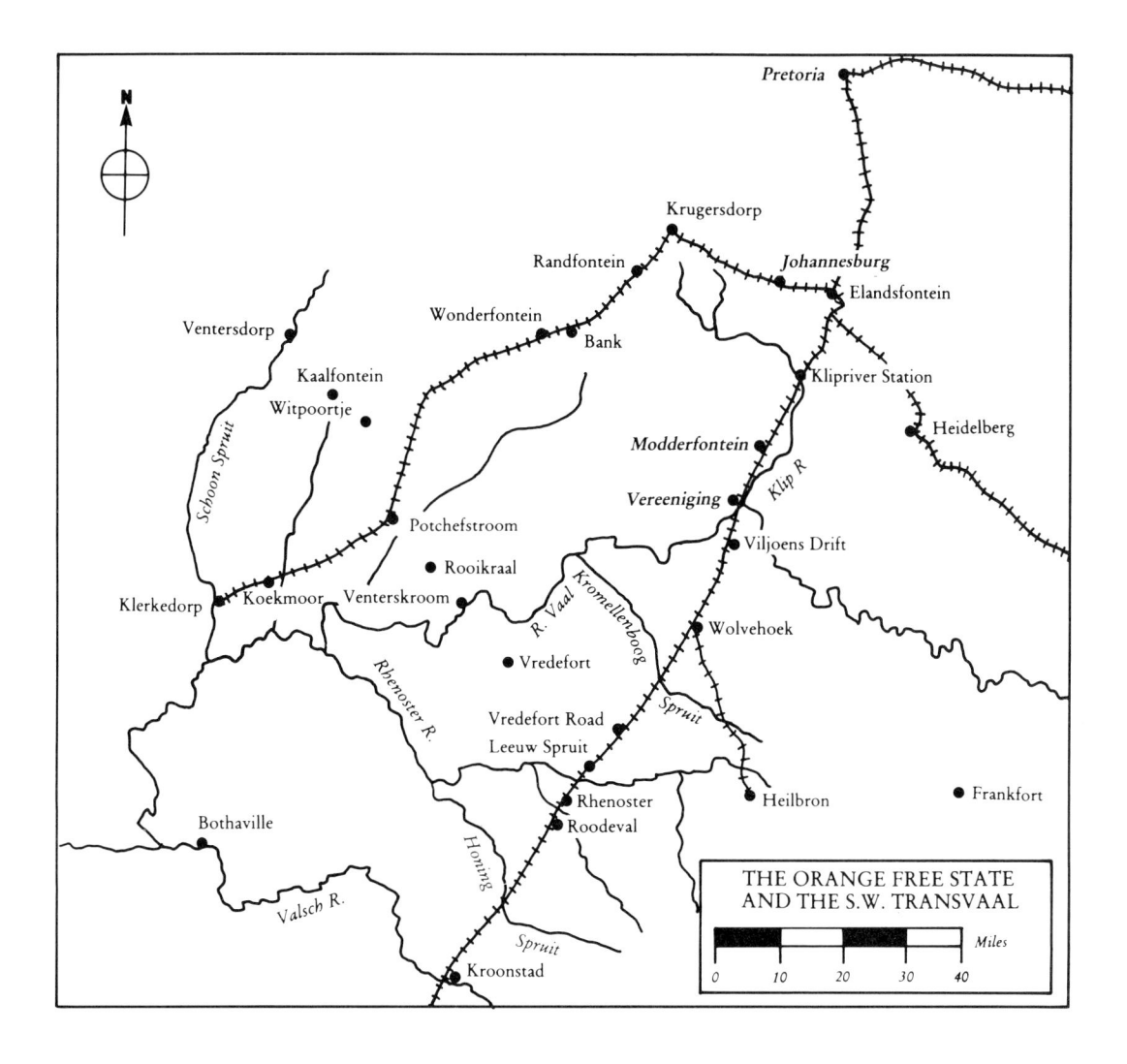

containing black muddy pools already trampled by mules were eagerly sought by the thirsty men. The absolutely uninteresting country greatly added to the fatigues of those terrible marches. A vast great undulating plain, as featureless as a calmly-swelling ocean, bright yellow in colour, owing to its burnt-up long grass, never cut, never grazed; no houses, no fences, ditches or trees, often not even a rocky kopje in sight; no wonder Tommy marched along in silence with his eyes fixed on the ground... As the men always marched in extended order, conversation was impossible. No martial tramp of hundreds of feet as on the roads at home, for soft dry grass deadened all sound of movement. They were silent marches in a silent country...

The night of 10th May which we spent at Reitspruit Siding was not a comfortable one. It was quite dark when we reached the bivouac ground, and it soon began to rain hard. The wagons were delayed and did not reach us until between 10 and 12 at night. The men had only the blanket they carried. The officers did not get their valises at all, and the scotch carts carrying their food enabled them to dine at the rather late hour of 11 p.m. round a fire on the open veldt, with ten degrees of frost, and after that sleep as best they could in their scanty coverings.

[After another two weeks and 166 miles, the force marched into Johannesburg on 31st May. For the first time both South Wales Borderers and Welch were together.] On Thursday, 31st, we marched off at 10.30 along a broad dusty road for Johannesburg, which city had been surrendered by the Boers the previous evening . . . Our approach to the Golden City now lay along a broad boulevard which passed through a suburb that had almost been destroyed by a dynamite explosion . . . A short distance from the Market Square the division halted; each company formed [column of] sections and fixed bayonets. About 2 p.m. the British flag was hoisted amid great cheering, and the division marched past Lord Roberts. The Welch were preceded by a very small Angora goat that had been obtained from a farm on the line of march.

There was a sharp little engagement on 4th June at Zwart Kop, eight miles south of Pretoria, where the Boers made one of their rare stands. As usual, after putting up a brave show of musketry and pom-pom fire, they melted away when their flanks were threatened, and The Welch had only three men wounded.

On 5th June Kruger and Botha fled their capital, and once more there was a bloodless and triumphal entry. All that Colonel Banfield has to say of this momentous event is that 'an excellent photograph was taken of the Welch, with the smart little goat, just as they were saluting Lord Roberts'. Unfortunately this excellent photograph does not seem to have survived.

'All say the war is now over', wrote a Dorset Yeomanry subaltern, and indeed Lord Roberts himself was sanguine that the Boers would capitulate. Cronje had been captured, Joubert had died and Kruger was soon to flee to Holland. But these leaders were replaced by implacable fighters like Louis Botha, de la Rey, De Wet and Jan Smuts, all of whom contemptuously rejected Roberts's demands for unconditional surrender. The struggle was to drag on for another two years.

On 11th June Botha made a gesture of defiance by massing some 6,000 men in a rugged position 20 miles from Pretoria, and to dislodge them Roberts sent out a strong force of cavalry and infantry. The Battle of Diamond Hill lasted two days, during which nine British cavalry regiments were pinned down by continuous fire, suffering many casualties. It was only when the infantry managed to work round a flank that the Boers repeated their customary tactics, and withdrew without allowing their opponents to come to grips. 1 Welch were engaged in this affair, but as Colonel Banfield makes clear, they saw little serious business. On the contrary, they spent a night in unwonted comfort billeted in and around 'a charming house occupied by Mr S. Marks, a South

African millionaire . . . a naturalised Englishman'. This gentleman not only provided wood, coal and cooking facilities for the soldiers, but 'invited the officers to dine with him . . . a welcome surprise in the middle of the veldt to sit down in a luxuriously furnished room lighted by electricity, to a well-cooked dinner, with a game of billiards afterwards in an excellently appointed billiards room'. Later the Welch's generous host was to become associated with a Mr Spencer in London. Needless to say, the Regiment suffered no casualties at Diamond Hill, In fact the entire British force lost only 28 killed and 145 wounded.

Diamond Hill marked a turning poing in the campaign. It was the last major confrontation of British and Boers, and thenceforth followed the 'Guerrilla War' with Botha and De Wet never risking an encounter in force, but harrying their enemy over thousands of miles of veldt, cutting communications, laying ambushes, pouncing on convoys and melting away again. The experiences of the 2nd Battalion The South Wales Borderers in this phase are well described by Atkinson. Joining a mobile Column under Major-General Fitzroy Hart, they, with the rest of the infantry:

> . . . had heart-breaking work; it fell to them to escort the wagons, which frequently had to be man-handled across drifts or over especially bad bits of track, while they were constantly liable to attack by parties of Boers who had eluded the mounted troops and seemed almost to hop up and out of the ground whenever any difficulty occurred. The columns toiled along, always hoping to corner some commando and force it to fight. In this they rarely succeeded, but they kept the Boers on the move, forced them to keep at a distance from the railway, and harassed them considerably.

Marching out of Krugersdorp on 29th August, the Column was 'on trek continuously for a month, covering more than 300 miles', or 'the length of England from Portsmouth to Scotland', as General Hart put it. On one attempt to surprise a commando, the column set out at 10.30 p.m., trekked continuously until 4.30 a.m., halted for thirty minutes, then marched for another five hours, only to find the commando had vanished. However, the month's exertions resulted in the capture of eighty Boers together with large stocks of supplies, ammunition, and herds of cattle – all for the loss of thirty men killed or wounded. The South Wales Borderers escaped without a single casualty.

In October Field Marshal Lord Roberts who had 'won the war' at Pretoria was replaced by his Chief of Staff, Major General Lord Kitchener, who was given the job of finishing it. To the troops it seemed incredible that 'Bobs', victor in Afghanistan, conqueror of the Transvaal and idol of the British public, should apparently be sent packing. The fact is, since the Boers were refusing to admit defeat, the Government were resolved on a scorched-earth policy of ruthless aggression. 'The last of the gentlemen's wars' was over, and the kindly Lord Roberts with his inherent gentlemanly nature had to be replaced by the tough, no-nonsense Kitchener, a man of very different mettle. However, on returning home 'Bobs' was rewarded with the supreme appointment of Commander in Chief of the British Army, and an Earldom.[4]

The final stage of the campaign was one of arduous marching across the seemingly limitless veldt in pursuit of a wily enemy who seldom allowed himself to be cornered. It was an unrewarding war for the infantryman: no heroic assaults on impregnable positions, few gallant stands against overwhelming odds. Mostly it was monotonous footslogging: 'Boots – boots – boots – movin' up and down again!', as Kipling wrote.

At home the public were regaled with the idealised pictures by the several war artists, such as Melton Pryor of *The Illustrated London News*, depicting spruced, immaculately-clad soldiers looking as though they were about to march on to the parade ground for Commanding Officer's inspection. The reality was rather different. 'The whole Brigade looked perfect scarecrows, our clothes were all in rags and dirty isn't the word for it . . . the only time we can get undressed is when we have time to wash our underclothing – which isn't very often.' So wrote a sergeant of a 'crack' cavalry Regiment, the 7th Dragoon Guards. More explicit is a letter from a corporal in the 1st Battalion The Border Regiment, who marched with The Welch:[5]

> We are, I think, in the most degenerate state of unpicturesque vagrancy – worn-out boots and clothing, men unkempt, dirty and rarely washed, subsisting on a bare ration that never satisfies the appetite . . . where you can never buy, beg or steal anything eatable . . . I'm now smoking a raking-up of pockets – tobacco dust, biscuit dust and shreds of khaki, not a very fragrant mixture, but better than nothing.

While no comments from The South Wales Borderers or The Welch seem to have survived, their experiences were undoubtedly similar. During the whole of the year 1901 both Regiments were continuously employed on wearisome 'sweeps' and cordons over most of the Transvaal and the Orange Free State, with their enemy eluding any serious confrontation.

Occasionally detachments were detailed as escorts to trains ferrying up supplies or evacuating wounded, and on 20th May, 2nd Lieutenant D. L. Campbell of The Welch was in command of such an escort when the train was ambushed and halted by a Boer commando. Campbell and his four men were in an open truck behind the locomotive (whose driver was killed), and came under heavy fire from Boers on the roof of the adjoining coach and also from their position on a bluff overlooking the line. Ignoring summonses to surrender, the five held out for nearly two hours. At length a patrol of The Welch led by Lance Corporal Isaacs arrived on the scene and drove off the fifty Boers. For this action 2nd Lieutenant Campbell was awarded an immediate DSO (gazetted 5th July 1901) and Lance Corporal Isaacs was promoted sergeant by special order of Lord Kitchener.

At this period the British troops in the eastern Transvaal were being stricken down by a mysterious fever which, though seldom proving fatal, saw hundreds incapacitated, on the sick list. Later it turned out to be dengue fever, common enough in India but then unfamiliar to the medical officers in South Africa, who were mostly home-service doctors. The Welch were so severely smitten that they could parade only 350 effectives out of the 900-odd who had marched from Pretoria.

The 1st Battalion The Welch Regiment entering Pretoria, May 1900 (led by the Goat).

While the name 'Modderfontein' may not be familiar to the general public, this small outpost, some thirty miles south of Johannesburg, was the scene of a gallant defence by a detachment of the 2nd Battalion The South Wales Borderers and other details. The post was located on a broad, flat-topped kopje, so broad that a complete perimeter defence was impossible, and there were only a series of detached stone sangars. In January (1901) the garrison consisted only of 150 rifles, 80 of these being A Company of 2 SWB under Captain Hugh Casson. On 29th January a convoy carrying wire for the defences arrived from Krugersdorp, having fought off a Boer attack en route. The escort included forty men of 2 SWB under Lieutenant Crawley, who was wounded in the affray. During the following night the Boers surrounded the post, and their intermittent outbursts of small arms fire allowed no rest for the defenders. Next morning it was evident that the enemy were in force, especially on a commanding kopje within range on the east, and now to the whine and crack of bullets were added the eruptions of HE shells and the thudding of pom-poms. When daylight came it was possible to contact Krugersdorp by helio, and Captain Casson flashed an urgent signal for reinforcements. This signal was acknowledged, but the day passed with no help sighted. Meanwhile the 200-odd garrison could only crouch in their sangars and take pot-shots at whatever targets they could sight on the surrounding kopjes, any movement on their own part bringing down storms of musketry, machine-gun fire and shell-fire. The water-cart was destroyed, and raging thirst was added to the other difficulties. On the second, moonless, night heavy rain pelted on the defenders. Taking advantage of this, the Boers managed to work up the kopje unobserved, and shortly after midnight rushed the position. The garrison was hopelessly outnumbered, and the sangars fell one by one.

Although Kitchener in his subsequent despatch referred to the capture of Modderfontein as 'a regrettable incident', he might have acknowledged that the little garrison of 240 men had held out for 40 hours against the assaults of some 1,500 Boers, commanded by Smuts himself. Four officers and sixty-five men were killed or wounded, 2 SWB losing ten men killed and nine wounded. The remainder were taken prisoner, but later Smuts chivalrously released them and sent for a British ambulance to evacuate the wounded. On 2nd February an attempt was made to recapture the position, but plans went awry, and B and F Companies of 2 SWB were pinned down in the open for eleven hours, losing nine men killed and twenty-nine wounded. For his gallantry in aiding a wounded man under fire Lance Corporal H. Blair was awarded the DCM.

The rest of the campaign saw few more such actions for our two Regiments. The Welch, smitten by the fever epidemic, were consigned to garrison duties in and around Johannesburg, while The South Wales Borderers trekked hundreds of miles across the Orange Free State and the Transvaal after an enemy who was becoming even more reluctant than ever to stand and fight. Now and then detachments were subjected to the distasteful and sometimes harrowing tasks of surrounding Boer settlements and carrying off women and children and old patriarchs to the new concentration camps set up by Kitchener. The latter's ruthless policy was now having effect. Constantly harried by the 'sweeps', their mobility restricted by the chains of blockhouses, the Boers began to lose heart. In March 1902 De Wet organised a referendum among all the leaders and their commandos, and on 31st May surrender terms were agreed upon at Vereeniging.

Despite the jingoism and victory bells at home, Britain had little to be proud of. It had taken 450,000 troops (including 256,000 regulars) two and a half years to defeat the 'rabble' of some 87,000 Boer farmers. The war had cost £20 million and 20,721 British lives (of whom 13,130 died of disease). The Boers lost an estimated 4,000 killed.[6]

As for The South Wales Borderers and The Welch Regiment, their casualties, as below, were relatively light considering their lengthy period of active service.

	2nd Battalion The South Wales Borderers		1st Battalion The Welch Regiment	
Killed in Action	Officers 2	Other Ranks 32	Officers 5	Other Ranks 67
Died of Disease	1	94	4	113
Wounded	4	83	13	242
Total Casualties	7	209	22	422

The Welch Regiment gained the Battle Honours 'Relief of Kimberley' and 'Paardeberg' besides the theatre Honour 'South Africa 1899–1902', but The South Wales Borderers had to be content with 'South Africa 1900–1902', since they were not present in force at any of the major actions. Among the many personal awards were four DSOs and eleven DCMs for The South Wales Borderers; eight DSOs and fifteen DCMs for The Welch. In addition CBs went to Lieutenant Colonel U. de R. Roche of The South Wales Borderers, and to Lieutenant Colonel R. J. F. Banfield and Majors H. d'A. Harkness and W. Wath of The Welch.

The end of the war did not mean immediate return home for either Regiment, both being retained in South Africa for internal security duties. The 2nd Battalion The South Wales Borderers eventually sailed for England in May 1903 and took up quarters in the newly-established Tidworth garrison. The 1st Battalion The Welch Regiment followed in Juy 1904, posted to ancient, fog-ridden barracks at Gravesend.

While these two Battalions were earning Battle Honours in South Africa, the other two regular Battalions had been serving peacefully in India. On 23rd January 1901, they were shocked to learn of the death of Queen Victoria. Having been on the throne for longer than any of them had been in this world, the Queen-Empress was an almost legendary figure, seemingly immortal. A General Order from Army Headquarters Simla directed that all flags were to be flown at half-mast, officers were to wear mourning armlets, and the playing of Bands was forbidden. Eight days later another General Order was published from Army Headquarters, announcing the accession of King Edward VII.

These events seem to have passed without any form of ceremonial, but a year later both The South Wales Borderers and The Welch were involved in the most lavish and spectacular ceremony ever witnessed in India since the days of the Mughal Emperors. This was the Delhi Durbar, master-minded by the extrovert, pomp-loving Viceroy, Lord Curzon, to celebrate the Coronation of Edward VII as King-Emperor. A vast tented 'City' was specially erected to accommodate 45,000 British and Indian troops from all quarters of the subcontinent, in addition to all the Indian ruling Princes with their own forces and hordes of retainers. The Viceroy entered Delhi in state on 29th December, when both the 1st Battalion The South Wales Borderers and the 2nd Battalion The Welch Regiment formed part of the street-lining contingent. The great Durbar itself took place on 1st January, with all 45,000 troops, in review order, drawn up on the huge arena to hear the Viceroy read the Proclamation.[7] Later Field Marshal the Duke of Connaught, representing the King, presented the South African medal to the officers and men of The South Wales Borderers and The Welch who had served in that campaign, and on 8th January a grand review was held by the Viceroy, at which 2 SWB were the first of the infantry battalions to march past His Excellency.

In 1906 the 1st Battalion The South Wales Borderers were stationed at Karachi, and on 17th March they formed a Guard of Honour for the visiting Prince and Princess of Wales. While inspecting the Guard, His Royal Highness showed great interest in the Wreath of Immortelles on the King's Colour, and expressed a wish to see the original, presented by his grandmother. Accordingly the precious emblem was removed from the Officers' Mess and sent under escort to Government House, where it was shown to

The South Wales Borderers Regimental arch for the Royal Tour to Karachi by the Prince and Princess of Wales, 1906.

the Prince by Captain Yates, who was commanding the guard.[8] Later Lieutenant Colonel Francis Hunter, Commanding Officer, was received by the Prince in a private interview. After detailing the history of the Immortelles, he was bold enough to request that this distinction should be recorded in the Army List along with the Battle Honours. 'This most certainly ought to be done', replied the Prince, 'but I cannot do it myself, you must make an official application.' However, he promised Colonel Hunter that when forwarding the application he was at liberty to say that the matter had 'his sympathy'.

Whether Colonel Hunter ever made his application is not recorded, but if he did, even the Prince of Wales's support was evidently unavailing. It was not until 1932 that the distinction first appeared in the Army List, and that it did so was entirely due to the indefatigable Colonel of the Regiment, General Morgan-Owen (who also won the battle with the church authorities of Warwick for the removal of the Chilianwala

The Boer War and After 1899–1914

Colours to Brecon (see Appendix 5). Since the Prince of Wales of 1906 had then become King George V, one might presume to imagine that the Colonel took the liberty of reminding His Majesty of his former 'sympathy'.

In the Records of Service of 1 SWB for 2nd June 1909 appears the terse entry: 'A set of silver drums arrived from George Potter, Aldershot.' This firm (still at the same address today) had been supplying drums, bugles and fifes to the Army since 1742, and Mr George Potter told a representative of *Sheldrake's Military Gazette* that these drums formed 'the most magnificent and unique set in the whole of the British Army'. The set comprised one bass drum, two tenors and fifteen side-drums, all with Battle Honours, crests and other repoussé work on the sterling silver shells. The drum-sticks were of ebony, with silver mounts. The cost, reported the *Gazette*, 'is estimated to run into four figures' – as well it might. Potter's report that today a single silver side-drum could not be supplied for less than £5,000. Happily, this unique set is still with the 1st Battalion The Royal Regiment of Wales, though naturally, it is paraded only on very special ceremonial occasions. In the 1960s it was found that the shells had become too weak for the skins to be correctly tensioned, so with a bequest from the former Colonel, General Sir Reade Godwin-Austen, they were strengthened, and at the same time the tensioning system was changed from ropes to the modern metal rods.[9] The 1st Battalion The South Wales Borderers were stationed at Quetta when their Corps of Drums received the splendid set, and probably the first time that they were seen in

Corps of Drums of 1 SWB, with their silver drums, Rawalpindi, 1936.

Wet Canteen of 2 Welch; field training, Pembrokeshire, 1910.

public was on 12th May 1910, when the whole garrison paraded in Review Order for the Proclamation announcing the succession of the King-Emperor, George V.

In December that year the Battalion completed its eighteen-year overseas tour and sailed from Karachi for Southampton. It so happened that their ship berthed just in time to see the 2nd Battalion embarking for South Africa. There was a convivial meeting of the officers on board the 2nd's ship, and when she steamed out 'a scene of the greatest enthusiasm followed, the Buglers of both Battalions sounding the Regimental Call and the troops cheering heartily' (Regimental Records). The last time the two Battalions had seen anything of each other was on those memorable days of January 1879 in Zululand.

Meanwhile The Welch Regiment were soldiering with the 1st Battalion in India and the 2nd on their home ground of Pembroke Dock. During the annual autumn manoeuvres it was the practice for the Foot Guards to be relieved of their Buckingham Palace and St James's Palace guard duties for field training, and Line battalions were selected to take their place. From 23rd August to 13th September 1910 The Welch were so honoured. There had been earlier ceremonial in July when the Battalion paraded at Caernarfon Castle for the Investiture of Edward, Prince of Wales.

During this period there were several important organisational changes, affecting regulars, Militia and Volunteers. As a result of the Haldane[10] reforms of March 1908, the Militia battalions were converted to a Special Reserve, for draft-finding and garrison duties; the Volunteers became a new body known as the Territorial Force (later

The Boer War and After 1899–1914

Territorial Army). As far as The South Wales Borderers and The Welch were concerned, these changes can be summarised as follows.

The South Wales Borderers lost their Montgomeryshire Militia, or 4 SWB, which was disbanded (the county being too thinly populated to produce recruits); their three Monmouthshire Volunteer Battalions became an entirely separate Territorial unit, 'The Monmouthshire Regiment', while the 5th Volunteer Battalion, (Montgomeryshire) transferred to The Royal Welch Fusiliers as their 7th Battalion. Only the Volunteer Breconshire Battalion remained with the Regiment, designated (but not numbered) the 'Brecknockshire Battalion The South Wales Borderers'.

The Welch Regiment's Militia Battalion (Royal Glamorgan) retained its name but became the Special Reserve Battalion, based at Cardiff. The Volunteer Battalions were retitled as follows, as part of the Territorial force: The 1st (Pembrokeshire) became 4th Battalion The Welch Regiment; the 3rd became the 5th Battalion, and the 3rd Glamorgan Volunteer Rifle Corps emerged as the 6th (Glamorgan) Battalion. The old 2nd Volunteer Battalion was divorced from the Regiment, being converted to Territorial artillery. However, in May 1908 a novel Territorial battalion was created, titled the '7th (Cyclist) Battalion The Welch Regiment'. This reflected the recently developed interest in the use of the bicycle for military purposes, and numerous cyclist battalions were formed before 1914. None went overseas; they were employed much as the mounted units of the Home Guard in World War II – patrolling and watching vulnerable areas on the coast and elsewhere.

If the pedal cycle had little impact on military tactics or strategy, between the 1880s

Married Quarters of 2 Welch; Llanion Barracks, Pembroke Dock, 1911.

and 1914 there appeared two technological developments which were to revolutionise warfare: the motor car and the aeroplane. By 1912 some of the more mechanically-minded (and wealthier) officers were proudly parking their Sunbeams and Lanchesters or De Dions outside the Mess, and when the newly-formed Royal Flying Corps called for suitable volunteers from the Army there was an immediate response. The Welch Regiment provided four officers, of whom Captain C. A. H. Longcroft was to have a distinguished flying career. In August 1913 he gained the record for the longest British flight, from Aldershot to Montrose. On the outbreak of war Longcroft commanded No. 1 Squadron of The Royal Flying Corps and continued to serve in (or over) France and Flanders until 1919, when as Air Commodore he was given command of the new RAF officers' training college at Cranwell. Having become Director of Personal Services at the Air Ministry, he retired in 1926, as Air Vice-Marshal.

The South Wales Borderers also produced an intrepid aviator of those early days, in the person of Andrew George Board, who joined the Regiment from Sandhurst in 1900. Board had a fascination for flying and learned to fly by taking a fortnight's course with Louis Bleriot's flying school at Hendon in 1910. At that time an Army Order was in force forbidding officers to learn to fly except with the Air Battalion RE, for which there was a long waiting list. He therefore took a fortnight's leave and did not tell his Commanding Officer his intentions. He received a reprimand, but also Pilot's Certificate No. 36.

In January 1913 he was posted as Instructor, Central Flying School, Netheravon, and in 1914 carried out what is believed to have been the first take-off and landing in darkness using a full moon and a torch tied to his belt for instrument reading. He was a member of the Army Air Contingent which flew to France to support the BEF in 1914, and spent the whole war in active flying on the Western Front, for which he was awarded the CMG and DSO. After the war his promotion was rapid. He was Commandant RAF Apprentices School, Halton; Deputy Director Personnel at the Air Ministry 1922–23; Commander RAF, Iraq, 1923–7 and Chief Air Staff Officer, Middle East, until he retired in 1931.

Re-employed by the Air Ministry during World War II he organised dummy airfields, factory sites, etc. to encourage German night bombers to unload their bombs harmlessly.

Although his service with the 24th virtually ceased in 1913 he never lost his love of the Regiment and attended all regimental functions almost to the time of his death. This occurred at the age of 94 in February 1973, when he had become Air Commodore A. G. Board, CMG, DSO, DL.

Since the earliest days of the British Army, infantry battalions had deployed at least eight (and sometimes more) companies, besides Headquarters. In October 1913 this somewhat cumbersome organisation was simplified and there came into being the four-company system which was to remain virtually unchanged down to the present day. The contemporary eight companies had been lettered A to H, and these were now amalgamated by pairs, emerging as A, B, C and D companies, each with a War Establishment strength of six officers and 221 other ranks. Each company had four platoons, these being subdivided into four sections. Each company was commanded by

The Boer War and After 1899–1914

a Major, with a Captain as Second in Command, while platoons were led by subalterns. Since the Commanding Officer (and Adjutant) and his company commanders were reckoned to require greater mobility than their men, they were provided with horses, but the platoon subalterns had to make do with their own legs. Previously each company had two Colour Sergeants: the senior now became Company Sergeant Major, the other, Company Quartermaster Sergeant. But the CSM still ranked as senior NCO, and it was not until 1915 that he became a Warrant Officer Class 2 (the only WO1s in the battalion were the RSM and the Bandmaster).

By now the time-honoured red coat (or tunic) was seen only on ceremonial occasions. Khaki service dress was the rule for all other duties, and it had evolved into the pattern that is still familiar to white-haired Old Comrades of today. The serge tunic (quaintly described as 'frock') with stand-up collar was common to the other ranks of all arms, but the infantryman's nether limbs were clad in puttees with the trousers folded over at the knee to give a sort of 'plus-four' effect. Most soldiers abominated puttees: although affording excellent protection, they were irksome to apply correctly, each fold to be exactly the same depth, and not too tight to constrict the calf muscles but not too slack to work loose. All dismounted officers, i.e. below company commander, were also afflicted with these, but of course, theirs were of finer-quality material. The old leather ammunition pouches and equipment gave way to the webbing equipment in 1908, and this too was to last until World War II. But, except on active service, it still had to be blancoed with the regulation shade of green, cakes of which the soldier purchased in the Dry Canteen. After that short-lived absurdity, the Brodrick Cap[11] – a pancake-shaped article with no peak – both officer and soldier received the peaked cap with chinstrap (worn under the chin if mounted) which has survived in one

A selection of uniforms worn by 2 Welch; Agra, India, 1906.

Officers of the 2nd Battalion The South Wales Borderers; Aldershot, 1907.

form or another to the present day. Introduced in 1908, this was described as 'Cap, General Service'.

As we have seen, the 2nd Battalion The South Wales Borderers had been posted to South Africa in 1911, being stationed at Pretoria. While here it was proposed that a memorial should be erected on the site of the Isandhlwana massacre. The project aroused keen interest and support, not only within the Regiment, but among the British settlers in Natal, and the necessary funds were quickly raised by subscription. The memorial was to be unveiled on the anniversary of the battle, in January 1913, but unhappily the Battalion were unexpectedly posted to join the international force in China in October 1912, and thus could not be present. The ceremony, however, was eventually performed on 4th March 1914, the memorial being unveiled by the Commander in Chief South Africa, Lieutenant General Sir Reginald Hart, VC.

In July 1914 the 1st Battalion The South Wales Borderers were preparing for autumn manoeuvres at Bordon in the Aldershot Command; the 2nd Battalion were still in China, dispersed between Peking and Tientsin. Also at Bordon were the 1st Battalion The Welch Regiment, while their 1st Battalion were enjoying relief from the Indian hot-weather season at the hill-station of Chakrata in the foothills of the Himalayas. The year had passed uneventfully enough, with routine 'collective training', interchange of drafts, and comings and goings of officers from or to leave. In June the newspapers had carried reports of the assassination of some Austrian Archduke at a place called

Sarajevo, but this aroused little interest in regimental Messes, and of course went quite unnoticed in the barrackrooms.

Away in Tientsin the Welshmen of The South Wales Borderers had established very friendly relations with their German comrades in the international force, as indeed had all the British troops, and it was somewhat of a surprise when on 1st August the entire German contingent loaded their transport and unceremoniously marched out. A letter from their commander to his British counterpart regretted that the unexpected haste of their departure precluded any personal farewells; he could only express his appreciation of the 'friendship and comradeship extended by all the British soldiers'. In his reply Brigadier General Barnardiston sincerely regretted the severance of the very cordial relations – 'a severance which we earnestly hope will only be a temporary one'.[12] There was little to suggest that the severance would last four years, and that the British Army was about to be flung into the bloodiest conflict of its whole history.

The South Wales Borderers wildebeest and their keeper, who is wearing the Brodrick hat.

The Boer War and After 1899–1914

Notes

[1] The pom-pom was a Vickers-Maxim automatic gun firing 1 lb. shells at the rate of 300 per minute. The nickname was derived from its distinctive 'pumping' sound. It was used both by Boers and British, but became obsolete after the South African War.

[2] *History of the Services of the 41st (the Welch) Regiment (Now 1st Battalion The Welch Regiment) from its Formation in 1719 to 1895.*

[3] Driefontein, which opened the way to Bloemfontein, was surely as significant a victory as the indecisive Paardeberg, yet strangely no Battle Honour was awarded.

[4] The last person to hold the post of Commander in Chief of the Army, Field Marshal Earl Roberts, VC, KG, died in France in 1914, while visiting the troops.

[5] Quoted in *Tried and Valiant. The History of the Border Regiment* (Douglas Sutherland, 1972).

[6] These figures are taken from the *Official History of the War in South Africa* (1906–10).

[7] From that date, until the last British troops left India in 1947, 1st January was celebrated as Proclamation Day, with ceremonial parades and reviews.

The 24th Regiment memorial at Isandhlwana unveiled in 1914.

[8] Today it might seem strange, not to say hazardous, for the unique and priceless wreath to be carried around with the Battalion on all its far-flung travellings. Nevertheless, it was not until 1st April 1934, that it was laid up in the Regimental Chapel of Brecon Cathedral, together with the Isandhlwana Colours.

[9] The rod-tensioners relieve the drummers of laborious chores of blancoing, but they lack the panache of those brilliant white ropes and braces.

[10] Richard Haldane (later Viscount) was Secretary for War 1905–12.

[11] Named after the then Secretary for War, St John Brodrick, who was said to have devised it.

[12] These letters were published in full in 2 SWB's Battalion Orders for 5th August 1914.

CHAPTER THIRTEEN

The Great War (1914–18)

In 1931 Professor C. T. Atkinson published his history of The South Wales Borderers in the Great War. This covers 601 pages and includes the services not only of the two regular and four Territorial battalions (among them The Monmouthshire Regiment and the Brecknocks) but also those of fourteen 'Service' or hostilities-only battalions. A year later appeared Major General Marden's record of The Welch Regiment's war services, embracing two regular, four Territorial, a 'Special Reserve' and no fewer than twenty-seven service and reserve battalions.

Thus it will be seen that during World War I the antecedents of The Royal Regiment of Wales deployed a total of four regular, eight Territorial and forty-one hostilities-only battalions. Some of these earned hard-won Battle Honours for the Regiment, together with VCs and numerous other decorations; some were on active service for the entire four-year duration of the war; others saw little or no actual campaigning. Obviously, it is impossible to cover adequately the activities of fifty-four battalions within a single chapter: only an outline can be attempted, leaving the reader to refer to the previously published histories for the detail.[1]

The declaration of war on 4th August saw mobilisation carried out with remarkable speed and enthusiasm on the part of reservists and recruits, who flocked to the Depots at Brecon and Cardiff in such numbers that the staffs could scarcely cope. At Brecon 381 reservists reported on 5th August and 470 the following day. By 8th August the 1st Battalion The South Wales Borderers and the 2nd Battalion The Welch, both at Bordon, were completed to War Establishment, and on the 12th both embarked at Southampton as elements of the 3rd Brigade, 1st Division. 1 SWB were commanded by Lieutenant Colonel H. E. B. Leach, 2 Welch by Lieutenant Colonel T. O. Marden (later Major General, author of the wartime history).

For their invasion of France the German High Command had planned a huge enveloping movement through Belgium, aiming to encircle Paris and penetrate behind the French forces positioned on the Franco–German frontier. On the left of the French line, the British Expeditionary Force was assaulted by heavy enemy attacks on 23rd August, but neither The South Wales Borderers nor The Welch were seriously engaged,

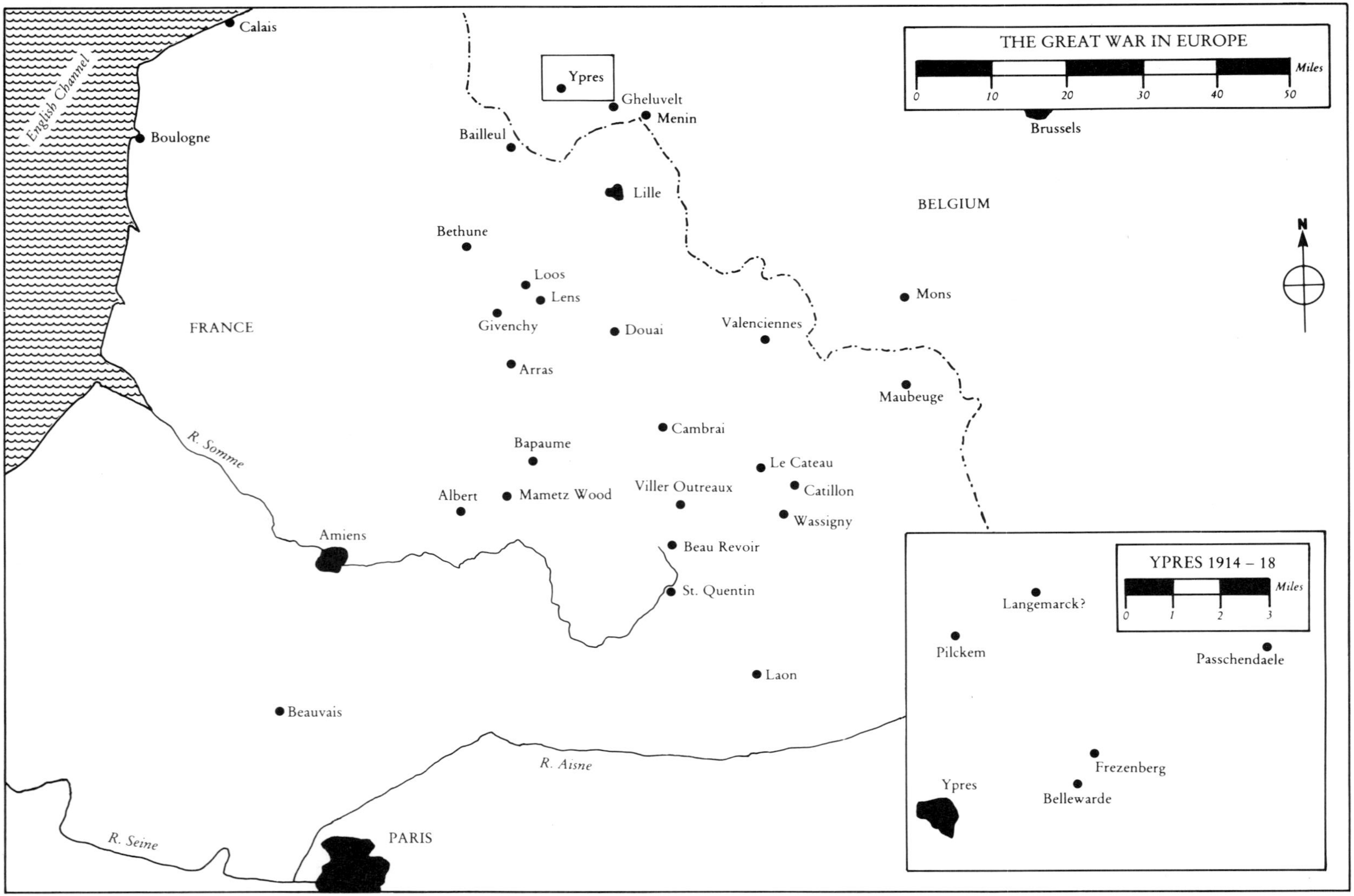
THE GREAT WAR IN EUROPE
0 10 20 30 40 50 Miles
Calais
English Channel
Boulogne
FRANCE
R. Somme
Amiens
Beauvais
R. Seine
PARIS
R. Aisne
Ypres
Gheluvelt
Menin
Bailleul
Lille
Bethune
Loos
Lens
Givenchy
Douai
Arras
Valenciennes
Bapaume
Albert
Mametz Wood
Cambrai
Villers Outreaux
Le Cateau
Catillon
Wassigny
Beau Revoir
St. Quentin
Laon
Brussels
BELGIUM
Mons
Maubeuge
N
YPRES 1914 – 18
0 1 2 3 Miles
Langemarck?
Pilckem
Passchendaele
Frezenberg
Bellewarde
Ypres

Captain Mark Haggard.
'Stick it The Welch!'

Lance Corporal William Fuller, 2 Welch, holding the bullet which wounded him, VC, 14 September 1914, France.

meeting only skirmishing cavalry patrols. However, the French line on their right was driven back and the whole of the BEF were forced to conform. Then began the exhausting and demoralising Retreat from Mons, during which both The South Wales Borderers and The Welch marched more than 200 miles in 13 days. Unlike some British infantrymen,[2] these two Battalions maintained admirable discipline and morale. A stand was made in early September, and after the forcing of the Marne the BEF effected the crossing of the Aisne, to attack the Chemin des Dames ridge. It was here on 13th September that both Battalions met ferocious German opposition on the ridge. The Welch, on the right of The South Wales Borderers, suffered heavy casualties as they advanced up the open slopes, and one of the first to fall was Captain Mark Haggard who was hit as he personally led a charge on a machine-gun emplacement. Though mortally wounded, he waved his men on, shouting 'Stick it the Welch!' Under heavy rifle and machine-gun fire, Lance Corporal William Fuller managed to drag his Company Commander back to safety, for which gallant act he was subsequently awarded the Regiment's first VC of the war.[3]

Captain Haggard died the following day, but his inspiring cry lives on. In gilt lettering below the clock at Maindy Barracks, Cardiff, the words 'STICK IT THE WELCH!' still remind us of his indomitable spirit. This inscription was the gift of Colonel Alfred Donald The Mackintosh, CBE, who owned the country seat of Cottrell near Cardiff, and whose wife hailed from Glamorganshire.[4]

The death of Captain Mark Haggard.

On 31st October 1 SWB and 2 Welch were once more together, exposed to the determined German assault on the British positions around Gheluvelt. After a dawn 'hate' of artillery bombardment, repeated infantry attacks by the Germans were repelled, but then superior enemy numbers began to tell. At about 10 a.m. Colonel Morland of The Welch told Colonel Leach of The South Wales Borderers that his Battalion had virtually been destroyed by shell-fire and the situation was desperate. Shortly afterwards Morland himself was mortally wounded by a shell-burst while trying to rally the remnants of his command. For the next six hours The South Wales Borderers stubbornly held on to their position around the Chateau of Gheluvelt, constantly assaulted by artillery, machine-gun and rifle fire. At one stage Colonel Leach led a counter-attack which drove the enemy from the Chateau gardens and gave a brief respite to his men. But casualties were mounting, and when the Germans renewed their attacks the end seemed inevitable: it could only be last man, last round. At this critical juncture the Colonel spotted a line of khaki-clad infantry advancing through shell-fire out of the right-flank woods. They were the 2nd Battalion The Worcestershire Regiment led by their Major Hankey, who had been ordered to 'retake' Gheluvelt, presumed overrun. Surprise was mutual: Hankey, expecting nothing but corpses, greeted Leach with 'Fancy seeing you here!', to which Leach could only reply 'Thank God you've come!' A determined bayonet charge by The Worcestershires with the remnants of The South Wales Borderers finally repelled the Germans. Gheluvelt was secured, and with it the whole line of the 1st Division. In his subsequent book, *1914*, Field Marshal Sir John French paid handsome tribute to both The South Wales Borderers and The Worcestershires, especially praising 'the indomitable courage and dogged tenacity' of the former. But the cost was dear: The Worcestershires lost 187 officers and men killed and wounded; The South Wales Borderers lost 400, among whom was Colonel Leach, so severely wounded that he had to be invalided home and never resumed command. As for 2 Welch, they had indeed been 'virtually destroyed' in the initial phase. That night they could muster only 3 officers and some 50 men out of the 12 officers and 600 men who had gone into action. After the war it became the custom for The South Wales Borderers and The Worcestershire Regiment to exchange greetings telegrams on each anniversary of Gheluvelt. The Battle Honour borne today by The Royal Regiment of Wales and The Worcestershire and Sherwood Foresters Regiment is justly revered.

The name 'Gheluvelt' is well known to all students of World War I, but away on the other side of the world, around the same date, the 2nd Battalion The South Wales Borderers were earning a Battle Honour that is virtually unheard of except to the present Regiment, for it is unique in the British Army. After the German contingent of the international force at Tientsin had bade fond farewells to their British friends in August 1914, they occupied the port of Tsingtao on the Yellow Sea. This caused concern to our Japanese allies, and a joint British-Japanese expedition was mounted to

'Stick it The Welch'; Maindy Barracks, Cardiff.

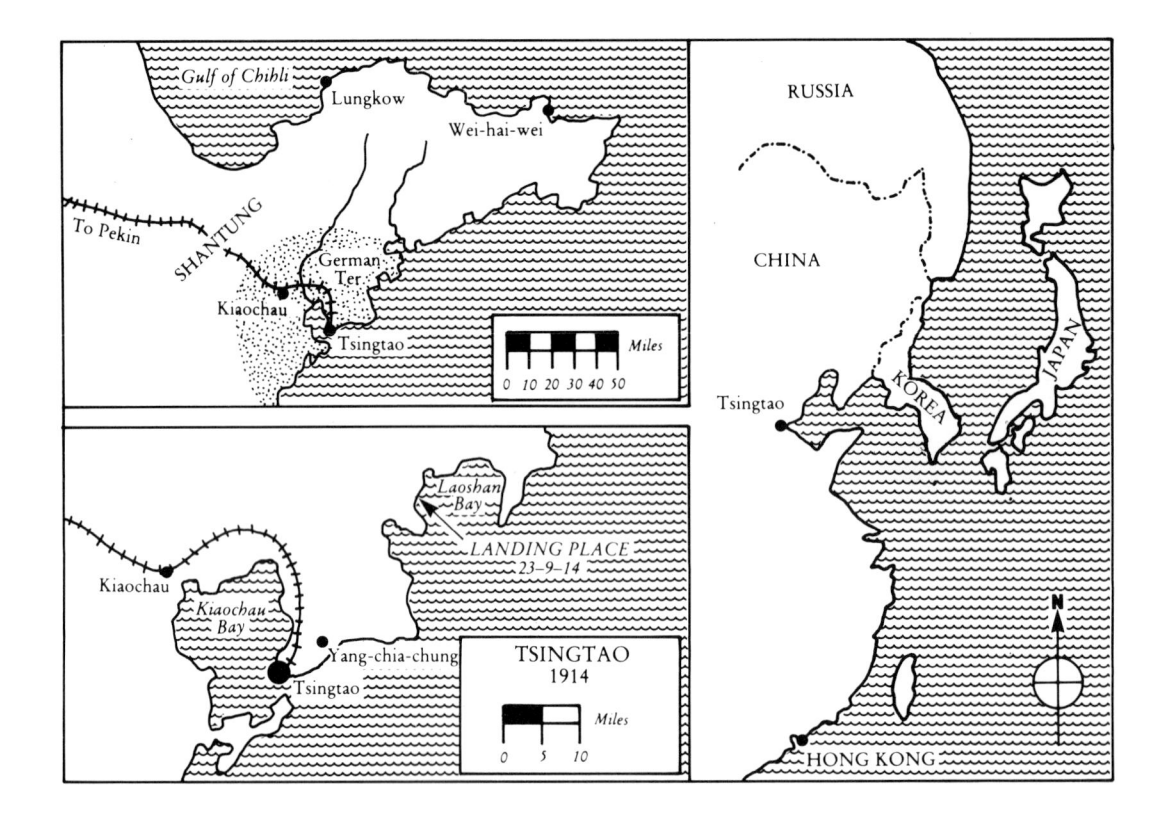

expel them. This operation proved to be a long-drawn-out siege, from 2nd October to 7th November, during which The South Wales Borderers, in their tropical kit, suffered more from the bitter weather, and shortage of rations, than from the enemy. Another problem was that of attempting to co-operate with the Japanese, whose methods, and ideas of discipline, were not those of the British Army, while few of either contingent could speak the other's language. When the Germans tamely surrendered on 7th November, the Battalion had lost fourteen men killed and thirty-four wounded, mostly by artillery and machine-gun fire. Among the enemy prisoners the Welshmen recognised many with whom they had been sharing cigarettes and drinks in Tientsin two months previously.

The 36th Sikhs (later 4th Battalion 11th Sikh Regiment) were also engaged in this operation, but the 2nd Battalion The South Wales Borderers were the only British unit present, and thus today the Battle Honour 'Tsingtao' appears only on the Colours of The Royal Regiment of Wales.

Back in Flanders, Battalions of The South Wales Borderers and The Welch were heavily engaged throughout the bloody Battles of Ypres. Among them were the three Battalions of the Monmouthshire Regiment. Although these former Volunteer Battalions of The South Wales Borderers had been divorced from the Regiment as

'The Battle of Isandhlwana', 22 January 1879, by C. E. Fripp. COURTESY OF THE NATIONAL ARMY MUSEUM

'The Defence of Rorke's Drift', by A. de Neuville.

2 SWB landing at Laoshan Bay, Tsingtao, 23rd September 1914. IMPERIAL WAR MUSEUM
2 SWB at Laoshan Bay, 23rd September 1914. IMPERIAL WAR MUSEUM

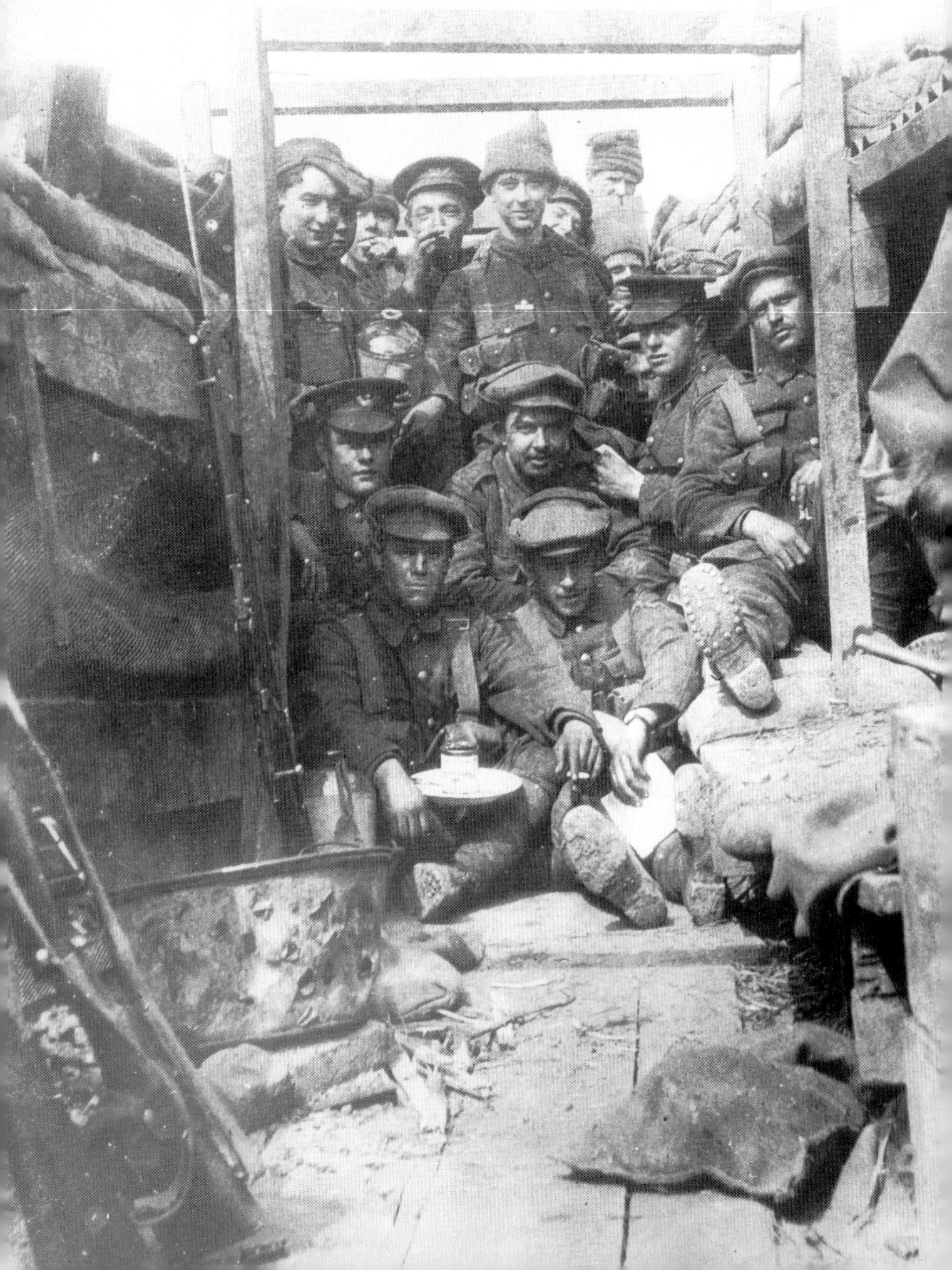

LEFT: *Men of 2 Mons in the trenches near Ypres; 2nd Battle of Ypres, 1915.*   B. OWEN COLLECTION
ABOVE: *Men of B Company, 2 Welch, in billets near Neuve Chappelle, March–April 1915.*

separate Territorial units in 1908, officially they were described as forming 'part of the corps of The South Wales Borderers', so their doings are very relevant.

In April 1915 the second Battle of Ypres opened with the first gas attack of the war (by the Germans), and the unprepared and unprotected British and French troops suffered heavily. On 8th May 1 and 3 Mons near Frezenberg bore the brunt of a heavy artillery bombardment, followed by an infantry attack in force. B Company of 3 Mons was left isolated and with two companies of the King's Own Yorkshire Light Infantry made an heroic stand that was described in the Official History (*French and Belgium 1915*) as 'among the historic episodes of the War'.

Of 1 Mons the war historian Sir Arthur Conan Doyle wrote:[5]

The shattered remains of the brigade (83rd) were compelled to fall back . . . This was about 11.30 in the morning. The 1st Monmouths on the left of the line, however, kept up their resistance till a considerably later hour, and behaved with extraordinary gallantry. Outflanked and attacked in the

Officers of 2 Welch in trench at Givenchy, 1915: Captain Aldworth, Lieutenant Leycester, Lieutenant Betts and Lieutenant Jones.

rear... they still, under their gallant Colonel Robinson, persevered in what was really a hopeless resistance. The Germans trained a machine-gun on them from a house which overlooked their trench, but nothing could shift the splendid miners who formed the greater part of the regiment. Colonel Robinson was shot dead while passing his men down the trench in the hope of forming a new front. Half the officers and men were already on the ground. The German stormers were on top of them with cries of 'Surrender! Surrender!' 'Surrender be damned!' shouted Captain Edwards, and died firing his revolver into the grey of them. It was a fine feat of arms, but only 120 men out of 720 reassembled that night.

On the night of 24th/25th May it was the turn of 1 Welch to distinguish themselves in the attack of Bellewaarde Ridge, which had been seized by the Germans. Supported by the Northumberland Fusiliers and the Suffolks, The Welch put in several attacks on the enemy position, and after losing heavily succeeded in occupying the ridge. Here the remnants held on until dawn, when the shattered force was compelled to withdraw. The attack had failed, and The Welch and their comrades had sacrificed themselves in the attempt. When 1 Welch was relieved by 2 Royal Scots, only five officers and thirty-nine other ranks marched back to Ypres.[6]

The Great War 1914–18

With the struggle on the Western Front developing into stalemate, Britain's war leaders, headed by Kitchener and Churchill (First Lord of the Admiralty), resolved to mount a diversion in the eastern Mediterranean, with the object of forcing the Dardanelles straits, wresting Constantinople from the Turks and relieving our Russian allies, hard pressed in the Caucasus. The First Lord insisted that the operation was to be entirely a naval one. But it proved impossible for the Fleet to secure their objectives unsupported, and in April Kitchener despatched a military force to '... take the Gallipoli Peninsula'. Commanded by General Ian Hamilton, this force included the last of the 'Old Army' divisions, the 29th, among whom were the 2nd Battalion The South Wales Borderers, lately returned home from Tsingtao. They were posted to the 87th Brigade, popularly known as 'The International Brigade', for it included, besides the Welshmen of The South Wales Borderers, Scottish, English and Irish regiments.[7]

The landing took place at Helles on 25th April, by which time the Turks had been fully forewarned by the previous naval bombardment, and all chance of surprise had been forfeited. On the extreme right of the assault, the 87th Brigade got ashore with relatively few casualties, but elsewhere there was carnage as men were mowed down by machine-gun fire and shell-fire as they struggled through concealed barbed-wire in the water. Over on the left flank The Lancashire Fusiliers lost half their strength before they were ashore, but also gained their six VCs (a record exceeded only by the 24th Regiment at Rorke's Drift). By the end of the day the 29th Division were established

Cape Helles, Dardanelles. IMPERIAL WAR MUSEUM

The Great War 1914–18

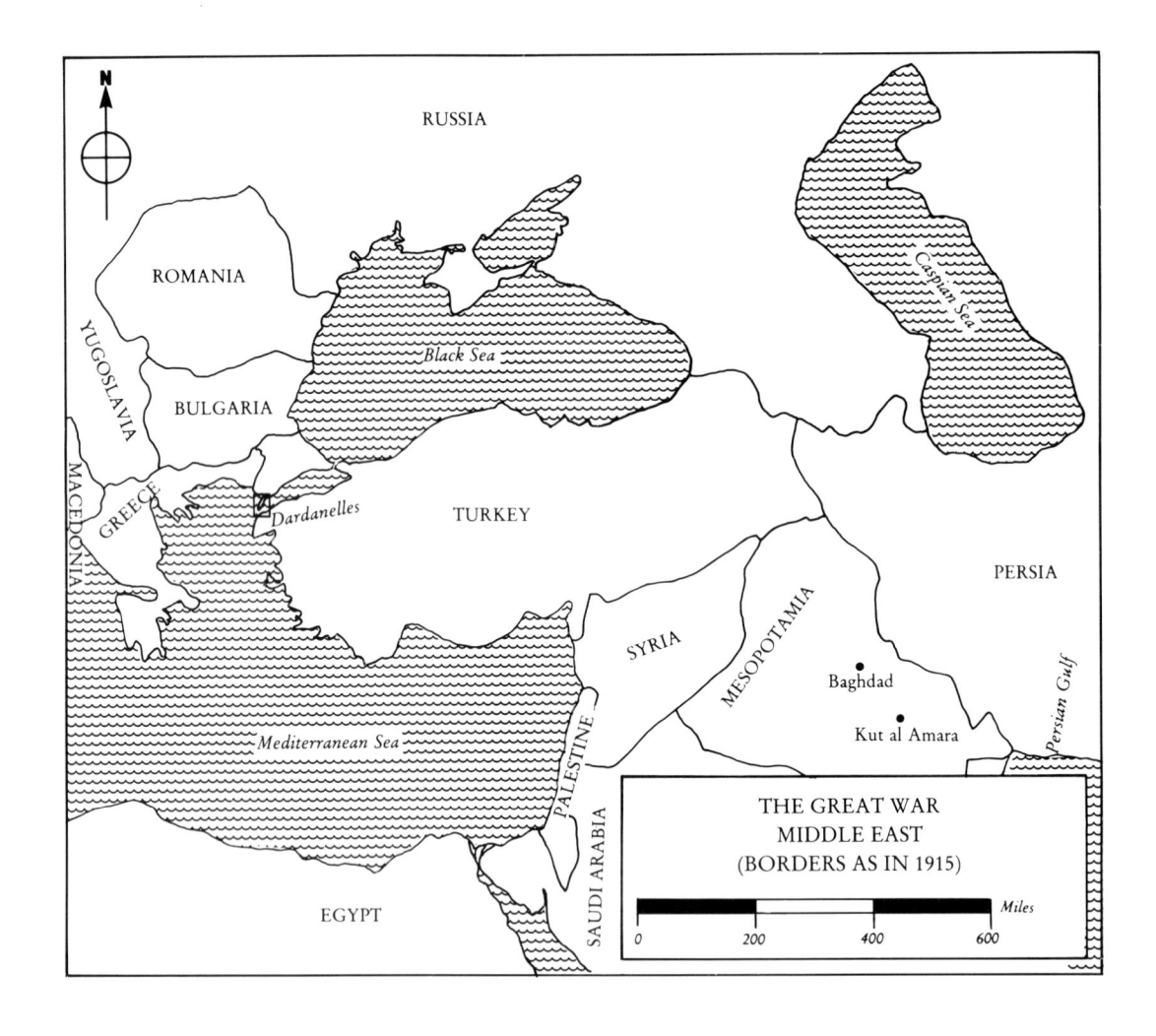

THE GREAT WAR
MIDDLE EAST
(BORDERS AS IN 1915)

above Cape Helles and the Anzacs at 'Anzac Cove', but neither force could link up with the other, while the Turks still held the dominating ground. The South Wales Borderers had lost two officers and twelve men killed, with two officers and forty wounded.

There followed a period of confused fighting for strongpoints on the peninsula as British and Anzacs strove to push back the dogged Turks, both sides suffering heavy casualties. On 11th June Captain Hugh Fowler of The South Wales Borderers led a gallant attack on a Turkish trench, personally hurling 'some thirty bombs, some of which were enemy bombs which he picked up and threw back at great personal risk'. When the initial attack failed, he, together with the RSM and two privates, coolly worked from traverse to traverse, hurling more grenades until the Turks bolted, leaving ninety-six dead. For this outstanding action Colonel Casson justifiably recommended

Captain Fowler for the VC, but authority transmuted it into a DSO, Privates Wood and Matthews received DCMs.

By early July the Helles beach-head had been extended inland for a mere 3 miles, at a cost of nearly 40,000 British and Commonwealth casualties. The 29th Division was depleted and exhausted. In response to General Hamilton's urgent signals, reinforcements were despatched from England, and on 17th July the 4th (Service) Battalion The South Wales Borderers, element of the 13th Division, disembarked at 'V' Beach, under Lieutenant Colonel F. M. Gillespie. The Battalion was soon in the thick of the fighting in the Suvla offensive, particularly distinguishing itself in the capture of a Turkish position at Damakjelik Bair on 6th August General Sir Ian Hamilton later wrote: 'The rapid success of this movement was largely due to Lieutenant Colonel Gillespie, a big fine man, who commanded the advance guard consisting of his own regiment – a corps worthy of such a leader.' On the following day Gillespie was killed while directing the fire of one of his machine-guns. Meanwhile 2 SWB had been routed round to the Suvla theatre with the 86th Brigade, and on 21st–22nd August were involved in the disastrous attack on Scimitar Hill, when they lost some 300 all ranks – nearly a third of their strength.

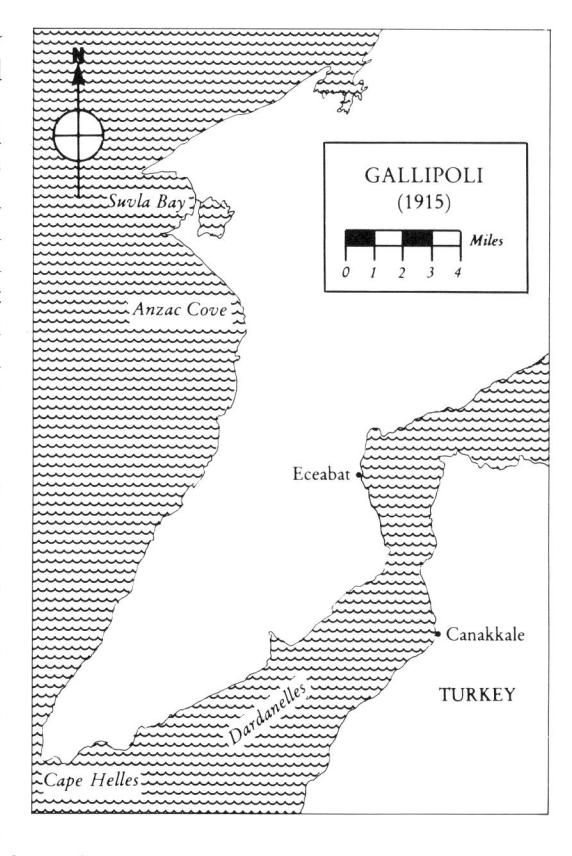

By October it was clear that the Suvla offensive had failed, and High Command were resigned to the fact that the whole Dardanelles venture had been a costly mistake, achieving little but casualties. When evacuation was orderd in December, 214,000 allied troops had been killed or wounded or had died of dysentery and enteric. 2 SWB suffered the shocking loss of nearly 1,600 all ranks; 4 SWB lost 500. In the later stages the 4th and 5th Battalions of The Welch were engaged, and between them they lost 480. Seven Battle Honours were awarded for the operations: the price paid for them was high.

While the Gallipoli debacle was gathering momentum, it fell to the Territorial Battalion of The South Wales Borderers to gain their less costly but unique Great War Battle Honour of 'Aden'. Mobilised and commanded by Lieutenant Colonel Lord Glanusk (late Major the Hon. J. H. R. Bailey, Grenadier Guards), the Brecknock Battalion arrived in the barren outpost in November 1914, their role being to assist the small Indian garrison in warding off potential Turkish threats to the Protectorate. In

Gallipoli, 1915: a view of Suvla Bay and the Salt Lake 'C' Beach. Lala Baba hill is at top left.

July the following year such threats became manifest, and a mobile column with 400 of the Brecknocks was ordered out to the desert post of Lahej, some 45 miles inland. This was the hottest period of Aden's notorious hot-weather season, with day temperatures soaring to 110°F, or even higher. Such conditions would have tried veteran troops accustomed to tropical soldiering. But the Brecknocks were nearly all raw young soldiers fresh from coast defence duties at Pembroke Dock, unused to long marches, and, of course, completely unacclimatised. By the time the little Column gained the desert outpost on their third day of marching, the bulk of the Battalion, officers and men, were smitten with heat exhaustion. When the Turks launched a vigorous attack the following day, only 100-odd men out of the 400 were capable of handling their rifles. Nevertheless the attack was beaten off, with no casualties. But then a supply convoy, approaching with medical stores, reserve ammunition and machine guns, was abandoned by its Arab camel-men and failed to arrive. The position now had to be evacuated, and the men were once more subjected to another exhausting march back to the security of Aden. The Battalion lost thirty soldiers from heat-stroke, three men had been wounded and four were missing, of whom one reappeared after the war, having been a prisoner of the Turks. Two officers and thirty men were invalided home as unfit for further duty. On being relieved by the 5th Buffs, the remainder of the Brecknocks were posted to Mhow in India, where they spent the rest of the war. There had been no heroics in this, the Battalion's only action. Nonetheless, it resulted in a Battle Honour not borne by any other regiment for 1914–18, while many officers and men found their way to 4 SWB in Mesopotamia, where they saw more serious fighting.[8]

In Flanders, the Loos offensive of September 1915 saw battalions of The South Wales Borderers and The Welch heavily engaged in the initial phases. At Hulluch

2 Welch, led by Lieutenant-Colonel A. G. Prothero, distinguished themselves by a dogged attack against fierce opposition, enabling their Brigade to capture an entire German regiment. The Official History remarked: 'The leading of the 2nd Welch after it had broken through . . . which resulted in the surrender of Ritter's force and enabled the 2nd Brigade to advance, was an exhibition of initiative only too rare on 25th September.' On the same day the 9th (Service) Battalion The Welch saw their first action in the same sector, and it was typical of so many gallant but costly actions on the Western Front. Ordered to advance over completely open ground in the face of concentrated machine-gun fire, they did so, and were mown down, losing 13 officers and 221 other ranks within a few minutes. The story was much the same in other sectors; in an attack with the Black Watch, 1 SWB suffered 100 killed and twice that number wounded within half an hour; at the Hohenzollern Redoubt 1 and 6 Welch suffered between them 322 casualties. Among the dead was Lieutenant Colonel Lord Crichton-Stuart, commanding 6 Welch.

The Loos offensive ended in stalemate and there followed months of the morale-

Fatigue parties loading 'Beetles' in the harbour at 'A' West Beach, Suvla Point, twenty-four hours before departure, 19th December 1915. IMPERIAL WAR MUSEUM

ABOVE: *2 SWB on their way to the trenches, Montsuban, October 1916.* IMPERIAL WAR MUSEUM
OPPOSITE: *The memorial to the 38th (Welsh) Division, facing Mametz Wood; Vallee de Gallois, Somme, (May 1987).*

sapping squalor and horrors of trench warfare when lives were sacrificed for the gain of perhaps 100 yards of ground. In July 1916, at Joffre's insistence, Haig launched the first of the bloody Battles of the Somme, with eighteen British divisions attacking on a fourteen-mile frontage. In the first day's fighting the British advanced a mile at the cost of 57,000 men. The bitter Somme struggle continued for four and a half months, when the front line was pushed forward seven miles, and Haig had suffered another 415,000 casualties. Throughout this carnage both The South Wales Borderers and The Welch were engaged with nearly all their Battalions: The South Wales Borderers were represented by their 1st, 2nd, 5th, 6th, 10th and 11th Battalions, besides the three Monmouthshire Battalions; The Welch had their 2nd, 6th, 9th 10th, 13th, 14th, 15th, 16th and 19th Battalions. Thus between them they contributed eighteen Battalions, or some 12,600 soldiers from South Wales (none of the Battalions were fully up to

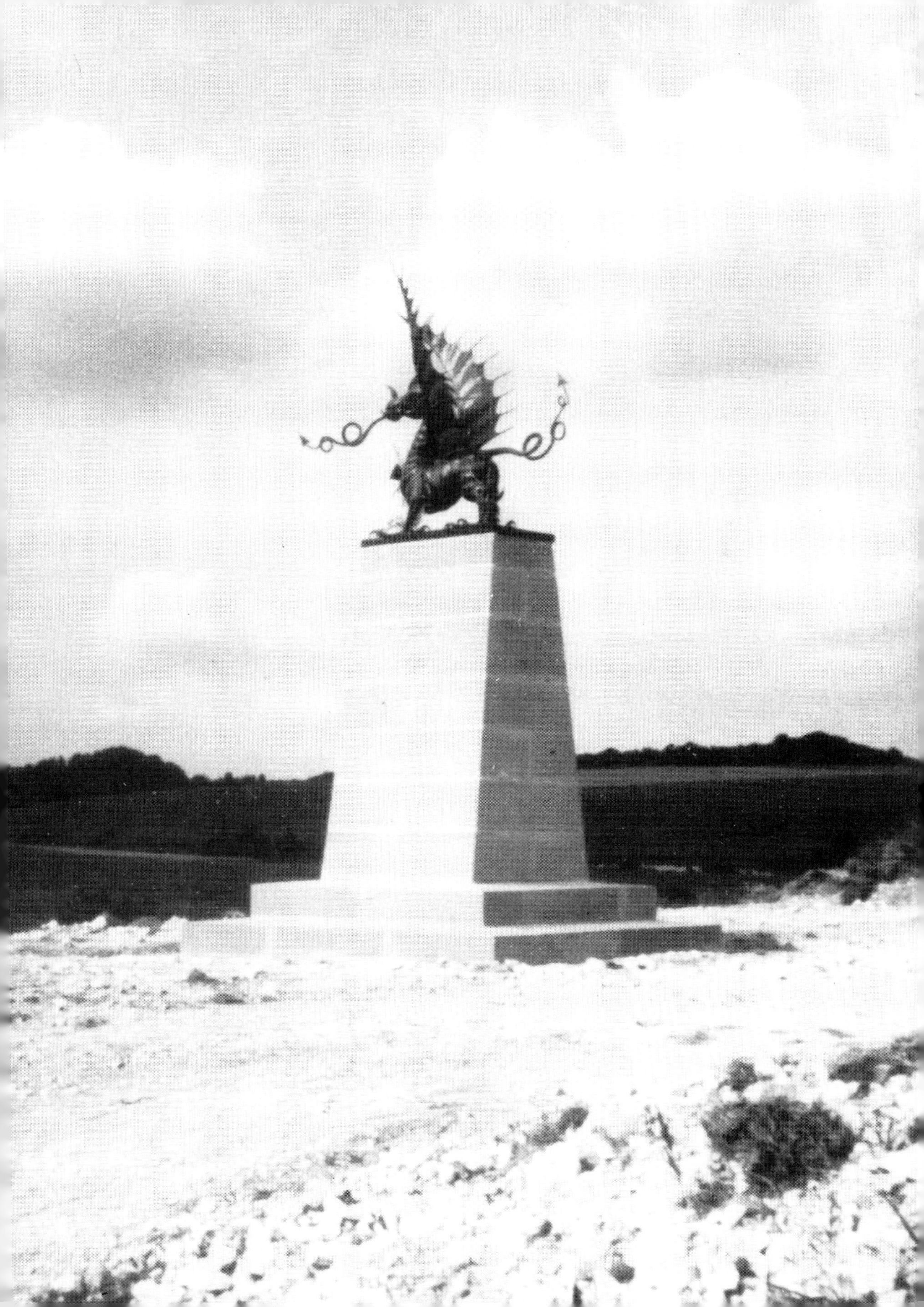

*Private James Finn,
4 SWB; VC, 9th April 1916, Mesopotamia.*

*2nd Lieutenant (Acting Captain) E. Kinghorn
Myles, DSO, The Welch Regiment;
VC, 9th April 1916, Mesopotamia.*

strength). Fewer than two-thirds of these survived to fight on. When the Somme offensive ground to a halt in November, 3,560-odd of both Regiments were lying in Flanders fields, or invalided with wounds, or prisoners-of-war.

On the initial advance, on 1st July, 2 SWB were virtually destroyed when they went 'over the top' near Beaumont Hamel. Before they could cover 500 yards to the German trenches, 235 were killed by machine-gun fire, and that night their casualties had mounted to 399 out of the 578 engaged. On 9th July it was the turn of two service Battalions of The South Wales Borderers and six of The Welch to suffer in the struggle to capture the strongpoint of Mametz Wood. After 48 hours of fierce fighting among thicket and wood, the position was secured, with the capture of 398 prisoners, 5 guns and numerous machine guns, but the cost had been heavy. The two Battalions of The South Wales Borderers lost 223 all ranks, while the six Welch Battalions' casualties totalled 1,673. 10 SWB lost their Commanding Officer, Lieutenant Colonel Wilkinson; in the final stages, Lieutenant Colonel J. A. Edwardes, commanding 13 Welch, was killed leading an attack on a machine-gun nest, and shortly afterwards his Second-in-Command, Major Bound, fell, command devolving on the 22-year-old Captain Johnson. In 14 Welch all senior officers were killed or wounded and the Battalion was led by Lieutenant J. Strange, who gained a DSO. Another young subaltern, Lieutenant J. Edwardes of 13 Welch earned a well-merited DSO by personally capturing a machine-gun post. Lieutenant Cowie, 10 Welch, also captured a machine-gun post, with his platoon, but was killed in doing so. In all, the two days' fight earned The South Wales Borderers and The Welch three DCOs, two MCs and 17MMs.[9]

The scene must now shift to Mesopotamia where General Townshend's attempt to wrest Baghdad from the Turks had been thwarted, and by December 1915 his 11,600 British and Indian troops had withdrawn to Kut-al-Amara on the Tigris. Here they were effectively surrounded and besieged by the Turks, and in February 1916 a relieving force was despatched from Egypt and India. This, the 13th Division, included the 4th (Service) Battalion of The South Wales Borderers and the 8th (Service) Battalion of The Welch, both of whom had been recouping in Egypt after the abortive Gallipoli operations. But The South Wales Borderers could still muster only 400-odd when they embarked at Suez; The Welch were twice that strength with 860.

The attempt to relieve Kut was unsuccessful. Confronted not only by dogged stands by the Turks, but by heat, thirst and tormenting myriads of flies, the Division failed to reach their objective before Townshend was forced to capitulate. In the advance both 4 SWB and 8 Welch were committed to several costly frontal attacks, losing heavily. After Kut fell, on 29th April, The South Wales Borderers had suffered 300-odd casualties, while The Welch were little better off. But these operations saw three VCs added to the Regiment's roll.

On 9th April Private James Finn[10] of The South Wales Borderers gallantly made several forays to succour wounded men lying in front of the Turkish trenches, and managed to carry two back to our lines, all this under continuous rifle and machine-gun fire. In the same action (at Sanna-i-Yat) 2nd Lieutenant Edgar Myles similarly distinguished himself by rescuing wounded men under fire. Myles was at that time attached to The Worcestershire Regiment, but his VC was rightly claimed by the Welch. On 5th April, at Falauyal, Captain Angus Buchanan, 4 SWB, performed yet another similar act of 'most conspicuous bravery' by bringing in wounded. Private Finn died of wounds in Mesopotamia, in March 1917. Captain Buchanan became blind through wounds suffered in the campaign and died at his home in Coleford, Gloucestershire, in 1944. Edgar Myles, promoted Captain, survived until 1977. In his later years he became destitute, and just before his death was discovered living in a converted railway wagon in Devon.

After the fall of Kut the 'Tigris Corps' spent a mainly inactive period regrouping and awaiting further reinforcements from India, the men suffering more from the temperature of 125°F than from the occasional brush with the enemy. The advance continued in December, 4 SWB and 8 Welch, still with the 13th Division, constantly engaged against stout Turkish opposition. On 11th March 1917 the Turks evacuated Baghdad and the British troops marched in to a warm welcome from the inhabitants, who had no love for their Ottoman masters. 4 SWB had the honour of leading the triumphal entry, behind General Sir Stanley Maude and his staff.

While these two service Battalions were confronting Turks in Mesopotamia, five others found themselves opposed to Bulgarians in the rugged mountains of Macedonia.

Captain Angus Buchanan, 4 SWB; VC, 5th April, 1916, Mesopotamia.

Corporal H. W. 'Stokey' Lewis, 11th (Service) Battalion The Welch Regiment (the Cardiff Pals); VC, 22–23 October 1916, Salonika.

'Imagine the hilliest part of Wales', wrote Captain Richards of 11 Welch, 'and extend the horizon to 5000 feet high. Take away all trees, roads and civilization . . . sear it with constant winds, freeze it in winter and scorch it in summer, and you have Macedonia.' In addition to 11 Welch ('Cardiff Pals'),[11] 1 Welch and 7 and 8 SWB joined the allied force at Salonika between October and November 1915, 23 Welch following in early 1916. But it was not until the following year that they saw serious action. When they did, it was the 'Cardiff Pals' who particularly distinguished themselves. In October 1916 the Battalion carried out a series of daring raids on Bulgarian and Austrian positions near Macukovo, capturing many prisoners and gaining valuable intelligence, which brought them congratulations from the Corps commander. It also earned them a VC which has seldom been better merited. Private Hubert Lewis[12] of A Company was one of a raiding party on Bulgarian trenches, and his actions are best described in the Citation (15th December 1916):

> . . . On reaching the enemy trenches, Private Lewis was twice wounded, but refused to be attended to, and showed great gallantry in securing enemy

dugouts. He was again wounded and again refused attendance. At this point three of the enemy were observed to be approaching and Private Lewis immediately attacked them, single handed, capturing all. Subsequently, during the retirement, he went to the assistance of a wounded man, and under heavy shell and rifle fire brought him to our lines, on reaching which he collapsed. Private Lewis showed throughout a brilliant example of courage, endurance and devotion to duty.

Lewis also received the Medaille Militaire and, surviving World War I, went on to serve in World War II as a sergeant in the Milford Haven Home Guard. He died in 1977, and was buried at Milford Haven.

As with Slim's 'Forgotten Army' in the Burma campaign of World War II, the operations of the allied forces in Macedonia went almost unnoticed at home. Yet in September 1918 there came one of the fiercest and most massive clashes of the four years of hostilities, when 28 allied divisions (four British) were launched against some 500,000 Bulgarians in the Doiran area. The dominating feature here was the rugged mountain named Grand Couronné, its heavily fortified crags rising to more than 3,000 ft. The brunt of the assault on this daunting strongpoint fell to the three Welsh service Battalions of the 67th Brigade – 11 RWF, 7 SWB and 11 Welch.

On 17th September a preliminary artillery bombardment with HE and gas shell succeeded in destroying some of the wire entanglements, but the gas lingered on, and next morning was to cause discomfort and exhaustion to the attacking infantry.

The Brigade advanced soon after dawn on the 18th. They immediately came under ferocious fire from artillery and machine guns. 11 RWF reached their first objective, but were then counter-attacked and driven back with many casualties. 7 SWB struggled to the lower slopes of the Grand Couronné, only to be met by a withering cross-fire from machine guns which bowled over whole platoons as they tried to extricate themselves from the wire entanglements. When the attack was called off, only some 50 survivors out of the original 470 managed to reach our own trenches; of these nearly half were suffering from the effects of the previous day's gas shells and had to be evacuated to hospital. Fourteen of the seventeen officers were missing, many known to have been wounded, among them the Commanding Officer, Lieutenant Colonel D. Burges. Only one of the three surviving officers remained unwounded. 11 Welch fared no better. Ordered to assault two features below the Grand Couronné, they too were almost destroyed by the murderous machine guns. 'By about 8 a.m. the Battalion had practically ceased to exist', wrote Lieutenant Colonel L. H. Trist, commanding. 'No reports came back and none of the messages I sent forward succeeded in getting through the storm of machine-gun fire. Not a single straggler and very few walking wounded returned from the assaulting companies.' Of the 15 officers and 409 other ranks who went into action on that morning, only one unwounded officer and 125 men were left by nightfall. Five officers and 64 men were killed, 8 officers and 217 wounded.

Meanwhile, 8 SWB had been in reserve and did not come into action until dawn on the 19th when they supported the 9th King's Own (Royal Lancaster) in an assault on one of the numerous rocky knolls, known as 'P4½'. The King's Own suffered as

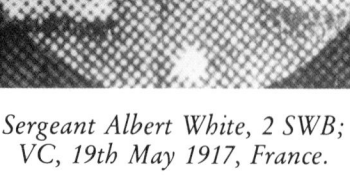

*Sergeant Albert White, 2 SWB;
VC, 19th May 1917, France.*

*Sergeant Ivor Rees, 11 SWB;
VC, 31st July 1917, Belgium.*

heavily as 7 SWB and 11 Welch, losing all but sixty of their number. But 8 SWB escaped relatively lightly with a total of fifty casualties including three killed.

The Battle of the Doiran sector dragged on until 22nd September when the Bulgarians broke and retreated, but our Welsh Regiments saw no further serious action before the enemy surrendered on 30th September. In all, the British forces suffered more than 5,000 casualties, but they captured over 100,000 prisoners, 2,000 guns and huge numbers of other weapons.

The two-day Couronné fight resulted in numerous decorations for 7 SWB and 11 Welch. For his great gallantry in personally leading attacks, Lieutenant Colonel Daniel Burges, commanding 7 SWB, was awarded the VC. Unhappily for The South Wales Borderers, however, this could not be credited to the Regiment, for Burges belonged to The Gloucestershire Regiment and was only attached to The South Wales Borderers. But 7 SWB received one DSO, three MCs, three DCMs and 6 MMs, while the Battalion itself was awarded the unit decoration of the Croix de Guerre – the only such award in the British Salonika force. 11 Welch received three DSOs, two MCs and a Croix de Guerre.

The Great War 1914–18

Back on the Western Front, both regular Battalions of The South Wales Borderers, the 2nd Battalion of The Welch and thirteen service battalions fought and suffered in the 1917 Flanders offensive known as 3rd Ypres, which became bogged down in the shell-torn mud of Passchendaele. On 19th May, D Company of 2 SWB were supporting the Inniskillings and the Border Regiment in an attack near Monchy le Preux when they were held up by a nest of machine guns. Sergeant Albert White promptly dashed forward to the nearest one, shot three of the Germans covering it, bayoneted a fourth and was almost on top of the gun itself when he was hit by a burst at pointblank range and fell riddled with bullets. This self-sacrifice momentarily diverted the enemy's attention, but it proved in vain, for renewed fire halted the attack and the shattered remnants had to take cover in shell craters until nightfall. Of the 116 South Wales Borderers men who went over the top only 61 got back to the Battalion, and half of these were wounded. But Sergeant White's bravery was subsequently recognised by the posthumous award of the VC (gazetted on 27th June 1917).

On 31st July there was heavy fighting for the capture of Pilckem Ridge, in which a German Guards division was smashed and an important objective gained. In the initial assault 10, 13, 14 and 15 Welch pushed forward against severe opposition, overrunning pill boxes and trenches and capturing some 300 prisoners. They gained their objective, but at the cost of 804 killed and wounded. The next phase was the crossing of the Steenbeck rivulet, strongly defended by pill-boxes and machine-gun emplacements in ruined buildings. 11 SWB were in the thick of this action, and at one point C Company was held up by close-range fire from an emplacement. Sergeant Ivor Rees (ex-steelworker from Llanelli) worked his platoon by short rushes to the rear of the position, then personally charged the gun; killing two of the team and silencing it. He next turned his attention to a nearby pill-box, hurling grenades through the slits, until two officers and thirty men emerged with their hands up, having left several dead inside. His well-earned VC was gazetted on 14th September.[13]

There were other heroics in the Battle of Pilckem Ridge which unaccountably went unrewarded. 2nd Lieutenant James Vizer led his platoon to silence a troublesome machine gun, capturing it together with one officer and fifty men. No award was forthcoming. At the Steenbeck crossing, Sergeant Brown of 16 Welch overran a German post and held it with his platoon against fierce counter-attacks for three days, during which all but four of his men were killed or wounded. In his Great War history, General Marden relates that Sergeant Brown was recommended for the VC 'but unfortunately was killed the day after his company was relieved'. Why his death should have precluded a posthumous award is not at all clear. But the four survivors of the platoon received the MM.

In October 1917 the 3rd Ypres offensive floundered to a halt in the quagmires around the village of Passchendaele, a name that has gone down in history as signifying mud, blood and appalling casualties. The ten Battalions of The South Wales Borderers and The Welch Regiment were in action almost continuously throughout the terrible three and a half months, and nobly acquitted themselves, as is borne out by the impressive total of immediate awards for bravery and distinguished service. In addition to the two VCs, between them these Battalions earned 9 DSOs, 27 MCs, 18 DCMs and

Cambrai, 1917.   THE TANK MUSEUM, BOVINGTON

127 MMs, besides 3 Croix de Guerre and 6 Medailles Militaire. But the cost was shocking: 739 officers and men killed, 2,453 wounded.[14]

There was little respite for the mangled regiments of Passchendaele. In November (1917) Haig launched the massive offensive of Cambrai, designed to pierce the Hindenburg Line and exploit northwards across the Sensee River to Valenciennes. Today this battle, which lasted from 20th November to 5th December, is remembered chiefly as the first operation in which massed tanks were employed – in fact 476 of them, or nearly the whole of the newly-formed Tank Corps. As surprise was a planned element, there was none of the usual preliminary artillery bombardment. In the early hours, waves of the steel monsters smashed through the wire entanglements on a six-mile front, overran trenches and were followed by six divisions of infantry who quickly overcame the demoralised enemy. 2 SWB in the 87th Brigade were among the first line of infantry and by nightfall had gained a position behind the Hindenburg Line with the loss of some eighty killed and wounded. But they had captured sixty prisoners together with two field guns and numerous machine guns. In fact the first phase had been a complete success: the advance had penetrated nearly 4 miles along the 6-mile front, while 6,000 prisoners and 100 guns were taken. The next two days saw The South Wales Borderers fighting desperately to hold a position by the Scheldt Canal where the Germans had massed reserves, and the Battalion suffered another 250 casualties.

Over on the left of the advance lay the strongly-held forest of Bourlon Wood which had to be taken before further progress could be made. The 40th Division was detailed for this task, and one of its Brigades was the 'all-Welsh' 119th, comprising 19 RWF, 12 SWB and 17 Welch. The 600 acres of thick wood and dense undergrowth became a death-trap as the struggling infantry were assaulted by artillery and machine-gun fire. 'The din of battle within the wood was awe-inspiring', wrote Colonel Whitton,[15] 'In front trees were falling wholesale from the shells of our guns, while around and behind German projectiles were crashing everywhere. The roar was amplified by the ceaseless chatter of enemy machine guns.' Losing men for every acre of wood gained, the 119th Brigade pushed stubbornly on until they had gained a ridge on the northern extremity of the wood, where they could advance no further. Here on 'Welsh Ridge', the remnants dug in and counted their losses. Between them, 12 SWB and 17 and 18 Welch had lost 1,077 all ranks killed and wounded. 12 SWB were the heaviest sufferers: 10 officers and 123 men were killed, 12 officers and 243 wounded.

Bourlon Wood was captured, and the 'Welsh' Brigade had played a significant part. But in the two days' fighting the 40th Division paid the appalling price of over 4,000 casualties.

This sacrifice proved in vain. By 28th November the Germans, recovered from their initial shock, had regrouped with their massive reserves, and on the 30th they put in a devastating counter-attack which regained nearly all their lost ground. During this onslaught 2 SWB distinguished themselves by tenaciously holding on to their position between Marcoing and Masnieres with enemy in front and rear. They were, writes Atkinson, 'inspired by the splendid fearlessness of their C.O., who exposed himself continuously and set a magnificent example'. Lieutenant Colonel Geoffrey Raikes was awarded a Bar to the DSO he had already won at Beaumont Hamel the previous year. In the same action his younger brother, Wilfred (acting Major), won the MC. When 2 SWB were finally relieved on 3rd December, all that remained to march out were the Commanding Officer, his Adjutant, the Medical Officer and seventy-three other ranks.

Today the Battle Honour 'Cambrai' is borne by every cavalry and infantry regiment of the British Army except the Gurkhas (and, of course, those units raised after World War I). But The South Wales Borderers and The Welch Regiment contributed as great a share as any – and more than some – to the dreadful cost.

While the grim battles were being fought out on the Western Front, another offensive was in spate in the Middle East theatre, where three British Divisions were attempting to drive the Turks out of Egypt and Palestine. With the 53rd Infantry Division were the 4th and 5th Battalions The Welch Regiment, who had been refitting in Egypt after the Gallipoli disaster. The first major confrontation came with the attempt to capture Gaza, in March 1917.

The 1st Battle of Gaza (on 26th March) failed through a breakdown of communications, but 4 and 5 Welch, together with the 4th Cheshire and 7 RWF, put in a spirited attack to capture a Turkish position at Ali el Muntar. In his Special Order of the Day, Lieutenant General Dobell praised the 'magnificent feat' of the 53rd Division, adding, 'The brunt of the fighting fell as usual on the infantry, and the Welsh Division more than lived up to the traditions of the British Army.' After another unsuccessful attempt to take Gaza, General Sir Edmund Allenby replaced General Murray as Supreme Commander, and it was this thrusting cavalryman with his Desert Mounted Corps who finally vanquished the Turks and sealed the fate of their Ottoman Empire. By a series of clever feints Gaza was captured in November 1917, 4 and 5 Welch being heavily engaged after the seizure of Beersheba during the first phase. By now another Battalion of The Welch – the 24th – had joined the offensive; this had been formed in Egypt the previous February, from the dismounted 1st Pembrokeshire and 1st Glamorgan Yeomanry. But, being in the 74th Division, they saw little of their Welsh comrades of the 53rd. Their first action came on 31st October when they and 25 RWF gallantly stormed strong Turkish trenches, carried them, and advanced nearly two miles into enemy territory.

All three Battalions were engaged in the arduous pursuit to Jerusalem, during which the mountainous terrain proved more formidable than the enemy. '26 miles of rocky road . . .', recorded the War Diary of 24 Welch on 29th November '. . . men exhausted, enormous difficulty in taking over outpost line in jumble of steep rocky hills falling precipitously into deep wadis and rising in places to over 2000 feet. Only means of progress was by native tracks . . . along which only one man could move at a time.'

General Allenby and his General Headquarters entered the Holy City on 11th December. But he had been preceded by 4 and 5 Welch. Unknown to the General, the Turks had evacuated the city on 7th December, and when the two Welch Battalions, with two squadrons of the Westminster Dragoons Yeomanry, headed the advance the following morning, they were met at the walls of Jerusalem not by enemy fire, but by enthusiastic throngs of inhabitants who were obviously pleased to see their Turkish oppressors replaced by British soldiers.

Although the loss of Jerusalem was a severe blow to the Turks' morale, they were by no means beaten, and the Palestine campaign was to be fought out for another year. With reinforcements from India, and with Lawrence and his Arabs creating havoc in the rear, Allenby pushed on through Jordan and into Syria. While his Yeomanry and Indian cavalry continued to display remarkable mobility and dash, putting in several spectacular charges with the sword, as always it was the infantry who bore the brunt of the slogging matches which resulted in the capture of successive strategic objectives. The present Regiment's Battle Honours 'Jericho', 'Tell 'Asur', 'Megiddo' and 'Nablus', bear tribute to the no less remarkable (if less spectacular) exertions of the 4th, 5th and 24th Battalions The Welch Regiment. The 24th Battalion, however, were deprived of any part in the final pursuit, for in March 1918 they were withdrawn with their 74th Division to France. By August, the 4th and 5th Battalions had been so depleted by battle casualties and sickness (sandfly fever was the besetting scourge) that they were amalgamated as the 4th/5th Battalion. On 21st September they took part in the last infantry action of the campaign, between Tell 'Asur and Nablus, which resulted in the virtual destruction of a Turkish division. Their 53rd Division was retained in the area while elements of the Desert Mounted Corps swept on to capture Aleppo and with it 75,000 prisoners and 360 guns. On 31st October the Turks conceded defeat and the Palestine campaign was at an end. It had cost the three Battalions of The Welch Regiment 258 officers and men killed and 922 wounded. But it also earned them five DSOs, thirteen MCs, eight DCMs and twenty-four MMs.

The end of the campaign was also the end of the war for 4 and 5 Welch. In November they were withdrawn to the UK, in time for the Armistice and demobilisation.

Meanwhile, on the Western Front the collapse of the British offensive at Cambrai was followed by another winter of stalemate, with Allies and Germans enduring bitter months in the trenches, casualties steadily mounting from artillery 'hates', raiding parties and patrol activity. At home the Prime Minister, Lloyd George, had conceived an antipathy towards Haig, and when the latter demanded 605,000 reinforcements only 100,000 were sanctioned, which precluded any possibility of a determined British offensive.

Suffering the 1917–18 'winter of discontent' were seven Battalions of The South Wales Borderers and five of The Welch. Of these only three were regular (1 and 2 SWB, 2 Welch) but by now there was little difference in the make-up of regular, territorial or service battalions, for the devastating casualties of the Somme, Ypres and the rest had seen all filled with raw young officers and men, many in their teens, and with minimal training. When a draft of replacements joined 1 SWB in February 1918 they were reported to be 'mostly boys'. New subalterns had, perhaps six months previously, been cadets in their school OTCs. Nevertheless, the spirit and steadiness of these youths was remarkable. In a large-scale German raid on 1 SWB's trenches in March, 18-year-old 2nd Lieutenant J. E. Seager (joined in December) 'did splendid work, moving across the open from post to post under heavy fire, directing the men's fire most effectively and inspiring them by his magnificent example' (Atkinson). He was rewarded with the MC. In the same action the newly-promoted Lance Corporal Turton gained the DCM for similar displays of courage. 2nd Lieutenant A. J Owen (19) joined 10 Welch in August 1917, and in January 1918 won his MC for a daring raid on a German trench.

In January of the new year all British infantry brigades were reduced from four to three battalions, and for The South Wales Borderers this meant the disbandment of their 11th and 12th (Service) Battalions, and for The Welch, of their 10th and 16th. Most of the officers and men were transferred to other battalions of their Regiments, the remainder being consigned to pick-and-shovel 'entrenching battalions' – essential but unrewarding chores.

While the allied commanders were bickering about strategy, and Lloyd George was quarrelling with his Commander-in-Chief, the Germans had been massing immense reserves for a spring offensive, which in March burst with unprecedented ferocity on the British sector between Arras and the Oise. By the end of April, when Haig issued his famous 'Backs to the Wall' Order of the Day, the British forces had lost 240,000 men and the Germans were within 40 miles of the Franco–Belgian coast. But they themselves had lost more than 350,000, their reserves were dwindling, and the Allies, stiffened by more American and Canadian reinforcements, were preparing for the counter-offensive which was to end the war.

During this final phase in which the Germans were driven back beyond their vaunted Hindenburg Line, The South Wales Borderers and The Welch were engaged throughout and played a worthy part – at a cost of steadily mounting casualty figures.

Between them the two Regiments deployed fourteen Battalions[16] in the fierce struggles between August and November: struggles that finally brought Germany to her knees, and earned for the Regiment such costly Battle Honours as 'Beau Revoir', 'St Quentin Canal', 'Sambre', 'Hindenburg Line' and many more.

Today we view such Honours with pride, as symbolic of the contribution to final victory made by those fourteen Battalions. But they do not immediately call to mind the innumerable examples of splendid leadership, courage, tenacity and acts of heroism 'beyond the call of duty' which lie behind the names.

After the capture of the Beau Revoir line in October 1918, the 10th Battalion The South Wales Borderers took part in the attack on the nearby strongpoint of Villers-Outreaux. As so often, the advance across open ground was temporarily checked by murderous machine-gun fire. Thereupon CSM John Williams of B Company acted on his own initiative.

The Great War 1914–18

WO2 John Henry Williams, DCM, MM (and Bar), 10 SWB; VC, 7–8th October 1918, France.

Major General D. G. Johnson, CB, DSO (and Bar), MC, who gained his VC on 4th November 1918, commanding 2nd Royal Sussex Regiment. He later became Colonel of The South Wales Borderers.

> ... Observing his company was suffering heavy casualties from an enemy machine gun, he ordered a Lewis gun to engage it, and went forward under heavy fire to the flank of the enemy post, which he rushed single-handed, capturing fifteen of the enemy. These prisoners, realising that Williams was alone, turned on him and one of them gripped his rifle. He succeeded in breaking away and bayoneted five enemy, whereupon the remainder again surrendered. By this gallant action and total disregard of personal danger he was the means of enabling not only his own company but also those on the flank to advance.

Thus ran the Citation for the VC with which CSM Williams was presented by King George V on 22nd February 1919. Williams had already won the DCM at Mametz Wood, the MM at Pilkem Ridge, and a Bar to the latter at Armentieres. All these medals were presented at the same Investiture, marking the first occasion on which the King had decorated the same man four times in one day. And with the award of the Medaille Militaire from the French, John Henry Williams became the most-decorated Welsh soldier in history.[17]

On 4th November the 1st Battalion The South Wales Borderers fought their last action of the war – the forcing of the Sambre-et-Oise Canal and capture of the village of Catillon. With them in the 2nd Infantry Brigade were the 2nd Battalion The Royal Sussex, whose Commanding Officer was well known to them. He was Lieutenant Colonel D. G. Johnson, who had been transferred from 1 SWB to take temporary command of the Sussex the previous February. While 1 SWB, with 1 Glosters, successfully took their objective, the Sussex and accompanying RE bridging party were assaulted by heavy artillery and machine-gun fire which held up the Sappers' operations.

At this moment Lt-Colonel Johnson arrived, and realising the situation, at once collected men to man the bridges and assist the Royal Engineers, and personally led the assault. In spite of his efforts, heavy fire again broke up the assaulting and bridging parties. Without any hesitation he again reorganised the platoons and led them at the lock, this time succeeding in effecting a crossing, after which all went well. During all this time Lt-Colonel Johnson was under a very heavy fire, which though it nearly decimated the assaulting columns, left him untouched. His conduct was a fine example of great valour, coolness and intrepidity which, added to his splendid leadership and great offensive spirit that he had inspired in his battalion, were entirely responsible for the successful crossing.

Colonel C. V. Trower, CMG, of the 24th Regiment. He joined the Regiment in 1876 and fought in the Kafir, Zulu and Boer Wars. He trained and commanded the 5th Battalion The South Wales Borderers and at 59 years of age took the Battalion to France, where he spent three hard years in the trenches before bringing them home again in 1918. 'We shall never see his like again.'

The above VC Citation was gazetted in January 1919. Colonel Dudley Graham Johnson had spent all his previous service (since 1903) with The South Wales Borderers, and although his supreme award was gained while with another regiment, it is justifiably added to The South Wales Borderer's roll. He had already won a DSO with

Bar, and the MC. Serving during World War II, he retired as Major General in 1944 and in the same year became Colonel of his old Regiment.[18]

Deeds of individual heroism and gallantry naturally shine like beacons in a regiment's records. But we ought not to forget the many other displays of corporate courage, or 'fighting spirit', which have won battles, but earned little public acclaim. The name 'Mortho Wood' will surely mean nothing to present-day readers. But in October 1918 this heavily-defended objective, near Cambrai, was attacked in two days' dogged fighting by the 38th Division, which included three service Battalions of The Welch Regiment. It was carried with the capture of some 500 prisoners, 20 guns and numerous machine guns, but 'Casualties were unfortunately heavy', reported Major General Cubitt, Divisional Commander. Among them were 447 officers and men of 14 and 15 Welch. Later General Cubitt wrote to their Brigade Commander expressing his 'unbounded admiration of the bravery and determination of the troops' and went on to 'thank and congratulate personally the 14th and 15th Welch for their brilliant courage and determination and most skillful fighting throughout the action. No praise can be too high for their performance.' Such instances, recorded only in War Diaries and official documents, were multiplied many times by many battalions.

After the eleventh day of the eleventh month of 1918 it fell to only four Battalions of The South Wales Borderers and The Welch Regiment to take part in the triumphant march across the German frontier into the Rhineland. These were 1 and 2 SWB and 2 and 6 Welch, who were to form elements of the Army of Occupation. The remaining Battalions were dispersed in far-flung theatres: in Macedonia, Turkey, Mesopotamia, Egypt and India, besides the war-ravaged landscape of France and Flanders. In the same theatres, and elsewhere, lay those who 'gave our today for your tomorrow': 5,777 officers and men of The South Wales Borderers, 7,779 of The Welch Regiment. Their names are inscribed in the Books of Remembrance in the Cathedrals of Brecon and Llandaff.

Notes

[1] Atkinson, C. T. *The History of The South Wales Borderers 1914–1918* (1931). Marden, Major General Sir Thomas O. *The History of The Welch Regiment, Part II 1914–1918* (1932).

[2] There was an unhappy incident at St Quentin on 27th August when some 500 men staged a 'sit-down' and were only persuaded to move by the efforts of Major Tom Bridges of the 4th Dragoon Guards with his 'Toy Drum and Tin Whistle'.

[3] Gazetted 23rd November 1914. Fuller, of Laugharne, Carmarthenshire, had enlisted in 1 Welch in 1902. Badly wounded at Gheluvelt, he was invalided home and discharged unfit for further service in 1915. He died at Swansea in 1974, aged 90. Captain Mark Haggard was the nephew of the novelist Sir Rider Haggard.

[4] The inscription and tablet were designed by the celebrated architect Sir Edwin Lutyens, and unveiled by Major General Sir Thomas Marden, Colonel of the Regiment, on Armistice Day 1924.

[5] *The British Campaigns in France and Flanders, 1915*, by Arthur Conan Doyle (1917).

[6] Many of those 'missing' eventually rejoined. The actual casualties on 24th/25th May were six officers and 123 other ranks killed; 12 officers and 266 other ranks wounded. Among the wounded was Lieutenant Colonel T. O. Marden.

[7] 1st King's Own Scottish Borderers, 1st Border Regiment, 1st Royal Inniskilling Fusiliers.

[8] Eventually some 300 officers and men were transferred to other units in India and took part in the 3rd (and last) Afghan War of 1919. It was only in November of that year that the remnants of the Brecknockshire Battalion arrived home for disbandment.

[9] The Battalions engaged at Mametz Wood were: The South Wales Borderers, 10th and 11th; The Welch Regiment, 10th, 13th, 14th, 15th, 16th, 19th. All these were service, or hostilities-only Battalions, consisting mostly of men from Cardiff, Swansea and the Rhondda.

[10] In Army records the name is incorrectly spelt 'Fynn'.

[11] 11 Welch were recruited exclusively in Cardiff.

[12] In the Citation the forename is erroneously given as Herbert.

[13] Having served as CSM in the 2nd Carmarthenshire Home Guard in World War II, Ivor Rees died at his home in Llanelli in March 1967.

[14] These figures are compiled from C. T. Atkinson's and General Sir Thomas Marden's wartime histories of The South Wales Borderers and The Welch. The Battalions engaged were: 2, 10, 11 SWB and 2 Mons; 10, 13, 14, 15, 16 and 19 Welch.

[15] Whitton, Lieutenant Colonel F. E. *History of the 40th Division* (1926).

[16] These were: The South Wales Borderers: 1, 2, 5, 6, 10; The Welch Regiment: 2, 6, 9, 13, 14, 15, 18, 19, 24.

[17] Severely wounded, Williams was discharged unfit for active service in October 1918, and was employed as commissionaire in an Ebbw Vale steelworks. During World War II he served as Captain in the Ebbw Vale Home Guard. He died in March 1953, aged 67, and was buried in Ebbw Vale cemetery.

[18] He was one of only two Colonels on the present Regiment's roll to have won the VC, the other being General Sir Alexander Cobbe, who gained his in Somaliland in 1902.

CHAPTER FOURTEEN

Interlude (1919–39)

'Battalion non-existent except on paper...'. So ran one of the first post-war entries in the 1st Battalion The South Wales Borderers' Digest of Services (May 1919). Demobilisation had reduced all regular infantry battalions down to minimal cadres: when 2 SWB arrived at Brecon in June they were represented by the Commanding Officer (Lieutenant Colonel G. T. Raikes), four subalterns and forty-four other ranks. 1 and 2 Welch, at Pembroke Dock, were similar skeletons. All service battalions had ceased to exist.

By the end of the year, however, the four regular Battalions had been made up to establishment with transfers from other regiments and drafts of new recruits from the Depots. It was purely coincidental that the 1st Battalion the 24th (late '2nd Warwickshire') should receive 235 men from The (1st) Royal Warwickshire Regiment. 1 Welch were joined by drafts from The Royal Welch Fusiliers, among them a goat kindly presented by the 7th Battalion and known as O. O. Jenkins. Thus up to strength, the Regiments could recommence peacetime soldiering, and by 1920 the two were widely dispersed on their postings. The 1st Battalion The South Wales Borderers received an unwelcome posting to southern Ireland where the pre-Republic 'Troubles' were in full spate. This term was really a euphemism for the all-out campaign of murder and terrorist outrages perpetrated by the Sinn Feiners, forerunners of the even more barbaric IRA and INLA gangsters to be confronted by a later generation of British soldiers. However, the Battalion was located in County Meath, one of the less disturbed areas, and their escort and patrol duties were largely uneventful. But on one occasion brevet Lieutenant-Colonel R. F. Gross, Second-in-Command, was nearly blown up by a mine which exploded only seconds after his lorry had passed. While this has a ring of modern times, the sequel would be unlikely in the 1980s. The next day a young Irishman approached the Colonel with profuse apologies. It had all been a mistake, he explained: the mine had not been intended for the soldiers at all, it was meant to get the 'bloody police'. The two-year spell passed with only one casualty: a sergeant whose strangled body was discovered in a river. In February 1922 the Battalion left Ireland for the more peaceful environs of Hampshire, at Blackdown. Meanwhile,

"REFORCE"
(INDEPENDENT BRIGADE, CHINA)
Hdqrs 15th Inf. Bde
4th Light Brigade R. A.
56th Field Company R. E.
15th Inf. Bde Signal Section
2nd Battn Scots Guards
1st Battn The Queen's Royal Regt
2nd Battn The Welch Regt
1st Bn The Northamptonshire Regt
No. 38 M. T. Coy, R. A. S. C.
Supply Unit, R. A. S. C.
10th Field Ambulance
'Y' General Hospital
B2 Fd Sec. Ordnance Mobile Workshop
Base Depot, R. A. O. C.

HONG KONG
CHRISTMAS
1927

Reforce Christmas card, 1927. In May 1927, 2 Welch arrived in Hong Kong to join Reforce, a special China Defence Force formed as a result of the serious situation then existing in North China. The Battalion saw service with the force in Shanghai and Wei-Hai-Wei before moving on to Singapore in November 1928.

the 2nd Battalion The South Wales Borderers had been soldiering in the untroubled station of Jhansi in Central India. Also in India, but further north at Ferozepur in the Punjab, were the 1st Battalion The Welch Regiment, who had left their 2nd Battalion home based at Pembroke Dock.

In June 1920 the 2nd Battalion was posted to Dublin, where it remained for nearly two and a half years. Although there were no serious incidents, the arduous tasks of day and night patrolling, arms searches, and escort duties among a sullen and largely hostile populace were severe tests of discipline and morale. 'Nevertheless the troops behaved with a loyalty and impartiality which drew the admiration of all with whom they came in contact', Captain J. de Courcy recorded. After the creation of the Irish Free State, on 14th December 1922 the Welch handed over their Dublin barracks to Irish soldiers and marched out of the city with drums beating, bayonets fixed and Colours flying.

The following few years brought notable events and developments. Among them was official recognition of The Welch Regiment's dogged insistence on their 'c' spelling, which for nearly ninety years had been as doggedly rejected by authority. On 27th January 1920 the following letter was addressed to 'The Officers Commanding 1st and 2nd Bns. The Welch Regiment':

> The War Office
> Whitehall
> London, S.W.1
>
> Sir,
> I am directed to inform you that the spelling of the word 'Welch' in the titles of The Royal Welsh Fusiliers and The Welsh Regiment is approved, but that the change is to take effect at once only in regard to the spelling in the Army List and official correspondence.
> I am to say that large stocks of cap badges, titles etc. are on hand and that immediate change cannot take place until such stocks are used up.
> I am to add that no public expense can be sanctioned in connection with the Colours until new ones are required in the ordinary course.
> I am, Sir
> Your obedient Servant
> (Sd) F. J. MOON, Captain
> *Staff Captain*
> For Director of Personal Services

No doubt this letter was as gratifying to The Royal Welch Fusiliers as it was to all ranks of The Welch, for the former had unofficially persisted with their 'c' since 1727.

Two years later it was the turn of The South Wales Borderers to enjoy even keener satisfaction, and pride. On 11th August 1922 *The London Gazette* announced that the King had been graciously pleased to appoint HRH Edward, Prince of Wales, as Colonel in Chief of the Regiment. This honour was doubly gratifying, for not only was this the first time in their history that they had been honoured with a Colonel-in-Chief, but for a Welsh regiment who could be more fitting in that appointment than the Prince of Wales? Moreover, the charisma and winning manners of the handsome young Prince had made him the most popular public figure of the day. In reply to a message of appreciation by General Sir Alexander Cobbe, VC (Colonel of the Regiment), the Prince's Private Secretary (Sir Alexander Lascelles) wrote from St James's Palace on 31st August to say that 'His Royal Highness is himself deeply proud of his association

HRH Prince Edward, Colonel in Chief, The South Wales Borderers

with your distinguished Regiment, and hopes sincerely that an opportunity of making its acquaintance may present itself before long.'[1]

In fact, the opportunity did not present itself until 1928, when the Prince, on his way to a tour of East Africa, called in on the 2nd Battalion at Aden 'and played tennis with the officers and watched the final of the inter-Company football . . .'. Two years later, the 1st Battalion in Egypt were able to welcome their Colonel-in-Chief, who paid them an informal visit in Cairo citadel. Typically, the Prince expressly declined any formalities or ceremonial. He watched the men at work in clean fatigue dress, asked to see the four Rugby balls with which the Battalion had won four successive Army Cups (1925–8), and in the Mess expressed keen interest in the Isandhlwana Colours. He departed to rousing cheers from the men lining the route.

On 20th January 1936, King George V was eased out of his suffering, and this world, by his private physician, and the Prince succeeded to the throne as King Edward VIII. With enhanced pride The South Wales Borderers learned that His Majesty had graciously agreed to continue as their Colonel-in-Chief. But the pride was short-lived. On 10th December that same year, the King announced his abdication and left the country for France, there to join his American bride-to-be, the controversial Mrs Simpson. In renouncing the throne he also renounced his Colonelcies-in-Chief. And so, after the brief span of fourteen years the Regiment was bereft of its only Colonel-in-Chief, and remained so for the remainder of its corporate existence. As for The Welch Regiment, they were one of the few who throughout their loyal services never succeeded in acquiring a Colonel-in-Chief, royal or otherwise.

In the preceding pages there have been many references to the Regimental Journals. These 'family magazines' form an invaluable source for the regimental historian, for amidst much trivial gossip, funny stories, cricket and Rugby scores and so forth, they offer contributions of great historical interest, not to be found even in published regimental histories. In fact, the following notes are culled from the pages of *The Men of Harlech*, to which, and to *XXIV The Journal of The South Wales Borderers*, the author gladly acknowledges his debt.

The Welch Regiment were the first of The Royal Regiment of Wales's antecedents to produce a Journal, albeit with very humble beginnings. In March 1893 the 2nd Battalion at Trimulgherry, in southern India, published the first issue of a 'Newspaper

1 SWB, the Citadel, Cairo, 1930.

for the men of the 2nd Battalion The Welch Regiment', the laudable object being to 'bring all ranks into close companionship and to foster Esprit de Corps', as the editorial announced. The half-dozen stapled sheets cost 3 annas (about 1½d.). The title chosen was that which the present Regiment has inherited, *The Men of Harlech*. Two years later the 'newspaper' had expanded to eighteen pages, and in 1899 it paid deference to the Welsh-speakers of the Regiment (of whom there were many) by including the two-page *Y Golofn Cymraeg* – The Welsh Column. After a lapse during the Great War, it was resuscitated in 1924 as the official Journal of The Welch Regiment, professionally printed and illustrated. There was another gap between 1939 and 1946, and then production continued regularly until it became *The Journal of The Royal Regiment of Wales* in 1969, with the original title.[2]

The South Wales Borderers were rather more laggard with their Journal. The first issue, in the form of a modest news-sheet, appeared in Newport in 1926, and the editorial stated: 'It has been suggested that some small pamphlet such as this which gives shortly the Regimental news of the year, would be welcomed by many Old Comrades.' Unlike The Welch Regiment's prototype, this one was thus directed primarily to the Old Comrades, and was in fact produced by their own Club, and issued free. Later a wider readership within the Regiment was aimed at, and a charge of 2d. per copy was made. In June 1932 the humble 'pamphlet' was transformed into a well-illustrated magazine, printed by *The Western Mail & Echo*, Cardiff, with the title *XXIV The Journal of The South Wales Borderers*. It carried a foreword by the Colonel of the Regiment, Brigadier (later General) Llewellin Morgan-Owen, in which he

Colours of 1 SWB, the Citadel, Egypt, 1930.

Section of Mounted Infantry Company, 3rd Battalion The South Wales Borderers; South African War, 1899–1902.

3rd Battalion The South Wales Borderers at the River Vaal, South Africa, 1900; Lieutenant Colonel C. Healey, Commanding Officer.

1 SWB, Mena Camp, Egypt, 1930.

expressed the hope that by spreading news of all battalions, including those of The Monmouthshire Regiment, it would serve to 'weld the Corps into one family'. However it was only in 1942 that the title was expanded to *Journal of The South Wales Borderers and Monmouthshire Regiment*. The successive editors, first at Newport and then at the Brecon Depot, maintained the regular biannual issues throughout World War II and down to amalgamation, when the Journal merged with, and assumed the title of, *The Men of Harlech*.

We must now revert to 1922. In that year the 'Geddes Axe' smote the armed forces, and the Army in particular.[3] Sixteen cavalry regiments were reduced to eight by the process of amalgamation; five infantry regiments of southern Irish origins were disbanded; those English infantry regiments with four regular battalions lost two each, while overseas garrisons were reduced.

However, this drastic retrenchment had little impact on either The South Wales Borderers or The Welch Regiment, both of whom had only two regular Battalions. For them the only effect was the absorption of a few redundant officers and soldiers from the axed regiments. But there was reorganisation in the Territorial Army, and in 1922 The South Wales Borderers lost their only Territorial Battalion when the Brecknockshire was amalgamated with the 3rd Battalion The Monmouthshire Regiment to form the 3rd (Brecknockshire and Monmouthshire) Battalion The Monmouthshire Regiment. But although the latter were not yet officially 'part of the Corps of The South Wales Borderers', Monmouthshire was an important recruiting area, and with The South Wales Borderers providing Adjutant and permanent staff, the severance was no great bereavement. The Welch Regiment retained their 4th (Carmarthenshire) and 5th and 6th (Glamorgan) Battalions. The 6th had already absorbed the 7th (Cyclist) Battalion, who, after pedalling dutifully round the coasts of Wales and Northumberland during the early part of the war, had been relegated as a draft-finding unit for infantry regiments in France.

Immediately after the war both Regiments set about commemorating their thousands who had fallen. With the approval of the church authorities, The South Wales Borderers resolved that a fitting memorial should be the restoration of the Havard Chapel in the Priory Church of Brecon,[4] and its dedication as the Regimental Chapel in which all the names of their dead would be preserved, together with the old Colours. In addition, the Regiment endowed beds in the Royal Gwent Hospital at Newport and in the Brecon Infirmary, to which ex-members of the 24th and their dependants were to be given prior claim. The work was completed in 1922, and on 5th May the Havard Chapel was consecrated by the Bishop of Swansea and Brecon. Immediately afterwards, General Sir Alexander Cobbe, VC, unveiled a tablet recording the restoration as a memorial to the 5,777 officers and ranks who gave their lives in the Great War. Later, in April 1924, the Colour pole of the 2nd Battalion, lost at Isandhlwana and subsequently recovered was also deposited in the Chapel.

In July 1924 The Welch Regiment's memorial was unveiled in Llandaff Cathedral by Field Marshal Lord Plumer and dedicated by the Bishop of Llandaff. It took the form of a mural tablet, with beneath it a prayer-desk containing the Regimental Roll of Honour.[5] In addition, a smaller replica of the Whitehall Cenotaph was erected at the entrance to the Regimental Depot at Cardiff in memory of the 1st and 2nd Battalions' war dead. This was unveiled in November 1924, in the same ceremony as the unveiling of the 'Stick it the Welch' tablet on the barracks clock.

Since General Sir Alexander Cobbe was one of the most distinguished 20th-century Colonels of either Regiment, and one of only two to win the VC, he deserves more than the previous passing mentions. 2nd Lieutenant Cobbe was commissioned from Sandhurst and joined the 1st Battalion The South Wales Borderers in 1889. But his service with the Regiment was very brief, for three years later he transferred to the Indian Army – understandable, perhaps, since he had been born and brought up in India. Joining the 32nd Sikh Pioneers, he fought in the operations for the relief of Chitral in 1895. Further active service followed in the 'Small Wars' in Nyasaland and Ashanti (1900), where as Captain in the West African Regiment he earned a DSO (and a wound). In 1902 he was again in action, in Somaliland, and it was at Erego on 6th October that he won his VC for personally fighting off enemy rushes with a Maxim gun and subsequently rescuing wounded under fire. After promotion to Colonel, with staff

The Regimental Chapel of The South Wales Borderers (The Havard Chapel) in Brecon Cathedral.

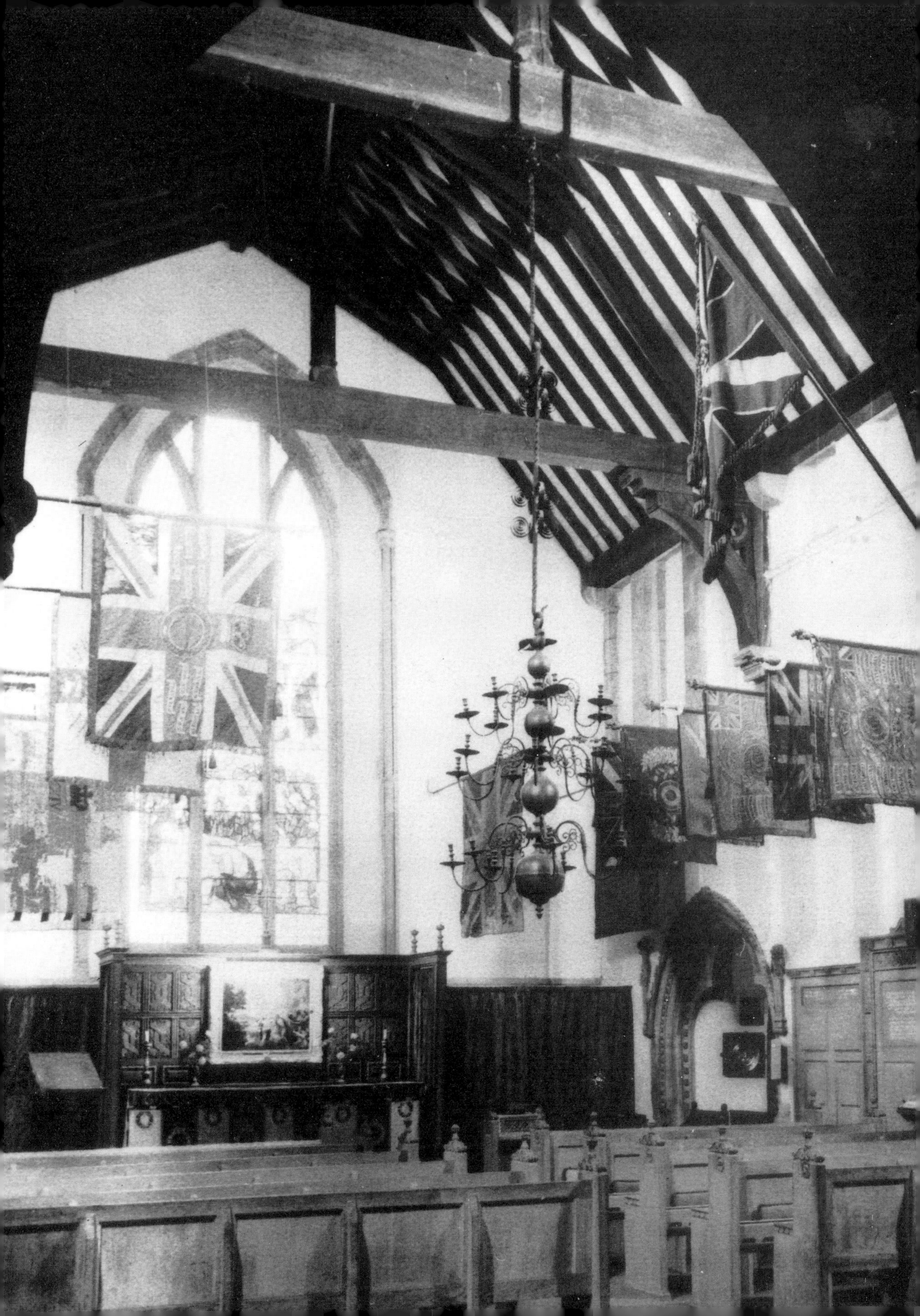

Unveiling of World War II inscriptions at Maindy Barracks Cenotaph, Cardiff, Sunday, 20th July 1947.

appointments at the War Office, he went to France in 1914 as GSO of an Indian division. In 1916, as Brigadier General, he took over the 7th Indian Division in Mesopotamia, and in August of that year, as Major General, succeeded General Sir Stanley Maude in command of III Indian Corps. In this post he directed the operations for the recapture of Kut and the final successful advance to Mosul, which saw the surrender of the main Turkish field force. Promoted Lieutenant General in 1919, he was successively appointed Military Secretary at the India Office (1920–6), GOC-in-C Northern Command, India (1926–30) and then returned to his former post at the India Office. When promoted full General in 1924 he was, at 54, the youngest officer to hold that rank.

General Sir Alexander Cobbe, VC, GCB, KCSI, DSO, died in June 1931, aged 69. Present at the funeral service in St Margaret's, Westminster, were representatives of the King and the Prince of Wales, besides officers and ex-officers of The South Wales Borderers, while the cortège included detachments of the Life Guards, Grenadier Guards, Coldstream Guards and Welsh Guards. Since both Battalions of his old

Lieutenant General Sir Alexander Cobbe, VC, KCB, KCSI, DSO; Colonel The South Wales Borderers, 1922–31.

Interlude 1919–39

Major General Sir Thomas Owen Marden, KBE, CB, CMG; Colonel The Welch Regiment, 26th May 1920–16th January 1941.

Regiment were overseas, neither could be present in strength, but the bearer party was formed of eight NCOs of the 2nd Battalion

From 1920 to 1941 The Welch Regiment paid respect to another distinguished officer as their Colonel. Major General Sir Thomas Owen Marden, KBE, CB, CMG, was born in 1866 and was commissioned 2nd Lieutenant in The 22nd (Cheshire) Regiment in 1886. After active service in Burma and South Africa, followed by staff appointments, Marden was given accelerated promotion to Major in the Northumberland Fusiliers. In 1908 he transferred to The Welch Regiment, and four years later assumed command of the 1st Battalion, which he led to France in 1915. After recovery from wounds, Colonel Marden took over an Infantry Brigade in the 38th (Welsh) Division. It was this Division, and Marden's Brigade in particular, that was heavily engaged at Pickem Ridge. Marden finished the war as commander of the 6th Division. In 1920 he was promoted Major General. His last command was that of the 53rd (Welsh) Division, which he held from 1923 until his retirement in 1927.

Known affectionately as Tom (T. O. M), Marden was a dedicated soldier and inspiring leader. He always cherished a loyalty to his own Regiment, and during his twenty-one years' service as Colonel proved indefatigable in its interests. It was he who was largely responsible for the erection of the War Memorials at Llandaff and the Cardiff Depot, while, as already noted, amidst all his other duties he found time to write the history of The Welch in the Great War. He died in September 1951, aged 85.

Until the late 1930s there was very little change in the infantry soldier's conditions of service, or his training, or his dress. In fact, the Army the recruit joined in that period was virtually a replica of the one that crossed the Channel in 1914. The infantryman's weapons were still the trusty SMLE .303 rifle, the Lewis light machine gun and the Vickers medium machine gun. Although The Royal Tank Corps was now well established, and most officers (other than the more impoverished subalterns) drove their Armstrong-Siddeleys, Vauxhalls or Austin 7s (according to rank), their battalions were still dependent on oats rather than petrol for their A and B Echelon transport, and theoretically, officers of field rank were still expected to ride to war on their Government-issue chargers.

Major General Frank Brooke, last Colonel of The Welch Regiment (1965–9) recalls the gentler side of soldiering in what most people fondly believed was the era of 'peace in our time'.[6]

> ...The two-Battalion system provided a very firm base for Regimental organisation with one Battalion at home, usually at low strength, supplying the overseas Battalion with sufficient drafts to keep it up to War Establishment. This resulted in a somewhat placid life in the home Battalion...
>
> Fatigues often swallowed up almost the whole Battalion – QM's fatigues, Garrison fatigues, coal fatigues, church fatigues, etc., leaving the officers largely free to hunt or shoot. A subaltern who could hire one or two cavalry troop horses for 15/- a month could hunt four or five days a week and the subscription to five packs of hounds (arranged by Aldershot Garrison) was 2/6d per month.

Interlude 1919–39

Horses, of course, provided our only form of transport. Apart from the 11 official chargers, horses drew such diverse vehicles as the 4-wheeled G. S. wagon, the 2-wheeled Company cart, the Vickers MG limbers, the Battalion water cart and even the field-cooker, where stew and tea for the whole Battalion were cooked on the move, the cooks marching stoutly behind, stirring and savouring as they went. Cookhouse food could only be described as appalling. Breakfast might be one sausage, bread-and-margarine and tea, mid-day dinner one ladle of watery stew, boiled potatoes and cabbage, and suet pudding, and the evening meal one small slice of corned beef, bread-and-margarine and tea . . .

In spite of it all, morale was high. Church parades every Sunday were compulsory, with the Field Officer of the week in command, two Companies, each commanded by a subaltern, and the entire Band and Drums – including Taffy in his No. 1 coat – marched to the Garrison church to join another dozen Regiments in their devotions and to march past the GOC Aldershot Command afterwards. A fine military spectacle.

On one occasion the Goat Major found himself in close arrest thanks to

Church parade; 1st Battalion The Welsh Regiment, Aldershot, c. 1898.

Bacchus, and a Drummer was deputed to do the job. Taffy was sent to join the parade, but on realising that his old pal was not to accompany him he lay down and refused to move, and the parade had to march round him...

Some tactical manoeuvres were to require revision a few years later. For example, if a column of infantry marching in fours along a road was threatened by ground-attack aircraft, the commander was to order 'Halt. Aircraft action front (or rear, or whatever)!' The men were to aim their rifles skywards in the appropriate quarter and on the command 'Fire!' to engage the foe...

The cavalry (horsed) operated as a Cavalry Brigade and had nothing to do with anyone else. There were no tanks with which to practise cooperation, and Gunners (with horse-drawn 18 pounders) and Infantry each went their separate ways... The traditional amateur approach to soldiering still held sway, and only a small minority of officers aspired to the Staff College. Indeed, in some Regiments, to do so was regarded as implied disloyalty to the Regimental family.

Life in India was different. In many respects it was 'cushy', as the soldier termed it, in that he had become a 'sahib', with native servants to perform the menial chores and fatigues, a 'bearer' to clean his kit, a 'nappi' to shave him as he lay on his charpoy at Reveille, a 'char-wallah' squatting on the barrack-room verandah to supply him with mugs of 'gurum char' (at 2 annas a mug), while Thursdays were sacrosanct as holidays.[7] But even in 'the sloth belt' of southern India, communal riots could erupt, with the British infantrymen called out 'in aid of the Civil Power': a thoroughly distasteful task. The target for a variety of missiles (often including excrement hurled from verandahs and roofs), he was allowed to use only the minimum of force, and his officer in command could not order fire unless a civil magistrate were present to sanction the order. The unhappy officer was still in a dilemma. The 'Amritsar Incident' of 1919 had demonstrated that a commander who employed excessive force could suffer a court of enquiry or a court-martial, with possible dismissal from the service. On the other hand, if a young, inexperienced subaltern were dilatory in his attempts to quell the disturbance, he could be reprimanded, and perhaps suffer loss of seniority.

There were no such inhibitions on the North West Frontier of India, where for nearly a century the wilderness of barren mountains and the warlike Pathan tribesmen had provided the British Army with a training ground unequalled anywhere else. Old 'Frontier hands' claimed that the Pathan was the finest umpire in the world, for he never allowed a mistake to go unpunished. Failure to picquet a narrow *tangi* (defile) might result in one more 'Frontier incident', ambush and casualties.

The 41st Regiment had first encountered these tribesmen when they withdrew from Afghanistan in the abortive campaign of 1842. Their descendants met them again when 1 Welch spent a year in Razmak, 1923–4; ten years later it ws the turn of the 2nd Battalion to sample Frontier life.

In December 1934 the Battalion were relieved at Rawalpindi by their future partners, the 1st Battalion The South Wales Borderers, and travelled by train to

Landi Kotal Camp, Khyber Pass, North West Frontier, India (c. 1934).

Peshawar, and thence by the Khyber railway to Landi Kotal, where they in turn relieved the 2nd Battalion The Border Regiment.[8] The highest point in the Khyber Pass, and only some six miles from the Afghan Frontier, Landi Kotal was one of the farthest-flung outposts of the British Empire, and in many respects resembled a 'Beau Geste' fort of fiction. The ancient fort itself was mud-built, housing hospital, Brigade Headquarters and magazine. When first occupied by British soldiers in 1919 (after the 3rd Afghan War), the so-called cantonment area were merely a tented camp with no amenities. By the 1930s it had become more sophisticated, with brick-built 'bungalows' (single-storey barrack blocks), electric light, running water and even a cinema. The sports 'fields', however, hardly merited that term, for they were merely bare, compacted earth, of the same dust-coloured or khaki hue as the Battalion parade ground (nostalgically named 'Trafalgar Square') and the harsh, jagged mountain ridges that surrounded the post. The whole perimeter was protected by a high barbed-wire fence (floodlit after dark), and no one was allowed in or out without authority. On strategic rocky knolls beyond the perimeter were stone-built, castellated 'blockhouses', similar to those throughout the Khyber, and here detachments of eight men and two NCOs were incarcerated for two-week spells, 'in observation'. There was no wireless, and communication with Battalion Headquarters was by telephone, with helio or Aldis lamp as standby if the line were cut, as it frequently was, by pilfering tribesmen.

In Rawalpindi, The Welch had imagined that life in the notorious Khyber Pass was going to be much like that of the French Foreign Legion, with constant sniping and periodic full-scale attacks by Paradise-seeking tribal fanatics. In fact it turned out to be very different. The local Shinwari tribesmen were 'friendly', in that apart from the odd pot-shot from some hot-headed youngster, they offered no hostility, and even welcomed the presence of the Raj as a source of income from their produce of chicken, eggs, mutton, and employment as Khassadars[9] with the troops on schemes and exercises. The Brigade at Landi Kotal comprised, besides the one British Battalion, two Indian Sappers and Miners detachment. The Brigadier was so pleased with the result that Signals, Sappers and Service Corps.

One of the first tasks that befell The Welch was not the expected punitive forays against recalcitrant tribesmen, but employment as navvies. The Brigade commander decided that communications with a local strategic mountain summit named Pisgah Spur should be improved by the construction of a metalled road, and who better for the job of digging and hewing than Welshmen from South Wales? So for six strenuous days the whole Battalian laboured with pick and shovel, and a little explosive help from the Indian Sappers and Miners detachment. The Brigadier was so pleased with the result that he ordered the new route to be named 'Welsh Road'. And thus it has remained, no doubt to the puzzlement of today's Pakistani soldiers of the Khyber Rifles at Landi Kotal.

A patrol from D Company, 1 Welch; Razmak, Waziristan, North West Frontier, 1923.

TOP: *Transport lines; Razmak Camp, Waziristan, North West Frontier, 1923.*
ABOVE: *Pitching bivouacs, Waziristan, 1923.*

However, this achievement was as nothing to the historic event that followed in October 1935. For The Welch, the most serious shortcoming of Landi Kotal was the lack of a suitable Rugby football ground. The hard, unyielding *matti* surfaces of the soccer and hockey grounds were quite out of the question. So with the approval of the Brigadier, himself a rugger enthusiast, the Battalion set about remedying the situation. In the spring an area was dug, turves were transported from Peshawar, the Military Engineering Services were co-opted to divert water, and by October the drab khaki of the cantonment landscape was relieved by a beautiful field of green grass. On 25th October 1935, the first, and only, Rugby football ground in the Khyber Pass was ceremonially declared open by Brigadier Molesworth (escorted by the Battalion's mule-mounted Indian Platoon). The huge concourse of spectators included some specially-invited (and bemused) tribal chiefs, and the Khyber's first rugger match was played between the 2nd Battalion The Welch Regiment and RAF Peshawar. The result was, appropriately, a victory for the home XV, by 5 points to 3. Afterwards another record was achieved when a dance was held by the Battalion, with ladies imported from Peshawar and from the married-families hill-station of Cherat. 'And so ended an enjoyable and notable day', reported *The Men of Harlech*, 'with what is believed the creation of three "records" – the first game of rugger, the biggest crowd of spectators, and the first dance in the Khyber.'

There were other unlooked-for diversions in the Khyber. In January 1935 the Battalion found itself studying the 1893 manual, *Infantry Training*, reverting to the Victorian Slade-Wallace equipment, drilling with the obsolete 'Long' Lee-Enfield rifle, and glueing moustaches to hairless upper lips. All this was in aid of the Gaumont British Film Corporation, who were making an epic based on Kipling's *Soldiers Three*, and who had obtained War Office approval for 2 Welch to beat off tribal attacks in a typical Frontier incident. The scenes were enacted with great gusto, particularly by the local Shinwari 'enemy', who (co-opted by the Khassadars), were persuaded to replace their private arsenal of live rounds by Government-issue blanks. 'They think we are mad', wrote the Battalion scribe in *The Men of Harlech*, 'but they like the money'. Among distinguished visitors who came to watch the battle were HRH Princess Alice and the Earl of Athlone, who were touring India.

2 Welch left Landi Kotal for the soaring temperatures and prickly heat of Agra in March 1936, but just before departing they managed a final rugger fixture, when Welsh met Welsh. Their opponents were their partners-to-be, the 1st Battalion The South Wales Borderers, whose XV had travelled all the way from Rawalpindi, to be rewarded with victory: 10–6.

On the abdication of King Edward VIII, his brother ascended the throne as King George VI, and in the Coronation ceremony of 9th May 1937 The South Wales Borderers and The Welch Regiment were represented by street-lining detachments. Each provided three officers and fifty other ranks, dressed in the new blue patrol uniforms specially issued for the occasion. Reporting the event, The Welch's Regimental Records add that a deluge of heavy rain caused the dye from the tunics to run 'and turn everyone's shirts to a vivid shade of blue'.

While 2 Welch had been diverting themselves in the Khyber Pass, elsewhere on the

Frontier that turbulent Pathan mullah, the Fakir of Ipi, was providing other diversions for the troops. Stirring up the fiercely independent tribesmen in Waziristan, he organised raids, ambushes, murders and kidnappings, and the Government was forced to launch large-scale operations to curb him and his followers. Thus in February 1937 the 1st Battalion The South Wales Borderers were moved by lorry convoy from Rawalpindi to Mir Ali fort in Waziristan, there to join the 1st Indian Brigade with three Battalions of Gurkha Rifles. For the next ten months the Battalion was almost constantly engaged in the arduous tasks of escort to convoys, picqueting mountain features, building perimeters and sangars, interspersed with deep-range patrols and attacks on (and by) tribal lashkars – in fact, the typical Frontier warfare familiar to so many British infantrymen for more than a century. By the time the Battalion were withdrawn to Rawalpindi in late December, they had marched some 800 miles over some of the world's most rugged terrain (climbing many thousands of feet), and had fought numerous actions and skirmishes. As always, their 'Johnnie Gurkha' friends proved staunch comrades, and a splendid camaraderie was established between the battalions. '. . . The Welshmen and the Gurkhas are great friends. Each seems to find a lot to admire in the other, while a great deal of laughter and leg-pulling goes on in no known language.' So wrote the Battalion's correspondent to the Journal of the 24th.[10]

The Waziristan operations of 1937 cost the 1st Battalion The South Wales Borderers three privates killed and one officer and twenty-three other ranks wounded, one of whom subsequently died of his wounds. However, the campaign brought a Bar to the Commanding Officer's DSO (Lieutenant Colonel A. E. Williams, DSO, MC), the MC to Captain D. Rhys, and two MMs. But most gratifying to the Battalion was the honour of being dubbed 'The White Gurkhas' by their Nepalese brothers-in-arms of the Brigade. In the following year the Battalion took up residence in Landi Kotal, where they also took advantage of the rugger facilities inaugurated by their predecessors, 2 Welch.

As we have seen, General Sir Alexander Cobbe, VC, had been Colonel of The South Wales Borderers since the end of World War I. On his death in 1931 he was succeeded by Brigadier (later General) Llewellin Morgan-Owen, who had joined the Regiment as 2nd Lieutenant in South Africa, in 1900. He was to remain Colonel for thirteen years, a period in which his Regiment underwent many changes before being committed to yet another World War. As related in Appendix 5, it was General Morgan-Owen who in 1936 finally defeated the church authorities of Warwick in the long-drawn-out battle for the removal of the treasured Chilianwala Colours to their rightful resting place in Brecon Cathedral.

In the two decades preceding World War II, both The South Wales Borderers and The Welch Regiment achieved memorable distinction on the sports field. For soldiers from South Wales, 'sport' means Rugby football, and it was in the nature of things that members of both Regiments should have been closely involved in the establishment of the game in the Army. The formation of the Army Rugby Union in 1906 was largely the brainchild of Lieutenant (later Lieutenent Colonel) J. E. C. Partridge of the 1st Battalion The Welch Regiment, while the first Secretary was Lieutenant (Lieutenant Colonel) G. H. Birkett, 2nd Battalion The South Wales Borderers. The two Regiments

The laying up of the Colours of 1 SWB in Brecon Cathedral, 1st April 1934.

first met in the Army Cup final in 1909, when The Welch were the victors. Further details of sporting matters will be found in Appendix 8.

For the 24th, the year 1934 was memorable for the laying-up of their revered Isandhlwana Colours. These worn and faded emblems had been in service since 1866, and at the time of their retirement were claimed to be the oldest carried by any regiment. They were also among the last to be borne in action, for this ancient practice was discontinued shortly after the Zulu War. With impressive ceremony the Colours were laid up in the Regimental Chapel of Brecon Cathedral on 1st April 1934, the original Wreath of Immortelles being deposited at the same time. Besides the Colonel of the Regiment (General Morgan-Owen) and representatives of both Battalions, the congregation included Lord Glanusk (Lord Lieutenant of Breconshire), Viscount Hereford, and members of the Coghill family whose name was so closely linked with what had then become the King's Colour. The ceremony attracted a leader in *The Times* of 4th April and a lengthy report in *The Morning Post* of the same date.

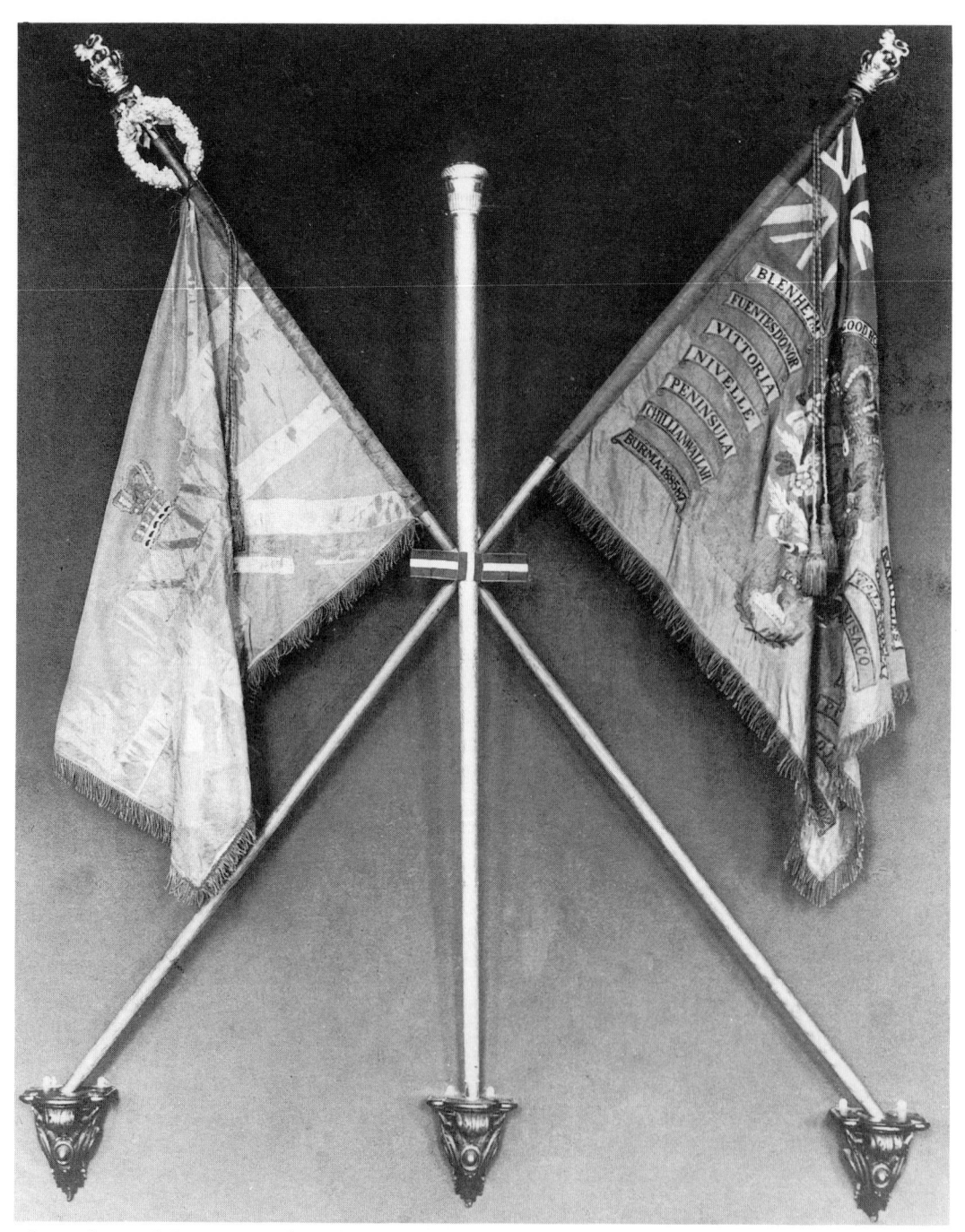

The Colours of the 1st Battalion the 24th Regiment which were carried from June 1866 to March 1933. The silver staff was used by Drum Majors of the Battalion from 1829.

Less than two years before this event the Regiment had mourned the death of their last surviving Zulu War VC hero. Ex-Private John Williams, a defender of Rorke's Drift, died at Cwmbran, Monmouthshire, in November 1932, aged 75. Not all the Zulu War VCs died natural deaths. Besides Lieutenants Melvill and Coghill, slaughtered trying to save the Queen's Colour after Isandhlwana, Captain Bromhead died of enteric and Private Henry Hook succumbed to TB. The death of Private Robert Jones, VC, was tragic for another reason.

After his discharge to the Reserve in 1888, Jones acquired a smallholding at Vowchurch in the Golden Valley of Herefordshire, also obtaining part-time work as a farm labourer on the estate of Major de la Hay at neighbouring Peterchurch. During the summer of 1898 he complained of frequent headaches, and is reported to have suffered some form of convulsion. On 6th September of that year he persuaded the Major to lend him a shotgun 'to shoot crows'. That evening a horrified maid found his body in her employer's garden at Peterchurch, the head almost blown off. He had shot himself in the mouth. The well-kept grave in Peterchurch churchyard bears an ornate marble headstone: 'In loving memory of Private Robert Jones V.C. late of The 24th Regt. South Wales Borderers Who Died Sept. 6th 1898 Aged 41 Years'.

The 1930s saw a somewhat overdue interest in the preservation of regimental memorabilia. Of course, volumes of regimental history existed, wherein, if so inclined, one could read all about one's predecessors and their achievements, how they lived, fought, were dressed and armed. But nothing had been done to bring those often dry pages to life by collecting and displaying the actual weapons, uniforms, trophies and other relics of centuries of service. A battered bugle picked up among the corpses at Isandhlwana, the actual assegais hurled by the Zulus at Rorke's Drift – these convey more than words. Such treasures of regimental history were lurking here and there, forgotten and unseen among the odds and ends accumulated by old soldiers, their fathers and grandfathers, or in hidden private collections.

It was The Welch Regiment's Colonel, and war historian, Major General Sir Thomas O. Marden, who took the first steps to gather together such relics for display in a regimental museum. In July 1929 a notice in *The Men of Harlech* announced: 'It is proposed to start a Regimental Museum at the Depot, and as a nucleus Maj. Gen. Sir Thomas O. Marden has presented a collection of trophies of the Great War.' There followed a plea for gifts of other articles of Regimental interest '. . . belts, badges, gorget plates etc.' As a result of this, and with the continued encouragement of the Colonel, objects of all description began to accumulate – among them the cap badge worn by Captain Mark Haggard when he fell crying 'Stick it the Welch' in September 1914. However, many years were to pass before the collection could be properly displayed in anything resembling a regimental museum. The 'bits and pieces of history' were housed wherever space could be found at the Cardiff barracks, being moved around to storerooms, Officers' Mess, Sergeants' Mess and elsewhere. And there was, of course, no official curator. This unsatisfactory state of affairs continued, in fact, until long after the Welch Regiment had ceased to exist as such.

It was only in May 1978 that the greatly-expanded collection was moved from its storage in the old Sergeants' Mess in Maindy Barracks, Cardiff, to its present august location in the Black and Barbican Towers of Cardiff Castle. These premises had previously been occupied by the University School of Music and Drama, and when this faculty moved to new quarters in the Civic Centre, the Regiment was allowed to take them over. Set in the historic centre of the Principality's capital, flanking the main entrance to the Castle, a more fitting home for The Welch Regiment Museum would be difficult to find. It was also fitting that the formal opening ceremony on 4th May 1978 was performed by HRH the Prince of Wales, Colonel in Chief of The Royal Regiment of Wales.

Appropriately too, the Regimental Museum of The South Wales Borderers has always been in Brecon, home of the 24th. But, like The Welch, the Regiment had to wait several decades before satisfactory accommodation could be found. Prior to 1934 there was no museum as such: the few relics that had come together more by chance than design were housed here and there in Messes and Regimental Institutes. In June 1934 Lieutenant Colonel Sir John Lloyd, Hon. Curator of the Brecknock County Museum in the town, offered a room for the Regiment's collection. This, of course, was gladly accepted, although the display came to be regarded more as part of the town's history than the 24th's. In 1947 the expanding County Museum became pressed for space, and the Regiment was obliged to hand back the room. The collection was then moved to the 24th's old Depot at the barracks in the Watton, where it was housed in the imposing 19th-century keep which had been the mobilisation store. Here it remained until 1961, when the final move was made across the square to the former NAAFI block. This was highly satisfactory: not only were four spacious rooms available for public display, with storage rooms above and adequate office space, but the building had historic associations with some of the Regiment's antecedents, having been erected in 1805 as an armoury for the Brecknock Militia. The Regimental Museum of The South Wales Borderers was declared open to the public in April 1962 – though without the ceremony enjoyed by that of The Welch Regiment.

Today the entrance to the Museum, fronting the Watton, one of the main thoroughfares into the centre of Brecon, is graced by an elegant pair of bronze gates bearing the badge of the 24th. Erected in 1967, these were the gift of the 5th Battalion The South Wales Borderers, in memory of Lieutenant Colonel C. V. Trower, CMG, who had commanded the Battalion throughout World War I. Courtenay Vor Trower was first commissioned in the 2nd Battalion in 1876, and later commanded the 1st Battalion. Having served in the Kaffir and Zulu Wars, and in the Boer War, he retired on half-pay in 1905, but on mobilisation in 1914 he immediately rejoined, to raise and take command of the 5th (Service) Battalion. Colonel Trower lived long enough to read of the doings of his old Regiment in World War II, for he died in November 1947, at the ripe age of 91.

A word must now be said about the Territorial battalions of our two Regiments. As already noted, The South Wales Borderers lost their only Territorial Battalion, the Brecknocks, in 1922, when it was merged with The Monmouthshires, to become the 3rd (Brecknockshire and Monmouthshire) Battalion The Monmouthshire Regiment. However, since the latter Regiment now officially formed 'part of the Corps of The South Wales Borderers', as stated in the Army List,[11] to all intents and purposes they

The South Wales Borderers and Monmouthshire Regiment Museum in Brecon Barracks.

were the The South Wales Borderers' Territorial comrades. The Monmouthshires had a 1st (Rifle) Battalion based at Newport and a 2nd Battalion at Pontypool, while the 3rd (Brecknock and Monmouth) had their Headquarters at Abergavenny.

The Welch Regiment's 'Terriers' still comprised the 4th Battalion (Llanelli), 5th Battalion (Pontypridd) and 6th (Glamorgan) Battalion (Swansea). In 1938 came the Munich Crisis, and with it the realisation that Britain was woefully lacking in air defence. Consequently a number of Territorial infantry battalions found themselves converted to an anti-aircraft role, among them being the 6th (Glamorgan) Battalion. In November 1938 they exchanged weapons for search-lights, to become the 67th Searchlight Regiment, based at Cardiff. Theoretically, they now owed allegiance to The Royal Engineers, but in fact they continued to wear their Welch cap badges and continued to report their doings to *The Men of Harlech* ('The citizens of Cardiff have seen our beams in the sky on numerous occasions, and on three occasions we have illuminated an aeroplane for them'). But in 1940 the 67th became a unit of the Royal

Buglers of 1 Mons, Armistice Day (11th November), 1936, Newport.
PERMISSION OF NEWPORT MUSEUM & ART GALLERY GWENT

Artillery, who had taken over all AA defence, and so they were finally lost to The Welch.

During the same period the 1st (Rifle) Battalion of The Monmouthshire Regiment was similarly converted, acquiring the subtitle '(68th Searchlight Regiment)', with headquarters at Newport. Later they too were divorced from the Corps of The South Wales Borderers, on transfer to the Royal Artillery. It is worth mentioning that the first Adjutant of 68th Searchlight was Captain D. P. Yates. He was to become Lieutenant General Sir David Peel Yates, last Colonel of The South Wales Borderers and first of The Royal Regiment of Wales.

The transformation of the regiments of 1914–18 into those of 1939 was a gradual process, for the mills of Government and the War Office ground slowly. The first hint of a new model Army came in 1928 when two distinguished cavalry regiments, 11th Hussars and 12th Lancers, were ordered to abandon their horses and take to armoured cars. But, of course, this was of no concern to the infantry soldier, who could not foresee any means of locomotion in his own world but those of his own feet. In February 1936 came a sweeping reorganisation. All infantry battalions were to lose their Machine Gun companies (usually D Company), and thirteen regiments were to have both their regular battalions converted to 'Machine Gun battalions'. The remainder would be classed as 'Rifle battalions', with no Vickers MGs. This was really a harking back to the old Machine Gun Corps of the Great War, except that the converted regiments still retained their individual identities, badges and distinctions. Each infantry brigade now comprised three Rifle battalions and one Machine Gun battalion. The Rifle battalions deployed four Rifle companies and a Headquarters company (including a mortar platoon and a (light) machine-gun platoon). Both The South Wales Borderers and The Welch were classified as Rifle Battalions, which meant that for them the only result of this change was the loss of their Vickers, and the

Lieutenant Colonel J. A. Wilson inspecting the Guard of Honour, 1 Mons, Royal Visit to Newport, 1937.　　　　　　　　　　　　　　　　　　　　　　　　B. OWEN COLLECTION

Kit laid out for Inspection; Depot, Maindy Barracks, Cardiff, 1937.

retraining of their gunners as riflemen. With the mechanisation of eight more cavalry regiments, to form the Tank Brigade, a 'mechanised Mobile Division', this reorganisation could be regarded, said the RUSI Journal of February 1936, 'as the greatest development since Parliament passed the Ordinance of 15th February 1645, creating the New Model Army.'

Mechanisation even touched the infantry, for the changes included the total banishment of the horse from the battalion transport and its replacement by 3-ton lorries and 15-cwt trucks. Perhaps of greater import to the officers, however, was the loss of their Government chargers, which '... is bound to make hunting and polo more expensive', bewailed a correspondent in the 24th's Journal.

In the same year the cumbersome, stoppage-prone Lewis light machine gun was superseded by the Bren, which like the Vickers medium machine gun, was to remain a respected weapon down to 1968.[12] Complete with its bipod it weighed only 21 lb., compared with the 31 lb. of the Lewis. With a special tripod it could also be used against low-flying aircraft. As Rifle Battalions, The South Wales Borderers and The Welch Regiment were each issued with eight Brens for the LMG platoons in their Headquarters Companies, but all riflemen were also trained to fire the Bren.

Of more direct concern to the soldier were revised rates of pay. Since 1922 the

Boy Soldier Hill, 2 Welch in his barrack room; Murree Hills, India, 1937.

basic rate of a private had been 2s. a day, with an increase of 6d. after three years' service. A sergeant received 6s., the RSM 14s. In 1937 the basic rate for a private was raised to 2s.9d., with an extra 6d. if he passed his Second Class Certificate of Education and qualified as a Second Class shot, while after three years he received an increment of 9d. Thus the fully-trained soldier now saw a total of 4s. a day. There were of course *pro rata* increases for NCOs and WOs. Officers did not fare so well: a 2nd Lieutenant's daily pay was raised from 10s. to 11s., a lieutenant's from 11s.10d to 13s. – after three years' service in that rank. Higher ranks got no increase at all, or even suffered a loss. Previously, a Major with five years' service as such received 33s.6d., now he had to make do with 28s.6d. The Lieutenant Colonel remained static on 43s.

This may sound like a crafty Government robbing the unfortunate officers to pay their soldiers. But the New Conditions of Service introduced by the Secretary of State for War in August 1938 also specified lower retirement ages for field officers and above: a Major, for example, was to retire at 47 instead of 50, a Lieutenant Colonel at 50 instead of 55, and so on. The effect, ran the directive, was to accelerate promotion and give increased pay at lower ages: '... In future, subject to efficiency, every subaltern will become a captain in 8 years, and every captain a major in a further 9 years.'[13]

One of the most radical innovations of the inter-war years was the introduction of the 'Y' cadetship scheme, whereby suitably qualified NCOs could be accepted as Cadets at Sandhurst. Thus for the first time the private soldier was granted the opportunity of becoming an officer through the normal channels. Moreover, the 'Y' cadet paid nothing for his Sandhurst course, and, if commissioned, was granted an initial uniform allowance of £100. At first the scheme (introduced by Army Order 254 of 1922) was limited to cavalry and infantry cadets at Sandhurst, but in 1928 it was extended to candidates for the Royal Artillery and Royal Engineers at the Royal Military Academy, Woolwich. Another novelty for NCOs was the introduction in October 1938 of the rank of Warrant Officer Class 3, which meant that Platoon Sergeants now became Platoon Sergeant Majors and could take command of platoons in place of subalterns. But this expedient was short lived. With the huge influx of young officers on the outbreak of war, vacancies for WO platoon commanders were drastically limited, and the rank was abolished, never to be revived.

In the same month the Journal of The South Wales Borderers reported: 'A new dress for training and war on the lines of that suggested by the Braithwaite Committee two years ago is to be brought in before Christmas.' General Sir Walter Braithwaite had chaired a committee appointed by the War Office in 1934 with the task of devising a more practical pattern of service dress than the tunic, 'plus-fours' and puttees style that had hardly changed since the Boer War. The committee came up with a two-piece suit of 'blouse' (based on skiing attire) and trousers, with short ankle-puttees. The prototype material was denim, but, as might have been foreseen, this was held to be insufficiently warm for wear in European winters, and so the existing khaki serge was adopted, while canvas gaiters were substituted for the puttees. The proposed head-dress was a floppy, deerstalker-style hat, which was considered a little too unmilitary, so the familiar side hat or 'Cap Field Service' was introduced. The new attire was, of course, the battledress familiar to soldiers down to the 1960s. The home-based Battalions, 2 SWB and 1 Welch, first paraded in it in November 1938, and a company scribe in *The Men of Harlech* described the effect as 'a cross between motor mechanics and factory hands'. But at least, he added, 'we have said goodbye to those infernal puttees'. There was soon to be general condemnation of the short 'blouse' which gave no protection below the waist, while the side hat was not only as useless as its 19th-century forage-cap predecessor, but was prone to fall off in energetic activity.[14]

In January 1939 *The Men of Harlech* reported that 'another novelty has appeared in the last few days – the Bren carrier'. This lightly-armoured, open topped vehicle on tracked running gear borrowed from the light tank was, as the name implied, primarily intended for the transport of the Bren LMG and its crew on the battlefield, but until the advent of the Jeep it became a general workhorse, ferrying ammunition and supplies, evacuating wounded, and sometimes serving as the Commanding Officers' runabout. Each infantry battalion now had its Carrier platoon (in Headquarters Company), consisting of ten Bren carriers. Since infantrymen were expected to defend themselves

Rail-mounted armoured car, 2 SWB, Palestine, 1936

against tanks, the battalions were issued with that curious, short-lived weapon, the Boys anti-tank rifle. Devised in 1936 by a Mr C. H. Boys of the Woolwich Arsenal Design Department, this looked like a grossly-overgrown rifle (which it was). It was a single-shot weapon, firing what was hopefully described as an 'armour-piercing' round of .5 in. calibre. It was to have little effect on the Panzers in the 1940 Battle of France and was soon withdrawn.

In the midst of training with unfamiliar weapons and equipment, and undergoing instruction in driving and maintenance, The South Wales Borderers did not overlook the fact that 28th March 1939 marked the 250th anniversary of the founding of the 24th Regiment. The 2nd Battalion, in Londonderry, held a ceremonial parade in which the Colours were trooped, and the Governor of Northern Ireland, the Duke of Abercorn, took the salute. In May there were ceremonies at Brecon, Newport, Pontypool and Tredegar, attended by the Band and Drums and Colour Party from Londonderry. Away in their Khyber Pass fortress of Landi Kotal, the 1st Battalion could hold no special parades, but they sent a telegram of anniversary greetings to their comrades of the 2nd Battalion.

The previous September had been marked by the Munich Crisis, when Prime Minister Neville Chamberlain returned from his meeting with the Führer of the 3rd Reich, flourishing his piece of paper and assuring the British public that 'Mr Hitler has no further territorial ambitions', and there would be 'Peace in our time.' However,

The Great Western Railway Castle Class locomotive 'The South Wales Borderers', 1937–62.

there were many not so ready to trust the Nazi dictator. In the same month that the 24th Regiment were celebrating their 250th birthday, German Storm Troopers goose-stepped into Prague. There were rumours of imminent pacts between Hitler, Stalin and Mussolini. Only those blind to events failed to suspect that 'our time' was running out.

Meanwhile, the Depots of The South Wales Borderers at Brecon and The Welch Regiment at Cardiff had been occupied with their routine tasks of training the normal intakes of recruits. Then in March 1939 came the creation of the new 'National Militia Force', in which all young men between the ages of 18 and 20 were to serve for six months' training in the Regular Army, followed by three-and-a-half years in the Territorials. This expedient, combined with the impetus in regular recruiting, posed problems of accommodation, particularly at Brecon. Thus a temporary hutted camp was hastily set up on the slopes of Slwch Hill, beyond the eastern suburbs of the town. We do not know who was responsible for naming this complex 'Dering Lines', but it was a happy inspiration, for of course it commemorated the founding-Colonel of the 24th Regiment, Sir Edward Dering. As mentioned in Chapter I, the modern hutments of Dering Lines are still very much in use, housing the NCOs' Tactical Wing of the School of Infantry.

Readers may recall that in 1922 The South Wales Borderers had lost their only Territorial Battalion, The Brecknockshire, when it was absorbed by the 3rd Battalion The Monmouthshire Regiment. With the augmentation of the Territorial Army in the spring of 1939, the Brecknockshire Battalion was revived in its own right, once more becoming a unit of The South Wales Borderers. Energetic recruiting around Crickhowell, Hay, Builth, Ystradgynlais and Brecon itself, resulted in full War Establishment being achieved by August. At the same time The Monmouthshire Regiment recruited their new 4th Battalion with a nucleus of some 200 all ranks from the 2nd Battalion. This too was up to strength by August.

The Welch Regiment were also busy expanding. Between April and June they produced two new Territorial Battalions, the 2nd/4th and 2nd/5th. The former, however, was redesignated the 15th Battalion shortly after its formation.

In the splendid summer weather of August 1939 the Territorial battalions went into camp as usual, at Porthcawl, Tenby, Weston-super-Mare and other pleasant seaside locations. For many of the officers and soldiers, these were the last such diversions they would ever see.

On 1st September Hitler launched his Panzers and Stukas across the Polish frontier, and two days later the British public around their wireless sets heard the sad voice of Neville Chamberlain declaring '. . . consequently, this country is at war with Germany'.

Notes

[1] The original letters are reproduced in the MS 'Digest of Services' of the 1st Battalion The South Wales Borderers, now in the Regimental Museum, Brecon.

[2] Although of venerable origins, *The Men of Harlech* was not the earliest Regimental Journal. This distinction was claimed by The Somerset Light Infantry whose 1st Battalion produced their news-sheet (forerunner of *The Light Bob Gazette*) in India, in October 1857.

[3] Named after Sir Eric Geddes, Chairman of a committee appointed by Lloyd George to cut public expenditure by £86 million.

[4] The Church was elevated to Cathedral status in 1923, after the creation of the new diocese of Swansea and Brecon.

[5] In January 1941 Llandaff Cathedral was virtually destroyed by the Luftwaffe, and it was not until 1956 that it, and the Memorial Chapel, were restored.

[6] Quoted in *The Men of Harlech*, May 1982.

[7] Since 1947 the Anglo-Hindustani argot, once so common throughout the Army, has now been almost forgotten. But readers will probably recognise 'char' (*chae*) as 'tea'. 'Nappi' (barber) was derived from *nai*, while 'gurum' (*garm*) signified 'hot'. Some soldiers of today may still refer to their rifles as 'bundooks' (*banduk*).

[8] A personal aside: It so happened that the present author was serving with the 2nd Battalion The Border Regiment at that time, and he recalls the Band and Drums 'playing in' The Welch to a lilting tune later identified as '*Ap Shenkin*'. The hand-over went with much conviviality. In the Sergeants' Mess The Borders' RSM nobly consumed a leek (specially imported from Peshawar)

and was made an honorary 'Welchman'. Taffy of Poonch (goat), as befitting his status, was entertained briefly in the Officers' Mess. All in all, it was a most cordial *Croeso i Khyber* for The Welch.

[9] Khassadars were paramilitary tribal levies, recruited for escort and liaison duties.

[10] The Gurkhas in the Brigade were 2nd/5th, 1st/6th and 2nd/6th Gurkha Rifles. The latter two are now represented in the British Army as 6th Queen Elizabeth's Own Gurkha Rifles. The 5th went to India on Partition.

[11] This was confirmed in Army Orders of 1929.

[12] The name was derived from *Br*no, Czechoslavakia, where it originated, and *En*field, where it was made for the British service.

[13] The New Conditions of Service were published in full in the RUSI Journal for November 1938.

[14] With their unerring sense of epithet, the soldiers coined a term for this object which cannot be reproduced in these pages.

CHAPTER FIFTEEN

The Second World War (Part I) (1939–45)

1. *Norway*

The outbreak of war found all but one of our two Regiments' regular battalions remote from the European theatre. The 1st Battalion The South Wales Borderers were still in that North West Frontier outpost, Landi Kotal; the 1st Battalion The Welch Regiment were in Palestine, whither they had moved in April; their 2nd

Mobilisation telegram received at Cardiff, Depot The Welch Regiment, 1939.

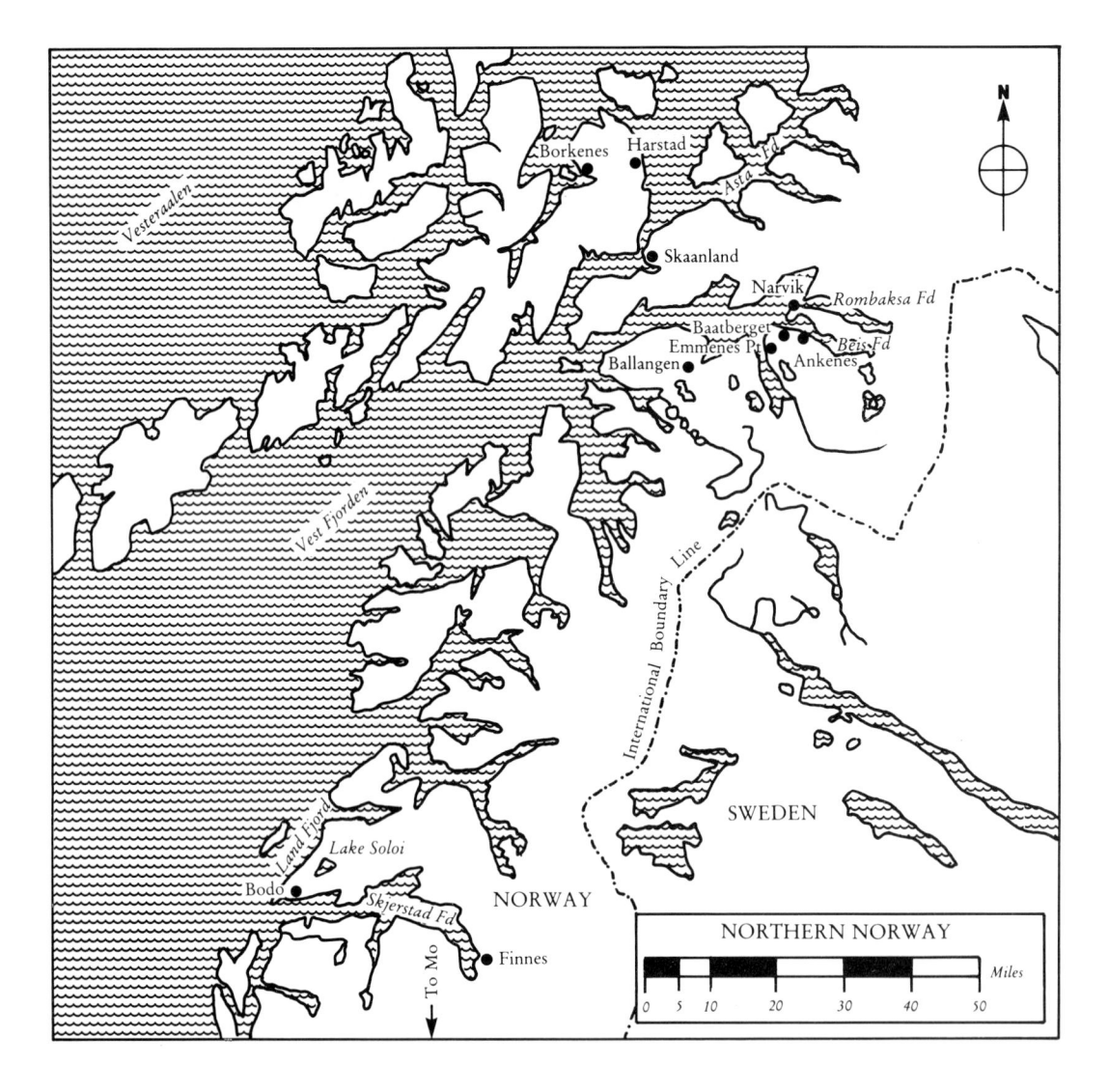

NORTHERN NORWAY map (showing Vesteraalen, Borkenes, Harstad, Skaanland, Narvik, Rombaksa Fd, Baatberget, Emmenes Pt, Beis Fd, Ballangen, Ankenes, Vest Fjorden, International Boundary Line, Land Fjorden, Lake Soloi, Bodo, Skjerstad Fd, To Mo, Finnes, SWEDEN, NORWAY)

Battalion were within sight of the Taj Mahal in Agra. Only 2 SWB were on the home front, at Londonderry.

The crisis in Europe had little impact in India. The *XXIV Journal* on 3rd September briefly noted that there had been 'a declaration of war (with Germany)', and then went on to describe the final of the Inter-Company Rugby Competition. At Agra 2 Welch were preoccupied with relief work among the local populace after an unprecedented 17-in. rainfall that caused disastrous flooding.

The reader will be generous enough to concede that this chapter, like that dealing with World War I, can be little more than a very selective digest of the services of the two Regiment's numerous battalions in diverse theatres. By 1940 both Regiments were

2 SWB on the quayside at Gourock, before embarking for Norway, 1940. IMPERIAL WAR MUSEUM

represented by their two regular Battalions, four Territorial and four hostilities-only or Service Battalions. Not all of these saw action, but nine of them did, and added 54 Battle Honours to the roll. For a more detailed account of this period the reader must refer to the previous war histories.[1]

In September 1939 the expected gave way to the unexpected. There was no immediate clash of arms; neither side took any offensive action. The British Expeditionary Force sat in their defensive positions along the Belgian frontier, and the strange 'twilight war', as Churchill described it, the 'phoney war' of the media, continued throughout the winter. It was only in the spring of 1940 that Allies and Germans came to grips, and the 2nd Battalion The South Wales Borderers gained the distinction of becoming the first unit of our two Regiments to confront the enemy.

From the outset Hitler had cast covetous eyes on neutral Norway. This was the peacetime source of his war machine's much-needed iron ore, imported from Sweden, and it was vitally necessary that the supply should not be interrupted. To the Allies, of course, it was equally important that it should be. But there could be no actual invasion of neutral territory, and Churchill's first plan was to mine the Norwegian coastal

2 SWB landing from 'Puffers' in Norway, 1940. IMPERIAL WAR MUSEUM

waters, thus denying Germany's shipping lane. However, Hitler was not one to observe such niceties as neutrality, and the whole situation changed when in early April his land forces occupied Denmark and swept on towards Oslo, while his warships steamed up the Norwegian coast to land troops at Narvik and other northern ports. Britain was now free to react.

At this juncture 2 SWB, commanded by Lieutenant Colonel P. Gottwaltz, were at Barnard Castle (County Durham), fully expecting to join the BEF in France. On 9th April they entrained for Glasgow and the following day embarked on a converted cruise liner. With them were the 1st Battalions of the Scots Guards and Irish Guards, forming the 24th Guards Brigade, under orders for Norway. The total allied force included three other British brigades, one Polish brigade, and battalions of the French Foreign Legion and Chasseurs Alpins. Their task was to make landings at three Norwegian ports: Narvik, Namsos and Aandalsnes. Subsequently there was much criticism of High Command for the inadequate planning and organisation of this hastily mounted campaign. Air cover was virtually non-existent, for the RAF was busy elsewhere;

Gheluvelt, 31st October 1914.

The 2nd Battle of Ypres, 8th May 1915. 1 Mons lost 21 officers and 439 other ranks.
NEWPORT MUSEUM AND ART GALLERY, GWENT

artillery support was limited to a single battery of 25-pounders; not all the troops were fully kitted out with Arctic clothing. It was obvious that movement in the snow-clad terrain would pose problems, but the only unit equipped for such conditions was the single battalion of Chasseurs Alpins ski-troops. Difficulties of transport would have been greatly eased by pack animals: none were embarked. Finally, 'the confusion of strategic and logistic planning made the task of the troops difficult on many occasions ... The Services, whose cooperation with each other was essential, had to respond to different orders from different Departments at home.'[2]

The 24th Guards Brigade, with 2 SWB, disembarked at Harstad on 16th April. This port, on one of several islands, was some 40 sea-miles from Narvik, their objective. The plan called for a heavy naval bombardment, after which the Irish Guards were to secure a beach-head and 2 SWB were to pass through and 'mop up'. But the plan proved abortive. Narvik was held in greater strength than suspected, and the initial shelling had little effect – partly because the Navy was reluctant to pulverise the port and inflict casualties on the Norwegian populace. The assault was temporarily abandoned. Instead, on 28th April, 2 SWB were ordered to occupy positions on the Ankenes Peninsula, only a couple of miles south of Narvik across the Beis fjord. Escorted by destroyers, the Battalion was landed from 'Puffers'[3] that evening near the port of Ankenes, meeting no opposition. This was fortunate, for the roads were some 18 in. deep in snow, while movement off-road was impossible, with 4 ft of snow. The Battalion was now joined by the Chasseurs Alpins and one section (two 25-pounders) of the RA Battery – one-third of the total artillery in the force.

So far there had been no contact with the enemy. The first brush was an anti-climax. One night Colonel Gottwaltz, Commanding Officer, heard movement outside his Headquarters hut, and on glancing out beheld a patrol of six German ski-troops within a hundred yards. His sentry fired a single round and the Germans vanished as suddenly as they had appeared. A more serious confrontation came on 30th April when an advanced Platoon under 2nd Lieutenant Holt, in position near the fjord, came under very heavy fire from mortars and a small naval gun from a German patrol boat. To avoid unnecessary casualties, the Platoon was ordered to withdraw, but in so doing Holt, his sergeant and a private were wounded and immobilised. Taking command, the Platoon Sergeant Major withdrew the rest to safety and then returned to the wounded, dressed their wounds and, still under fire, carried them back one by one. For this gallant act PSM R. F. Richards was subsequently awarded the DCM.

All this while, 2 SWB's companies and platoons were strung out over a frontage of more than eight miles on snow-clad peaks overlooking Narvik, forward posts in stone-built sangars, others in barns and farm buildings. With constant blizzards imposing virtual 'white-outs', and sub-zero temperatures at night, the natural conditions were as formidable as the enemy. To maintain communications between advanced posts and Tac HQ, the Signal Platoon under Sergeant Adams[4] laboured eighteen hours a day manhandling all their heavy gear and laying telephone lines in 'impossible' terrain. A single pack-pony would have eased their struggles, but not one was available. Nor were snowshoes: 'boots ammunition' are not ideal footwear in the Arctic Circle.

The Battalion had suffered its first three casualties on 30th April without being able to hit back. But on the following night they took revenge in full measure. D Company under Captain C. F. Cox were in position on a ridge between the villages of Ankenes and Baatberget, overlooking the mouth of the Beis fjord. Shortly before midnight Captain P. St.M. Sheil returned from a patrol towards Baatberget with the report of some enemy activity in the area. What neither he nor Captain Cox could know was that a strong German force had crossed the fjord from Narvik and were concentrating for an attack on D Company's sector.

At about 0300 hours a hail of tracer bullets whistled among and over the position, coming from the mountain slope on the right flank. In the dim light (the midnight sun did not rise for another couple of weeks) white-coated ski-troops could be made out, and the Company returned fire. Fortunately the enemy's aim was inaccurate and most of the rounds fell harmlessly into the sea behind. With all their rifles and Brens, the Company had no difficulty in keeping the ski-troops at a respectful distance. But these were merely creating a diversion. Soon heavier fire developed from woods on the left flank and to the crack and whine of bullets were added explosions of HE shells. At this critical moment one of our patrolling destroyers, attracted by the din, steamed close inshore and, hoping to be of assistance, signalled 'Have all your patrols returned?' Captain Cox takes up the story:[5]

> Cursing the Navy for worrying me in the middle of a battle with what I thought was a routine signal, I replied in the affirmative. Whereupon the destroyer proceeded to within a few yards of the shore and opened up with everything she possessed. It was then just light enough to see the main German attack coming in on the left flank. Fortunately the left forward platoon was well equal to the situation, but had it not been for the Navy's vigilance and timely assistance, both material and moral, we might well have been hard pressed.
> ... As it became lighter it was an amazing sight to see the ship firing 4-inch shells at single Germans from point-blank range, and at barns in which they had taken shelter. One shell went through the front of a big barn and out at the back; at the same time the roof rose in the air and descended again, apparently in the proper place ...

As Captain Cox later observed, it was rather unusual for an infantry company commander to have a Royal Navy warship 'attached' for close support.

In large measure owing to the Naval intervention, the Germans conceded the day and fled. In the fierce fire-fight, D Company had lost three men killed and three wounded. They took seven prisoners (one of whom was so demoralised that he fled to the Company's lines and surrendered); five dead Germans were buried, but many more were undoubtedly killed to lie hidden in the snow, and possibly to be discovered later by the Norwegians. The spoil captured included much enemy equipment, mortars, automatics, ammunition, and a wireless set.

On the morning after this action a Stuka flew over the Battalion position and dropped a stick of bombs which exploded around the Headquarters billets and the

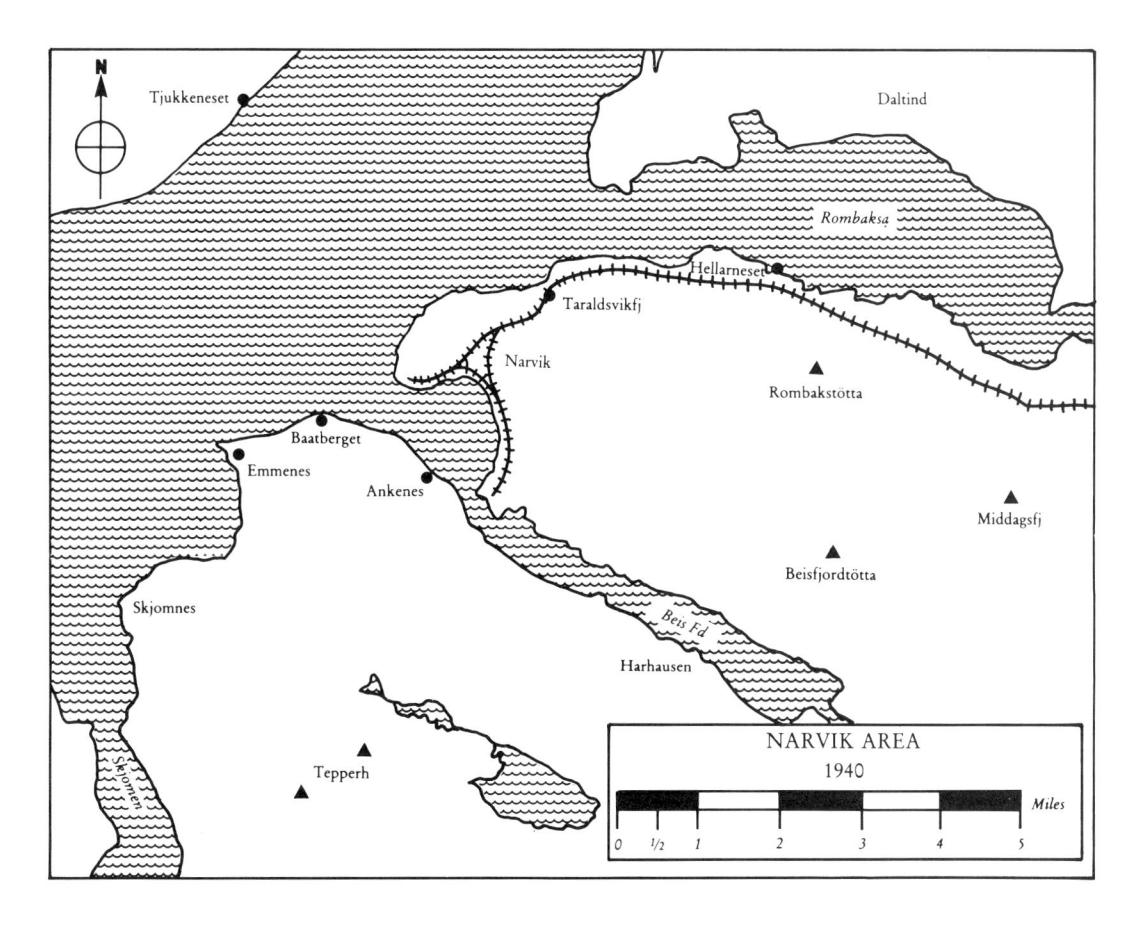

Officers' Mess barn. Three men were killed, three wounded, and 'one old Norwegian woman died of shock' as the Battalion correspondent reported in the 24th's Journal.

For the next fortnight 2 SWB remained virtually unmolested in their Ankenes position, but elsewhere things were not going according to plan. At Trondheim, 400 miles south of Narvik, the allied attack had ended in repulse and disaster, with heavy casualties. At Namsos a British brigade had been driven back without even coming to grips. At Narvik itself the Germans were still in force, as they were further north.

On 15th May 2 SWB were ordered to hand over to a Polish battalion and embark in the cruiser *Effingham* for 'an unknown destination'. After embarkation they learned that this was Bodo, 100 miles south, where their 24th Guards Brigade were to defend a hastily-built airfield from developing German threats. Already at Bodo was a company of the Scots Guards, with the remainder at Mo, some sixty miles further south. The Irish Guards had also been routed to Bodo, but their ship was bombed and set on fire en route, and with the loss of all their equipment the Battalion was returned by destroyer to base at Harstad. Hence there was some urgency for 2 SWB to reinforce the Scots Guards' Company.

Effingham had been at sea for only fifteen hours when, steaming at full revolutions, she struck one of the many uncharted rocks and began to sink. There followed what might have become another heroic *Birkenhead* incident. On the bridge, Colonel Gottwaltz was told that the ship must be abandoned: all ranks formed up at their boat stations with perfect discipline and awaited orders. As the stricken vessel listed, an escorting destroyer came alongside and the whole Battalion, together with Marines, were trans-shipped without fuss or casualty. But as there was no possibility of recovering *Effingham*, she was sunk by a destroyer's torpedo, and down with her went all the Battalion's stores and equipment. Like the Irish Guards, they were then taken back the the Harstad base. Re-equipping the Irishmen after their disaster had exhausted the base stores, and 2 SWB were forced to call on the base units. Even so, they remained short of many essentials, including mortars and signalling equipment.

When on 25th May the Battalion eventually concentrated (by 'Puffer' and destroyer) at Bodo they were made solely responsible for the defence of the airfield, which was still uncompleted. They found that the RAF was represented only by three obsolescent Gladiator biplanes. Despite rumours of German landings, no enemy troops appeared, but the Luftwaffe soon made up for that deficiency. On 27th May squadrons of bombers came over, to be confronted by the three gallant Gladiator pilots. One machine overturned in a bomb-crater before take-off, but the other two managed to shoot down five of the enemy. Meanwhile 2 SWB could only remain as spectators, for their sole AA defence were their Brens, not very effective against high-flying enemy. Next day an even stronger force with fighter escort appeared and utterly devastated the airfield and Bodo itself. The two remaining Gladiators valiantly met them: one was shot down; the other managed to account for one bomber before making good his escape to an airfield near Harstad. As the 2 SWB account in the Journal remarked, the pilots of these three antique machines had 'put up a very stout show'.

Although the Battalion had endured two days of intensive bombing, they had escaped with but a single casualty – one man wounded. By now, events elsewhere were diverting attention from Norway. On 10th May German Armies invaded the Netherlands and Belgium, and with this threat to France, perhaps Britain itself, the British and French Governments conceded that the Norwegian campaign must be abandoned.

On 29th May Colonel Gottwaltz received orders for evacuation; 2 SWB were to be responsible for covering the withdrawal of the Brigades. On three successive days the Scots and Irish Guards passed through the 2 SWB position with no interference from the enemy. On the final day, C Company with one company of Scots Guards had to fight off German patrols pushing foward, and Platoon Sergeant Major W. G. Johnson, in the one remaining Bren carrier, distinguished himself by repelling the more aggressive enemy. On the previous day Johnson had evacuated a demolition party of Sappers under heavy fire. For these actions he was awarded the second of the two DCMs gained by the Battalion in the campaign.

On 5th June, 2 SWB embarked at Borkenes in a destroyer which trans-shipped them at sea to a converted cruise liner. After an unmolested voyage via the Orkneys they were landed at Greenock five days later.

So ended the first chapter in The South Wales Borderers' war service. If it had not been a victorious one, that was no fault of theirs. The 2nd Battalion had done everything asked of them, and if their casualties had been remarkably light – six killed, thirteen wounded – they had the satisfaction of knowing they had accounted for a far greater number of the enemy.[6]

2. *Crete and North Africa*

From the snows of Norway our scene now shifts to the sands of the Western Desert and the mountains of Crete, where the 1st Battalions of The South Wales Borderers and The Welch Regiment were both to suffer severely. After trying to keep the peace between Jews and Arabs in Palestine, 1 Welch were routed to Egypt, arriving at Mersa Matruh in November 1939. In the following June Mussolini's forces in Libya became the new enemy, and the Battalion eagerly awaited the chance of showing 'the Eyeties' what Welsh soldiers could do. But that chance was not yet to come, for they were moved back to Alexandria, soon to confront a more formidable enemy elsewhere.

The threat to the strategic island of Crete, valuable as a refuelling base for the Royal Navy and the RAF, became serious in early 1941 when the Germans occupied Greece. Reinforcements for the British and Anzac garrison were hastily sent in from Egypt. Among these were the 1st Battalion The Welch Regiment who disembarked on 18th February. Commanded by Lieutenant Colonel A. Duncan, MC, they mustered 21 officers and 830 other ranks. The next few months were spent peacefully enough, preparing defensive positions and digging slit trenches. The expected onslaught came on 14th May – saturation bombing by 600 Luftwaffe aircraft which destroyed airfields, pulverised defences and silenced nearly all the 60-odd AA guns on the island. Well dug-in in the Suda Bay area around Force Headquarters, The Welch endured six days of this ordeal with remarkably few casualties. On 20th May the Germans launched their airborne assault with waves of Junkers 52 troop-carriers spewing out their hordes of paratroops, and swarms of gliders crash-landing throughout the island. Six of these planed down about 400 yards from B Company's position: Captain Evans personally shot up two with a Bren and the troops in the other two were effectively dealt with on deplaning by the rest of his Company. When fifty parachutists occupied a deserted monastery nearby, these were overcome by three platoons of D Company who took twenty-five prisoners. Bitter and confused fighting followed in all sectors. Advancing on a building believed to be held by paratroops, C Company came under heavy machine-gun fire. Corporal McTiffin located the gun and boldly led his section to silence it. All his men fell, but he went on unscathed and with his bayonet killed the entire crew of seven, thus allowing his company to continue. In World War I similar acts of valour won VCs. As it was, Corporal McTiffin was later awarded the MM.[7]

Undeterred by heavy casualties, the Germans continued to send in wave after wave of fresh airborne troops, and within a week they were virtually in control of Crete. Our own losses were equally heavy. By 20th May B Company had lost more than half its strength while the other companies were in little better shape.

Suda Bay, Crete.   IMPERIAL WAR MUSEUM

    The Battalion's last stand came on 28th May when, virtually isolated in their Suda Bay position, they were overwhelmed by the onslaught of nine German battalions. After a desperate fire-fight, the remnants withdrew in scattered groups, but not all of them managed the forty-mile mountainous trek to the British base at Sphakia. The Pioneer Platoon was surrounded and captured; C Company was reduced to two officers and twenty men. Lieutenant Colonel Duncan was last seen firing a Bren to cover the withdrawal: he too was captured. Some 300 survivors, many of them wounded, eventually reached Sphakia where the Navy was organising evacuation. But here Major Gibson, now in command, was ordered to send a composite company of 200 men to support the commando battalion holding the last rearguard position. These marched off under Major Griffiths and were not seen again. Subsequently it was learned that after holding off attacks they received orders from Force Headquarters to surrender. On 1st June all that remained of 1 Welch disembarked at Alexandria: they numbered 7 officers and 161 other ranks. They had left behind in Crete some 250 dead, while 400-odd had been marched into captivity.[8]

    In July the Battalion received a new Commanding Officer (Lieutenant Colonel

The Second World War, Part 1, 1939–45

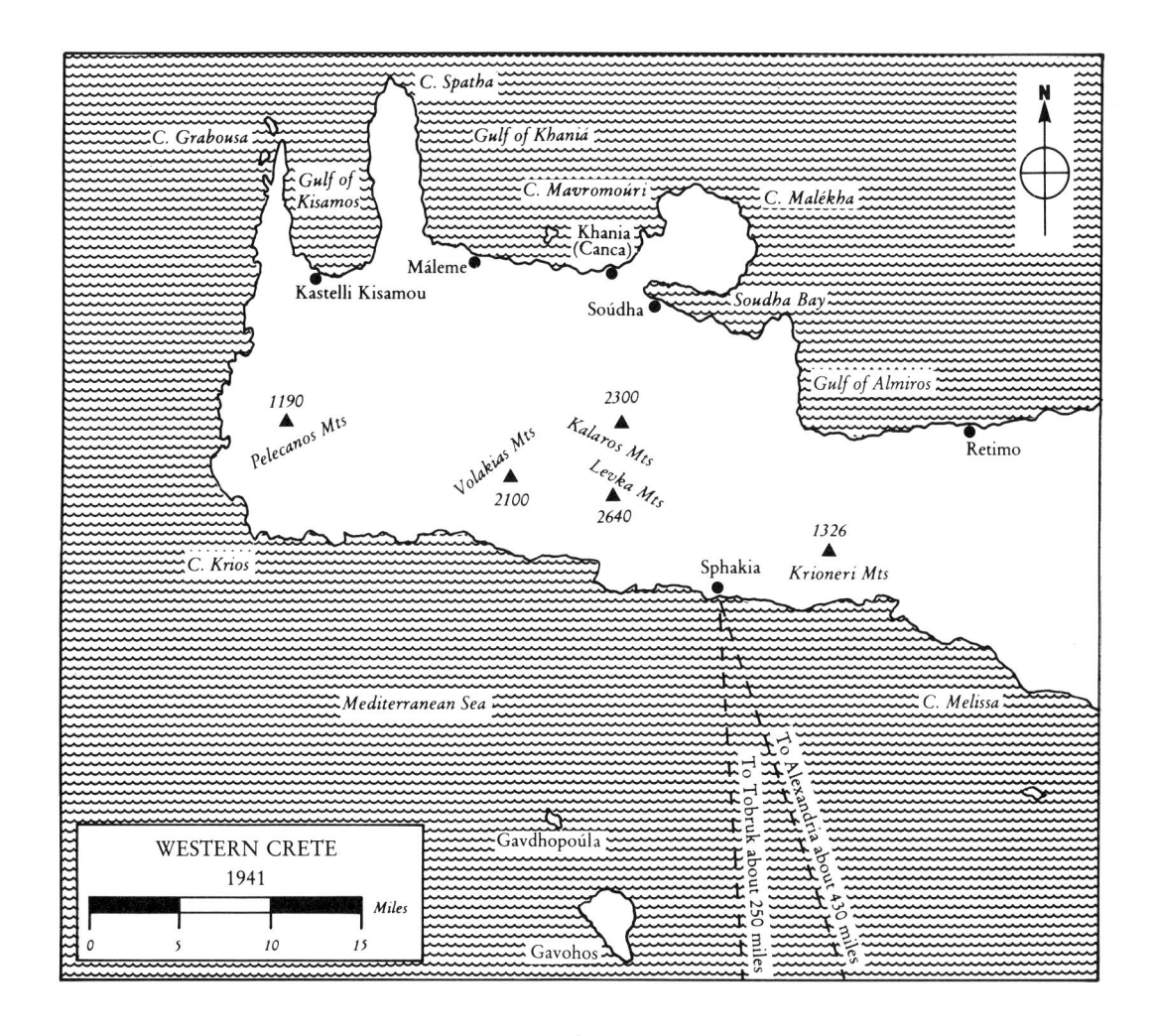

V. J. L. Napier, MC, of The South Wales Borderers) and in September the strength was made up with a draft of 700 officers and men from home.

It was now the turn of Colonel Napier's old Regiment to suffer disaster. In Libya the Italians whom 1 Welch had been hoping to vanquish were largely replaced by the more formidable Afrika Korps under Erwin Rommel. The 1st Battalion The South Wales Borderers arrived at Bir Hamid, a few miles east of Tobruk, on 5th June. They had come from Iraq, and had covered the 1,500 miles by truck and lorry in 12 days, which, as Colonel Jack Adams observes, must have been the most remarkable 'approach march' in history.[9] Lieutenant Colonel F. R. G. Matthews was in command, and with the 1st/6th Rajputana Rifles and 3rd/18th Garhwal Rifles they formed the 20th Indian Brigade. After one night at Bir Hamid they moved to form a defensive 'Box' at Bel Hamid.

Constant patrols were made outside the Box, though at first there was little argument with the enemy other than some artillery and mortar exchanges. On 16th June a strong Panzer attack on the 'Rajrif' Battalion's position at Sidi Rezegh overran them, leaving the Brigade with only two battalions. Tobruk was under imminent threat, and orders were to defend the Box to the bitter end. But on 17th June came fresh orders: withdraw to Sollum, now Salum, 70 miles to the east across the Egyptian frontier. The move was to commence after dark, at 2200 hours, and after marching twelve miles across the desert the Battalion was to rendezvous with waiting transport, which would motor them across the remaining sixty-odd miles to Sollum. But in war, events do not always conform to plans. The Intelligence Officer sent to recce the route ran into a German patrol and was captured, so that Colonel Mathews with his Headquarters Group could only march on compass bearings, trusting to luck that no minefields would be encountered. Luck held, but it took the weary Column nearly five and a half hours to cover the twelve miles to their RV point in the empty desert. At 0330 hours they embussed in the waiting lorries and trucks, and set off on what proved a journey into virtual extinction.

Just before dawn, the convoy encountered a force of thirty Panzers and lorried infantry across their front. Well knowing that an attack against armour without any artillery support was out of the question, Colonel Matthews took evasive action and led his command on a wide detour to bypass the opposition. This was accomplished, but as 18th June dawned over the escarpment of Trigh Capuzzo, 'We began to see that all along our flank were enemy tanks . . . As we dropped into the Trigh Capuzzo we came under shellfire from our rear, tanks moved on us from our left and ten enemy tanks were directly ahead of us on the far side of Trigh. A number of vehicles got knocked out here, and the convoy scattered and dispersed.' So wrote Colonel Matthews.[10] He, with his Adjutant and one other officer, managed to navigate unscathed to Sollum. There he found Captain Parry, the MT officer, with three trucks and some thirty men. 'Of the rest', he wrote, 'I have no news.' Later a few more straggled in, bringing the strength of the survivors to just 4 officers and 100 other ranks. This disastrous withdrawal had practically destroyed the Battalion. Fourteen officers and 500 other ranks were reported 'missing', subsequently proved to be prisoners-of-war.

After the fall of Tobruk (on 21st June), the remnants were withdrawn to Quassassin in the Canal Zone, there receiving reinforcements to bring their strength to 15 officers and 300 other ranks. The reconstituted Battalion was then posted to the 4th Indian Division in Cyprus, where a German invasion was threatening. Fully equipped with carriers, mortar platoon, motor-cycle platoon and an anti-tank platoon with 25-pounder guns, they were to operate as a mobile striking force. This was in early August, and they were eagerly awaiting the opportunity to prove that the Western Desert disaster was only a temporary setback. That opportunity never came. It was with stunned disbelief that on 15th August orders were received for the complete disbandment of the Battalion. By the end of the month all officers and men, except a small cadre sent home, were transferred to the 1st King's Own Royal Regiment, also in Cyprus, and the 1st Battalion The South Wales Borderers had ceased to exist. As recorded later, it was to be reborn; but it saw no further action in the war.

Tobruk, 1942. IMPERIAL WAR MUSEUM

    By the curious fortunes of war, the Western Desert saw 1 Welch undergoing a very similar experience to that of 1 SWB, though this did not result in extinction. Having refitted after the Crete debacle, the Battalion, commanded by Lieutenant Colonel Napier, was involved in the fierce struggles for Benghazi in January 1942. In the face of Rommel's onslaught, Benghazi was evacuated and on the 28th The Welch, with the remainder of the garrison, were ordered to withdraw to the Egyptian frontier. The Battalion had already been split into individual companies and detachments, and each group was forced to make its own way across hundreds of miles of mine- and German-infested desert. Colonel Jack Napier, with seventy men of Headquarters and B Companies, had only covered some twenty-five miles when they were completely surrounded by German tanks and lorried infantry and compelled to surrender. C Company had joined up with other units of the 7th Indian Infantry Brigade, and after eluding enemy patrols in the night, managed to motor 250 miles in 30 hours without opposition, eventually arriving within the lines of the Free French and Polish Brigade at Mechili on 30th January.

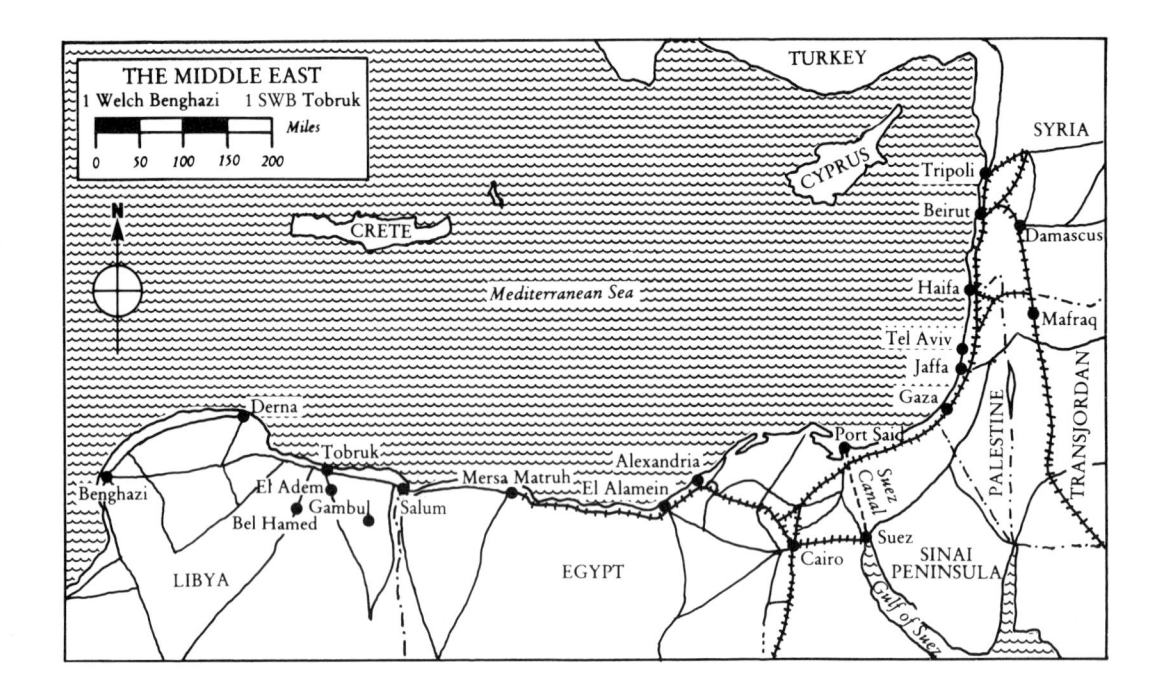

Meanwhile, at 2045 hours on the 28th, A and D Companies, already mauled in the defence of Benghazi, set out under Major J. T. Gibson (Second-in-Command of the Battalion) to break through the German lines. The column of 150 'soft' vehicles and carriers was unmolested until at 0300 hours next morning they encountered a formidable road block. It was heavily covered by mortars, machine guns and armoured cars. With his rifle platoons backed up by the Punjabis and the carriers of the Central India Horse, Major Gibson made several valorous attempts to break through, but the only result was loss of his own men and vehicles. By 0400 hours it became obvious that further attack was suicidal, and the only option to avoid surrender and capture was dispersal and a *sauve qui peut* footslog across the desert. And so, after destroying vehicles, those fit to face the gruelling task split into small parties and set off into the dark waste (many, both British and Indian, had already reached the limit of endurance and had to be left to fall into enemy hands). The epic feats of some of the scattered groups of officers and men marching more than 200 miles through hostile territory, enduring heat, cold, thirst and hunger, are recounted in detail in General Lomax's history.

Sample of 'Jon's' humour. Jon, or W. J. Jones, was commissioned into The Welch Regiment in 1941.

STILL IN SUNNY ITALY

"Give me a sandstorm anyday."

"Remember the week without water at Wadi Zem-Zem?"

Lieutenant V. J. B. Silvester and two privates escaped when Colonel Napier was captured on 30th January. Constantly evading German patrols, they walked for 14 days until finally being picked up by Polish troops, when they estimated they had covered some 300 miles. Major Gibson and his party, including Captain David Hammond and three soldiers, marched nearly 200 miles in 18 days, and for much of the time Gibson, suffering from fever, had to be carried by his companions. They were fortunate in bumping into a patrol of the Long Range Desert Group on 14th February. Captain A. G. Comer's party had similar experiences in their 200-mile march: by 13th February, after 15 days on the run, they were utterly exhausted, mentally and physically, and were resigned to giving themselves up to the first German patrol that approached them. When three armoured cars appeared, they hailed them, '... and to our great joy we recognised them as Marmon-Harringtons. They turned out to be South African, and we were safe.'[11]

Of the 700-odd officers and men of 1 Welch who fought at Benghazi, 214 survived to face the task of refitting and building up anew for the second time in a year. But unlike the unhappy South Wales Borderers, there was no humiliation for them. Reinforced, they were posted to the Sudan and spent a quiet spell at Khartoum. In March 1943 they went to Palestine where they immediately began training for their special role in the invasion of Sicily and Italy. This was one of the 'Beach Brick' units tasked with the organisation and flow of men and materials on the beaches in an assault landing. After full-scale 'wet' exercises in the Gulf of Akaba, the Battalion, now known as 34 (Welch) Brick, carried out their unglamorous but essential duties in the successful Operation 'Husky', the landing on Sicily on 9th July. The Italian opposition was minimal, and there were no casualties, although in the run-in Colonel's Gibson's Headquarters landing craft was shelled and sunk.[12] With Sicily occupied, the next objective was the landing on the 'toe' of Italy across the Messina Straits. This took place on 3rd September, with 34 (Welch) Brick performing their beach tasks. Again there was virtually no resistance, other than long-range German shelling. The Italians, now utterly demoralised, surrendered in droves, and five days later their High Command formally capitulated. But Hitler was by no means prepared to see his southern flank breached, and with the more formidable Wehrmacht adversary the bitter fighting of the Italian campaign was only just beginning. While the 8th Army were slowly pushing up the peninsula, 1 Welch were dismayed to find themselves (with the other 'Bricks') despatched back to Egypt for guard duties. Here at least they were gratified to provide an escort for Winston Churchill, attending a three-power conference in Cairo.

The Welch then became involved in a little-known episode of the war in the Middle East. Stationed at Alexandria were some Greek troops evacuated from their homeland when it was overrun. They were known as the 1st Greek Brigade Group, and comprised three infantry battalions, one AA Battery, a troop of field guns, three Stuart tanks and some Bren carriers. In April 1944 the whole group 'mutinied': that is, they refused to take any orders from the British, and shut themselves up in their camp. A spokesman declared that they merely wished to be left alone to conduct their own affairs; but if force were used against them, they would reply in kind. Since all attempts at negotiation failed, Operation 'Rabbit' was mounted, in which the mutineers were attacked by a force including 1 Welch, battalions of the London Scottish and London Irish Rifles, and some squadrons of the Royal Tank Regiment. At dusk on 20th April the infantry advanced; B Company of The Welch took their objective without loss, capturing several Greeks and putting the rest to flight. A half-hearted counter-attack by Greek carriers and two armoured cars was driven off by rifle fire and showers of grenades from A and B Companies, and contact was established with 2 RB, who had also captured their objective. But a hard core of mutineers was still holding out, and at midnight the Royal Tanks mounted a tank attack. In the pitch blackness the squadrons strayed off course and ran into a salt marsh, where their vehicles became bogged. However, the resultant din and roar of engines as they extricated themselves so over-awed the remaining Greeks that they surrendered unconditionally. The only British casualty in 'Rabbit' was one officer of The Rifle Brigade killed by a stray bullet.

3. *Italy*

The 1st Battalion The Welch Regiment were soon to see more serious fighting. In May 1944, at Alexandria, they received the welcome orders to abandon their 'Brick' duties and resume their normal role as a combat Battalion, joining the 168th Infantry Brigade in the 56th (London) Division. By now, despite fierce German opposition, the Allies had succeeded in their steady advance up the Italian peninsula, and when 1 Welch landed with their Brigade at Taranto on 17th July, Rome had been occupied by US forces. But this seemed only to stiffen opposition in the north, where the natural features of ravines, mountains and rivers, offered ideal defensive positions for Kesselring's twenty divisions. The main barrier to the 8th Army's advance was the series of defences known at the Gothic Line, running some 200 miles from La Spezia on the western coast to Rimini on the Adriatic Sea. The task of the 8th Army under General Sir Oliver Leese was to break through the Line at the Rimini 'Gap' and then join up with the US 5th Army for an advance to the Po valley.

The Welch were now commanded by Lieutenant Colonel O. G. Brooke, MBE, and with their 168 Brigade comrades of London Scottish and London Irish they were to endure bitter fighting for the next eight months. Their first serious action came in early September with the 'push' of 56 Division in the Croce area, south of Rimini. On 6th September the Battalion was ordered to support 7 Armoured Brigade in an attack on Croce itself. The Germans were in a formidable craggy position, difficult for tanks, and the armour was held up both by the terrain and the fearsome 88 mm. anti-tank guns. As a result, 1 Welch could only sit it out under heavy shellfire, which killed four men and wounded ten – their first casualties of the Italian campaign. Two days later there was a more successful, if more costly, action when the Battalion attacked the strongly-held village of Casa Menghino, near Croce. In the face of very fierce fire from Spandaus and mortars, C Company drove out the enemy, to capture the position and with it many prisoners and eleven Spandaus. But they lost twenty-five killed and twenty-eight wounded. Croce itself was finally occupied, and 168 Brigade had succeeded in establishing a springboard for the advance of their 56 Infantry Division. The operations had lasted six days, during which the Brigade was under almost constant shellfire. The Battle Honour 'Croce' was well earned. For the next two weeks 1 Welch and 168 Brigade were continuously engaged in overcoming enemy strongpoints in the San Marino–Rimini sector, during which they suffered heavy casualties, but captured several hundred prisoners and much equipment, arms and stores.

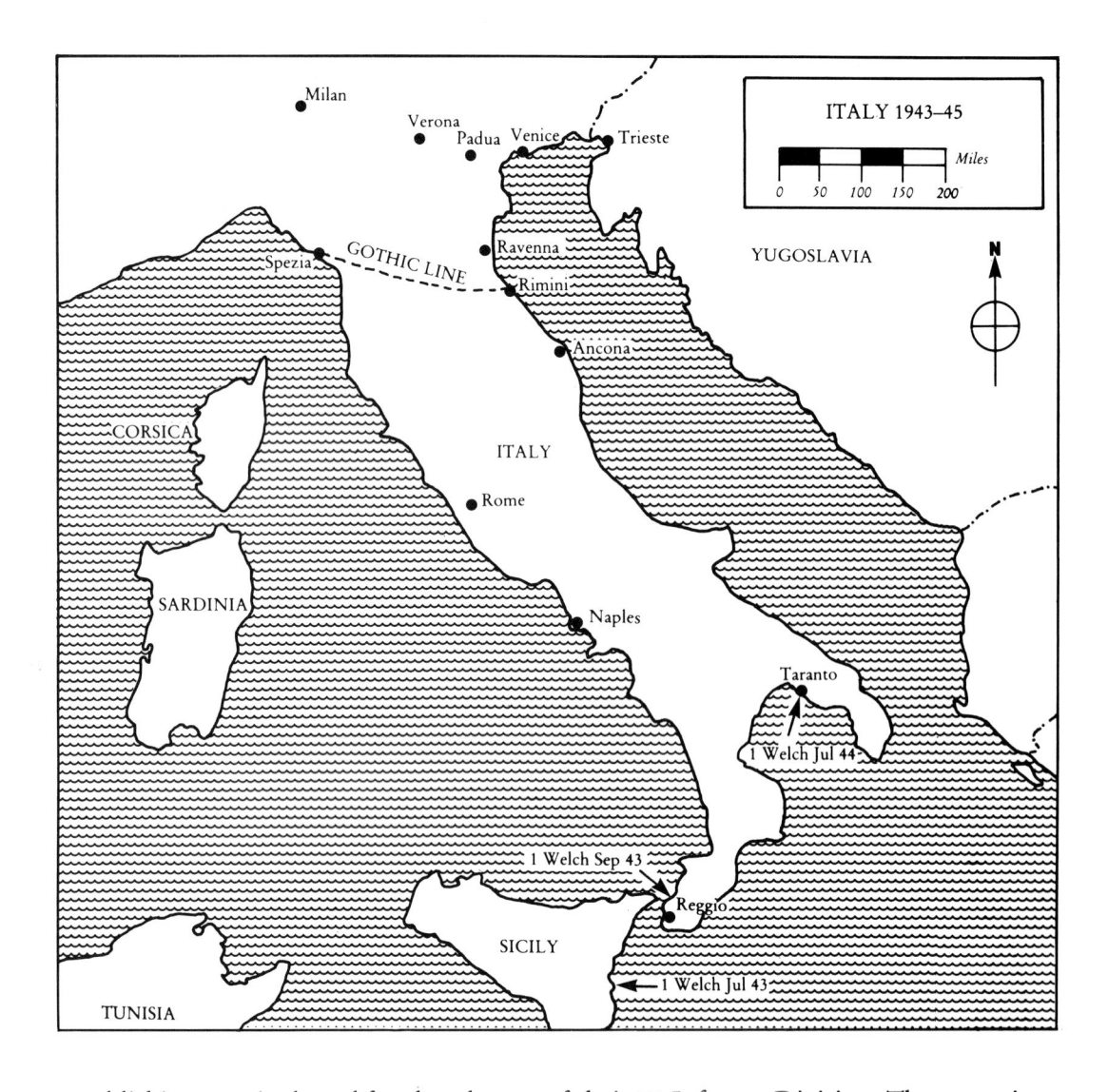

On 21st September the depleted Brigade was withdrawn into reserve. By now 1 Welch could parade only 320-odd all ranks. Two days later Colonel Brooke was aghast to receive orders from the Divisional Commander that his Battalion was to reduce to a cadre of five officers and sixty other ranks, which would be sent home to reform. The remainder would be transferred as reinforcements to The London Scottish, London Irish and The Queen's in 169 Brigade. In other words, 1 Welch were being 'cannabilised' to repair the rest. Amid gloom and despondency the Battalion dispersed, Colonel Brooke with the cadre moving to billets on the Adriatic coast south of Ancona, where they spent two unhappy months speculating on the future. But if the Commanding Officer could only obey orders, he felt he had a duty to fight for his Battalion. In October, command of 8th Army passed from Leese to Lieutenant General Sir Richard McCreery, with whom Colonel Brooke succeeded in obtaining an interview. To his intense gratification the new Army commander rescinded the reduction and ordered 1 Welch to reform as a combat Battalion. There followed a flurry of re-transfers of those transferred, while reinforcements came from the Infantry Training Depot at Caserta and a disbanded LAA Regiment which had many Welshmen from South Wales. By 13th December, 1 Welch were again operational with 37 officers and 738 other ranks. Another boost to Regimental pride was the announcement of several immediate awards for bravery in the Croce fighting: MCs went to Major J. A. Watkins and Lieutenants D. Davis and E. L. Jones, while Private Groves, Wilcox and Coster received the MM.

The end of 1944 saw a period of static warfare set in throughout northern Italy. In the face of stubborn opposition, the Allies had not been able to break out into the Po valley, nor to break through along the Adriatic plain, and it seemed that stalemate had been reached. The bitter winter of snow and rain evoked cynical comments about 'sunny Italy' from the British soldiers. For the next four months the Battalion was occupied in defensive positions along the Senio River, beating off constant enemy thrusts. On the night of 16th/17th January B Company, with supporting troop of the 4th Hussars, were heavily attacked by SS troops who had crossed the Senio river under cover of darkness. After a fierce fire-fight lasting nearly five hours, the Germans were put to flight, leaving behind thirty dead and sixty wounded in the Company position. B Company suffered only fourteen men wounded. This was just one of several similar actions which, together with constant patrolling, gave little respite to the Battalion. When relieved and withdrawn to billets in Ravenna on 6th February, 1 Welch had been almost continuously engaged for thirty-nine days. They had lost ten men killed, two officers and 76 ranks wounded.

The final allied offensive was launched in April, when, in his Special Order of the Day, Field Marshal Alexander, Supreme Allied Commander, assured his troops that the Germans were now 'very groggy and only need one almighty punch to knock them out for good'. 1 Welch now had the honour of being transferred to the elite 1st Guards Brigade, with 3rd Grenadier Guards and 3rd Welsh Guards, an element of 6th Armoured Division, and with this formation they added their weight to the final 'punch'.

The offensive opened on 9th April with the assault crossing of the Senio River. This had been preceded by saturation bombing and artillery concentration which crushed all opposition, so that the 8th Army were able to push on through the Argenta Gap towards the next formidable obstacle, the River Po. For the 1st Guards Brigade this proved something of an anti-climax, for when 1 Welch in their DUKWs (amphibious vehicles) were ferried across the 500-yard stretch of water on the morning of 25th April, the enemy seemed to have vanished. 'The Po that morning presented an astonishing sight . . . the river was alive with every variety of craft: DUKWs pounding along like paddle-steamers, storm boats whipping to and fro at high speed, and the large rafts, constructed by the Sappers in record time, ploughing their erratic course with heavy loads of vehicles and returning with batches of very surprised German prisoners.'[13]

Next day, from their position around Saguedo, just south of the Adige River, 1 Welch were able to see the dust clouds raised by the US 5th Army columns as they pushed on eastwards from the newly-captured Verona. The Germans were now indeed 'very groggy', caught between the pincers of the 5th and 8th Armies.[14] As 1 Welch raced ahead in their lorries with 6th Armoured Division, they met only pockets of easily-overrun resistance, but also droves of surrendered enemy who had no stomach for further fighting.

By 28th April New Zealand forces had entered Padua; the next day they reached Venice. On the 30th, 1 Welch crossed the Adige River, unopposed, and that night billeted peacefully in the town of Noale, having covered nearly ninety miles since noon. The Wehrmacht now seemed to have disappeared, apart from groups of dejected prisoners, and the last few days of the campaign proved more of a triumphal progress than the climax of a hard-fought offensive. Motoring on through Udine and along the fine Highway 13, the Battalion was greeted not by enemy fire, but with volleys of flowers and bottles of wine by the cheering Italian populace, who had long since abandoned any regard they might have had for their former allies.

Taking the lead of the 1st Guards Brigade, 1 Welch entered Cividale on 2nd April, This town, only some six miles from the Yugoslav frontier, was found to be already occupied by Marshal Tito's troops and some Italian partisans (together with 1,000 German prisoners), and a delicate situation arose when the Yugoslav commander demanded the withdrawal of the British soldiers. But by the exercise of great tact and patience, Colonel Brooke persuaded his new-found 'friends' that the town should be amicably shared. When the rest of the Brigade arrived, 1 Welch moved forward to Caporetto, where the inhabitants were predominantly Serbs, and pro-Tito. There was no welcome here, only sullen stares, and more dispute with the Yugoslav General. However, Brooke's tact secured another victory, and that evening the Union Flag and the Red Star of Tito flew side by side.

On the evening of 5th May the Battalion wireless picked up the BBC announcement that Germany had surrendered unconditionally. The Italian campaign, and World War II in Europe, were over. The ten months of fighting from the toe of Italy to the frontier of Yugoslavia had cost 1 Welch 14 officers and 157 other ranks killed or died of wounds or sickness.

In addition to the decorations already mentioned, Lieutenant Colonel O. G. Brooke was awarded the DSO; Major P. Ellis received the MC; while MMs went to Sergeant F. W. Dunn and Lance Corporal C. Jones.

4. *Burma*

In February 1942 the 'impregnable fortress' of Singapore fell to the Japanese; by May they had driven a British Army out of Burma, and were threatening the very frontier of India. From Hong Kong to Rangoon, and beyond, the Rising Sun had ousted the Union Flag and British prestige throughout the Far East was at its lowest ebb in history. But a year later the heroic battles of Kohima and Imphal inflicted the first serious defeat on the Imperial Japanese Army and smashed the legend of its 'invincibility'. By February 1944 Lieutenant General Sir William Slim and his 14th Army were poised for the victorious Burma campaign – the most arduous and bitterly contested ever fought by British soldiers in the East. Two antecedents of the present Regiment played significant roles in the triumph of Slim's 'Forgotten Army', and the first to see action was an hostilities-only battalion of The South Wales Borderers.

In July 1940 the 6th Battalion of The South Wales Borderers was raised in the gracious purlieu of Glanusk Park in the Usk Valley, near Crickhowell. Lieutenant Colonel V. J. F. Popham was appointed to command. Apart from a small cadre of regulars and Territorials from Dering Lines, Brecon, the successive intakes of 800-men were 'green' civilians who had never handled any weapon, other than, perhaps, a 12-bore. But these same recruits were to match the fanatic courage of Japanese soldiers and earn prestige for 6 SWB in the jungles of Burma. They formed the backbone of the Battalion for the whole of its war service.

After moves to Swansea and then East Anglia, the Battalion were posted to Felixstowe in April 1942, where they learned that they were to relinquish their infantry role and convert to a tank unit. A hectic period of MT and D & M training followed, with more than half the strength away on courses at the Royal Armoured Corps training centre at Bovington and the Lulworth gunnery ranges. In July, at Southend, 6 SWB ceased to exist as such: the Battalion had become a 'Regiment', its companies 'squadrons', its title altered to 158 Regiment Royal Armoured Corps (The South Wales Borderers). The first tanks, American Grants and Lees, arrived while most of the Regiment were away and were bravely driven from the railway sidings by inexperienced young officers. The only damage was one pillarbox, demolished.

Hardly had retraining been completed and all tank crews formed, than the Regiment found itself under orders for embarkation. This was effected at Liverpool on 29th October (1942), and after a cruise which took them to Bahia in Brazil and Durban in Natal, the Regiment disembarked at Bombay on 17th December.

For the next few months troop and squadron training followed, interspersed with some live-firing with the 75 and 37 mms. of their Grant and Stuart tanks (the latter, only recently delivered to the British, seemed such an excellent AFV that it was dubbed the 'Honey'). By March, 158 Regiment RAC had emerged as a fully-operational armoured unit, eager to prove its newly-acquired skills in battle. But this was not to be. On 29th March Colonel Popham was informed by Army Headquarters, Delhi, that the Regiment was to abandon its armoured role and reconvert to infantry, with its original title. Even though there were comforting remarks about the RAC's loss being the infantry's gain, this was a traumatic episode. All ranks had become attached to their

'Honeys' and Grants, and were even proud of their black berets. Moreover, all those months of intensive training in the mysteries of tank gunnery and the arcane intricacies of fighting vehicles now seemed utterly wasted.

Dutifully, they went about reconversion to their new, or rather, original role, with their rightful title, 6th Battalion The South Wales Borderers – the loss of which had caused some heart searching. In June 1943 Lieutenant Colonel Popham, founding Commanding Officer, was promoted Colonel and posted away. He was succeeded by his Second-in-Command, Major R. S. Cresswell, who as Lieutenant Colonel was to command the Battalion throughout the Burma campaign. The Battalion was allotted to the 72nd (Infantry) Brigade of the 36th Division, earmarked as an amphibious assault formation, and strenuous training in assault landings with amphibious Jeeps and DUKWS, together with jungle warfare exercises, occupied the rest of the year in India.

Meanwhile, after their repulse at Kohima and Imphal the Japanese had regrouped to confront the 14th Army in Arakan, the mountainous, jungle-clad area of Burma bordering the Bay of Bengal. Once more the enemy were beaten back, but not defeated. To continue his offensive General Slim requested reinforcements, and in February 1944 the 36th Division was ordered to join his Army.

For the third time 6 SWB found their special training wasted, for, the Japanese having been pushed well back from the coast and the port of Akyab, no assault landing was necessary, and they and the rest of the Division arrived peacefully at Chittagong. From here, on 24th February, 6 SWB were ferried by steamer down the coast, to disembark at Cox's Bazaar, whence they marched across the Burmese frontier to Bawli Bazaar.

The dominant feature of Arakan is the Mayu Range of hills, running parallel to the coast, about five miles inland, its crests rising to some 1,500 feet and, like the terrain elsewhere, covered with dense scrub and bamboo thickets. Even without any enemy opposition, movement in such country is difficult, to say the least. The only roads for wheeled traffic were one along the coast and another piercing the Mayu Range through tunnels. Committed to constant patrolling, 6 SWB were totally dependent on what could be carried on their own backs, or on mules led by Indian sepoys. In addition to his personal weapons, each man had 3 days' rations, spare clothing, 100 rounds of SAA, spare Bren magazines, 2 grenades, an entrenching tool and whatever 'comforts' he might manage to stuff into pack or haversack. The No. 1 of Bren sections was also burdened with the 32 lb. of that weapon. But even the sturdiest soldier could not be expected to stuggle under the weight of a 3-in. mortar and its bombs; the mortar platoons were aided by their mule teams.

Under such conditions the Welshmen of 6 SWB were opposed to an enemy who was not only adept at jungle warfare but whose tenacity, endurance and blind courage bordered on fanaticism. It was well known that few Japanese prisoners had ever been captured, for in their Samurai code, to surrender was the ultimate disgrace, incurring ostracism from regiment, family and country. 'Better death than dishonour' was a motto rigidly adhered to by most Japanese soldiers.

A month's patrol activity brought no contact with the enemy, but on 18th March the Battalion was ordered to relieve a battalion of the Royal West Kents, who had been trying unsuccessfully to evict a strong force in possession of the Mayu Tunnels area. As already mentioned, these tunnels carried the only road (originally a railway) through the Mayu Range, linking the strategic port of Maungdaw with the inland town of Buthidaung on the Mayu River. There were two tunnels, each about 200 yards long, cutting through a knife-edged, scrub and bamboo-clad ridge and surrounded by other similar ridges. The first tunnel was believed to contain a gun emplacement and stocks of ammunition and supplies; its entrance was covered by one of the spurs on which were numerous well-concealed Japanese bunkers defended by machine guns and mortars.

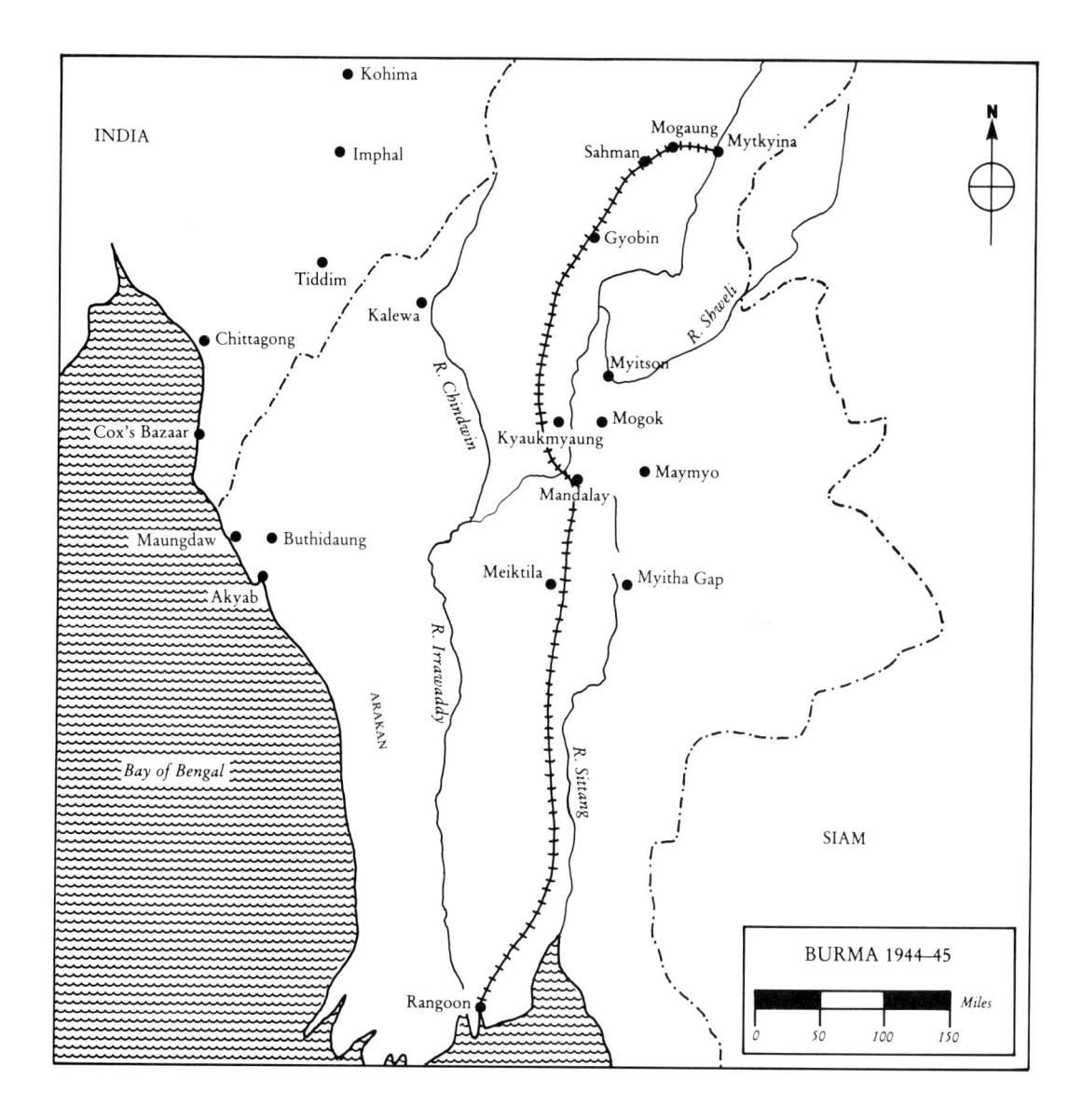

The sharp crest was no more than 5 ft wide, severely restricting the frontage of any attackers, while dense bamboo covered the steep slopes.

In an attempt to soften up the position, artillery was called forward and blasted the crest with HE, while US 'Hurribombers' flew over and added to the devastation. After three days of this onslaught it was judged expedient for 6 SWB to put in their attack. Led by Major Crewe-Read, B Company struggled up through the bamboo thickets and, hurling grenades, advanced slowly along the crest. In such constricted conditions the attack developed into a series of fierce hand-to-hand engagements by individual sections. Sergeant Woodhouse's leading section was virtually wiped out by automatic fire, but he himself pressed on alone, lobbing grenades into the bunkers and spraying them with his sten. Single-handed he captured a complete enemy position, killing all its defenders. This valiant action enabled the rest of B Company to continue their assault, and after two hours' fierce contest the whole of the defences over the first tunnel were in our hands.

Meanwhile D Company were scaling the ridge on their own front, but this proved to be more stubbornly held, and with the loss of many casualties the attempt had to be abandoned. Most of the killed (including the first officer casualty, 2nd Lieutenant A. N. Stephens) came from Tredegar in Monmouthshire, and thenceforth the position was known as 'Tredegar Hill'.[15]

By nightfall on 26th March the enemy were still in their dominating position on this hill, while although B Company's ridge had been cleared, the tunnel underneath was still occupied by the Japanese with their gun emplacement and stores. Any attempt to drive them out by an infantry attack down its constricted 200-yard length would surely be suicidal.

Next morning another unsuccessful assault was made on Tredegar Hill with 'Wasps' (carriers armed with flame-throwers), which shot forth their jets from the road below. But the range was too great, and the only effect was an impressive display of blazing bamboo. Attention was now turned to the tunnel itself. A Sherman tank was summoned up from an Indian armoured regiment and took up position at the mouth of the tunnel, with orders to shoot its 75 mm. gun straight into it. At pointblank range it fired one HE round, and the result was spectacular. There was a thunderous explosion in the depths of the tunnel, with stonework and debris hurled out of the mouth, and the Sherman, as if astonished at what it had done, rocked back on its suspension. The tunnel then belched out clouds of black smoke, and further explosions followed as the ammunition dump went up. It was not until the following morning that the raging fire died down and a patrol was able to enter the scorched cavern. All they found were bits and pieces of Japanese bodies and the remains of a burnt-out 150 mm. howitzer.

On the following morning D Company again struggled up Tredegar Hill, only to be surprised by the absence of any opposition. Perhaps demoralised by the holocaust in the tunnel, the enemy had withdrawn to a feature known as 'The Hambone', another spur. A couple of days later this positon was utterly devastated by bombing and artillery fire. There were no Japanese prisoners: only mangled bodies.

The two-day battle for 'The Tunnels' – the first action of 6 SWB – cost the Battalion one officer (2nd Lieutenant Stephens) and ten other ranks killed, three officers

6 SWB, Mayu or '24th' Tunnel, Burma.

and twenty-six wounded. Major R. O. Crewe-Read was awarded the MC for his leadership in B Company's initial attack, while Sergeant W. G. Woodhouse received the DCM. An unusual award was that of the MM to an Indian bhisti (water carrier), one Allah Bakhs, who, like Kipling's 'Gunga Din', succoured several of B Company's casualties under fire. Before leaving the area, the Battalion erected a large plaque at the scorched mouth of the first tunnel, proclaiming it 'XXIV Tunnel'.

Today the Battle Honour 'Mayu Tunnels' is borne only on the Colours of The Royal Regiment of Wales and The Gloucestershire Regiment, who gave covering fire in the attacks.

The Arakan area was now cleared of Japanese, and 6 SWB were withdrawn with the 36th Division for refitting and regrouping in Assam. This was in June, and on the 6th they heard the BBC announcing: 'This morning strong Allied forces established themselves on the mainland of France.' The term 'D-Day' had meant nothing to them, on the other side of the world, but the opening of the 2nd Front was heartening news. At home little had been heard of the operations in Burma, and now that the war correspondents and the media were devoting all their attention to the dramatic events in Normandy, the soldiers in jungle-green became well and truly a forgotten Army.

In July 1944 relays of US Dakotas flew the 36th Division back to Burma, and 6 SWB were landed (amid intermittent shelling) at Myitkina airfield, recently captured from the Japanese. This was some 250 miles north of Mandalay, and on the 27th the Battalion set out on a march which was to continue for nine months. Their 36th Division was now allotted to the Northern Combat Area Command under the vitriolic US General, Joseph Stilwell, or 'Vinegar Joe'.

Thrusting south down the 'Railway Corridor' from Mogaung, on 5th August the Battalion met fierce opposition at Sahmaw, where the Japanese were dug in along a narrow *chaung* (river-bed). Attacking on a three-column front, with little cover, they came under heavy fire from machine guns and automatics, and two of the columns were held up. The right Column under Major E. J. Jones was similarly checked, but a gallant bayonet charge led by Lieutenant I. L. Tibbs overran the bunker and the advance continued, only to be held up again. The struggle continued for nearly two days: it was only after a heavy artillery concentration from the supporting Gunners that the Japanese lost heart, allowing A and B Companies to rush the position with slight opposition.

The Battle of Sahmaw Chaung was the most costly action yet. Three officers and seventeen other ranks were killed, four officers and fifty-four wounded, four of the latter subsequently dying. The Japanese left behind forty dead, but many wounded must have been carried off. Only two prisoners were captured – both wounded.

For the rest of August 6 SWB were constantly feeling forward, sending out patrols, occupying 'Boxes', and enduring not only enemy harassment but the endemic hazards of jungle and climate. Malaria was the chief enemy, and to combat it every man was supposed to swallow one Mepacrine tablet each day. The soldiers bore an antipathy towards Mepacrine: not only did it produce a jaundiced yellow hue, but there were rumours (baseless, of course) that it rendered a man impotent. However, all Commanding Officers had strict orders from General Slim himself about the daily 'Mepacrine parade', and anyone found defaulting was in for trouble.[16] Little could be done to combat those other scourges, dysentery and typhoid, for battle conditions in monsoon jungle are not conducive to good hygiene.

By the end of August the fighting strength of 6 SWB was down to 350 all ranks, and they were withdrawn to recuperate. A couple of weeks later they were back, and continuing with the push of 36 Division down the 'Railway Corridor'. The next trial came at Gyobin Chaung near the town of Pinwe, situated on the railway line itself. This confrontation with the 128th Japanese Infantry lasted for five days, cost heavy casualties, and gained the Battle Honour 'Pinwe'.

Lieutenant (later Major) Arnold James was then a platoon commander in B Company and he subsequently wrote:[17]

> It was November 1944 and the Battalion was lead Bn of 72 Bde, pressing down the Railway Corridor. We – the 36th Div. – were being opposed by the Jap 53rd Division, trying to prevent our link-up with 19 Div at Sittang...
>
> By 9 Nov. the Bn had passed through Mawlu – site of 'White City' fame[18] – and was pressing on to Pinwe. Opposition began to harden. The 6th were moving astride the jungle track while the Sussex were astride the railway track and roughly parallel. We quickly uncovered the Jap defensive positions just south of the Gyobin Chaung, and a series of patrol clashes and skirmishes took place. Eventually B and D Coys took up positions around the chaung while HQ, A and C Coys were located some distance away. The Japs, employing their classic encircling movements, cut in between B & D Coys and the rest of the Bn, and also between the Bn and Bde.
>
> The Sussex were also attacked on the railway line and their forward Coy was forced to fight its way back to the main body.
>
> A real jumbo sandwich of troops!
>
> At the beginning of this encounter, with B Coy pressing forward, I was blown up by grenades and left for dead. Fortunately as the Japs counter-attacked and drove B and D Coys back to the Gyobin Chaung, none of them bothered to stick a bayonet in me, and when I recovered I managed to struggle back to the Coy. By that time I had been noted 'missing, believed killed'.
>
> Events now took the usual jungle warfare form of attrition. Jap attacks on all our positions came in three times a day and though we had a lot of casualties we managed to hold on...
>
> Eventually (on the fourth day) it was decided to make a night withdrawal to the main body. Major Vivian was OC B Coy and senior officer. He delegated me (then i/c 11 Platoon) and Lt. Littleford to be path-finders and, after the usual early evening attack, the Column quietly formed up and set off through the jungle on a planned compass route. We were assisted by the Bn firing a mortar on the hour, for direction. As dawn broke – nearly 10 hours later – we hit the Bn HQ spot on...
>
> Next day attempts were made to clear the Jap block, open the track for much needed supplies and ammo and to evacuate the wounded. Captain Dennis Lord took the west of the track, I took the east with 11 Platoon and the Sussex on the north. The 'squeeze' was effective: a few well placed rifle grenades caused casualties to the main Jap MG positions, the Sussex rushed the position and the track was open (the Sussex Major got an MC here).

Field Marshal Sir Claude Auchinleck inspecting 6 SWB; Burma, 1944.

The convoy of Jeeps and 15-cwt trucks, with Indian drivers, came up at high speed, overshot Headquarter's 'Box' and bumped straight into the Japanese block beyond. Lieutenant Davies of B Company immediately rushed forward with his Platoon, engaging the enemy with rifles, automatics and mortars. The leading truck was being driven off by the Japanese when a lucky hit from a 3-in. mortar wrecked it. Private Harber of Davies's Platoon bravely took over the second truck and reversed it out of danger – with seventeen bullet holes in the cab. Meanwhile a sudden determined rush by all men with Stens and Brens swept through A and B Companies' original positions, took the Japanese by surprise and recaptured the positions. Fifty Japanese dead were counted; many more must have been wounded. But as usual there were no prisoners.

The opposition had now crumbled, and when on 19th November 6 SWB were withdrawn to recoup, 29th Brigade took over the advance, and the pipers of the Royal Scots Fusiliers headed the march into the remains of Pinwe village.

The name 'Gyobin Chaung' does not appear in the roll of Battle Honours: instead, 'Pinwe' was selected. The five-day battle cost 6 SWB one officer (Lieutenant P. W. Tyson) and twenty-five other ranks killed. Eight officers and 123 other ranks were wounded, 6 of whom died later. There were many awards for bravery. Major C. J. Vivian received the DSO and MC; Major J. A. Lloyd and Lieutenant N. L. Davies, the

MC. The DCM was awarded to CQMS V. Croker for his gallantry in rescuing the wounded Major Lloyd under fire. Six MMs went to private soldiers.

In December the Battalion, still with the NCAC, took part in the advance down the Shweli River which culminated the following February in a hard-fought struggle at Myitson, where the Japanese fiercely contested the river crossings. Attack and counter-attack followed almost continuously for seven days, and it was only after the enemy had suffered more than 400 killed and twice as many wounded that they conceded the bridgeheads and withdrew. It was here that Lieutenant A. Cave-Brown-Cave displayed outstanding leadership in beating off repeated attacks on his position, thereby earning an immediate DSO – a rare distinction for a subaltern officer. Here also the Battalion lost eighteen all ranks killed or died of wounds, and forty wounded.

In March 6 SWB and their Division were detached from the NCAC to rejoin the 14th Army for the pursuit of the retreating Japanese along the road to Mandalay. That city fell on 21st March, but the Battalion hhad no share in the capture, being engaged further north. They were then flown by detachments to Myituge (a few miles south of Mandalay), poised for their final push to Rangoon. But this was not to be. There was still a troublesome pocket of resistance around Kubyin in the souther Shan States, and 72 Brigade was detached to 'clean up' the area. For the first three weeks of April there was hard slogging through dense jungle as 6 SWB pushed from position to position, frequently clashing with enemy patrols and outposts, but never encountering opposition in strength. The Japanese in this area were the remnants of the Army cut off on the British capture of Meiktila. Many had made good their escape into Thailand, where they were glad of the railway built by British prisoners-of-war; but many others were prepared to stand and fight it out.

6 SWB fought their last battle on 29th April when they were ordered to clear the Myittha Gap. Some 50 miles east of Meiktila, the Gap was a strongly-defended pass between jungle-clad mountains, the enemy commanding the road from fortified heights and caves. Supported by artillery and mortars, three companies pressed the attack most gallantly; but although they inflicted casualties, they could make little progress in the face of heavy fire and the difficult terrain. They spent the night dug in where they were, while the Gunners' 25-pounders continued to send their HE screaming over. At first light next morning patrols felt forward, only to find the enemy had vanished. Perhaps this final action was a somewhat tame end to the campaign, but it was not a bloodless one; the Batalion lost seven killed and eight wounded.

Meanwhile 72nd Brigade had been under orders for withdrawal to India, and in early May 6 SWB were evacuated by air to Imphal, whence they travelled by rail to Poona. Moving to Bangalore, they set about refitting and training for the projected recapture of Singapore and Malaya – an operation which was precluded by the devastation of Hiroshima and Nagasaki by the American atom bombs. But VJ Day did not mean home and demob for 6 SWB. In the Dutch East Indies a tense, if somewhat Gilbertian, situation had arisen since the capitulation of the Japanese occupiers. Strong 'nationalist' factions of the native Indonesians saw this as the opportunity to rise against their former overlords, the Dutch, with consequent outbreak of murder and terrorism. Under the terms of the Armistice, the Japanese forces strove to maintain law and order, protecting their erstwhile enemies from the latter's subjects, but of course this could only be a temporary measure, and in October 1945 British and Indian troops were sent to take over. Among them were 6 SWB, a unit of the 26th Indian Division.

The Battalion was centred on Medan, capital of Sumatra, where many thousands of Japanese troops had to be disarmed and evacuated. This was effected with surprisingly willing co-operation from the Japanese themselves: as the previous historian records, it was a strange experience to see these former inplacable foes bowing and saluting instead of hurling grenades and loosing off automatics from behind bunkers. There then followed months of guard and escort duties, varied with constant patrolling, when there were many encounters with insurgents armed with weapons ranging from ex-Japanese machine guns to blow-pipes with poisoned darts.

By the end of December order had been restored. And with it came the run-down of 6 SWB. On 26th December, 250 men were repatriated, not replaced; by 5th March the strength was down to 393 effectives, and D Company was disbanded. Finally, on 15th March 1946 orders came for the formal disbandment of the Battalion.

During their six years' service the 6th Battalion The South Wales Borderers had fought through some 500 miles of the Burmese jungles, leaving there 8 officers and 81 other ranks killed in action, while 18 officers and 251 were wounded. They had added six Battle Honours to the Colours of the 24th, and had earned two DSOs, six MCs, four DCMs, seventeen MMs, and several American decorations. For a unit that had not existed before 1940, this was a record to be proud of.

It was sad that there was no fitting *Nunc dimittis* for this splendid representative of The South Wales Borderers. After a valedictory Special Order of the Day by the Allied Commander in Sumatra (Major General Hedley, DSO), the Battalion, like old soldiers, simply faded away. Personnel due for release were sent home in successive drafts; those with low 'demob numbers' were posted to other units. By the end of April 6 SWB had ceased to exist.[19]

We must now revert to 1939, and to the 2nd Battalion The Welch Regiment who, as related at the beginning of this chapter, were serving at Agra, in India, when war was declared. If there was a flurry of initial excitement at the prospect of active service, this soon evaporated. Weeks passed into months with no hint of an overseas posting: routine remained virtually unchanged and the only effect of war was the loss of more experienced officers, WOs and NCOs drafted to units earmarked for the Middle East or elsewhere. Meanwhile the Battalion moved from Agra to Bombay, from Bombay to Bangalore, and normal peace-time training continued. In October 1941, at Bangalore, all the transport mules were handed over, to be replaced by 15-cwt trucks and '3-tonners'. This seemed to presage active service; but no orders arrived. Next February, however, after the Japanese had overrun Malaya and invaded Burma, there was a surge of excitement when 2 Welch were rushed to Calcutta, there to embark with 2 Border and 1 Northants, under orders for Rangoon. The Brigade sailed on 7th March and had scarcely cleared the mouth of the Hooghly when Rangoon fell to the Japanese and the

Comrades of 6 SWB with guests, attending the 40th annual dinner at Newport in October 1986. Lieutenant Colonel Cresswell, Commanding Officer of 6 SWB in Burma, is in the centre of the front row.   PHOTOGRAPH: JEFFREY F. MORGAN

operation was aborted. Frustrated, 2 Welch returned to Bangalore, and thence to Conjeevaram in Madras – 'a place noted for its terrible humidity and frogs' as Captain de Courcy recorded. By now the overriding question seemed to be not so much 'When shall we go?' but 'Shall we go?' It was almost unbelievable that a fully-trained, regular Battalion should be kept virtually kicking its heels in India when their comrades of the 1st Battalion had been heavily in action for more than a year. Nevertheless another two years were to pass before 2 Welch confronted an enemy.

    By March 1943 the Battalion had been allotted to its fighting formation, the 19th (Indian) Division, the 'Dagger' Division, under the inspiring leadership of Major General T. W. Rees (a Welsh-speaking Welshman). Together with the 4th/4th and 4th/6th Gurkha Rifles they formed the 62nd Indian Infantry Brigade, and during the arduous months of intensive jungle training firm bonds of friendship and mutual respect were established between Welshmen and Gurkhas. Preparations for the Burma operations went ahead. Mules reappeared to oust the heavy MT vehicles; American Jeeps were issued; Sten guns, 2-in. and 3-in. mortars were added to the weaponry; slouch hats and jungle-green dress replaced topis and khaki drill.

At long last the years of frustration were over: in October 1944, 2 Welch and their Gurkha comrades arrived at a perimeter camp at Mile 13 on the Imphal–Kohima road. The Battalion was commanded by Lieutenant Colonel D. L. C. Reynolds, OBE. The 19th Division now formed part of the 14th Army, its task being to drive eastwards across the Chindwin to Katha where the Mandalay road and railway met the Irrawaddy. The Chindwin crossing was unopposed, and the columns pushed ahead along the jungle tracks. From now on all supplies were dropped by air, which meant additional hard labour clearing the dropping zones. On entering the Zibyu mountain range there was more wearisome toil as precipitous tracks had to be made up to allow the pack-animals to scale them. No enemy was met until the end of November (after some fifty miles of jungle slogging), when 2 Welch contacted a small Japanese rearguard. The subsequent brief fire-fight was 'more strenuous than dangerous' (de Courcy); no casualties were suffered by the Battalion and the Japanese withdrew without leaving any dead behind. This seemed a tame introduction to an enemy held to be ferocious and unyielding, and when 2 Welch, leading 62 Brigade, entered the Division's first objective, the town of Pinlebu on 16th December, they found it abandoned by the Japanese. But more serious business was soon to come. On 20th December the Brigade had secured the Kawlin airfield, some 30 miles west of the Irrawaddy, when 2 Welch were ordered to push east and cut off a Japanese force withdrawing towards the village of Kyaukpyintha, nearer the Irrawaddy. On approaching the area A and B Companies were held up by heavy machine-gun fire; an attempt to outflank the enemy failed, and with nightfall both sides resigned themselves to sitting it out and hurling grenades. One officer and six men of 2 Welch were wounded. On the following day artillery and mortar concentration enabled D Company to work round the rear of the enemy position, but they too became pinned down by machine-gun fire on their flanks, eventually withdrawing after dark. Next morning a patrol pushed forward to find the enemy gone. This action cost 2 Welch three men killed and one officer and eleven men wounded. By now jungle ulcers and fever were taking their toll: so much so that at the end of December C Company had to be temporarily disbanded, the few fit men being distributed among the other three companies.

The next objective of 19 Indian Division was to clear the Shwebo area and establish bridgeheads on the Irrawaddy River, preparatory to an all-out thrust on Mandalay. On 5th January 1945 2 Welch arrived within twelve miles of the Irrawaddy. Since the previous November they had covered some 350 miles from the plains of Imphal, nearly all of it on their own feet. Next day, B and D companies moved forward and a patrol of D under Lieutenant A. Murrow crossed the river to carry out a reconnaissance on the east bank. This small body of 2 Welch were the first British troops to cross the Irrawaddy since the retreat from Burma in 1942. They returned with valuable intelligence, but Lieutenant Murrow was killed by a sniper. On 14th January the 19th Division established a bridgehead on the east bank of the river, and next day a second bridgehead was secured eight miles downstream at Kyaukmyaung. The actual crossings were affected without casualties, but consolidation proved more difficult. Suspecting (erroneously) that the whole of the British IV Corps would follow 19 Division, the Japanese concentrated all available forces in the area, consisting of two infantry divisions supported by regiments of artillery and tanks.

The battle of the Kyaukmyaung bridgehead was fought out for a whole month, from 14th January to 14th February, and 2 Welch were constantly engaged with their 62nd Brigade. At first holding positions on the west bank of the river, they suffered severely from artillery fire, but launched several attacks across the river. On one of these Major J. B. Brown and A Company captured a strongly-held Japanese position, with much ammunition, stores and valuable documents, losing only four men wounded. For his outstanding leadership in this action Major Brown was awarded the MC. Among the Japanese dead were discovered the horribly mutilated bodies of two of the Battalion's men who had been taken prisoner earlier.

With the arrival of reinforcements from Imphal on 20th January, it was possible to reform C Company, who promptly carried out a successful reconnaissance on the far side of the river. On the night of 28th/29th January 2 Welch crossed the Irrawaddy at the Kyaukmyaung bridgehead and two days later took over a section of the perimeter at Yeshin, two miles into the jungle. Continuously opposed by enemy ambushes, and the difficult terrain, the Battalion took nearly ten hours to cover those two miles. For the next fortnight the dispersed companies were subjected to almost continuous shelling and sniping, while movement between the positions nearly always involved clashes with parties of Japanese who remained exceedingly active by night as well as by day. On 3rd February the 4th/6th Gurkhas passed through The Welch, and with tank support attempted to clear the main enemy position. But the Japanese put down such a devastating concentration of artillery fire, from 105 mm. and 150 mm. guns, that both Gurkhas and tanks were halted, with heavy casualties. The Welch, too, suffered as the shelling fell among their positions, but this did not deter them from going to the aid of their Gurkha friends, and there were several acts of gallantry as wounded Gurkhas were brought back under fire. Later, Sergeant H. G. Jones and Private Telke were awarded the MM for such acts. This day's action cost 2 Welch 19 killed (including Major J. B. Brown, MC) and 32 wounded, while the 4th/6th Gurkha Rifles lost 22 killed and 87 wounded.

It was not until 14th February that the Battalion was relieved and pulled back for a much-needed rest. The final two weeks at Yeshin proved the most trying period of the campaign. As General Lomax wrote:

> Shelling was almost continuous ... The water supply was contaminated by Japanese corpses and the bodies of 120 mules ... There were clouds of flies, breeding as fast as only flies can. The mosquitoes were merciless. Constant harassment by small parties of Japanese made it almost impossible to use mosquito veils. The stench of decomposing flesh was overpowering and repulsive. It was impossible to bury all the bodies, and paraffin was used for speedy cremation. The health of the Battalion began to suffer.

To add to these sufferings, the air drops included Indian and not British rations, for the rear supply base was under the mistaken impression that the Gurkhas had relieved 2 Welch. Thus the Welshmen had to make do with a strange diet of dried fish, lentils, peas, nuts and hard biscuits.

At this juncture Lieutenant Colonel D. L. C. Reynolds, who had led the Battalion since the outset of the campaign, was posted home under the 'Python' scheme,[20] his place being taken by Lieutenant Colonel B. T. V. Cowey.

By March the 14th Army had the Japanese on the run. But, though retreating, the Japanese still showed plenty of fight, as 2 Welch discovered in several major clashes. On 5th March their 62nd Brigade was ordered to capture Maymyo, some 25 miles from Mandalay, two other brigades being tasked with an attack on the latter. The approach march of sixty miles through the mountainous area of the Shan Hills was one of the stiffest tests the Battalions had yet experienced. The route (along opium-smugglers' trails) involved a climb of 4,000 ft up an almost precipitous track wide enough for only single file. Even mules slipped and fell; the men were struggling under 70-lb. loads and the ascent took a whole day to complete. On the fourth day the 4th/6th Gurkhas took over the lead and on 11th March entered the Maymyo cantonment area and began to clear the town. Meanwhile 2 Welch were ordered to outflank the town and take up a 'long-stop' position to cut the Maymyo–Mandalay road. In this they were eminently successful. At dusk a convoy of some 300 Japanese in assorted vehicles ran straight into the ambush and the Battalion opened up with everything they had – rifles, Brens, mortars, and grenades for good measure. The result was a haul of thirty-six 3-ton lorries, nine staff cars, a Jeep and a 75 mm. gun, together with cash chests, rations, spare tyres and equipment and marked maps and confidential documents. Only a few dead bodies were found, but pools of blood everywhere betokened many other casualties. 2 Welch lost not a single man. In Maymyo itself the Gurkhas had been equally successful, and on the following day both Corps and Divisional commanders flew in to congratulate the Brigade.

During the ten days' respite at Maymyo a parade service was held in All Saints Church – the first since the Japanese occupation in 1942 – and the names of all 2 Welch killed and wounded during the campaign were read out. Later the Battalion presented a lectern to the Church, bearing the inscription: 'Presented to All Saints Church, Maymyo by 2nd Battalion The Welch Regiment, to commemorate the liberation of Maymyo and the first Divine Service held in this church after three years of Japanese occupation, on Sunday 18th March 1945.'

While 62nd Brigade were capturing Maymyo, the remainder of 19 Division with 2 British Division had advanced on Mandalay, and on 21st March the Union Flag was hoisted over the city in the presence of Lieutenant General Sir William Slim. The 14th Army had won the battle for central Burma and now followed the final drive on Rangoon. While 4 Corps, with 19 Division, forged ahead down the road from Meiktila, 26 Indian Division prepared for a seaborne assault on Rangoon. This Division, whose assault troops landed there unopposed on 4th May, was commanded by Major General C. E. N. Lomax, who had been Commanding Officer of 2 Welch in India from 1935 to 1939, and whose wartime history of the Regiment has been one of the principal sources for this chapter.

The race to Rangoon began on 1st April, 19 Division's chief role being one of mopping up and consolidating behind the spearhead of the 14th Army. Besides the constant patrolling and hard marching, this meant several fierce clashes with delaying

Japanese diehards who, true to their code, refused to surrender. During the whole Burma campaign 2 Welch took only half a dozen prisoners, some of whom were badly wounded.

In early May the Battalion crossed the Sittang and began vigorous operations east of Toungou. Everywhere they met stubborn opposition, for the Japanese fought every inch of the ground, laying ambushes covered by machine guns and artillery. During the period 15th–20th May they pushed forward only six miles and lost twelve killed and fifty-two wounded, but in the same period they captured twelve field guns – which brought them a congratulatory message from the Divisional commander. For his leadership in this operation Lieutenant Colonel Cowey was awarded the DSO; Major A. C. Tyler received the MC. General Lomax remarks that the fighting in this phase, while not spectacular, was a severe test of physical and moral endurance. To the usual hardships of jungle warfare against a fanatical enemy was added the incessant deluging of monsoon rain, which soaked everyone and everything and transformed tracks into quagmires of mud, rivulets into raging torrents. While crossing one of these by raft, C Company lost six men drowned. By early July, battle casualties and sickness had reduced the effective strength of 2 Welch to 320 officers and men.

But the end was near. By 28th July, some 4,000 Japanese had been killed in the Meiktila–Toungou area, of which 1,500 were claimed by the 19th Indian Division. The Battalion was now patrolling the lines of communication from Toungou to Thandaung, between the Sittang and Salween Rivers. Although they did not suspect it, World War II had only a fortnight to run. They suffered their final casualties on 28th July when a convoy was ambushed on the Thandaung road and twenty men of the Battalion and four Indian soldiers were killed. One of the survivors was Private G. Tanner who, although wounded, dragged others to cover, and then struggled three miles to Thandaung for help. He was awarded the MM.

On the Japanese surrender on 15th August 1945, 2 Welch were at Toungou, where, on the 26th, they attended a service in the Church, to witness the dedication of a memorial to their dead. During the Burma campaign they had lost 10 officers and 140 other ranks killed, most of whom lie in unmarked graves in the jungle.

Notes

[1] Brett, Lieutenant Colonel G. A. *et al. History of The South Wales Borderers and The Monmouthshire Regiment 1937–1952* (5 vols., Pontypool 1953–6); Lomax, Major General C. E. N. *The History of The Welch Regiment 1919–1951* (Cardiff, 1952).

[2] Fraser, General Sir David. *And We Shall Shock Them: The British Army in The Second World War* (1983).

[3] These were co-opted Norwegian fishing vessels. No purpose-built landing craft were available at this date, and as the previous historian observes, the troops were fated later to travel many scores of miles in the humble 'Puffers'.

[4] Later as Lieutenant Colonel Jack Adams he wrote the history of the 24th for the 'Famous Regiments' series.

[5] Published in the 24th's Journal, April 1941. Charles Cox retired as Brigadier in 1958.

[6] In 1945 the French government created Brigadier Philip Gottwaltz a Chevalier de Legion d'Honneur, and awarded him the Croix de Guerre avec Palmes.

[7] It is generally agreed that the standards of 'valour' required for the VC award became progressively stricter. As early as 1918 Colonel Graham, DMS at the War Office, said: 'You cannot compare the VC in this war with any previous war. People are now getting the MM for what would have won the VC in the South African war.' (*The Evolution of the Victoria Cross*, by M. J. Crook, 1975).

[8] These figures were reported in *The Men of Harlech*, May 1969. They were not available to General Lomax when he published his *History of The Welch Regiment 1919–1951*.

[9] Adams, Lieutenant Colonel J. Q. *The South Wales Borderers* (1968).

[10] His detailed account of this last operation of 1 SWB was published in the October 1942 issue of *XXIV The Journal of The South Wales Borderers*.

[11] Captain Comer survived to become Lieutenant Colonel, MBE, and his unpublished account of the Benghazi 'walk-out' relates a remarkable coincidence. In 1962 he participated in a Staff College 'Study Group' tour of the Gazal Line, and there he met the German officer who nearly captured him at Benghazi.

[12] After Benghazi Major J. T. Gibson was promoted Lieutenant Colonel and given command of the Battalion in place of the captured Colonel Napier.

[13] Major General Lomax, op. cit.

[14] The US and British Armies finally linked up on 23rd April at a village with the appropriate name of Finale (near Ferrara).

[15] In 1946 a casket of earth was brought home from the hill and lodged in the offices of the Tredegar Urban District Council. It was later consecrated and placed in Tredegar Parish Church.

[16] In December 1944 Slim actually sacked one Commanding Officer for failing in this duty.

[17] Unpublished letter from Major A. James, OBE, to author, 11th May 1987.

[18] A valiantly-defended Chindit 'Box', March 1944.

[19] But the comradeship of 6 SWB officers and men forged in the Burmese jungles has lived on to the present day with annual Reunion dinners in Newport, when tales of how they licked the Japs are told and retold. At the 1987 Reunion 140 members of the old Battalion were present.

[20] A system of repatriation by groups, according to length of service overseas.

"D" Day, 6th June 1944; by Terence Cuneo. BY KIND PERMISSION OF TERENCE CUNEO

The 53rd (Welsh) Division Memorial at s'Hertogenbosch.

CHAPTER SIXTEEN

The Second World War (Part II) (1944–45)

1. *D-Day–VE Day*

Before arriving at the momentous date of 6th June 1944, the reader may find it helpful to glance at the dispositions of our two Regiments' various Battalions. As we have just seen, in June 6 SWB and 2 Welch were heavily engaged in Burma. 1 Welch were in Egypt, preparing for their Italian experience. Only six combatant Battalions were home based, available for the long-awaited assault on Hitler's 'Atlantic Wall', or what Montgomery termed 'the Great Crusade'.[1] Of these six only two were regular – the 1st and 2nd Battalions The South Wales Borderers. As recounted earlier, the 1st Battalion had suffered 'suspended animation' after the Libyan disaster in 1942. It was subsequently reformed with an influx from the 4th Battalion The Monmouthshire Regiment, but for reasons known only to High Command, it remained uncommitted to active service for the duration of the war. After returning from the abortive Norwegian campaign, the 2nd Battalion had also spent frustrating years at home, engaged in such homely tasks as lifting potatoes in East Anglia. But in March 1944 morale soared when the Battalion was ordered to form, with the 2nd Battalions of The Gloucestershire and Essex Regiments, the 56th (Independent) Infantry Brigade, earmarked for Operation 'Overlord'.

The remaining Battalions who landed in Normandy in June 1944 were all Territorial: 2 and 3 Mons and 4 and 1/5 Welch. Although mobilised in 1939, none of these had yet fired a shot in anger. But their moment was approaching.

To sum up, the Order of Battle for the two Regiments in June 1944 was thus:

```
2 SWB     – 56 (Ind.) Inf. Bde
2 Mons    – 160 Inf. Bde, 53 (Welsh) Division
3 Mons    – 159 Inf. Bde, 11 Armoured Division
4 Welch   – 160 Inf. Bde, 53 (Welsh) Division
1/5 Welch – 160 Inf. Bde, 53 (Welsh) Division
```

Despite top secrecy, long before the first week of June, everyone, soldier and civilian, knew the Second Front was about to be launched with an invasion of occupied France. But what no one except a select few knew, was exactly when and where that assault would take place.

Overt preparations were made for an attack in the Pas de Calais, and this deceit, named Operation 'Fortitude', was largely successful in diverting German attention from the real objective, the coast of Normandy. The plan, devised over some five months by allied High Command, was to land British, US and Canadian forces along a fifty-mile sector of the coast in the bay of Seine between Le Havre and the Cherbourg peninsula. After establishing a firm 'lodgement' (Monty's term), the British would attempt to contain the German forces in the Caen area on the left flank, while the Americans on the right would break out and put in a pincer movement. The allied assault force comprised 40 divisions: 23 in Bradley's 2nd (US) Army Group and 17 in Montgomery's 21st Army Group: a total of some 800,000 men and 324,000 vehicles, tanks, guns, transport and others. Naval support included 284 warships, while 7,700-odd bombers and fighters provided air cover.

The assembly of this massive force and its movement across the Channel on D-Day was a *tour de force* of staff work which has never been equalled in the history of warfare. Since this is a regimental history, it is unnecessary to go into details, but those seeking such an in-depth study could profitably refer to Max Hastings's *Overlord: D-Day and the Battle for Normandy*.[2]

Only one representative of our two Regiments was privileged to land with the spearhead of the assault force on 6th June 1944. This was the 2nd Battalion The South Wales Borderers, who were further distinguished by being the only Welsh unit in action on the D-Day beaches.[3] Their 56 (Independent) Brigade had been training as lorried infantry, to work with an armoured division, but for the assault landing they were attached as a fourth Brigade to 50 (Northumbrian) Division. The Battalion was commanded by Lieutenant Colonel R. W. Craddock, MBE, with Major F. F. S. Barlow as his Second-in-Command. It so happened that both the other two Battalions in the Brigade – 2 Glosters and 2 Essex – bore a Sphinx in their badge, like The South Wales Borderers, and so this was adopted as the Brigade sign, worn on battledress and painted on vehicles. Thus the 'Sphinx Brigade' acquired its distinctive cachet.

The unprecedented degree of planning and painstaking attention to detail that preceeded D-Day were such that by 3rd June every officer and man of 2 SWB in their sealed camp in the New Forest was not only equipped for all eventualities (even down to sea-sickness tablets) but knew exactly what his task was. Low-level RAF photographs and sand models enabled all to become familiar with the actual features they would see on the ground. At the final briefing it was revealed that 56 Independent Brigade would go ashore in the second wave, on the British Gold Beach about a mile east of Arromanches, then push inland, seizing the bridge at Vaux-sur-Aure, to secure the high ground north of Bayeux. They would be the right-flank element of the entire British assault force, and would endeavour to link up with the US 1st Army elements on the British right.

The D-Day landing was the most critical operation of World War II and the

D DAY 6 JUNE 1944

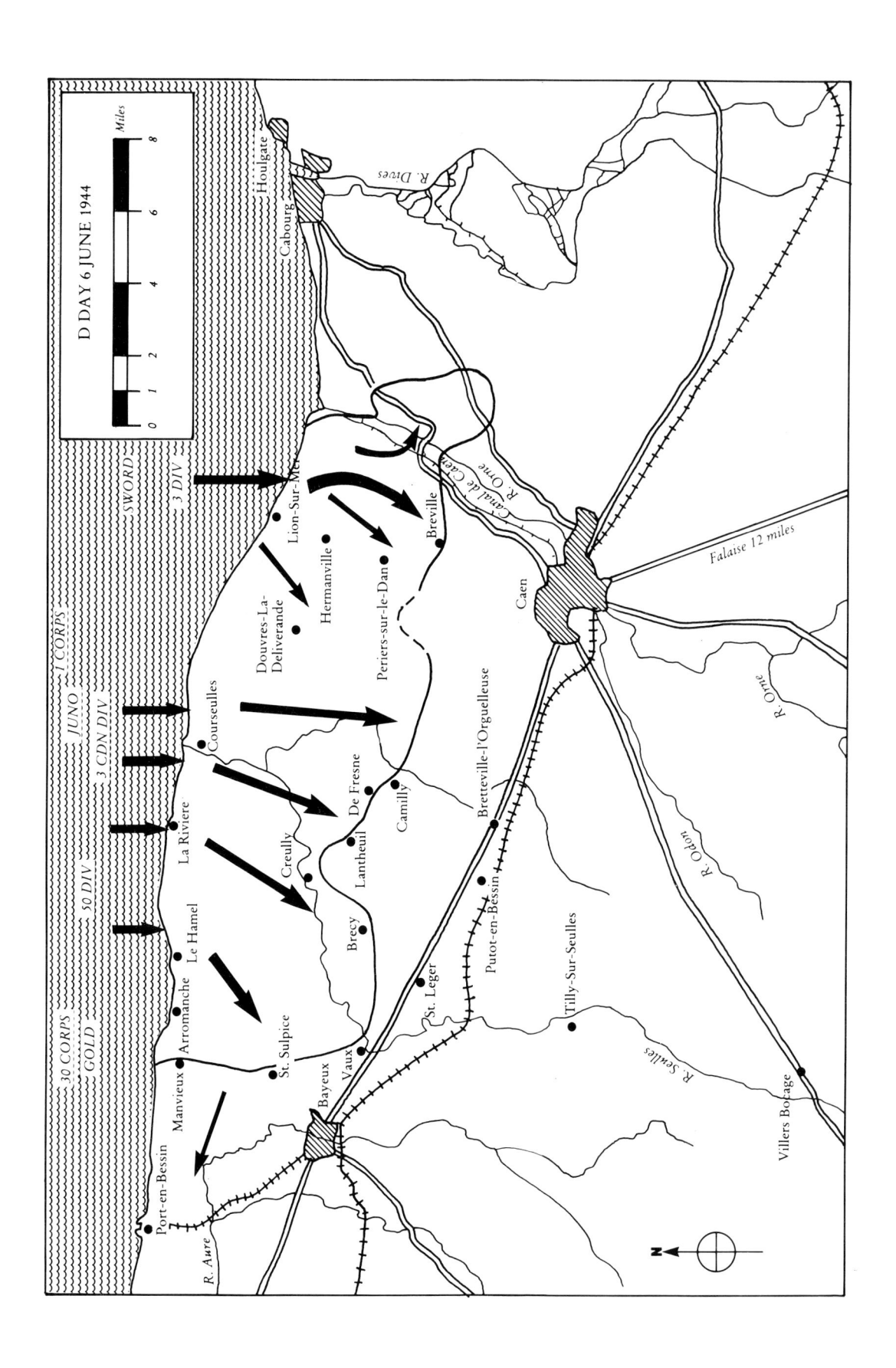

subsequent campaign in North-West Europe was the victorious climax. With the possible exception of 'The Hundred Days' of the Waterloo campaign, no other operations have produced such a vast body of literature, from general histories down to personal reminiscences. The present Regiment's archives contain six published volumes recording in detail the services of the five Battalions who added twenty-eight Battle Honours to the Colours. Within the limitations of this single volume it is impossible to do more than single out some of the more significant actions and to reproduces a few first-hand accounts.

First, D-Day: Major J. T. Boon was commanding B Company of 2 SWB, and his eminently readable account of the Battalion's operations throughout the campaign was published as Part II of The South Wales Borderers' war history.[4]

> We arrived off the coast on 6th June at around ten o'clock. In places clouds of smoke were rising and a few destroyers were shelling strong-points in a desultory fashion. Every now and then through the clouds flights of aircraft could be glimpsed (ours) . . . Just before mid-day the three landing craft began their run-in, and as their engines accelerated a thrill of excitement ran through the decks. Gathered in the bows stood the 2/24th, a truly fantastic sight, laden with guns, ammunition boxes, stretchers, wireless sets and pistols, and wearing, like extended 'Long Johns', stretched waders reaching to the armpits. Soldiers of other wars may smile, but the Battalion had to advance at least fifteen miles, and nothing reduces marching efficiency more than wet, sore feet.
>
> About noon the craft rammed the beach at Hable de Heurtot and with the cry 'Down Ramps' the two gangways extending beyond the bows were lowered. It was a freakish sort of landing. A few hundred yards to the east the 2nd Essex walked ashore dry shod. One Company of the 2/24th had water only up to its ankles. The others, in particular the craft in which the CO's Battalion HQ was carried, had less luck. The craft could not get close into the beach and between them and dry land a deep channel formed, swept by a heavy cross sea . . . Lt. Col. Craddock, with typical dash, seized the landing line and leapt into the sea, only to disappear from sight. Handicapped by his heavy load, he was swept right across to the next landing craft to port before he reached the shore.

Captain J. N. Somerville[5] was Adjutant and kept a diary from D-Day. Of the landing, he wrote:

> We went in line abreast, full speed ahead, and everybody felt a sort of quickening of the pulses with the surge of the engines vibrating through the ship. We grounded some way out . . . and had to wade ashore up to our necks in water, and sometimes out of our depth. Luckily there was no serious opposition from the beaches. We were lucky to have no casualties from drowning . . . the waves were picking men up and throwing them forward on

their faces. The worst loads to carry ashore were the 18 sets,[6] PIATS and about 100 airborne bicycles . . . [On the way up to the Assembly area] we passed numbers of our dead, as 231 Bde had had a fair number of casualties . . . we had twelve casualties from mortar fire and a couple from snipers. Snipers seemed to be everywhere. The man behind me marching up was hit in the head and just fell down, which rather shook me . . . We reached our assembly area at about 1500 hrs. It had been shelled and bombed previously and there were six very dead and rather disgusting horses and cows slap in the middle of it, and the stench was appalling.

It will be noted that 2 SWB met little of the fierce opposition they had been expecting. This was due partly to the saturation naval and air bombardment which preceded the landings, and partly to the fact that their Brigade was in the second wave and missed much of the initial resistance. Pushing on from the assembly point, the Battalion successfully cleared their first objective, a radar station which the Germans fired and abandoned in the face of an attack by D Company. They then moved on to secure the day's final objective, the important bridge at Vaux-sur-Aure which carried one of the main roads to Bayeux. This, surprisingly, was found to be undefended and intact, and the Battalion dug in for the night. So ended D-Day. Colonel Craddock could be well satisfied. His Battalion had done everything asked of it in the planning; it had secured its objective, and in doing so had covered more ground than any other battalion in the assault force – some fifteen miles. Twenty-odd prisoners had been taken, many more enemy had been killed, all this for the loss of only three men killed and half a dozen wounded. But more serious business was soon to follow.

At dawn on D+1 (7th June) 2 SWB pushed forward to the ridge north of Bayeux, which patrols reported clear of Germans. The Americans were now advancing after their costly landing on Omaha Beach, and to effect a link-up with them 2 SWB were ordered to capture the strongpoint of Sully, just east of Bayeux. Here was a bridge over the Drome and a large chateau, which was reported to be heavily fortified and occupied by the Headquarters of a German regiment (equivalent to a British brigade).

For close support of the Battalion, a field regiment of Gunners, a platoon of 4.2 in. mortars and troops of tanks were ordered up, while off Gold Beach a naval cruiser was prepared to add the weight of its 6-in. guns. This might have evoked memories of the Battalion's 'attached warship' in Norway, but unhappily the cruiser proved unable to help. Her FOB (Forward Officer Bombardment) was unable to direct her fire because it was impossible for him to find a clear OP in the close, thickly-wooded area.

While A Company took up position along the road leading to the bridge and the chateau, B Company (Major Boon) passed through them and deployed for attack. The Gunners' 25-pounders were now sending over HE, but unfortunately several shells burst in the trees, causing casualties in both Companies. Soon B Company were held up near the bridge by heavy fire from an 88 mm. gun and an assortment of other weapons. Realising that further advance down the narrow road would be costly, Major Boon took Corporal Thomas and a few men and worked round the flank of the gun position. What followed is described by the Company Second-in-Command, Captain A. F. Thompson:

With no more than three or four men in support, he stalked the 88mm gun which was firing at almost pointblank range at the main body of the Company. Bursting through a hedge on the right flank, he came upon the gun's tracked vehicle, its driver and a few German stragglers who, completely surprised, were quickly forced to surrender. Guided by the noise of the firing he worked forward again to within close range of the gun itself. Throwing grenades and firing bursts with his Sten, he demoralised the crew who fled back towards the river and the Chateau. As we moved forward from our 'bottled-up' position astride the road we met him behind the deserted 88mm, reconnoitring the ground for the Company's main advance . . .

Major Boon's bold action enabled the rest of B Company to cross the river and establish a bridgehead in the grounds of the chateau, followed by A Company. Then a storm of machine-gun fire and grenades drove both to ground in the orchards. The Gunners could no longer give covering fire without hazarding friends, while the tanks had been unable to make headway through the thickly-enclosed bocage. It was now realised that the chateau was more strongly defended than supposed, and to make matters worse, more enemy appeared along the river banks, withdrawing before the Americans' advance. A group with an SP gun blasted one of A Company's platoons, wounding the commander, and then took up a dominating position at the bridge, thus effectively cutting off the Companies and Tac HQ from the rest of the Battalion across the river. Shortly afterwards the platoons near the chateau were heavily attacked by infantry supported by tanks. It was now clear that in view of the new threat, the taking of the chateau was more than a two-company task. They could not be reinforced, because the remainder of the Battalion were still in position on their Bayeux objective. Lieutenant Colonel Craddock had been badly wounded, and, assuming command, Major Barlow resigned himself to a withdrawal. Under cover of smoke put down by our guns this was accomplished without serious loss, although two carriers were knocked out, the Gunner FOO's tank was shot off the bridge, and he and his crew were drowned. Next morning, patrols reported that the chateau had been evacuated. It had been held by at least 250 enemy in formidable defences, subsequently reinforced by many more with tanks and guns. This first 'blooding' of 2 SWB may not have been a resounding victory, but it was initial proof of the splendid fighting spirit of all ranks which was to be so often demonstrated in the long months ahead. It also enabled the US forces to advance unopposed beyond this strategic feature. The booty included fifty prisoners, three 88 mm. guns, a 20 mm. Flak gun and some transport vehicles.

Besides the Battle Honour 'Sully', the action earned the Battalion four MCs and six MMs. In view of the fierce opposition, casualties were relatively light: six men were killed, three officers and forty-six wounded. The wounded Lieutenant Colonel Craddock was evacuated, and on 9th June Major F. F. S. Barlow was promoted and officially took over command. Colonel Craddock's tenure had been brief, but his stout leadership was later recognised by the award of the DSO.

On 10th June, 2 SWB (and their 56 Independent Brigade) came under command of the 7th Armoured Division, the 'Desert Rats', and formed their motorised (or lorry-borne) infantry Brigade, for which role they had been trained in England. They were committed to the fighting in the difficult bocage country and the expansion of the bridgehead to Villers Bocage. But now it is time to glance at the other, Territorial, Battalions of The South Wales Borderers and The Welch, who were to prove fully equal to regulars in the ardours of the North-West Europe campaign.

The first of these to see action was the 3rd Battalion The Monmouthshire Regiment. Like 2 SWB, the Battalion had been training as lorried infantry for work with an armoured division, and in April 1944 it concentrated at Aldershot as a unit of 159 Infantry Brigade of the 11th Armoured Division – a formation with which it fought throughout the campaign. Lieutenant Colonel H. G. Orr (ex-Durham Light Infantry) was in command, with Major W. P. Sweetman as Second-in-Command. The Brigade was landed on the Normandy coast near Courseulles-sur-Mer on 14th June. Apart from some distant artillery fire, the periodic thud of a cruiser's 6-inches, and the wreckage on the beach, there was little evidence of the critical struggle that was in progress inland. But 3 Mons were soon to receive their costly baptism. The British 7th Armoured Division had been unable to extend the bridgehead beyond Villers Bocage and German reserves had poured into Caen, the hinge-pin of the advance eastwards. In an attempt to break this stronghold, Operation 'Epsom' was launched on 26th June. After an attack by the 15th (Scottish) Division, tanks of the 11th Armoured were to establish a bridgehead on the Odon River west of Caen, where its Infantry Brigade would take over and allow the tanks to advance to the high ground beyond, known as Hill 112. The bridgehead was duly established, but it was not until darkness had fallen on the 26th that 3 Mons moved up, to find that they had strayed off course and were in the deserted village of Mouen. Unknown to them, this was the objective of a dawn advance by the Germans. Discovering their error, the Battalion left C Company there as a flank guard and moved to their correct position between the villages of Tourville and Mondrainville. At first light the German attack, with tanks and Panzer Grenadiers, swept upon C Company, completely overwhelming them. After a hopeless struggle, Major H. F. Richards, Company commander, fought his way out with his few unwounded men. Only he and fourteen other ranks eventually rejoined the Battalion. C Company temporarily ceased to exist. Two days later Major Richards himself was killed by a shell-burst.

The remainder of the Battalion spent the next eight days in defensive positions below Hill 112, while the armour tried unsuccessfully to evict the enemy from that feature. On 6th July they were relieved by the Dorsets and withdrawn to rest and refit. During their nine days' first battle, 3 Mons had lost nearly a quarter of their strength. Two officers and thirty men had been killed; some sixty had been captured, of whom many were wounded, and the other wounded amounted to more than a hundred. It had been a costly 'battle inoculation'.

Meanwhile, other battalions of The South Wales Borderers and The Welch had also been baptised. Between 26th and 28th June elements of the 53rd (Welsh) Division were landed near Arromanches. These included 2 Mons, 4 Welch and 1/5 Welch, and all three were soon in action as the Division was hastily moved up to take over from hard-pressed battalions of the 15th Scottish. On 29th June 2 Mons (under Lieutenant

N.W. EUROPE
1944–45

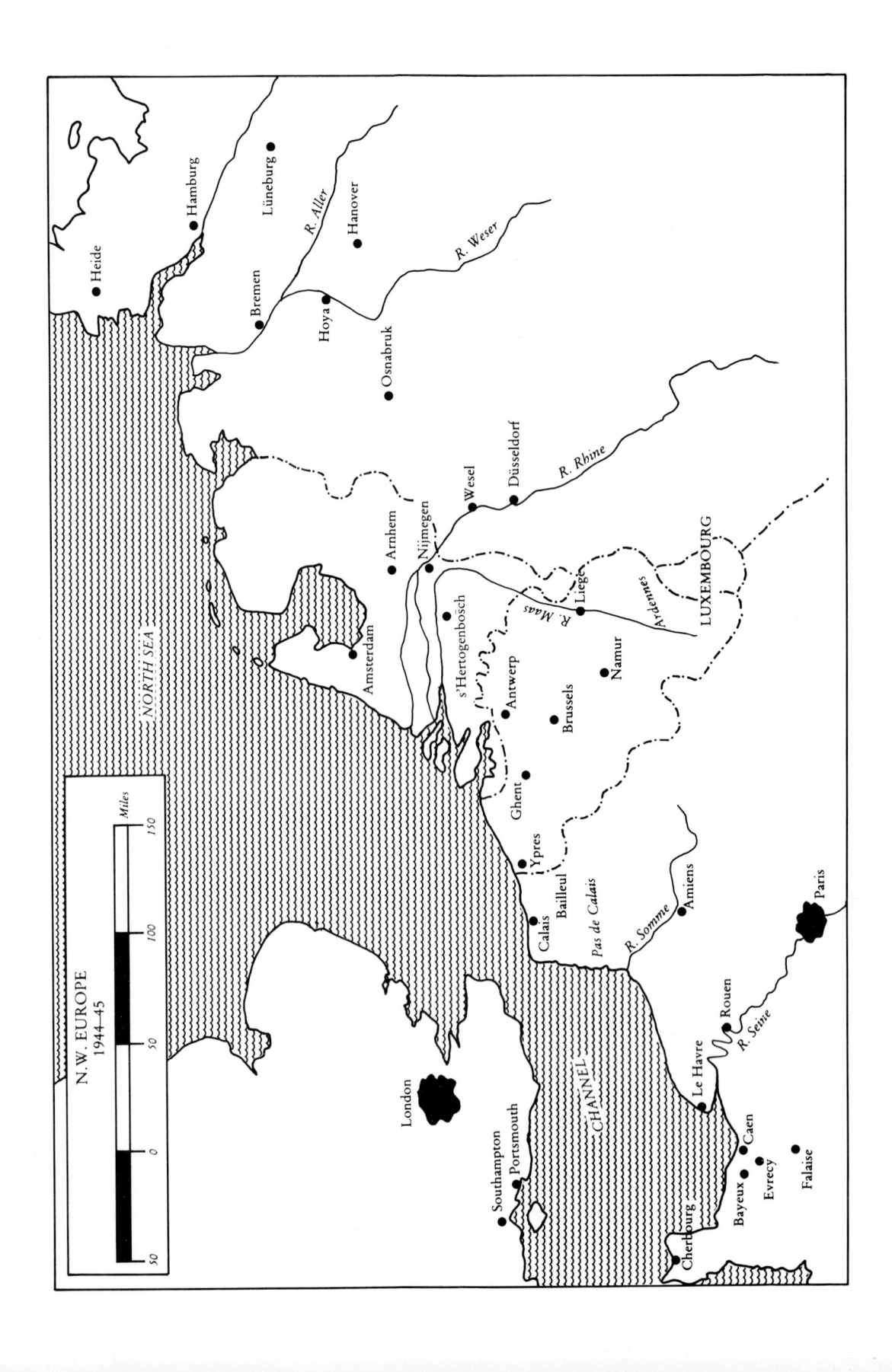

Colonel W. F. H. Kempster) had just dug in at Mesnil le Patry, five miles west of Caen, when they were subjected to a concentration of 105 mm. HE which erupted among S and Headquarters Companies. Two men were killed and several wounded, including Headquarters Company commander, Captain Herbert, and Lieutenant G. Edwards, who died shortly afterwards. Two days later the Battalion again suffered from artillery fire when Colonel Kempster's TAC HQ received a direct hit, killing his Second-in-Command, Major John Price, and wounding the Adjutant, Captain Baker, together with one other officer and nine signallers.

The 4th Battalion The Welch Regiment was brought to Normandy (with 53rd (Welsh) Division) by Major G. A. Burnett, since the true Commanding Officer, Lieutenant Colonel C. F. C. Coleman, had been appointed to command the Brigade.[7] 4 Welch had a lively experience. On 1st July they relieved 9 Cameronians at the Odon bridgehead of Grainville-sur-Odon, to meet an inferno of fire from heavy and light guns, phosphorous shells, 'moaning Minnies' (multi-barrelled mortars), machine guns and grenades. The Germans then mounted a full-scale attack, but though they penetrated one of the forward positions they were driven off. One of the Battalion's 6-pounder anti-tank guns had the satisfaction of making the first 'kill' on enemy armour when it knocked out a Mk IV Panzer with three rounds. Miraculously, the Battalion came through this initial twelve-hour battle with no fatal casualties. On the same day command was assumed by Lieutenant Colonel J. W. C. Williams (late of The South Staffordshire Regiment) – whose arrival was greeted with a direct hit on his command post. Apart from being buried in debris, he suffered no hurt.

On 3rd July, 4 Welch relieved their sister-Battalion 5 Welch, who had suffered heavily in their first action. Commanded by Lieutenant Colonel E. R. G. Ripley (ex-KSLI), they had moved up from the coast on 30th June, and the following day were ordered to take over the Seaforth Highlanders' position at the village of Le Valtru, near Mondrainville. Colonel Ripley and his company commanders went ahead to recce the positions, but they had scarcely reached the sector when Ripley was killed by a shell-burst. When the Battalion arrived they were met by an inferno of shell-fire and mortaring, and suffered fifty casualties before they could dig in. This onslaught continued for their 48 hours' spell at Le Valtru, and on being relieved by 4 Welch they had lost about 150 killed and wounded.[8] On 18th July the Battalion relieved the Glasgow Highlanders at the ironically-named village of Le Bon Repos, on the slopes of Hill 112, and here they were once more ferociously attacked, this time by Panzers and SS infantry. On the right flank, A Company was completely overrun and all contact with them was lost. Later the bodies of Major Northcott, Captain Pickton and thirteen other ranks were discovered; the rest were presumed captured. The remainder of the Battalion grimly held their ground in the battle of attrition for Hill 112 until 25th July, when, sadly mauled, they were withdrawn, to receive messages of congratulation from Corps and Divisional Commanders for their stubborn resistance. Subsequently Private L. George was awarded the Battalion's first DCM for his valour in stalking and 'killing' a Tiger tank with his PIAT.[9]

Meanwhile on 18th July Operation 'Goodwood' was launched, its objectives to seize the Bourgebus Ridge south of Caen and push on to Falaise. Only 11th Armoured

Division made any real progress, but then had to call forward their infantry. Led by 3 Mons 159 Brigade took several villages, captured many prisoners and finally consolidated around Hubert-Folie, some four miles south of Caen. Here the advance was halted after the Division had suffered heavy tank losses. For his splendid leadership Lieutenant Colonel Hubert Orr of 3 Mons was awarded the DSO.

On 31st July 11th Armoured began a wide flanking movement west of Falaise which brought them holding a salient on the Bas Perrier Ridge between Vassy and Vire. Here, until 6th August 3 Mons were subjected to massive attacks by waves of SS Panzers and their Panzer Grenadiers. For a period of forty-eight hours they were virtually cut off, with companies overrun. Casualties were heavy: many platoons were reduced to little more than large sections – one platoon of D Company had only fifteen men under a lance-corporal. In B Company the only officer still effective was a Lieutenant. After firing Brens and hurling grenades in the face of the oncoming enemy, Major J. France of C Company was killed by a shell-burst. His fearless conduct and inspiring leadership brought a posthumous DSO.

When withdrawn on 7th August, the Battalion had lost five officers and fifty-one other ranks killed, with more than twice that number wounded.

But with the intervention of the 3rd British Division, the Germans lost heart and the Falaise Gap was closed, allowing the break-out of the British and American Armies from their Normandy bridgehead.

While 3 Mons were hotly engaged with 11th Armoured, away to the east 2 Mons and 4 and 5 Welch were operating with their 160 Brigade to contain the left flank of the Falaise pocket. On 25th July 5 Welch had been joined by a 26-year-old Lieutenant, who, having received his emergency commission in 1941, had been serving at home. His name was Tasker Watkins, and he was soon to gain distinction for himself and his Regiment.

On 16th August Lieutenant Colonel Gibson was ordered to take 5 Welch and cut the main road to Falaise from the west. They arrived near the village of Bafour, and observing enemy on their front, resolved to attack with two companies up and tanks in support. 'Then unfortunately the situation became disjointed', wrote Sergeant Machin.[10] There was a complete breakdown of wireless contact between the two Companies and Tac HQ. Just after the Companies had advanced, Colonel Gibson received fresh orders from Brigade: the Battalion was to stand fast and on no account to cross the Falaise road. But in the absence of wireless, this order could not be relayed to A and B Companies who were now well ahead. B Company (including Lieutenant Watkins) were last spotted crossing the Falaise road and heading straight for their objective. At Headquarters the atmosphere was one of tenseness and helplessness: it was impossible to restore the situation. By 0100 hours B Company had been given up as lost, but just then (wrote Sergeant Machin) '. . . to the expressed delight of everyone, Lieutenant Watkins and the remainder of his Company, which I regret to say numbered only 27, returned to our lines. They had actually reached the objective after crossing fields strewn with booby traps, repelled an enemy counter-attack and killed some 50 Germans.'

On 2nd November 1944, *The London Gazette* announced the award of the VC to

Lieutenant Tasker Watkins: the official Citation fills in details that are lacking in Machin's somewhat bald account:

> In North-West Europe on the evening of 16th August 1944, Lieutenant Watkins was commanding a company of the Welch Regiment. The battalion was ordered to attack objectives near the railway at Bafour. Lieutenant Watkins' company had to cross open cornfields in which booby traps had been set. It was not yet dusk and the company soon came under heavy machine-gun fire from posts in the corn and farther back and also fire from an 88mm gun; many casualties were caused and the advance was slowed up.
>
> Lieutenant Watkins, the only officer left, placed himself at the head of his men and under short range fire charged two posts in succession, personally killing or wounding the occupants with his Sten gun. On reaching his objective he found an anti-tank gun manned by a German soldier; his Sten gun jammed, so he threw it in the German's face and shot him with his pistol before he had time to recover.
>
> Lieutenant Watkins' company now had only some 30 men left and was counter-attacked by 50 enemy infantry. Lieutenant Watkins directed the fire of his men and then led a bayonet charge, which resulted in the almost complete destruction of the enemy.
>
> It was now dusk and orders were given for the battalion to withdraw. These orders were not received by Lieutenant Watkins' company as the wireless set had been destroyed. They now found themselves alone and surrounded in depleted numbers and in failing light. Lieutenant Watkins decided to rejoin his battalion by passing round the flank of the enemy position through which he had advanced, but while passing through the cornfields once more, he was challenged by an enemy post at close range. He ordered his men to scatter and himself charged the post with a Bren gun and silenced it. He then led the remnants of his company back to battalion headquarters.
>
> His superb gallantry and total disregard for his own safety during an extremely difficult period were responsible for saving the lives of his men, and had a decisive influence on the course of the battle.

The main road to Falaise from the west was effectively cut by this action, and was never after used by the enemy.

In the following October Acting Major Watkins was badly wounded in his Battalion's action at s'Hertogenbosch and was invalided home. No longer fit for active service, he spent the rest of the war as instructor at Officer Cadet Training Units, and was finally released from the Army in 1946. Having earned the first of the Regiment's two VCs in World War II, Tasker Watkins went on to earn high distinction in his civilian career. Called to the Bar in 1948, he became a Queen's Counsel in 1965, was knighted in 1971, and in 1974 became Presiding Judge, Wales and Chester Circuit. At the time of writing, Major The Rt Hon. Lord Justice Watkins, VC, is a Lord Justice of

Major Tasker Watkins, 5th Welch; VC, 16th August 1944, Normandy.

Appeal for England and Wales. He is the only holder of that high office ever to have won the supreme award for gallantry.

By the middle of August the Falaise Gap had been closed and the way was now open for the breakout through France and Belgium, resulting in what the troops dubbed 'the Great Swan' as they raced for Antwerp and Brussels. The astonishing 550-mile advance was led by the 11th Armoured Division, with 3 Mons and their Brigade comrades of the KSLI and Herefordshire Regiment riding on the Shermans of the 15th/19th Hussars, 23rd Hussars and Fife and Forfar Yeomanry. A well-tried drill had been established for tank–infantry co-operation. Companies were allotted to squadrons, platoons to troops, and if the leading group met opposition the infantry would leap off the tanks and deploy while the tanks covered them with their 75 mms. and Besas. Should the opposition prove tough, further squadron–company groups could be quickly summoned up by wireless, usually to outflank the enemy. All this called for close liaison between company and platoon commanders and squadron leaders, together with fluid, independent action. Often sub-units could be ten miles or more away from their Battalion or Regimental Headquarters. It also demanded a high degree of operating skills from the wireless-operators of the 'Big Brothers' and the signallers of their 'Flatfooted Friends'.[11]

After several actions with diehard rearguard units of the retreating Germans, 11th Armoured reached Antwerp on 4th September, having covered the last 340 miles in 6 days – a feat claimed as a record. 3 Mons were sent through the city to clear the dock area, and this they did after a hard fight which cost them sixteen killed and some forty wounded.

The capture of Antwerp was of tremendous significance to the allied forces: it meant that material and supplies for the further advance through the Low Countries and into Germany could now be landed here, instead of having to be perilously ferried up from the 'Mulberry Harbour' remote on the Normandy coast.

Meanwhile, at the end of August 2 SWB and their 56th Brigade were transferred from their 'independent' status to form an integral element of the 49th (West Riding) Division. On 20th August the Battalion moved through Falaise to join their Division.

'Falaise was in a terrible state', wrote Captain Somerville, 'every house burning and the whole place littered with bomb craters, dead horses,[12] dead Germans, dead civilians. It made one wonder just how long it would take to clear up this terrible battlefield with its fires, its dysentery and the stench of death and destruction. The only thing left standing in Falaise was the statue of William the Conqueror on his horse.' By this time the Battalion was so much below strength through casualties and sickness that C Company had to be disbanded and its men distributed among the other three companies to bring them to fighting efficiency.

The next objectives of 49 Division were the crossing of the Seine and the capture of the port of Le Havre at its mouth. After cleaning up a pocket of German resistance in the forest of Bretonne on the south bank of the Seine, 2 SWB swept through to the crossing points. Some 400 prisoners had been captured, for only 10 men killed. The crossing of the 500-yard-wide river was effected without opposition, but one of the storm-boats ferrying men of A Company capsized in the strong current and fourteen men were drowned.

The investment of Le Havre began on 10th September. After saturation bombing by waves of Lancasters, 2 SWB with 56 Brigade attacked the outer defences from the north. Captain Somerville wrote:

> We attacked in the afternoon, and supported by tanks and flame throwers pushed through the gaps that the flails had made through the minefields, crossed the anti-tank ditch over bridges that the AVRES[13] were carrying and went into the objective behind six Crocodiles, actually treading in the flames. D Coy under Maj. Talmage took their objective... but A Company who were to pass through them came under concentrated 88 fire and suffered very heavy casualties on their start line. Eventually, only ten men of A Coy managed to reach their objective. OC B Coy who was waiting to pass through A Coy's objective, realised that all was not well and so assaulted A Coy's position, found some enemy and the ten men of A having a hand-to-hand fight. Having mopped up the enemy he proceeded to assault and capture the third objective. Major Collin's initiative and courage on this occasion earned the MC... Next day the final mopping up of the Bde objective was completed, but instead of pushing the two other bdes through the town, the General decided on one of his bold strokes, and 56 Bde, with the infantry riding on the tanks, advanced in three columns straight into the heart of the city, with the crowd roaring its applause.

On the following day, 12th September, all resistance petered out and Le Havre was in British hands. Some 13,000 Germans had been captured, of which 2 SWB claimed at least 1,100. After a pleasant respite enjoying the spoils of victory (including stocks of champagne and brandy) 2 SWB continued on their marathon to the Belgian frontier.

While 49 Division were enveloping Le Havre, 53 (Welsh) Division, with 2 Mons and 4 and 5 Welch, were racing ahead towards the Netherlands. There was fierce fighting for the bridgeheads on the Escaut Canal, and here on 19th September 5 Welch lost their Commanding Officer, Lieutenant Colonel Gibson, who had only been in command since July. He was replaced (in October) by Lieutenant Colonel Nelson Smith, MC, from the Hampshires. At Vorheide, on 24th September, both 2 Mons and 4 Welch were heavily engaged. In pitch darkness and heavy rain 2 Mons fought off a determined counter-attack by paratroops, losing eighteen killed and twenty-two wounded, but inflicting some 70% casualties on the enemy and earning the Divisional commander's message 'Well done, 2nd Mons!' On 25th September 4 Welch were involved in the bitter and confused fighting for the village of Reusel, just over the Dutch border. Companies and platoons were cut off from each other by infiltrating Germans, and for three days there was a house-to-house struggle, often with the Germans in one part of a building, Welshmen in another. When ordered to withdraw, half of D Company were cut off in the Church, with no wireless: the only means of relaying orders to them was to shout across the street from Tac HQ. The Germans would certainly have understood the gist of orders in English, so Sergeant J. H. Williams yelled the orders in Welsh. Happily there were fluent Welsh speakers in D Company, and the orders were acted upon. Almost certainly this was the only occasion during the war when the Welsh language was used to tactical advantage.

All three Battalions of The Monmouthshire and The Welch were engaged in the fight for s'Hertogenbosch, near the Maas, a fight which lasted for three October days of struggling through minefields under infernos of shelling and mortaring and wicked Spandau fire. In their advance of five miles 2 Mons destroyed 2 German battalions, took 255 prisoners and earned 2 MCs and 4 MMs. Another 200 prisoners were 'bagged' by 4 Welch, among them the German commader. 5 Welch were among the leading troops to enter s'Hertogenbosch on 27th October, and that evening the Welsh Dragon of 53 (Welsh) Division flew over the Town Hall.

Among 2 Mons's casualties was an officer with a somewhat exotic name for a member of a Welsh regiment: Captain the Prince Dimitri Galitzine. 'Cossack', as he was familiarly known, was fatally wounded while gallantly leading his platoon on an enemy position. The son of a Colonel in the Imperial Russian Hussars, killed in the Great War, Prince Galitzine was educated in England and had been employed with a petroleum company on the outbreak of war. He immediately volunteered for service and was given an emergency commission in The South Wales Borderers.

After the capture of Antwerp, 3 Mons pushed on through the Low Countries with their 'Big Brothers' of the 3rd Royal Tanks in the 11th Armoured Division. On 25th September the leading group flushed out four enemy half-tracks which sped away down the road leading from the village of St Anthonis. A mile or so down this road the Brigade commander was holding an O Group with his unit commanders, and the half-tracks ran straight into them. Lieutenant Colonel Silvertop of 3 RTR was killed outright, and Colonel Orr of 3 Mons and the Brigade Major were seriously wounded, the Brigadier being slightly wounded. The half-tracks paid the penalty for their aggression when they bumped into some 'Big Brothers' who shot them up. Lieutenant Colonel H. G. Orr, DSO, died the following day. He had commanded the Battalion since the early days of training in October 1942 and his personal courage, inspiring leadership and unfailing good humour had earned him the respect (and affection) of all ranks. His loss was a severe blow, and 3 Mons halted their war for an hour to hold a memorial service in the little village Church of Westerbeek, near St Anthonis. On 30th September Lieutenant Colonel R. C. Stockley, from The Royal Welch Fusiliers, arrived to take command.

The Battalion were soon to lose not only their second Commanding Officer, but many other officers and men. By 30th November they had advanced to the River Maas, where on the western bank lay the village of Broekhuizen with its Kasteel, an old moated fortress. Here a stubborn pocket of German paratroops were holding out. On the morning of the 30th, Colonel Stockley was ordered to eliminate this pocket. Supported by Shermans of the 15th/19th Hussars, A Company was directed on to the Kasteel and C Company to the village of Broekhuizen itself, with D in reserve. Confined to narrow paths through minefields, A Company met murderous fire from Spandaus and Flak guns. Major Nodwell, Company commander, was killed, as were two other officers and the CSM, while the only other officer was wounded. Most of the senior NCOs were also killed or wounded, together with many of the men. C Company fought their way into the outbuildings of the village but were then beaten back by fire from the houses. Major Hall, Company commander, was mortally wounded, and two other officers were killed outright, while nearly 70% of the other ranks became casualties. Meanwhile D Company, in rear, suffered from artillery fire, and the ambulance in the Regimental Aid Post received a direct hit. Colonel Stockley, at his Tac HQ, could get no news from the attacking Companies, for their wireless had been destroyed. So he sent up his Intelligence Officer, Captain Gibbs, who never came back (he was shot by a sniper). The Battalion Second-in-Command, Major Allen, then tried to reach C Company, but was badly wounded. Finally Stockley himself went forward: he contacted the remnants of A Company and attempted to lead an attack across the moat round the Kasteel. He fell in a burst of Spandau fire, and so did most of his men.

These sacrifices were not in vain. The 15th/19th Hussars brought up all their squadrons, and concentrated fire from their 75 mms., 17-pounders and Besas enabled D Company to overcome the village defences, while the combined survivors of A and C Companies forced the surrender of the Kasteel. Next day, what remained of the Battalion were relieved by 4 KSLI.

The capture of Broekhuizen had cost 3 Mons dear. They suffered 140 casualties, including the Commanding Officer and 7 other officers killed. The Second-in-Command was severely wounded; A and C Companies were reduced to skeletons. But, as ordered, they had 'eliminated' the enemy pocket, and had taken more than 200 prisoners.

After the failure of Operation 'Market Garden' at Arnhem and the bitter winter of 1944–5 in 'the island' around Nijmegen, the major offensive of Montgomery's 21 Army Group (including 53 (Welsh) Division) was the 'cleaning' of the Reichswald forest area between the Maas and the Rhine and the breaching of the Siegfried Line's northern flank. In the Reichswald operations, which commenced in early February 1945 and continued for almost a month, 2 Mons and 4 and 5 Welch were constantly engaged, and a hard struggle they had of it. The weather was appalling, with perpetual heavy rain and sleet adding to the other hazards of some fifty square miles of enemy-infested woodland. In some areas the going was so bad that even tanks and other tracked vehicles became bogged down.

Whereas crews of the 'Big Brothers' enjoyed some protection from the elements (and missiles), the foot-soldier had to bear the brunt of everything. All his arms, equipment and immediate needs had to be carried on his person. With the ever-present odds that at any moment he might drop with a bullet through his head or a shell fragment in his guts, he had to force his way through thick undergrowth and 'paths' ankle-deep in mud. On reaching his position he first had to dig in, and then spend four hours of the night on sentry. If lucky he might be able to doze the rest of the night in his slit trench – a waterlogged hole in the ground.

Major A. J. Lewis, MC, was commanding D Company, 4 Welch, in the Reichswald, and later wrote a graphic account of his experiences, of which the following is a typical extract:

> When I arrived at Bn Command Post I found that B Coy had been counter-attacked and badly cut up. At that moment there was nothing between our HQ and the enemy. I was ordered to capture B Coy's original objective. After I had laid on a sharp artillery stonk, we set off determined to give the enemy hell. I was feeling a little mad with them, as B Coy Commander had just been killed: he was a very fine fellow...[14] We went into the final assault, bayonets fixed, firing from the hip. The enemy did not stand up to this determined charge, and leaving their weapons where they were, they ran... We were now on the far edge of the forest and we killed large numbers as they tried to escape across the open. Once on the objective we dug slit trenches feverishly, in readiness for the inevitable counter-attack. Just as we finished there arrived one of the worst artillery and mortar bomb stonks I have ever experienced; within our tight area of about 100 yds by 50, hundreds of shells and mortar bombs must have fallen. It is extremely unpleasant being shelled when one is surrounded by trees. The shells burst in the trees with a two-fold effect: the burst comes straight down into the trenches and also has a lethal effect over a wide area...
>
> Throughout the night self-propelled guns continually moved up, fired rapid at point-blank range and then withdrew before we could stalk them. Just before first light heavier tracks were heard, which could only come from a heavy tank. The whole Company stood to: were the enemy about to launch a dawn attack with tanks? Gradually the darkness thinned, and we could just discern the profile of a Tiger tank. The crew were securing a tow-chain to an SP gun which was firmly embedded in the mud. 'Look sharp – get an anti-tank gun forward through the trees! And get the PIATs up!'
>
> It was difficult to get the A/Tk gun into position because of the dense trees and undergrowth. Brens began to rattle and the Tiger crew dived for cover. The PIAT fired, but the tank was just out of range. The Tiger then started up and began to withdraw, leaving the SP to its fate. At last the A/Tk

gun was in position: too late to catch the Tiger, but the SP was a sitting target. With two rounds it burst into flames. That gun would not worry us again ...

I returned to my Coy HQ to find a number of casualties awaiting evacuation. The Bren carrier and my Jeep had already gone back loaded with wounded, as also had the stretcher bearers. It was a hell of a task getting back to the R.A.P. through mud and under constant fire. One of the walking wounded passed us taking a German prisoner with him. Just as he passed a shell landed, killing him and blowing off the German's leg. He lay there crying for help in an agonising voice, but there was nothing I could do with all my transport away. Every spare man was helping our own wounded, and they came first. His cries became weaker and within ten minutes ceased altogether. We were so hardened that such incidents meant little to us. The only comment I heard was, 'He's had it.'

What Major Lewis omits to mention in his account is that his leadership and complete disregard of personal danger throughout D Company's attacks in the Reichswald won him an immediate MC.

There were many other examples of bravery and leadership among our four Battalions. Here, only one must suffice. On 24th February 2 Mons were committed to a costly attack on the small town of Weeze, stoutly defended by SS and paratroops. Advancing over open ground, B Company suffered heavily from machine-gun and mortar fire, and the right-flank Platoon lost their subaltern-commander and all NCOs except one, a 19-year-old Lance Corporal. This lad immediately took command, rallied the remainder and led a bold attack on a fortified farmstead. For four hours he and his puny command fought among the buildings until all the defenders were either killed or wounded, by which time the Platoon was reduced to fifteen men. The Lance Corporal then led them through fire-swept zones to rejoin the Company on their final objective. For this splendid performance Lance Coropolal J. H. Christian was awarded the DCM, one of only three for 2 Mons in the war. Of the 120 men of D Company who took part in this action only 40 were left effective. Unfortunately the casualties of 4 Welch are not detailed, but those of 5 Welch were given as two officers and seventeen other ranks killed, one and fifty-one wounded, with one officer and fifty-three other ranks 'sick and shell shock'.

In the meantime 2 SWB with 56 Infantry Brigade had seen hard fighting in 'the Island' around Arnhem and Nijmegen. In early January 2 SWB distinguished themselves in what they termed 'the Battle for the Castle'. The 'castle' was in fact a strongly-built and moated mansion at Hemmen, which had to be occupied in order to prevent the Germans using it as a base for their attack on the neighbouring town of Zelten. Lieutenant Kernick was ordered to take his Platoon and hold the castle for twenty-four hours. The only approach lay over an exposed stretch of open road leading to the narrow bridge across the moat. The Platoon crossed without let or hindrance, and proceeded to search the outbuildings. Then from behind barricaded windows came a storm of Spandau fire and stick grenades. The Germans had forestalled them. After an inconclusive fire-fight, Lieutenant Kernick ordered up a section of the Battalion's

Wasps, led by Corporal Cook. Despite a hail of fire, the corporal was able to bring his carrier to within fifty yards of the castle walls and began to spray the windows with his jets of flame. Inspired by his example, the other two carriers rattled over the bridge and did likewise, all the while under close-range small-arms fire. Flame-throwers were horrific weapons against infantrymen in foxholes or flammable cover, but against stout masonry they could have little effect. The castle refused to ignite. Under cover of fire from a 6-pounder anti-tank gun, Corporal Cook withdrew his carriers. This was the first time that 2 SWB had used their Wasps in anger, and though they had no chance against the stone walls, Corporal W. G. Cook's bold leadership earned him the MM. Meanwhile, enemy reinforcements were approaching, Lieutenant Kernick's position was perilous. One of his sections was pinned down in the castle grounds, while he and the other two at the bridge were subjected to a cross-fire from the castle itself and the advancing reinforcements. He fought off all attacks, and as dusk fell his platoon, having been in action for twelve hours and now running out of ammunition, was withdrawn, covered by Shermans of the Royal Tanks. Lieutenant R. Kernick survived an eventful day unscathed, and was rewarded with the MC. Although next morning the castle was reduced to rubble by pounding with HE, mortars and AVREs, it was again to figure largely in 2 SWB's operations.

On 20th January they and their Essex comrades of 56 Brigade were ordered to recapture the town of Essen which had been occupied by the Germans after 'the Battle for the Castle'. 2 SWB found themselves on all too familiar ground when A Company, supported by 'Big Brothers', crossed the bridge over the moat and cleared the outbuildings and stables. Then some 120 Germans emerged from the ruins of the castle mansion and surrendered to a platoon of 30 men. Sergeant M. Jones, commanding, was awarded the MM. In all, the final 'Battle for the Castle' resulted in the capture of 208 prisoners, with large quantities of arms and supplies, for the loss of only 6 men killed and 40 wounded.

On 23rd March came Operation 'Plunder', the crossing of the Rhine, and the final advance, or what Monty termed the 'crack-about in Germany'. Thanks to an unprecedented artillery and air bombardment (witnessed by Winston Churchill in person), the Rhine crossing was effected with virtually no opposition, and the 53rd (Welsh) Division suffered no casualties (2 SWB were still in 'the Island'). By now most of the hordes of Wehrmacht prisoners, seemed resigned to their country's ultimate defeat, but there were still diehards, particularly among the SS, Paratroops and Marines, who were to provide bitter resistance for the next couple of months. And this period brought more examples of heroism.

On 12th April C Company of 4 Welch were attacking the village of Barnstedt, between the Weser and the Aller, when they were met by heavy Spandau fire. Working forward to one of the machine-gun posts, CSM Finch charged it single-handed and killed all the crew with his Sten, though not before he had been wounded in the arm. Heedless of the wound, he rushed another enemy post and destroyed that in similar fashion. This enabled the following Platoon to advance, but as he too was advancing, a grenade landed beside him, smashing his leg and blowing off the fingers of one hand. Immobilised, but not out of action, he got one of the men to reload his Sten and, with one hand, gave covering fire as the Platoon rushed the objective. CSM Roy Finch received a well-merited DCM.

A few days before this incident, 2 Mons put up a smart, if punishing fight in their assault on the town of Rethem, commanding one of the strategic crossings of the River Aller. It was said to be held by between 500 and 1,000 Marines, with artillery. The plan was to attack on a two-company front, supported by tanks, artillery and aircraft. Under artillery cover, which seemed to silence the enemy guns, B Company managed to reach outlying buildings, when all their forward platoons were raked by fire from the murderous Spandaus and mortars. The leading platoon commander, Lieutenant Mackenzie, was wounded, but he carried on. Smoke shells from our guns enabled the advance to continue, and led by Mackenzie the men overcame several enemy posts held by the dogged Marines, who fought to the last. But then the advance was checked by well dug-in enemy on a railway embankment, and the men could only take cover in shell-holes. By now Lieutenant Mackenzie had suffered five more wounds, in arms, back, chest and face, but he still retained command. Meanwhile D Company had suffered also, and when darkness fell the Commanding Officer (Lieutenant Colonel Brooke) was forced to order a withdrawal. But the operation had not been a failure. The two Companies had given the Germans more than they received, to such an extent that next morning the Battalion was able to enter the town without opposition, collecting 150 prisoners, and the German commander later admitted that only 60 of his original 500 men had survived. The town and the important bridge were thus secured. Lieutenant H. C. H. Mackenzie (posted from The Border Regiment) received a well-earned DSO. Lance Corporal Dawson and Private Wild were given MMs for their gallantry in evacuating wounded under fire.

During all this period 3 Mons had been operating with their 11th Armoured Division, who by 1st April had forced a crossing of the Dortmund-Ems Canal, on the east bank of which lay the thickly wooded hills of the Teutoburger Wald. 'The enemy were not expected to yield this dominating feature without a struggle', as The Monmouths' history observes. And indeed they did not. But the bitter struggle brought its reward for the Battalion.

Their attack went in on 2nd April and proved abortive. As later discovered, the enemy were an élite force of officer-cadets with their seasoned NCO instructors, all fanatical Nazis, and after fierce and confused fighting in thick forest, when platoons and sections lost touch with each other, the attack had to be called off, with the loss of four officers and thirty-seven other ranks killed and many times that number wounded. However, it was later some compensation to learn that it subsequently took three days for a full brigade of 7th Armoured Division to clear the Teutoburger Wald. And shortly afterwards it also was learned that this, the last battle of 3 Mons, had earned them a VC.

During the confused initial stages of the battle:

> ... Corporal Chapman was advancing with his section ... along a narrow track when the enemy suddenly opened fire with machine guns at short range, inflicting heavy casualties and causing some confusion. Corporal Chapman immediately ordered his section to take cover, and seizing a Bren gun, he advanced alone firing the gun from his hip, and mowed down the

enemy at point-blank range... At this point, however, his company were ordered to withdraw, but as Corporal Chapman and his section were still in their advanced position the order could not be got forward to them.

The enemy then began to close up... and under cover of intense machine gun fire they made determined charges with the bayonet. Corporal Chapman again rose with his Bren gun to meet the assaults, and on each occasion halted their advance.

He had now nearly run out of ammunition. Shouting to his section for more bandoliers, he dropped into a fold in the ground and covered those bringing up the ammunition by lying on his back firing the Bren gun over his shoulder. A party of Germans made every effort to eliminate him with grenades, but with reloaded magazine he closed with them and once again drove the enemy back with considerable casualties.

During the withdrawal of his company, the company commander had been severely wounded and left lying in the open a short distance from Corporal Chapman. Satisfied that his section was now secure... he went out alone under withering fire and carried his company commander for fifty yards to comparative safety. On the way a sniper hit the officer again, wounding Corporal Chapman in the hip, and when he reached our lines it was discovered that the officer had been killed [he was Major P. Taylor]. In spite of his wound Corporal Chapman refused to be evacuated and went back to his company until the position was fully restored two hours later...

Corporal Edward Chapman, 3 Mons; VC, 2nd April 1945, Germany.

The above is extracted from the Citation for the VC,[15] with which Sergeant Edward Thomas Chapman was presented at Buckingham Palace on 31st July 1945.

Edward Chapman continued with the Battalion until released to the Reserve in 1946. He then re-enlisted in the Territorial Army (Monmouthshire Regiment) and served until discharged as CSM in 1957. For his devoted service in the Territorials he was awarded the BEM in June 1953. On 2nd April 1985, the 40th anniversary of the Teutoburger Wald Battle, a diorama of the VC incident, and a portrait of Chapman, were unveiled in The South Wales Borderers and Monmounthshire Regiment Museum, Brecon. The unveiling, attended by Ted Chapman himself and many of his old

En route for Blighty; 5 Welch casualty, Reichswald, February 1945.
Char up; 5 Welch group, Reichswald Forest, February 1945.

comrades of 3 Mons, was performed by the Colonel of the Regiment, Major General L. A. H. Napier.

The Teutoburger Wald action had so depleted 3 Mons that they were in no state to continue operations. The historian of the 11th Armoured Division wrote:

> During the campaign the Mons had been in the forefront of many bitter encounters and they had suffered cruel losses; their casualties to officers since D-Day now stood at well over 100 per cent. After this latest battle they could hardly have been expected to make a further effort for some time, and they were left behind, passing eventually to command of 115 Brigade. We were sorry to see such a fine Battalion leave us.[16]

At the beginning of May the 53rd (Welsh) Division were poised along the Elbe, awaiting the final drive on Hamburg. A week previously the 53rd had been joined by 2 SWB, transferred from their 49th (West Riding) Division and posted to 158 Brigade where they found 1/5 Welch. Though pleased to be alongside fellow-Welshmen, they regretted the loss of their Sphinx flashes and vehicle insignia which they had proudly borne since D-Day.

If the beginning of World War II had been 'phoney', its end in Europe was similar. As the battalions advanced, their Commanding Officers would frequently telephone the German commander in the next village ahead demanding surrender in order to avoid unnecessary bloodshed. These demands were generally complied with, and mixed hordes of Wehrmacht, Marines, Volksturm, and even U-boat crews, were constantly passed to the rear. Our Gunners were ordered to withhold fire on specified roads so that the German envoys could approach safely. On 1st May unit wirelesses picked up the BBC news that Hitler had committed suicide amid the ruins of Berlin. As 4 Welch marched into the village of Winsen, twelve miles from Hamburg, a company commander expressed the general sentiment when he remarked: 'It's a bit too near the end of the war to be killed now.'

It was with some relief, therefore, that on 3rd May all units were officially informed that the German commander in Hamburg had surrendered. Germany's second largest city and most important port was open for a bloodless entry.

At 0500 hours next morning, 2 SWB, led by B Company's Carrier Platoon, were among the first British troops to march in. 'The city was quite lifeless', wrote Major Boon, 'street after street was lined by empty shells of buildings or by heaps of rubble. Great concrete road blocks barred the main roads, but there was no sign of life, only a few faces at windows . . .'. 2 SWB, 2 Mons and 4 and 5 Welch were all allotted sectors of the city, with the onerous and unfamiliar tasks of sorting out and administering to the motley throngs of released prisoners-of-war, German captives, and 'displaced persons'. Captain Somerville of 2 SWB recalled that as a company commander he was responsible for about a square mile of the city, in which he had to look after and feed some 30,000 ex-POWs and DPs, including '15,000 Russians, 2000 Poles, 10,000 assorted lost souls and a POW Camp of Italian officer-deserters, plus some 800 Polish women in a fish factory'. 4 Welch were fortunate in being allotted quarters of unaccustomed luxury in a Dutch cruise liner which had been used as Headquarters and central Mess for U-boat officers.

Of our five Battalions only 3 Mons were absent from Hamburg. As already related, they were so depleted after their last battle at the Teutoburger Wald that they were withdrawn to join 115 Independent Infantry Brigade guarding the Rhine bridges, and their war ended at Haldern where, like their other Welsh comrades, they dealt with the hordes of DPs.

On 4th May Montgomery accepted the unconditional surrender of the German armed forces, and the 'Great Adventure' was over. It was not a spectacular finale to the eleven months of bitter conflict. As the historian of 2 Mons wrote: 'The cease-fire order brought with it a sense of anti-climax, in which the prevailing memory was that of the many gallant comrades who had died on the long road between the dusty orchards of Normandy and the shattered cities of the Elbe.'

The five Battalions of The South Wales Borderers, The Monmouthshires and The Welch had paid a heavy toll on that long road. 2 SWB lost a total of 7 officers and 157 other ranks killed, 42 officers and 452 wounded, 2 officers and 156 missing. 2 Mons lost 7 officers and 188 other ranks; 3 Mons lost 23 officers and 242. 4 and 1/5 Welch between them lost 18 officers and 474 other ranks killed or died of wounds.[17]

The Commanding Officer and officers of the 89th Quartermaster Battalion, US Army, who occupied Maindy Barracks 1943–4. LIEUTENANT COLONEL JOSEPH FLEISCHER, US ARMY

Postscript

It is very seldom that historians of Line regiments give due acknowledgement to the supporting arms to which all at 'the sharp end', and the infantry in particular, owe so much. Thus it was a rare gesture of 2 Mons's historian (Lieutenant-Colonel G. A. Brett) to conclude his account with a generous tribute to the Royal Artillery Battery who had fought with them in some forty actions, major and minor. 'Throughout all these actions the speed and accuracy with which any call for fire was answered bred in the infantry complete confidence that whatever happened 'the Gunners would compete'. And compete they did, often firing concentrations 100 yards in front of forward platoons, sometimes beating off counter attacks by skilfull and defensive fire, always ready to give the utmost support at any time and in any conditions. To all of them, and to those at the guns, the Battalion now says "Thank You".'

Surely, all British infantry soldiers of World War II would echo those sentiments.

Notes

[1] There were in addition eight hostilities-only battalions, but these were purely draft-finding and training units who saw no active service as such. Although their roles were essential, if unheroic, they are not dealt with in this chapter.

[2] Michael Joseph Ltd (London, 1984).

[3] 2 Mons, 4 and 5 Welch, in 53 (Welsh) Division, were not put ashore until 27th June. 3 Mons, with 11 Armoured, landed on 14th June.

[4] *History of The 2nd Battalion South Wales Borderers D-Day 1944–1945* (1955).

[5] Later Brigadier Sir Nicholas Somerville, CBE.

[6] No. 18 Wireless Sets. For PIAT see below (9).

[7] Colonel Coleman was later to become Lieutenant General Sir Charles Coleman, KCB, CMG, DSO, OBE, Colonel The Welch Regiment.

[8] Unlike The South Wales Borderers' war history, that of The Welch Regiment is regrettably imprecise about casualties. Figures seldom appear in the text; there is no complete Roll of Honour; all killed, died of wounds or 'Died of sickness or from Natural Causes' are merely summarised by theatres in an appendix.

[9] Projector Infantry Anti-Tank – basically a steel tube firing a hollow-charge projectile. Since its maximum range was only about 100 yards, great courage and strong nerves were demanded of its aimer in order to get close enough to penetrate the thick armour of a Tiger, or a Panzer IV or V. In Normandy each infantry platoon had one PIAT. The German equivalent was the Panzerfaust, while the Americans had their Bazooka.

[10] Sergeant J. Machin served as Intelligence Sergeant throughout the campaign, and his account of 5 Welch's operations was published as Chapter XII of General Lomax's *History of The Welch Regiment 1919–1951*.

[11] These code-words were employed in an attempt to confuse enemy listeners-in to radio traffic. There were others, such as 'Sunray' for a unit commander. But it is doubtful whether such subterfuge continued to fool the Germans throughout the campaign.

[12] It was odd that the Germans, leading exponents of mechanised warfare, should have employed huge numbers of horses throughout the war. Most were employed in transport and artillery units, but the elite SS Corps deployed five horsed cavalry divisions. After the surrender, 58,000 German horses were handed over to the British.

[13] Armoured Vehicle Royal Engineers was a Churchill tank armed with a formidable 90 mm. mortar. Its projectile was known as the 'Flying Dustbin'. The Crocodile was a flame-throwing tank.

[14] He was Major C. L. Rosenheim, MC.

[15] *The London Gazette* 13th July 1945.

[16] Anon. *Taurus Pursuant. A History of 11th Armoured Division* (1945).

[17] As remarked earlier, casualty figures published in previous histories leave much to be desired. The Welch Regiment's historian does not distinguish between 4 and 1/5 Welch and includes in his total those 'who died of Sickness or from Natural Causes . . .'. 2 and 3 Mons do not list wounded or missing. Only Major J. T. Boon's history of 2 SWB gives a complete breakdown. Even the present Regiment is unable to supply the missing figures.

CHAPTER SEVENTEEN

End of an Era (1945–68)

As in 1919, the end of hostilities in 1945 brought about the inevitable demise of hostilities-only and Territorial units, which were either peremptorily disbanded or euphemistically consigned to 'suspended animation'. We have already seen that The South Wales Borderers had suffered the disbandment of their gallant 6th Battalion in Sumatra. In February 1946 came another loss for the 24th when the 3rd Battalion The Monmouthshire Regiment went into suspended animation. A year later they re-emerged with the cumbersome title, 637 Heavy Anti-Aircraft Regiment (3rd Monmouths) Royal Artillery (TA). Though the name '3rd Monmouths' lived on for a while, the Battalion had been lost to the Regiment.

The same year also witnessed the disbandment of 2 Mons and 4 and 5 Welch, but happily this was only temporary. With the reconstitution of the Territorial Army in 1947, all three Battalions were reformed: 2 Mons were based at Pontypool (later Newport), 4 Welch at Llanelli and 5 Welch at Pontypridd.

Before the war, India (and particularly its North West Frontier) had provided a splendid training ground for the British Army, and there were never fewer than 40,000 British soldiers garrisoning the subcontinent – in addition to some three times that number of Indian troops. But in 1947 India gained her independence and in February the last British troops sailed from Bombay.[1] Then came the evacuation of Palestine and the planned withdrawal from Egypt. The Empire was dwindling, and the Army's overseas commitments were progressively curtailed. The old Cardwell system of 'linked' battalions, one at home providing drafts for the one overseas (usually India), finally came to an end. A consequence of all this was that most regular infantry regiments with two battalions were ordered to reduce to single-battalion regiments.

Thus The South Wales Borderers and The Welch Regiment were sad to say farewell to their 2nd Battalions which had fought so nobly in far-flung theatres from Norway to Burma. It was ironic that 2 SWB received their orders for 'suspended animation' on the very day – 22nd January – that they were celebrating the anniversary of B Company's stand at Rorke's Drift. The valedictory in the *XXIV Journal* expressed the hope that 'the Battalion will in the future emerge from its retirement to add further

Visit of HRH Princess Elizabeth to Cardiff: the Regimental goat was trained to kneel at the opening bar of the National Anthem and to rise on the closing bar, when in the presence of a member of the Royal Family.

pages to its record of brave and loyal service'. This was a vain hope. Both 2 SWB and 2 Welch passed into a limbo from which they have so far not emerged. Their epitaph might well be 'Faithful We Served'.

By now The Welch Regiment's 1st (and only) regular Battalion had returned from Italy, and were to remain home-based until they once more saw action on the other side of the world, as recounted later.

Since their disbandment in 1942 the reconstituted 1 SWB had been no further overseas than the Orkneys, but their turn for more demanding service came in October 1945 when they sailed for that strife-torn Holy Land of Palestine. Here they spent a trying winter dealing with Zionist terrorists and carrying out the distasteful tasks of guarding those unfortunates, the illegal Jewish immigrants, many of whom were survivors of the Nazi death-camps. Following a brief spell in Cyprus, with a similar role, the Battalion were posted to the Sudan in early 1949. Here they spent over a year in garrison duties based in Khartoum and Kebeit in the Red Sea hills. Many officers and NCOs were attached to the Sudan Defence Force during this tour.

At this period there was an eruption of terrorist activity in neighbouring Eritrea, a former colony of Mussolini's Empire but now under British rule. To reinforce the security forces, 1 SWB moved to Asmara in 1950, and for the next two years they were constantly scouring mountain and wadi in pursuit of the murderous gangs of dissidents, or *Shifta*. Their task was made the more arduous by daytime temperatures of 115°F. Many *Shifta* were captured, some killed, but the Battalion suffered no serious casualties. In 1952 the United Nations decreed that Eritrea should be handed over to Ethiopia, and on 15th September a detachment of the Battalion formed a Guard of Honour at Asmara when the Union Flag was hauled down. The last British soldiers to serve in Eritrea, 1 SWB (under command of Lieutenant Colonel Charles Cox), embarked for home a few days later, and arrived at Sennybridge near Brecon in October. When they entered Brecon itself, they were given a civic welcome, marching through the bedecked streets with Colours flying, drums beating and bayonets fixed. This privilege had been conferred on the 24th in June 1948, when the Regiment was granted the Freedom of the Borough of Brecon. The Welch Regiment had been granted the Freedoms of Cardiff and Carmarthen in June 1944, as part of the 'Salute the Soldier Week'.

Apart from the traumatic disbandments and 'suspended animations' in the immediate post-war years, there were other significant reorganisations for the infantry. Even before 1939 some military pundits had been advocating a 'Corps of Infantry', analogous to the other corps (and to The Royal Regiment of Artillery). Under this scheme, officers and soldiers on joining, and throughout their service, would be posted to any unit within the 'corps', where most needed. This, of course, seemed the death-knell of the time-honoured and cherished regimental system with its 'tribal' loyalties. Predictably, the proposal met with fierce opposition, not least from Montgomery, who declared: 'We must be very careful what

WO1 (RSM) Albert Edward Visick, MBE, Scots Guards, 1926. He transferred to 1 Welch in Italy on St David's Day 1943, as RSM. He retired in 1973 as RSM, Depot, The Welch Regiment and died in January 1983. Many a recruit, and others, trembled under his ever-watchful eyes.

we do with the British Infantry . . . their fighting spirit is based largely on morale and regimental *esprit de corps*. On no account must anyone be allowed to tamper with it.' Proponents of the scheme pointed to the cavalry's newly-formed Royal Armoured Corps which had come into being without any hard feelings or dispute. But apart from the fact that the RAC provided a common training centre, it was really no more than a 'Corps' on paper. All the regiments preserved their identities and distinctions, recruits could opt for the regiments of their choice, and there was little or no cross-posting except when wartime battle casualties demanded.

The 'Corps of Infantry' idea died an unlamented (if temporary) death, but in 1946 a modified, less drastic variant came into operation. This was the infantry 'Group System' under which three or more regiments were grouped together with a common centre. Theoretically, officers and soldiers were to be interchangeable among the regiments of their group. In practice, however, they were usually allowed to express their preferences. In all, thirteen groups (soon renamed 'Brigades') were established, each based on a central Depot and training centre.[2]

And so in 1946 The Welsh Group (Brigade) came into existence. It was located at Dering Lines, Brecon, and logically enough comprised the three Line Regiments of Wales: The Royal Welch Fusiliers, The South Wales Borderers and The Welch Regiment. As yet there was no 'tampering' with the component Regiments: each retained its own identity, badges and distinctions. The system seemed to work harmoniously, at least within The Welsh Brigade. For Brecon, one result was that this home of the 24th now became familiar with the Bursting Grenade of The Royal Welch Fusiliers and the Prince of Wales's Plumes of The Welch Regiment.

Although Attlee's Labour Government was determined to disengage from military commitments overseas, Britain still had responsibilities to fulfil, and with the wholesale 'demobbing' of wartime soldiers it became necessary to maintain some form of conscription (the recent disbandment of all the infantry's 2nd battalions now seemed somewhat precipitate). In July 1947 the National Service Act was passed, becoming effective the following year. This was not wholeheartedly welcomed, either by the conscripts or the hard-pressed Services. For the regiments it meant recurring intakes swamping their training centres, month after month, all having to be documented, kitted out, trained and transformed into good soldiers. And by the time they had become fully competent riflemen, machine-gunners, signallers, driver-mechanics, Orderly Room clerks, or whatever, their eighteen-month term (later two years) would be up and they would depart back to civvy street.

In June 1948 1 SWB reported (in the *XXIV Journal*) a total effective strength of 892. Of these, no fewer than 488 were National Servicemen. But there is no denying that by the time the scheme was abolished in 1963, thousands of these temporary soldiers had proved themselves fully worthy of their cap badges in the trials of active service. And 'peacetime' or no, the decades following World War II brought plenty of real soldiering.

As we have seen, 1 SWB fired their weapons in anger against the *Shifta* in Eritrea – and were later to do so against the 'CTs' in Malaya. But it was 1 Welch who became involved in a full-scale war.

In June 1950, Communist forces of North Korea, aided and abetted by China, invaded the Western-inclined Republic of South Korea, which had been set up by the United Nations after the Japanese defeat. For the first and only time in its undistinguished history, the UN resolved to combat force with force, and four American divisions were hastily sent out to aid the puny South Korean forces. Later Britain contributed her 28th Commonwealth Division, under UN command. This comprised British, Australian, New Zealand and Canadian troops, supported by naval and RAF elements.

In November 1951 the 1st Battalion The Welch Regiment, under Lieutenant Colonel H. H. Deane, disembarked at the South Korean port of Pusan. Before leaving home, the Commanding Officer had taken the precaution of enquiring from the South Korean Legation in London whether there were any restrictions on the import of live goats. None at all, replied the Minister, adding his 'Best wishes and grateful thanks to the Regiment'. And so the usual curious throngs of locals at Pusan docks were bemused to see the newly-arrived British soldiers led down the gangway by Taffy IX.

The Battalion mustered 38 officers and 746 other ranks and was allotted to 29 British Infantry Brigade, commanded by Brigadier A H. G. Ricketts, DSO, OBE. The two other Battalions were 1 Royal Norfolk and 1 Royal Leicesters, with the 5th Royal Inniskilling Dragoon Guards providing armour support. Also under Brigade command were batteries of 14 Field Regiment RA and troops of 55 Field Squadron RE.

Within seventy-two hours of disembarking, The Welch were ordered to take over a reserve sector from 1 Glosters who, the previous April, had won renown and two VCs for their heroic stand on the Imjin River. But although the year that 1 Welch spent in Korea was marked by many individual acts of dash and bravery, the Battalion as a whole had no opportunity for such heroics. Instead, after moving up to a forward position around Yongdong, they were to endure four bitter winter months of arduous, if often unrewarding, patrol activity in conditions not unlike those in the Western Front in World War I. In temperatures down to forty-five degrees of frost, officers and men lived and slept in their bunkers, under constant shelling and mortaring. Daily and nightly fighting or 'lay-up' (ambush) patrols and wiring fatigues took up most of the time; all too often the wily Chinese did not allow themselves to be caught, and the report was 'NTR' (nothing to report) or 'NC' (no contact). But on occasions there was contact that resulted in casualties to both sides, and awards for 1 Welch.

On 10th January 1952 Corporal M. J. Keogh was second-in-command of a daylight patrol under 2nd Lieutenant A. R. Bentham when, on reaching their first objective, they were ambushed by about twenty enemy who killed four men and wounded the patrol leader. Corporal Keogh now found himself in command without any wireless contact, for the No. 88 set had been damaged and its operator killed. Having scattered the enemy with his Bren and Stens, he sent back a runner to Company Headquarters and remained in position for four hours, beating off further attacks until a relieving party arrived, whom he covered on to the objective. He then led his surviving men to the scene of the ambush, collected the wounded subaltern and the dead and brought them back to Company lines. 'From the time his patrol commander was wounded Cpl Keogh showed a high degree of initiative in what was a very difficult

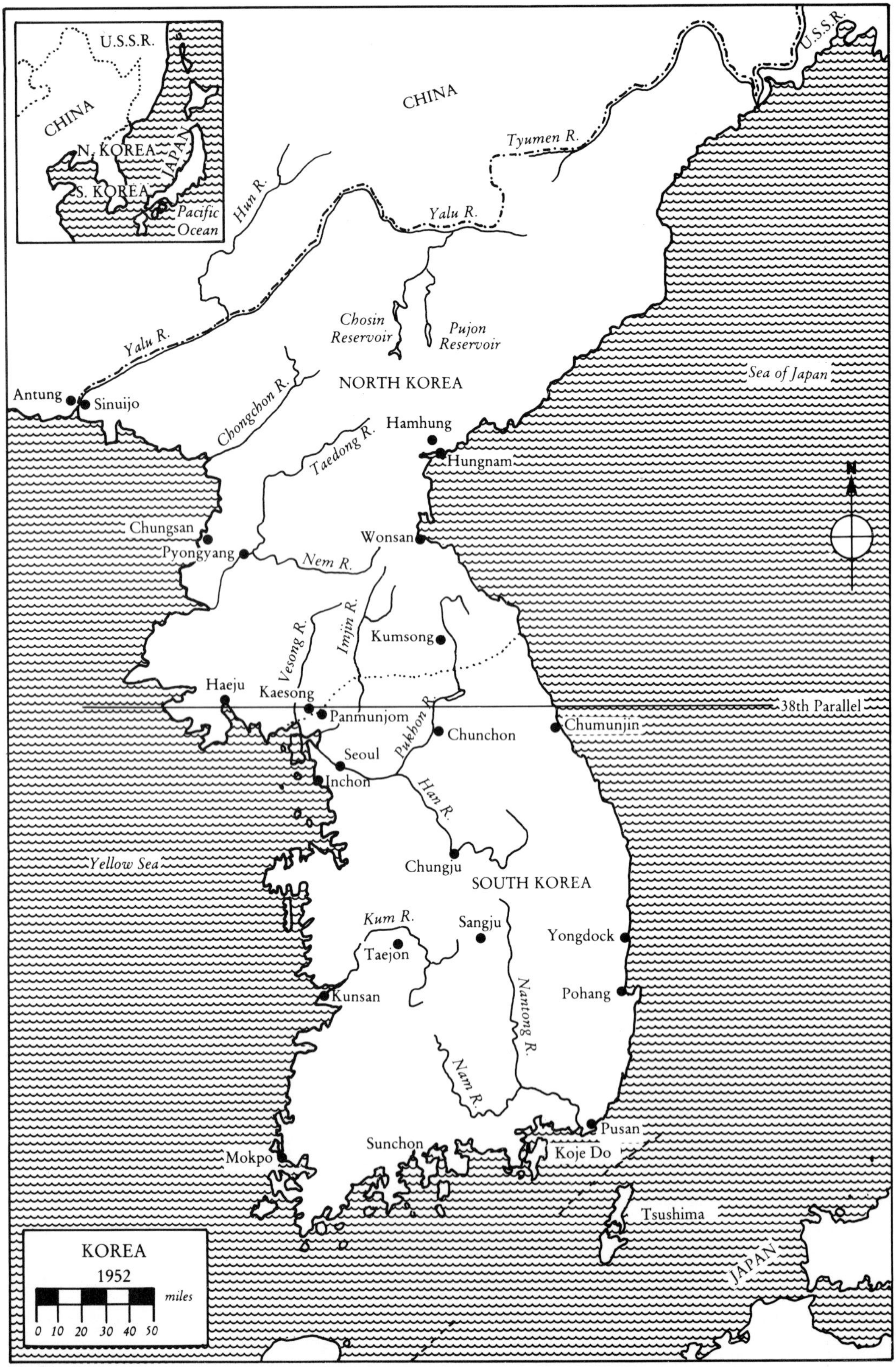

U.S.S.R.
CHINA
N. KOREA
S. KOREA
JAPAN
Pacific Ocean
CHINA
U.S.S.R.
Tyumen R.
Hun R.
Yalu R.
Yalu R.
Chosin Reservoir
Pujon Reservoir
NORTH KOREA
Sea of Japan
Antung
Sinuijo
Chongchon R.
Taedong R.
Hamhung
Hungnam
Chungsan
Wonsan
Pyongyang
Nem R.
Vesong R.
Imjin R.
Kumsong
Haeju
Kaesong
Panmunjom
38th Parallel
Pukhon R.
Chunchon
Chumunjin
Seoul
Inchon
Han R.
Yellow Sea
Chungju
SOUTH KOREA
Kum R.
Sangju
Yongdock
Taejon
Kunsan
Nantong R.
Pohang
Nam R.
Pusan
Sunchon
Koje Do
Mokpo
Tsushima
JAPAN
KOREA
1952
miles
0 10 20 30 40 50

Taffy VII in Berlin during 1 Welch' tour, 1961–3.

Amalgamation Parade, Cardiff Castle, 11th June 1969.

A Company, 1 Welch; Samichon Valley, Korea, 1951.

situation. His men were naturally shaken after the ambush, but he rallied them and encouraged them and in every way set the highest example . . .'. Thus wrote Colonel Deane when recommending this NCO for an MM. Corporal Keogh in fact received a Mention in Despatches. There were several other instances when acts of gallantry and leadership were similarly transmuted by War Office from the Commanding Officer's recommendation.

On the night of 24th/25th May a fighting patrol led by Captain R. C. Taverner was engaged in a fierce fire-fight at close range, Captain Taverner and his corporal, second-in-command, being severely wounded. The young Bren Gunner, Lance Corporal Ellaway, was blown down the hillside by a grenade, but, quickly recovering, he assumed command, drove the enemy back and then organised the evacuation of Taverner and the corporal. Although he had strained his back in the early fall, he personally helped to carry Taverner ('a heavily-built officer') to a stretcher in rear, and then returned to recover two more wounded. Utterly disregarding his own safety, '. . . his first concern was to get to grips with the enemy, and later to get the wounded back . . . There is no doubt that he was directly instrumental in saving his Officer.' So ran the Citation for the MM which Lance Corporal T. P. Ellaway subsequently received.

The Korean conflict has been described as a platoon commander's war, for the encounters were mostly fought out by small sub-units on patrol between the forward lines. Many of the young subalterns in 1 Welch were National Service conscripts who earned great respect for the way they proved their qualities of leadership in challenging situations. 2nd Lieutenant John Davey took out numerous fighting and 'lay-up' patrols during his twelve months in Korea, and was later rewarded with an MC and a regular commission. Today he has become Brigadier K. J. Davey, CBE, MC, DL. Other National Service platoon commanders included 2nd Lieutenants John Bowler and Ian Powys, both of whom received the MC for their patrolling endeavours.

The strength of patrols naturally varied according to tasks, from one officer and half a dozen soldiers for a short-range recce to one and twenty-five or more for a fighting patrol. The latter would be armed with six LMGs (Brens) besides Stens, rifles and grenades, while three signallers were laden with their No. 88 wireless sets. For rations each man carried two tins of American-issue C7 rations and two tins of self-heating soup, together with six bars of chocolate and six packets of chewing gum. During the heat of the summer months the chocolate tended to melt, and also induced thirst, so boiled sweets were substituted. In addition to each man's field dressing, a supply of morphia tablets was carried by the patrol leader.

While patrolling was the main operational task of the Battalion throughout the campaign, there were rare occasions when a large-scale, all-arms attack was undertaken. One of these was appropriately code-named Operation 'Maindy', which took place on the night of 23rd/24th June 1952. B Company, commanded by Major T. J. Jackson, was ordered to attack a strong Chinese position on a feature known as Hill 227. It was believed to be held by about 140 enemy in a complex of bunkers, and an assault by another unit in January had been repulsed with many casualties. The Company was supported by a squadron of 5 DG and three batteries of Gunners, together with a detachment of Sappers from 55 Field Squadron RE. The attack went in just before first light on the 24th, with two platoons 'up', the other in reserve with Tac HQ. The left Platoon succeeded in capturing their bunker objective after a fierce exchange of LMG fire and grenades, during which the Platoon commander was wounded, but remained in action. While consolidating, they were subjected to further assaults by machine guns and grenades. Meanwhile the right Platoon had cleared three bunkers, but on exploiting they came under a hail of grenades which killed the leading section commander. While the two leading sections were thus engaged, the right Platoon commander moved up in support but as he was about to attack another bunker he was severely wounded by 'burp' fire.[3] By this time the other Platoon commander had received a second wound which put him out of action. The Platoon Sergeant was likewise hit and the wireless operator was killed by a mortar bomb. Learning that both Platoon commanders were casualties, the Company commander went forward and consolidated the survivors of the platoons, before organising a section-by-section withdrawal which was successfully carried out. Operation 'Maindy' cost B Company two men killed and twenty-two wounded, including two subalterns. During the early stages of the attack the artillery put down supporting fire to silence some long-range mortars, but their FOO, with Company Headquarters, was killed and the wireless operator was wounded. The

Hill 355; Korea, April 1952; Major David Salmon, 1 Welch, having substituted the Battalion Battle Flag for the Stars and Stripes, takes over the position from the United States Army Company Commander. ON LOAN FROM MAJOR DICK TAVERNER

Lieutenant Colonel Deane, DSO, presents leeks to 1 Welch; Korea; St David's Day, 1952.

enemy casualties were estimated to be sixteen killed and many more wounded. These could only be estimated, for the Chinese always made every effort to evacuate casualties – as did 'own troops'. In fact all B Company's dead and wounded were safely brought back to base. For his part in this action, Major T. J. Jackson received an immediate DSO.

After a 'rest' period in reserve (when the opportunity was seized to organise a Rugby match with a battery of New Zealand Gunners), the Battalion moved back to the front line along the Imjin River. This was in July, and apart from clashes with enemy patrols, it was High Explosive that became the chief threat. The PLA (Chinese People's Liberation Army) were well equipped with artillery, much of it 122 mm. calibre, and seemingly inexhaustible stocks of ammunition, and throughout July and August they appeared to be concentrating their 'hates' on 1 Welch. The War Diary reported that one morning seventy-six shells fell in C Company's position within thirty minutes, while 'about 120 shells fell in A Coy's area between 1500 and 1845.'

On 17th July 'the three fwd Coys received about 300 shells, mostly of 122mm calibre'. Such laconic entries occur and recur, and one can only marvel that the Battalion was not destroyed. But thanks to all the back-breaking work on bunkers with their revetted walls and turf and stone covered roofs, casualties were slight. Some bunkers survived direct hits without any hurt to occupants.

Soldier of 1 Welch eating the leek; Korea, St David's Day, 1951.

The Korean summer brought another hazard with the arrival of the monsoon. In June the Imjin River rose 40 ft, washing away roads and bridges. Bunkers were flooded, 'fighting bays became swamps, and communication trenches resembled miniature rivers'. Bunkers that had withstood all that shelling succumbed to the assaults of nature and collapsed. One soldier was buried and drowned as he lay asleep after his spell of 'stag'. Yet another endemic threat in the summer months was malaria, but this was combated by the new Paludrine drug, much more effective than the Mepacrine of the Burma campaign, and with none of the unpleasant side-effects. As in Slim's Army, every officer and soldier was ordered to swallow one Paludrine tablet every morning with the result that malaria was never a problem.

On 26th October 1952, The Welch found themselves withdrawn to a staging camp by the Imjin River, actually astride the 38th Parallel. Two days later the Commanding Officer of the 1st Duke of Wellington's Regiment arrived, and, having handed over to him and his Battalion on 2nd November, 1 Welch moved by train to Pusan, where they had disembarked for their campaigning almost exactly twelve months previously.

The Korean conflict was the last full-scale war to have been fought by antecedents of the present Regiment, and the Battle Honour 'Korea 1951–52' seems unlikely to be superseded by a later grant as this history is written. Those twelve months had brought their inevitable casualties, and their well-earned decorations. Perhaps 1 Welch were fortunate in losing only one officer (2nd Lieutenant Stephen Burgess), but they also lost thirty other ranks killed and five officers and fifty-nine other ranks wounded (two of the latter subsequently died). Decorations included three DSOs (Colonel Deane, Major Jackson and Major A. G. Roberts), two MCs (2nd Lieutenants Davey and Powys), three MMs and numerous Mentions in Despatches.

On 16th November, at the United Nations Military Cemetery overlooking Pusan harbour, 1 Welch paraded for a solemn memorial service to their thirty comrades who now lay buried there. After wreaths had been laid by Colonel Deane and the RSM, Last Post and Reveille were sounded by the Battalion's buglers.

During the 1950s both The South Wales Borderers and The Welch Regiment saw changes of distinguished Colonels. In January 1950 Major General D. G. Johnson, VC, CB, DSO, MC, resigned the Colonelcy of The South Wales Borderers, which he had held since 1944. One of only two Colonels of either Regiment to earn the supreme award for gallantry (the other being General Alexander Cobbe, also 24th), Dudley, as he was familiarly known, had enjoyed the esteem and affection of all ranks, not only for his proven soldierly qualities, but for his deep understanding of, and regard for, men

A cheerful group of 1 Welch officers at mess in inclement weather; Korea, 1952. 2 Lt K. J. Davey (later Brigadier) is in the centre.

under his command, whether senior officers or humble privates. Dudley Johnson lived to the ripe old age of 91, dying at his Hampshire home in December 1975.

His successor was General Sir A. Reade Godwin-Austen, KCSI, CB, OBE, MC. His family name had long been familiar, not only within the Regiment but far outside it, among geographers and Himalayan explorers. His uncle, Colonel Henry Godwin-Austen, had served as a subaltern in the 24th in the 1850s before becoming attached to the Trigonometrical Survey of India. As a topographical officer he carried out exploration and surveying of the then unknown Karakoram ranges on the borders of India, China and Afghanistan. In 1863 he discovered and mapped the world's second highest mountain in this 'Roof of the World', which was at first named after him as 'Mount Godwin-Austen' (28,250 ft). But, ignoring the precedent of Mount Everest, the Government of India decreed that personal names were inappropriate for Himalayan peaks, and so today this distinguished mountain bears the undistinguished, cipher-like designation, K2.

Sir Reade Godwin-Austen (his first forename was Alfred, but he preferred the second) was commissioned into The South Wales Borderers in 1909, at the age of 19. During the Great War he served on the Staff of 40 Infantry Brigade and 13 Division, eventually becoming AAG and QMG, and gaining the OBE and MC. After command of the 2nd Battalion the Duke of Cornwall's Light Infantry, and then further staff appointments between the wars, Major General Godwin-Austen commanded the British forces which drove the Italians out of Somaliland in 1940, and in the following year commanded 13 Army Corps in the relief of Tobruk. As Vice QMG in 1944 he was responsible for much of the logistic planning of Operation 'Overlord'. General Godwin-Austen retired from the active list in 1947. He was knighted in 1957.

In January 1958 The Welch Regiment bade farewell to Major General C. E. N. Lomax, CB, CBE, DSO, MC, who had assumed the Colonelcy exactly nine years earlier. We have already met him as author of *The History of The Welch Regiment 1919–1951*, and as such he enjoys the distinction of being one of only two Colonels of either Regiment to have produced a regimental history (the other was Major General Sir Thomas O. Marden, who wrote the World War I history of The Welch).

Lomax was replaced by Lieutenant General Sir Charles F. C. Coleman, KCB, CMG, DSO, OBE. The new Colonel had

Major General Sir A. Reade Godwin-Austen, KCSI, CB, OBE, MC, Colonel The South Wales Borderers, 3rd February 1950–18th April 1954.

Colours on parade for the Freedom of the Borough of Brecon to The South Wales Borderers, 11th June 1948.

joined 1 Welch as a 2nd Lieutenant in 1923. After service in China and Malaya, and at the Cardiff Depot, he was made Adjutant of the 2nd Battalion and went with them to Landi Kotal. As related on p. 269, 2 Welch had set records in this Kyber outpost when they played the first Rugby match and held the first dance. Another rather different record was achieved when Lieutenant Cyril Coleman (as he was then known) was married at Landi Kotal's tiny garrison Church (to Miss Margaret Petrie) on 7th December 1935. This was the first such ceremony to take place in the Khyber Pass. Promoted Major in 1940, Coleman took over command of 4 Welch the following year, and was responsible for the training up to D-Day. Just before the landings, however, he was given command of their Brigade (160 Infantry Brigade), and led them with great distinction throughout the North-West Europe campaign, earning a DSO. After the war he became successively GOC 43 (Wessex) Division and SE District, and GOC Berlin (British Sector). This latter command was during the tense period of the Soviet blockade, and his services were rewarded with the CMG. In 1956, as Lieutenant General, he became GOC Eastern Command, and the following year was made KCB.

Although the Army of the 1950s had become more sophisticated than its predecessor of the 1930s, particularly as regards artillery, fighting vehicles and transport, its infantry soldiers were still armed with weapons that had changed little since their fathers' days. They still trained with the venerable Lee-Enfield .303 rifle, or SMLE, and the Vickers MMG, both of which dated from the turn of the century. Only the Bren LMG and the mortars were relative newcomers. But since World War II deeper thought had been given to the infantryman's means of defence against his main threat, the battle tank with its increased fire-power and armour protection. By 1954 the Soviets had fielded their fearsome JS series and the T54, protected by 120 mm. of armour plate. To combat such threats, Britain introduced the BAT anti-tank gun, issued to battalion anti-tank platoons.[4]

This deadly weapon fired a 120 mm. HESH projectile (High Explosive Squash Head), a post-war British development used by tank gunners themselves, and reckoned capable of 'killing' any enemy tank likely to be confronted. But there was a price to pay for the infantry users. The weapon on its wheeled carriage was heavy, weighing more than a ton, while the projectiles themselves in their steel transport cases each weighed 100 lb. This was more than could be towed by a Jeep, and one of the transport 'soft trucks' had to be employed.

Major General C. E. N. Lomax, CB, CBE, DSO, MC, Colonel The Welch Regiment, 8th January 1949–7th January 1958.

In March 1954 1 SWB were in Brunswick, Germany, and their Anti-Tank Platoon laid on a demonstration of the BAT for the benefit of officers of 11 Armoured Division. When the Platoon succeeded in removing the turret from a target tank, one senior RTR officer was heard to remark: 'This is the moment at which I retire.' However, when The South Wales Borderers next saw active service, they had no need of their BATs.

After the Japanese surrender in Singapore, the British rubber planters returning to their Malayan estates fondly believed that life could now go on as before. But they had not reckoned with the Chinese Communist element who, ironically enough, had been staunch supporters of the British against the Japanese during the war. In 1948 they began their campaign of terrorism and intimidation in their attempt to oust the British and take over the Malayan peninsula. This Malayan 'Emergency' was to drag on for nine years and to cost the lives of some 500 British and Gurkha soldiers, besides more than 2,000 civilians, many of whom were brutally murdered.

By 1955 the guerrillas, or 'CTs' (Communist Terrorists) had been largely forced on

Lieutenant General Sir Charles Coleman, KCB, CMG, DSO, OBE, Colonel The Welch Regiment, 8th January 1958–19th November 1965.

the defensive, thanks to the tactics of General Sir Gerald Templer, but there were still 2,000-odd hard-core Marxists operating from their camps hidden deep in the *ulu*, ambushing convoys, raiding rubber estates and forcing Malayan villagers to supply their needs. It was the task of the security forces to eliminate these diehards by deep-range jungle patrols and surprise attacks on their camps, forcing surrender by denying supplies, or by employing the CTs' own tactics of ambush. It was to such gruelling jungle-warfare operations that 1 SWB were committed in October 1955, when the Battalion, fresh from their spell in BAOR, landed at Singapore. They were commanded by Lieutenant Colonel R. C. H. Miers, DSO, who not only led them with conspicuous initiative and personal courage throughout the following two and a half years, but who later, as Brigadier, wrote an absorbing account of the operations under the title *Shoot to Kill*.[5]

Before being committed to active operations the Battalion underwent an intensive 'crash course' in jungle warfare at the Kota Tinggi Training Centre (near Johore Bahru). The last British troops to fight in Malaya had been those who were harried down the peninsula by the Japanese, from whom they learned nothing and to whom the jungle itself was anything but 'neutral'. Now, under tough Australian and British instructors, the Battalion were taught to use the jungle to their advantage, as did the CTs. They learned all the elements of patrolling. Each member of an eight-man patrol had his allotted tasks: the leading scout, carbine or shotgun at the ready,[6] advanced cautiously, senses strained for any tell-tale crackle of undergrowth or sudden flurry of disturbed bird life ahead. Behind came two men, one watching the track to the left, the other to the right. The fourth man kept an eye aloft, into the branches of the trees which could conceal a CT with grenades; then came the section leader and the Bren-gunner and last of all was the man responsible for watching the rear. Groups were taken into the jungle and shown how to erect their 'poncho' capes to make a reasonable shelter; how to cook their meals and to navigate with map and compass, and how to clear DZs (Dropping Zones) with *parangs* (long Malay knives) for the supply helicopters. The soldiers of 1941–2 had been taught none of these skills.

In December 1955 the Battalion relieved 1 East Yorks in the Kluang area, becoming responsible for an extent of jungle and swamp the size of Kent. Among the most notorious terrorist leaders in this area was one Kok Fui, Branch Committee Secretary of the Malayan Communist Party. So far he had eluded all attempts at 'elimination'.

Early in January, Special Branch Intelligence reported that some of Kok Fui's gang would be crossing a jungle road to pick up supplies on a certain date. And so Colonel Miers laid an ambush. After dark on 12th January, 2nd Lieutenant Jeremy Barnes (the youngest officer in the Battalion) led out his patrol, and after some very skilful navigation reached the location at dawn and took up position. Almost as soon as it was light they spotted four figures moving through the trees. They were CTs, carrying rifles. But the range was rather long, and the group were moving farther away:

> Jeremy collected a few men and silently moved after them. Ten minutes later he and the Bren-gunner topped the rise of the hill. Fifty yards away two figures were standing behind a tree. One was a tapper, the other, on the instant, put his rifle to his shoulder and opened fire. Bullets clipped the tree above Jeremy's head.
> 'Charge!' yelled Jeremy and his Bren-gunner together as they returned the fire and dashed forward.
> 'Charge!' shouted the rest of the men breasting the hill . . . Two figures lay silent on the ground, three more, a long way off, scuttled into the jungle.

The troopship Dilwara *which took 1 SWB to Malaya in 1955 and brought them home in 1958.*

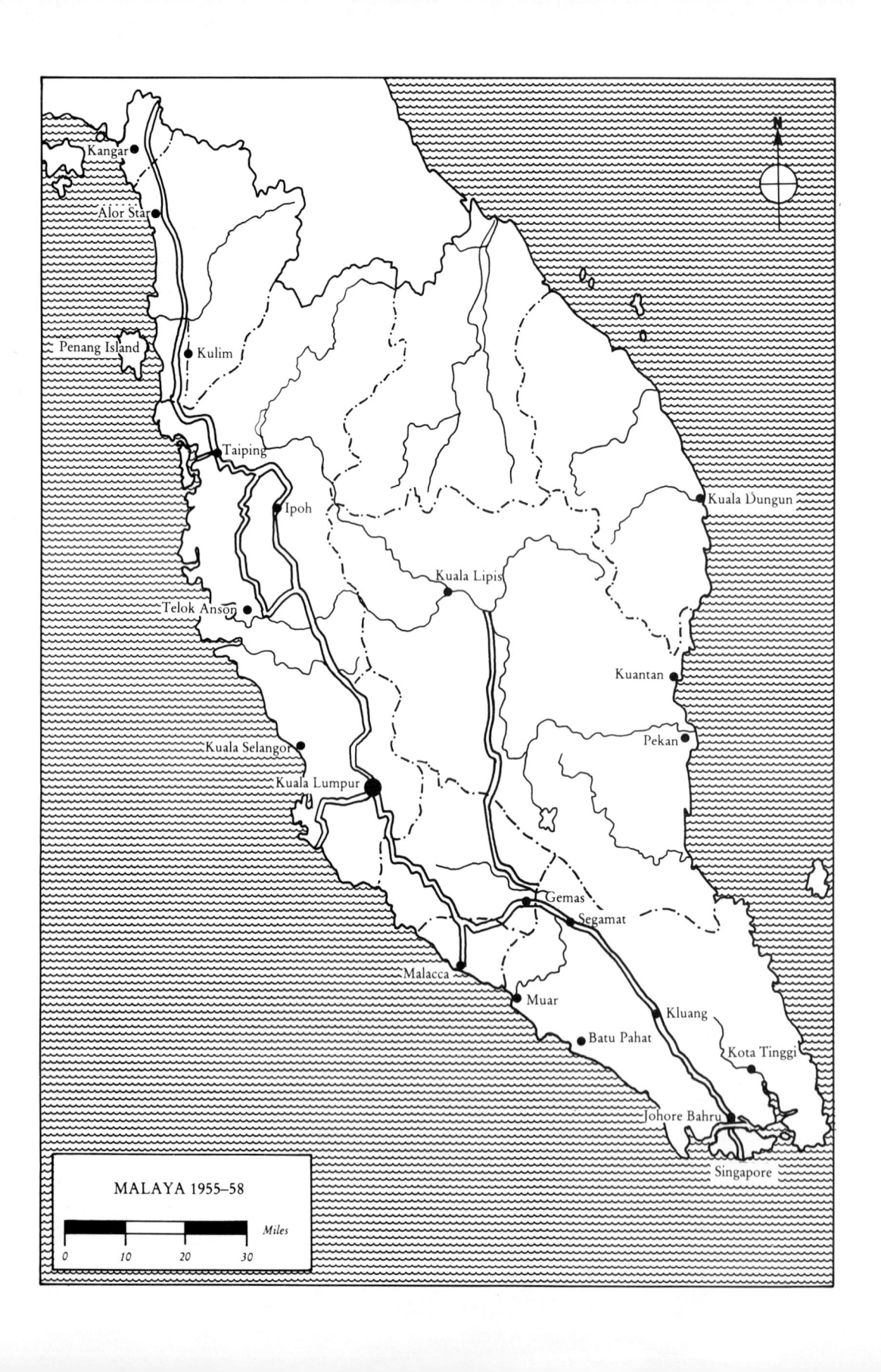

MALAYA 1955–58

Soldiers of 1 SWB on patrol in mangrove swamp in Malaya, 1956.

> Jeremy returned to where the two bodies, one a CT, the other a tapper, lay on the ground. The CT was already dead, the tapper died on the way home (somewhat to our relief he proved to be one of the chief CT civilian contacts in the area, and as bad as any of them) ...
>
> We put the body in a jeep and rushed back to the police station, there to dump it on the lawn ready for identification ... Even in death the ugly distorted little face bore the stamp of cruelty and evil, and stirred little feeling of compassion.[7]

Shortly afterwards, when the Brigade commander had arrived, the body was identified. It was Kok Fui himself. The Battalion had bagged their first CT, and a very important one he was.

This incident was typical of many that followed, though all too often the quarry got away, leaving only trails of blood. But in February the Battalion took part in an unusual operation in the form of a massive air strike against a large CT base camp remote in thick Kluang jungle. This was known to be the headquarters of the much-wanted Political Commissar, Goh Peng Tuan, and was said to house a hundred or so of his gang. Previous attempts at pinpointing the exact location had failed. But in the first week of February, Major John Margesson (Battalion Second-in-Command) took out a 'search-and-locate' patrol, and after two days of struggle through virgin jungle, succeeded in spotting the camp. Its position in the middle of a vast swamp, protected by a formidable zareba of felled thorn bushes and numerous sentry posts, rendered it

A Sikorsky S55 helicopter of the Royal Navy landing soldiers of 1 SWB in a Malayan jungle clearing.

virtually impossible to capture by the normal method of ground attack. To Miers, the only answer seemed to be an air strike.

After much debate at the joint Army/Air Headquarters in Kuala Lumpur, Colonel Miers managed to persuade his superiors to accept his proposal, and planning went ahead. At first Miers had intended to throw a cordon of his men around the camp to block escape routes, but since they would need to be dropped by helicopter, thus forfeiting surprise, this plan was modified: the men would be dropped immediately *after* the bombing raid.

At 0900 hours on 21st February, aircraft detailed from as far away as Singapore in the south and Penang in the north rendezvoused somewhere in the sky west of Kluang, while the men of 1 SWB squatted beside their helicopters. Half an hour later the first wave of bombers roared over Miers's Headquarters. 'All at once', he wrote, 'a great rectangular rent opened in the backcloth of the jungle, the ground trembled under our feet, and through my field-glasses I could see in the cloud of dust and rubble, broken lengths of tree being tossed in the air as though they were matchsticks.' Then the helicopters took off and, hovering low over the devastated position, allowed their passengers to swarm down knotted ropes – into fetid swamp and chaos of bomb-craters and uprooted trees. When the men struggled into the ruined camp they found only thirteen dead CTs and one badly wounded, who died later. Among the dead was the Political Commissar, Goh Peng Tuan.

Although one officer remarked that the raid had been rather like taking a very large sledgehammer to crack a very small nut, the bag, including one of the CT hierarchy, was the largest yet achieved in local operations, and it resulted in a flood of congratulatory signals from all over the Federation. While the RAF deserved the highest credit for their pinpoint attack, there was no doubt that Major Margesson, who had located the camp, and Colonel Miers, who had conceived the operation, were entitled to their share.

For the next year 1 SWB were continuously occupied in hunting down the elusive CTs up and down the peninsula, sometimes rushing a camp to find it deserted, sometimes laying ambushes to kill one or two. Here are extracts from a digest published in the *XXIV Journal*:

Captain (later Major) J. A. Ll. Mitchley, left; and the Commanding Officer of 1 SWB in Malaya, Lieutenant Colonel (later Brigadier) R. C. H. Miers, DSO, OBE, right.

On the evening of 12th September [1956] an ambush party commanded by the Adjutant, Major A. K. Sharp . . . killed three out of 4 CT. The dead included Mun Leong, District Committee Member, his wife and another male member of the branch

On 1st December an ambush party of B Company commanded by Major A. Gwynne-Jones . . . killed two male Chinese CTs.

On 19th June a patrol of A Company, led by Captain I. G. B. Goad, attacked a camp occupied by ten CT. During a short battle one CT was killed. Throughout the next three days the escaping CT group was tracked by the Mortar Platoon . . . one CT was killed.

On 16th April a recce patrol of Support Company killed a member of a party of 3 CT whom they met in the Selumpur smallholdings. He was Low

Bok Pin, a member of the Selumpur Branch. The following morning an ambush party laid on the jungle edge after the contact killed Kim Hua, another member of the Selumpur Branch. On 22nd April the third member of the original party, Ng Kim Choon, surrendered.

The Selumpur Branch (of the Malayan Communist Party), mentioned above, was one of the most troublesome in the Segamat area, where 1 SWB spent the last few months of their tour. The leader, Ming Lee, had acquired a reputation for brutality, ruthlessness and an uncanny cunning which time and again had seen him through numerous near escapes from killing or capture. The Battalion was now under orders to withdraw to Singapore in ten days' time, for return home, and Colonel Miers was determined that they should not depart without accounting for 'the scourge of Segamat'.

Miers split his task force into a large number of four-men groups and sent them into the jungle to form a 'pepper-pot' of ambushes, confident that the quarry must stumble into one of them. On the second day an ambush party spotted two CTs and opened fire. One was killed, but the other jinked among the trees and disappeared. Evidence showed that he was none other than Ming Lee himself, who seemed to have more lives than any cat.

The Battalion tracking team was then unleashed. This consisted of three Sarawak or Iban trackers, two dogs and six soldiers with rifles, shotgun, Bren and wireless, all commanded by a subaltern. Starting at the ambush point, the Ibans quickly picked up Ming Lee's tracks, and for some twelve hours they followed the trail, twisting and turning through undergrowth and swamp. At nightfall they seemed to be closing in on their quarry: the tracks were fresh, reported the trackers, and the man appeared to be limping. Tracking was impossible in the dark, so the team lay up for the night.

Back at the Battalion Headquarters next morning, Colonel Miers was greeted by the report that Ming Lee had run slap into one of his ambushes – and they had missed him. The man was surely superhuman. Despondently Miers radioed to the tracking team to switch to the site of the latest ambush. But inwardly he was

Major (later Lieutenant Colonel) J. E. Margesson, MBE, Second-in-Command, in Malaya.

resigned to his Battalion having to leave Malaya with their last operation a failure.

Shortly afterwards came a telephone call from the local Special Branch officer. Ming Lee had surrendered. Interviewed by Miers and a bevy of Special Branch officers, the insignificant-looking terrorist admitted that after the bombing raid, when he lost most of his trusted 'officers', he found that escape was impossible because of the Battalion's cordon of ambushes, and burying his rifle in a swamp, he walked into the nearest police station.

Colonel Miers received numerous congratulatory signals, including one from General Sir Roger Bower, Director of Operations. But that which pleased him most was one from 'The People of Segamat' who invited him and his Battalion to a celebration to mark the declaration of the new 'White Area'.

As for Ming Lee, the terror of Segamat, he underwent a sojourn in the Government Rehabilitation Centre, and became employed as groundsman to the Segamat Cricket Club. As Miers observed, the ways of the British were just as inscrutable as those of the Chinese CTs.

Major A. Gwynne-Jones, now the Rt. Hon. Lord Chalfont, OBE, MC, PC.

With this successful finale, 1 SWB embarked at Singapore and sailed for home in September 1958. Incredibly enough, their two and a half years' duty in the 'Emergency' had cost not a single fatal casualty; only half a dozen men were wounded. But it brought its awards. Colonel Miers received a Bar to his DSO; MCs were awarded to Major A. Gwynne-Jones (later Lord Chalfont), Captain L. A. H. Napier (future Colonel of The Royal Regiment of Wales) and Captain R. I. Hywel-Jones. Major (QM) J. Q. Adams was made MBE, and many officers and soldiers received Mentions in Despatches.

In bidding farewell to Malaya, 1 SWB were sad to do likewise to their Commanding Officer. Lieutenant Colonel Richard Miers was promoted Brigadier, to take command of 24 Independent Infantry Brigade in East Africa.[8]

As related on p. 350, The Welsh Brigade (Royal Welch Fusiliers, South Wales Borderers and Welch) had come into existence in 1946. Now in 1958, as a result of War Office direction, there came further reorganisation, with the closer association of all three Regiments. At a meeting of the three Regimental Colonels in January, it was agreed that the Brigade Depot of the Regiments should be located at Cwrt-y-Gollen,

The new cap badge, 1958.

just outside Crickhowell (Breconshire), and this would be responsible for training all recruits for the three Regiments. Despite the former cautions about 'tampering' with regimental identities, authority had decreed that all regiments within a Brigade should share a common cap badge, as well as a Depot. After much debate among themselves, and with the Battalions, the Colonels resolved to submit a design incorporating the Welsh Dragon surrounded by the Garter scroll and surmounted by the Crown. But as will be seen, this design was not adopted.

Writing of these changes in the *XXIV Journal* (for May 1958), the Colonel of the 24th, Major General F. R. G. Matthews, hoped that they would see a Brigade loyalty superimposed on Regimental loyalty. Then, with uncanny but surely unwitting premonition, he went on to suggest that at some future date the three Battalions might be united 'under some such title as The Royal Regiment of Wales'. Though only two of the Battalions were to become thus united, this was a remarkable forecast of things to come.

On return from Malaya, 1 SWB were based in Dering Lines, Brecon. After well-earned leave they found themselves busy brushing up their ceremonial drill and being kitted out in blue No. 1 Dress.[9] The Territorial Battalion, 2 Mons, were similarly occupied. All this was in preparation for the Presentation of new Colours to both Battalions. The ceremony (in pelting rain) took place at Ebbw Vale on 25th July 1958, when the Colours were presented by HRH the Duke of Edinburgh, deputising for the Queen, who was unfortunately taken ill shortly before. Later, on 14th September, the old Colours were laid up with due ceremony in the 24th Regimental Chapel in Brecon Cathedral.

In August 1958 The Welch Regiment carried out similar ceremonial duties on the occasion of the visit of the Queen to Pembroke. Stationed at Pembroke Dock, the 1st Battalion provided a Guard of Honour for Her Majesty as she arrived at Haverfordwest on 6th August, while a street-lining contingent in Pembroke was found from men of B and D Companies. The Guard of Honour included the Colour Party, and by special invitation of the Council, the whole detachment (headed by Taffy X and the Goat Major) marched through the streets of the borough 'Colours flying, bayonets fixed, and drums beating'.

Meanwhile, after a period as a home-defence Battalion, in June 1956 1 Welch began a tour of duty in BAOR. The Battalion was accommodated in surprisingly pleasant and spacious barracks on the outskirts of Luneburg, and immediately underwent a reorganisation, to deploy only three Rifle companies. The fourth (D Company) was reduced to Headquarters and instructional staff, with the task of continuation training for drafts from the Depot. The remainder of the Company were absorbed by the other three. The Support Company disappeared into Headquarters Company and the Anti-

National Servicemen under training at Brecon barracks, 1956.

Tank Platoon was split among the Rifle companies, each having one detachment with its BAT. The Machine Gun and Assault Pioneer platoons became part of Headquarters Company. All this was intended to provide a 'more flexible' structure, as authority had it.

With intensive training, battalion and brigade schemes, large-scale exercises, and the acquisition of such linguistic skills as 'Zwei Bier bitte' and 'Wie geht's Fräulein?' weeks and months passed quickly; so quickly, in fact, that no sooner had they settled down to BAOR life than they found themselves posted home to Worcester, under orders for Cyprus, whither they moved by troop-ship in October 1957. The Battalion was commanded by Lieutenant Colonel J. R. L. Traherne.

But before noticing their activities in that unhappy island, we must revert to September 1956. On the 22nd of that month The Welch Regiment Memorial Chapel in Llandaff Cathedral was consecrated by the Lord Archbishop of Wales. As related earlier, the Cathedral had been virtually destroyed by the Luftwaffe during the war. In 1945 the Colonel of The Welch, Major General Douglas Dickinson, proposed that the Regiment should assist in the restoration of the Cathedral by building a Chapel as a memorial to those who fell in the two World Wars. A subscription list was opened, with such generous response by serving and past members of the Regiment, allied

Regiments, families and friends, that within a year the sum of £6,303 had been received. By 1956 the total had risen to £21,245, and further donations were promised. Designed by the Cathedral architect (who incurred some criticism for his inclusion of the ultra-modern Epstein figure of 'Christ in Majesty' on its concrete arch in the nave), the Chapel abutting the north wall is a blend of traditional and contemporary. (A detailed architectural description of the Chapel was published in *The Men of Harlech* for October 1956.) The solemn Consecration ceremony was attended by representatives of all battalions, regular and Territorial, the then Colonel of the Regiment (Major General C. E. N. Lomax), the Lord-Lieutenant of Glamorgan, the Home Secretary and the Minister for Welsh Affairs, besides numerous civic dignitaries including the Lord Mayor of Cardiff. Also present were the four living VCs and a next-of-kin representative of an officer, a Warrant Officer, sergeant, corporal and private who had been killed

RIGHT: *The Welch Regiment Memorial Chapel, Llandaff Cathedral, Cardiff.*
BELOW: *The Welch Regiment Memorial Chapel, Llandaff Cathedral, Cardiff: interior.*

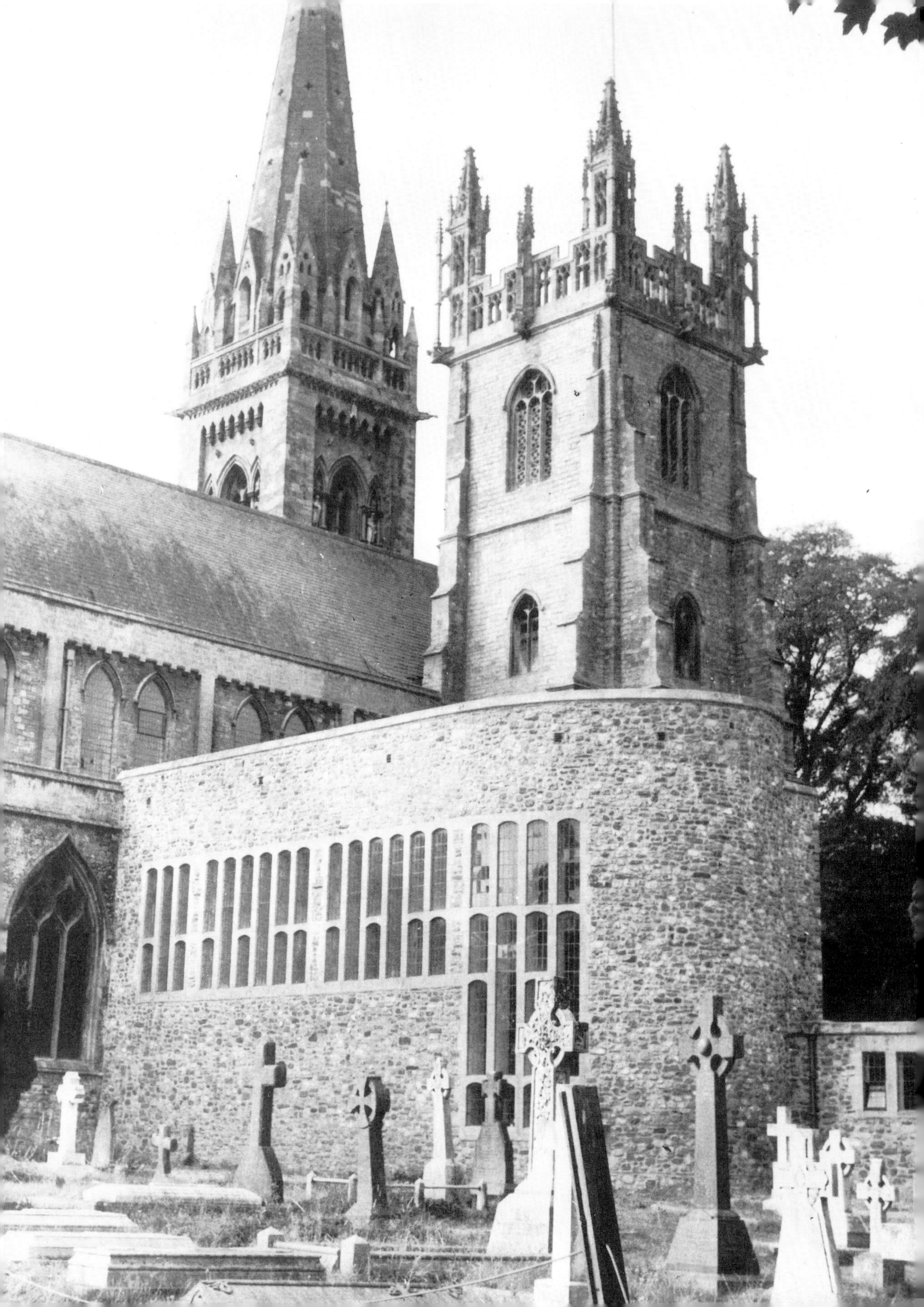

in World War II. The choir was accompanied by the Band of the 5th Battalion, whose trumpeters sounded the Last Post and Reveille. It was a most impressive and moving ceremony, and as the correspondent to *The Men of Harlech* wrote: 'The vast congregation had one thing in common – they belonged to the family of The Welch Regiment... and their heads were bowed together in prayer for those who had worn the same cap badge, but whom death had prevented from being on parade that day.'

On 28th September 1957 the old Colours of the 1st and (disbanded) 2nd Battalions came to their rightful resting place when they were laid up in the new Chapel.

Meanwhile, 1 Welch had been doing their duty in Cyprus, stationed first at Xeros and then at Dhavlos, 35 miles from Famagusta. In fact only three Rifle Companies were in Cyprus, one being detached for a tour of duty in Cyrenaica – at Benghazi and Tobruk. The Battalion's operational area was divided among the three Companies, each one having some hundred square miles to look after, the terrain varying from sandy coastal beaches to rugged mountains and thick scrub. The situation in Cyprus was not unlike that encountered by 1 SWB in Malaya, CTs being replaced by the murderous gangs of Greek EOKA terrorists whose main targets were the security forces. Laying ambushes and mining roads, they proved a menace to all but their Greek-Cypriot brethren. EOKA's aim was '*Enosis*', or union with Greece and the complete subjugation of the Turkish population.[10] It was the thankless task of the British soldiers to try to maintain law and order among the opposing factions, though the Turks were no great threat, fearing the EOKA as their real enemy. Constant patrolling in the rugged terrain was varied by the periodic 'Snatch Party' – a dawn raid on suspected terrorists' hideouts, in village or mountain cave. Then there were the cordon and search operations when a village suspected of harbouring EOKA gangs would be surrounded and every inhabitant 'screened' by Intelligence. In one week in July the Battalion rounded up a hundred-odd suspects (sent to 'cages') and captured a haul of 1,600 rounds of .303 ammunition together with sticks of dynamite, petrol-bombs, rifles and shotguns. Like the Malayan CTs, the EOKA seldom risked a face-to-face confrontation with the troops, but relied chiefly on such clandestine tactics as ambushes and road mines. Only one man of 1 Welch was killed during the Cyprus tour, and that was when his vehicle was blown off the road by a mine, which wounded his two companions. Corporal W. P. Jones received the MM for several acts of bravery and initiative in capturing terrorists.

In Cyprus the Battalion leaned to handle new weapons and new vehicles. The long-serving SMLE .303 rifle had been replaced by the Belgian FN self-loading weapon with its standard NATO 7.62 mm. rounds. This had been accepted for the Army in 1954. The Sterling sub-machine gun had superseded the World War II Sten. On patrol some additional fire-power, and armour, were provided by the useful little Ferret scout cars with their turret-mounted Browning MGs. In was also in Cyprus that The Welch were introduced to the vehicle that was to become the Army's mechanical workhorse – one which, in successive models, has survived to the present day. Officially designated 'Truck ¼ ton 4 × 4', it was more familiar as the Land Rover, Britain's worthy answer to the American Jeep. The Battalion MT Section were most impressed with their new acquisitions, as their scribe revealed in *The Men of Harlech*: 'These blunt-nosed, plucky little vehicles clock more mileage and more running time than any other vehicle in the Platoon . . . they will carry you over the roughest country and the steepest hill tracks with little or no trouble at all.' The Rover Company, then fighting their Jeep rival in export markets, would have seized on those comments for publicity.

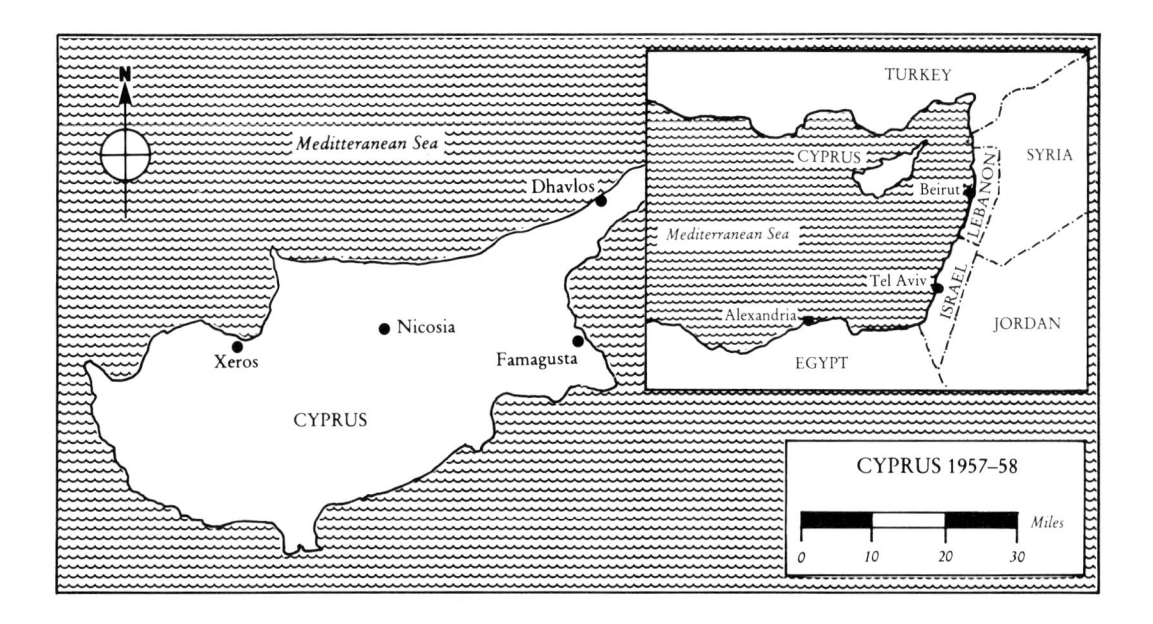

Having spent nearly two years in the turmoil of Cyprus, 1 Welch were confidently expecting a home posting, but instead they found themselves routed to Benghazi in Libya. Since 1951 Libya had been an independent federal state under its Amir, Mohammed Idris. This potentate was at first anxious to see the departure of all British forces who had been granted training facilities in his Kingdom. But in July 1958 his fellow-Arab monarch, King Faisal II of Iraq, was assassinated in a coup led by his own Army officers, and his country was declared a Republic. Fearing for his own security, Idris decided that it might be advisable to allow the 5,000-odd British soldiers to remain, for the time being.

And so in December 1958, 1 Welch concentrated in Benghazi, which was to be their Headquarters for the next eighteen months. Soon after arrival, Lieutenant Colonel A. G. Roberts, DSO, took over command from Lieutenant Colonel Traherne, who had been given a War Office appointment. There was no insurrection during the Battalion's Libyan tour (but it was to come later), and routine training was varied only by large-scale desert exercises and visits of VIPs, including the Secretary of State for War (The Rt Hon. Christopher Soames), the CIGS (General Sir Francis Festing), and Lieutenant General Sir Charles Coleman, Colonel of the Regiment. Each Rifle company took it in turns to perform security duties around King Idris's palace at Tobruk, which inspired *The Western Mail* (Cardiff) to come out with the headline: 'Welshmen Guard A Desert King'.

Cwrt-y-Gollen, Crickhowell, c. 1960.   PHOTOGRAPH: MAJOR R. P. SMITH

    Before 1 Welch left for home, Colonel Roberts was gratified to receive a laudatory signal from the Commander Libya, Brigadier N. J. Dickson: 'You are one of the best Battalions out of the 32 I have had under my command in the past 5 years.'

    When the Battalion arrived on their home ground of Maindy Barracks, Cardiff, in October 1960, they were wearing a new cap badge. As mentioned earlier, the formation of The Welsh Brigade in 1955 had entailed not only the move to the new Brigade Depot at Cwrt-y-Gollen (Crickhowell), but the adoption of a common Brigade cap badge for all three Regiments. After consideration and rejection of several proposals by the three Colonels, final approval was given to a design incorporating The Prince of Wales's Plumes, the Coronet and the Motto *'Ich Dien'*. The Royal Welch Fusiliers and The South Wales Borderers were the losers, for the former lost their Bursting Grenade, the latter their Sphinx. The Welch still displayed the Plumes, even though their own Motto had disappeared. However, each Regiment was permitted to wear individual collar badges, so that The South Wales Borderers were glad to retain their Wreath of Immortelles encircling the numeral XXIV, while The Welch wore their Dragon.

    There were appropriate 'Rebadging parades' to retire the old and welcome in the new. At Cwrt-y-Gollen on 8th April (1960) the three Colonels[11] witnessed the symbolic handing-in of the old Regimental badges and the adoption of the new. Away in Benghazi, in April, 1 Welch held their own ceremonial. First the 'Old Guard' wearing the Regimental badges marched on with the Regimental Colour, which was handed over to the 'New Guard' wearing the new badges. The 'Old Guard' then marched off to 'Auld Lang Syne' as the Battalion presented arms. On 2nd April a similar ceremony was performed by 1 SWB at Minden, in BAOR.

By January 1960 The Welsh Brigade had become fully established in their Cwrt-y-Gollen Depot, although the planned complex of permanent buildings was by no means completed. As already mentioned, the site, one and a half miles along the Abergavenny road from Crickhowell, had been chosen by the three Regimental Colonels as the most suitable location. It was certainly handy for The South Wales Borderers with their Regimental Headquarters a mere twelve miles away at Brecon, while The Welch had less than an hour's drive to or from Cardiff. But perhaps The Royal Welch Fusiliers might not have regarded it as 'central', for their Headquarters was far off in North Wales, at Wrexham.

Cwrt-y-Gollen ('Hazel Court') had once been an elegant 18th-century mansion, its gracious setting of oak-studded park backed by wooded heights running up to a spur of the Black Mountains. In 1895 the property was bought by the wealthy landowner Mr Sandeman, of Dan-y-Parc near Llangattock. He started to rebuild and extend his residence, but in the course of the work a disastrous fire destroyed everything. The house was never rebuilt and no trace of it remains. But the spacious parkland remained, and in 1940 this was taken over by the War Office for the use of American forces who erected the hutted camp which, after the war, was periodically occupied by successive British units. The uninviting 'prefabs' of concrete and asbestos huts were the only accommodation to be seen when the contractors moved in to build what became the model group of barracks and amenities that exists today. However, it was not until 16th May 1963 that Her Majesty the Queen, accompanied by the Duke of Edinburgh, came to declare The Welsh Brigade Depot formally open. The Guard of Honour was formed by detachments from the 1st Battalions of all three Regiments, commanded by Major M. W. F. Dyer (Welch). The Regiments were represented by their Colonels and selected personnel, including five holders of the VC: Major General D. G. Johnson (South Wales Borderers), Major Tasker Watkins (Welch), Ex-Sergeant J. Davies (Royal Welch Fusiliers), Ex-Private H. W. Lewis (Welch) and Ex-Corporal E. T. Chapman (South Wales Borderers).

With the Welsh Brigade commencing business in April 1960, all the individual Regimental Depots were formerly closed as such. They became (as they are today), the locations of Regimental Headquarters and 'outstations', with retired officers acting as Regimental Secretaries, assisted by small staffs of ex-servicemen and clerks. Thus the Regimental Headquarters of The Royal Regiment of Wales is located in the old Welch Depot at Cardiff, while the former 'home' of the 24th at Brecon forms an outstation. In addition, these two centres accommodate bases and Headquarters for other units, such as Home Headquarters of The Queen's Dragoon Guards at Cardiff, and Headquarters Wales at Brecon.

The 24th's recruit training Depot at Brecon had been set up in 1873 by Colonel

The three Colonels of Regiments of The Welsh Brigade, in 1963. FRONT ROW (LEFT TO RIGHT): *Lieutenant General Sir Charles Coleman (Welch), General Sir Hugh Stockwell (RWF) and Major General 'Mark' Matthews (SWB). Also shown,* REAR (LEFT): *Colonel J. E. T. Willes (RWF) and Lieutenant (later Major General) R. M. Llewellyn (RWF).*

Edmond Wodehouse, formerly Commanding Officer of the 1st Battalion and later to become Colonel of the Regiment. It was a strange but happy coincidence that when, on 7th January 1961, the last intake of recruits passed out from what had become the Welsh Brigade Depot at Brecon, they were commanded by Lieutenant A. Wodehouse, Royal Welch Fusiliers, a great-nephew of the Colonel.

The year 1960 was also marked by the Presentation by the Queen of new Colours to the 4th, 5th and 6th Battalions The Welch Regiment. This ceremony took place on 6th August in the splendid setting of Bute Park, Cardiff. Her Majesty, with the Duke of Edinburgh, was received by the Colonel of The Welch Regiment, Lieutenant General Sir Charles Coleman, who presented the three Honorary Colonels: Lieutenant Colonel

Sir Grismond Philipps (4 Welch), Major General C. E. R. Hirsch (5 Welch) and Brigadier E. W. C. Hurford (6 Welch). The parade was commanded by Lieutenant Colonel J. R. Vaughan Roberts of 4 Welch, and the music was performed by the massed Bands and Drums of all three Battalions.

This is an appropriate moment to glance at the Territorial Battalions of both Regiments, some of whom had undergone strange metamorphoses. In 1960 (and until 1969) The South Wales Borderers could claim only one TA Battalion, the 2nd Battalion The Monmouthshire Regiment, based at Newport. This had emerged from its post-war 'suspended animation' in 1947 and remained the only representative of The South Wales Borderer's T.A. units who had won so many Battle Honours (and a VC) in World War II.

As seen above, The Welch Regiment were less deprived. Their 4th and 5th Battalions, like 2 Mons, were reactivated in 1947. The 4th remained in being until after amalgamation, but 5th and 6th were merged in 1967 to form 5/6th Battalion The Welch Regiment, with Headquarters at Pontypridd. The 6th had seen a chequered career. Originally (pre-war) the 6th (Glamorgan) Battalion The Welch Regiment, it became the 67th Searchlight Regiment RE in 1938, then in the same role was transferred to the Royal Artillery in 1940, and so was divorced from the Regiment. Having dutifully served as 608 Garrison Regiment RA and 602 HAA Regiment (Welch) RA, TA, it then took to the air under the designation of 16 (Welch) Battalion The Parachute Regiment. Surely few units could boast such multifarious roles. It finally came back to The Welch in October 1956, with the old title, 6th Battalion The Welch Regiment. Its Battalion Headquarters was established at Cardiff.

When The Welsh Brigade's new Depot at Cwrt-y-Gollen began to function, both Regiments' 1st Battalions were in Germany: 1 SWB were just completing their tour at Minden, with BAOR; 1 Welch were in Berlin. While in Minden, 1 SWB received their first issue of the new generation of infantry vehicles, officially designated 'Truck 1-ton Armoured 4×4', but immediately dubbed 'Pig'. This Humber-built machine was in fact the original form of the now familiar APC (Armoured Personnel Carrier). It could carry a complete section of eight men, plus driver, and its cross-country performance, in four-wheel drive, was equal to the Land Rover's. But its armour was proof only against small arms, and it had no mountings for machine guns or other weapons. Fifty of these armoured 1-tonners were received, so that, with each section mounted in its own vehicle, the Battalion was fully mobile in the field. As a member reported to the *XXIV Journal*: 'To watch a Company riding into battle supported by a troop of tanks is a stirring and impressive sight.' With the wholesale introduction of the APC during the next decade, the infantrymen no longer had to cling precariously to turrets and engine-decks of his supporting tanks.

The year 1962 saw the phasing out of the National Service scheme. 'For the first time for almost 25 years we are an all-Regular Battalion', wrote the 1 Welch scribe in *The Men of Harlech* (he was, of course, including the wartime conscription). His counterpart in 1 SWB penned a more generous valedictory in the *XXIV Journal*:

This is a suitable time to reflect upon the debt which the Regiment owes to its

National Servicemen. Since the War the First Battalion has been supported by a complete cross-section of the youth of Wales between the ages of 18 and 20. We have had the best and the worst, the clever and the simple ... On balance, these men have been magnificent. They have proved themselves in Palestine, Cyprus, Eritrea, Malaya and BAOR as fit for war with the minimum of training. The quantity and quality of the good far outweigh the reputation of the bad. There exists in Wales today a large band of young men who have had an experience of common loyalty, comradeship and shared endeavour which brings smiles of recognition and good fellowship wherever they meet ...

At Minden 1 SWB's last contingent of sixty-four National Servicemen paraded as a separate Company at the Administrative Inspection by the Brigade commander. They had the honour of taking the right of the line and leading the march past.

At home there was honour of a regal nature for The South Wales Borderers' Territorials, the 2nd Battalion The Monmouthshire Regiment. On 26th October, 1962, Her Majesty the Queen visited Llanwern, near Newport, to open the vast new steelworks, and 2 Mons were privileged to parade a Guard of Honour at Newport station. Commanded by Captain Peter Morgan, the Guard consisted of ninety-six men (who had all volunteered for the weeks of drills and rehearsals), and Band and Drums received Her Majesty with the Royal Salute. This was the first time that 2 Mons had been so privileged.

Until 1954 the oldest specimen of Colours possessed by either The South Wales Borderers or The Welch Regiment was the Regimental Colour of the 24th brought out of action at Chilianwala in 1849 and laid up in Brecon in 1936 (see Appendix 5). But in January 1954 The Welch were delighted to acquire the King's Colour of the 41st Foot which had been presented to that Regiment in May 1773. This precious relic was generously given to The Welch by Mr W. N. D. Lang, a great-great-grandson of Lieutenant General William Thomas, who had commanded the 41st during the West India operations of 1794–6. The Colour, now restored, is exhibited in The Welch Regiment Museum at Cardiff Castle, and takes pride of place as the oldest extant Colour of The Royal Regiment of Wales.

Ten years later The South Wales Borderers were equally gratified to acquire a complete stand of Colours – King's and Regimental – of an earlier date than their Chilianwala Colour. These were given to the Regiment by the Hon. Mrs Fleming, widow of the grandson of Lieutenant General Edward Fleming who, as Lieutenant Colonel, commanded the 1st Battalion the 24th Regiment from 1823 to 1833. It was established that the Colours had been carried by the 1st Battalion from 1812 to 1825. In September 1964 they joined the other laid-up Colours in Brecon Cathedral.

Ever since 1879 the 24th had celebrated 'Rorke's Drift Day' (as the present Regiment still does), and it was of great interest when in 1964 they learned that the Natal Provincial Administration were to unveil a Zulu War Memorial on the site of Isandhlwana. The ceremony took place on 5th July and was attended by a vast concourse of Government officials, guests, and the local Zulu populace. Among those invited were some descendants of the Zulu warriors who overran the 24th on that very spot, and were repulsed eleven miles away at Rorke's Drift. The very modern Pavilion of Remembrance, built of stone and concrete, stood on 'Black's Kopje', looking across the scene of the slaughter to the towering 'sphinx' of Isandhlwana mountain. It housed a diorama showing the dispositions of the opposing forces, and a museum with exhibits of the uniforms, weapons and other relics which had been picked up on the battlefield. A Union Flag covered the diorama. As this was withdrawn, trumpeters of the South African Police sounded the Last Post and Reveille, and then the flag of the Republic of South Africa was raised over the Memorial. In his speech Mr Mervyn Wood, a senior member of the Natal Administration, stressed that the memorial commemorated all those who fell at Isandhlwana and Rorke's Drift – British, Zulus and South Africans: 'Supreme bravery is not the prerogative of any one race of men of any one colour. Here on this famous battlefield men of different races, creeds and cultures stood and fought and fell. They attacked with fearless ferocity, they defended with unwavering determination. They faced death and accepted it, fighting desperately to the last.' Mr Wood paid handsome tribute to the heroic conduct of the 24th Regiment, and added that they were pleased and honoured to have present with them a former member of that same Regiment. This was Brigadier O. M. Wales, CB, CBE, MC, who with his wife had been visiting Cape Town when he received a cable from Regimental Headquarters at Brecon asking him to represent the Regiment. This was a happy coincidence. In 1923, as Captain Wales, this officer had commanded the Colour Party who received the 2nd Battalion Colour Pole from King George V and conveyed it to the Regimental Chapel.

With Harold Wilson's Labour Government in power, the year 1967 brought radical retrenchment and reorganisation in the armed forces. This had all started at the top in 1964 when the three service ministries were amalgamated to form the single Ministry of Defence, with scaled-down 'Departments' for Navy, Army and RAF. Now the axe smote the Territorial Army, whose loyal part-time volunteers had provided such a valuable second line for the Regular Army since 1908. On 1st April 1967, Denis Healey, Secretary of State for Defence, virtually destroyed the Territorial Army (as *The Daily Telegraph* bewailed): many units were disbanded, others merged. The Yeomanry lost twelve regiments with origins dating back to the 1790s; some survived as single squadrons of new polygenic regiments, such as 'The Royal Yeomanry'. There were similar destructions in the infantry. Formerly the Territorial Army could deploy 120,000 officers and men. Now the new attenuated force, with the augmented title 'Territorial and Army Volunteer Reserve' was just 50,000 strong.

The effect of all this on our two Regiments was not as disastrous as elsewhere. It was briefly thus: a Territorial formation known as The Welsh Volunteers TAVR was created, consisting of one Battalion from The Royal Welch Fusiliers and one each from The South Wales Borderers and The Welch Regiment. The South Wales Borderers Battalion came into being in April 1967, with the title Monmouthshire (Territorial) Battalion The South Wales Borderers, and, like its predecessors, had its Headquarters at Newport. At the same date The Welch Regiment was represented by the 4th (Territorial) Battalion at Llanelli, and a merger of the 5th and 6th Battalions was effected to form the 5th/6th (Territorial) Battalion with Headquarters at Pontypridd.

Thus although all these units officially formed part of The Welsh Volunteers, they still bore allegiance to their regular parents. But, as will be seen, they were to have brief lives.

The old pre-war recruiting slogan 'Join the Army and see the World!' still had much relevance even in 1967. After returning home from Hong Kong in 1966, and spending a year at Lydd in Kent (not far from the 24th's birthplace), 1 SWB found themselves sweltering in the heart of the city of Aden. Commanded by Lieutenant Colonel J. N. Somerville (whose wartime reminiscences were quoted in the previous chapter), the Battalion was flown out from Lydd in January 1967, for a nine-month operational tour. While all were well aware that they were flying into a hornets' nest of terrorists, they could not know that this would be the last tour on which the 24th Regiment as such would fire its weapons in anger.

Aden, the last surviving British outpost between England and Hong Kong, had been promised independence by 1968. This was taken as a sign of weakness by the rival nationalist organisations, the NLF and FLOSY,[12] who, with the active encouragement of Nasser and his new United Arab Republic, redoubled their efforts to speed the British on their way by a campaign of murder, bombing, sniping and intimidation of the local populace.

When 1 SWB arrived they were given responsibility for the Ma'alla district between Steamer Point and Crater. Here were blocks of flats occupied by some 900 British families; behind was a densely-packed native quarter of narrow streets and

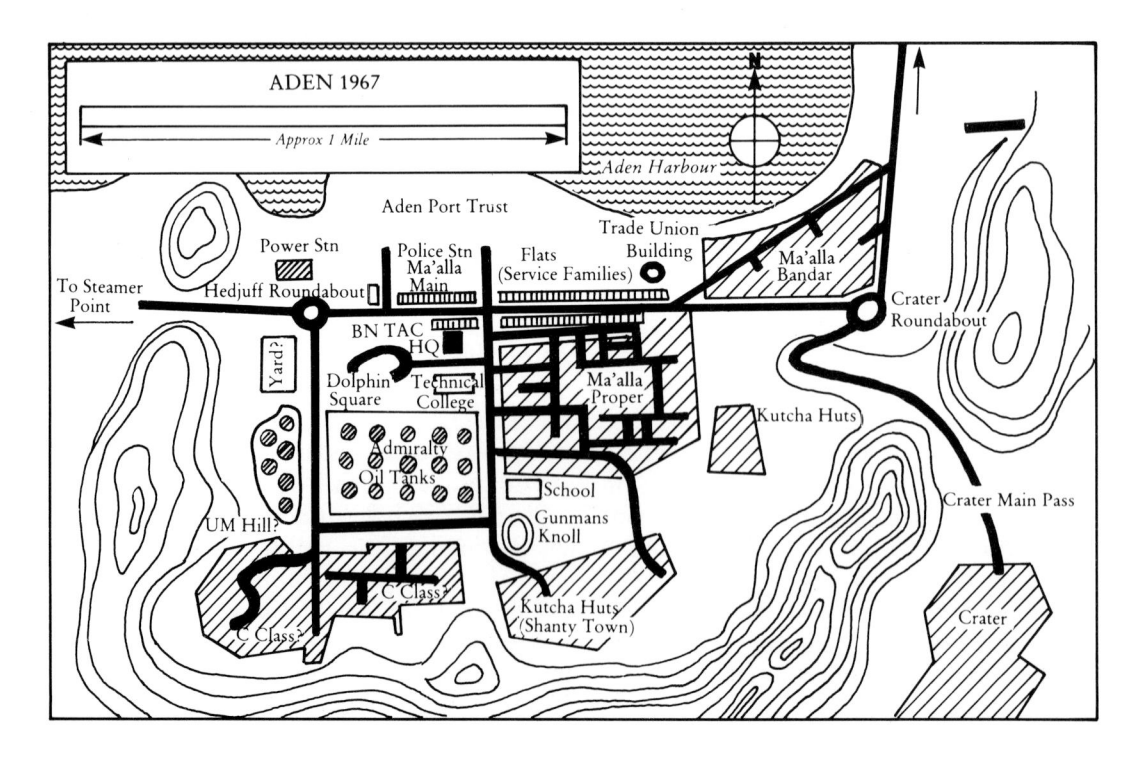

Lance Corporal Lane of 1 SWB on picquet duty in Ma'alla, Aden, 1967.

alleys. The Battalion's main task was to protect the families and important installations, such as a power station and oil depot, and to carry out anti-terrorist patrols.

Before leaving home, Colonel Somerville had been ordered to detach one company at a time for duty in the newly-emerged African Republic of Botswana. His operational command post was set up in Ma'alla, but as no barracks were available there, the Battalion's base was in Little Aden. Thus, as he wrote, his Orderly Room and Reserve Company were 25 miles from his own Headquarters, while his fourth Company was 4,000 miles away in another continent. 'This was quite a thought', he wrote.

The operations in Aden can only be summarised here.[13] In addition to providing security for the Ma'alla families, the three Companies, on foot, or in Ferret scout cars and Land Rovers, were engaged in some 300 small arms and grenade attacks. They killed at least forty terrorists, and wounded many more. They discovered numerous arms caches. Their casualties were two men killed and thirty-three wounded. On 8th September the Ma'alla district was handed over to 45 Commando, Royal Marines, and by the 19th the Battalion was safely back at Lydd.

Meanwhile the detached companies at Francistown in Botswana had each enjoyed peaceful spells of 'protecting' the BBC Central Africa Relay Station, with such

Soldiers of 1 SWB discover a hoard of weapons in Aden, 1967.

The first Colours of The Royal Regiment of Wales (24th/41st Foot).

Freedom scroll recording the granting of the Freedom of Cardiff to the Regiment, 11th June 1969.

diversions as safaris into the local bush, visits to game reserves, and soccer fixtures in Pretoria. During their tours, both A and B Companies managed to organise Land Rover expeditions to visit Isandhlwana and Rorke's Drift, where they were received with lavish hospitality by the local white population.

Soon after the Battalion had once more settled down at Lydd, in December 1967 Colonel Somerville departed to the Joint Services Staff College. He was replaced by Lieutenant Colonel L. A. H. Napier, MBE, MC, who as a Major had been his Second-in-Command. Colonel Napier was to be the last Commanding Officer of The South Wales Borderers and the first of The Royal Regiment of Wales.

Meanwhile, 1 Welch had also been seeing the world. In June 1966 the Battalion flew out to Hong Kong where they relieved their future partners, 1 SWB, and took over their excellent quarters in Stanley Fort. Lieutenant Colonel L. A. D. Harrod, MBE, was in command. The first twelve months of the two-year tour passed with nothing untoward to interrupt the normal routine of training, exercises and ceremonial duties, together with playing host to visiting Royal Navy ships. But this was the period of China's Cultural Revolution, and in May 1967 Communist elements within Hong Kong and from the mainland began to provoke riots, strikes and general opposition to the British presence. The situation became serious in July, with increasing acts of violence, and the Battalion was heavily committed to 'anti-intimidation' patrols, cordons, searches and escorts to bomb disposal teams. Most of these activities were carried out in support of the (Chinese) Hong Kong Police, with whom very firm rapport and respect were established. On one occasion a successful Welch–police raid was mounted on a twenty-seven storey building which housed an illegal Communist printing press, D Company and the policemen being dropped on the roof-top by helicopters from HMS *Hermes*. This was the first time that an airborne raid had been carried out in the Colony. Before leaving Hong Kong the Battalion were proud to see the George Medal awarded to one of its members. At extreme personal danger, Sergeant J. H. Matchett rescued three policemen from a minefield after one mine had exploded and severely wounded ont of them.

The bonds of friendship with the police were marked by reciprocal presentations: the Battalion presented a silver trophy to be competed for among the divisions on the island and to be known as 'The Welch Trophy', while the police responded with a handsomely mounted and inscribed baton.

In July 1968 1 Welch were flown home to their UK posting at Gravesend. While here the Battalion took part in Exercise 'Attract' in Ghana. Their two and a half weeks' series of schemes in this former British Colony were carried out in co-operation with the Ghanaian Army, and proved valuable not only as operational experience, but for the very real mutual esteem developed between the two nations' soldiers. The Ghanaians 'went out of their way to make our tour a success', wrote Colonel Harrod (in *The Men of Harlech*), 'nothing was too much trouble for them, and their obvious liking for Britain and the British way of life was a tonic. We all left feeling that exercises of this nature could do nothing but good.'

In the *XXIV Journal* for August 1965 the Colonel of the Regiment (Major General David Peel Yates) had commented on the policy of the MOD of creating 'large

Regiments' by amalgamating numerous individuals. In 1964 The Royal Anglian Regiment had been formed, representing nine previous Regiments. Now it was decreed that The Rifle Brigade ('Left of the Line') should be merged with The King's Royal Rifle Corps and the Oxfordshire and Buckinghamshire Light Infantry (43rd and 52nd), to emerge as The Royal Green Jackets.[14] However, the Colonel of the 24th reported that his fellow-Colonels of The Welsh Brigade could 'see no advantage in making any change in our present constitution within the forseeable future', and he hoped that this news would 'set at rest any doubts about the destiny of the three Regiments'. This was to prove wishful thinking.

In November 1967 Major General F. H. Brooke, Colonel of The Welch Regiment, revealed (in *The Men of Harlech*) that in the previous May the Army Board had declared that The Welsh Brigade should be reduced to two Regiments, either by disbandment or amalgamation, or by the formation of a 'large Regiment'. At the same time it was announced that the Brigade would form an element of one of the new infantry divisions, to be known at The Prince of Wales's Division and including the Mercian and Wessex Brigades. The three Colonels of the Welsh Brigade formulated a unanimous submission to the Army Board, strongly advocating that the status of Wales should be recognised by the continued existence of The Welsh Brigade and its component Regiments. There was no response to this submission; the Army Board peremptorily demanded a decision about the reduction by 15th June. General Brooke for The Welch, and General Sir David Peel Yates for The South Wales Borderers, both favoured the 'large Regiment' option, a merger of all three Regiments as truly representative of the Principality. General Brooke flew out to his 1st Battalion in Hong Kong, from whom he received overwhelming support for this option. Returning on 4th June, he met the other two Colonels for a final decision. By now General Stockwell had been replaced as Colonel of The Royal Welch Fusiliers by Colonel J. E. T. Willes, MBE, and he strongly resisted the proposal of a large Regiment. The Royal Welch Fusiliers had borne their title for nearly 250 years; they were one of the few regiments never to have undergone amalgamation, and they had no wish to submit now. This left two alternatives. Either the other two Regiments must amalgamate, or the junior must accept complete disbandment. After further discussion, General Peel Yates and General Brooke finally agreed to submit to the Army Board their recommendation that The South Wales Borderers and The Welch Regiment should amalgamate 'to create a new Regiment for Wales'. In his Notes for *The Men of Harlech* of November 1967 General Brooke wrote: 'There is no Regiment with which we would sooner join than our old friends the 24th. As a Regiment they will be affected by amalgamation every bit as much as we shall be, and I wish to place on record our deep appreciation of their sympathetic and unselfish attitude.'

The recommendation was accepted by the Army Board, and an official announcement was made on 18th July. The South Wales Borderers and The Welch Regiment would merge to form a new Regiment. It was forecast that the actual ceremony of

Lieutenant General Sir David Peel Yates, KCB, CVO, DSO, OBE, Colonel The South Wales Borderers and The Royal Regiment of Wales, 1st January 1962–25th September 1977.

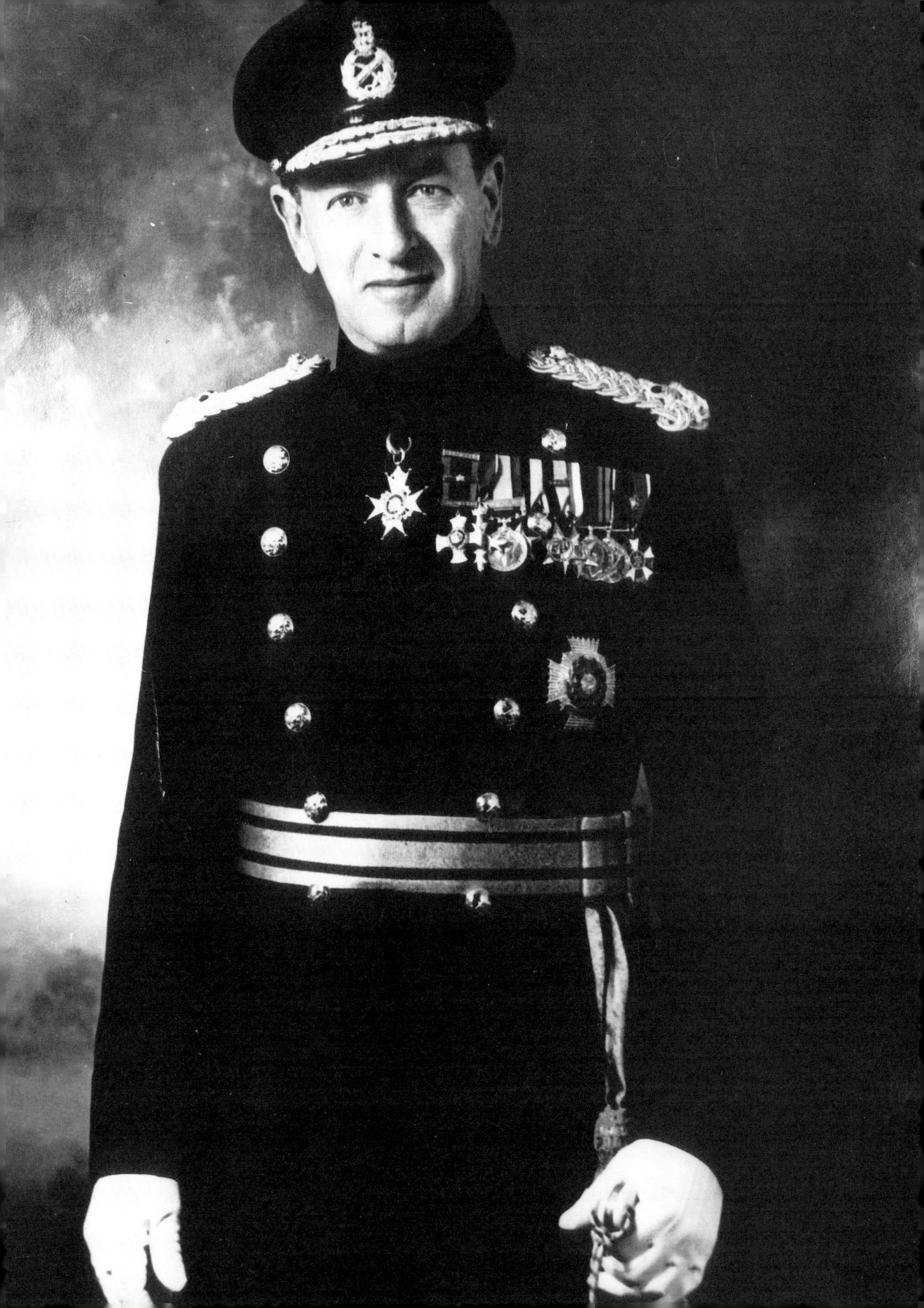

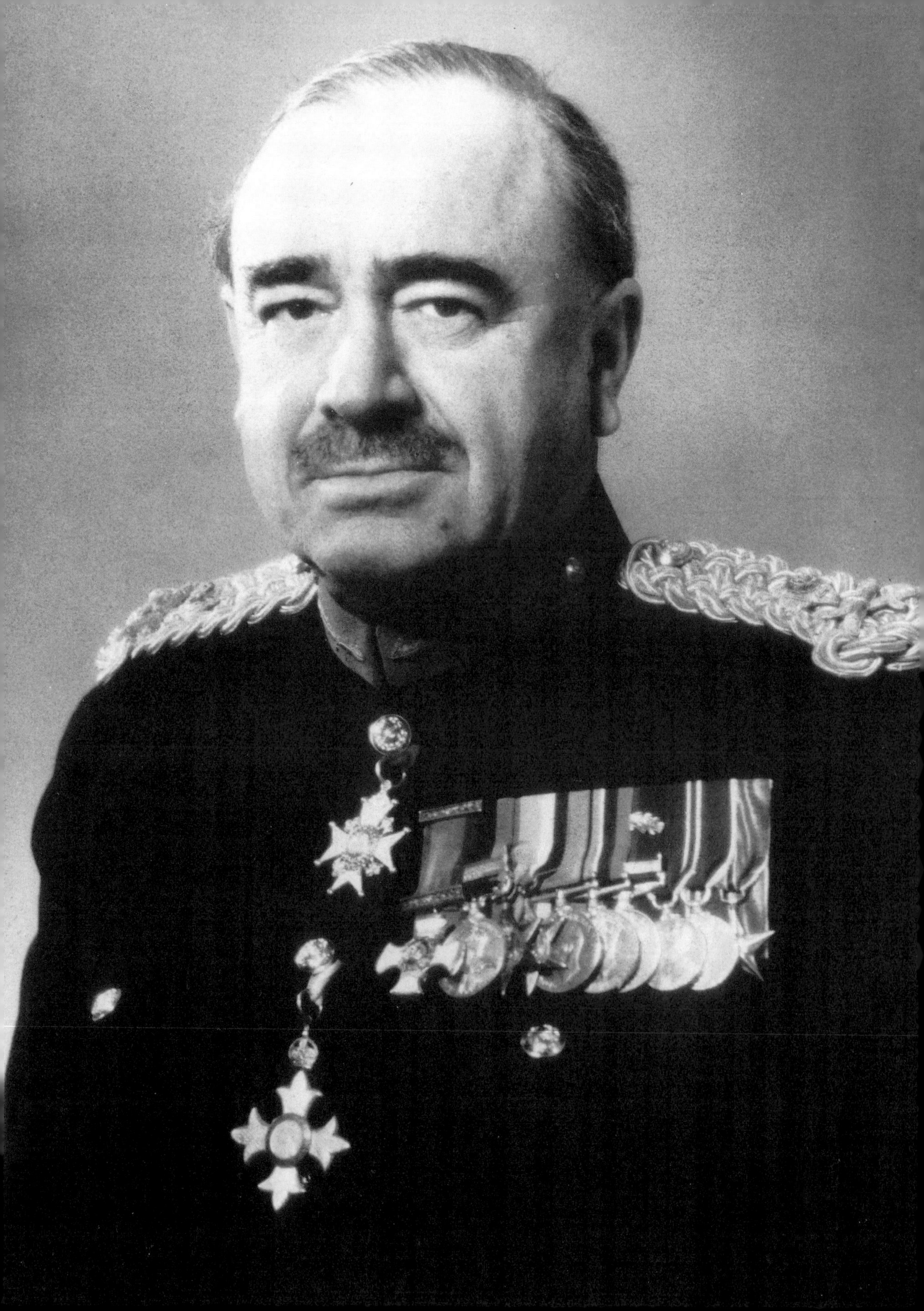

amalgamation would take place at some date in the middle of the following year. In the past there had been unhappy examples of forced marriages between disparate partners, having nothing in common with each other; but if two of the three Welsh Regiments had to be joined together, the present choice was undoubtedly the most felicitous. Unlike The Royal Welch Fusiliers, who were traditionally a North Wales Regiment, both 24th and 41st had been truly representative of the south of the Principality for generations, and had enjoyed close associations with each other. They were indeed, as General Brooke remarked, 'old friends'. On the other hand, The Royal Welch Fusiliers had seen no such close acquaintance until the end of National Service and the creation of The Welsh Brigade twenty years previously. Although at this stage The Royal Welch Fusiliers claimed recruiting rights throughout Wales, they still had priority in the north.

With amalgamation finally agreed, there were, of course, innumerable details to be debated and mutually approved, before submission for royal approval – not least the title of the new Regiment. For this purpose General Peel Yates and General Brooke set up a working party which drew up recommendations on every aspect of the merger, even down to such minutiae as Regimental collect and Regimental tie.

It was with the utmost pride and satisfaction that in August 1968 the two Regiments learned from the official announcement:

> Her Majesty the Queen, to mark the Investiture of The Prince of Wales, has been graciously pleased to approve that the name of the new Regiment to be formed by the amalgamation of The South Wales Borderers and The Welch Regiment shall be 'The Royal Regiment of Wales (24th/41st Foot)'.

On 19th August the two Colonels despatched a joint letter to Her Majesty, on behalf of all ranks of both Regiments, conveying their thanks and deep appreciation of this honour. It was indeed an honour; for the first time in their combined history they were to become distinguished as a 'Royal' Regiment.

In March 1969 there was further honour when Her Majesty appointed HRH the Prince of Wales to be Colonel in Chief of the new Regiment. For a 'Royal Regiment of Wales' there could have been no more fitting appointment. On 18th March General Peel Yates and General Brooke were invited to Buckingham Palace to meet His Royal Highness, and there they presented him with an appropriately inscribed sword. The Investiture of the Prince of Wales at Caernarfon Castle had been arranged for 1st July 1969, and in order that the new Regiment could be represented at that ceremony, the date of amalgamation was fixed for 11th June of that year.

If anyone had imagined the pre-amalgamation months would see a rundown in normal duties, they were sharply disillusioned. In fact the period was as busy as any, for both regular Battalions. Hardly had 1 SWB settled down at Lydd after their Aden tour than they went to Norfolk for a large-scale exercise. Then in the summer of 1968 they found themselves further afield on Exercise 'Pond Jump' in Canada, operating with,

Major General F. H. Brooke, CB, CBE, DSO, Colonel The Welch Regiment, 20th November 1965–11th July 1969. He was the last Colonel of The Welch Regiment.

1 Welch undertaking Public Duties, London, 1969.

and against, units of the 3rd (Canadian) Infantry Brigade Group on the vast training area near New Brunswick. On return from the 'Pond Jump', A and B Companies played a spectacular role in the Cardiff Tattoo when they re-enacted the defence of Rorke's Drift, expending huge quantities of blank.

Arriving home from their exercises in Ghana in October 1968, 1 Welch returned to Gravesend. In the midst of normal training and sundry schemes and cadres, their main preoccupation was with drill and turnout in preparation for forthcoming ceremonial. On 10th February 1969, the well-rehearsed B Company took over The Queen's Guard from compatriots of the Welsh Guards at Buckingham Palace, also finding the Guards at St James's Palace and the Tower of London. B was followed by C and D Companies until, Public Duties completed, the Guard was handed over to the Irish Guards. The high standard of drill and turnout earned fulsome praise from the media, and later the Commanding Officer, Lieutenant Colonel P. L. Cutler,[15] was most gratified and honoured to receive a message of congratulation from Her Majesty the Queen Mother.

This was the first occasion since 1911 that The Welch Regiment had been honoured with these duties. Inevitably, it was also the last.

But there was more ceremonial to come. In 1719 Colonel Edmund Fielding had raised the Regiment of Foot which was to become the 41st or The Welch Regiment. It was perhaps sad, therefore, that the 250th anniversary of that event should fall on 14th March 1969 – less than twelve weeks before The Welch Regiment ceased to exist. But it was fitting that as the Regiment was originally formed from 'invalids' or out-pensioners of the Royal Hospital at Chelsea, the celebrations should be held at that venerable establishment. This proposal was readily accepted by the Governor of the Hospital, and by the authorities of the Ministry of Devence, and the anniversary parade duly took place there on 14th March. The Battalion was commanded by Lieutenant Colonel Cutler, and the parade was formed of three Guards from the 1st Battalion, and one composed of representatives of the Welsh Depot at Crickhowell, together with the Glamorganshire and Carmarthenshire Army Cadet forces. At the march-past before Field Marshal Sir Gerald Templer (Constable of the Tower of London), the parade was led by Taffy XI and the Goat Major accompanied by Sergeant Ernest Vaughan, one of the Regiment's inpensioners.

Lieutenant Colonel L. A. D. Harrod, Commanding Officer of 1 Welch (later Major General L. A. D. Harrod, OBE, Colonel The Royal Regiment of Wales, 1977–82) with RSM Pennington, greeting Taffy during Buckingham Palace duties, 1969.

Although sporting matters are dealt with in Appendix 8, here it must be recorded that the splendid Rugby achievements of the affianced pair of Regiments were crowned in April 1969 by the 1 SWB XV who carried off the Army Cup by defeating 7 Signal Regiment, Royal Signals. The victory was the more gratifying since it was the last time that a team could be fielded by The South Wales Borderers.

By 1969 radical changes had taken place in The Welsh Brigade Depot at Cwrt-y-Gollen, Crickhowell. As we have seen, in 1967 it was decided for economic and administrative reasons ('to provide a more flexible and economical structure', as the Army Order had it), to group all the existing infantry brigades into larger formations, known as divisions. Each division would absorb a number of the brigades, with common recruit training centres and separate divisional Headquarters. They were to be

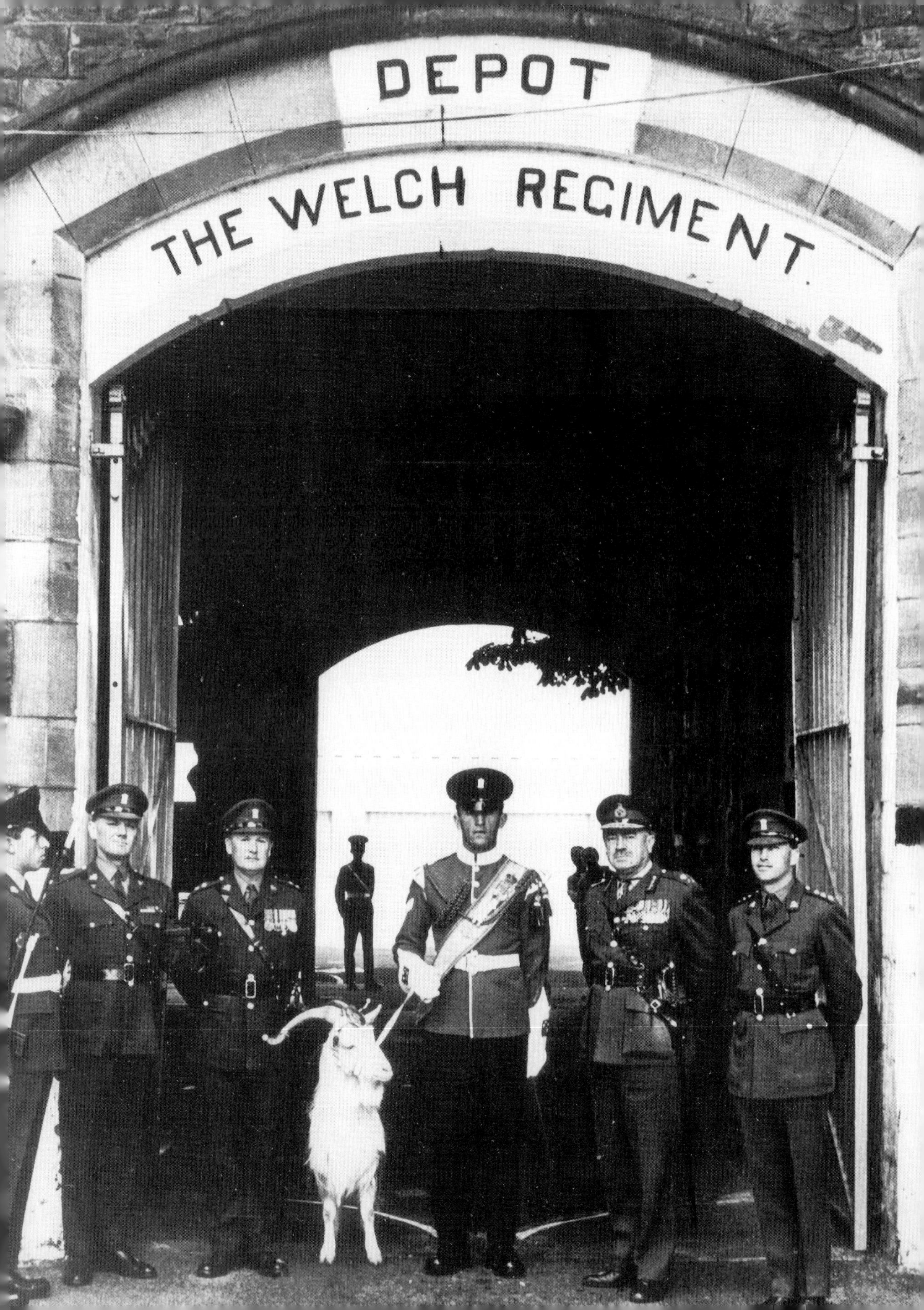
DEPOT
THE WELCH REGIMENT

purely administrative and training formations, bearing no relation to operational divisions formed in time of war.

And so on 1st July 1968 there came into being the six new infantry divisions which have existed to the present day. On that date The Welsh Brigade at Cwrt-y-Gollen lost its identity to become part of The Prince of Wales's Division.[16] The earlier plea by The Welsh Brigade's Council of Colonels that the Brigade should be allowed to continue as a separate entity within the new organisation had fallen on deaf ears at the Ministry of Defence. However, the three Welsh Line Regiments (soon to be only two) would retain their common Depot at Cwrt-y-Gollen, and the only noticeable change was the new title, 'Welsh Depot Prince of Wales's Division'. With eleven component Regiments the Prince of Wales's was the largest of all the Divisions, and remained so when eleven became nine after amalgamation.

Apart from the original three Welsh, the other Regiments were (and are): Devonshire and Dorset, Cheshire, Gloucestershire, Worcestershire and Sherwood Foresters, Royal Hampshire, Staffordshire and Duke of Edinburgh's Royal Regiment. Divisional Headquarters was established at Whittington Barracks, Lichfield, in Staffordshire.

Meanwhile, June 1969 was drawing near. The end of an era was at hand and the old order was about to change.

Notes

[1] They were the 1st Battalion the Somerset Light Infantry.

[2] These were: Lowland (four regiments); Home Counties (seven); Lancastrian (eight); Yorkshire (seven); Midlands (four); East Anglian (five); Wessex (five); Light Infantry (six); Mercian (four); Welsh (three); North Irish (three); Highland (six); Green Jackets (two).

[3] The 'Burp' gun was the Chinese equivalent of the Sten.

[4] The name was a contraction derived from '*Burney Anti-Tank*', after Sir Dennis Burney, a War Office armaments engineer who had been designing anti-tank weapons since the 1940s.

[5] This was published by Faber and Faber in 1959, and was immediately hailed as a worthy addition to the literature of the little-publicised 'Emergency'.

[6] The Remington 12-bore pump-action shotgun was issued to British and Commonwealth forces for counter-terrorist operations between 1950 and 1970. It had a five-round magazine.

[7] Miers, Brigadier, R. C. H. *Shoot to Kill*.

[8] In 1962 Brigadier R. C. H. Miers, DSO, OBE, was appointed DQMS at Headquarters Rhine

Major General F. H. Brooke, CB, CBE, DSO, last Colonel of The Welch Regiment; Lieutenant Colonel P. L. Cutler, MBE, last Commanding Officer of 1st Battalion, The Welch Regiment; RSM Pennington and others at the gate of the Depot, Cardiff, June 1969.

Army. Shortly afterwards, The South Wales Borderers and his many friends elsewhere were shocked to learn that he had taken his own life.

[9] Comprising blue tunics and trousers, peaked cap and white waistbelts, this was fomerly known as blue patrols and before World War II had been worn only by selected personnel. In 1947 it was issued to all units as ceremonial dress, and still serves as such.

[10] The word 'EOKA' was derived from the initials of the Greek words meaning 'National Organisation for the Cyprus Struggle'.

[11] General Sir Hugh Stockwell (the Royal Welch Fusiliers), Major General F. R. G. Matthews (The South Wales Borderers), Lieutenant General Sir Charles Coleman (The Welch Regiment).

[12] National Liberation Front; Front for the Liberation of Occupied South Yemen.

[13] A detailed account was published in the *XXIV Journal* for August 1967.

[14] This was effected in January 1966. And in December of the same year The Queen's Regiment was added to the Army List, representing no fewer than ten original Regiments.

[15] Colonel Cutler had taken over from Colonel Harrod on 18th February.

[16] The other Divisions created were (and are) The Guards Division (five regiments); The Scottish Division (eight); The Queen's Division (three 'large' regiments); The King's Division (eight); The Light Division (two 'large' regiments').

CHAPTER EIGHTEEN

The Royal Regiment of Wales (1969–78)

At Cardiff the morning of Wednesday 11th June 1969 dawned bright and sunny. Within the bailey, or courtyard, of the Castle the vivid green of the freshly-mown lawns contrasted with the grey stonework. There was just enough breeze to set the Standard of the Prince of Wales lazily flapping on the keep's turret. It was a perfect day for the ceremonial about to be witnessed by some 10,000 spectators gathered around the courtyard and on vantage points along the Castle walls and towers. Among these spectators were distinguished invited guests: the Lords-Lieutenant of Glamorgan, Monmouth, Brecon and Carmarthen, Members of Parliament for South Wales constituencies, Honorary Colonels of TAVR battalions, Councillors of town and county boroughs – and five holders of the VC, formerly of The South Wales Borderers and The Welch Regiment.

At 1035 hours the massed Bands struck up 'Men of Harlech', and from the south gate of the Castle marched on the two Guards of the 1st Battalion The South Wales Borderers, 184 officers and soldiers with their Colours. They were commanded by Lieutenant Colonel L. A. H. Napier, MBE, MC, and having formed line, they took up position in front of the ancient Castle keep (which had no doubt witnessed Roman, Norman and Plantagenet soldiers performing much the same evolutions). Then the Bands swung into 'Ap Shenkin', and a similar contingent of the 1st Battalion The Welch Regiment marched on from the north gate, to take post on the left of The South Wales Borderers. Commanded by Lieutenant Colonel P. L. Cutler, they were led by Taffy XII wearing for the last time his ceremonial coat with The Welch badge and Colours. A General Salute signalled the arrival on parade of the GOC-in-C Western Command, Lieutenant General Sir Anthony Read, KCB. The parade then stood at ease.

As the Castle clocks chimed the hour of eleven, the two contingents were called to attention. They presented arms and the Bands played a Royal Salute as HRH the Prince of Wales was driven on parade in a Land Rover. Accompanied by Lieutenant General Sir David Peel Yates, Colonel The South Wales Borderers, and Major General F. H. Brooke, Colonel The Welch Regiment, the Prince was wearing the No. 1 Dress uniform of Colonel in Chief of The Royal Regiment of Wales and carrying the sword

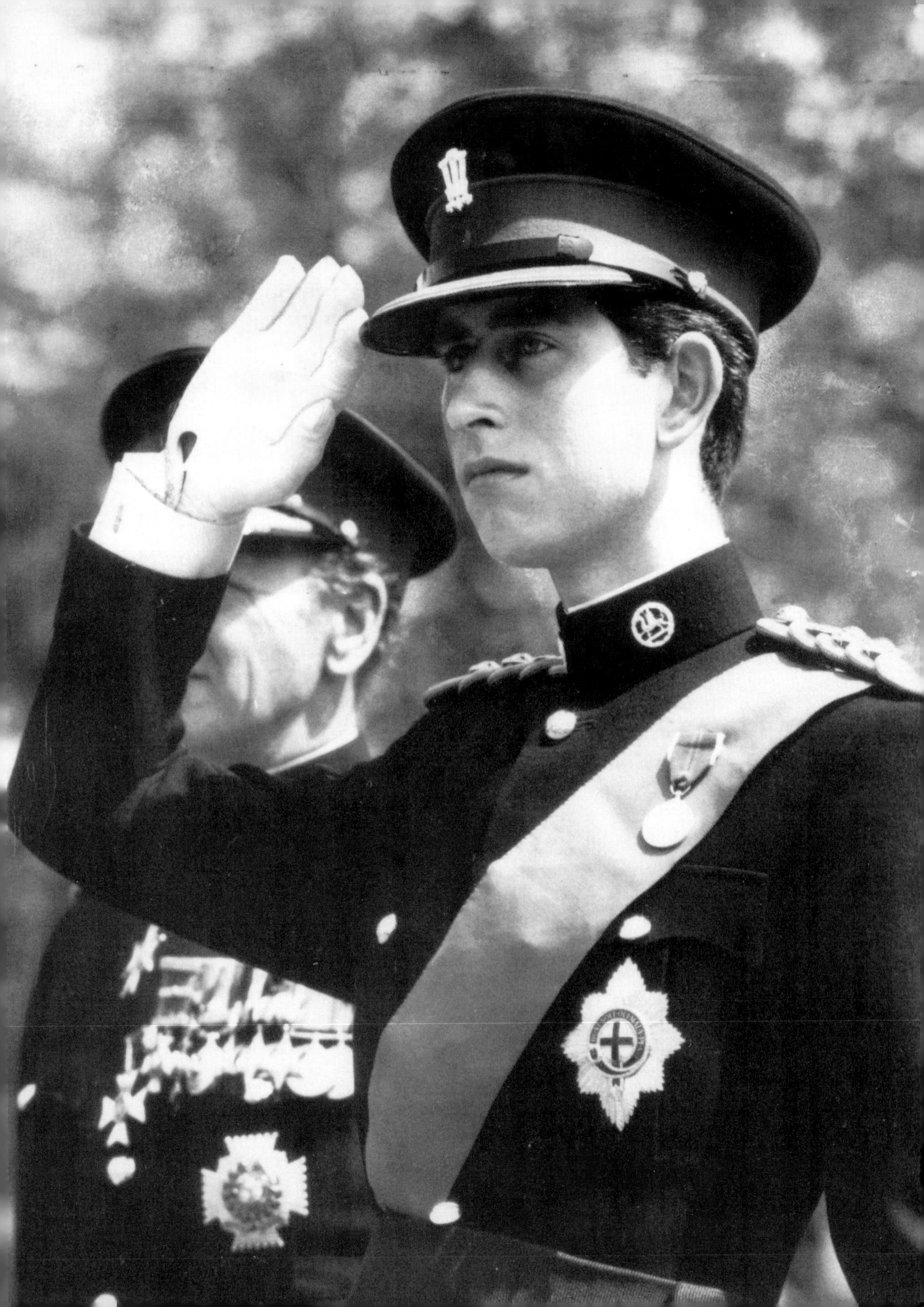

which had been presented to him by the two Regiments a few weeks earlier. After inspecting the parade, His Royal Highness took up his position on the Saluting Base.

From his post in front of The South Wales Borderers, Lieutenant Colonel Napier gave the final words of command to that Regiment: 'The South Wales Borderers will lay down their arms – ground arms!'

Then Lieutenant Colonel Cutler: 'The Welch Regiment will lay down their arms – ground arms!'

There was a moment of tense silence as the disarmed ranks stood motionless. The spectators had risen to their feet.

Then from Colonel Napier came the first words of command for the new Regiment: 'Royal Regiment of Wales will take up arms. Take up – arms!'

And so, in the historic setting of the Principality's capital, two Welsh Regiments had passed away, to hand on their traditions to their new-born successor.

Next came the marching-off of the Old Colours (to 'Auld Lang Syne') and the Presentation of the New. After consecration by the Chaplain-General, The Ven. Archdeacon J. R. Youens, OBE, MC, the New Colours were handed over by the Prince of Wales to the two Ensigns, Lieutenants P. D. Gordon and J. D. Wilson, who took post with their Escort.

The Colonel in Chief presents the new Queen's Colour to Lieutenant P. D. Gordon. MAIL NEWSPAPERS PLC

Returning to the dais, the Prince on behalf of his Regiment received from the Lord Mayor of Cardiff the Scroll recording the grant of the Freedom of the City to the Regiment. The Battalion then marched past in column, reformed, and advanced in Review Order to give their Colonel in Chief a Royal Salute.

As the Prince was driven away in his Land Rover, the Battalion removed head-dresses and gave him three resounding cheers, while the Bands played 'God Bless the Prince of Wales'. When the Battalion had marched off to the Regimental march, 'Men of Harlech', the Keepers of the Ground reformed and left their posts. These were twenty-eight NCOs and men of the affiliated Regiments, The Ontario Regiment from

LEFT: *The Colonel in Chief takes the salute at the Amalgamation Parade.* MAIL NEWSPAPERS PLC

The Colonel in Chief with Taffy XII of 1 Welch (later Taffy 1 of 1 RRW)

Canada and The Royal New South Wales Regiment from Australia.

The following days brought many messages of congratulation and well wishing for the new Regiment. The Prince wrote to say: 'how very proud I am to be made Colonel in Chief of a Regiment that acquitted itself so well yesterday. Without exception everyone played his part magnificently and the standard of drill, to my way of thinking, was carried out superbly.' Lieutenant General Sir Anthony Read declared: 'your parade on Wednesday was quite superb. It was faultless in every way and really was the most magnificent start to your Regiment.' Colonel E. R. Hill, Lord-Lieutenant of Monmouthshire, was no stranger to such ceremonial, for he had commanded the Coldstream in their Tercentenary celebration, and he wrote to express his admiration of the drill and all the administrative and organisational details that had preceded 'the wonderful Parade'. The Colonel of The Royal Welch Fusiliers, Colonel J. E. T. Willes, wrote that he had 'never witnessed a more impressive ceremony: it was a really splendid send-off for The Royal Regiment of Wales, and there is no doubt that your young Colonel in Chief won all our hearts. You must be very proud indeed.'

And proud they were on the next day to exercise their newly-granted right to march through the streets of Cardiff with Colours flying, drums beating and bayonets fixed.

At this historic date it is fitting to record the names of the officers who held key posts in the new Regiment.

The Royal Regiment of Wales (24th/41st Foot)
(As at 11 June 1969)

Battalion Headquarters
Commanding Officer	Lieutenant Colonel **L. A. H. Napier, MBE, MC**
Second-in-Command	Major **I. D. B. Mennell**
Adjutant	Captain **T. S. Brown**
RSM	WO1 **G. I. Amphlett**

Headquarters Company
Officer Commanding	Captain **T. M. E. Brown**
Second-in-Command	Captain **M. J. H. Harry**
Quartermaster	Captain (QM) **K. D. Roberts, MBE**
Bandmaster	WO1 **D. Dawson**

A Company
Officer Commanding	Major **B. J. Hanley**
Second-in-Command	Captain **M. M. Howes**

B Company
Officer Commanding	Major **K. J. Davey, MC**
Second-in-Command	Captain **J. O. Crewe-Read**

C Company
Officer Commanding	Major **N. O. Roberts**
Second-in-Command	Captain **M. G. R. Roberts**

Support Company
Officer Commanding	Major **D. E. Cox**
Second-in-Command	Captain **R. H. Tyler**

With the passing of the old and the birth of the new, there were inevitable changes, all of which had been amicably agreed by the two Colonels. The matter of the new Colonelcy was settled by the retirement of Major General F. H. Brooke, CB, CBE, DSO, of The Welch, leaving the first Colonelcy of The Royal Regiment of Wales to be assumed by his counterpart of the 24th, Lieutenant General Sir David Peel Yates, KCB, CVO, DSO, OBE.

In the first issue of the new Regimental Journal for November 1969 (with the title *The Men of Harlech*, inherited from The Welch), there was a fitting 'thank you' to General Brooke for all his work for The Welch Regiment during his three and a half years of office, and particularly for his efforts in ensuring a smooth and harmonious merger, preserving the traditions and customs of both Regiments. 'Thanks to his tactful handling of the negotiation with the South Wales Borderers, and their sympathetic approach to the problem, there was never any feeling of senior and junior partner, and everyone was anxious to see the other side's point of view.'

Other changes or modifications resulting from the amalgamation were as set out below.

The Colours
The Queen's Colour was, as always, the Union Flag. In the centre was the figure 1 on a red background, surrounded by the title of the Regiment, the whole surmounted by the Royal Crown. Thirty-five Battle Honours of the previous Regiments were emblazoned to left and right and below the central device. The silver Wreath of Immortelles inherited from the 24th continued to be borne on the pike.

The Regimental Colour had a ground of grass green (colour of the uniform facings). The central device was the Welsh Dragon in red superimposed in the centre of a silver Wreath of Immortelles and surrounded by the title of the Regiment, all surmounted by the Crown. Around the whole device was the Union Wreath with, at bottom, the Motto 'Gwell Angau na Chywilydd' (inherited from The Welch). The Colour bore 41 Battle Honours of both former Regiments, and in the corners were the Royal Cypher with the figure 1, the Union Badge and Garter, the Sphinx superscribed Egypt, and the Naval Crown superscribed '12th April 1782'.

The Regimental Crest was the Dragon within the Wreath of Immortelles, with the Welsh Motto beneath. The whole surmounted by the Crown.

The Cap Badge The Prince of Wales's plumes and Motto inherited from The Welsh Brigade.[1] The Collar Badge was the Wreath of Immortelles with the Dragon superimposed.

Regimental Marches The Quick March was 'Men of Harlech' (from the 24th); the Slow March 'Scipio' (Handel).

Regimental Mascot The Goat Mascot of The 1st Battalion The Welch Regiment was adopted. Having been Taffy XII, he was now renamed Taffy I.

Full Dress Worn only by the Band and Drums and by selected personnel on special occasions: scarlet tunics with grass-green facings, blue trousers with red welts. Helmet with chain and spike.

Regimental Headquarters This was established at Maindy Barracks, Cardiff, in the former headquarters of The Welch. An out-station was set up in the old 24th Depot at Brecon. The two previous Regimental Museums remained at Cardiff and Brecon.

Regimental Magazine This continued as *The Men of Harlech*.

As their Territorial force, The Royal Regiment of Wales shared The Welsh Volunteers with The Royal Welch Fusiliers. The Volunteers had been formed in the TA reorganisations of April 1967 and now consisted of A Company (RWF) and B and C Companies (RRW).

After the amalgamation there came more ceremonial, on the occasion of the Investiture of the Prince of Wales by Her Majesty the Queen. This splendid ceremony took place at Caernarfon Castle on 1st July 1969, and all the Welsh Regiments were represented – the Welsh Guards, The Royal Welch Fusiliers, and the 1st Battalion The Royal Regiment of Wales. The latter provided a Guard of Honour and street-lining duties, while strong detachments of The Welsh Volunteers were also on parade. Following the Investiture, the Regiment was honoured to be granted the Freedoms of Newport, Brecon and Carmarthen, at each of which ceremonies the Colonel of the Regiment, General Sir David Peel Yates, received the Scrolls. He was accompanied by B Company with the Colours, and the Band and Drums.

During all this pomp and pageantry 1 RRW had been based at Lydd, where they took over the barracks previously occupied by 1 SWB. The first move as a formed Battalion provided a highly-contrasted form of activity. In August 1969 they were posted to Belfast, with Lieutenant Colonel Napier still in command, and were immediately committed to the thankless task of 'IS' or Internal Security in streets that were erupting with violence and arson by the warring factions of Catholic and Protestant. By 15th August mob rule had taken over, and B and C Companies' patrols were in the thick of it, in the notorious Falls Road area. 'Small arms, fire bombs and other missiles were used by both sides [i.e. Catholic and Protestant]; rows of houses and large factories, schools and other buildings were ablaze . . . certain areas looked as if they had suffered a severe air attack.' So wrote the correspondent to *The Men of Harlech*, who added that the 'incredible situation' was reminiscent of Aden.

Yet here they were confronting fellow-Britons, in the United Kingdom. At this stage the murderous gangsters and thugs of the so-called Irish Republican 'Army' were not yet the main enemy, and the two factions were more intent on slaughtering each other than British soldiers. And although some of the Belfast inhabitants proved friendly and hospitable, others displayed a sullen hostility. When the Battalion was withdrawn in mid-September, the only casualty was one private peppered with gunshot pellets. Nevertheless, their first tour in this unhappy part of the 'Emerald Isle' was an experience which no one wished to repeat, as the Battalion scribe wrote. But, they were to repeat it within less than a year and many times later.

Having returned to Lydd, the Battalion had hardly settled in, when in November (1969) they were posted to BAOR, arriving at Osnabrück at the end of the month, to join 12 Infantry Brigade as a fully mechanised Battalion. For this rôle they were mounted with eighty armoured personnel carriers, or APCs, of the FV432 type. These vehicles, introduced in 1963, were tracked, so that they could accompany tanks over virtually any cross-country terrain, and each accommodated ten men plus the driver. They had a top road-speed of about 35 m.p.h., faster than any tank, but were not amphibious: for 'swimming' a special flotation screen had to be erected (as with the DD tanks of D-Day). Each Rifle company had fifteen APCs, four per platoon and three in Company Headquarters. The remainder were allotted to Battalion Headquarters and Support Company.

In July 1970, while at Osnabrück, the Battalion said farewell to their first Commanding Officer when Lieutenant Colonel L. A. H. Napier, OBE, MC, was posted away to the Joint Services Staff College. He was succeeded by Major I. D. B. Mennell, promoted Lieutenant Colonel. Lennox Napier's tenure of command had been very brief; but it had involved the difficult and delicate task of creating and training a completely new Battalion from two previous Battalions, with all the concomitant problems of setting standards and establishing a new morale, or *esprit de corps*. It so happened that just after his departure the Battalion was selected to host a study visit from officers attending the JSSC, and later a senior RAF officer paid handsome tribute:

> Frankly, this was the best visit ever, and the Royal Regiment of Wales could not have produced a more impressive performance. That you have a well-equipped fighting force with efficiency and morale second to none was everywhere apparent, and you and your men have done more good in fostering inter-service understanding and in putting over what the British Army is all about, than 20 terms spent in the class-room.

Although this letter was addressed to the new Commanding Officer, credit for achieving such results in just over twelve months was surely due to his predecessor. Colonel Napier's efforts were recognised by his being created OBE in that year's Honour List. and in due course the Regiment were to welcome him as their Colonel.

By 1970 the situation in Northern Ireland had deteriorated to such an extent that some 12,000 troops were needed to maintain a semblance of the Queen's Peace among a populace bitterly divided among themselves and either apathetic or fiercely hostile to the presence of British soldiers. The IRA 'freedom fighters' (or terrorists) had now spawned a splinter group known as 'Provisionals', whose declared object was full-scale guerrilla warfare against the representatives of British Government, the security forces. From now (and until beyond the end of this history), practically every regiment of the British Army was destined to serve repeated tours of duty in this disunited province of the United Kingdom.

October 1970 saw 1 RRW commence their second tour among the riot-torn streets of Belfast. This one lasted four months – four months of ceaseless patrolling on foot or

RIGHT: *Training, 1970s. The vehicles are Armoured Personnel Carriers.*

PHOTOGRAPHS: MAJOR R. P. SMITH

The Royal Regiment of Wales 1969–78

in vehicles with the ever-present threat of a sniper's bullet or a petrol-bomb, constant showers of bricks and stones, and, of course, yells of abuse from taunting youths, many no older than some soldiers' sons. There were confrontations with riotous mobs in the ghettos of the Shankill and Ardoyne when the soldiers stood and endured the hail of 'missiles ranging from simple stones and paving stones to chisels, knives, bottles, nail-bombs and petrol bombs', as *The Men of Harlech* reported. In days long past such mobs would have been quickly dealt with by a couple of rounds of controlled fire, or perhaps a determined bayonet charge. But in these more enlightened times when destructive, blood-thirsting rioters have become 'demonstrators' and any aggressive retaliation by the troops is liable to censure by left-wing MPs at Westminster (and slanted reporting by TV news editors), such tactics are condemned. The soldiers could only resort to firearms in self-defence. In other words, the enemy must be allowed to shoot first. During the tour the Battalion suffered its first Ulster casualties when three soldiers were wounded by small-arms fire and eight by home-made bombs and other missiles. But the tour also brought the first gallantry award for The Royal Regiment of Wales. Just after midnight on 8th February 1971, Private Bennett was patrolling in an APC with four other men in the Falls Road area where there had been serious rioting. When the vehicle came under attack by nail-bombs and grenades, Bennett dismounted and drove off the bombers with rifle-fire. While doing so, he was felled by a bullet in his arm. Quickly recovering, he engaged another group of rioters who were attacking with small arms and bombs. Although suffering from his wound, he refused to be evacuated until another rifleman had arrived to take his place. Subsequently Lance Corporal D. Bennett, as he became, was awarded the George Medal.

The Battalion returned to Osnabrück in mid-February, but before they could resume normal BAOR duties they welcomed their Colonel in Chief on his first visit to the Regiment since the amalgamation parade. The Prince spent three days with the Battalion, during which he drove an APC, fired several of the Battalion weapons, took part in an exercise – and dutifully consumed a leek in the Officers' Mess. In August 1971 when His Royal Highness qualified as a pilot at the RAF College, Cranwell, the Colonel of the Regiment, Sir David Peel Yates, sent him a congratulatory message 'on his high class qualification in another element'. Replying, the Prince declared that 'from now on Colonels have to follow the Colonel in Chief's example'. But they have been shamed: to date, none has done so.

At home there was yet another reorganisation for the Regiment's Territorial representatives. In June 1970 the Conservative Party returned to power, with their commitment to repairing some of the ravages inflicted on the reserve Army by the previous Labour Government. As a result, on 1st April 1971, the TAVR in Wales was augmented. The Welsh Volunteers as such were disbanded, and in their place three separate Battalions were created: one for The Royal Welch Fusiliers and two for The Royal Regiment of Wales. Thus there came into existence the Battalions that have survived down to the publication date of this history: 3rd (Volunteer) Battalion and 4th (Volunteer) Battalion The Royal Regiment of Wales. The 3rd Battalion's Regimental Headquarters was established at Cardiff, the 4th's at Llanelli.

In March 1972 the 1st Battalion were detailed for their third tour of duty in unhappy Ulster. In the contemporary *The Men of Harlech* the Commanding Officer, Lieutenant Colonel Mennell, expressed his view that: 'there are now signs of reason prevailing among the hard-liners on both sides, and a peaceful Ulster is just on the horizon. However, these are early days, and in this hard area of the Ardoyne it may take some time before passions are finally cooled.' As these lines are written, fifteen years later, there is not much evidence of cooled passions.

The Battalion arrived in Belfast on the day that Direct Rule was announced from Westminster. Overnight the Army's tactics changed to the 'Low Profile' (in less Parliamentary language, kid glove) role introduced by William Whitelaw, who began his policy of winning 'hearts and minds' by releasing scores of detainees. As Colonel Mennell wrote (in *The Men of Harlech*) this 'proved to be a very difficult tour, not so much because of the heavy gun battles with their inevitable casualties, but as a result of the severe restraints imposed upon the Battalion and the changing emphasis required by Low Profile...'.

Sentry post, Northern Ireland.
PHOTOGRAPH: MAJOR R. P. SMITH

The small, hard core of gunmen in the Ardoyne and Boyne districts was soon reinforced by many of those set free, while their weapons were now far more sophisticated than those the Battalion had faced in their previous tours. With the shameful support of United States sympathisers (NORAID), they possessed a formidable armament of Armalite rifles firing armour-piercing rounds, M1 carbines, Thompson sub-machine guns, rockets, and a variety of modern hand guns, besides plentiful supplies of ammunition. This was the enemy the British soldier had to confront. Colonel Mennell again: 'We had great difficulty in locating the IRA gunmen, particularly within the limits imposed upon us by the Low Profile. We could only search houses for men and weapons on good 'hard' intelligence, and this was not easy to come by once internment ended – or in 'Hot Pursuit' of a gunman if a patrol saw one running into a house.' The gunmen never actually lived in their areas of operations; they changed locations every couple of days, and moreover enjoyed support among the Catholic inhabitants. Another recently created menace was the paramilitary Ulster Defence Association, or UDA, which emerged as a Protestant protest against the Government's lack of aggressive policy against the IRA. Thus the troops were often caught in the cross-fire of inter-sectarian battles, while still striving to maintain the Low Profile. And this role was further complicated by continual shifts of emphasis: 'each day brought further restraints or changes in direction in dealing with the IRA gunmen or militant Protestants'.

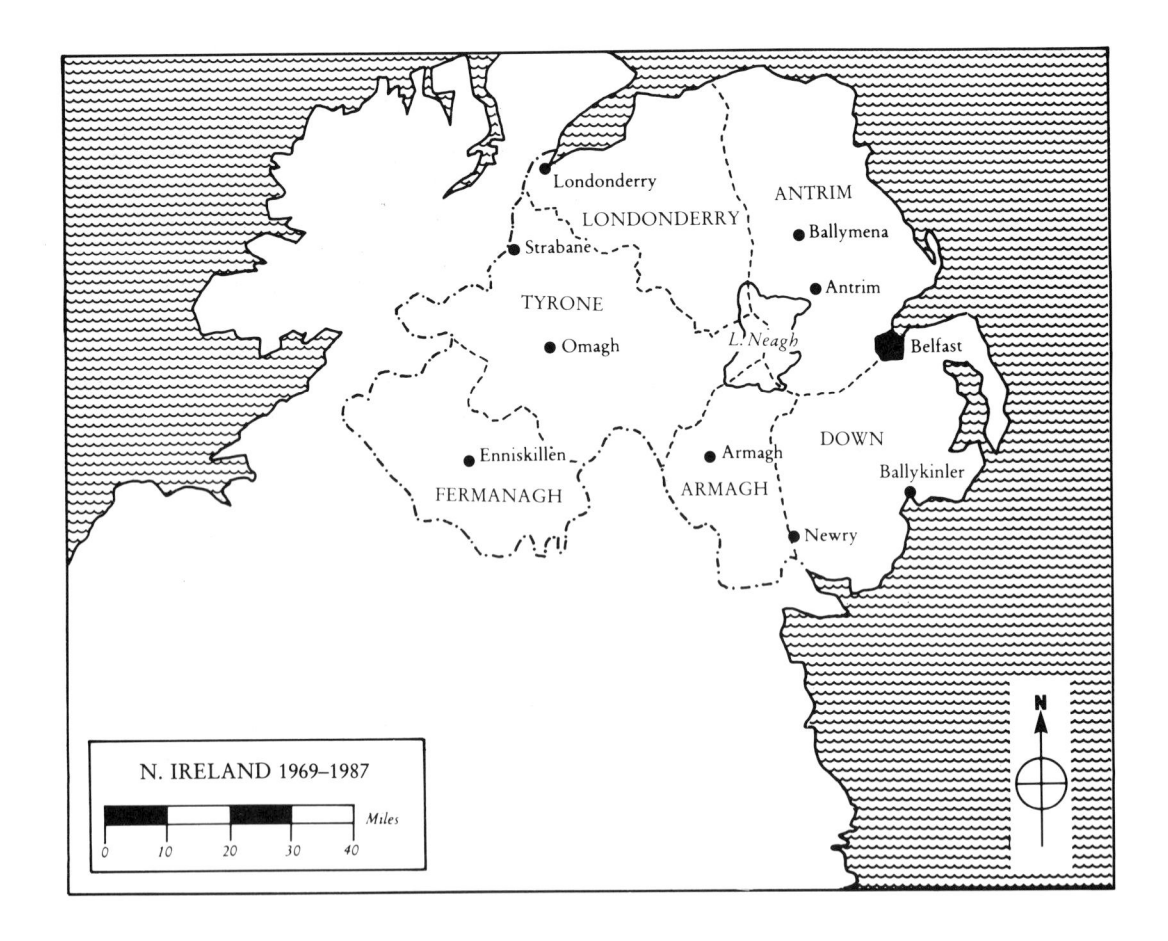

Within ten minutes of 1 RRW companies being deployed in the ugly Ardoyne and Shankill areas of the city, shooting broke out between Catholics and Protestants and for nine hours the Battalion was at full stretch dealing with riotous mobs from both sides, curbing looters and endeavouring to extinguish blazing cars and buses. This set the pattern for the rest of the tour. In April the first casualty was suffered when a private of A Company was wounded. In the same period Mr Whitelaw visited the Battalion, to be received with the courtesy always accorded by regiments to Ministers of State. A month later a lance corporal was killed by a sniper while on duty in his OP overlooking the Ardoyne. At the end of May there was a general escalation of violence, with bombings, shooting and arson. The Protestants, and the UDA, were becoming increasingly angry and antagonised by the continued release of internees, which the IRA hard-liners interpreted as a sign of failing resolve. The Battalion Medical Officer, Captain Mackay, was shot in the stomach while tending wounded after a bomb explosion. Shepherding local children home from school, a corporal was hit in the leg; a few days later another corporal was critically wounded in the spine as he confronted a mob. And so it went on, day after day, while the IRA established 'no-go' areas in Londonderry and the UDA erected their barricades throughout Belfast. A typical Battalion sitrep[2] read: 'A hard night. 76 shooting incidents. 550 rounds fired at Bn. 369 fired by Bn. Bn suffered two killed and one wounded. Bn definitely hit 8 gunmen.' By the end of the statutory four months' tour in August 1972, the Battalion had lost six men killed and twenty-five wounded. This was the costliest tour yet, and when they handed over their area to the 1st Battalion The Light Infantry, there was no sign of any improvement in the situation. The 'Emergency' tours in Northern Ireland became an occupational hazard, disrupting normal training schedules and courses and commitments to BAOR duties. Welsh and Scottish soldiers subjected to the bombs, bullets and booby traps in this weed-infested 'back garden' of the United Kingdom may sometimes have wondered why their fellow-Celts, the Irish, could not live in peace with each other and with England, as their own countrymen had done for centuries. After a particularly ferocious gun battle in the Shankill Road ghetto one wounded infantry soldier (not from The Royal Regiment of Wales) was heard to remark: 'The best thing they could do with this f------ country is to tow it out to the middle of the Atlantic and scuttle it.'

In August 1972 the 1st Battalion thankfully exchanged the back streets of Belfast for the peaceful north German plains, resuming their BAOR role of a mechanised Battalion at Osnabrück. December that year saw a change of command, when Lieutenant Colonel I. D. B. Mennell handed over to Lieutenant Colonel R. H. Godwin-Austen. Ian Mennell had seen two demanding tours in Ulster as Commanding Officer and had earned a high reputation for his Battalion and himself. 'We were all delighted', wrote *The Men of Harlech* correspondent, 'to see the announcement that he had been awarded what we consider a well deserved OBE.' Ian Mennell's new job was quite a contrast: he was posted to the Trucial States in the Persian Gulf, as Chief of Staff to the Abu Dhabi Defence Force.

The new Commanding Officer's surname had been very familiar to the old 24th Regiment, for Robin Godwin-Austen was a nephew of the former Colonel of the Regiment, General Sir Reade Godwin-Austen, and great-nephew of the surveyor-explorer, Henry Godwin-Austen, after whom the world's second highest mountain was named. His father, Captain Annesley Godwin-Austen, had served with the Regiment in World War I.

In January 1973 the 1st Battalion at Osnabrück were honoured by the second visit from the Colonel in Chief, who was accompanied by the Colonel of the Regiment, Lieutenant General Sir David Peel Yates. As on his previous visit, His Royal Highness displayed a keen (and knowledgeable) interest in the Battalion's weapons and vehicles, firing and driving several of them. After being briefed on the recent tour in Northern Ireland, he was given a demonstration of a typical VCP (Vehicle Check Point) in a Belfast back street, at which a most realistic mob of yobbos and Belfast 'ladies' was provided by C Company. The Prince's visit served to confirm what everyone already knew: that their Colonel in Chief was no remote figure-head, but a warm, approachable personality who obviously cherished a lively interest in the Regiment that bore his

Plumes in their cap badge, and was determined to maintain contact. That His Royal Highness is still doing so as this history goes to press, fifteen years later, is proof of his sincerity.

We must now shift our scene to South Africa. Early in 1973 came distressing news that the graves of the two VCs, Lieutenants Melvill and Coghill, at Fugitives Drift near Isandhlwana, had been broken open by vandals, who had also damaged the cross. It so happened that a Mr Dacre Watson, OBE (father-in-law of Captain A. J. Martin, Royal Regiment of Wales), was about to travel to South Africa, and he agreed to visit the site. When he arrived there in March 1973, he found that most of the desecration had already been put to rights by the South African Historical Monuments Commission and the War Graves Commission. Only the broken cross was awaiting a replacement from Dundee (Natal). The two coffins, in a single grave, had been exposed by the vandals: both had practically disintegrated and one showed evidence of having been smashed open. The Natal authorities believe that the vandals were after a nickel-plated revolver which was supposed to have been buried with the bodies. There was no trace of the weapon. The Commissioners' representatives were unable to distinguish between the two skeletons: the only differing features were a set of still perfect teeth in one skull, while the other had several missing. The uniforms had, of course, decayed beyond recognition, but the thick leather braces were still in good condition, as were the boots. The two skeletons were placed together in one new coffin which was re-interred and covered with rocks cemented in position.

At home, each issue of *The Men of Harlech* inevitably contained obituaries of old soldiers, of both high and humble rank (after all, the Regimental Journal is 'the family magazine'). Thus the issues for 1973 included the usual tributes to the departed, and while it might seem invidious to single out any one, two of them should be recorded.

On 30th August there passed away, at the age of 80, Major General C. E. N. Lomax, CB, CBE, DSO, MC. Readers will recall him as Colonel of The Welch Regiment, 1949–58, and author of *The History of The Welch Regiment 1919–1951*, a work to which the present author is greatly indebted. In the field of regimental history he was following his father's example, for in 1899 Captain D. A. N. Lomax had produced the first history of the 41st[3] just before he sailed with the 1st Battalion for the Boer War, in which he was killed.

'Sonny' Lomax joined 1 Welch as a 2nd Lieutenant in 1913. Serving with the Battalion in many of the early Western Front battles, he was transferred as Major to the Manchester Regiment in 1916, and a year later was promoted Lieutenant Colonel and given command of the 21st Manchesters. At the age of 24, he was one of the youngest Battalion commanders in France and Flanders (if not *the* youngest).

He emerged from the war with the DSO and Bar, MC, Croix de Guerre and several Mentions in Despatches. After serving as Adjutant to the reformed 6th (Glamorgan) Battalion (TA), in 1936, he took over command of 2 Welch in India. The outbreak of World War II found him as Brigadier commanding the 16th (Infantry) Brigade in the operations against the Vichy French on the Palestine–Syria border. As we have seen in the previous chapter, by 1944 he had become Major General in command of the 26th Indian Division, fighting in the Arakan. These services earned him the CB and CBE. During his tenure of the Colonelcy General Lomax directed the committee set up to raise funds for the Llandaff Memorial Chapel. He laid its foundation stone in 1953, and saw it consecrated in September 1956. In September 1973 his memorial service was held in the same Chapel.

To have given sixty years' loyal service to the Crown is a record of which few can boast. Ex-RQMS J. H. Keefe was one. 'Jimmy' Keefe was truly a 'son' of the 24th Regiment. He was born in the Brecon barracks in 1891, his father having fought with B Company at Rorke's Drift. He enlisted in the 24th as a drummer in 1905 (at the age of 14) and went to France with 1SWB in 1914. Fighting in the retreat from Mons, he then went to Gallipoli with the 2nd Battalion. Later he returned to France with the Battalion and served there until the Armistice. After leaving the Army in 1930 'Jimmy' took up a civilian post in the Brecon barracks until the outbreak of World War II, when he immediately rejoined The South Wales Borders, finishing as RQMS. Demobbed again in 1945, he rejoined the Brecon Headquarters staff as Barrack Inventory Accountant and finally retired in October 1965, aged 74.

If few individuals could match Jimmy Keefe in their service to King, Queen and country, surely few families could equal 'the remarkable Raikes'. Standing near the banks of South Wales's largest natural sheet of water, Llangorse Lake, (Powys), is an 'Elizabethan Gothic' mansion, known as Treberfydd, erected by one Robert Raikes in the 1840s. In the late 1890s his descendant, Robert Taunton Raikes, produced six sons, one of whom died in infancy. The other five flourished to serve their country in Army and Navy, and between them earned one DSC and one Bar, four DSOs and three Bars, and two MCs and two Bars. The eldest, Laurence Taunton (born 1882), was a Gunner and earned the first of the brothers' DSOs while commanding a Field Battery in January 1916. After the war he commanded the 20th Field Brigade RA and then became Chief Instructor at the School of Artillery, Larkhill (1928–32). His final post was as Colonel commanding the 4th Divisional Royal Artillery. He died soon after assuming these duties, in October 1932.

The second son was Geoffrey Taunton, born in 1884 and commissioned in The South Wales Borderers in 1903. The outbreak of war in 1914 found him serving with the Egyptian Army as Captain, but in 1916 he joined 2 SWB in France and in the same year was awarded the DSO. Just over a year later he had risen to command the Battalion, and in February 1918 he gained a Bar to his DSO. In September he greatly distinguished himself by rallying the remnants of two badly mauled brigades and repelling frequent enemy attacks. The Citation for the second Bar declared that: 'it was entirely due to his absolute disregard of danger, capacity for command and powers of organisation that the line held to the last'. A DSO and two Bars is not a unique achievement, but it is a rare one.[4] Colonel Geoffrey was also awarded the French Croix de Guerre and five times received Mentions in Despatches. After the war he served as a Chief Instructor at the Royal Military Academy, Woolwich, and then commanded the 1st Battalion The South Wales Borderers from 1931 to 1934, after which, as Brigadier, he was appointed to command the 9th Infantry Brigade. In 1937 he was promoted Major General, and in 1939 he was given command of the 38th (Welsh) Division. But as he had now passed the age considered acceptable for senior officers on active service, he had to spend the war on home-based staff appointments. Having reached his sixtieth year in 1944, he finally retired from the Army – after forty-one years' service. From 1948 to 1959 Major General Raikes served his county as Lord-Lieutenant of Breconshire; his devotion to such duties brought its reward with a Knighthood in 1960. Sir Geoffrey died in March 1975, at the age of 91.

The third of the Raikes 'quintet' was Robert Henry Taunton, born in 1885. Unique among his brothers, he chose the Senior Service rather than the Army, gaining his Sub Lieutenancy in the Royal Navy in 1900. During World War I he served as a submariner and in 1916, as Lieutenant Commander, he was awarded the DSC for sinking a German U-boat in the Western Approaches. In June 1917 he sank another U-boat and was given a Bar to his DSC. He was also created Chevalier de Legion d'Honneur by the French Government in the same month. Between the wars Raikes served as Director of the Royal Naval College, Greenwich (1932–4), Commodore and Chief of Staff, Mediterranean (1934–5), and Rear Admiral Submarines (1936–8). On 1st February 1937 he became the first officer to be appointed CB by King George VI. On the outbreak of World War II, Vice Admiral Raikes was commanding Northern Patrol; he was then appointed Commander in Chief South Atlantic Station and finally Flag Officer Aberdeen. He had been advanced to KCB in 1941; he retired with Admiral's rank and died in 1953.

Admiral Raikes's son followed in his father's footsteps (or, rather, in his father's ship's wake). At the time of writing Vice-Admiral Sir Iwan Raikes, KCB, CBE, DSC, lives in retirement on the banks of the Usk near Brecon. He had held the posts of Flag Officer Submarines and Commander Submarines Eastern Atlantic.

The fourth of 'the remarkable Raikes' was Wilfred Taunton (born 1892) who, like his elder brother Geoffrey, chose to serve in The South Wales Borderers, which he joined as 2nd Lieutenant in August 1914. Wilfred won his MC at Cambrai in November 1917, when he was temporary Major attached to the newly formed Tank Corps. His Bar came in September 1918 after the Battle of Lys. He was the last of the five brothers to win the DSO, which was awarded in June 1919. Lieutenant Colonel Wilfred Taunton Raikes died in 1957.

The fifth and youngest of the brothers, David Taunton Raikes, was born in 1897 and was the third to spend his early service with The South Wales Borderers, fighting with them in France and Flanders 1916–17. Like his brother Wilfred, he was then attached to the young Tank Corps, with which he distinguished himself by winning the MC in September 1917, the DSO in February 1918 and a Bar to his MC in 1919. Captain David Raikes left the Army in 1919. In World War II he was employed as Chief Inspector of Fighting Vehicles. He died in July 1966.

In November 1973 the 1st Battalion The Royal Regiment of Wales underwent their fourth tour in Northern Ireland, this time as the reserve Battalion for 39 Infantry Brigade. This meant being called upon for tasks anywhere in the Brigade area, which included Belfast city, its suburbs and the rural hinterland, besides deploying companies or platoons across the whole of the Province. It was the mixture as before, with ceaseless patrolling, manning VCPs, searches for arms, and the periodic confrontation with missile – and obscenity-hurling gangs of yobbos: nothing seemed to have changed since their last tour. On this tour, however, the Battalion were fortunate enough not to lose any of their members to bullets or bombs. Before leaving for a new posting in BAOR, in March 1975, the Commanding Officer, Lieutenant Colonel Godwin-Austen, was gratified to receive a laudatory letter from the Secretary of State for Northern Ireland. On 10th March 1975, Mr Merlyn Rees wrote:

Dear Colonel Godwin-Austen,

As the 1st Battalion the Royal Regiment of Wales draws near the end of its long term of duty in Northern Ireland, I would like to say how much the work of the whole Battalion has been appreciated, and it has been with a great deal of pride as a fellow Welshman, that I have heard of the work of the Battalion, in particular in the field of community relations. It is almost a cliché to say that the British soldier is one of our best ambassadors, but never truer than in Northern Ireland, and of the soldiers of the Royal Regiment of Wales. The easy ability of Welsh soldiers to chat to people in the streets of Belfast has helped to keep me informed of local feelings and has certainly helped to bridge the gap between the man in the street and the Security Forces...

There is one aspect of the work done by the Regiment which I would not wish to pass unremarked: it is the work performed by the five senior NCOs of your Community Relations Team. I have great admiration for these men who, working alone and unarmed, have built up a marvellous contact with youth groups, community and tenants' associations, old age pensioners and the handicapped. The day to day help that they provide is, I know, much appreciated by the citizens of Belfast...

Without the sort of community work undertaken by the men of your Battalion, the problem of returning to normality and the building of a worthwhile life in Belfast would be infinitely more difficult

Yours sincerely
MERLYN REES
Secretary of State

When the above letter was written, Lieutenant Colonel Robin Godwin-Austen was no longer Commanding Officer. On 6th March he was ceremonially towed out of Palace Barracks, Belfast, in an APC, on appointment as GSOI HQ (IBR) Corps in Germany. He had handed over to Lieutenant Colonel K. J. Davey, MC.

While in Northern Ireland 1 RRW managed to keep their 1st XV in training for the Army Cup, which they won in March 1974, defeating 7 Signal Regiment by 15 points to 12. This was their first victory as The Royal Regiment of Wales, and it was to be repeated twice more within the next three years.

The period 1973–4 brought ceremonial parades for the 3rd (Volunteer) Battalion.

> REDEDICATED
> BY THE DEAN OF MONMOUTH
> ON THE 22ND OCTOBER 1986
> AND UNVEILED BY
> H.R.H. THE DUKE OF GLOUCESTER G.C.V.O.

ABOVE: *Rededication tablet, St Cadoc's Church, Trevethin, Pontypool.*
RIGHT: *The Regimental Chapel of the 2nd Battalion The Monmouthshire Regiment in St Cadoc's Church, Trevethin, Pontypool.*

On 27th October 1973, HRH the Prince of Wales as Colonel in Chief presented the Battalion with new Colours. The setting was Cardiff Castle, and as at the amalgamation parade four and a half years earlier, the Prince's personal Standard flew from the keep while a capacity crowd of some 4,000 spectators witnessed the ceremony. His Royal Highness was accompanied by Lieutenant General Sir David Peel Yates, Colonel of the Regiment, Colonel Sir William Crawshay, Honorary Colonel of the 3rd Battalion, and Colonel Sir Cenydd Traherne, Lord-Lieutenant of Glamorgan.

In the same month a Colour Guard from A and B Companies, together with Band and Drums, laid up the Colours of the disbanded 2nd Battalion The Monmouthshire Regiment in Trevethin Parish Church near Pontypool. January 1974 witnessed a similar ceremony when the Colours of 5th Battalion The Welch Regiment (TA) were laid up in St Catherine's Church, Pontypridd.

The Royal Colonel in Chief continued indefatigable in his efforts to maintain a close personal association with his Regiment. Just before presenting the new Colours to the 3rd Battalion in October 1973, the Prince paid a lengthy visit to the Welsh Depot at Cwrt-y-Gollen. Earlier that summer he had piloted his helicopter to Knook Camp, near Warminster, there to watch various activities of the 4th (Volunteer) Battalion in their annual camp. By now the Prince had also been appointed Colonel in Chief of the Welsh Guards; but this, and the fact that he was still a serving Naval officer, in no way prevented him from making every effort to maintain the contact and interest that he had promised to The Royal Regiment of Wales on its formation. Ever since that event the Prince had expressed his wish to attend the annual Reunions, but his Naval and numerous other duties interposed until October 1973, when he was able to attend the

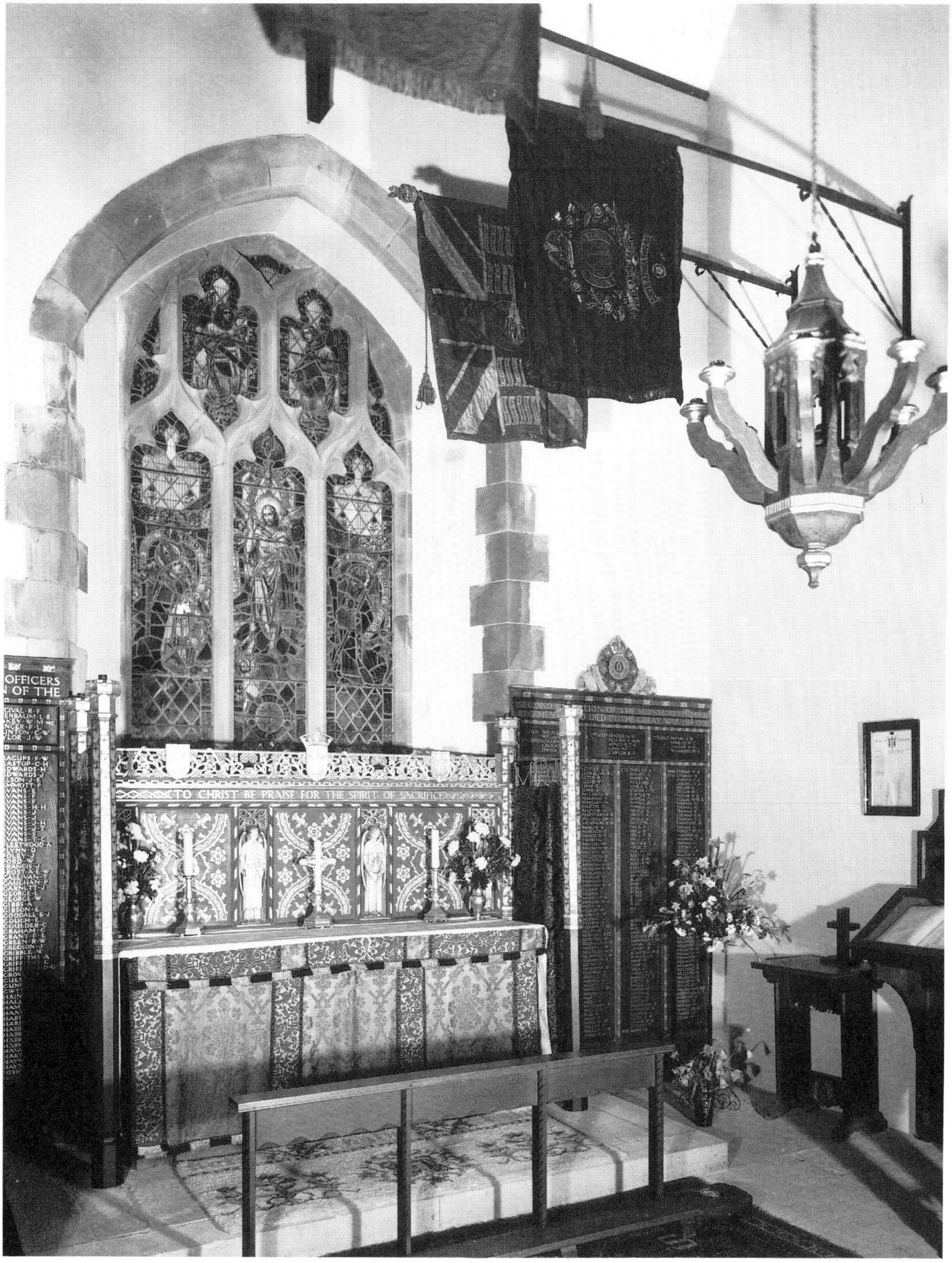
OFFICERS
TO CHRIST BE PRAISE FOR THE SPIRIT OF SACRIFICE

Reunion in Cardiff's City Hall. When the 1974 Reunion was planned for August at Dering Lines, Brecon, it seemed too much to hope that the Regiment could again be honoured. However, not only did the Prince spend two days at Brecon and preside at the dinner, but, to the delight of the Comrades, and the throngs of spectators, he marched behind the Band and Drums of the 1st Battalion through the streets from Dering Lines to the Cathedral, and back. While at Brecon the Prince was inroduced to two of the surviving VCs, Major General D. G. Johnson and Mr Edward Chapman.

A detail that had not escaped the Colonel in Chief's notice, and mild disapproval, was the fact that the cap badge worn by his Regiment (and inherited from The Welsh Brigade) did not conform to the traditional design of The Prince of Wales's Plumes which he himself wore. In The Royal Regiment of Wales's Badge, all three plumes rose stiffly upright, whereas in the official crest the two outer plumes inclined gracefully to left and right. Accordingly in 1973 steps were taken to rectify the design. This proved no simple matter. A number of draft sketches were prepared and rejected for one reason or another, never progressing beyond the Regimental Committee. 'Finally, the 1st Battalion produced a sketch which having been recommended by the Regimental Committee, was approved by the Colonel in Chief' (*The Men of Harlech*, November 1974).

But there is an interesting story behind that 'Finally', as is revealed by Lieutenant Colonel Robin Godwin-Austen, then commanding the 1st Battalion. He relates that one evening in October 1973 (at Osnabrück) he visited the Sergeants' Mess and was chatting with the RSM and Bandmaster about sundry topics, including the thorny question of a new badge, when a sergeant approached, bearing a paper parcel. 'Sir', said the Sergeant, 'look what I've got here'. He took out from the parcel a larger, solid silver badge – the Prince of Wales's Plumes and Motto. This, he said had been inherited from his grandfather. Unfortunately Colonel Godwin-Austen cannot recall the Sergeant's name, nor how his grandfather came to possess the badge, which looked as though it might have been an old helmet plate of one of The Welch's battalions. At all events, it was agreed that here was a splendid prototype for the new badge. The Commanding Officer then got his attached REME craftsman to work: an exact replica was produced in plastic, and this was sent home to the Regimental Committee, who had a drawing prepared, and it was this that was approved by the Colonel in Chief. But this was by no means the end of the badge story. The design had next to be submitted for approval to the Army Dress Committee in Whitehall. Since the Prince of Wales had already approved, this body could hardly do otherwise, and the design was then forwarded to the College of Arms for consideration by Garter King of Arms. On his approval the College artists prepared a detailed painting for submission to Her Majesty the Queen. Her gracious approval being granted, the hundreds of individual badges (in anodised aluminium) had to be manufactured by the Government contractor and distributed to the three Battalions. Thus it was not until November 1975 that The Royal Regiment of Wales at last bore on their headdress their Colonel in Chief's own version of the Prince of Wales's Plumes and his Motto.

In that same year the Colonel in Chief yet again demonstrated his interest in his Regiment. In July 1975 the 3rd (Volunteer) Battalion went to camp at Jurby in the Isle of Man, and on the 27th the Prince flew in to spend four hours with them, witnessing a platoon attack, and then, as always, chatting informally with officers, NCOs and men. Later that month His Royal Highness went to Llanelli in South Wales, there to receive the Freedom of the Borough on behalf of the Regiment, which was represented by the Band and Drums of the 1st Battalion, Colour Parties of all three Battalions, and a composite company of 3rd and 4th Battalions. At this date the 1st Battalion, under Lieutenant Colonel K. J. Davey, MC, were serving in the British sector of Berlin.

When The Royal Regiment of Wales was formed, it was a simple matter to combine the Battle Honours of both former Regiments for publication in the Army List and display on Colours. But there was the question of The Monmouthshire Regiment, which although 'part of the Corps of The South Wales Borderers', had its own separate Battle Honours. In this it differed from

The new cap badge, 1975.

most Territorial infantry units, which bore the titles of their regular Regiments and enjoyed those Regiments' Battle Honours and distinctions. At the time of the amalgamation, The Monmouthshire Battalion The South Wales Borderers existed only in cadre form, and was the only representative of the former 2nd Battalion The Monmouthshire Regiment.

On 1st April 1971 this cadre was finally disbanded, being absorbed by the new 3rd (Volunteer) Battalion, The Royal Regiment of Wales (together with the cadre of 5th/6th Battalion The Welch Regiment). Since the 3rd (Volunteer) Battalion inherited the property and funds of the disbanded cadres and could in every way be regarded as their legitimate successors, it seemed only right and proper that the Battle Honours earned by The Monmouthshire Regiment should also be handed on, otherwise they would be lost to posterity. Accordingly a case was prepared and forwarded by the Colonel of the Regiment, Lieutenant General Sir David Peel Yates, to the Ministry of Defence, who after checking by the Battles Nomenclature Committee, submitted the request to the Queen for formal approval. This was granted in November 1974, with the result that The Royal Regiment of Wales was then able to add no fewer than sixteen Battle Honours to their World War II roll. All these had been earned by 2 Mons on that long road from the Normandy beaches to Hamburg. It would have been shameful indeed if they had been allowed to vanish into the limbo that had swallowed up the Battalion itself.

The 1970s saw the passing of three more of the dwindling band of VC survivors. Major General D. G. Johnson, VC, CB, DSO, MC, died on 21st December 1975, at the venerable age of 91. As we have seen, Dudley Johnson was Colonel of The South Wales Borderers from 1944 to 1950, and was one of only two Colonels to gain the supreme award 'For Valour'. which he did on the Sambre-et-Oise Canal in November 1918. He was then commanding the 2nd Battalion The Royal Sussex Regiment, but he had spent all his early regular service with the 24th, which he joined in 1903. He first saw action with the 2nd Battalion in that little-known Chinese operation, the capture of Tsing-Tao, in November 1914. After being badly wounded in the Gallipoli landings, he served as Second-in-Command of the 1st Battalion in France, but in March 1918 he was transferred to The Royal Sussex as Commanding Officer of the 2nd Battalion. The outbreak of World War II found him commanding the 4th (Infantry) Division, as Major General, and he led this formation to France and Belgium with the BEF, returning via Dunkirk. He was then 56, an age considered somewhat advanced for further field commands, so that his next four years were spent as GOC Aldershot Command followed by staff appointments at General Headquarters. He retired, aged 60, in 1944, and immediately accepted the Colonelcy of The South Wales Borderers.

William Fuller, VC (former Lance Corporal, The Welch Regiment), died at his home in Swansea on 29th December 1974. Like General Johnson, he had reached the age of 91. As related on p. 221, he won his VC in 1914 when he rescued under heavy fire the mortally-wounded Captain Mark Haggard who had uttered the immortal cry now to be seen inscribed on the Cardiff barracks clock tower: 'Stick it the Welch!' Fuller had enlisted in The Welch Regiment in December 1902, aged 18, and after serving in South Africa and India was discharged to the Reserve in 1909. Recalled to the Colours in August 1914, he went to France with the 2nd Battalion. Promoted Lance Corporal after his VC action, he was severely wounded at Gheluvelt one month later and was invalided home, to be discharged as unfit for further service in December 1915. In June 1938 Fuller was again distinguished by the award of the Royal Humane Society's Medal for Lifesaving, gained when he saved two children from drowning off Swansea beach. During World War II he served as Air Raid Warden in Swansea.

Hubert William Lewis, VC, died at Milford Haven on 22nd February 1977, aged 80. 'Stokey' Lewis joined the 11th Service ('Cardiff Pals') Battalion The Welch Regiment in September 1914, aged 18, and served with them in France and Salonika. He won his VC in Macedonia on the night of 22nd/23rd November 1916, when, although twice wounded, he continued his attack on German-held trenches, and during the withdrawal brought in one of his badly-wounded comrades under heavy fire. 'Private Lewis showed throughout a brilliant example of courage, endurance and devotion to duty', as the Citation recorded. He was also awarded the Médaille Militaire by the French authorities. Lewis was discharged in 1919. In World War II, when he served as sergeant in the Milford Haven Home Guard, one of his three sons was killed in action while flying with the RAF.

Although sporting achievements are dealt with in Appendix 8, due mention must here be made of 1 RRW's continued success on the Rugby field; on 17th March 1976 their XV won the Army Cup by defeating the 1st Battalion The Duke of Wellington's Regiment by 10 points to 4. Almost exactly a year later (23rd March 1977), the team was again victorious, beating 8 Signal Regiment by 22 points to 9. This was the third

1988 EQUIPMENT
ABOVE: *Private with SA80 rifle. The new rifle was first issued in 1988.*
ABOVE RIGHT: *Private with SA80 rifle.*
RIGHT: *Private in full Nuclear Biological and Chemical Warfare Equipment.*

ABOVE: *General purpose machine gun sustained fire.*
RIGHT: *Light anti-tank weapon: Sennelager, May, 1987.*
BELOW: *The 1st Battalion training with Warrior, the new Armoured Personnel Carrier, 1988.*

time in four years that the Army Cup had been carried off by the The Royal Regiment of Wales.

After completing their Berlin tour in May 1977, the 1st Battalion returned home, to Aldershot, but only for a brief spell. On arrival they found they were detailed for a six-month tour in the sub-tropical posting of Belize, in the Caribbean, to commence in August. The interim period was a busy one, with packing of stores and hand-over in Berlin, then unpacking in the new Normandy Barracks at Aldershot, followed by repacking for the next move, together with restructuring and retraining for their jungle role. However, time was found to give an appropriate welcome to the Colonel in Chief who managed to fit in yet another flying visit in July, while D Company provided a Guard of Honour for Her Majesty the Queen during her visit to Cardiff on 24th June.

The tiny enclave of Belize in the Central American isthmus was originally British Honduras, before being renamed and granted self-government in 1964. Since then the neighbouring dictatorship of Guatemala had been threatening invasion, and though Belize was an insignificant member of the British Commonwealth, unimportant strategically or commercially, its mixed population of 120,000 less than that of Cardiff, Britain felt a duty to defend its loyal citizens from aggression. Thus by 1977 some 1,500 British soldiers were serving their 'tours' in Belize, supported by units of the Royal Navy and RAF. The 1st Battalion The Royal Regiment of Wales arrived in early August 1977, and immediately underwent a ten-day jungle-training course in which they acquired skills similar to those put into practice by 1 SWB in Malaya, twenty-two years earlier. They were now commanded by Lieutenant Colonel M. T. O. Lloyd, who had taken over from Colonel K. J. Davey, MC, at Aldershot the previous June.

1 RRW, Belize, 1977. (Air-portable Land Rover). (PHOTOGRAPH: MAJOR R. P. SMITH)

Perhaps deterred by the presence of the British Army, the Guatemalans never carried out their threats of invasion, and as far as 1 RRW were concerned, the tour passed off peacefully and even with a modicum of enjoyment. 'The country is fascinating', wrote A Company's correspondent to the Journal; 'already the soldiers are discovering the many varied opportunities existing here. Some have been into the jungle, some to the almost European landscape of Mountain Pine Ridge, and some to the coral reefs near the Cays (islands). A small group are at sea with HMS *Scylla* and visiting Kingston, Jamaica among other places. Bird and animal life abounds. Exotic leave schemes to places such as Mexico and San Salvador are already being planned.' The main drawbacks compared with life in BAOR were the somewhat primitive hutted accommodation and the absence of the families, for Belize was of necessity an 'unaccompanied' tour.

No shots were fired in anger during the tour, but the Battalion gained an award for bravery. Just two weeks after their arrival, Colour Sergeant Edwards was travelling in a Land Rover along the Western Highway when his attention was called to a large petrol tanker which had crashed on a sharp corner, overturned, and rolled down a steep bank to the edge of a river. When Edwards approached the engine was still running and petrol was leaking from the tanks. Ignoring the imminent danger of fire and explosion, Edwards and his driver gave first aid to one of the injured occupants lying on the river bank. He then spotted two others struggling in the water. Immediately he plunged in, brought ashore one who was unconscious and then dragged out the second, also badly injured. With the three casualties in the back of the Land Rover, Edwards and his driver motored them to the nearest hospital. For his initiative and courage, Colour Sergeant Anthony Edwards received the Commander in Chief's Commendation.

In September 1977 the Regiment said *ave atque vale* to new and old Colonels. General David Peel Yates had served as Colonel of The South Wales Borderers and the The Royal Regiment of Wales for a total of fifteen years. He was 66 and felt that 'the time is now ripe for me to hand over to a younger man', as he revealed in the November 1977 issue of the Journal. The 'younger man' was Major General L. A. D. Harrod, OBE (aged 53), who took up the appointment on 25th September. Unlike his predecessor, General Harrod had seen little of 'the family' until 1964, when he became Major, Second-in-Command of 1 Welch, rising to command the Battalion two years later. All his early regimental soldiering had been with the Grenadier Guards, in which he received an emergency commission as 2nd Lieutenant in 1944. He continued to wear the cap badge of the 1st Foot Guards until 1963, holding various staff appointments as Major, before his posting to The Welch. But that Regiment saw no more of him after he relinquished command of the 1st Battalion in 1969, for more senior staff appointments followed, in Washington, SHAPE, Baghdad and elsewhere. Promoted Brigadier in 1970, he was advanced to Major General in 1976.

In saying farewell to their former Colonel, the Regiment wished him 'Many happy years of peaceful retirement'. Tragically, this was not to be. Just over one year later, on 8th October 1978, Lieutenant General Sir David Peel Yates, KCB, CVO, DSO, OBE, DL, suffered a stroke and died while on a visit to his married daughter in the United States. This news came as a stunning shock to the Regiment, to whom and to its predecessors he had given such devoted service.

General David was well and truly of 'the family'. His father, Lieutenant Colonel Hubert Peel Yates, DSO, had entered the 24th in 1896 and risen to command the 2nd Battalion from 1923 to 1925, when he retired. David was commissioned in the same Battalion in 1931, but transferred to the 1st in 1933, seeing active service with them in the Waziristan operations of 1937. On the outbreak of World War II he was Adjutant of 1 Mons, but was immediately appointed a Brigade Major, and the first two years saw him in staff posts in North Africa. In 1944 he was given command of the 6th Battalion The Lincolnshire Regiment, whom he led with distinction throughout the Italian campaign, gaining a DSO and Bar. After the war he became instructor at the Joint Services Staff College and at the NATO Defence College in Paris. In 1953 he returned to the 24th, to command the 1st Battalion in BAOR until 1955, when, as Brigadier, he was given command of 27 Infantry Brigade in Hong Kong.

Major General L. A. D. Harrod, OBE, Colonel, The Royal Regiment of Wales, 25th September 1977–31st December 1982.

Next came sundry other appointments (and promotion): Assistant Commandant, Staff College (1957–60); Chief of Staff Eastern Command (1960–2); GOC, British Sector, Berlin (1962–6); GOC Eastern Command (1966–8); GOC Southern Command (1968–9). He retired in 1969, after thirty-eight years' continuous service. Meanwhile, of course, he had become Colonel of his old Regiment, the 24th, in 1962.

General David's military career was one of high distinction and devotion to duty, in war and peace. But he is remembered by the present Regiment essentially for those outstanding qualities of tact, understanding and wise counsel that, as Colonel of The South Wales Borderers, allowed him to play his leading role in the traumatic episode of amalgamation. As his counterpart of The Welch Regiment (Major General Frank Brook) wrote: 'It was David as much as anyone who ensured that the marriage should be a happy one.' And since then there has been no happier union than that represented by The Royal Regiment of Wales.

General Peel Yates was one of the few Colonels of the Regiment to make his home in his Regiment's territory. His country house lay among the foothills of the Black Mountains, outside the hamlet of Llanbedr, near Crickhowell.

One of the last acts performed by General David before giving up the Colonelcy was to write a foreword to a new history of the Regiment, which was published in the very month that he handed over (September 1977). This modest booklet is entitled *A Short History of The Royal Regiment of Wales (24th/41st Foot)*. 'Short' it may be, comprising only eighty-nine pages and lacking any illustrations, but it is a model of what a short history should be; clearly, concisely and accurately covering all the salient details in the centuries of service of 24th, 41st, 69th and the subsequent amalgam up to the 1970s, not omitting the reserve battalions. The present author's guide and *vade mecum*, this little book has been constantly at his elbow, and his debt to it is gratefully acknowledged. Its title page bears no author's name, but the foreword reveals that 'the painstaking and often frustrating work' was carried out by Colonel John Margesson, fitted in amidst his multifarious tasks as Regimental Secretary at Cardiff.

Colonel J. E. Margesson, MBE, had joined The South Wales Borderers as 2nd Lieutenant in 1933, following the example of his father who had been killed at Gallipoli with the 2nd Battalion. Most of John's service was spent with the 1st Battalion, of which he was successively Adjutant, Company commander and Second-in-Command. It was in the latter capacity that he served in the Malayan Emergency when, as related in Chapter 17, he led a search patrol to locate a notorious terrorist's camp in remote jungle, thereby enabling a successful air strike to be carried out.

Colonel Margesson performed the duties of Regimental Secretary of The Royal Regiment of Wales for seven years, retiring in 1976. At the present date his son is serving with the Regiment as Major H. D. Margesson.

Notes

[1] This was later modified: see p. 414.

[2] Situation Report.

[3] *History of the Services of the 41st (The Welch) Regiment.*

[4] During World War I a total of 8,981 DSOs were awarded. Seventy-one officers gained two Bars, while only seven gained three.

[5] Lieutenant Colonel Davey had won his MC while serving as Second Lieutenant with 1 Welch in Korea, 1951.

CHAPTER NINETEEN

To the Tercentenary (1978–89)

After their six-month tour in Belize, 1 RRW returned home, to Normandy Barracks, Aldershot, still under command of Lieutenant Colonel M. T. O. Lloyd. This was in May 1978, and a month later the Battalion were off overseas again, this time to Canada for Exercise 'Pond Jump West' in Alberta. Taking with them a detachment of Junior Soldiers from Crickhowell and some members of the 3rd and 4th (Volunteer) Battalions, they spent a month on intensive training and field-firing exercises. On the latter they were able to experiment with their new anti-tank guided missile system, the MILAN (but at £4,000 a missile, firing was somewhat limited). A short spell of leave also enabled parties to witness the Calgary Stampede and to see something of the National Parks in the Rocky Mountains.

Meanwhile, as already noted, The Welch Regiment Museum had moved to its present location in the Black and Barbican Towers of Cardiff Castle, where on 4th May 1978, it was formally opened by HRH the Prince of Wales as Colonel in Chief.

No sooner had 1 RRW returned once more to Aldershot than they found themselves deploying in the rain-sodden plains of Schleswig Holstein on the large-scale NATO Exercise 'Bold Guard'. This was 'quite an experience', wrote the Commanding Officer, 'as none of us had taken part in an exercise of such size before. We all learned a great deal...' Back again in Aldershot, C Company with Band and Drums and the Milan Platoon were detailed to carry out the 1978 KAPE tour of South Wales. Based in Cardiff, the team visited several major centres, including Builth Wells for the Royal Welsh Agricultural Show, and finishing in Caerphilly. At each stage they put on static displays and demonstrations, expended large quantities of blank in mock battles, and the Band and Drums beat Retreat. Their efforts certainly did much to 'keep the Army in the public eye', as was evidenced by the crowds of enthusiastic spectators. The correspondent to *The Men of Harlech* declared: 'I do not think recruits rushed to join, but the thought that there is a future in the Army was planted in the minds of many 14 and 15 year olds who, hopefully, will join us in a few years' time.' And that, of course, was one of the objects of the exercise.

The year was a busy one for the Territorial battalions. On 3rd June, the 3rd

Normandy Barracks, Aldershot. PHOTOGRAPH: MAJOR R. P. SMITH

Battalion played their part in the ceremonial at Cardiff Castle to mark the Queen's Birthday, when they fired a *feux de joie* and were inspected by the Lord Mayor of Cardiff, afterwards entertaining the GOC Wales, Major General Arthur Stewart-Cox, in the Banqueting Hall of the Castle. In July Lieutenant General Sir Peter Hudson, KCB, CBE, Commander in Chief UKLF, expressed his wish to visit a typical TAVR unit on one of their drill nights, and 3 RRW were selected. After witnessing the normal training sessions in the Cardiff Barracks, the General wrote a highly complimentary letter to the Commanding Officer, Lieutenant Colonel B. T. John.

The highlight of any Territorial unit's year is the annual camp, and in September 3 RRW spent their fortnight's field training in Scotland, at Barry Buddon, near Dundee. The fact that 396 all ranks out of 417 establishment attended was perhaps due to the pre-announced visit of the Prince of Wales. Ever conscious of his obligations as Colonel in Chief, His Royal Highness spent a day with the Battalion and lunched with the officers. Meanwhile, the 4th Battalion, under Lieutenant Colonel R. M. Scott, had also camped at Barry Buddon (in June), and while there they managed a liaison with HMS *Zulu*, in the Firth of Tay. This enabled some members of the Battalion to become temporary sailors on a Fishery Protection patrol.

In December 1978 the 1st Battalion (under Colonel Lloyd) commenced yet another operational tour in Northern Ireland. While no such tours could be described as welcome, in one respect this was particularly unwelcome, for it meant that the Regiment's only regular component was unable to be represented at the ceremonies to mark the most celebrated event in their history. As the Battalion scribe observed in *The Men of Harlech*: 'Fate played a cruel trick in placing us in Armagh for the 100th anniversary of the Immortal Defence of Rorke's Drift.'

Few readers will need reminding that the centenary of Isandhlwana and Rorke's Drift fell on 22nd–23rd January, 1979. On Sunday, the 21st, an impressive commemorative service was held in Brecon Cathedral. Led by the Colonel of the Regiment, Major General L. A. D. Harrod, and the Band of the 3rd (Volunteer) Battalion, the Regiment was represented by officers and men of both 3rd and 4th Batallions, a contingent from Crickhowell, and a large turn-out of Comrades who marched from the barracks to the Cathedral. The Colours of all three Battalions were laid upon the High Altar for the service, which was conducted by Major the Revd G. H. Roblin, RA ChD. As a young National Service subaltern this chaplain had served with 1 SWB throughout their operations in Malaya. Among the packed congregation were 60 direct descendants of the officers and soldiers who won VCs one hundred years before.

As early as 1973 plans were being formulated for a full-scale centenary ceremony of Remembrance at Isandhlwana and Rorke's Drift, at which it was hoped that the Regiment could be represented by the 1st Battalion Band and Drums and B ('Rorke's Drift') Company. But unhappily political and financial problems proved insurmountable: at one stage even the Colonel of the Regiment was informed that he would not be allowed to attend in his 'official' capacity. In the end, a compromise was reached, whereby a 'private' party of thirty-one members of the Regimental Association flew out to South Africa at their own expense. This contingent was headed by the Colonel, Major General Harrod ('not in his official capacity') and included Major General F. H. Brooke (last Colonel of The Welch Regiment), together with many ex-members of the old 24th and several descendants of those who fought at Isandhlwana and Rorke's Drift.

Although it had been hoped to hold the ceremonies on 22nd January, the date finally agreed was 25th–26th May, which avoided the rainy season. However, it so happened that Brigadier Charles Cox (ex-24th) and his wife were visiting South Africa in January, and on the 21st he was able to lay wreaths on the Regimental memorials at

To the Tercentenary 1978–89

Isandhlwana and Rorke's Drift at roughly the same time that the service of commemoration was taking place in Brecon Cathedral.

Arriving in Natal on 19th May, the main party were met by the Hon. Colonel of The Natal Carbiniers, Colonel P. C. A. Francis, MC, whose Regiment generously hosted the visit and made most of the arrangements. Like the 24th, the former Royal Natal Carbiniers had fought and suffered at Isandhlwana. After a church service in Pietermaritzburg conducted by the Lord Bishop of Natal, and attended by a uniformed detachment of the Carbiniers, the party were conducted on a tour of the battlefields and Fugitives Drift, where they stood in silence around the grave of Lieutenants Melvill and Coghill, marked by the restored plaque and a black granite cross. The climax of the visit came with the memorial ceremonies on 25th May. Beneath the distinctive Sphinx-like hill of Isandhlwana former enemies were united in wreath-laying ceremonies and a short religious service. As Colonel of the Regiment, General Harrod laid the wreath on the 24th's memorial, watched by the Kwa Zulu King, Zweilithini Goodwill Ka Bhekuzulu, and 150 of his warriors dressed in their old Impi regalia. A similar ceremony then followed at Rorke's Drift. Here the mass graves of the Zulu dead are dispersed in three different locations around the perimeter, and as a chivalrous gesture the plaques were simultaneously unveiled by three ex-members of the 24th, led by Lieutenant Colonel Jack Adams.

The fortnight's events culminated in lavish receptions and dinners: first a reception by the Mayor of Durban, who was presented with a plaque bearing the Arms of Brecon, then entertainment in the Officers' Mess of the Durban Light Infantry and finally, on 1st June, a centenary dinner laid on in Durban's Royal Hotel. As the Regimental party left for Heathrow on 3rd June they felt that their visit had been doubly worth all the planning, effort and expense. Not only had they paid the Regiment's respects to its soldiers lying on those remote battlefields, but they had cemented the warmest bonds of friendship with members of a country which, despite political differences, had shown them such generous hospitality. And not least memorable was the spirit of goodwill and respect established between the representatives of the old 24th Foot and their enemies of a century ago.

To set the seal on the Zulu War Centenary, on 22nd January 1979, the Colonel of the Regiment received the following telegram from the Colonel in Chief:

> On the occasion of the 100th Anniversary of the immortal defence of Rorke's Drift I send my very best wishes to all ranks of The Royal Regiment of Wales. I am certain that the courage, spirit and devotion to duty which were so evident 100 years ago at Rorke's Drift, and which earned the Regiment seven Victoria Crosses, are still to be found in the Regiment today, and I am proud to be your Colonel in Chief in this 10th Anniversary year of the foundation of The Royal Regiment of Wales.
> CHARLES
> Colonel in Chief

Ignoring proper chronology, mention must here be made of the restoration of the

3 RRW, training with SA 80 rifle.

3 RRW, training; 12-ft wall.

Queen's Colour that had been recovered from Isandhlwana, to be hung in the Regimental Chapel at Brecon. By 1979 this colour was in a poor state, with the fabric seriously deteriorating. Its preservation was due to Major A. J. Martin, formerly of the 24th and now serving with 1 RRW. He personally designed and produced a set of commemorative cover issues for the centenary and sold 13,000 worldwide. 'The interest shown was remarkable', he related, 'from train drivers in Australia to ex-members of the 24th in the USA'. This venture resulted in a fund of £1,500 which, with the approval of the Regimental Committee, was devoted to the restoration of the Colour. This was carried out by the Textile Conservation Centre at Hampton Court Palace, and in January 1984 the restored Colour was returned to its resting place in Brecon Cathedral.

As already noted, 1 RRW could play no part in the centenary, for they were otherwise engaged in Northern Ireland. Their tour was in a tactical area of operations covering some 460 square miles in East Tyrone, and their charter was to support the Royal Ulster Constabulary, which meant that, as before, they were Low Profile troops, providing check-points, covering police patrols and manning barricades. As always, the 'active service' elements, or terrorists, of the IRA and the Provos never came face to face with their enemy: indiscriminate bombs, mines and booby-traps were their tactics. However, this tour cost no casualties to the Battalion. While those inflicted on the terrorists were always difficult to establish, patrol and check-point vigilance resulted in several arrests being made and caches of arms and ammunition being discovered. These

To the Tercentenary 1978–89

Ulster tours imposed a tremendous physical and moral strain on all ranks. In a basically hostile environment, restricted by rules and procedures, they were fighting a campaign that was not officially a war, against a vicious, usually unseen enemy who could move freely among a population that was not always 'innocent', an enemy they could not attack unless attacked first.

> ... Despite it all, morale remains high, there is a tremendous comradeship and a grim determination to overcome the hardships and maintain the high standards of professionalism that have been a feature of the army's image over the past ten years. The weight of responsibility that lies on the shoulders of young officers, NCOs and soldiers is often immense. The calm and efficient way that these young men cope cannot be praised too highly, and I have the greatest possible admiration for them. Surely there can be no finer soldiers in the British Army than those I have the privilege to command. We should all be immensely proud of them...

Thus wrote Lieutenant Colonel Martin Lloyd shortly before returning with his Battalion to Aldershot, in April 1979. His words must surely be echoed by all readers of this history. And coincidentally, that same year marked the tenth anniversary of the creation of the Battalion with the raising of The Royal Regiment of Wales. The young offspring had inherited in full measure the centuries-old traditions and spirit of its two forebears.

On their return to Aldershot, 1 RRW indulged in very different activities. On 28th July 1979 they exercised their rights of Freedom of the City of Cardiff by marching through the streets with Colours flying, the salute being taken by the Lord Mayor. In August they were in Cardiff once more, this time to re-enact the Defence of Rorke's Drift, which formed the centre-piece of the Cardiff Searchlight Tattoo. Appropriately, B Company were the valiant defenders, while the other Companies deployed a highly realistic impi of Zulus, led by 2nd Lieutenant Robert Aitken.

The advent of 1980 saw 1 RRW heavily committed. First, the Battalion was placed on 'Worldwide Spearhead', which means that it could be flown at short notice for any 'fire brigade' operation in trouble spots. Then from December 1979 to March 1980 it was called upon to provide a contingent for the Monitoring Force tasked with supervising the cease-fire in Rhodesia, soon to become Zimbabwe. The contingent comprised four officers and twenty-one other ranks under Major M. G. R. Roberts – one of the largest sent by any regiment – and their handling of a delicate and often dangerous situation among the rival Zipra and Zanla terrorists and the Patriotic Front was carried out with characteristic tact and firmness. The result was a peaceful hand-over to the emergent independent Zimbabwe and, as Major General Akland, force commander, wrote in a valedictory signal: '... success in what most people in Rhodesia and indeed in many other parts of the world, saw as an impossible task'. Among the awards made to the force were well-earned MBEs for Major W. R. M. Watson and CSM Harris.

1 RRW undertaking Public Duties; Buckingham Palace, 1980.

PHOTOGRAPH: MAJOR R. P. SMITH

On 4th February 1980 a detachment of 1 RRW under Major R. J. Ashwood took over from the Scots Guards a fortnight's spell of Public Duties in London, finding the Guards at Buckingham Palace, St James's Palace and the Tower of London. This was the first time since amalgamation that the Regiment had been selected for these 'Senior Guard' duties, and as on the occasion in February 1969 when 1 Welch were so honoured, their drill and turn-out evoked many congratulatory signals. In the Officers' Mess of the St James's Palace Guard the officers were able to entertain HRH the Colonel in Chief to dinner, when the Secretary of State for Wales, Nicholas Ridley, MP, was among other guests.

In the same month of February the Battalion saw a change of command. Lieutenant Colonel M. T. O. Lloyd was posted away to Headquarters UKLF, being succeeded by Lieutenant Colonel S. R. A. Stocker who had been serving as Training Major with 11 Ulster Defence Regiment.

In August of the same year there was also a change at the Brecon Regimental Headquarters outstation, when Major G. J. B. Egerton retired after serving the Regiment and its predecessor, the 24th, in various capacities for forty-four years. George Egerton had joined 2 SWB in 1938. After service with 1 SWB in India he was captured in Tobruk in 1942. Repatriated after the war, he was appointed to command the Brecon Depot from 1956 to 1960 when he retired from the Active List to become Regimental Secretary of the 24th. On amalgamation he became Assistant Regimental

Secretary of The Royal Regiment of Wales. But this was only one of the hats he wore. In addition to editing *The Men of Harlech* from 1969, he was also Curator of The South Wales Borderers Museum. On his retirement he became the first President of the Comrades Association. His duties at Brecon were taken over by Major R. P. (Bob) Smith, who was still in office when this history went to press. Major Bob Smith could truly claim to represent The Royal Regiment of Wales, for, having joined The Welch Regiment in 1944, he was posted to 1 SWB in 1948 and served with them in Cyprus, the Sudan and Eritrea. His horizons were broadened by tours with The King's African Rifles and Malaysia Rangers.

Sadly, George Egerton did not live long to enjoy his retirement: he died at his home near Hay-on-Wye in 1985.

The 3rd and 4th Battalions were soldiering well up to strength, and displaying the enthusiasm and zest for which the TA had always been noted. The old image of 'Saturday afternoon soldiers' was long outdated. With modern weapons and equipment and realistic large-scale training exercises, often on the Continent of Europe, the volunteer battalions could claim to be as professional as their regular brothers, and at the sacrifice of their own spare time. In October 1979, 3 RRW under Lieutenant Colonel T. S. Brown and 4 RRW under Lieutenant Colonel R. M. Scott spent a gruelling weekend on Headquarters Wales FTX 'Dragon's Teeth' on the Sennybridge training area and acquitted themselves with credit. Colonel Brown commented: 'Much of this credit goes to those of our TA soldiers who finished their shift work at midnight on the Friday, were in the exercise area by 0600 hrs on the Saturday, had no sleep, and were back in time for their night shift on Sunday evening.' This is, surely a shining example for some sectors of today's youth. Almost immediately after the exercise, 3 RRW organised and ran the first TA Junior NCO's Cadre at Crickhowell, for all TA infantry units in Wales.

In April 1980 a composite company of 130 all ranks, mostly from 4 RRW but including men from 1 RRW, 3 RRW and 3 RWF, was flown out to Gibraltar for Exercise 'Marble TOR', involving Border Duty and Frontier Defence, combined with Adventure Training.

In September came the much-publicised major Exercise 'Crusader', in which some 30,000 men, including 20,000 TA units, were 'mobilised' and rushed out to reinforce BAOR 'under threat of attack'. This was the biggest British military operation since World War II and many valuable lessons were learned during the fortnight's activities. Lieutenant Colonel Trevor Brown of 3 RRW learned that he could mobilise his 450 soldiers and deploy them in their operational role on the Continent within 72 hours. After defending important supply dumps at Antwerp, the Battalion carried out exercises in the Belgian Army training area near Leopoldsburg, where they were visited by the Colonel of the Regiment, Major General Harrod, and the GOC Wales, Major General Napier.

To return to our regular element, after another sortie to Canada for exercises in Alberta, 1 RRW (under Lieutenant Colonel Stocker) flew out to Hong Kong in mid-September for a three-month tour as Land Frontier Battalion, the task being to help stem the flood of illegal immigrants from Communist China. The Battalion were deployed along some twenty miles of frontier from Lok Ma Chau in the west to the Tolo and Sai Kung peninsulas in the east. Quite apart from the moral aspect of having to arrest or repel abject would-be refugees from an oppressive regime, the physical strain of those three months was severe. The operations were conducted round the clock, seven days a week, with continuous manning of observation posts, deployment of patrols, check-points, ambushes, and instant reaction to any violence offered by the 'IIs' (Illegal Immigrants). Soldiers were lucky to enjoy more than five hours sleep in any twenty-four-hour period. Nearly all operations were carried out at night, so that the soldiers became nocturnal animals, snatching their sleep during the 'quiet' daytime hours. When the tour ended on 14th December, 1 RRW had been responsible for arresting 2,700 of those unhappy immigrants. The Battalion was thankful to return home in time to celebrate Christmas with their families.

In February 1981 the Regiment was granted the Freedom of the City of Swansea at which ceremony representatives of all three Battalions were present to witness the Scroll being received by the Colonel in Chief. This Freedom was in fact a transfer of that previously enjoyed by The Welch Regiment.

We now reach July 1981, and with it the pageantry and ceremonial of the Royal Wedding, when HRH the Prince of Wales was married to Lady Diana Spencer in St Paul's Cathedral on 29th July. It was a singular but fitting privilege for The Royal Regiment of Wales to provide the Army element of the tri-service Guard of Honour at the Cathedral, the whole Guard being commanded by their own Commanding Officer, Lieutenant Colonel S. R. A. Stocker. Perhaps it was no surprise to learn that this privilege had been conferred by their Colonel in Chief himself. The Regiment was also represented by a street-lining contingent of eighty soldiers under Major David Bromhead, together with the Colour Party and Taffy II. Among the guests in the Cathedral were Major General L. A. D. Harrod, Colonel of the Regiment, and Lance Corporal and Mrs Edwards. It was typical of the Prince that he should express his wish for a soldier of the Battalion and his wife to be specially invited. He also directed that one of the several wedding cakes should be given to his Regiment, and the following day all ranks (including Taffy II) partook of it. Earlier the following telegram had been received by Major General Harrod:

> Please convey our warmest congratulations to all ranks of my Regiment for the superb way in which they performed their duties today. They helped to make our wedding day so memorable.
>
> CHARLES and DIANA

As wedding gifts for the royal couple, the Regiment presented a solid silver Welsh Dragon on a walnut plinth, and, for Princess Diana, a brooch formed of the Regimental Crest in gold, diamond and enamel. These had been subscribed for by the three Battalions, retired officers and Comrades and the Glamorgan Army Cadet Force. An illuminated book containing all subscribers' names accompanied the presents.

Prior to all the London pageantry, 1 RRW had been committed to less pleasant duties. In May, as the Spearhead Battalion, they were put on twenty-four hours' notice

Graffiti; Northern Ireland.

to move yet again to Northern Ireland. The decision to deploy arrived at 1445 hours on the 6th; by dawn the next morning Colonel Stocker had moved his 650 officers and soldiers to Belfast and patrols were out on the streets. There followed five weeks of 'the mixture as before', as an A Company scribe wrote in the Journal: petrol-bombs, sniping, stone-throwing yobbos, blazing cars and buses – nothing had changed since the days of William Whitelaw and his 'hearts and minds' policy nine years before. On this deployment the Battalion co-operated with their fellow-Welshmen from 1 RWF, and although the level of rioting and violence was as brutal as ever, both units were fortunate in escaping serious casualties. On being withdrawn back to Aldershot on 8th July, Colonel Stocker paid tribute to the young officers and NCOs 'who carried the greatest burden . . . and did marvellously well in what was an extremely unpleasant and violent period'. On leaving, he received many complimentary messages on his Battalion's performance.

May 1981 saw the 40th anniversary of the Battle of Crete in which 1 Welch suffered so heavily. On 16th May a party of twenty-seven ex-members of The Welch Regiment and some serving members of 1 RRW flew out to Crete to take part in the memorial ceremonies. They were led by the last Colonel of The Welch, Major General F. H. Brooke, CB, CBE, DSO, who was in his 72nd year and not in the best of health. Sadly, this was the last service that General 'Frankie' was able to perform for his old Regiment: in the following January he succumbed to his illness. A memorial service was held in Llandaff Cathedral on 7th May 1982.

Lance Corporal Molloy, A Company; West Belfast Hunger Strike tour, 1981.

In January 1982, 1 RRW were earmarked for a posting to BAOR as a fully mechanised Battalion, and were in the midst of training for this role when in April the Argentinians invaded the Falkland Islands and South Georgia. Being otherwise committed, the Battalion could play no part in the dramatic events which saw the splendidly-mounted task force eject the invaders and force the enemy to surrender. However, The Royal Regiment of Wales was represented by one officer, Major M. M. Howes, who commanded 601 Tactical Air Control Party attached to 5 Infantry Brigade. With him was a fellow-Welshman, Major A. Hughes of 1 RWF, who was commanding 602 TACP. Landing at San Carlos, Michael Howes was present at most of the actions, finishing at Tumbledown Mountain. His experiences were fully related in *The Men of Harlech* for May 1983. Here his concluding summary will suffice: 'We had sailed 8000 miles... landed on the Falklands and joined battle alongside 3 Cdo Bde. Within two weeks we won a decisive victory against odds of three to one in a climate and on a terrain as bad as can be found anywhere in the world. I am glad I was part of it.'

To the Tercentenary 1978–89

Meanwhile his parent Battalion were busy at Aldershot acquiring expertise in the driving and maintenance of the variegated armoured vehicles deployed in a mechanised infantry battalion, from tracked AFV 432s, wheeled Stalwarts and Spartans to the numerous 'soft-skinned' trucks. The move of 1 RRW to Lemgo in BAOR was scheduled for August, and on 11th June they were honoured with a 'farewell visit' by their Colonel in Chief. Once more His Royal Highness evinced his very real and abiding interest in his Regiment. Before the move there was a change of command when Lieutenant Colonel S. R. A. Stocker handed over to Lieutenant Colonel J. M. Grundy, who had been an instructor at the Warminster School of Infantry. Colonel Stocker's successful tour in command was rewarded by his appointment as OBE in the Birthday Honours List.

The Battalion arrived at Lemgo, in the Lippe district of West Germany, in early August 1982, and took over the barracks from their old friends, 1 RWF. As a mechanised Battalion, their BAOR job was to provide the infantry element of 20 Armoured Brigade whose Headquarters was some ten miles away at Detmold. Lemgo was to be the 1st Battalion's home for five years, and a pleasant one it proved: a typical small German town with attractive half-timbered buildings and most friendly inhabitants. There had always been close liaison between British units stationed here and the townspeople, and Colonel Grundy and his men saw to it that these links were strengthened. The Stornoway Barracks complex itself offered luxury undreamed of by old soldiers; in fact, the term 'barracks' was hardly appropriate to describe the 'accommodation blocks' over which *The Men of Harlech* correspondent eulogised. 'Gone are the highly-polished corridors and rooms with metal lockers and steel beds, replaced by wall-to-wall carpeting and modern furniture. Each block is divided into a number of flats, each flat containing rooms for between two and four men, a sitting room and a kitchen fully equipped with fridge and cooker'. On the ground floors were locker rooms where soldiers could change out of their working clothes before taking their ease in their flats. These locker rooms were dubbed 'the Pithead Baths'. The complex boasted its own amenities such as a cinema, community centre, post office and library, and even a ladies' hairdresser. Only the constant scream of APC transmissions and odour of fuel and grease served as reminders that Stornoway Barracks *were* the barracks of a mechanised infantry unit. The ceremony of raising the Regimental Flag, on 6th August, was attended by hordes of local journalists, who were given a hand-out on 1 RRW and its Commanding Officer. Among other facts this mentioned that Colonel Grundy had done his basic training with The Royal Green Jackets before being commissioned into The Welch Regiment. Either the journalists did not bother to read beyond the first paragraph, or their command of English was unequal to the task; next morning the Commanding Officer was dismayed to learn from the local newspaper that

ABOVE LEFT: *Major D. de G. Bromhead, Commanding A Company 1 RRW, also Lance Corporal Farquaher, Lance Corporal Molloy and Lance Corporal Halfpenny; West Belfast Hunger Strike tour, 1981.*

LEFT: *Private Coundley, Anti-Tank Platoon, Support Company 1 RRW; West Belfast, 1983.*

Stornoway Barracks had been taken over by 'a distinguished English regiment, The Royal Green Jackets'.

At home the Volunteer battalions were again demonstrating their keenness and professionalism. The 3rd Battalion (Lieutenant Colonel O. M. Roberts) spent their fortnight's annual camp in Belgium where they acquitted themselves with credit on exercises in the Ardennes and elsewhere. Out of a total establishment of 514 all ranks, 469 had found time to attend. The 4th Battalion (Lieutenant Colonel M. G. R. Roberts, MBE) went farther afield. In March a platoon flew out to Gibraltar; in July a composite company flew to the USA to participate in field exercises with the National Guard. In September the Battalion underwent a hard fortnight's training on the Otterburn ranges in Northumberland.

This brings us to January 1983, and with it a change in the Regimental hierarchy. In that month Major General L. A. H. Napier, CB, OBE, MC, took over as Colonel of the Regiment, Major General Harrod having retired. We have already met Lennox Napier as last Commanding Officer of The South Wales Borderers and first of The Royal Regiment of Wales. He was of the 24th 'family', for he had been commissioned into The South Wales Borderers (1st Battalion) in 1948, serving with them in Egypt, Sudan and Eritrea, besides the UK and Germany. After instructing at the Small Arms Wing, School of Infantry, and at the Royal Military Academy, Sandhurst, Napier served as Second-in-Command and company commander in 1 SWB in Hong Kong and Aden. Promotion to Major followed in 1960, and in 1967, as Lieutenant Colonel, he took over command of 1 SWB, a command which became 1 RRW two years later. His next appointment, in 1970, was to the Directing Staff of the National Defence College; then after two years at the Ministry of Defence, Brigadier Napier became Brigade Commander, Berlin Infantry Brigade (1974–6). Returning to the UK in 1976, he was appointed Divisional Brigadier, The Prince of Wales's Division. Promotion to Major General followed in 1980 and with it the post of GOC Wales with his Headquarters in the old barracks of the 24th at Brecon. At the same time he was made Colonel Commandant The Prince of Wales's Division. These posts he held until his retirement in 1983, when he achieved the distinction of becoming Colonel of the Regiment whose forebear he had joined as a raw young 2nd Lieutenant thirty-five years previously.

The period 1982–3 saw an important reorganisation in the training of recruits for The Prince of Wales's Division. The Depot at Cwrt-y-Gollen (Crickhowell) ceased to take adult recruits as it had done since its formation, and was now responsible for training Junior soldiers only. All adult intakes were trained at the other Divisional Depot in Whittington Barracks just outside Lichfield, former home of The Staffordshire Regiment and still housing their Regimental Headquarters. But for Cwrt-y-Gollen this change was merely a prelude to more drastic reorganisation. In 1984 the Ministry of Defence proposed that the Depot should be closed down completely. This provoked strong protests, not only from the military concerned but also from the local MP and the Welsh media. As the Colonel of The Royal Regiment of Wales lamented (in *The Men of Harlech*): 'It will be a sad day for Wales, the Regiment and the Army if the only sizeable Regular Army unit in Wales was to close, particularly as Wales supports the Army so well.' Eventually a compromise was reached. The Cwrt-y-Gollen barracks

Major General Lennox Napier, CB, OBE, MC, DL, Colonel of the Regiment 1983–9 (Commanding Officer of 1SWB 1967–9 and 1 RRW 1969–70), and Mrs Jennifer Napier, at their home in Gwent.

would remain in being, but not as a Depot for The Prince of Wales's Division. On 17th October 1986 the Depot ceased to function as such, becoming a training camp for Territorial units and centre for Adventure Training. All Junior Soldiers (Welshmen or no) would train with the Infantry Junior Leaders' Battalion in far-off Shorncliffe, followed by a period at Lichfield.

Since 1959 Cwrt-y-Gollen had come to be regarded as the UK military 'home' of The Royal Welch Fusiliers and The Royal Regiment of Wales, besides the seven other

Soldiers training at the Depot, Prince of Wales's Division, Crickhowell, 1980.

English regiments making up The Prince of Wales's Division. Now they had to transfer loyalties to a Midlands city.

From September 1983 to February 1984 the 1st Battalion under Lieutenant Colonel Grundy endured yet again a tour in unhappy Ulster, being deployed in West Belfast with the now familiar task of providing back-up for the Royal Ulster Constabulary. This tour was relatively 'quiet', in that members were merely shot at, bombed and stoned without getting involved in any serious rioting. 'We made a few significant discoveries of arms, ammunition and bomb-making equipment', wrote Colonel Grundy, 'and we arrested a large number of suspected terrorists, most of whom were later released for lack of evidence.' Casualties were suffered in November when a remote-controlled bomb was detonated in Beechmount, wounding Lieutenant Brayshaw, five soldiers and six civilians. Brayshaw and four of the soldiers later recovered fully, but the sixth, Private Andrew Bull, tragically lost the sight of both eyes. After discharge from the Queen Elizabeth Military Hospital at Woolwich, he was admitted to St Dunstan's.

Returning to Lemgo in February 1984, 1 RRW reverted to their normal mechanised infantry role, at the same time keenly looking ahead to an event planned for July. This was the visit of His Royal Highness the Colonel in Chief, who flew in on 11th July

The Lord Mayors and the Mayors of the cities, boroughs and towns of which the Regiment has the Freedom, Cwrt-y-Gollen, 1966: Cardiff, Swansea, Newport, Dinefwr, Brecon, Carmarthen, Llanelli, Taff Ely (3 RRW) and Brecknock (host borough) (Brecknock is to confer the Freedom of the Borough on the Regiment in 1989).

to spend a busy twenty-four hours with the Regiment that was so truly his own. Among the ex-members present was the blinded Andrew Bull, and it was yet another example of the Prince's genuine interest in and concern for his soldiers that he had arranged for Bull to be flown to and from Germany in his own aircraft.

In September came the NATO Exercise 'Lionheart' which outdid even the 1980 'Crusader' in its massive scale, involving 56,500 British troops, of whom 35,000 were Territorials. With participating Germans, Dutch and Americans, the total opposing forces amounted to 131,560 troops of all arms. The Regiment was represented by the 1st and 3rd (Volunteer) Battalions, the former operating in the Springe area near Hameln, the latter in the Belgian Infantry Training Area around Leopoldsburg, familiar to some from 'Crusader'.

In December 1984 1 RRW were invited to participate in celebrations in Ravenna marking the 40th anniversary of that city's liberation from the Germans. Since The Welch Regiment had contributed to the liberation, it was fitting that their descendants should be present. Led by Major J. Quinton-Adams, members of A Company and the

Drums took part in the ceremonial in the city when wreaths were laid on the Italian memorial. They then marched to the Commonwealth Cemetry for more wreath-laying and the sounding of Last Post and Reveille by the Drummers. After being wined and dined that evening, the contingent travelled to the Argenta cemetery in the morning where they were met by the Deputy Mayor of Ravenna and the Mayoress of Argenta, who had brought an immense wreath inscribed to the Regiment whose soldiers lay buried there. Throughout their visit all ranks were greatly impressed by the warmth of the reception, both from officials and from the crowds of Italian people.

The year 1985 was ushered in with a change of command for 1 RRW at Lemgo. In January Lieutenant Colonel D. de G. Bromhead, LVO, took over from Lieutenant Colonel Grundy who was posted as British Liaison Officer to the US Army Infantry Centre in Georgia. David Bromhead, of the same family as the Rorke's Drift hero, was well known to the Colonel in Chief, for he had just completed a tour of duty as his Equerry. As usual, in BAOR, the Battalion was heavily committed during the year: exercises in the Soltau Training Area, field firing on the Sennelager ranges, one company despatched for a fortnight's schemes in Denmark, and then in July the large-scale 'Medicine Man' exercise in the live-firing area of Suffield on the Alberta prairie of Canada. In addition to all this, time was snatched for sundry 'non-khaki' diversions of Adventure Training. In January a course of skiing instruction, termed Exercise 'Snow Queen', was started in the Bavarian mountains and here 120 soldiers learned the basic techniques. 'It is heartening too, to see that some of our young officers have, on their own initiative, taken platoons/soldiers away on a host of outings and adventurous training, ranging from skiing in the Hartz to a Corsica visit' (Colonel Bromhead in the Journal).

Perhaps not strictly classifiable as Adventure Training, a remarkable 'non-khaki' event took place in September 1985. This was the truly 'marathon' run from John o' Groats to Lands End, performed by four members of 1 RRW. The scheme was mooted by Colour Sergeant Herbert and with the willing co-operation of the Commanding Officer, Colonel Bromhead, plans went ahead. The team, all of roughly the same age and proven running ability, comprised the RSM himself, WO1 Harrhy, Sergeant Foley, Colour Sergeant Hampton and the founder, Colour Sergeant Herbert. There were two objectives: to raise money for charity, and to beat the world record of six days, seven hours and twenty-one minutes set by The Parachute Regiment. Colonel Bromhead approached the Colonel in Chief to ask if he had a preferred charity. The prompt answer was, St David's Foundation, a hospice for cancer patients in Newport, recently visited by the Prince and Princess Diana. Since the 1st Battalion were preoccupied in BAOR they could not provide the necessary back-up. This was enthusiastically undertaken by 4 (Volunteer) RRW, 'without whom the run could not have taken place'. They contributed support in the form of two Land Rovers and trailers, a minibus and a cook, all food, and fuel vouchers. The team met their support in 4 RRW's lines at Neath, and on 23rd September the convoy set off for John o' Groats, arriving the following day.

At 0600 hours on the 25th, in rain and fog, Colour Sergeant Hampton began the first leg of the world record attempt. It had been agreed that each member would run for one hour, then rest in the minibus for three hours, thus completing five hours' running in a twenty-four-hour period. He was expected to cover at least eight miles in each running hour. This scheme worked well and by 0200 hours on the following day the team had passed south of Aviemore. The English border was reached on Day 3, after negotiating the streets of Edinburgh, and Day 4 saw the runners pounding through the dreary built-up areas of Greater Manchester. Although there had been some problems with dehydration, and the RSM's leg was giving him pain, there was no cause to modify the relentless routine. On Day 5 the team reached the Severn Bridge, across which the RSM had the honour of running while the remainder waited on the English side to greet him with cheers. After passing the famous Jamaica Inn on Bodmin Moor there was a hiccup in the routine when the 'resting' team fell asleep in the minibus, leaving the gallant RSM to run for two hours and fifteen miles. Day 6, from Penzance, brought the triumphant finish. As Colour Sergeant Hampton passed under the archway at Land's End, the clock was stopped at six days, three hours and fourteen minutes. The previous record had been beaten by four hours and seven minutes. The Royal Regiment of Wales were the new World Champions for the John o' Groats–Lands End marathon.

On 28th January Colonel Bromhead at Lemgo received a letter of thanks and congratulations from Sir Maynard Jenour, Chairman of the St David's Foundation, which was richer by £1,708 as a result of sponsorship of the run.

In October 1985 the Burgomaster of the Dutch city of s'Hertogenbosch invited survivors of the 53rd (Welsh) Infantry Division to celebrate the 41st anniversary of the liberation of the city by that Division. The contingent of 450 veterans included Old Comrades of 1/5th Welch, 2 Mons, 4, 6 and 7 RWF, besides those from supporting arms. Among honoured guests were two holders of the VC, Major Sir Tasker Watkins and Mr Edward Chapman. Through thronged streets decked with Welsh and Union Flags and posters proclaiming 'Thank you, Liberators in 1944!' the parade made a ceremonial entrance to the city square where the salute was taken by the GOC Wales, Major General P. E. de la C. de la Billiere. There followed a dinner and a liberation ball and on the next day there were commemoration services in the Cathedral and at the 53rd memorial and the Uden War Cemetery. The hospitality of the Dutch citizens was overwhelming. 'Strong men were reduced to tears by the welcome and gratitude of the citizens of s'Hertogenbosch... who represent the city that never forgot' (*The Men of Harlech*).

At home, the great event of the year was the visit of the Colonel in Chief to Llandovery, there to accept the Freedom of the Borough of Dinefwr on behalf of his Regiment. The ceremony, on 1st June, was attended by the Colour Parties of the 3rd and 4th Battalions, the Band and Drums of 3rd, and detachments of both Battalions. In the afternoon the Prince visited the Sennybridge Training Area to watch the Battalion on exercise. On this memorable day His Royal Highness was accompanied by Major General L. A. H. Napier, Colonel of the Regiment, and the Commanding Officers of the two Battalions – Lieutenant Colonel C. B. Jones (3 RRW) and Lieutenant Colonel D. C. Bromham (4 RRW).

Since the disbandment of the 2nd Battalion The Monmouthshire Regiment, their

The Colonel of the Regiment and the Commanding Officer of 4 RRW accompanying the Colonel in Chief at the Freedom of Dinefwr parade, 1985.

Colours, Rolls of Honour and Books of Remembrance had been lodged in the Memorial Chapel at Trevethin Church, Pontypool. In 1984 it was learned that the fabric of the Chapel was badly invaded by damp, posing a threat to the Colours and other memorials. Accordingly an appeal was launched by the Regiment for a contribution towards the cost of rendering the Chapel damp-proof, and in the spring of 1985 a cheque for £3,000 was presented to the Church Council. This sum had been raised by serving and past members of The Royal Regiment of Wales, generously supported by Headquarters Wales and TAVR (Wales). By October 1986 the sum had risen to £4,000, and on the 22nd of that month the restored Chapel was rededicated by the Dean of Monmouth in the presence of the Duke of Gloucester, who unveiled a memorial plaque.

In Germany 1 RRW were distinguishing themselves on the Rugby field. Having carried off the BAOR Cup, their XV fought their way to the Final of the Army Cup. This was played at Bad Lippspringe on 19th March against 7 RHA, and resulted in a 7 points to 6 victory. Curiously enough, this was an exact reversal of the previous year's Final, when they lost to 7 RHA.

Once more the Battalion was engaged in another 'Medicine Man' Exercise in Canada (in April 1986), and schemes and exercises continued apace in Germany. 'We as a Corps are the only combat arm which has to re-role every time we move from one theatre to another', wrote Major Kerruish in the Journal. 'Tank men merely apply their commanding, signalling, gunnery and driving and maintenance skills to different vehicles. We have now been in the mechanised role for four years and have much experience in armoured warfare... As I write we are training up for a totally different role in Northern Ireland.' This was really nothing new. Over the centuries the infantry, 'maid of all work', had been called upon to perform multifarious tasks, while cavalry, Gunners and the rest went about their own business.

In the old inter-war days the infantryman's life was relatively simple. The only battle skills he needed were the ability to reach the required standard of marksmanship with his .303 SMLE rifle, to yell fearsomely as he plunged his bayonet into a straw dummy, and to burrow into the ground with his entrenching tool. His mobility was provided by his own two feet. Of course the MG company and the signallers required their special expertise, but this was not very demanding. The battalion commander was responsible merely for some 700 soldiers, their rifles and machine guns, and an assortment of horse- and mule-drawn transport vehicles.

The infantryman of the 1980s has developed into a very different being: he is just as much a master of multifarious skills as his supporting comrades in the more technical arms. And nowhere is this more true than in a mechanised infantry battalion, such as 1 RRW in BAOR. Although the manpower has not changed much, with 36 officers and 718 other ranks, the scope and complexity of 'hardware' would surely boggle the mind of a 1930s officer or soldier. The most important vehicles are the tracked AFV 432s or Armoured Personnel Carriers which enable the soldiers of the mechanised companies to be transported through fire-swept zones, across virtually any terrain, to objectives where they can dismount and fight on foot with their self-loading rifles, their GPMGs, their Light Anti-Tank Weapons, and their mortars. The mechanised battalion deploys ninety of these 'battlefield taxis', four in each platoon, seventeen in a company. Others carry the Mortar Platoon with their 61 mm. and 88 m. weapons, and the Anti-Tank Platoon armed with their MILAN guided missiles. The Reconnaissance Platoon is mounted in eight Scimitars ('Combat Vehicle Reconnaisance Tracked'), which are virtually fast light tanks, armed with turret-mounted 30 mm. Rarden cannon and grenade launchers. The long-serving Ferret scout cars and Land Rovers are still in evidence, as are the Bedford transport vehicles, varying from 1 ton to 8 tons. But the most impressive of the 'tail' transport are what the Army designates 'High Mobility Load Carriers' or HMLC, but which were named by the Alvis manufacturers as 'Stalwarts'. This is an apt pseudonym, for with six-wheel drive (the front four steerable) these mechanical monsters can transport five tons of ammunition and supplies not only everywhere Challenger tanks can go, but where they cannot, for they are amphibious. Modern technology has also introduced aids undreamt of by The Royal Regiment of Wales's predecessors – such as laser range-finders and Mortar Fire Data Computers, while computer jargon is now familiar in the Orderly Room and company offices, all of which boast their Amstrad computer/word processors.

All this complexity of vehicles, armament and equipment (not to mention ammunition) is the responsibility of the modern battalion commander. In the old days cavalrymen and Gunners would refer to the infantry as 'Gravel-Crushers' or 'the Feet', and in World War II they were 'Flat-Footed Friends' to supporting tankmen. These terms are hardly applicable today.

Naturally, a mechanised battalion is required to operate closely with armour, and there were frequent exercises in Germany and Canada when companies of 1 RRW formed a Battle Group with armoured regiments and ancillaries. In the 1986 BATUS (British Army Training Unit Suffield) exercises in Canada, A and C Companies plus Mortar and Milan Platoons spent an energetic three weeks operating with the Blues and Royals, who were part of their Brigade in Germany. A very happy relationship was established between Household Cavalrymen and Welshmen, both in Germany and Canada. Major G. P. Kerruish of 1 RRW acted as Second-in-Command of the Battle Group and on returning to Lemgo he wrote (in the Journal): 'If permanent groupings of Armoured Infantry were ever to come about in the British Army, a combination of Household Cavalry and the Welsh would be unbeatable.'

BAOR life provided plenty of variety, and opportunity to see how other people did their jobs. In January a platoon of B Company spent a week attached to 212 Panzer Grenadier Battalion (equivalent to our mechanised battalions); in May another platoon attended a three-week course at the French Army Commando School near Nancy, being attached to 110 Régiment d'Infanterie.

Also in May, a flurry of signals between Captain Bryan Forbes, RN, commanding HMS *Cardiff*, and 1 RRW resulted in a party of one subaltern and twelve soldiers from the Battalion enjoying an 'attachment' to that ship in the Mediterranean. In between instructive tours of all departments on board from bridge to engine room, the Welsh 'pongos' were treated to traditional naval hospitality and were able to do some sightseeing at sundry ports of call, including Naples and Gibraltar. The opportunity was taken to remind their hosts that they had a certain 'right' to be on board, for their Regiment boasted a Naval Crown awarded for active service in HM ships – a little earlier. To commemorate the 'attachment' a Regimental plaque was presented to Captain Forbes just before *Cardiff* docked at Portsmouth.

Meanwhile, back at Lemgo there took place Exercise 'Welsh Amazon'. This was a two-day scheme (in atrocious weather) in which the twenty participants had to 'bivvy' for the night and then lay on a fighting patrol and ambush. There was nothing very remarkable in that, perhaps – except that the 'cammed-up', combat-clad patrol were all wives of the Battalion's soldiers, who had volunteered as 'Amazons'. 'A tremendous performance, ladies', wrote the Commanding Officer in *The Men of Harlech*, '... lads, take note!'

In 1982 the 'Home Service Force' was formed. At first only four companies were formed, in England and Scotland, but in 1985 three more companies were enlisted in Wales. Two of these were attached to 3 and 4 RRW, becoming their 'E' (HSF) companies – both Battalions already had four Rifle Companies, A–D. Although the HSF soldiers may have been somewhat aged compared with the TAs and Regulars, there was nothing of the old 'Dad's Army' image about them. A high proportion were ex-regular soldiers and they brought with them their former skills and a sense of professionalism that helped to weld their companies into efficient units which fully participated in the Battalions' activities.

At the other end of the age-scale is a category we have so far overlooked – the boys of the Army Cadet Force. Somewhat similar to the old school OTCs (later CCFs), but organised by the Army, the ACF enables lads under 16 to be given some military training and first-hand experience of Army life. The hope is, of course, that the promising ones will mature into recruits for the regulars or Territorials. For administration and training the various county ACF battalions are affiliated to regular regiments, those for which The Royal Regiment of Wales is responsible being Dyfed, Glamorgan, Gwent and South Powys.

A notable extra-mural annual event for services teams is the Three Peaks Yacht Race, perhaps a somewhat mystifying title, for even Services yachts are not normally expected to ascend mountains. But their crews can and do. The competing vessels put to sea at Barmouth in Cardigan Bay and sail to Fort William in the Great Glen of Scotland, a distance of 389 sea miles. En route they put in at Caernarfon where two of the crews of five race up and down Snowdon (24 miles, 3560 ft); on reaching Ravenglass on the Cumbrian coast, the two runners tackle Scafell (32 miles, 3210 ft) and from Fort William they attempt Britain's highest peak, Ben Nevis ($17\frac{1}{2}$ miles, 4406 ft). In June 1986, 3 RRW decided to enter with a 26-ft flat-bottomed monohull craft 'Men of Harlech', which was skippered by a Flight Lieutenant from RAF St Athan, the Mate being Captain Michael Maguire of 3 RRW, with Sergeant G. Williams (4 RRW) as Second Mate. The two runners from 3 RRW were Sergeant G. Finlayson and Lance Corporal M. Owens. The team did well as far as Ravenglass, achieving second place up and down Scafell, but a spell of bad weather set them back ('Men of Harlech' proved to be a fast ship in flat seas, but 'was a pig in a heavy swell') and the final placing was 15th out of 26. Nevertheless, for a crew who had little experience of off-shore racing or running up and down mountains, it was an achievement not to be lightly dismissed.

The 3rd (Volunteer) Battalion did, however, distinguish itself by winning the TA Welsh 1000 m. Race (originally 'Welsh 3000s'), thus becoming 'Kings of the Mountains'.

The 4th (Volunteer) Battalion had meanwhile been seeing the world beyond South Wales. One hundred and twenty men of A and B Companies were despatched to Gibraltar 'where we all managed to carry out some adventurous training in addition to normal military exercises'. Fifty men went to the Aviemore Ski Centre in the Highlands, two to Canada with 1 RRW and four to Lemgo. One officer and a soldier spent an instructive week in the USA, attached to the National Guard. In addition, six soldiers went on attachment to 1 Cheshire in Belize. 'Join the Territorial Army and see the World!'

OP Cara Cara, Northern Ireland; Clogher, September 1986–February 1987.

In September, 1 RRW once more interrupted their mechanised role in BAOR for yet another four-month tour in Ulster. This was the eighth in seventeen years and the situation had changed little. The Battalion was deployed as an Incremental Reinforcement Battalion in 8 Infantry Brigade area, and this saw companies and platoons widely dispersed in the counties of Londonderry, Tyrone, and Fermanagh, all facing hard-line IRA and Provo gunmen and bombers. Thus there followed the now-familiar gruelling tasks of round-the-clock patrolling (mostly on foot), manning VCPs, supporting the RUC and protecting their police stations, deploying by helicopter into 'target areas' for spells of twelve hours at a time. A Company's scribe in *The Men of Harlech* wrote:

> This tour, even more than previous ones, has been an NCOs' and Privates' campaign. Young corporals and lance corporals led their teams on patrol in appalling conditions... A good many hours – roughly 97,000 – were spent pounding the Clogher Valley, on foot. Patrols varied from a few hours up to

OP Cara Cara, Northern Ireland; Clogher, September 1986–February 1987.

six days in length. Although the skies were clear in the early weeks, we were soon introduced to Fermanagh weather – non-stop rain. The countryside is deliberately designed to trap the unspecting soldier. Fields are bordered by drystone walls or thick blackthorn hedges with a hidden barbed-wire fence and a deep muddy ditch on the far side, ready to catch the unwary. Creature comforts out on the ground became essential parts of life – the bivi bag, peak stove, sleeping mats, and fresh supplies of cigarettes and rations – leading to many a covert midnight rendezvous.

There were no battle casualties on this tour, but several successes. In November Corporal Michael Edwards and his team on a night patrol in Londonderry captured three heavily armed terrorists who were about to gun down a policeman. B (Rorke's Drift) Company's patrol in Carrickmore discovered caches of 500 rounds of ammunition in assorted calibres. The unearthing of a firing device for a terrorist bomb later enabled the RUC and UDR to discover a complete bomb-making 'factory' with more than 600 kg. of explosive. As always, the reaction of the local populace to the presence of soldiers striving to keep the fragile peace was unpredictable. In some areas the public proved friendly and would welcome a chat with members of a patrol; in others, particularly the hard-line Republican districts, patrols were constantly assaulted by bottles, stones, bricks and obscenities. As *The Men of Harlech* reported, there was a notable 'first' on this 1986–7 tour: for the first time the Battalion mustered a female member on its staff. She was 2nd Lieutenant Mary Eccles, WRAC, who served as Assistant Adjutant.

With no regrets, 1 RRW returned to their APCs, Scimitars, Stalwarts and the rest at Lemgo in January 1987.

The new year was the usual busy one for all three Battalions. On 12th March His Royal Highness the Colonel in Chief flew in to 1 RRW while they were operating on a local exercise near Lemgo. In his brief visit of three and a half hours, the Prince fired the 81 mm. mortar, and the Milan simulator, drove a Scimitar and a Stalwart and met a wide cross-section of all ranks.

For the Band there was an interesting 'away' engagement when they travelled to Höchstadt for the opening of the new town museum. Höchstadt is only a few miles from Blenheim, where in 1704 the 24th Foot gained their earliest Battle Honour, and it was for this reason that the Band of their descendants had been invited. After a concert in the town, the bandsmen enjoyed lavish Bavarian hospitality from the townspeople. Before returning to Lemgo, the Band were presented with one of the cannon balls picked up on the site of the battle.

3 RRW (Lieutenant Colonel D. G. Morgan) and 4 RRW (Lieutenant Colonel M. J. H. Harry) occupied themselves with exercises on Salisbury Plain and SENTA (Sennybridge Training Area). In November (1986) both Battalions took part in Exercise 'Triple Crown' involving most of the Welsh TA units in an 'advance to contact' scheme across the SENTA impact area. This saw companies leapfrogging by Chinook helicopter. In the following June a composite Company of 3 RRW spent a fortnight at Gibraltar attached to 1 Royal Anglian Regiment. In the same month the whole of 4 RRW took part in Exercise 'Hardbottle' on SENTA where, under the eye of the GOC Wales (Major General de la Billiere), they had to search and locate cunning enemy forces represented by the Welsh Squadron of 21 SAS.

Earlier that year The South Wales Borderers Museum at Brecon had received foreign visitors of some importance, at very short notice. At 0900 hours on 8th February Major Bob Smith, Curator and Assistant Regimental Secretary, was informed that the King and Queen of Kwa Zulu were in England and had expressed the wish to see the Museum with its Zulu War exhibits the following day. With his customary aplomb Major Smith made the necessary arrangements, which included a luncheon in the Officers' Mess attended by the GOC Wales. He even managed to acquire a full-size Kwa Zulu Flag which replaced the Welsh Flag on the Keep. The royal party arrived at lunchtime on the 9th – a little late, as they had been informed that Brecon was 'only a short distance down the M4 from London'. King Goodwill Zweilitini Zulu Ka Bhekezulu and Queen Mantfombe were accompanied by the Crown Prince Gideon and Princess Dhlamini, the Queen's sister. They were met by the Colonel of the Regiment,

To the Tercentenary 1978–89

Major General Lennox Napier. Naturally they evinced keen interest in the exhibits in the Zulu War Room, and afterwards they were taken to the Regimental Chapel in the Cathedral to see the Isandhlwana Colour.

Over the years since 1879 numerous parties and individuals from the Regiment had visited the Zulu War battlefields (as during the centenary celebrations mentioned earlier) but this was the first occasion that the reverse had occurred, with the visit of Zulus to Brecon.

It should here be recorded that although the Zulu War Room of The South Wales Borderers Museum has always attracted much attention and publicity, the Weapons Room boasts the most comprehensive collection of military firearms (British and foreign) to be found anywhere outside the Pattern Room of The Royal Small Arms Factory at Enfield. It was the Custodian of that Pattern Room who described the display as 'the finest of any regimental museum in Britain'.

On 7th July 1916 the 38th (Welsh) Division began their assault on Mametz Wood on the Somme battlefield. In the four days that followed, Battalions of The Royal Welch Fusiliers, The South Wales Borderers and The Welch Regiment were all but decimated. On 11th July 1987, seventy-one years later, a fitting memorial was unveiled at Mametz Wood. It took the form of a Red Dragon of Wales, clawing a strand of barbed wire, its tongue spitting out defiance at the former enemy positions, the whole mounted on a plinth bearing the Regimental Crests of all three Regiments. Appropriately, the Dragon had been sculpted of Welsh steel. After Last Post and Reveille had been sounded by Royal Welch Fusiliers buglers, wreaths were laid by Brigadier A. Vivian, Colonel The Royal Welch Fusiliers, Colonel J. E. J. Lane, representing the Colonel of The Royal Regiment of Wales, and Brigadier Le Blanc Smith, representing GOC Wales.

Also in July 1987 there was a change of command for 1 RRW at Lemgo. Lieutenant Colonel D. de G. Bromhead, LVO, handed over to Lieutenant Colonel C. H. Elliott who had been instructing at the Staff College. In addition to normal training and the ever-recurring Exercise 'This' and Exercise 'That', the 1st Battalion mounted the most ambitious and demanding Adventure Training scheme yet indulged in. Named 'Ex Welsh Quadrant', the plan was to motor overland from Lemgo to Athens and thence by ferry to Crete, where the 1941 actions of 1 Welch and their subsequent withdrawal were to be followed. The party of thirteen selected NCOs and men was led by Major C. W. Wilks of A Company, with Lieutenant I. R. Williams as 'Battlefield Study Project Officer'. Mounted in two 4-tonners with eight sea kayaks secured to the roofs, the expedition left Lemgo on 28th March (1987), arriving in Crete four days later. The first phase traversed the battle sites from Maleme eastwards, while a kayak party of eight paddled the fifty-nine sea miles from Maleme to Kalives in three days. For the last few miles they were escorted by a Greek Navy minesweeper who gave encouraging signals (hand). Next, a trekking party of twelve, led by Lance Corporal Fyfield, followed the withdrawal route of 1 Welch over the mountains to the evacuation beaches at Sphakia (now Khora Sfakion). Although this was only a distance of some forty miles, it led over 6,000-ft peaks and, heavily laden with equipment, the members had a gruelling time of it – in temperatures over 70° F. Here and there they encountered fearsome-looking locals whom they would have preferred to avoid. But these proved to be offspring of the partisans who had fought with the British against the German invaders, and when they discovered the identity of these strangers their welcome was embarrassing. The final days of 'Ex Welsh Quadrant' were spent in canoeing and rock climbing. The return journey to Lemgo was covered in three days. The total round trip amounted to roughly 5,000 miles, all this without a single breakdown or casualty, and 'the whole expedition proved a worthwhile and extremely enjoyable project', wrote Major Wilks in *The Men of Harlech*. Perhaps he might have added that the Battle Honour 'Crete' on the Regiment's Colours was now more than just a name to some of the successors of the 1st Battalion The Welch Regiment.

At home, laurels were won by 3 (V) RRW in the annual WALSAAM or Wales Skill at Arms Meeting on the Sennybridge ranges. With their SLR rifles in competition against the new SA80s, the twelve-man shooting team won the TA Championship and several other awards. In October 1987 4 (V) RRW were pleased to move their Headquarters, and Headquarters and D Companies, from ageing quarters at Llanelli to the modern custom-built TA Centre at Morfa, Swansea.

We now reach the year 1988, which though only some twelve months short of the date which sees the Regiment celebrating 300 years of service to Crown and country, must, by reason of printing requirements, mark the end of this history.

Before closing, however, it is fitting to record some details of the deployment of The Royal Regiment of Wales as it stood in February 1988.

The 1st Battalion, under Lieutenant Colonel C. H. Elliott, were still serving in Germany, at Stornoway Barracks, Lemgo. One of several mechanised infantry battalions in BAOR, they formed the mechanised infantry element of 20 Armoured Brigade, their cavalry comrades being the 4th/7th Royal Dragoon Guards and the 15th/19th The King's Royal Hussars. 20 Armoured Brigade formed part of 4 Armoured Division, which in turn was a formation of 1 (British) Corps of the NATO forces. All units of the Brigade are kept at six hours' notice to move out of barracks fully manned, armed and equipped for war. The establishment (or 'Orbat') for 1 RRW allowed 36 officers and 718 other ranks, with 162 assorted vehicles. Foremost among these were the tracked 'battle taxis', ninety AFV432 Armoured Personnel Carriers (now with turret-mounted GPMG), while other armour included the Scimitar light tanks or 'Combat Vehicle Reconnaissance (Tracked)'.

In August 1988 the 1st Battalion will relinquish its BAOR role to return home to Warminster, where it takes on the tasks of Infantry Demonstration Battalion at the School of Infantry. Here among other commitments it supports courses held by the School and Junior Division of the Staff College, prepares demonstrations of infantry weapons and vehicles, and carries out trials of new equipment as required by the Infantry Trials and Development Unit.

The 3rd (Volunteer) Battalion, commanded by Lieutenant Colonel D. G. Morgan, TD, was based at Maindy Barracks, Cardiff. It was designated as a four-Rifle Company Milan Battalion committed to a wartime role with NATO forces in the British Communications Zone of Belgium and Holland. In peacetime, and for administrative purposes, the Battalion is brigaded with the other Welsh Territorial infantry battalions

1 RRW Band and Drums on parade, Lemgo.

The Goat Major of 1RRW with Taffy III, 1987.

(3 RWF and 4 RRW) in 160 (Welsh) Infantry Brigade.

Under Lieutenant Colonel M. J. H. Harry, the 4th (Volunteer) Battalion had their Headquarters in the new TA Centre at Morfa, Swansea. Unlike the 3rd, they were roled entirely for home defence, and in time of war would become a reserve unit for GOC Wales. It is envisaged that their tasks would be to depoly 'mobile reaction' forces and to provide guards on key points and vital installations.

Both 3rd and 4th Battaions had one HSF (Home Service Force) company attached, but on mobilisation these would be detached from command to carry out independent guard duties in their respective areas.

Envoi

In March 1689 Sir Edward Dering raised the Regiment that was to become the 24th Regiment of Foot, later The South Wales Borderers. In 1719 a regiment of 'Invalids' was raised by Edmund Fielding, soon to be ranked as the 41st Foot. Then in 1758 the 69th Foot was created, and in 1881 these two merged to become The Welch Regiment.

'The South Wales Borderers' and 'The Welch' were titles which enjoyed honour and respect not only in their South Wales homeland but throughout the Army and among the general public, as typifying the sterling qualities of the British infantrymen of the Line, worthily carrying on the traditions of Marlborough's and Wellington's redcoats.

Titles of regiments may change; they may undergo metamorphoses undreamt of by their predecessors. But throughout the history of the British Army there is one characteristic that has abided unaltered. We may call it *esprit de corps*, pride of regiment or 'tribal loyalty', but it simply means that no matter where a regiment's name appears in the official Army List precedence, it is *The* Regiment to its members, superior and unique.

In 1988 The Royal Regiment of Wales had been in existence for only nineteen years, a mere eyeblink in the life of the Army. Yet during that short span its members had fully inherited the spirit of their forbears and were as jealous of their youthful title and badges as any of their predecessors were of theirs. While much of this happy state of affairs must be accredited to the Colonel of the Regiment, successive Commanding Officers and their subordinates, surely much must also be due to a natural sense of pride in belonging to a venerable 'family' that has distinguished itself during very nearly three centuries, has earned so many Battle Honours, so many VCs – and has left so many of its members lying in foreign fields. It was that valiant soldier-monarch, Frederick the Great, who once remarked: 'The spirit of a soldier, a regiment, an army, feeds on and is nourished by tradition'. This is just as true of the British Army as it may have been of the Prussian – probably more so.

And now all that remains to be said is, the year 1989 will witness the celebration of 300 years of tradition and service to Kings, Queens and country. The climax will come during the summer, in Cardiff Castle, when HRH the Prince of Wales as Colonel in Chief will present new Colours to the 1st Battalion The Royal Regiment of Wales, with guards from the 3rd and 4th Battalions also on parade.

These Colours will bear that unique emblem of valour, the Wreath of Immortelles, and the Motto that symbolises the spirit of a very fine Regiment of British Infantry
GWELL ANGAU NA CHYWILYDD.

APPENDIX ONE

The Victoria Cross

Won by Officers and Soldiers of the former Regiments of The Royal Regiment of Wales

1854	Sergeant A. Madden	41st Regiment	Crimea
	Major H. Rowlands	41st Regiment	Crimea
1867	Assistant Surgeon C. M. Douglas Private D. Bell Private J. Cooper Private W. Griffiths Private T. Murphy	2nd/24th Regiment	Andaman Islands
1873	Lieutenant Lord Gifford	2nd/24th Regiment	Ashantee
1879	Lieutenant T. Melvill Lieutenant N. J. A. Coghill	1st/24th Regiment	Zululand (Isandhlwana)
	Lieutenant G. Bromhead Corporal W. Allen Private F. Hitch Private H. Hook Private R. Jones Private W. Jones Private J. Williams	2nd/24th Regiment	Zululand (Rorke's Drift)
	Lieutenant E. S. Browne	1st/24th Regiment	Zululand
1914	Lance Corporal W. Fuller	2 Welch	France
1916	Captain A. Buchanan Private J. H. Finn	4 SWB	Mesopotamia
	2nd Lieutenant E. K. Myles	Welch (att. Worcesters)	Mesopotamia
	Private H. W. Lewis	11 Welch	Macedonia
1917	Sergeant A. White	2 SWB	France
	Sergeant I. Rees	11 SWB	Flanders
1918	Company Sergeant Major J. H. Williams, DCM, MM	10 SWB	France
	Lieutenant Colonel D. G. Johnson, DSO, MC	South Wales Borderers (att. Royal Sussex)	France
1944	Lieutenant Tasker Watkins	1/5 Welch	Normandy
	Corporal E. T. Chapman	3 Mons	Germany

APPENDIX TWO

Titles of the Regiment

Note: Until 1751 all regiments were known by the names of their Colonels, shown in Appendix Three.

1689	Colonel Sir Edward Dering's Regiment of Foot		
		1719 Colonel Edmund Fielding's Regiment of Invalids	
1751	24th Regiment of Foot	41st Regiment of Foot (Invalids)	
1756			(2nd Battalion 24th Foot)
1758			69th Regiment of Foot
1782	24th (2nd Warwickshire) Regiment of Foot		69th (South Lincolnshire) Regiment of Foot
1787		41st Regiment of Foot	
1831		41st (The Welsh) Regiment of Foot	
1881	The South Wales Borderers	41st and 69th amalgamated to form The Welsh Regiment (in 1920 spelling officially altered to 'Welch')	
1969	The South Wales Borderers and The Welch Regiment amalgamated to form		

THE ROYAL REGIMENT OF WALES
(24th/41st Foot)

APPENDIX THREE

Colonels of the Regiment

24th Regiment
(From 1881 The South Wales Borderers)

8th March 1689	Sir Edward Dering, Bart
27th September 1689	Daniel Dering
9th June 1691	Samuel Venner
13th March 1695	Louis James le Vasseur Cougnee, Marquis de Puisar
1st March 1701	William Seymour
12th February 1702	John Churchill, Earl (later Duke) of Marlborough
25th August 1704	William Tatton
9th March 1708	Gilbert Primrose
10th September 1717	Thomas Howard
27th June 1737	Thomas Wentworth
21st June 1745	Daniel Houghton
1st December 1747	William Kerr, Earl of Ancram (afterwards 4th Marquis of Lothian)
8th February 1752	Hon. Edward Cornwallis
15th January 1776	William Taylor
13th November 1793	Richard Whyte
13th July 1807	Sir David Baird, Bart, GCB, PC
7th September 1829	Sir James Lyon, KCB, GCH
2nd November 1842	Robert Ellice
19th June 1856	Hon. Daniel Finch, CB
26th November 1861	Pringle Taylor, KH
6th April 1884	Sir Charles Ellice, GCB
13th November 1888	Edmond Wodehouse
29th May 1898	Richard Thomas Glyn, CB, CMG
22nd November 1900	Henry James Degacher, CB
26th November 1902	George Paton, CMG
27th February 1922	Sir Alexander Stanhope Cobbe, VC, GCB, KCSI, DSO
30th June 1931	Llewellin Isaac Gethin Morgan-Owen, CB, CMG, CBE, DSO
30th June 1944	Dudley Graham Johnson, VC, CB, DSO, MC
1st January 1950	Sir Alfred Reade Godwin-Austen, KCSI, CB, OBE, MC
18th April 1954	Francis Raymond Gage Matthews, CB, DSO
1st January 1962	Sir David Peel Yates, KCB, CVO, DSO, OBE

41st Regiment

11th March 1719	Edmund Fielding
1st April 1743	Tomkins Wardour
4th March 1752	John Parsons
16th May 1764	Alexander Leslie, Lord Lindores
6th September 1765	John Parker
5th August 1771	Jordan Wren
14th January 1784	Archibald McNab
13th January 1790	Sir Thomas Stirling, Bart
16th May 1808	Hay Macdowall
22nd February 1810	Sir Josiah Champagne, GCH
14th June 1819	Hon. Sir Edward Stopford, GCB, KTS
26th September 1837	Sir Ralph Darling, KT, GCH
5th February 1848	Sir Charles Ashe a'Court Repington, KH, CB
20th April 1861	Sir Richard England, GCB, KH
20th January 1883	Julius Edmund Goodwyn, CB

69th Regiment

28th April 1758	Hon. Charles Colville
8th September 1775	Hon. Philip Sherard
17th September 1790	Sir Ralph Abercromby, KB
26th April 1792	Henry Watson Powell
20th June 1794	Sir Cornelius Cuyler, Bart
11th March 1819	William Carr, 1st Viscount Beresford, GCB, GCH
15th March 1823	Sir John Hamilton, Bart, KCB, KCH
2nd January 1836	John Vincent
5th February 1848	Sir Ralph Darling, KT, GCH
3rd April 1858	Ernest Frederic Gascoigne
19th July 1876	Sir William Montagu Scott McMurdo, GCB
23rd August 1877	David Elliot MacKirdy

The Welch Regiment (41st and 69th Foot)

1st July 1881	David Elliot MacKirdy
16th February 1894	Francis Peyton, CB
31st January 1904	William Allan
13th July 1918	Sir Alexander Bruce Tulloch, KCB, CMG
26th May 1920	Sir Thomas Owen Marden, KBE, CB, CMG
17th January 1941	Douglas Povah Dickinson, CB, DSO, OBE, MC
8th January 1949	Cyril Ernest Napier Lomax, CB, CBE, DSO, MC
8th January 1958	Sir Cyril Frederick Charles Coleman, KCB, CMG, DSO, OBE
20th November 1965	Frank Hastings Brooke, CB, CBE, DSO

The Royal Regiment of Wales (24th/41st Foot)

11th June 1969	Sir David Peel Yates, KCB, CVO, DSO, OBE
25th September 1977	Lionel Alexander Digby Harrod, OBE
1st January 1983	Lennox Alexander Hawkins Napier, CB, OBE, MC, DL

APPENDIX FOUR

Commanding Officers 1945–88
(Regular Battalions and Territorial Battalions of The Royal Regiment of Wales)

1st Battalion The South Wales Borderers

September 1945	Lieutenant Colonel J. L. Jordan
September 1945–June 1948	Lieutenant Colonel C. F. Cox, OBE
August 1948–February 1950	Lieutenant Colonel J. W. Hope, OBE
May 1950–August 1951	Lieutenant Colonel D. C. Campbell-Miles, MBE
August 1951–November 1953	Lieutenant Colonel C. F. Cox, OBE
November 1953–May 1955	Lieutenant Colonel D. Peel Yates, DSO, OBE
May 1955–March 1958	Lieutenant Colonel R. C. H. Miers, DSO, OBE
April 1958–July 1960	Lieutenant Colonel P. J. Martin
August 1960–January 1963	Lieutenant Colonel A. K. Sharp
January 1963–January 1966	Lieutenant Colonel A. R. Evill
January 1966–December 1967	Lieutenant Colonel J. N. Somerville
December 1967–June 1969	Lieutenant Colonel L. A. H. Napier, MBE, MC

2nd Battalion The South Wales Borderers

May 1945–August 1946	Lieutenant Colonel J. O. Crewe-Read
August 1946–January 1947	Lieutenant Colonel A. J. Stocker, DSO
January 1947–March 1947	Lieutenant Colonel D. L. Rhys, MC

1st Battalion The Welch Regiment

November 1945	Lieutenant Colonel D. L. C. Reynolds, OBE
March 1947	Lieutenant Colonel E. M. Davies-Jenkins, OBE
December 1950	Lieutenant Colonel H. H. Deane
January 1953	Lieutenant Colonel J. N. Goodwyn
July 1953	Lieutenant Colonel B. T. V. Cowey, DSO
March 1956	Lieutenant Colonel J. R. L. Traherne
December 1958	Lieutenant Colonel A. G. Roberts, DSO
June 1961	Lieutenant Colonel M. C. P. Stevenson, MC
November 1963	Lieutenant Colonel E. A. Priestley
May 1966	Lieutenant Colonel L. A. D. Harrod, MBE
April 1969	Lieutenant Colonel P. L. Cutler

2nd Battalion The Welch Regiment

February 1945   Lieutenant Colonel B. T. V. Cowey
December 1947   Lieutenant Colonel S. Griffith

1st Battalion The Royal Regiment of Wales

June 1969–July 1970   Lieutenant Colonel L. A. H. Napier, MBE, MC
July 1970–January 1973   Lieutenant Colonel I. D. B. Mennell
January 1973–March 1975   Lieutenant Colonel R. H. Godwin-Austen
March 1975–June 1977   Lieutenant Colonel K. J. Davey, MC
June 1977–February 1980   Lieutenant Colonel M. T. O. Lloyd
February 1980–July 1982   Lieutenant Colonel S. R. A. Stocker
July 1982–January 1985   Lieutenant Colonel J. M. Grundy
January 1985–July 1987   Lieutenant Colonel D. de G. Bromhead, LVO
July 1987–   Lieutenant Colonel C. H. Elliott

3rd (Volunteer) Battalion The Royal Regiment of Wales

April 1971–September 1971   Lieutenant Colonel R. L. Spurrell, OBE
September 1971–March 1974   Lieutenant Colonel B. M. Pim
March 1974–September 1976   Lieutenant Colonel D. E. Cox, MBE
September 1976–March 1979   Lieutenant Colonel B. T. John, TD
March 1979–September 1981   Lieutenant Colonel T. S. Brown
September 1981–April 1984   Lieutenant Colonel O. M. Roberts
April 1984–October 1986   Lieutenant Colonel C. B. Jones
October 1986–   Lieutenant Colonel D. G. Morgan, TD

4th (Volunteer) Battalion The Royal Regiment of Wales

March 1971–August 1973   Lieutenant Colonel G. R. Miles, TD
August 1973–March 1976   Lieutenant Colonel F. C. Batten
March 1976–August 1978   Lieutenant Colonel M. Davies
August 1978–March 1981   Lieutenant Colonel R. M. Scott, TD
March 1981–September 1983   Lieutenant Colonel M. G. R. Roberts, MBE
September 1983–March 1986   Lieutenant Colonel D. C. Bromham
March 1986–October 1988   Lieutenant Colonel M. J. H. Harry
October 1988–   Lieutenant Colonel A. J. de Lukacs-Lessner de Szeged

APPENDIX FIVE

The Chilianwala Colours

As related in Chapter VIII, the Regimental Colour brought out of action at Chilianwala by Private Perry remained in service with the 24th until it was replaced by a new Colour in June 1866. On 4th December 1868, this Colour, together with the Queen's Colour presented in 1849 to replace that lost at Chilianwala, were deposited in the Beauchamp Chapel of St Mary's Church, Warwick. At that date the Regiment still bore the title '2nd Warwickshire', so it seemed fitting that the Colours should be laid up in the county town – even though the Regiment itself had only slight connections with that county.

By 1881 the 24th had become The South Wales Borderers with its Depot at Brecon, and all tenuous links with Warwickshire were severed. In 1922 the Regimental Chapel was dedicated in the then Priory Church of Brecon, wherein all the 'retired' Colours, including the cherished Isandhlwana Colour and the Queen's Wreath of Immortelles, were laid up. But there was a sad omission. The equally cherished Regimental Colour which had faced the Sikh guns at Chilianwala was still at Warwick, as was the later Queen's Colour. It was not until 1925 that initial steps were taken to bring these revered relics to their rightful resting place in what had become Brecon Cathedral. The complex story of the eleven-year struggle with the church authorities of Warwick is revealed in a bulging file of 112 letters and numerous other documents preserved in the Museum of The South Wales Borderers at Brecon. The following is, necessarily, a résumé

The battle began in August 1925 when, at the instigation of the Colonel (General Sir Alexander Cobbe, VC), Major John Bradstock, commanding the Depot, approached the Vicar of Warwick, the Rev. Canon Wood. This elderly ecclesiastic was not only quite ignorant of military matters, but seemingly had scant regard for the sentiment attached to the Colours by the Regiment. Described by Bradstock as 'an obstructive old man', he flatly refused to part with what he maintained was the property of his Church. Although his superior, the Bishop of Coventry, took the Regimental view, and agreed that the laying-up of Colours in a church for 'safe custody' did not invalidate a regiment's rights to them, Canon Wood remained obdurate. Bradstock then sought legal opinion from a member of the King's Bench. In his letter of 14th November 1925, Maurice Healey, KC, declared that the Vicar of Warwick was totally wrong in his views: 'there is no doubt that a Regiment cannot surrender its Colours to anyone other than the King who gave the Colours, or the Country as represented by the King, Lords and Commons in Parliament assembled'. Although, he went on, 'it would be possible to obtain a declaration from the High Court that the Colours in question are the property of the Regiment, of course nobody wants it to come to that'. Healey's suggestion was that some of the senior officers might approach the King privately, so that 'a hint from that august quarter' could be conveyed to the Vicar, who would surely be amenable to the wishes of his sovereign.

There is now an unfortunate hiatus in the correspondence, so that we cannot tell whether the above suggestion was followed. But it seems unlikely, for 'the battle for the Colours' was joined again in 1934. By now Major General Morgan-Owen had succeeded to the Colonelcy and he was determined to renew the fight with all his energy. Having established that a precedent existed, with the removal of several of the Essex Regiment's Colours from various churches to their Regimental Chapel, he approached the Assistant Chaplain-General, the Rev. J. J. E. O'Malley, who agreed to intervene with the parochial authorities of Warwick. As O'Malley reported in his letter of 23rd November, he first met the Vicar, now the Rev. A. D. Henwood, who proved more sympathetic than his predecessor, and appeared willing to accede to the Regiment's wishes. But then followed discussions with three members of the Parochial Church Council, including the Mayor of Warwick and the Council's solicitor, all of whom 'were of an obstinate nature and determined to hold, at all costs, to what they have . . .'. Their objections were based on two mistaken views: that the Colours had been 'a gift' to the Church, and that The South Wales Borderers was 'quite separate and distinct' from the 24th Foot, 2nd Warwickshire Regiment. After unsuccessfully trying to educate them, O'Malley left without achieving his object.

Having been refused a meeting with the Church Council, General Morgan-Owen then enlisted the support of a friend who happened to be one of Warwick's distinguished parishioners, General J. G. Turner (retired). His response was to publish a lengthy letter in the local newspaper, disabusing the Church Council of their mistaken views and correcting other fallacious statements that had previously appeared – such as that the 2nd Warwickshire Regiment had been 'a second battalion' of the true Warwickshire Regiment (6th Foot). Turner's private letter to Morgan-Owen (13th May 1935) assured him that neither the people of Warwick nor the church congregation had any sentiment in the matter and 'not one in a thousand has even heard of the Colours'. Though the soldier – Sergeant Perry – who had retrieved the Regimental Colour at Chilianwala was a Warwick man and lay buried in the churchyard, so little interest had been taken in him that the grave was unmarked and no one could say where it was. Finally, as all were aware, The Royal Warwickshire Regiment disclaimed any right to the Colours and fully supported the 24th's case. Turner's opinion was that the Vicar himself would willingly surrender: it was only the 'obstinate, narrow-minded Church Council who refuse to budge'.

Morgan-Owen's next approach was to higher authority. In May he presented his case to the Bishop of Coventry, the Rt Rev. M. G. Haigh. Recently Chaplain to the King, this dignitary had served as a padre during World War I, and proved both understanding and helpful. He advised that the only solution to the problem was for the Regiment to petition for a 'Faculty', or official authorisation, to remove the Colours.

Major General Ll. I. G. Morgan Owen, CB, CMG, CBE, DSO, Colonel of the Regiment 1931–44.

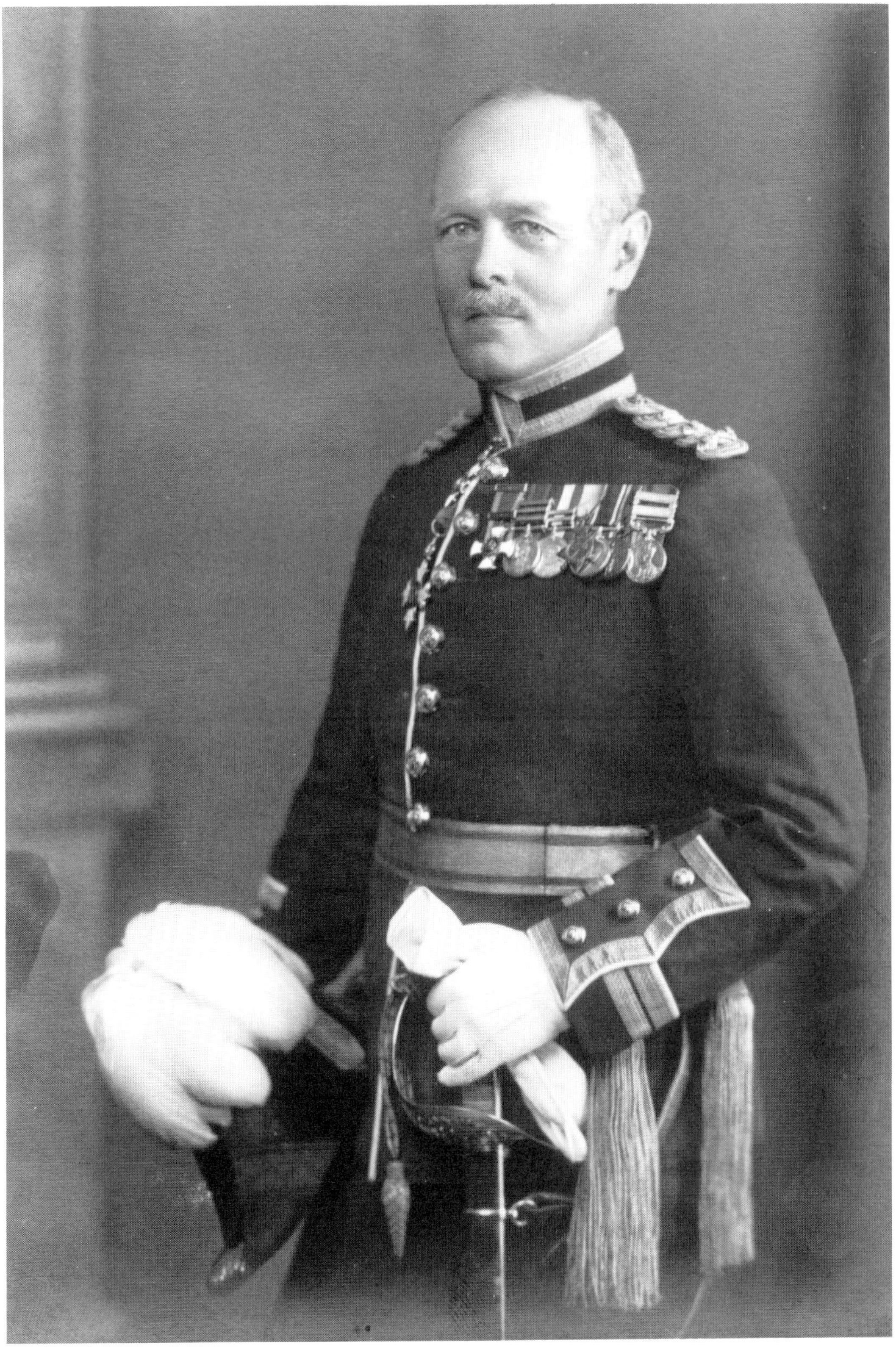

His Legal Secretary would co-operate in drawing up the Petition and forwarding it.

And so in November (1935) the Petition was duly prepared and placed before the Diocesan Chancellor. As foreseen, the Warwick opposition immediately lodged an objection. After the curious reasoning that 'the Petitioners have no status to petition for a Faculty since they are not parishioners,' the main plea was that the Colours had been the property of the then Colonel of the Regiment who 'gave them to the church in accordance with the desire expressed by the regiment'. It was also claimed that they formed 'an integral part' of the memorial to two officers of the 24th, which was also 'a gift to the church'.

Essentially, therefore, the point at issue was the question of whether, in 1868, the Colonel had merely deposited the Colours 'for safe custody', or whether, as the objectors claimed, he had handed them over as a gift, If so, had he any right to do so? There was then a flurry of correspondence between Morgan-Owen, the War Office and Mr C. T. Atkinson, who was just completing his history of the Regiment. From this it transpired that prior to 1855 Colours were usually presented by the Regimental Colonel, and were thus his property, to dispose of as he wished when replaced. This, of course, was exactly what the Warwick Church Council had claimed. But there were complications. Although both the Colours in question had been acquired prior to 1855, by 1868 Queen's Regulations had laid down that Colours were the property of the State, which paid for them, and they could only be presented by or on behalf of the sovereign. Further, they could not be surrendered or 'given' to any person or persons but the sovereign himself. Thus the Regiment's case was that if the 1868 Colonel (Major General Pringle Taylor) had intimated that he was handing over the Colours to St Mary's, Warwick, as a gift, he had no power or authority to do so, and such 'gift' was invalid.

The case 'Morgan-Owen v. Parochial Church Council of St Mary's Church, Warwick' was heard by the Diocesan Chancellor of Coventry in the Shire Hall, Warwick, on 6th May 1936. The full proceedings are no longer available, but the reasoned Petition was presented by General Morgan-Owen himself. In it he 'prayed', first, that The South Wales Borderers were the true, lineal descendants of the '24th or 2nd Warwickshire Regiment of Foot,' and had no connection with The Royal Warwickshire Regiment. The original Regiment had no link with the county of Warwick other than its subtitle, and at no time had they or the present Regiment established a Depot or permanent base in Warwickshire. He then disposed of the objectors' claim that the Colours had been presented to the Church as a gift. Finally he stressed that since 1873 the Regiment had been associated with Brecon, where its Depot was established in 1881. Its own Regmental Chapel had been dedicated in the Cathedral, and 'that sacred shrine of the Regiment' now housed all the old Colours and memorials of service. He went on:

> It is recognised that the sentimental association of the said Colours with Warwick for over 60 years is strong, and the fact that they have been housed by the Vicar and Churchwardens of the said Church for over 60 years is remembered with gratitude by the Regiment. The removal, however, of the

said Colours is not prayed for by reason of their sentimental value to the people of Brecon, but because of their value to the Regiment. It is considered that the said Colours have a greater sentimental value to the Regiment as a whole than to the people of Warwick ... The present members of the Regiment inherit the traditions of service and self-sacrifice passed on from men of the Regiment who had fought and died under the Colours of the Regiment from the year 1689 ... The said Colours, therefore, (which form an essential link in the succession) when hung with the other Colours of the Regiment in the Cathedral Church of Brecon will be a living symbol of such continuity, and will be a constant source of inspiration and incentive ...

Mr C. T. Atkinson also appeared and read a lengthy memorandum outlining the services of the Regiment since 1689, proving that The South Wales Borderers were the rightful inheritors of the Colours presented to the 24th (2nd Warwickshire) Regiment.

The objectors' response is not recorded, but on 4th June 1936, the Chancellor issued his judgement: he found in favour of the Regiment. And so, after a battle that had begun eleven years previously, the Chilianwala Colours were won back. But there was now another ecclesiastical hurdle to surmount. Before the Colours could be physically removed to Brecon Cathedral, approval for their deposit therein had to be sought from he Governing Body of the Church in Wales (although the Cathedral authorities had agreed). The Secretary was one Canon B. Davies, to whom Morgan-Owen wrote on 11th June. The Canon's curt, scribbled reply merely said that the matter would be brought up at the next meeting of the Governing Body. No date was revealed. An element of urgency now arose, for it was hoped that the Colours could be formally laid up at Brecon on 23rd August when a Regimental Reunion was being held. Moreover the Colours were in a poor state, and repairs were needed. There was no further response from Canon Davies by 8th July, so Morgan-Owen wrote again, informing him of the urgency. A six-line scrawl in reply stated that a meeting of the Governing Body was arranged for 24th July when the matter would be discussed. Meanwhile, the Colonel had received a note from the Vicar of St Mary's, Warwick, saying that 'the Colours cannot be released until the decision of the Governing Body of the Church in Wales is known'.

Despite further prodding, the Reverend Canon bided his time until the meeting of his Governing Body. Thus it was only on 27th July 1936 that Morgan-Owen received the following:

> The Vicarage,
> Wrexham.
>
> July 26th 1936
>
> Dear Sir,
> I am instructed by the Standing Committee of the Governing Body of the Church in Wales to say that the Governing Body is

prepared to receive and accept for the Regimental Chapel in Brecon Cathedral the Colours of the South Wales Borderers which are now at St. Mary's Church, Warwick.

Yours faithfully,
(Sd) *B. Davies*
Hon. Secretary

There must then have followed some creditable industry on the part of The Royal School of Needlework, for the Colours were 'preserved' (at a cost of 12 guineas) and handed over to the Depot at Brecon ready for the ceremony on 23rd August.

The laying-up of the Colours on that date is fully described in the issue of *XXIV The Journal of The South Wales Borderers* for October 1936. Here a summary must suffice. Fittingly, the detachments of the Regiment were commanded by General Morgan-Owen. The Queen's Colour was borne by Lieutenant A. G. D. Home and the Regimental – the actual Chilianwala Colour – by Lieutenant W. R. D. Vernon-Harcourt. After being escorted from the Barracks through the crowded Brecon streets, the Colours were received in the Cathedral by the Bishop of Swansea and Brecon (The Rt Rev. John Morgan) who declared: 'I receive these Colours for safe custody within the Cathedral walls. They shall be placed in the Memorial Chapel set aside for your Regiment.' He then laid the Colours on the Chapel altar.

Later the two Colours were hung where they can be seen today, to the left of the altar and almost opposite the Isandhlwana Colours and the Queen's Wreath of Immortelles.

It is scarcely necessary to add that it was entirely due to the determined, untiring efforts of Major General Llewellin Morgen-Owen that the hallowed relics of the Battle of Chilianwala came at last to their rightful resting place.

APPENDIX SIX

Regimental Music
1. *The Bands*

From the earliest days of the Standing Army, and indeed long before, the footslogging infantryman's marching was enlivened by the regiment's drummers and fifers. These were enlisted soldiers and twelve were allowed on the establishment. But until the formation of The Royal Military School of Music at Kneller Hall in 1857, there was no such establishment for regimental bands, although all regiments had acquired them by the 18th century. These early Bands were in fact very much *ad hoc* ensembles, entirely dependent on the officers for their funding, while the 'Master' was invariably a hired civilian musician, often German or Italian.

The authorities at Horse Guards (later War Office) took no account of these unofficial Bands, apart from occasionally noting that 'the Regt. has a band of Musick' in the periodic Inspection Returns. But when it became apparent that soldiers were being co-opted from the ranks to be trained as musicians, Horse Guards issued a series of mandatory restrictions. In 1803 a battalion Band was allowed one private soldier from each company, plus one NCO as 'Master'. Some niggardly increases followed: by 1846 the permitted establishment had risen to twenty players with a 'Sergeant Master' in charge. This NCO was really equivalent to the later Band Sergeant, responsible chiefly for discipline and turnout; all musical matters were still in the hands of the civilian 'Master', while all expenses were still met by the regiment (or battalion). Neither the Master nor the sergeant had any authority over the drummers, who were a quite separate 'corps' under their Drum Major.

In view of the unorganised (in fact, disordered) state of Army music in the 18th and early 19th centuries, it is hardly surprising that information about the Bands of The Royal Regiment of Wales's predecessors during that period is sadly lacking.

For the 24th Regiment the earliest reference appears in the MS Regimental Records for 16th May 1771 with the usual laconic statement 'the regiment has a band of Musick'. In 1801, however, we learn that it consisted of eleven bandsmen, two fifers and a drummer – the youngest member being aged 11 years, the oldest 50 with thirty-six years' service. In 1792 an Inspection Return for the 41st Regiment showed seventeen musicians (generous for the period), with twelve drummers. In the same year the 69th were reported to have only nine bandsmen – but the usual twelve drummers. The periodic issues of Regimental Standing Orders lay down explicit instructions for the sergeant in charge ('. . . he must be attentive to the Dress, Behaviour and Morals of the Musicians . . .'), but there is seldom any reference to the Bandmaster himself: being a civilian he was not subject to military discipline. One imagines that this must often have been the source of friction between him and the sergeant – and the Commanding Officer.

The later term 'military band' was (and is) applied to an ensemble of both brass and woodwind instruments, as opposed to the 'brass band' (with no woodwind). This description arose because from the earliest days of military music, regimental bands always included woodwinds with their brass. Thus in 1792 the instrumentation of the 69th's Band was given as one trumpet, two horns, two clarinets and two bassoons – and that curious wooden bass instrument, the serpent. At this date both trumpets and horns (or 'French' horns) were valveless and so had only limited melodic scope. Unusually, no hautboys are mentioned. These precursors of the modern oboe generally figured largely in 18th-century bands.

The bands were expected to accompany the regiments wherever they went, on active service or no, and there is plenty of evidence to show that they did (though without their civilian Masters). At least one bandsman is reported to have been present on a man-o'-war with the 69th at the Battle of St Vincent in 1797. The Band of the 2nd/24th served throughout the Battalion's campaigning in the Peninsula (1809–14), when they not only acted as stretcher-bearers, but gave performances when occasion demanded. In his *Recollections of a Peninsular Veteran* (1913), Lieutenant Colonel Joseph Anderson relates that at Santarem the nuns of a convent sent gifts of fruit and cakes to the officers billeted nearby, '. . . and in return for all these favours we sent our band to play under the convent walls every other evening'. Quite an experience for both parties. One hopes that the Band had a suitable selection in their repertoire.

In 1854 the bandsmen of the 41st were under fire as stretcher-bearers at the Battle of the Alma and Inkermann. In the Kaffir War of 1877–8 the Band of the 1st/24th performed not with instruments or stretchers, but with ordnance. Having been drilled as artillerymen, they employed their 7-pounder guns to good effect with the newly-arrived 2nd/24th in the final stages of the campaign. Sadly, a year later the same Band were slaughtered at Isandhlwana, while the 2nd Battalion's Band lost several members, including their Bandmaster, H. T. Bullard. By this time Bandmasters were enlisted soldiers, qualified at Kneller Hall and ranking as staff sergeants. It was not until 1881 that Warrant rank was granted. Until 1873 bandsmen's uniforms were distinguished by a reversal of the colours of those of the rest of the regiment. Thus, if the latter wore red tunics with green facings (as in the 24th), the Band had green tunics with red facings. At the above date this practice was discontinued and bandsmen were attired like their rank-and-file comrades.

During the Boer War of 1899–1902 most Bands accompanied their regiments, as did those of 2 SWB and 1 Welch. The Great War was the last in which Bands as such went on active service: some as stretcher-bearers, others as runners and orderlies.

Among distinguished Bandmasters of the Regiments, the O'Donnells, father and sons, were especially noteworthy. Mr Patrick O'Donnel qualified at Kneller Hall in 1884 and was posted to 2 SWB, with whom he served until 1905. He had three sons, all of whom enlisted as bandsmen in the Regiment and then went on to become Directors of Music Royal Marines.[1] P. S. G. O'Donnell served in the Chatham Division, R. P. O'Donnell in the Portsmouth and B. Walton O'Donnell at Plymouth. All three were awarded the MVO. The last-named later achieved wide recognition as Director of the BBC Military Band. Another, who gained celebrity as a composer of light music, was

Charles Ancliffe (1 SWB, 1900–18) whose waltz 'Nights of Gladness' was a popular 'hit' of the 1920s and is still performed. Ancliffe was also distinguished by being the youngest Bandmaster ever to be appointed in the Army – at the age of 20. In 1932, 1934 and 1935 the Band of 2 SWB gained the distinction of an 'Outstanding' report from the annual Kneller Hall Inspection, a record believed to be unique. This was largely due to the efforts of Mr G. H. Willcocks (1926–37), who was later appointed Director of Music Irish Guards.

An old Band Sergeant of the 1st/24th, from 1869 to 1878, was Harry Rattray who, having escaped the Isandhlwana debacle through retirement, lived to become the oldest Chelsea Pensioner of the Regiment at the age of 102 – only to be killed by Hitler's Luftwaffe in 1941.

Kneller Hall and Regimental Records show the following Bandmasters serving with the 24th, 41st, 69th and Royal Regiment of Wales.

24th Regiment of Foot (later The South Wales Borderers)

1st Battalion		2nd Battalion	
J. McBride	1793–1802	P. Waters	1865–78
J. Clarke	1863–9	H. Bullard	1878–9
H. A. Rattray	1869–78	R. Goodings	1879–84
G. Tamplini	1878–82	A. Preece	1884
G. C. Burck	1882–9	P. O'Donnell	1884–1905
J. A. Caborn	1889–1900	F. Ripp	1905–6
C. W. Ancliffe	1900–18	J. C. Roberts	1906–15
T. Taylor	1918–22	H. Fenner	1915–23
J. L. Gecks	1922–34	D. J. Plater	1923–26
C. Eldicott	1934–41	G. H. Willocks	1926–37
W. J. Hickman	1946–55	S. V. Hays	1937–46
O. R. Whiting	1955–69		

41st (The Welch) Regiment of Infantry (later 1 Welch)

T. McArdle	1862–72	T. Clegg, ARCM	1941–51
Sam Rolandson	1872–95	G. W. Bennett, ARCM	1951–2
J. W. Monk	1895–1909	R. A. Verrall	1952–8
A. E. Shaw	1909–30	T. A. Kenny, ARCM	1958–65
F. J. Davidson	1930–9	D. Dawson, ARCM	1965–9
T. G. Dought, ARCM	1939–41		

69th (South Lincolnshire) Regiment (later 2 Welch)

W. C. Lamont	1863–73	C. L. P. Ward	1920–33
T. Barley	1874–86	T. G. Dought, ARCM	1933–9
A. Shackleford	1886–1910	F. J. Davidson	1939–48
K. S. Glover, LRAM	1910–20		

The Royal Regiment of Wales (24th/41st Foot)

D. Dawson, ARCM	1969–73	A. O'Connor	1981–5
J. G. Lewis, LRAM, LTCL, A(Mus)LCM, BBCM	1973–80	P. D. Shannon, LRAM, ARCM	1985–
M. Pegram, ARCM	1980–1		

In 1988 the Band of 1 RRW mustered the official establishment of twenty-one musicians, including the Band Sergeant Major, plus the Bandmaster (WO1). Strangely enough, although a Drum Major is allowed, there is no longer any establishment for a Corps of Drums in an infantry battalion.

The Drums Platoon, as it is termed, is therefore made up of eighteen NCOs and privates taken from the three mechanised companies. The Platoon is 'double-hatted' – that is, in addition to their acquired skills on drums, bugles and fifes, the men are fully trained to operate as machine-gunners with the GPMG, and form a Sustained Fire Platoon which is deployed among the companies on exercises, and, of course, in the event of war.

The wartime role of the bandsmen is solely that of medical assistants, for which they undergo frequent training. This does not apply to the Bandmaster, who would not accompany the Battalion on active service.

The instrumentation of 1 RRW Band in 1988 was as under:

Flute/Piccolo	1
B flat Clarinet	3
E flat Alto Saxophone	1
B flat Tenor Saxophone	1
Horn	2
B flat Cornet	5
Tenor Trombone	3
Bass Trombone	1
Euphonium	1
Bass	2
Percussion	1
Total	21

In the recent years Westminster has tended to regard military music as an unnecessary luxury: witness the abolition of the centuries-old Royal Military Academy Sandhurst Band Corps and the proposed closure of that alma mater of Army musicians, Kneller Hall. In this climate it is hardly surprising that the Territorial Army is not generously established for Bands. In fact, The Royal Regiment of Wales is permitted only one Band for its Territorial battalions, and that is maintained by the 3rd (Volunteer) Battalion at Cardiff. Since this ensemble is the only official Territorial Band in Wales, it is allowed a more generous establishment than usual, of thirty-six performers in addition to the Bandmaster.

From what has just been said, it will be obvious that the 4th (Volunteer) Battalion of The Royal Regiment of Wales is not entitled to parade any musicians. But such is the 'volunteer' spirit that the Battalion has created what is known as the 'Band Club'. This consists of musically-inclined soldiers who give up their time voluntarily to form what is acknowledged to be a very professional Regimental Band, for both parade and concert duties. Most of the bandsmen provide their own instruments; uniforms are purchased out of fees for private engatements, of which there are many in the Swansea area.

2. *Regimental Marches*

It is impossible to say when regiments first adopted some melody as their own distinctive March, to be accorded almost the same veneration as the National Anthem. Many such Marches have been taken from traditional songs, such as 'Lilliburlero'; from the world of opera, such as 'Daughter of the Regiment'; or even from the enemy, such as 'Ça Ira'.

It was only in 1882 that War Office approval was given to the Quick Marches of the infantry, and this came to pass in a curious fashion. Prior to the 1870s, on big ceremonial parades of brigades or larger formations, each regiment was played past the saluting base by its own Band. But then arose the practice of massing the Bands, so that it became necessary for all to be able to play each others' Marches. Accordingly, in order that the scores could be available at short notice, every regiment was ordered to submit its March to Kneller Hall for approval and subsequent publication. This took time, for some were considered 'unsuitable' and alternatives had to be offered. Thus it was not until February 1882 that War Office finally approved, and all the Marches were then printed and issued on the handy little 'March Cards' still in use today.

No account was taken of any Slow Marches that infantry regiments might have owned, for, of course, infantry always marched past in quick time (the reverse applied in the cavalry, whose Slow Marches were authorised in 1903).

The following are the Regimental Marches of The Royal Regiment of Wales:

Men of Harlech (Quick March)
This well-known Welsh ballad had previously been the Quick March of The South Wales Borderers from 1881, and (with altered tempo) was also the Slow March of The Welch Regiment. As with so many venerable tunes, its composer is unknown. It first appeared in print in 1794 when it was included in the *Musical and Poetical Relics of the Welsh Bards*, compiled by the celebrated Welsh harpist, Edward Jones. It may seem paradoxical that two South Wales regiments should select an essentially North Wales melody, while their North Wales counterpart, The Royal Welch Fusiliers, should prefer a South Wales one for their Slow March ('War March of the Men of Glamorgan')!

Scipio (Slow March)
Shared with The Grenadier Guards, this was adopted on amalgamation in 1969. It is a setting of the *maestoso* march which opens the first act of Handel's opera *Scipione*, first performed in 1726. There is a tradition that Handel originally composed it specifically for the Grenadiers, and only later incorporated it in the opera to bolster what is acknowledged as a very dull score.

Prior to 1881 the 24th Regiment's subtitle was '2nd Warwickshire', so the song 'The Warwickshire Lads' was an obvious choice for their Quick March, probably adopted in 1782 when the Regiment was thus designated. Equally obvious, it was also the quickstep of the 'true' Warwickshire Regiment (6th Foot). It was written by the prolific composer and dramatist, Charles Dibdin, for the Shakespeare Jubilee at Stratford-upon-Avon in 1769.

As noted above, The Welch Regiment's Slow March was a version of 'Men of Harlech'. Their Quick March was the equally well known *'Ap Shenkin'* (strictly '... *Siencin*'), though there is no record of when this was adopted. The song was written about 1803 by John Parry of Denbigh (another North Wales choice!), who served for a time as Bandmaster of the Denbighshire Militia, and went on to become composer of light music in London and music critic of *The Morning Post*. He conducted several eisteddfodau, including one at Brecon in 1822, and was given the title 'Bardd Alaw' (Master of Melody).

'Ap Shenkin' was also the Quick March of The Monmouthshire Regiment ('Part of the Corps of The South Wales Borderers'). It is still frequently played as The Royal Regiment of Wales's 'second' Quick March.

Before the creation of The Welch Regiment by the merger of the 41st and 69th in 1881, the latter had been known as 'South Lincolnshire'. Inevitably, their Quick March was 'The Lincolnshire Poacher', of which all one can say is, it was a very popular ditty and dance tune in the 18th century. It was also, of course, the Quick March of The Lincolnshire Regiment (10th).

Although never attaining the status of a Regimental March, the well-known melody 'God Bless the Prince of Wales' has long been among the repertoire of 'regimental music'. It is performed on certain ceremonial functions and in the St David's Day ceremonies. The song was composed in 1862 by the Carmarthen-born Henry Brinley Richards (1817–85), and immediately achieved extraordinary popularity throughout the country. The then Prince of Wales succeeded his mother Queen Victoria as King Edward VII. The music was adopted by several 'Prince of Wales's' regiments as their Quick or Slow March, among them being The Carabiniers (6DG) and 12th Royal Lancers, and of course the present regiment, The Prince of Wales's Own Regiment of Yorkshire.

Notes

[1] In 1898 Queen Victoria approved that Directors of Music (i.e. Bandmasters of Guards and Corps) should be granted commissions as Lieutenants.

APPENDIX SEVEN

Regimental Customs, Traditions and Affiliations
1. *The Goat Mascot*

Regiments of the British Army have always been prone to adopt some member of the animal world as their mascot: bears, apes, dogs, geese, ponies and rams, are just a few that have graced ceremonial parades. Only two Regiments parade goats – The Royal Welch Fusiliers and The Royal Regiment of Wales.

The wild goat was once common among the mountains of Wales, and while it did not quite achieve the status of that other beast, the dragon, as a national emblem, it was nevertheless regarded as typical of Welsh wildlife. Thus it was natural that our two Welsh Regiments should take it as their mascot. The Royal Welch Fusiliers claim that they were parading a goat as early as 1777, if not earlier, but the origins of The Royal Regiment of Wales's counterpart are undoubtedly much later, even though there has always been dispute about the exact period.

It is, however, undisputed that the custom arose in the 41st Foot, or The Welch Regiment. One story goes that while that Regiment was serving in the 1st Afghan War of 1842 they adopted one of the tribesmen's goats as a pet, and it marched with them to Kabul. But there is not a shred of evidence to support this assertion. We are on much firmer ground when we reach the Crimean War of 1854–6 in which the 41st were engaged. Indefatigable researching by Lieutenant Bryn Owen, RN, Curator of The Welch Regiment Museum, unearthed a photograph, probably one of Roger Fenton's (the earliest official war photographer), showing a group of 41st officers posing outside their Mess hut at Sebastopol in the winter of 1855–6. In front of the group a goat kneels to consume some offering from a bowl. There are two stories about how this 'Russian goat' was acquired. The first says that it was picked up by a Sergeant Major and brought home with the 41st to Aldershot, where it was paraded before Queen Victoria (committing *lèse-majesté* by butting her). The second, more romantic, alleges that one of the Irish soldiers acquired a small goat kid with which he intended to supplement his meagre rations. He was on sentry duty at the time and tucked the live kid under his greatcoat. During the night he fell asleep, to be suddenly awakened by the agitated bleating of the animal. As he came to, he espied a Russian patrol advancing and was able to warn the forward picquet, who drove off the enemy. Thus, like the Roman geese, the goat had averted disaster. Later, when the Adjutant inspected the animal he enquired whether it was a billy or a nanny. 'Sorr, he be a he', replied the Irishman, whereupon the Adjutant ordered that it should be kept as a pet, and named 'Hebe'. In the 1920s a battered and faded old painting of a goat was discovered among some rubbish in the Museum store at Maindy Barracks, Cardiff. On the back someone had scribbled

Lieutenant J. E. Goodwyn, officers of the 41st Regiment and the first Regimental goat mascot; Sebastopol, 1855.

REPRODUCED BY GRACIOUS PERMISSION OF HER MAJESTY THE QUEEN

'Hebe'. An old lithograph depicting the 41st camp at Dover Heights in 1857 clearly shows a goat. Whether all these are one and the same animal is problematical: the goat shown in the photograph at Sebastopol could scarcely be the Irish soldier's kid, Hebe, for it is obviously fully grown, and not even the burliest Irishman could have concealed it under his greatcoat.

While it seems most probable that The Welch Regiment's original goat mascot was certainly acquired in the Crimea, the whole question is further confused by three silver teapots formerly held in the Officers' Mess and now in the Museum at Cardiff. The earliest, dating from 1846, is crowned with a statue of a small *couchant* goat; the next (1847) has a larger specimen; and the third, presented to the Mess in 1848, is adorned with a very fine animal indeed, with lengthy horns. Obviously, the goat appears to have become a Regimental emblem, if not mascot, long before the Crimea, which might lend credence to the Afghan theory.

At all events, the first goat to be officially recorded was that presented by Queen Victoria from her royal herd at Windsor around 1860. He was known as Billy. The next was a singularly intelligent animal presented by the Sultan of Lahej when the Regiment was serving in Aden in 1874. Not only did he kneel when the National Anthem was played, but he actually marched by himself, unled by Goat Major, on ceremonial parades and on Battalion route marches.

Queen Victoria had set the precedent of presenting the goat mascots from the Windsor royal herd, and this was followed by her successors until the herd was dispersed, the remnants being sent to Regent's Park Zoo. However, when the Regiment was overseas, replacements were obtained from local sources (as in Aden).

The 69th Regiment had no official mascot, but on becoming the 2nd Battalion The Welch Regiment in 1881 they quickly adopted their senior partner's custom. Their first Taffy was presented by the Queen in 1889, only to die the following year, when it was replaced by another from the same august source. One of the 2nd Battalion's most imposing goats was acquired while they were serving on the North West Frontier in 1899. Presented by the Amir of Tirah (a district of Chitral), it was of a splendid Himalayan species with long silken coat, and when persuaded to stand on its hind legs it stood taller than the 6-ft tall Goat Major.

In 1906 2 Welch were joined by Taffy IV (actually the fifth), presented by King Edward VII. He was the only goat of either Battalion to see active service in World War I, accompanying 2 Welch in the Retreat from Mons and at the Battles of Ypres, Gheluvelt, Festubert and Givenchy. At the latter place, in 1915, he died and was buried there, but his horns were removed and are now preserved in the Regimental Museum at Cardiff.

In 1924 2 Welch were stationed at Colchester, and in March their Band and Drums, led, of course, by Taffy VI, were required to 'play in' to the cavalry barracks the 3rd/6th Dragoon Guards, just arrived from India. Now this Regiment had only recently been amalgamated and still retained both previous cap badges, that of the 3rd's being the Prince of Wales's Plumes – which, of course, also figured in The Welch's badge and on Taffy's ceremonial coat. Thus when the populace beheld the arrival of a cavalry regiment led by a goat bearing the Regimental badge, some mistaken conclusions were drawn. Next day the local Press came out with the headline 'Dragoon Guards Get Their Goat'. Commenting on this episode the historian of the (later) 3rd Carabiniers remarks: 'It was perhaps a little odd of the Welch to parade their goat at the head of another regiment, but it was no doubt intended as a compliment.'

The last of the 2 Welch goats was acquired in an unusual fashion. When his predecessor died, in 1933, the Battalion was serving in India, in the Murree Hills (foothills of the Himalayas), and as by then the home authorities had dictated that goats from UK sources should not be subjected to the Indian climate, a local replacement had to be found. The word was spread throughout the bazaars that the *Gora Paltan* ('White Battalion') was in need of a goat. In due course an aged tribesman trudged into the lines leading a large, shaggy white goat. The two had walked for many days over the mountains from their home in the state of Punch ('Poonch') after hearing the bazaar rumours. The goat seemed to be a fine specimen of the mountain breed, with twisted horns, and when he was groomed and spruced 'Taffy of Poonch' (or Goat No. 8) proved a worthy successor to the departed one. After serving at Agra and Landi Kotal

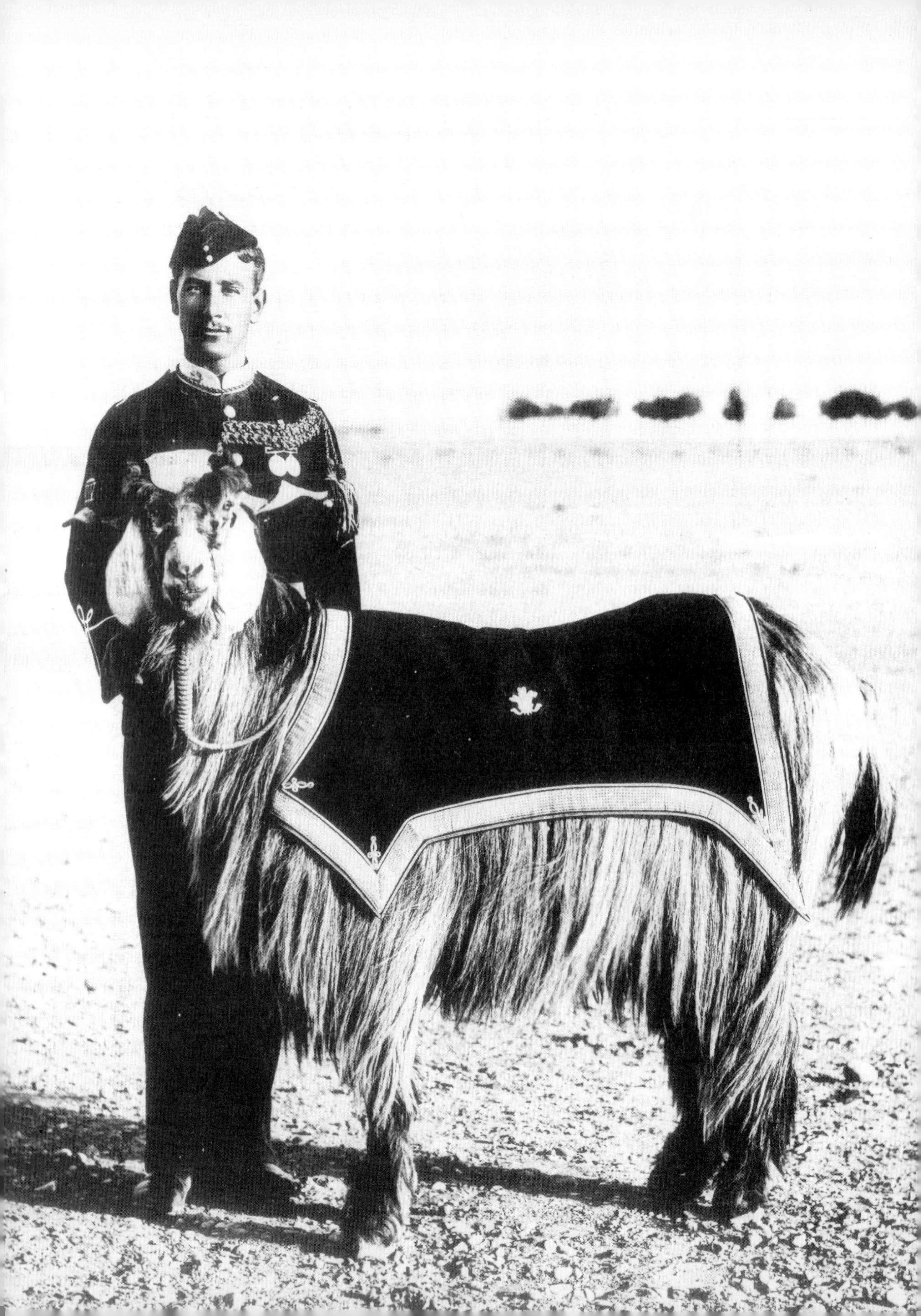

he died in February 1939. This was the eve of war and there was no replacement before 2 Welch were disbanded in 1948.

The last goat to be received from the Royal herd was Taffy VI of the 1st Battalion, presented by King George V in 1933. After that the animals came from the London Zoo for the home-based Battalion or from local sources for their overseas partner.

On 11th June 1969 the last goat mascot of the 1st Battalion The Welch Regiment led his Battalion on to the parade ground at Cardiff Castle for the amalgamation with The South Wales Borderers. During the ceremony his scarlet coat was replaced by one of green and he became Taffy I of The Royal Regiment of Wales.

Since the earliest days of the Regimental goat mascots it has been traditional for the

LEFT: *Taffy, the massive goat mascot of the 2nd Battalion The Welch Regiment, 1899–1905; obtained by Captain A. G. Prothero from the Emir of Tirah as a gift to the Battalion.*

BELOW: *Taffy IV, goat mascot of the 2nd Battalion The Welch Regiment, 1906–15. A royal goat, it saw service with the Battalion in India, South Africa and the United Kingdom. In August 1914 it embarked with the Battalion for France, and saw active service during the Retreat from Mons, the Battle of the Aisne and the 1st Battle of Ypres. It died and was buried at Bethune in 1915 – a loss greatly felt by the few remaining survivors of the old pre-World War I Battalion.*

animal to be cared for by a member of the Drums (usually a corporal or lance-corporal), known as the Goat Major. He is entirely responsible for all the duties of feeding, watering, exercising, grooming and, of course, instilling the necessary parade discipline into a young entry. As NCO in charge of the Drums, the Drum Major bears overall responsibility for the mascot.

Although the above has dealt only with regular battalions, the Territorials also have their goat mascots. In 3 (V) RRW he has traditionally been named Dewi (David), and in 4 (V) RRW, Sospan. The latter is taken from the popular Welsh ditty *'Sospan Fach'* (Little Saucepan) which was, and is, in great vogue among Rugby clubs in South Wales, particularly in Llanelli, former home of 4 RRW.

There is no record of the 24th Regiment, or The South Wales Borderers, ever having acquired an 'official' mascot, goat or otherwise.

2. *The Leek*

Like the goat and the dragon, the leek has long been symbolic of Wales; indeed when the Welsh Guards were raised in 1915 this humble vegetable was adopted as their badge. It had been worn much earlier, however: by the Royal Carmarthen Fusiliers Militia between 1808–16, by the London Welsh Rifle Volunteers in the 1850s and by The Welsh Horse (Yeomanry) 1914. Between 1844 and 1855 it even figured on the officers' shako plate of the 41st (Welch) Regiment.

There are conflicting theories about the origin of the leek as a Welsh emblem. The earliest claims that it stems from Cadwallader's victory over the Saxons in the 7th century, when his Celtic warriors wore leeks as distinguishing badges. Possibly the best known story is that referred to by Shakespeare in *Henry V*, Act IV, when Fluellen, the Welsh Captain, reminds the King of Crècy, where 'Welshmen did good service... wearing leeks in their Monmouth caps'. The King replies that he too wears the leek 'for a memorable honour'. Whatever the true origins, the wearing of the leek by Welshmen on St David's Day was well established by the 16th century.

All this refers only to the *wearing* of the leek: the custom of consuming it is another matter, about which there is little to go on. While The Royal Welch Fusiliers boast that their Leek Eating Ceremony dates back nearly 300 years, there is no firm evidence that anything similar was practised in The Welch Regiment until after World War I. It was then kept up every year on St David's Day (1st March), military commitments permitting, and has been inherited by The Royal Regiment of Wales.

The ceremony, in the Officers' Mess, differs slightly among the three Battalions, but that of the 1st Battalion may be taken as standard practice.

THE LEEK EATING CEREMONY
1. The President, normally the senior subaltern, makes a short (and not too serious) speech explaining the significance of St David and the leek.

A SELECTION OF REGIMENTAL SILVER

Centrepiece – ex-SWB.

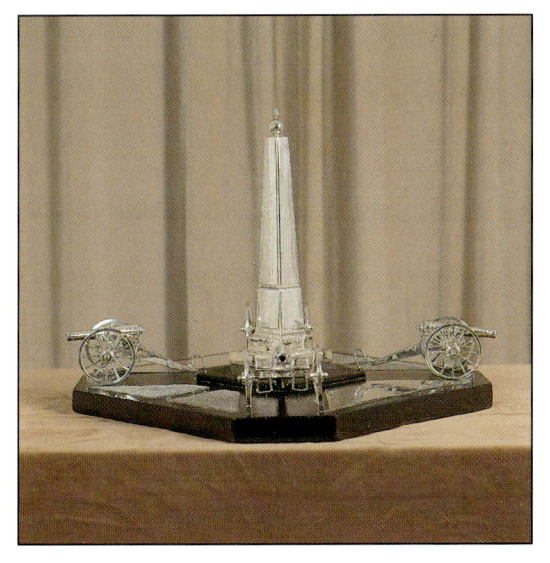

Centrepiece – ex-Welch.

The Chilianwala memorial, Chelsea Hospital – ex-SWB.

Regimental silver drums.

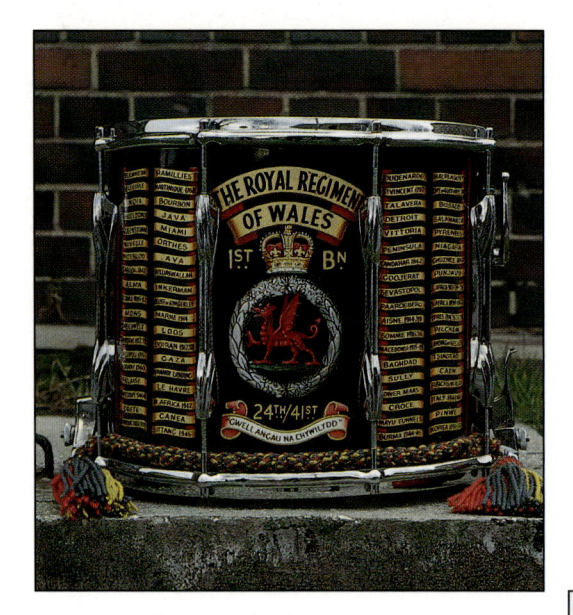

Regimental issue side drum.

The Regimental Association Service Medal is awarded to members of the Regiment Association for "Valuable and Meritorious Service" to Regimental Comrades. It was first awarded in 1986.

3rd Battalion; the "Druid" recites the history of the leek.

2. The President signals for the following to march into the Dining Room, while the Band plays 'Men of Harlech':

>Taffy and the Goat Major
>The Drum-Major bearing a silver salver of leeks.
>The Mess Sergeant carrying a tray of silver goblets filled with beer.
>Two drummers.

(All the above are in Full Dress, Taffy in his ceremonial coat.)

3. The President calls upon serving members of the Battalion who are leek-eating 'virgins' to undergo the necessary transmutation. Commencing with the most junior, he calls up each officer in turn. The officer stands upon his chair and places his right foot on the table. The Drum-Major then hands him a leek. Holding the leek in his right hand, the officer lifts

up his voice in song (or as near as he can get to it). He must sing at least one verse of his chosen *opus*, with a chorus, in which, he hopes, he will be assisted by the assembled company. This ordeal over, he devours the leek as quickly as possible, without taking it from his lips. As he does so the drummers beat a roll. Next, the Drum-Major hands up a goblet of beer. The officer raises it in his right hand with the toast '*A Dewi Sant*' (To St David), while another drum roll is beaten. He then consumes the beer in one draught and resumes his seat. Should there be a large number of leek-eating 'virgins', the President may select a group to perform the ceremony simultaneously, all singing the same ditty.

4. Officers attached to the Battalion are then invited to eat the leek. Needless to say, it is very bad form to decline the invitation.

5. When all serving officers have qualified as leek eaters, guests are encouraged to perform. They need sing only one verse of a song (with or without chorus) and will do so collectively.

6. At the conclusion of the leek eating, the Drum-Major, Taffy and drummers march out while the Band plays 'God Bless the Prince of Wales'.

7. The names of all officers who have qualified as leek eaters are inscribed in the Leek Eating Book, preserved in the Mess.

A very similar ceremony is conducted in the Warrant Officers' and Sergeants' Mess on St David's Day, and another ceremony is performed for the youngest soldiers of each company in their Dining Hall.

3. *The Vesper Hymns*

The custom of playing what are known as three Vesper Hymns after First Post (2130 hours) on Sundays arose in The Welch Regiment, but as with so many other customs, the origin is obscure. It has been suggested that it dates from the Crimea, but evidence is entirely lacking. The hymns are 'Sun of My Soul', 'Spanish Chant' and 'Vesper Hymn'. The first-named appeared in *Katholisches Gesangbuch* (Catholic Songbook), published in Vienna, c. 1775. The origin of 'Spanish Chant' is unknown, though it appears under different titles in hymnals dating from the 1820s. 'Vesper Hymn' is said to originate from the Russian Orthodox Church, but it has appeared in several English hymnals, the most familiar being the version composed by Sir John Stevenson of Dublin in 1818, and set to the words of Thomas Moore: 'Hark, the Vesper Hymn is stealing . . .'.

Until well into the present century the hymns were regularly performed by the Band on Sunday evenings immediately after the duty bugler had sounded First Post. But with the demise of routine bugle calls by 1939, the custom fell into abeyance. In

1963 the Colonel of The Welch (General Sir Cyril Coleman) expressed his concern about the lapse of old customs and was determined that the playing of the Vesper Hymns should be revived, if only on certain occasions. As he recorded in *The Men of Harlech* for October 1963, he therefore gave authority for the Band of the 1st Battalion to play the three hymns: '(1) At the Officers' Dinner Night in Mess just before the Band plays off. (2) Whenever the Battalion is on parade for a Commanding Officer's Drill or Ceremonial Parade... This Ceremony will take place at the start of the parade immediately after the Officers have fallen in. The Battalion will stand to attention.'

With the passage of the years this ancient custom became entirely subject to the whims of Commanding Officers. It has not been performed by 1 RRW for the past ten years.

4. *Regimental Anniversaries*

St David's Day (1st March)
Naturally, in a Welsh regiment, this 'Day' takes precedence over all others. Military duties permitting, the programme in 1 RRW is usually as under:

0700 hours	'Gunfire' served to the soldiers by the Commanding Officer and his company commanders.
0900	Battalion parades for presentation of leeks (worn, not eaten).
1000–1100	Visit to companies by Colonel of Regiment, Commanding Officer (or Colonel in Chief if visiting).
12 noon	Colours escorted to soldiers' Dining Hall (now known as Regimental Restaurant).
1215	Soldiers' Leek Eating Ceremony in Dining Hall.
1230	Colonel of Regiment or Commanding Officer gives address to Battalion.
Afternoon	Sport. Seven-a-Side Rugby match.
Evening	Guest Night in Officers' Mess, with Leek Eating Ceremony (see above). Party in Warrant Officers' and Sergeants' Mess, with similar ceremony.

Rorke's Drift (22nd January)
Soldiers are given a guided tour and explanation of the Colours and silver in the Officers' Mess. Very often, depending on commitments, there will be functions such as 'Ladies Night' and balls in the Officers' Mess and parties in the Warrant Officers' and Sergeants' Mess.

Gheluvelt Day (31st October)
After that fateful day in 1914 when 1 SWB and 2 Welch were virtually destroyed, the remnants saved by the intervention of 2 Worcesters, it became customary for The South

Wales Borderers and The Worcesters to exchange greetings telegrams on each anniversary of the action. Today The Royal Regiment of Wales sends greetings (by post) to The Worcestershire and Sherwood Foresters Regiment, who reciprocate in like manner.

5. *Officers' Badges of Rank*

The Eversleigh Star and Large Crown
From about 1890 officers of The South Wales Borderers took to wearing a distinctive, and unique pattern of 'Eversleigh' Star and large (Edward) Crown on their badges of rank. These remained unique until about 1928, when with the approval of the 24th, the Middlesex Regiment adopted the same design. The practice continued with their descendents, so that today only The Queen's Regiment and The Royal Regiment of Wales wear the Eversleigh Star and Crown, though The Royal Regiment of Wales wears the 'staybright' or polished type.

Despite extensive research by previous and present Regiments, the origin of this custom is shrouded in mystery: even the identity of 'Eversleigh' is unknown, and we do not know why or exactly when these distinctive designs came into being. However, what is certain – and somewhat surprising – is that the wearing of these rank badges remained quite unofficial and unauthorised for some sixty years. It was only in 1956 that the matter came to the notice of the (then) War Office Dress Committee, and the Colonel of The South Wales Borderers, Major General F. R. Matthews, was asked to

The Eversleigh Star.

justify this departure from Dress Regulations. Although he could find no chapter and verse in the Regiment's archives, he was able to plead 'long-established custom' to such good effect that on 11th July 1956 the War Office Dress Committee gave official approval to 'the wearing of the Eversleigh Star and of a larger Crown than the standard pattern'. A follow-up to this letter, dated 17th August, cautioned that 'this measure is NOT to be at public expense'; in other words, the officers must pay for their distinction. They continued to do so until 1988, when a generous MOD sanctioned free issue.

It should be added that there has been some confusion about the spelling of the name 'Eversleigh'. Owing to the fact that the 's' was always silent, the word often appears as 'Everleigh'.

6. Affiliated Regiments

It has long been the custom for regular regiments of the British Army to form alliances with counterparts in the armed forces of the Empire or Commonwealth. Formerly The South Wales Borderers enjoyed alliance with the Rhodesian African Rifles and The Welch Regiment with 4th Battalion The Baluch Regiment of the Pakistan Army. After these two countries left the Commonwealth, however, such links were regrettably severed. Today the overseas affiliated Regiments are as under:

Australian military forces: The Royal New South Wales Regiment
Canadian armed forces: The Ontario Regiment,
Royal Canadian Armoured Corps

7. Regimental Collect

The Royal Regiment of Wales (Catrawd Frenhinol Cymru)

O God, our Heavenly Father who gave Thy Son, Jesus Christ, to die upon the Cross for us, and calls men to be ready to lay down their lives for their friends, grant that we, Thy servants of The Royal Regiment of Wales, choosing death rather than dishonour, may so follow the path of duty in this life that we may be found worthy of eternal life, through Jesus Christ Thy Son our Lord.

O Dduw, Ein Tad Nefol, a roddaist Dy Fab Iesu Grist i farw trosom ar y Groes, ac a elwi ddynion i fod yn barod i roi eu bywydau dros eu cyfeillion, nertha ni, dy weison o Gatrawd Frenhinol Cymru, i ddewis angau yn hytrach na chywilydd, fel y gellwn ddilyn llwybr dyletswydd yn y bywyd hwn a'n cael yn deilwng o fywyd tragwyddol, trwy Iesu Grist, Dy Fab, ein Harglwydd.

APPENDIX EIGHT

Sport

To a Regiment always firmly associated with South Wales (and with a former Depot and present Headquarters within easy reach of Cardiff Arms Park) sport is an activity in which Rugby football naturally takes pride of place. It has done so, in fact, since late Victorian times, when both The South Wales Borderers and The Welch Regiment were fielding victorious XVs. In 1894, for instance, 2 Welch, serving in India, not only won the Bombay Cup but held the trophy for eight consecutive seasons.

However, although the civilian Rugby Football Union had been formed in 1871, there was no similar organisation in the Army until 1906. In December of that year the Army Council approved the establishment of the Army Rugby Union, which has remained the governing body for the sport to the present day. Members of both The South Wales Borderers and The Welch Regiment were intimately associated with its inception. 'There is no doubt that the chief credit for the setting up of the ARU must go to Lieut. (later Lieut.-Colonel) Partridge', wrote Colonel John McLaren in *The History of Army Rugby* (1986). Lieutenant J. E. C. ('Birdie') Partridge, The Welch Regiment, first conceived the idea of an Army Union on a train journey after playing for the Blackheath XV in Scotland. With him were Lieutenant W. S. D. Craven (RA) and Lieutenant C. G. Liddell (Leicestershire Regiment) who enthusiastically supported Partridge's proposal to approach the War Office for sanction. On this being granted, the first ARU Committee was formed, with representatives for all arms. There were three for the infantry, one being Partridge himself, the second being Captain C. E. Wilson (The Queen's), and the third Lieutenant (later Lieutenant Colonel) G. H. Birkett (The South Wales Borderers). The last named was also elected as the first Secretary of the ARU, but was in office only a year, since in 1908 he was posted to India with 1 SWB.

The first inter-unit Army Cup Final was played at Aldershot in January 1907, when 2 Duke of Wellington's Regiment were the victors against a Royal Engineers XV. Since then the Army Cup has come to be regarded in military circles with the same cachet as the soccer Cup Final in the civilian sporting calendar. And The Royal Regiment of Wales and its forebears have worthily upheld the prestige expected of Regiments so closely associated with the origins of the game in the Army. Their first Regimental victory was gained by 1 Welch in 1909, when oddly enough their opponents were their future partners, 2 SWB, whom they beat 6 points to 0. Just before the Great War, The Welch (2nd Battalion) were victors again, against 1 Glosters, but there was then a hiatus from 1915 to 1919. After that, The Welch (2nd Battalion) came back with three consecutive wins from 1920 to 22, but between 1925 and 1928 The South Wales Borderers (1st Battalion) beat that with four wins in a row. Although this

2nd Battalion The Welch Regiment, Winners of the Army Rugby Cup and Aldershot Command Rugby Cup, 1912
STANDING: LEFT TO RIGHT: *Private G. Bristowe, Lance Corporal T. Fisher, Private T. Garrington, Lance Corporal C. Jones, Lance Sergeant W. Murphy, Private W. Thomas, Private T. Bagnall, Private W. Hows, Private D. Daley*
SEATED LEFT TO RIGHT: *Private C. Jones, Lance Corporal T. Davies, Lieutenant F. W. Gransmore, Lieutenant F. H. Lacy (Captain), Captain J. E. C. Partridge; 2nd Lieutenant J. A. Daniel, Corporal J. Baker, Lance Corporal T. Foreman*
SEATED FRONT LEFT TO RIGHT: *Lance Sergeant J. Edwards, Private J. Secombe*

achievement was later equalled by The Duke of Wellington's Regiment (1965–8), it has never been surpassed to date.

A complete record of Army Cup winners is given in Colonel McLaren's work quoted above; the following is a résumé restricted to the victories of The Royal Regiment of Wales and its predecessors:

1909	1 Welch	6	v.	2 SWB	0
1913	2 Welch	9	v.	1 Glosters	3
1920	2 Welch	9	v.	2 Life Guards	0
1921	2 Welch	31	v.	Training Bn RE	3

Sport

1922	2 Welch	27	v.	1 Glosters	8
1925	1 SWB	16	v.	Royal Horse Guards	3
1926	1 SWB	10	v.	1 Welsh Guards	3
1927	1 SWB	9	v.	RE (Aldershot)	8
1928	1 SWB	15	v.	1 King's Own Royal	14
1935	1 Welch	11	v.	2 SWB	0
1937	1 Welch	13	v.	1 Prince of Wales's	7
1939	1 Welch	6	v.	2 Glosters	3
				(1940–6; no fixtures)	
1956	1 Welch	9	v.	1 RWF	8
1969	1 SWB	11	v.	7 Signal Regiment	3

2nd Battalion The Welch Regiment, Winners of the Army Rugby Cup and Essex Priory Cup, 1923–4
STANDING LEFT TO RIGHT: *2nd Lieutenant C. E. R. Hirsch, Captain S. E. V. Quinn, Captain B. U. S. Cripps, MC, 2nd Lieutenant P. F. Pitt, Lieutenant D. L. C. Reynolds, Private A. Jacobson, Corporal Nuttall*
SEATED LEFT TO RIGHT: *Lance Corporal G. Williams, MM, Captain W. Y. Price, MC, Lieutenant Colonel A. Derry, DSO, OBE, Captain B. M. Dunn, MC (Captain), Lieutenant R. M. Phillips, Sergeant I. Beynon, MM*
SEATED FRONT LEFT TO RIGHT: *Private D. Jones (42), Private R. L. Jones (33)*
INSET LEFT TO RIGHT: *Private A. Payne, Staff Sergeant C. Jones, Lance Sergeant J. Brindle*

1st Battalion The South Wales Borderers' Rugby team; winners of the Army Rugby Union Challenge Cup for four successive years: 1924–5, 1925–6, 1926–7 and 1927–8.

1974	1 RRW	14	v.	7 Signal Regiment	12
1976	1 RRW	10	v.	1 Duke of Wellington's	4
1977	1 RRW	22	v.	1 Duke of Wellington's	9
1986	1 RRW	7	v.	7 RHA	6

In 1987 the 1st Battalion entered a Seven-a-Side team for the BAOR competition, and despite training being curtailed by commitments in Northern Ireland and on exercises, they beat the Welsh Guards team by 30 points to 22 in the Final, thus becoming BAOR Sevens Champions.

Readers may recall that when 2 Welch were stationed in Landi Kotal (Khyber Pass) in 1935 they set a record by laying out the first Rugby field and playing the first Rugby match in that North West Frontier outpost. Earlier, the same Battalion had created Rugby history while serving in the Shanghai Defence Force. In January 1928 Captain (later Brigadier) B. U. S. Cripps organised and led the first British Army team on a tour of Japan. Of the twenty-two players eighteen were from 2 Welch, two from the Northamptonshire and two from the Coldstream. The Welch members included

Sport

A "selection" of Welsh International players and Rugby stalwarts of The Welch Regiment
BACK ROW LEFT TO RIGHT: *Lieutenant (later Major) F. J. V. Ford, Major Bill Clement, Private W. C. Major*
FRONT ROW LEFT TO RIGHT: *Lieutenant (later Brigadier) B. T. V. Cowey, Lieutenant (later Lieutenant Colonel) B. E. W. McCall*

1st Battalion The South Wales Borderers; winners of the Army Rugby Union Challenge Cup, 1968–9 (in the year of Amalgamation).
BACK ROW LEFT TO RIGHT: *Corporal Paddy O'Brien, Private David Chown, Sergeant Bob Ralph, Private Harry Rundle, 2nd Lieutenant David Hodges, Corporal 'Porky' Long, Corporal Paul Beard.*
FRONT ROW LEFT TO RIGHT: *Corporal George Boden, Private Wyndham Lewis, Corporal Terry Coates, Lieutenant Tudor Williams, Lieutenant Colonel L. A. H. Napier, MBE, Major David Cox, Corporal Bwane Kucuve, Corporal Jim Jenkins, Private 'Killer' Llewellyn.*

Lieutenant Charles Coleman, who was later (1958) to become Colonel of the Regiment. Five matches were played against Japanese university teams, the Army XV winning four. Among the enormous and enthusiastic crowds of spectators was the Crown Prince of Japan who on one occasion brought along his whole Regiment to watch the sport. To commemorate this unique tour the British forces in Shangai presented the Japanese Rugby Union with a silver trophy to be competed for annually by the universities. Thirteen years later Japan had become an enemy, and sadly the trophy was destroyed in the American bombing of Tokyo in 1945.

Among outstanding Welch players in the pre-war days was Lieutenant (later Brigadier) B. T. V. Cowey, who as Captain of the 1st Battalion XV led them to victory in two Army Cup Finals. He was the first officer of the Regiment to play for Wales, and also became a Barbarian.

In The South Wales Borderers' 'Bun' Cowey's counterpart may be said to have been Captain (Major) C. A. Baker, whose inspiring leadership and personal prowess contributed largely to the 1st Battalion's feat in carrying off the Army Cup in four consecutive seasons. Today relics of this achievement may be seen in The South Wales Borderers' Museum at Brecon – the four age-blackened Rugby balls used in the Finals.

In the post war period, the BAOR Rugby Cup has been won four times by 1 RRW – 1970, 1972, 1976 and 1977 – while 1 SWB were victors in 1954 and 1955 and 1 Welch in 1957.

By now some readers may have the impression that Rugby football is the only sport acknowledged by the Regiment and its antecedents. This, of course, is far from the truth. All three Regiments have indulged in all the games and sports normally played on military fields, and in some, such as skiing, hang-gliding, yachting and Adventure Training which were virtually unknown to the pre-World War II soldier.

Since the earliest days of organised sport in the Army – that is, during the 1850s – the regular battalions had their cricket, soccer and hockey teams, while boxing was actively encouraged. In India, polo could be afforded by most officers so inclined, for it was possible to hire ponies from the cavalry at very cheap rates. When 1 SWB were serving in India in 1899 they fielded a very fine team which, among other victories, won that year's All-India Infantry Polo Tournament. In 1959 the officers of 1 Welch took the opportunity of forming a polo team while serving in Benghazi, but there were no tournaments in that part of the Western Desert. Golf was also regarded as an officer's sport, but after World War II not much interest was shown in it until very recently. In 1986 Colonel N. O. Roberts, Regimental Secretary at Cardiff, proposed the formation of a Regimental Golf Society. The response was unexpectedly gratifying: twenty-five serving and retired officers turned up at the Cardiff Golf Club to play in the Inaugural Meeting on 27th June. Among them were Major Sir Tasker Watkins, VC, and Major General Lennox Napier, Colonel of the Regiment. The Royal Regiment of Wales Golf Society is now flourishing.

While successes on the rugger field have always tended to overshadow others, the Regiment and its forebears have enjoyed their victories elsewhere, as the following random examples indicate.

The Regiment's first English Rugby International, 2nd Lieutenant W. D. J. Carling, 1988. (Durham University O.T.C.)

1901	1 SWB win the coveted Durand Cup – the All-India Trophy for Association Football
1910	1 SWB win the All-India Boxing Tournament
1925–6	2 Welch win Southern Command Hockey Tournament
1935–6	1 SWB win Rawalpindi District Athletics
	2 Welch win Peshawar District Boxing Tournament
1939	1 SWB win Durand Cup
1953	5 Welch win 53 (W) Infantry Division Association Football Cup
1963	4 Welch Football XI win TA Challenge Cup Competition
1966	1 Welch win Hong Kong Major Units Football Cup
1973	1 RRW win Infantry Football Cup
1974	1 RRW win Northern Ireland Hockey Cup
1977	3 RRW win Western Area TAVR Cross Country Championship (also won in 1983)
1985	1 RRW win BAOR Novice Boxing Championships, 4 Armd Div Boxing Championship
1986	1 RRW win 4 Armd Div Boxing Championship
	3 RRW win Western Area TA Cross Country Championship
1987	1 RRW win Army Novices (Grade 2) Boxing Championship

WO1 E. H. Richards.

During the period 1936–48 The South Wales Borderers produced one of the most outstanding boxers ever to enter an Army ring. Private Edward Richards joined the 2nd Battalion in 1934 and retired twenty-three years later, after becoming RSM of the 1st Battalion – and having earned the sobriquet of 'Killer' Richards. His successes in the ring are too numerous to catalogue fully here, but apart from representing the Army on numerous occasions, he beat the Light-Heavyweight Champion of Wales, won the Ulster Championships, fought for England against Germany in 1938 and defeated both the Heavyweight and Light-Heavyweight Champions of All-Ireland. All this was prior to World War II, and had it not been for that conflict he would almost certainly have represented Britain in the Olympics. In 1937 he had the unusual experience of boxing for a foreign team against his own country. Having disposed of his man in the contest between the Army and Denmark, he was asked to compete in the Danish team to

1 RRW boxing team, Lemgo, 1987; Army Novices (Grade 2) champions.

meet England. He won his bout against the then ABA Champion of Great Britain. During the war 'Killer' Richards served as CSM with his Regiment in North Africa and Italy, where he was wounded (and earned a Mention in Despatches). At Tunis, in 1943, he took part in an American Red Cross Tournament and defeated the American Ezzard Charles who later became World Heavyweight Champion. After the war further victories followed: Heavyweight Championship of CMF, and, in 1948, Light-Heavyweight Championship of Western Command. He then left the ring and after serving with 1 SWB as RSM, he became RSM at the Brecon Depot, finally retiring from the Army in 1957. At the time of writing, ex-RSM Edward ('Killer') Richards maintains his connections with the Regiment as Chairman of the Swansea Branch of the Comrades Association.

APPENDIX NINE

Regimental Association (As at 1st January 1988)

President: The Colonel of the Regiment
MAJOR GENERAL L. A. H. NAPIER, CB, OBE, MC, DL
Secretary: MAJOR P. L. CUTLER, MBE, JP.

Branch	Secretary
ABERDARE	Mr R. J. LUKER
ABERTILLERY	Mr T. EDWARDS
BIRMINGHAM	Mr D. J. ARTHURS
BRECON	Mr G. SMITH
BRIDGEND	Mr T. G. D. HARDING
CAERPHILLY	Mr W. T. BRAUND
CARDIFF	Captain T. ILES
DEE AND MERSEYSIDE	Mr E. C. JOHN
ISLWYN	Mr E. BARBERO
LLANELLI	Mr W. C. GRIFFITHS
LONDON	Mr L. G. MORGAN
MANCHESTER	Major W. A. PICKERING, MM
MERTHYR TYDFIL	Major T. PRICE, MBE
NEATH	Mr B. JENKINS
NEWPORT	Mr J. A. ASHWELL
PONTYPOOL	M. I. WILLIAMS
RHONDDA	Mr C. J. VAUGHAN
SWANSEA	Mr J. S. HARRIS
TONYPANDY	Mr J. G. TAYLOR

ASSOCIATED BRANCHES

BIRMINGHAM WELCH	Mr V. D. WILLIAMS
6 SWB	Mr M. S. THOMAS
3 MONS	Mr H. JONES

Badges of the Regiment

Badges and insignia of The South Wales Borderers (24th Regiment)

1. Helmet plate, officers' pattern, 24th Regiment 1879–91.
2. Breast plate, soldiers' pattern, 24th Regiment, c. 1820.
3. Helmet plate, soldiers' pattern, 24th Regiment, c. 1881.
4. Shako plate, soldiers' pattern, 24th Regiment, 1861–9.
5. Glengarry badge, soldiers' pattern, 24th Regiment, 1871–82.
6. Helmet plate, officers' pattern, SWB, c. 1881.
7. Shako plate, soldiers' pattern, 24th Regiment, c. 1812.
8. Breast plate, soldiers' pattern, 24th Regiment, c. 1824.
9. Clasp, belt, officers' pattern, SWB, c. 1881.
10. Badge cap, officers' pattern (silver), SWB, c. 1898.
11. Badge cap, soldiers' pattern (brass and white metal), SWB, c. 1898.
12. Clasp, belt, officers' pattern, 24th Regiment, c. 1879.
13. Shako plate, officers' pattern, 24th Regiment, 1861–9.
14. Helmet plate, officers' pattern, 24th Regiment, c. 1812.
15. Shako plate, soldiers' pattern, 24th Regiment, 1868–1880.

Badges of the Regiment

Badges and insignia, The Welch Regiment

1. Badge, collar, soldiers pattern, 41st Regiment, c. 1879.
2. Clasp, belt, officers' pattern, 41st Regiment, 1855–81.
3. Shako plate, officers' pattern, 41st Regiment, c. 1864.
4. Clasp, belt, officers' pattern, 69th Regiment, 1855–81.
5. Badge, collar, soldiers pattern, 69th Regiment, c. 1879.
6. Clasp, belt, soldiers pattern, 41st Regiment, c. 1879.
7. Badge for Glengarry cap, soldiers pattern, 41st Regiment, c. 1879.
8. Shako plate officers' pattern, 41st Regiment, c. 1875.
9. Badge for Glengarry cap, soldiers pattern, 69th Regiment, c. 1879.
10. Clasp, belt, soldiers pattern, 69th Regiment, c. 1879.
11. Helmet plate officers' Pattern, 41st Regiment, c. 1880.
12. Badge for Glengarry cap, officers' pattern, The Welch Regiment, c. 1885
13. Ornament, leather sabretache, 69th Regiment, c. 1875.
14. Badge for Glengarry, cap, soldiers pattern, The Welch Regiment, c. 1885.
15. Helmet plate, soldiers pattern, 69th Regiment, c. 1880.
16. Helmet plate, officers' pattern, The Welch Regiment, 1881–1902.
17. Badge for Glengarry cap, officers' pattern, c. 1890.
18. Shako plate, officers' pattern, 69th Regiment, c. 1875.
19. Badge, coloured, field service cap, officers', c. 1950.
20. Helmet plate, soldiers pattern, The Welch Regiment, 1881-1902.
21. Badge cap, soldiers pattern, The Welch Regiment, 1898–1920; spelling: 'The Welsh'.
22. Badges, collar, The Welch Regiment, soldiers pattern, Brass 1881–1909, white metal, c. 1952–69.
23. Helmet plate, soldiers pattern, The Welch Regiment, 1902–14.
24. Badges, collar, soldiers pattern, The Welch Regiment, 1909–1939.
25. Badge cap, soldiers pattern, 1920–60; spelling: 'The Welch'.

Badges of the Regiment

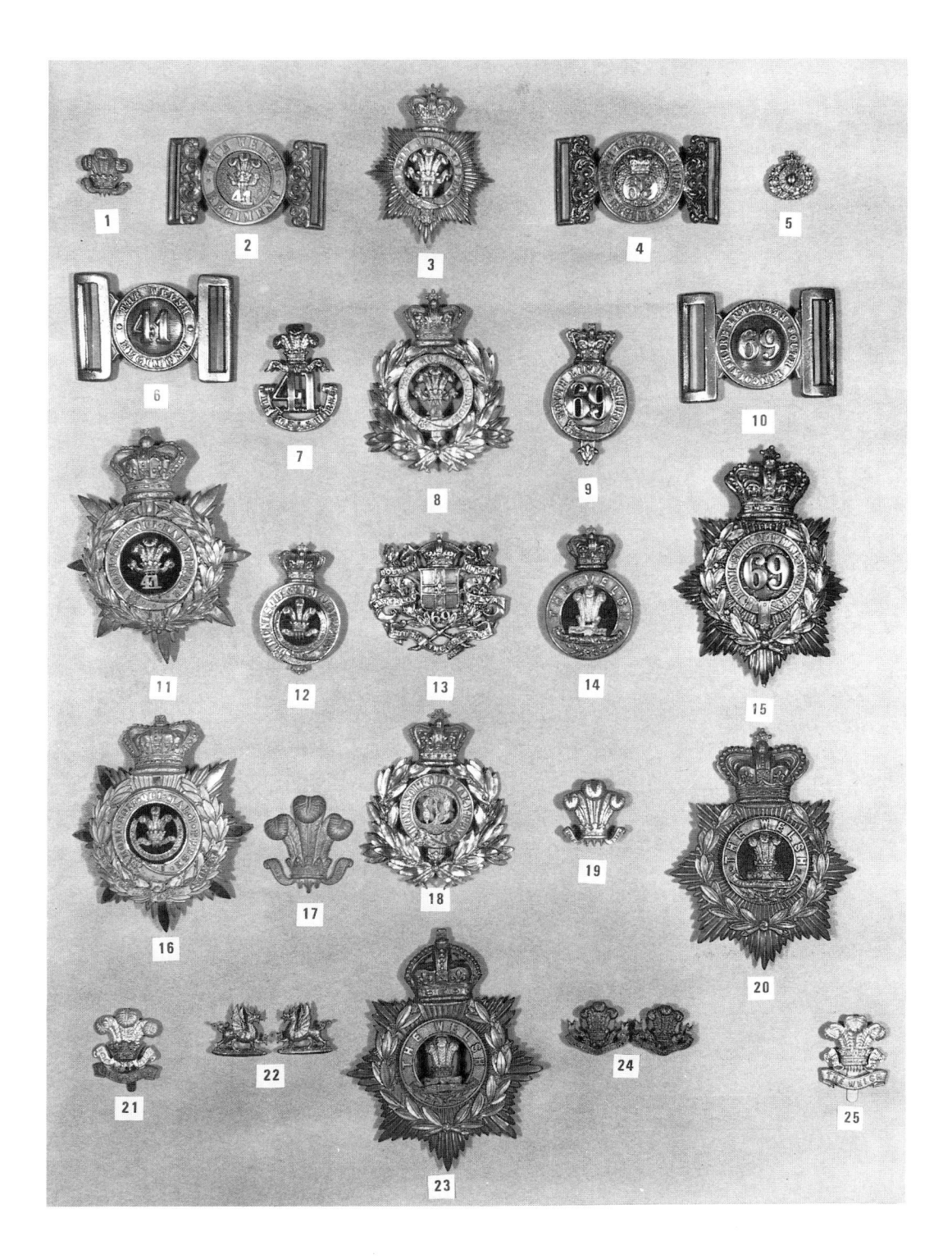

Badges of the Regiment

Badges and insignia, 41st and 69th Regiments of Foot

1. *Plate, shoulder belt, officers' pattern, 41st Foot, c. 1798.*
2. *Plate, shoulder belt, officers' pattern, 41st Foot, c. 1794.*
3. *Plate, shoulder belt, officers' pattern, 69th Regiment, c. 1850.*
4. *Plate, shoulder belt, officers' pattern, 41st Regiment, c. 1830.*
5. *Shako plate, universal pattern, c. 1803.*
6. *Plate, shoulder belt, officers' pattern, 41st Regiment, 1831–55.*
7. *Shako plate, soldiers pattern, 41st Regiment, c. 1844 (Battalion companies).*
8. *Shako plate, universal pattern, c. 1815.*
9. *Shako plate, soldiers pattern, 69th Regiment, c. 1844 (Battalion companies).*
10. *Shako plate, officers' pattern, 69th Regiment, c. 1842.*
11. *Skirt ornament, officers' regimental coat, 69th Regiment, c. 1840.*
12. *Shako plate, officers' pattern, 41st Regiment, c. 1854.*

Badges of the Regiment

503

Badges of the Regiment

Badges and insignia, The Monmouthshire Regiment

1. *Badge, cap, white metal, 1st Monmouthshire Regiment, soldiers pattern, rifle green walking-out dress, c. 1912.*
2. *Shako plate, Monmouthshire Rifle Volunteers (all corps); introduced 1864.*
3. *Badge, cap, brass, 1st, 2nd and 3rd Battalions, Monmouthshire Regiment; soldiers khaki service dress, c. 1914.*
4–6. *Badges, collar, brass, 1st, 2nd and 3rd Battalions, Monmouthshire Regiment; soldiers khaki service dress, c. 1914.*
5. *Helmet plate, 1st Monmouthshire Rifle Volunteer Battalion, c. 1880.*
7. *Badge, officers' pattern, 3rd Battalion The Monmouthshire Regiment; khaki service dress, c. 1945.*
8. *Badge cap, white metal, soldiers pattern, 1st Battalion The Monmouthshire Regiment, 1920–45.*
9. *Badge, cap, Monmouthshire Territorials, c. 1968.*

Badges of the Regiment

Index

Major campaigns, battles and actions are listed under BATTLES...
With a few exceptions, ranks shown are those ultimately attained and not necessarily current at the date of reference.

Abercromby, Lt-Gen Sir Ralph 57, 456
Adams, Lt Col J. Q. 289, 295, 320, 369, 424
Aden 231, 254, 382–83
Afghanistan *see BATTLES and CAMPAIGNS*
Affiliated Regiments 485
Afrika Korps 295
Agra (India) 269, 286
Alcock, Capt Charles 14
Aldershot, 140, 142, 146, 421
Alexander, F-M Earl 303
Allah Bakhs 309
Allan, Maj-Gen William 457
Allen, Cpl W., VC 168, 451
Allenby, Gen. Sir Edmund 243–44
Alma *see BATTLES and CAMPAIGNS*
Amalgamations
　41st and 69th 180
　SWB and Welch 386, 389
　Ceremony at Cardiff, 1969 395, 397–99
Amherstburg (N. America) 90
Amphlett, WO1 G. I. 399
Ancliffe, Charles (Bandmaster) 469
Ancram, Earl of 44–45
Andaman Is. 143–45
Anderson, Lt Joseph 70–73
Ankenes (Norway) 289 *et seq.*
Anne, Queen 25, 27
Anniversaries
　Gheluvelt 483
　Rorke's Drift 483
　St. David's Day 483
Arakan (Burma) 306 *et seq.*
Arcot (India) 59
Arms *see 'WEAPONS'*
Army Cadet Force 443
Army Medical School 145
Army Rugby Union 270, 487 *et seq.*
Articles of War 4
Ashwood, Maj R. J. 427
Asmara (Eritrea) 349
Assam Valley (Merchant ship) 143
Atkinson, C. T. xxx, 219
Auchmuty, Lt Gen Sir Samuel 63, 64
Ava (Burma) 100

Badges regimental 102, 187, 188, 370, 376–77, 400, 414–15

Badges of rank 43, 484
Baird, Gen. Sir David 58, 455
Band (and Drums) 19, 209, 467–70
Bandmasters 469
Banfield, Lt Col R. J. F. 191, 197, 200, 202, 207
Barlow, Maj F. F. S. 322–26
Barnes, 2/Lt J. 363–65
Barracks 108
Barrow, Capt 60, 61
Barrow, Ens. M. 14
Barthorp, Michael 173–75
Battledress *see UNIFORM*
BATTLES and CAMPAIGNS
　(including actions, combats etc.)
　Afghanistan (1842) 110–15
　Alexandria (1801) 58
　Alma 133–34
　Ashanti 151
　Battle of the Saints 53
　Belleisle 46–47
　Blenheim 30–33
　Burgos 74
　Burma (excl. WWII) 99–100, 185
　Cape of Good Hope 58
　Chilianwala 117–26
　Ciudad Rodrigo 73
　Detroit 90–92
　Erie, Fort 98
　Frenchtown 92–93
　Fuentes d'Onor 72
　Indian Mutiny 140–42
　Inkerman 136–38
　Ireland (William III's Campaign) 13 *et seq.*
　Isandhlwana 151–57
　Java 63–64
　Little Inkerman 134–35
　Lundy's Lane 96–97
　Malplaquet 38–39
　Miami 98
　Moravian Town 95
　Nepal (1814–16) 87–88
　Orthes 76
　Oudenarde 36–37
　Peninsular War 67–77
　Quatre Bras 77–79
　Ramillies 34–35
　Rorke's Drift 157–72
　St. Vincent 53–54

　Schellenberg 29–30
　Sebastopol 139
　Talavera 67
　Vellore 59–63
　Vittoria 75
　Warburg 49
　Waterloo 81–83
　Boer War
　Bloemfontein 199
　Driefontein 199
　Karree 199–200
　Modderfontein 205–06
　Paardeberg 193–97
　Pretoria 202
　First World War
　Aden 231–32
　Cambrai 242–43
　Chemin des Dames 221
　Frezenberg 227–29
　Gallipoli 229–331
　Gaza 243
　Gheluvelt 222–23
　Jerusalem 244
　Macedonia 237–40
　Mametz Wood 236–37
　Mesopotamia 237
　Nablus 244
　Passchendale 241
　Pilkem Ridge 241
　Sambre-et-Oise 247
　Somme 234–36
　Tel 'Asur 244
　Tsingtao 223–24
　Villers-Outreaux 245–46
　Second World War
　Antwerp 332
　Bafour 330–31
　"Battle for the Castle" (Hemmen) 337–38
　Bodo 291–92
　Broekuizen 335
　Burma 306–319
　Cividale 304
　Crete 293–94
　Croce 301–03
　D-Day 321–25
　"Great Swan" 332
　Hamburg 342–43
　Irrawaddy Bridgeheads 316–17
　Italy 301–304

507

Index

Le Havre 333
Maymyo 318
Mayu Tunnels 306–310
Mouen 327
"Overlord" 321 et seq.
Pinwe (Gyobin Chaung) 311–12
Po (River) 303–04
Reichswald 335–37
Sahmau Chaung 310
s'Hertogenbosch 331, 334
Sully 325–26
Teutoburger Wald 339–41
Toungou 319
Tredegar Hill 308
Western Desert 293, 295–301
Cyprus 374–75
Korea 351–58
Malaya 361–69
"Beach Bricks" 300
Belfast 401, 402–07, 410, 430, 436
Belize 417–18, 421
Bell, Pte David VC 144, 451
Beresford, 1st Visct. 456
Berlin 415, 417
Birkett, Lt Col G. H. 270, 487
Blachford, Capt 119
Blair, L/Cpl H. 206
Blakiston, Maj. John 62
Board, Air Cdre A. G. 212
Boon, Maj. J. T. 324, 325–26, 342
Botha, Louis 202
Botswana 383
Bottom, Pte Philip 61
Bradstock, Maj J. 461
Brady, Sgt 60, 62
Brecon See also 'Depots' and 'Dering Lines' 1, 87, 108, 130, 149, 187, 219, 258, 274, 282, 349, 377–78, 423
Bren Carrier see Vehicles
Brest 17
Brett, Lt Col G. A. xxx
Brickhill, Mr 160–61
Brock, Maj Gen Isaac 87, 88, 91, 92
Bromham, Lt Col D. C. 460
Bromhead, Capt Benjamin 46
Bromhead, Ensn, C. 142
Bromhead, Capt C. J. 151
Bromhead, Lt Col D. de G. 429, 438, 447, 460
Bromhead, Lt G., VC 163 et seq. 189, 451
Brooke, Maj Gen F. H. 263–65, 386-89, 395, 399, 423, 430, 457
Brooke, Lt Col O. G. 301, 304
Brookes, Lt Col R. 116, 119
Brown, Capt T. M. E. 399
Brown, Lt Col T. S. 399, 428, 460
Brown, Sgt (16 Welch) 241
Browne, Lt E. S., VC 176, 451
Brudenell, Lt Col T. 18
Buchanan, Capt A., VC 237, 451

Buckingham Palace (public duties at) 210, 390, 427
Bull, Pte A. 436, 437
Buller, Gen Redvers, VC 191–92
Burges, Lt Col D., VC 240
Burgess, 2/Lt S. 358
Burnett, Maj G. A. 329
Byng, Admiral 46

Cairo 254
Cambridge, F-M Duke of 132, 142, 179
Campbell, Brig Sir Colin (later Lord Clyde) 118, 120, 123
Campbell, 2/Lt D. L. 204
Campbell-Miles, Lt Col D. C. 459
Canada (training in) 389–90, 421, 428, 438, 442
Cardiff see also 'Depots' 130, 180, 221, 258, 273, 377, 412, 421–22, 426
Cardiff Castle 274, 395, 412, 421–22, 450
Cardiff HMS 442
Cardigan, Lt Gen Earl of 134
Cardwell, Edward 146–47, 148, 179
Carmarthen 130
Carpenter, Lt Col G. 131, 138
Casson, Capt Hugh 205, 206
Cavaye, Capt 159
Cave-Brown-Cave, Lt A. 313
Cetywayo, King 152, 160
Chamberlain, Maj Thomas 67, 70
Chambers, Lt Col P. 99, 100
Champagne, Sir Josiah 456
Chapman, Cpl E. T., VC 339–40, 377, 439, 451
Chard, Lt John, VC 163, 164, 168–72
Chelmsford, Maj Gen Lord 154, 155–57, 162, 172
Chelsea see Royal Hospital
Childers, Hugh 179
Chilianwala see under BATTLES
Chilianwala Colours (removal from Warwick to Brecon) 120, 270, 461–66
Christian, L/Cpl J. H. 337
Churchill, John see Marlborough
Churchill, Sir Winston 25, 229, 287, 300
Clark, Lt John 14
Clarke, Ensn Christopher 84
Clinkard, Capt Archibald 14
Coates, Maj James 59, 61
Cobbe, Gen Sir Alexander, VC 253, 258–61, 270, 358, 455
Cochrane, Lt James 90
Coghill, Lt Nevill, VC 159, 160–62, 173, 175, 408, 451
Coleman, Lt Gen Sir C. F. C. 329, 360, 375, 378, 457, 483
Collect, Regimental 485
Collis, Ensn 118, 120
Colonel of the Regiment 3, 4, 43

Colonel-in-Chief see also 'Prince of Wales' 253-54, 389
Colours (Regimental) 8–9, 45, 271, 380, 400, 425
Colville, Col the Hon. Charles 46, 456
Comer, Capt A. G. 300, 320
Commissions, purchase system 10–11, 24, 107, 146–47
Conan Doyle, Sir Arthur 227
Cook, Cpl W. G. 338
Cooper, Pte James VC 144, 451
Cornwallis, Lt Gen. Hon. Edward 45, 50, 455
Corps of Drums see Band (and Drums)
"Corps of Infantry" 349–50
Cowey, Brig B. T. V. 318–19, 459, 460, 492
Cox, Brig C. F. 290, 320, 349, 423, 459
Cox, Lt Col D. E. 399, 460
Craddock, Lt Col R. W. 322, 324, 325–26
Cradock, Lt Gen Sir John 59, 63
Cresswell, Lt Col R. S. 308
Crest, regimental 400
Crete (Exercise "Welsh Quadrant") 447–48
Crewe-Read, Lt Col J. O. 459
Crewe-Read, Maj R. O. 309
Crichton-Stuart, Lt Col 233
Cripps, Brig B. S. 490
Crofts, Lt George 14
Croker, CQMS V. 313
Cronje, Piet 193, 197, 202
Cutler, Maj (Lt Col) P. L. xxx, 390–91, 395-96, 459
Cutts, Lt Gen Lord 30, 32
Cuyler, Sir Cornelius 456
Cwrt-y-Gollen (Welsh Brigade and Prince of Wales's Division training centre) 369–70, 376–77, 391–93, 434–35

D Day see under BATTLES (Second World War)
Dalton, Charles 2, 13
Dalton, Asst Cmmsy. James, VC 172
Danube, Marlborough's March to 26–29
1 SWB's March to 33–34
Darling, Gen Sir Ralph 456
Dartnell, Maj 155–56, 162
Dauntless, HMS 129
Davey, Brig K. J. 354, 358, 399, 411, 415, 418, 460
Davies, Sgt J. VC (RWF) 377
Davies, Lt Col M. 460
Davies, Lt N. L. 312
Davies-Jenkins, Lt Col E. M. 459
Davis, Lt D. 303
Dawson, L/Cpl 339
Dawson, WO1 D. 399, 469–70
Dean, Pte 90
Deane, Lt. Col. H. H. 351, 353, 358, 459

Index

De Blaquiere, Lt 113–14
De Berry, Maj Gen G. F. 122–23
Degacher, Maj Gen H. J. 154, 455
Delhi, Durbar 207
de Lukacs-Lessner de Szeged, Lt Col A. J. 460
Depots (establishment of)
  Brecon 149
  Cardiff 180
  Cwrt-y-Gollen 369–70
  Fort Hubberstone (Haverfordwest) 149
De Puisar, Marquis de 18, 20, 21, 455
Dering, Col Daniel 4, 14, 15, 455
Dering, Col Sir Edward 1–3, 14, 15, 450, 453, 455
Dering, Capt John 16
Dering Lines (Brecon) 1, 282
Diana, Princess of Wales 429
Dibdin, Charles 472
Dickinson, Maj Gen D. P. 371, 457
Dinapur (Memorial in church) 89
Discipline 24, 57, 107, 146
Dooley, Pte 82
Douglas, Asst Surgn. C. M., VC 143–44, 451
Drake, Peter 23–24
Dress see 'Uniform'
Drummond, Lt Gen Gordon 96–97, 98
Drums, Silver (1 SWB) 209–10
Drums, Platoon 470
Dublin 252
Duncan, Lt Col A. 293–94
Dundalk 14, 15
Dunkirk (1692) 16
Dunn, Sgt F. W. 304
Durnford, Col (RE) 157, 162–63
Dyer, Lt 156–58, 159

Eccles, 2/Lt Mary 446
Edinburgh, HRH the Duke of 370, 378
Education (of the soldier) 6, 107, 146, 184
Edward VII, King 172, 207
Edward VIII, King see also 'Prince of Wales' 254
Edwardes, Lt J. 237
Edwardes, Lt Col J. A. 236
Edwards, L/Cpl and Mrs. 429
Edwards, Col. Sgt A. 418
Edwards, Lt G. 329
Edwards, Cpl M. 445
Effingham HMS 291–92
Egerton, Maj G. J. B. 427–28
Eley, Lt 60
Elizabeth II, Queen 370, 377, 378, 380, 389, 401, 417
Ellaway, L/Cpl T. P. 353
Ellice, Gen. Sir Charles 140, 141, 150, 455
Ellice, Lt Gen R. 120, 455
Elliott, Lt Col C. H. 447–48, 460

Ellis, Maj P. 304
Eman, Lt Col James 138
England, Gen Sir Richard 110, 112–13, 149 (footnote) 456
Eritrea 349
Eugene, Prince of Savoy 27, 30, 32–33, 36, 38
Eversleigh Star (rank badge) 484–85
Evill, Lt Col A. R. 459

Facings see UNIFORM
Falaise 332–33
Falkand Is. 431
Fancourt, Lt Col St John 59–60
Ferdinand, Prince of Brunswick 49
Fielding, Lt Gen Edmund 41–42, 391, 453, 456
Fielding, Henry 51
Finch, Lt Gen Hon. Daniel 455
Finch, CSM R. 338–39
Finn, Pte James, VC 237, 249, 451
Fitz-Simmons, Lt E. 14
Fleming, Lt Gen E. 380
Fleming, Hon. Mrs. 380
Flinn, Dmr Thomas, VC 190
Flogging (punishment) 57, 107, 146
Ford, Sgt Daniel 138
Fowler, Capt Hugh 230–31
France, Maj J. 330
Francis, Col. P. C. A. 424
Fraser, Brig. Simon 50–51
French, F-M Sir John 222
French Foreign Legion 142
Frere, Sir Bartle 152–53
Fuller, L/Cpl William, VC 221, 248, 416, 451

Galitzine, Capt Prince 334
Gascoigne, Gen E. F. 456
Gaumont British Film Corporation 269
"Geddes Axe" 257
George, Pte L. 329
George II, King 45
George V, King 176, 209, 254
George VI, King 269
Gerrard, Col 140–41
Ghana (exercise in) 385, 390
Ghazni (Afghanistan) 114
Ghent, Treaty of 98
Gibson, Maj J. T. 298, 300, 320
Gifford, Lt Lord, VC 151, 451
Gillespie, Lt Col F. M. 231
Gillespie, Maj Gen Sir Rollo 60–65
Glanusk, Lord 231
Glanusk Park 305
Glennie, Col F. xxx
Glyn, Lt Gen R. T. 154–55, 188, 455
Goats (Mascot) 140, 191, 475–80
Godwin, Lt Col H. 99–100
Godwin-Austen, Capt A. 407
Godwin-Austen, Col H. 359, 407
Godwin-Austen, Gen Sir A. Readé 209, 359, 455

Godwin-Austen, Lt Col R. H. 407, 411, 414, 460
Golf 493
Goodwyn, Gen, J. E. 139, 180, 456
Goodwyn, Lt Col J. N. 459
Gordon, Lt P. D. 397
Gore-Brown, Maj T. 110, 114, 130
Gottwaltz, Brig. P. 288–89, 292, 320
Gough, Gen Sir Hugh 115–118
Granby, Lt Gen Marquis of 49
Grand Couronne 239–40
Griffen, Lt P. 14
Griffith, Lt Col S. 460
Griffiths, Pte William, VC 144, 451
Gross, Lt Col R. F. 251
Grundy, Lt Col J. M. 436–37, 460
Gurkha Demonstration Company (Brecon) 87
Gurkhas 87–89, 317
Gwynne-Jones, Maj A. (Lord Chalfont) 367, 369

Haggard, Capt Mark 221
Haig, F-M. Sir Douglas 242, 244
Haldane, Richard (Visct) 210, 217
Halkett, Maj Gen Sir Colin 77, 81, 83
Hamburg 342–43
Hamilton, Gen Sir Ian 229, 231
Hamilton, Lt Gen Sir John 456
Hancock, Pte 90
Hankey, Maj (Worcesters) 222
Hanley, Maj B. J. 399
Harford, Lt Col F. 173, 178
Harkness, Maj H. d'A. 207
Harnage, Richard 3
Harrod, Maj Gen L. A. D. 385, 418, 423–24, 428–29, 434, 457, 459
Harry, Lt Col M. J. H. 399, 446, 449, 460
Hart, Maj Gen Fitzroy 203
Hart, Gen Sir Reginald, VC 151, 214
Harvey, Maj J. 185
Haslock, C/Sgt David 111–12, 114
Havard Chapel (Brecon Cathedral) 258
Healey, Denis 381
Hedderwick, Capt W. 74, 84
Herbert, Col Lord Henry (23rd Foot) 13
Higgenson, Lt 161
Hirsch, Maj Gen C. E. R. 379
Hitch, Pte F., VC 168–69, 172, 190, 451
Hitler, Adolf, 281, 283, 287–288
Höchstadt (Visit of RRW Band) 446
Home Service Force 442–43
Hong Kong 252, 382, 385, 428–29
Hook, Pte A. H., VC 165–66, 172, 190, 451
Hope, Lt Col J. W. 459
Horses (riding and draught) 19, 213, 263, 264, 278, 345
Houghton, Brig Gen D. 44, 455
Howard, Lt Gen Thomas 41, 43, 51, 455

Index

Howes, Maj M. M. 399, 431
Hull, General 90–91
Humphrey, Capt F. 14
Humphreys, Ens. H. 14
Hunter, Lt Col F. 208
Hurford, Brig E. W. C. 379
Hywel-Jones, Capt R. I. 369

Idris, King Muhammed 375
Immortelles, Wreath of 173–74, 178, 207–08, 217, 271
India, Services in 58–61, 87–89, 129, 207–08, 265–69, 270, 314–15, 347
Indian Mutiny *see also BATTLES etc.* 140–42
Infantry, School of 1, 448
Infantry, tasks and training xxix, 8, 24, 277–78, 349–50, 361, 441–42
Inkerman *see BATTLES*
"Invalids", Regiment of 41–42
Ipi, Fakir of 270
IRA 251, 402, 405–06, 425, 444
Isaacs, L/Cpl 204
Isandhlwana *see BATTLES*
Isandhlwana Colours (laying-up) 271
Istalif (Afghanistan) 114
Italy, campaign in, *see BATTLES*

Jackson, Maj. T. J. 354–56
Jalalabad (Afghanistan) 110
James, Maj A. 311, 320
James II, King 2, 9, 13, 15
Jeffreys, Lt F. 14
Jephson, W. 14
Jhelum (River) 117
Johannesburg 200–02
John, Lt Col B. T. 422, 460
John o'Groats – Lands End Marathon 437–38
Johnson, Maj Gen D. G., VC 247, 358–9, 377, 451, 455
"Jon" (Lt W. J. Jones) 299
Jones, L/Cpl C. 304
Jones, Lt Col C. B. 460
Jones, Maj E. J. 310
Jones, Sgt H. G. 317
Jones, Sgt M. 338
Jones, Pte R., VC 165, 167–68, 172, 273, 451
Jones, Pte W., VC 165, 167–68, 172, 451
Jordan, Lt Col J. L. 459
Journals, Regimental 254–57
Junior Leaders' Battalion (Infantry) 435
Junior Soldiers 434–35

Kabul 110, 112, 114, 126
Kalunga (Nepal) 88
Kandahar 110, 112, 114, 126
Karachi 207–08
Kathmandu 88
Keefe, RQMS J. H. 409
Keith, Ens C. 79

Kellerman, Gen F. 78–79
Keogh, Cpl M. J. 351–52
Kernick, Lt R. 337–38
Kerr, William Henry *see Ancram, Earl of*
Khaki *see UNIFORM*
Khalsa (Sikh army) 116
Khartoum 348
Khyber Pass 110–11, 115, 266, 269, 360
Kingsley, Ens W. 14
Kitchener, F-M Lord 185, 203, 229
Kluang (Malaya) 362 *et seq.*
Korea *see BATTLES*
Kruger, Paul 191, 200–02

Land Rover *see VEHICLES*
Landi Kotal (Khyber Pass) 266–69, 270, 281, 285
Leach, Lt Col. H. E. B. 219, 222–23
Lee-Enfield (rifle) *see WEAPONS*
Leek, traditions and ceremonial 480–82
Legard, Lt Col G. 55
Le Havre *see BATTLES (Second World War)*
Lemgo (BAOR) 433, 436, 446, 448
Le Mesurier, Capt W. 76
Leslie, Alexander *see 'Lindores'*
Lewis, Maj A. J. 336–37
Lewis, Pte H. W., VC 238–39, 416, 451
Libya, post-war service in 375–76
Lichfield (Depot) 434–35
Light Company 43, 52
Lindores, Maj Gen Lord 456
Lisle, Gerald 14
Llandaff Cathedral, Welch Regiment memorials in 258, 371–74
Lloyd, Lt Col. M. T. O. 418, 421, 423, 426, 427, 460
Lloyd George (Prime Minister) 244
Lomax, Maj Gen C. E. N. xxx, 359, 372, 408–09, 457
Lomax, Lt D. A. N. xxx, 199
Longcroft, Air V-M. C. A. H. 212
Lonsdale, Cmdt 156–57
Louis, Prince, Margrave of Baden 29
Louis XIV, King 21, 25
Lucan, Lt Gen Lord 132–33
Lundy's Lane *see BATTLES*
Lydd (Kent) 389, 401
Lyon, Lt Gen Sir James 455

McCreery, Lt Gen Sir R. 303
Macdowall, Lt Gen H. 456
MacKirdy, Gen D. E. 180, 188, 456–57
Maclachlan, Capt 60–61, 63
McManus, Sgt A. 61, 63
McMurdo, Gen Sir W. 456
McNab, Maj Gen A. 42–43, 456
Mcpherson, Lt A. J. 117, 118, 122, 126
Macedonia *see BATTLES (1st World War)*

Machine Gun Battalions, formation of 277
Mackworth, Sir Digby 104
Madden, Sgt A., VC 134–36, 451
Madras 58, 98–99, 101
Madrid 93–94
Maindy Barracks (Cardiff) 180
Malaya *see BATTLES*
Malplaquet *see BATTLES*
Malta 131
Manningham, Col Coote 55–56
March to the Danube (Marlborough) 26–30
Marches, Regimental 180, 471–72
Marden, Maj Gen Sir T. O. xxx, 219, 263, 457
Margesson, Lt Col J. E. xxx, 365, 367, 420
Marks, Mr. S. 202–03
Marlborough, John Churchill, 1st Duke of 25, 26–39
Marley, Maj Gen B. 88
Marsack, Lt H. 142
Martin, Maj A. J. 425
Martin, Lt Col P. J. 459
Matchett, Sgt J. H. 385
Maxim, Sir Hiram 183, 190
Maymyo *see BATTLES (2nd World War)*
Mayu Tunnels *see BATTLES (2nd World War)*
Meade, Capt P. 14
Mechanisation 276–78, 305, 441–42
Melvill, Lt T., VC 159–61, 173, 175, 451
Menzies, Lt R. 14
Mesopotamia *see BATTLES (1st World War)*
Miers, Brig R. C. H. 362 *et seq.*, 369, 393–94
Ministry of Defence, formation of 381
Modderfontein *see BATTLES (Boer War)*
Monmouthshire Regiment, Formation 211
"Part of Corps of SWB" 224, 227; Battle Honours 415
Montgomery, F-M Visct. 321–22, 338, 343, 349
Morgan, Lt Col D. G. 446, 448, 460
Morgan-Owen, Maj Gen Ll. I. G. 208, 270, 273, 455, 462–66
Morice, Col C. 77–78, 81
Motto, Regimental 102–04, 182
Mountain, Col 121–22
Much, Lt W. T. 143
Murphy, Pte T., VC 144, 451
Museums, Regimental 273–74, 421, 447
Music *see Bands and Marches*
Mutiny Act 4, 12
Muttlebury, Lt Col G. 81, 83
Myles, Lt E. K., VC 236–37, 451

Index

Napier, Maj Gen L. A. H. xxxi, 369, 395, 397, 399, 401, 402, 434, 439, 440, 447, 457, 459, 460
Napier, Lt Col V. J. L. 295, 297, 300
Napoleon Bonaparte xxix, 58, 70, 77, 81–83
Napper, Capt R. 14
National Service 350, 354, 379–80
Naval Honours 53–54
Nelson, Admiral Lord 53–55
Nepal 87–89
Nightingale, Florence 139
Nodwell, Maj 335
Normandy (2nd World War) 321 *et seq.*
North Africa *see Western Desert*
North America 50–51, 52, 89–98
North West Frontier (India) *see also Khyber Pass, Landi Kotal, Razmak, Waziristan* 265
Northcott, Maj 329
Northern Ireland 401, 402–03, 404–07, 410–11, 423, 425–26, 430, 444–46
Norway 287–293
Nott, Maj Gen Sir W. 110, 112, 114, 126

Officers, badges of rank *see Eversleigh*
O'Donnell, Lt B. Walton *(et al.)* 468-69
Oldfield, Capt T. 14
Orange, Prince of 38, 78–79
Orr, Lt Col H. G. 327, 330, 334–35
Orthes 76
Osnabrück 401–02, 404, 407
Oudenarde *see BATTLES*
"Overlord" Operation *see also BATTLES (2nd World War)* 321
Owen, 2/Lt A. J. 245
Owen, Lt Bryn RN (Retd) xxx, 65, 475

Paris, Treaty of 47
Parker, Maj Gen J. 456
Parker, Capt R. 28, 38, 40
Parson, Lt Gen J. 456
Partridge, Lt Col J. E. C. 270
Paton, Col G. xxx, 9, 455
Pay, rate of 9–10, 107, 147, 184, 278–80
Peel Yates, Lt Gen Sir D. 276, 385–86, 387, 395, 399–400, 407, 418–19, 457, 459
Pembroke Dock 188, 251, 370
Peninsular Campaign *see also BATTLES* 67–77
Pennycuick, Col (Brig) J. 116–17, 119, 120–22, 123–24, 126
Pennycuick, Ens A. 116, 120–22
Penn Symons, Maj Gen Sir W. xxx, 154–55, 157, 178, 192
Perry, Sgt R. 120, 462

Peyton, Gen F. 457
Pim, Lt Col B. M. 460
Pluckley (Kent) 2
Polo 493
Popham, Lt Col V. J. F. 305–06
Potter, George & Co (Aldershot) 209
Powell, Gen H. W. 456
Priestley, Lt Col E. A. 459
Primrose, Maj Gen G. 35, 36, 41, 455
Prince of Wales (later Edward VII) 472
Prince of Wales (later George V) 207–209
Prince of Wales (later Edward VIII) 253–54, 269
Prince of Wales, Charles (Colonel-in-Chief, RRW) xxx, 389, 395–97, 398, 401, 404, 407, 412–15, 421, 423, 424, 429, 433, 435, 438–39, 446, 450
Prince of Wales's Division 386, 391–93, 434–36
Princess of Wales (Diana) 429
Proctor, Lt Col H. 89–90, 92–93, 94–96
Prothero, Lt Col A. G. 233
Pulleine, Lt Col 155–56, 157–59, 162
Punishments *see Discipline*
Purdon, Capt A. 14

Quatre Bras *see BATTLES*
Quetta 110, 112, 209
Quinton-Adams, Maj J. 437

Raglan, F-M Lord 131–32, 139
Raikes, Capt D. T. 410
Raikes, Maj Gen G. T. 243, 251, 409–410
Raikes, Vice Admiral Sir Iwan 410
Raikes, Col L. T. 409
Raikes, Admiral R. H. 410
Raikes, Lt Col W. T. 243, 410
Ramillies, *see BATTLES*
Ravenna (liberation anniversary) 437–38
Razmak 265
Read, Lt Gen Sir A. 395, 398
Rebecca Riots 130, 149
Rees, Sgt I., VC 241, 249, 451
Rees, Maj Gen T. W. 315
Repington, Gen Sir Charles A. a'C. 456
Reynolds, Lt Col D. L. C. 316, 318, 459
Reynolds, Surg-Maj J., VC 163, 172
Rhodesia, Monitoring Force 426
Rhys, Lt Col D. L. 459
Richards, Capt E. 136
Richards, Henry Brinley 472
Richardson, Maj G. 90, 92, 94, 96
Roberts, F-M Lord 192–93, 197, 199, 202, 203, 216
Roberts, Lt Col A. G. 358, 375, 459
Roberts, Capt (QM) K. D. 399

Roberts, Lt Col M. G. R. 399, 434, 460
Roberts, Col N. O. xxx, 399
Roberts, Lt Col O. M. 460
Robinson, Capt N. L. G. 33
Roblin, Maj the Revd H. 423
Roche, Lt Col U. de R. 192, 207
Rorke's Drift *see BATTLES*
Rorke's Drift, Visit, 1979 centenary 423–24
Row, Brig A. 30–31
Rowlands, Gen Sir Hugh, VC 133, 136, 149, 176, 451
Roy, Pte W. 172
Royal Armoured Corps 305, 350
Royal Hospital, Chelsea 41, 42, 127, 391
Royal Military College (Academy) Sandhurst 147, 280
Royal Military School of Music, Kneller Hall 467–69, 470, 471
Royal Regiment of Artillery 344
Royal Regiment of Wales (Formation of) 386–87, 395–401 (title) 389
Royal Welch Fusiliers (23rd Foot) 3, 7, 13, 16, 350, 386, 389
Rufane, Brig W. 45, 48, 50
Rugby Football 269, 270–71, 391, 416–17, 441, 487–93

Sale, Maj Gen Sir R. H. 110
Sarajevo 214–215
Scheiss, Cpl F., VC 172
Schellenberg *see BATTLES*
Schomberg, Gen Frederick, Duke of 13, 14–15
School of Infantry (Warminster) 448
Scimitar *see VEHICLES*
Scott, Lt Col R. M. 460
Sennybridge (SENTA) 1, 349, 439, 446
Seymour, Lt Gen W. 21, 23, 25, 455
Sharp, Lt Col A. K. 459
Sheil, Capt P. St.M. 290
Sher Singh (Sikh general) 116–17
Sherard, Lt Gen Hon. P. 456
Shirley, Lt E. 14
Sikhs, war with *see also BATTLES – Chilianwala* 115–127
Slaper, Capt R. 14
Smelt, Lt Col W. 100, 105
Smith, Maj R. P. xxx, 428, 446
Somerville, Brig Sir N. 324–25, 333, 342, 382–83, 384, 459
Soult, Marshal N. 75–77
South Lincolnshire Regt (69th Foot): Formation 46
"South Lincolnshire" 51
Merger with 41st 180
South Wales Borderers (24th Foot): Origins 1–4
"2nd Warwickshire" 51
"South Wales Borderers" 179–80
Merger with Welch Regt 386–89

511

Index

Sport *see Rugby Football and Appendix 8* 487
Spurrell, Lt Col R. L. 460
Stevenson, Lt Col M. C. P. 459
Stilwell, Gen J. 310
Stirling, Gen Sir T. 456
Stocker, Lt Col A. J. 459
Stocker, Lt Col S. R. A. 427, 428–29, 430, 460
Stockley, Lt Col. R. C. 335
Stopford, Lt Gen Hon. Sir E. 107, 456
Strange, Lt J. 237
Surrenden (Kent) 1, 3
Sweetman, Maj W. P. 327

Talavera *see BATTLES*
Tanks *see VEHICLES*
Tanner, Pte G. 319
Tatton, Lt Gen W. 34–35, 455
Taverner, Capt R. C. 353
Taylor, Lt A. 136
Taylor, Gen P. 180, 455
Taylor, Lt Gen W. 455
Territorial and Army Volunteer Reserve 381, 404
Territorial Force (Army), Formation of 210–211
Teutoburger Wald *see BATTLES (2nd World War)*
Thompson, C/Sgt W. 188
Three Peaks Yacht Race 443
Tibbs, Lt I. L. 310
Tientsin 214–15, 223
Titles, Regimental 6, 7, 42, 45, 51, 101–104, 179–80, 253, 389
Tollemache, Lt Gen T. 17
Traherne, Lt Col J. R. L. 459
Trist, Lt Col L. H. 239
Trower, Col C. V. 274
Tsingtao *see BATTLES (1st World War)*
Tulloch, Maj Gen Sir A. 182, 457
Twistleton, Capt G 14
Tyler, Maj A. C. 319
Tyler, Capt R. H. 399
Tyson, Lt P. W. 312

Ulster *see Northern Ireland*
UNIFORM
  General 3, 7, 43, 64, 109, 147, 184, 213
  Battledress 280

Facings 7–8, 45, 109, 400
Blue Patrols (No 1 Dress) 269, 370, 394
Full Dress 147, 400
Gorget-plate 8
Headdress 7, 147–48, 213–14, 280
Khaki Service Dress 147, 184, 186, 213
Puttees 213, 280
Sam Browne belt 184, 190
Utrecht, Treaty of 41

Vaughan, Capt J. 130
Vaughan Roberts, Lt Col J. R. 379
VEHICLES
  Armoured Personnel Carriers 379, 433, 441, 448
  Bren Carriers 280
  Jeeps 306, 374
  Land Rovers 374–75, 441
  Load Carriers 278, 314, 433, 441–42
  Scout Cars (Ferret) 374, 441
  Tanks 305, 332, 441, 448
Vellore, sepoy mutiny at 59–63
Venner Col S. 16–17, 18
Victoria, Queen 140, 173, 207
Victoria Cross, institution of 135
  posthumous awards 172
Vigo (Spain) 41
Vincent, Gen J. 456
Vivian, Maj C. J. 311–12
Vizer, 2/Lt J. 241
Volunteer Battalions (RRW) 404, 448–49

Wales, first services in 130, 179
War Memorials SWB 258; Welch 258, 371–74
Warburg *see BATTLES*
Wardour, Col 42, 456
Warminster 448
Waterloo *see BATTLES*
Watkins, Maj J. A. 303
Watkins, Maj Tasker, VC 330–32, 451
Watson, Mr. D. 408
Watson, Maj W. R. M. 426
Waziristan 269-70
WEAPONS Anti-tank (BAT) 361, (Boys) 281, (Milan) 421, 441 (Piat) 344); Bayonets, 8, 56, 108; Grenades 7; Machine-Guns, (Bren) 278 (GPMG) 183 (Lewis) 278 (Maxim)

182–83 (Vickers) 183; Mortars 441; Muskets 8, 56, 108; Pikes 8; Pistols 148; Rifles (Lee Enfield) 182, 374 (Lee Metford) 182 (Martini Henry) 148 (SLR) 182, 374 (Snider) 148; Sub Machine guns (Sten) 374 (Sterling) 374; Swords 7, 8, 56
Welch Regiment (41st Foot) Origins of 41–42
  "Welsh Regiment of Infantry" 101–104
  Merger with 69th Foot 180
  Merger with South Wales Borderers 386–89
Wellesley (Wesley) Arthur *see Wellington*
Wellington, 1st Duke of 43, 67, 74–75, 76, 77, 79, 80, 83
Welsh Brigade 350, 377, 386, 391–93
Welsh Volunteers TAVR 381–82, 404
Wentworth, Lt Gen T. 43–44, 455
West Indies, mortality in 54–55
Western Desert 293, 295–301
White, Sgt A., VC 240–41, 451
Whitelaw, William 405-06, 430
Whyte, Gen R. 455
Willes, Col J. E. T. 386, 398–99
William III, King 2, 13, 15, 25
Williams, Col Sir E. K. 107–08
Williams, Pte J., VC 165–68, 172, 273, 451
Williams, CSM J. H., VC 245–46, 451
Williams, Lt Col. J. W. C. 329
Wilson, Lt J. D. 397
Witt, Otto 163
Wodehouse, Lt A. 378
Wodehouse, Gen E. 378, 455
Wolseley, Gen Sir Garnet 151
Wray, Lt C. 14
Wren, Lt Gen J. 456

Y Cadetships (Commissions from the ranks) 280

Zabange (Zulu warrior) 159–60, 178
Zimbabwe *see Rhodesia*
Zulu nation: military prowess 152
  King and Queen of Kwa Zulu visit Brecon 446–47 *see also BATTLES (Isandhlwana, Rorke's Drift)*